Michelle,

Happy reading and always stay
politically engaged!

Duane Bratt

BLUE STORM

ARTS IN ACTION

SERIES EDITOR:
Jennifer Pettit, Dean, Faculty of Arts, Mount Royal University

Co-published with Mount Royal University
ISSN 2371-6134 (Print) ISSN 2371-6142 (Online)

This series focuses on illuminating, promoting, or demonstrating the fundamental significance of the Arts, Humanities, and Social Sciences to public well-being and contemporary society—culturally, spiritually, socially, politically, and economically—with the aim of raising awareness of the essential skills, perspectives, and critical understandings of societal issues these disciplines cultivate.

No. 1   *Understanding Atrocities: Remembering, Representing, and Teaching Genocide*
        Edited by Scott W. Murray

No. 2   *Orange Chinook: Politics in the New Alberta*
        Edited by Duane Bratt, Keith Brownsey, Richard Sutherland, and David Taras

No. 3   *Signs of Water: Community Perspectives on Water, Responsibility, and Hope*
        Edited by Robert Boschman and Sonya L. Jakubec

No. 4   *Blue Storm: The Rise and Fall of Jason Kenney*
        Edited by Duane Bratt, Richard Sutherland, and David Taras

UNIVERSITY OF CALGARY
Press

BLUE STORM

The Rise and Fall of Jason Kenney

Edited by
DUANE BRATT,
RICHARD SUTHERLAND
AND **DAVID TARAS**

Arts in Action Series
ISSN 2371-6134 (Print) ISSN 2371-6142 (Online)

University of Calgary Press
2500 University Drive NW
Calgary, Alberta
Canada T2N 1N4
press.ucalgary.ca

LIBRARY AND ARCHIVES CANADA CATALOGUING IN PUBLICATION

Title: Blue storm : the rise and fall of Jason Kenney / edited by Duane Bratt, Richard Sutherland,
    and David Taras.
Names: Bratt, Duane, 1967- editor. | Sutherland, Richard, 1964- editor. | Taras, David, 1950-
    editor.
Series: Arts in action ; no. 4.
Description: Series statement: Arts in action, 2371-6134 ; no. 4 | Includes bibliographical
    references and index.
Identifiers: Canadiana (print) 20220445184 | Canadiana (ebook) 20220445273 | ISBN
    9781773854168 (softcover) | ISBN 9781773854175 (hardcover) | ISBN 9781773854205 (EPUB) |
    ISBN 9781773854199 (PDF) | ISBN 9781773854182 (Open Access PDF)
Subjects: LCSH: Kenney, Jason, 1968- | LCSH: Premiers (Canada)—Alberta—Biography. | LCSH:
    United Conservative Party. | LCSH: Alberta. Legislative Assembly—Elections, 2019. | LCSH:
    Alberta—Economic conditions—21st century. | CSH: Alberta—Politics and government—2015-
Classification: LCC FC3676.1.K46 B58 2023 | DDC 971.23/04092—dc23

The University of Calgary Press acknowledges the support of the Government of Alberta through
the Alberta Media Fund for our publications. We acknowledge the financial support of the
Government of Canada. We acknowledge the financial support of the Canada Council for the Arts
for our publishing program.

This book has been published with the help of a grant from Mount Royal University Library, through
the Mount Royal University Library Open Access Fund.

Cover image: Colourbox 6153926 and 8364348
Copyediting by Tania Therien
Cover design, page design, and typesetting by Melina Cusano

In memory of
David Taras

CONTENTS

Preface

In 2019, the United Conservative Party (UCP), under the leadership of Jason Kenney, unseated the New Democratic Party (NDP) to form the provincial government of Alberta, a restoration of conservative power in a province that had seen the Progressive Conservatives win every election from 1971 to 2015. Almost from its first days in office, the UCP began to create political waves, many of which have yet to subside.

Blue Storm is the first scholarly analysis of the 2019 election and the first years of the UCP government, with special focus on Jason Kenney's rise to power and his stunning fall. It brings together a wealth of original research from scholars, journalists, and political watchers, each with a unique methodological approach, to provide a well-rounded analysis of complex and ongoing political issues in Alberta, including the impacts of COVID-19.

It opens with an examination of the election from a number of vantage points, including the campaign, polling, and online politics. It provides fascinating insight into internal UCP politics with chapters on the divisions within the party, gender and the UCP, and the symbolism of Kenney's famous blue pickup truck. Explorations of oil and gas policy, the Energy War Room, Alberta's budgets, health care, education, the public sector, Alberta's cultural industries, and more provide unprecedented insight into the actions, motivations, and impacts of Kenney's UCP government in power. It concludes with a survey of the impacts of COVID-19 in Alberta and a comparison between Jason Kenney and Doug Ford.

Blue Storm is essential reading for everyone interested in Alberta politics and the tumultuous first years of the UCP government. Providing key insights from perspectives across the political spectrum, this book is a captivating deep dive into an unprecedented party, its often controversial politics, and its unforgettable leader. Unfortunately, not all policies or events could be covered with the same depth in a single volume. Nonetheless, *Blue Storm* provides what we believe will be the definitive account of the conservative restoration after four years of an NDP government, Alberta's political management of COVID-19, and the turbulent three-and-a-half-year reign of Jason Kenney as premier.

While the book features a distinguished roster of contributors from across the province and beyond, much of the expertise and indeed the financial support for this enterprise came from Mount Royal University. We are grateful to Jennifer Pettit, the dean of arts, for her support of the project, which is part of the Faculty of Arts' "Arts in Action" book series through the University of Calgary Press.

Just as the COVID-19 pandemic affected every aspect of the Kenney government's first three years in office, it also affected our work on the book. We benefitted from an intensive two-day workshop in June of 2021. Because of COVID-19, this workshop had to be held virtually. We're grateful that our authors were willing to spend two days online to bring the volume together as a cohesive whole, and for their perseverance in working on the volume at a time that was disruptive and difficult for many.

We are also grateful to Brian Scrivener and Helen Hajnoczky at the University of Calgary Press for their professionalism, encouragement, and advice. We also owe a great debt to Tania Therien for copy editing the manuscript and Alison Cobra for designing the promotion strategy for *Blue Storm*. This project has been a voyage of discovery and intensive but warm collaboration for the editors. We are indebted to our contributors and to the peer reviewers who helped us steer our course.

It is with deep sadness that we acknowledge the loss of our colleague and friend David Taras before *Blue Storm* was published. Several days before the contributor's workshop was to begin in June 2021, David informed the other editors that he had been diagnosed with cancer and would be immediately starting treatment. This meant that he would be unavailable to participate in the workshop. Over the subsequent year, David remained engaged with the project and read, when his strength allowed him to, draft chapters. In June 2022, roughly a year after his cancer diagnosis, David passed away. While an obviously massive tragedy to his family and friends, David's death also leaves a huge absence in Alberta's scholarly community and political analysis. David was an internationally renowned scholar, greatly admired teacher, public intellectual with many media appearances spanning decades, generous mentor to junior scholars, and, most importantly, a very kind man. Many of the contributors to *Blue Storm* had been friends and colleagues of David for years during his two decades at the University of Calgary and the decade that he spent working as the Ralph Klein Chair in Media Studies at Mount Royal University. The editors will miss the brainstorming sessions enjoying the lunch buffet at the Danish-Canadian Club, where David was a member and always, despite protests from others, picked up the cheque!

In our last conversation with David, less than a week before his death, he complained that he did not do enough work as editor to warrant his name on the book cover. He was kindly, but firmly, told that we were acknowledging his request, but denying it. It is no exaggeration to say that David was the driving force behind *Blue Storm* and its prequel *Orange Chinook*. Both books were David's idea. David helped to identify the themes and topics for *Blue Storm*, recruited the contributors, and planned the workshop.

In recognition of his contributions not only to this volume, but to understanding politics, government, and communication in Alberta throughout his distinguished career, *Blue Storm* is dedicated to the memory of David Taras.

Duane Bratt
Richard Sutherland

I.
Setting the Scene

Introduction: Jason Kenney and the Perfect Storm

Duane Bratt, Richard Sutherland, and Lisa Young

When Jason Kenney drove his blue Dodge Ram pickup truck into the convention hall on election night in April 2019, he was celebrating a landslide victory that returned the province to "normal." After two years of campaigning to win the leadership of both the Progressive Conservative (PC) and Wildrose parties, merging them into a new United Conservative Party (UCP), and then soundly defeating Rachel Notley's New Democratic Party (NDP) government, Kenney seemed poised to join the likes of Manning, Lougheed, and Klein in the pantheon of long-serving Alberta conservative premiers. Instead, only three years later, Kenney stood in front of a much smaller crowd of supporters to announce that he would step down as party leader after receiving only 51.4 per cent yes votes in the 18 May 2022 UCP leadership review.

This book tells the rise and fall story of the Kenney government's ambitious plans to return to "true" conservatism reminiscent of the early Klein years, and how these plans were received. It examines the Kenney government's efforts to will the province out of its sense of decline by taking on national and international forces calling for a shift away from fossil fuels. It traces the ways in which the COVID-19 pandemic laid bare the internal tensions in the UCP, and enumerates the tragic consequences of the government's inability to manage the situation.

Just as Jason Kenney was the centre of attention on election night in 2019, he remained a central and increasingly controversial figure in the government his party formed. Through many of the chapters, the book tells the story of hubris: excessive pride and self-confidence that left Jason Kenney resigning before finishing his first term.

From Orange Chinook to Blue Storm

In 2019 we, along with Keith Brownsey and David Taras, co-edited *Orange Chinook*.[1] We felt that the 2015 election of the NDP and Premier Rachel Notley was such a notable event that it needed to be documented in a major academic study. The NDP not only replaced the forty-four-year PC political dynasty, but also it represented a dramatic ideological turn for a historically dominant conservative province. *Orange Chinook* explained the breakthrough election victory and also examined the first three years of the Notley government. The Notley years saw the creation of the Climate Leadership Plan (CLP), fights over pipelines, changes to the tax structure, reforms to party financing, an ill-fated farm bill, and a host of other changes to Alberta's political and cultural system. The 2019 election, which saw the NDP lose to the new UCP, was initially seen as the second half of the same story.

If 2015–2019 was a dramatic shift away from conservatism, 2019 was the backlash and the restoration of conservative rule under the leadership of UCP Premier Jason Kenney. One of us was at the UCP election night victory party at Calgary's Big Four building. In speaking to UCP staffers at the end of the evening, they promised a return to Alberta conservatism. They did not just mean replacing the NDP, they were also referring to previous PC governments that they felt were insufficiently conservative (Stelmach, Redford, Prentice). In other words, they promised a return to the conservativism of Ralph Klein in the 1990s. The UCP would form government with a massive set of campaign promises that sought to reverse many of the NDP's policies, reclaim the glory days of oil and gas prosperity, cut back on the size of the public sector, confront the federal government, and institute more conservative social policies.

The first book had orange (NDP's colour) in its title, so we wanted blue (UCP's colour) in the title of this book. Within a year of the election, we realized that *Blue Storm* would be an appropriate title. This is because, by March 2020, the UCP's carefully crafted agenda was sideswiped by the arrival of the COVID-19 storm. This unprecedented health pandemic also had far-reaching economic consequences and social dislocation. The Kenney government had to reorient its scheduled agenda to address COVID-19. However, in other respects, they decided to persevere with their agenda, sometimes to disastrous consequences, in the midst of COVID-19. This book analyzes the UCP agenda in the context of COVID-19.

However, COVID-19 was not the only storm facing Jason Kenney and his UCP government; they also confronted substantial political turmoil. Prominent Alberta pollster and political commentator Janet Brown regularly says that a premier has three main audiences: 1) the public, 2) the party caucus, and 3) the party donors. On all three indicators, there were storm clouds that swirled around Kenney leading to his resignation. As Brooks DeCillia shows in his chapter, the NDP passed the UCP in public opinion polls in June 2020, but because of the vagaries of seat distribution was not in a position to form a majority government until March 2021. If an election had been held in May 2022, the NDP would easily have formed a majority government. Kenney's approval rating was the lowest of any Canadian premier and was stuck in the high 20 per cent (the lowest of any Alberta premier since just before Alison Redford resigned). When it comes to caucus, as David Stewart and Anthony Sayers describe in their chapter, two former MLA critics of Kenney were expelled from caucus, two MLAs have been demoted, and other MLAs have been openly critical of Kenney's leadership. Adding to Kenney's woes was the re-emergence of Brian Jean, the former Wildrose leader and failed 2017 UCP leadership candidate. In March 2022, Jean was elected as a UCP MLA in a by-election in Fort McMurray-Lac La Biche (Jean's old riding) on an explicit platform of Kenney resigning as UCP leader.[2] Finally, UCP donors appear to be abandoning the party. Even in the era of stricter party financing rules, governing parties usually have a huge fundraising advantage, and conservative parties usually have a huge fundraising advantage over progressive parties. Therefore, it is shocking that over the last two years, the opposition NDP has raised several million dollars more than the UCP (see Table 0.1).

Table 0.1. Party Fundraising (2020–2022)

	2020	2021	JANUARY–JUNE 2022
NDP	$5,059,537.66	$6,152,003.93	$2,467,675.38
UCP	$3,747,753.11	$3,795,701.01	$1, 409, 149. 70

Note: The 2022 figures do not include donations to UCP constituencies, because recent reporting changes only require those numbers at the end of the year. The NDP does not have separate donations to its constituencies.

Sources: Elections Alberta, "Financial Disclosure—Parties," accessed on 3 August 2022 at https://efpublic. elections.ab.ca/efParties.cfm?MID=FP.

Revisiting the 2019 Election

The book begins with three chapters on the 2019 election. Graham Thomson summarizes the election campaign that saw the UCP form a majority government. The formal campaign was twenty-eight days, but in reality the 2019 campaign began when Jason Kenney won the UCP leadership on 28 October 2017 and continued to election day on 16 April 2019. It was a battle between two parties, two very different ideologies, and two powerful politicians. Rachel Notley was an incumbent premier challenged by Jason Kenney, a former senior federal cabinet minister. Kenney ran on a slogan of "jobs, economy, pipelines" and fixated on ending the economic recession that dogged Notley throughout her time as premier. Given the weakness of the Alberta economy, Notley decided not to run on her record. Instead, the NDP, through the surrogate of Health Minister Sarah Hoffman, responded by attacking Kenney's past record as a social conservative as well as other UCP candidates. Kenney won the election by largely sweeping Calgary and rural Alberta seats. Thomson concludes, in a foreshadowing of the rest of the book, "Kenney was about to discover that winning the election was the easy part. Governing would prove to be much more difficult."

Peter Malachy Ryan and Kate Toogood follow with a chapter that examines the parties' digital campaign: websites, apps, and social media accounts (Facebook, Twitter, and Instagram). They make two key arguments. First, Alberta is turning from a historical one-party dominant system (the successive political dynasties of the Liberals, United Farmers of Alberta, Social Credit, and PCs) to a two-party system (UCP and NDP).

Second, there was a strategic communication framing with the NDP portrayed as a nurturing parent, while the UCP was seen as the strict parent.

Brooks DeCillia concludes the section on the 2019 election with a focus on public opinion polling. The election was not close (UCP won a majority government and had a 22-point lead in the popular vote), despite the media narrative in the last two weeks that the campaign was tightening. This is because the media was relying upon nine polls (half of the total that were publicly released) that showed the gap between the UCP and NDP was in single digits. DeCillia analyzes the accuracy of the public polls in the 2019 campaign to explain why they were so off the mark and critically analyzes the news media's reporting about the polls. He also goes beyond the 2019 campaign to demonstrate that the UCP government had a short honeymoon and by May 2022 were facing a massive loss in a 2023 election.

Inside the United Conservative Party

David K. Stewart and Anthony M. Sayers in their chapter detail some of the challenges that Jason Kenney faced within the UCP. Stewart and Sayers argue that COVID-19 did not create the divisions within the UCP; instead it amplified existing tensions of a party that is only a few years removed from its merger of the PC and Wildrose parties. Stewart and Sayers use surveys of party supporters in 2015 and 2019 and an analysis of party activists at the 2020 UCP policy convention to demonstrate that there are significant internal divisions within the UCP that go well beyond COVID-19 or the unpopularity of Premier Kenney's leadership. Changing unpopular leaders to present a new image with a new election on the horizon has been a frequent pattern of conservative parties in Alberta. All governing parties do this in Canada, but only in Alberta has it frequently led to electoral victory instead of an impending loss. During the last decades of the PC dynasty, the party replaced an unpopular Don Getty with Ralph Klein. When Klein started to become unpopular after over a dozen years in office, he was replaced by Ed Stelmach. When Ed Stelmach became unpopular, he was replaced with Alison Redford. And when Redford became unpopular, she was dumped in favour of Jim Prentice. Now the UCP is attempting the same trick by replacing Kenney.

In fall 2019, Justin Trudeau and the federal Liberals were re-elected, albeit with a minority government. However, the party was wiped out in Alberta, losing all four of the seats that it had won in 2015 with the lowest Liberal vote share in history (which is quite a feat, considering the party's unpopularity in the province). Trudeau's re-election sparked a noticeable rise in separatist sentiment in Alberta. In response, the Kenney government convened a Fair Deal Panel to hold town halls across the province and conduct research on a set of proposals to increase Alberta's autonomy within Canada. The most high-profile of these involved a referendum on the federal equalization program, creating an Alberta tax collection agency (replacing Revenue Canada), creating an Alberta provincial police force (replacing the Royal Canadian Mounted Police [RCMP]), and creating an Alberta Pension Plan (withdrawing from the Canadian Pension Plan). Jared Wesley's chapter analyzes these efforts. He makes clear that these fair-deal proposals did not emerge from thin air but had been first promoted in the famous firewall letter of 2001 (written to then-Alberta Premier Ralph Klein by Stephen Harper and other prominent conservative thinkers) and had circulated among Alberta conservative intellectuals for two decades. Western alienation is as old as Alberta, but Wesley argues that these populist approaches have become more aggressive in recent years and are not only out of step with public opinion, but also have a potential to backfire.

Wesley discusses broadly the fair-deal proposals, while Doug King focuses narrowly on one of them: the proposal for an Alberta provincial police force. King links legitimate fears of rural crime with the proposal to replace the RCMP with an Alberta provincial policy force. The case of Eddie Maurice, who shot a trespasser on his ranch outside of Okotoks, is highlighted to show the unique challenges of policing in rural Alberta and the response of the UCP government. In this way, the desire for greater provincial autonomy meshed with the other UCP goal of combatting rural crime. As King notes, replacing the RCMP is not popular among the public (including in rural Alberta), it would also be substantially more expensive for the province and municipalities, but there are clear indications that the UCP government will still pursue it because those who do support it constitute the UCP base. King also examines the enforcement of COVID-19 restrictions by the police, the defund-the-police movement, and the removal of UCP Justice Minister Kaycee Madu for calling the Edmonton police chief over a personal traffic ticket.

Melanee Thomas contrasts the approach to gender and women between the UCP and its predecessor NDP government. While Rachel Notley had a gender-equal cabinet with women in many senior positions, women were under-represented in Kenney's cabinet and caucus. This did not mean that gender and masculinity were insignificant to the Kenney government; instead, Thomas argues that, "like many conservative and populist parties," gender and especially masculinity are central to the UCP and explain its representation and policy priorities. Thomas empirically assesses the UCP's performance in four areas of gender and women representation (descriptive, substantive, symbolic, and affective). She does this through candidate/MLA/cabinet counts and content analysis of Hansard.

The back cover of *Blue Storm* includes a photo of Jason Kenney arriving at his election-night victory party in his famous blue Dodge Ram truck. This was chosen because it captures the sense of optimism by UCP supporters that the election of the Kenney government would mean a return to economic prosperity, but also because it included the iconic blue truck. Chaseten Remillard and Tyler Nagel dedicate an entire chapter to assessing the symbolism of the blue Dodge Ram. Kenney conducted three major tours of Alberta: 1) in 2016 as part of the PC leadership race, 2) in 2019 during the provincial election, and 3) in 2021 as part of "Open for Summer." For each tour, Kenney used the same blue truck, and it was no accident. As Remillard and Nagel write, "[t]he image of Kenney and his truck aligned his own personal political brand with the well-trodden symbology of the pickup truck, and brought together powerful myths of Alberta exceptionalism, sovereignty, anti-elitism, and populist homogeneity." However, critics would not see the blue truck as a positive symbol. Instead, they would see the truck as "a symbol of an antiquated, troubled (and troubling) reliance on old thinking about resource management, exclusionary and pugilist politics, and conservative (non-liberal) populist values and politics."

Oil and Gas Policies

The next section of the book explores, in different ways, the importance of the oil and gas sector in Alberta. Duane Bratt examines the climate policy of the Kenney government. The signature policy of the Notley government was the CLP. From the moment that it was announced in November 2015, Alberta's conservative opposition (Wildrose, PCs, and then the merged UCP) railed against the consumer-based carbon tax and the rest of the CLP. However, on closer examination there is a lot more continuity between the Notley and Kenney governments on climate policy than appears. Despite quickly repealing the carbon tax, Albertans continue to pay a different version because the federal government carbon tax backstop kicked in soon after the removal of the provincial one. The Kenney government, along with other allies among conservative provincial government, sued the federal government over its carbon tax backstop, but the Supreme Court upheld the federal government's jurisdiction. As for the other components of the CLP—coal phaseout, an emissions cap on oil sands production, and methane reduction—they remain in place, and in some cases are even more stringent. This is a good news story, but something that the Kenney government does not want to publicly acknowledge. This contraction between rhetoric (defending the oil and gas sector) and reality (an improving climate record) is explained with a contrast between the Public Kenney and the Private Kenney. The Public Kenney is a fierce defender of Alberta's oil and gas sector and critic of the Trudeau government, but the Private Kenney is working behind the scenes to reduce Alberta's carbon footprint and is working with the Trudeau government to do so.

The difficulties of building pipelines to get Alberta's oil to market has plagued successive governments. In his chapter, Jean-Sébastien Rioux uses the concept of hubris to explain why there was such a wide gap between Kenney's rhetoric on pipelines (only he could get them built) versus the sustained lack of success he has had in getting pipelines built. Kenney promised he would get Trudeau to repeal Bills C-48 (tanker ban off the northwest coast of British Columbia) and C-69 (which Kenney always referred to as the "no more pipelines" bill), as well as fight other Canadian provinces and environmental non-government organizations (ENGOs). This would revive the old Northern Gateway and Energy East pipeline projects. Unfortunately, despite Kenney's efforts, he was not able to re-peal federal legislation nor restart old pipeline projects. Rioux also traces the ill-fated decision to invest in the Keystone XL pipeline. Keystone XL would take Alberta crude through the United States to refineries along the Gulf of Mexico. The Obama Administration had refused to sign a permit for Keystone XL, then the Trump administration approved it. But, on his first day in office, newly elected US President Joe Biden revoked federal ap-proval. Over $1.5 billion of Alberta taxpayers' money went down the drain.

Rounding out the discussion of oil and gas, Brad Clark provides an analysis of the controversial war room. The war room (officially known as the Canadian Energy Centre) was created by the Kenney government to respond to the perceived misinformation being spread by ENGOs about Alberta's oil and gas sector. Modelled on political parties' war rooms dur-ing an election campaign, the war room was intended to respond quickly to ENGOs' claims and would defend and promote Alberta's oil and gas sector. However, Clark argues that the war room, since its launch in late 2019, "has become best known for its frequent missteps and belligerent tone, its credibility as the arbiter of lies and myths frequently shredded." Clark notes that the war room "has sought to take on the air of credibility associated with institutions associated with informational rigor, namely journalism and academic research." However, in practice the war room has been "highly selective in the voices and perspectives it incorporates, narrowly amplifying themes consistent with UCP rhetoric, attacking, discounting, or excluding legitimate points of view." For over two years, the war room has been such a constant source of ridicule that the Allan Inquiry into foreign funding of ENGOs was forced to acknowledge that it had "come under almost universal criticism."[3]

Alberta's Fiscal Situation

Is Alberta in decline? At one level that seems like a silly question. Despite a sustained economic downturn that started in late 2014, Albertans remain the richest people in Canada. But, by the time of the April 2019 prov-incial election, Alberta had had lingering high unemployment, increased personal and business bankruptcies, massive government budget deficits, large downtown vacancy rates in Calgary, and other negative economic statistics for over five years. Moreover, its primary industry (oil and gas) seemed to be under sustained attack from ENGOs, other governments, large private investors, and insurance companies. Reversing this economic decline was the centrepiece of the UCP election campaign and in Kenney's victory speech on 16 April 2019, he pledged, "[h]elp is on the way, and hope is on the horizon!" It is in this context that Trevor Tombe examines the fiscal situation in Alberta. Tombe notes that, "Alberta has been managing a steady fiscal decline for over four decades," but despite the illusionary aspects of good times at various points over this time, the challenge has worsened. The essential problem is an overreliance by the government on resource revenue. This was a challenge that both the Notley and Kenney governments (like previous PC ones) have ignored, in the hopes that resource revenue would rebound (which it did in 2022). However, Tombe argues that the UCP government has made the situation worse due to implementing tax cuts, making it even more dependent on natural resource revenue. Then COVID-19 exacerbated the strain on Alberta's finances. Tombe argues that these fiscal hurdles are not insurmountable, but it will take a combination of spending cuts and tax increases to properly address them.

Roger Epp's chapter focuses on rural Alberta, a region that he says has been in decline for over a generation. One of Epp's challenges is defining rural Alberta, which he says is not just the parts of Alberta outside of Edmonton and Calgary, but also outside of smaller cities (e.g., Red Deer or Lethbridge) and satellite communities on the edges of the big cities (e.g., Sherwood Park or Airdrie). It is also not homogeneous, "rural is agrarian, northern-boreal, industrial, Indigenous, acreage-residential, and mountain playground." For Epp, the major challenge facing rural Alberta is not just economic or political, but demographic disappearance. As young people increasingly move to the cities, small towns and villages fear the loss of hospitals and schools, and in some cases, the disappearance of the municipality itself. This has led to resentment similar to what is seen in the rural parts of the United States, but Epp argues that this narrative is insufficient for two reasons. First, the Kenney government has "demonstrated that its strongest interest in rural Alberta lies in resource extraction, not communities." This was best illustrated by the rural backlash against the UCP plan to re-institute coal mining in the eastern slopes of the Rockies. Second, Epp argues that rural Alberta is not just a place of decline; it is also a place that is adapting to reality, as evidenced by initiatives like renewable energy projects.

Alberta's economy is often described as a boom-bust cycle due to the volatility of the oil and gas sector. In periods of economic bust, there are loud calls for economic diversification to reduce the province's dependency on oil and gas. Richard Sutherland demonstrates that cultural industries have become one of the diversification targets by the UCP government. In particular, Sutherland examines film and television production and video game development. Soon after being elected in 2019, the UCP cut its financial assistance (grants and tax credits) to cultural industries. As Sutherland notes, this was part of a general repealing of the previous NDP government's policies. However, by early 2021, the UCP reversed course when Jobs and Economic Development Minister Doug Schweitzer announced new financial supports to film and television productions as part of its Economic Recovery Plan, which quickly succeeded. By November 2021, film and television production had become a rare bright light in Alberta's economy. The video games sector suffered the same initial drop in financial assistance when the UCP came to power, but unlike the case with film and television productions, there was no policy reversal. Explaining the differential treatment of these two main cultural industries is one of the themes of Sutherland's chapter.

Health Care, Education, and Public Sector Policies

Health care and education policy (K–12 and post-secondary) is in the jurisdiction of provincial governments. They represent, by far, the largest spending envelopes of any Alberta government. Surprisingly, when we published *Orange Chinook* we did not include any chapters on health care and education. This was because there was nothing really controversial or novel in the NDP's approach. That has not been the case with the UCP government, which set out to make fundamental structural changes to health care, K–12, and post-secondary education. One of the government's first acts was to appoint former Saskatchewan NDP Finance Minister Janice MacKinnon—who had instituted significant cuts to provincial spending in the 1990s—to lead a blue-ribbon commission to advise on the province's finances. The MacKinnon report laid out the blueprint for restructuring and reducing government spending, particularly in health care, post-secondary education, and public-sector compensation and bargaining.

Spending on health care comprises 42 per cent of the provincial budget; it is the single-largest spending item,[4] so wrestling with rising health care costs is a challenge for any provincial government. The MacKinnon report emphasized that Alberta spent more per capita on health care than other big provinces (Ontario, Quebec, and British Columbia) and recommended reducing the wages of doctors and nurses, and the contracting out of some hospital services. In her chapter, Gillian Steward notes that when then-Health Minister Tyler Shandro tried to implement these recommendations, it resulted in a fierce backlash with medical professionals responding by retiring, moving to different provinces, or withdrawing services. Rural clinics, in particular, were hard hit. Remarkably, the government did not abandon its efforts to reduce the compensation of medical professionals even in the midst of the COVID-19 pandemic.

Turning to education, Charles Webber examines Alberta's kindergarten to grade 12 system with a focus on the adversarial relationship between the Alberta Teacher's Association (ATA) and the UCP government, controversial changes to the school curriculum, and the COVID-19 response. The ATA is publicly opposed to certain aspects of Alberta's educational system, in particular, school choice (private and public charter schools), standardized testing, and certain curriculum decisions. The UCP also has sought to reduce the power of the ATA by aiming to split its accreditation role from its collective bargaining role. The UCP promised to overhaul the school curriculum to promote greater literacy, numeracy, and citizenship, but its draft changes to the social study curriculum for K–6 students became another storm of controversy. Many teachers, and university education professors, described it as ideological social engineering that was filled with age-inappropriate and Eurocentric content, but lacking Indigenous content (especially around the history of residential schools). Due to these pedagogical concerns, most school boards have refused to pilot the draft curriculum. School boards, teachers, and parents have also complained that there were insufficient precautions to address the COVID-19 pandemic in schools. For almost two years, students have shifted between in-person to remote learning and back (often making the transition within hours). Mask use, vaccination requirements, and extracurricular activities have been further COVID-19 issues. Webber discusses the long-term negative impact on learning, mental health, and socialization due to COVID-19.

In the case of post-secondary education, Lisa Young shows that, in successive budgets, the Kenney government has singled-out Alberta's universities and colleges for cuts to operating budgets. To compensate for this loss of revenue, Alberta's post-secondary institutions were encouraged to raise tuition (the NDP had frozen tuition for the four years it was in power but provided the institutions with a backfill grant), recruit international students (who pay higher tuition rates), and reduce employee wages. This approach is not unusual, as Young points out; for decades the funding of post-secondary education in Alberta has been on a fiscal roller coaster: "enjoying generous funding when times are good, and then hanging on while funding plunges in the harder times." But, this time is different because of the uncertainty that boom times will ever return combined with the expected rise in the number of Albertans in the prime age for post-secondary education.

Lori Williams turns to public-sector bargaining. She notes that for many decades Alberta governments (Notley's NDP notably the exception) have publicly dismissed and actively campaigned against socialism. When it comes to public-sector unions, Alberta's boom-bust economy is a critical variable. When times are good, Alberta has to pay public employees more than those in other provinces in order to retain them. However, when there is a downturn in the economy, one of the first targets of government restraint is public-sector wages. Given the long recession in Alberta, it was no surprise when Kenney formed government and declared war on labour. Williams carefully documents all of the anti-labour initiatives (legislation, contract negotiations, and control over pensions) pursued by the Kenney government. However, Williams also shows that the Kenney government has faced public pushback on these measures, due in no small measure, because his conception of Alberta's political history and culture is a caricature. In contrast, Williams argues that the reality of Alberta has presented "challenges for Kenney's vision that he did not anticipate, and has yet to effectively respond to."

COVID in Alberta and Ontario

Jonathan Malloy compares the Kenney government with the Ontario PC government led by Doug Ford. Ford and Kenney came to power within a year of each other, were both conservatives, campaigned as populists, replaced progressive governments, and aligned against the Trudeau government. The differences are just as striking. Kenney was a political lifer who had been a federal cabinet minister, while Ford had been a business owner before entering Toronto municipal politics. Kenney had merged two conservative parties, but Ford took over an existing PC party and moved it to the right. Malloy uses these similarities and differences to compare how Kenney and Ford handled COVID-19. He argues that there has been an ideological consistency to Kenney's approach, while Ford's reactions have been much more scattered. This helps to explain why Ford was easily re-elected with another majority government in Ontario, but Kenney was forced to resign before completing his first term.

The COVID-19 theme emerges in almost every chapter of this book, so it makes sense to conclude the book by pulling all of these threads together. Lisa Young's thesis is that COVID-19 "is a story of two mutually reinforcing failures." The health failure has resulted in over 4,300 dead Albertans, the postponement of tens of thousands of medical procedures, and the overwhelming of Alberta's health care system. In particular, the fourth wave (roughly August to November 2021) resulted in the highest COVID-19 case rates of any Canadian province. It emerged after Kenney prematurely announced that Alberta would be "Open for Summer," which led to the dropping of health restrictions and provided a disincentive for people to get vaccinated. The political failure was "a steady erosion in public support for the Kenney government, coupled with internal caucus strife that threatened the premier's hold on his office." The UCP caucus is split between those who opposed vaccine mandates and other health restrictions and those who believed that the Kenney government waited too long to respond and when it did its actions were confusing and incomplete.

Addressing COVID-19, largely unsuccessfully as Lisa Young writes, is *the* story of the Kenney government. The UCP's COVID-19 response was not the sole reason for Kenney announcing his resignation in May 2022, but it was the most important reason. Young argues that these failures ended Kenney's political career.

Future of Alberta Politics

What about the future? At the time of writing, we do not know who will be on stage when the party leaders meet to debate during the 2023 provincial election. The NDP's Rachel Notley will certainly be there, seeking to demonstrate that her party's 2015 victory was no accident and to establish the NDP as an alternative governing party in a province prone to multi-decade dynasties. She will face the winner of the UCP's 2022 leadership contest. Notley will surely want to confront her opponent with the baggage of the very unpopular Kenney government, but the novelty of a change in leadership may make this difficult to accomplish. With Kenney staying on as premier until the fall of 2022, Danielle Smith will have a relatively short time to distance the party from the unpopular Kenney legacy.

It is within the realm of possible that Notley will face not one but two conservative party leaders in 2023. There are real risks of the UCP splintering. Kenney was the principal architect of the PC-Wildrose merger that resulted in the formation of the UCP. Therefore, it would be highly ironic if he was also in place if the UCP splintered. Duane Bratt and Bruce Foster have written that conservative parties, especially in Alberta, have had a habit of splintering and merging.[5] Conservatives are a tough group to lead, and COVID-19 simply exacerbated the internal tensions within the UCP.

For the past two decades, the politics of Alberta have been tumultuous. Ernest Manning served for twenty-five years as premier, and Peter Lougheed and Ralph Klein each served for fourteen. But since Klein left office in 2006, there have been seven premiers in seventeen years. It remains to be seen whether a new UCP leader can move beyond the Kenney government's troubles and establish another conservative political dynasty, or whether this period of tumult has been a transition to some kind of competitive two-party system.[6]

NOTES

1   Duane Bratt, Keith Brownsey, Richard Sutherland, and David Taras, eds., *Orange Chinook: Politics in the New Alberta* (University of Calgary Press: Calgary, 2019).

2   Mark Vallani, "Brian Jean targets Jason Kenney, rallying member votes for UCP leadership after byelection victory," *CTV Calgary News* (16 March 2022), https://calgary.ctvnews.ca/brian-jean-targets-jason-kenney-rallying-member-votes-for-ucp-leadership-after-byelection-victory-1.5822115

3   J. Stephens Allan, Report of the Public Inquiry into Anti-Alberta Energy Campaigns (Government of Alberta, 30 July 2021), 655, https://open.alberta.ca/dataset/3176fd2d-670b-4c4a-b8a7-07383ae43743/resource/a814cae3-8dd2-4c9c-baf1-cf9cd364d2cb/download/energy-report-public-inquiry-anti-alberta-energy-campaigns-2021.pdf

4   Government of Alberta, *Blue Ribbon Panel on Alberta's Finances* (August 2019), 2, https://open.alberta.ca/dataset/081ba74d-95c8-43ab-9097-cef17a9fb59c/resource/257f040a-2645-49e7-b40b-462e4b5c059c/download/blue-ribbon-panel-report.pdf

5   Duane Bratt and Bruce Foster, "The fragility of a 'big tent' conservative party," *CBC News* (25 July 2019), https://www.cbc.ca/news/canada/calgary/conservative-party-splitting-merging-western-canada-1.5220417; Duane Bratt and Bruce Foster, "UCP caucus revolt latest in a long history of splintering conservative parties in Alberta," *CBC News* (13 April 2021), https://www.cbc.ca/news/canada/calgary/road-ahead-alberta-conservative-parties-splinter-history-1.5984055?cmp=rss; and Duane Bratt, "If Kenney can't unite the right in Alberta, then no future UCP leader will be able to either," *Globe and Mail* (21 May 2022), A6.

6   Duane Bratt, "Alberta's Transition to a Two-Party System: The 2015 and 2019 Elections," *Canadian Political Science Review* 16/1 (2022), 32–41.

II.
The 2019 Election

Two Combative Leaders, Two Disparate Parties, and One Bitter Campaign: The 2019 Alberta Election

Graham Thomson

It was a campaign seemingly unlike any in Alberta's history: more vicious, more personal, and more divisive. Alberta's 2019 general election was less like a political horse race and more like the chariot clash in Ben-Hur, but with less "civility."

This was not just a battle of political ideologies, but a personal confrontation between two very different politicians that had begun two years prior when former federal cabinet minister Jason Kenney became leader of the Progressive Conservatives (PC), beginning his remarkable journey to unite forces with the Wildrose to form the United Conservative Party (UCP). In that sense the campaign wasn't twenty-eight days long, or even twenty-eight weeks, but more like twenty-eight months.

Albertans who had been paying attention to the escalating confrontation were likely exhausted before the campaign even began. Premier Rachel Notley officially launched Alberta's thirtieth general election campaign on 19 March with election day set for 16 April, but the date that would prove most significant for Notley and her New Democratic Party (NDP) had already occurred on 31 August 2018. On that day, the Federal Court of Appeal quashed approval for plans to expand the Trans Mountain pipeline to ship more Alberta energy products to the West Coast. "Alberta has done everything right and we have been let down," said a frustrated Notley at the time. "It is a crisis."[1] A crisis not only for Alberta's battered economy, but a catastrophe for Notley's embattled NDP government that, in 2015, had had the misfortune of becoming government just in time for Alberta to sink into a four-years-and-counting oil-price recession.

Notley desperately needed at least a photo-op's worth of Trans Mountain pipe in the ground before the 2019 election to demonstrate to Albertans that their first-ever NDP government had not been an economic jinx. Instead, Notley was heading into the election campaign on a hobbled horse. On 18 March 2019, literally the eve of the election campaign, Notley unveiled a Speech from the Throne designed to defend her record while pointing the finger of blame at others: "Your government has fought to get new pipelines built, but, due to the failures of successive federal governments, Alberta's resources remain landlocked."[2] That same day, she tried to manufacture a fight with the UCP over health care by introducing a piece of legislation entitled Bill 1: The Protection of Public Health Care Act. Notley said the bill was about "defending Albertans from American-style health care."[3] Kenney refused to take the bait and the tactic fizzled.

Notley would instead campaign on her social justice victories: instituting $15 minimum wage, providing workplace protection for paid farmer workers, keeping anti-abortion protesters away from clinics, and safeguarding gay-straight alliances in schools. But not on her Climate Leadership Plan (CLP), which was arguably the signature achievement of her government.

Jason Kenney, leader of the two-year-old UCP, was facing troubles of his own on 18 March as he stoically endured an hour-long barrage from journalists about the renewed accusations of wrongdoing in the UCP's 2017 leadership race. Kenney denied doing anything wrong, or that he had unfairly colluded with another campaign candidate, Jeff Callaway, to defeat rival Brian Jean. But the news media and NDP were all atwitter with news that the RCMP had been called in to investigate by Alberta's election commissioner who continued to levy fines against several people associated with the Callaway campaign.[4]

Notley had likely wanted to see if the investigations led anywhere—and if the Trans Mountain pipeline project could be restarted—before calling an election, but she was hamstrung by Alberta's legislated electoral "window" that stipulated an election date be set between 1 March and 31 May every four years. This window was not legally binding, but Notley realized that delaying the election until later in 2019 would have unpleasant echoes of the PC's disastrous decision under Jim Prentice to call an election one year early in 2015. Notley therefore had the campaign thrust upon her at an inopportune time.

She entered the arena armed with a weak economic record that placed her on the defensive. So, to create an offensive narrative, she targeted what she thought were the UCP's weakest links: its socially conservative ideals and the socially conservative history of its leader. She focused on the character, history, and ethics of its candidates—but mostly the character, history, and ethics of Kenney. "It's a choice about who is going to be the premier of Alberta and who is fit to be the premier of Alberta," declared Notley on 19 March as she kicked off her campaign at Calgary's National Music Centre surrounded by a diverse audience of supporters. "Two days ago, we learned Mr. Kenney cheated to win his party's leadership. And when he was caught, he didn't tell the truth. Mr. Kenney looked Albertans in the eye and very casually and very comfortably lied to us, which in many ways goes to the heart of this issue: how comfortable Mr. Kenney is with lying."[5]

Shredding Kenney's character would become a major theme in the NDP campaign, but the party realized Notley should not be the one wielding the knife day after day, especially not after she declared on the opening day that "the politics of love and hope and optimism always trump the politics of anger, division, and fear, and that's why I'm running to be premier."[6] Instead, the NDP would have veteran politician Sarah Hoffman take charge of anger, division, and fear. "I believe Jason Kenney's unfit to be premier of Alberta and that Albertans deserve to know who the real Jason Kenney is," declared Hoffman, who on the third day of the campaign unveiled a ten-minute attack "documentary" against Kenney pointing, among other things, to his views against same-sex marriage while a university student in California decades before.[7]

Using Hoffman to aggressively attack Kenney would keep Notley insulated from the worst of the mud-slinging that, although damaging the target, often hurts the mud-slinger, too. Going negative hard and early in the campaign was a risk for the whole NDP campaign.

In keeping with his focus on the energy industry, Kenney launched his campaign in the lot of a Leduc-based drilling company, where he arrived in a blue Dodge Ram truck, the same prop he had used in the leadership race for the PCs and then later for the UCP. He accused the NDP of mismanaging the economy and blamed the Notley government's carbon tax for undermining Alberta's growth. "Tens of thousands of Albertans have given up looking for work," said Kenney. "Albertans are poorer because of NDP policy."[8] His message was simple, blunt, and easily articulated in three words: economy, jobs, pipelines.

Then Kenney introduced another character into the campaign, Prime Minister Justin Trudeau, who was disliked by many Albertans and happened to be a personal and professional nemesis of Kenney's. Kenney used the spectre of Trudeau to diminish the reputation of Notley who, according to opinion polls, was well liked by many Albertans but had worked closely with Trudeau over energy issues and climate plans. "This campaign is not about politics, it's about people, the people who have been damaged by the ideological job-killing policies of the NDP and their alliance with the Trudeau Liberals," declared Kenney.[9]

Not surprisingly, when the campaign began the news media focused on Kenney and Notley, and their respective parties. They were the front-runners by far according to just about every public opinion poll over the previous eighteen months. An Ipsos-Reid poll released on the opening day indicated the UCP enjoyed a large lead over the NDP: 52 per cent to 35. The other parties, including the Alberta Liberals, the Alberta Party, and the Freedom Conservative Party had a combined total of seven per cent[10] (see chapter by Brooks DeCillia). "For those that think that this is a multi-party race, it's not," said Mount Royal political scientist Duane Bratt. "I mean you add up all the smaller parties and it doesn't even reach double digits."[11]

Even though the UCP was far ahead, Kenney stumbled on the first day thanks to a strategically placed hurdle by the NDP-friendly website Press Progress, which published a story about controversial statements involving white supremacists made two years previously by one of Kenney's star candidates, Caylan Ford in Calgary-Mountain View. The story reinforced

a narrative that had plagued the UCP for months: a string of "bozo eruptions" by UCP members running to be candidates who were subsequently tossed from the party, or at least prevented from carrying the party
banner, because of racist or homophobic views posted online. Eruptions
can kill campaigns as Albertans had learned during the province's 2012
election after the Wildrose suffered the Mount Vesuvius of bozo eruptions
when a candidate's homophobic "lake of fire" comment helped sink the
party's election chances.

Ford angrily disputed the context of the quotes but abruptly resigned
nonetheless, perhaps realizing if she didn't voluntarily jump, she might be
pushed out by her party. When asked about Ford's resignation, Kenney
expressed shock and disappointment over her comments, but said she did
the right thing by tossing herself overboard.[12] Ford was just the latest embarrassment for the UCP, but Notley and her supporters hoped it wouldn't
be the last as they tried to trip up the social conservatives in the UCP
ranks. Kenney's challenge was to keep his candidates in line, on message,
and under control. And if they created a "distraction," he had to jettison
them overboard without a second thought, even if they were, like Ford,
star material destined for the cabinet. "It's really a fear versus loathing
campaign: Do you fear Jason Kenney more than you loathe the New
Democrats, or vice versa," said Faron Ellis, a political science professor at
Lethbridge College.[13] By having Ford leave the campaign quietly, Kenney
managed to defuse the controversy relatively quickly.

The UCP's campaign turned out to have no fatal "bozo eruptions,"
though one did surface that created a political headache for Kenney. On 2
April, UCP candidate Mark Smith was confronted by an audio recording
of comments he had made during a sermon five years previously where he
suggested that love between a same-sex couple was not love, and then he
went on to mention pedophilia. "You don't have to watch any TV for any
length of time today where you don't see on the TV programs them trying
to tell you that homosexuality and homosexual love is good love,"[14] said
Smith who was running for re-election in Drayton Valley-Devon, having
originally won the seat as a Wildrose candidate in 2015.

The audio recording was broadcast by a University of Alberta-based
radio station as part of a program dealing with 2SLGBTQA+ issues. When
questioned by reporters on the campaign trail, Smith said he couldn't

recall making the comment but he issued an apology of sorts by saying he was sorry if he had upset anyone: "Of course I do not believe that homosexuality is akin to pedophilia. I unequivocally apologize if anyone was offended or hurt. Obviously that would never be my intention."[15]

Kenney said he found Smith's comments offensive but stuck by his candidate, pointing out that Smith had apologized and Kenney had not heard Smith repeat similar comments in his four years as an MLA. The issue eventually dissipated but not before Kenney endured a headline-grabbing grilling from someone who considered himself an old friend of Kenney's: national radio broadcaster Charles Adler.

In a heated interview on 3 April that would turn out to be a foreshadowing of Kenney's troubled future as premier and his difficult relationship with once-sympathetic journalists, Adler pressed Kenney on the Smith affair, pointing out that even though Kenney had said the UCP was inclusive, it had no openly gay candidates. "I've considered you a friend for a long time and I know you're an intelligent person and you're politically astute," said Adler. "Don't you realize that right now, people are screaming back at the radio and they're saying, 'People who hate LGBT people are highly attracted to the (United Conservative) party and running for the party, but the people who are LGBT people—the targets of the hatred—they're not running for the party.'"[16] When Kenney argued that some openly gay Albertans had sought UCP nominations, Adler pointed out, "none of them are up for election right now as members of the UCP. Not a single one."[17]

Adler also took aim at Kenney's problematic personal history—raised repeatedly by the NDP during the campaign—where Kenney, as a university student in San Francisco in the 1980s, had championed an initiative removing the rights of same-sex partners to visit their loved ones suffering from AIDS in hospital.

"AIDs patients were dying alone, no visitors, no visitation allowed and in many cases, they couldn't even visit them at funerals," said Adler. "Mr. Kenney, we could put this to bed immediately if you could only offer a genuine, fulsome apology—I'll move on from San Francisco—have you ever offered a genuine, remorseful apology for the many people that you and your colleagues hurt with that initiative?"[18]

"Charles, I've said that I regret many things I did when I was a young man and I wouldn't take the same position," replied Kenney.

"That's not an apology, Mr. Kenney, that's not an apology," said Adler.[19] The interview made news across the country but it didn't knock Kenney off stride.

He was off and running with nary a glance backward as he renewed his attack on the NDP for introducing a carbon tax, for not getting a pipeline built, for running a record provincial debt, and for not creating more jobs. Kenney honed his "fight back" strategy designed to inflame anger at the federal Liberal government while positioning himself as the one person who could effectively oppose Prime Minister Trudeau.

In the first week of the campaign, Kenney unveiled a nine-point plan that he said would strengthen Alberta's position in Canada's federation by, among other things, holding a referendum against the federal equalization program, demanding Ottawa increase payments under the Fiscal Stabilization program, and setting up an Alberta parole board.[20] In the second week, the UCP released an ambitious, decidedly anti-NDP, and unapologetically pro-business 114-page platform that included promises to scrap Alberta's carbon tax, kill the NDP's CLP, cut the corporate tax rate, lower the minimum wage, and set up a "war room" to defend Alberta's energy industry.[21]

However, sensitive to complaints the UCP was a laggard on environmental issues—and no doubt realizing it could not ignore the dangers of human-made climate change—the party's promises included a technology innovation and emissions reduction program where a carbon tax on large emitters would help fund new technologies to reduce emissions (see Duane Bratt's chapter).

For its part, the NDP unveiled a platform that included promises to provide high-speed internet to all Albertans, help farmers buy energy-efficient equipment, lower the cost of prescription drugs for seniors, help families afford their first home, and expand the existing subsidized childcare system.[22] Perhaps realizing Albertans were more interested in jobs than in cheap drugs for grandpa, Notley continued to focus her attention on Kenney, arguing his platform policies were a tired echo of the past that would hurt Alberta in the future. "His plan to remove the cap on emissions from the oilsands, his plan to move back to coal, this will actually make our kids less healthy," said Notley. "It's a plan where the rich get richer. It's a compilation of failed old ideas that got Alberta into a whole heap of trouble in the first place."[23]

At the midway point in the race came the one and only leaders' debate that proved to be a microcosm of the whole campaign. Joining Kenney and Notley onstage for the televised event were Alberta Party leader Stephen Mandel and Alberta Liberal leader David Khan, whose parties each had one legislative seat when the election was called (neither of the seats were held by Mandel or Khan).

The debate was decidedly off kilter from the moment it started. Instead of Notley being the one under constant attack as the incumbent premier, the attention was focused on Kenney who was the campaign's clear front-runner according to virtually every opinion poll. "Your record in Ottawa is a decade of failure," said Notley of Kenney's time as a federal MP. "It is becoming clearer and clearer that people on Mr. Kenney's leadership team, at the very least, cheated for him to win the leadership," she continued, once again trying to keep the spotlight on controversies surrounding the 2017 UCP leadership race.[24]

But here Notley faced two problems. First, the leadership controversies had so far involved candidate Jeff Callaway and his campaign. Kenney was not directly implicated and as columnist Catherine Ford had pointed out at the beginning of the campaign, voters in Alberta were "yawning all over the province"[25] at leaked documents showing the Kenney and Callaway campaigns working together during the 2017 UCP leadership race. "I really don't think that this is going to have any effect whatsoever on the Alberta election," Ford told CBC Radio. "They won't care. They think that this is how politics is played, that there is always some chicanery going around."[26]

And the second problem for Notley was that voters probably didn't care about Kenney's political past record as a cabinet minister in federal politics. This was a provincial election dealing with current issues. Much to Notley's frustration, Kenney was a blank slate when it came to provincial politics. So, too, his UCP. Even though the UCP was formed from the ashes of the old PC Party that had governed Alberta for forty-four years, and from the right-wing Wildrose Party that had been viewed as too socially conservative by many Albertans in previous elections, the UCP was a new political entity and thus relatively baggage free (see the chapter by David Stewart and Anthony Sayers).

Kenney complained during the debate that he was being unfairly attacked by the other leaders, that he was being "defamed." But he, naturally, also launched his own attacks against Notley by lumping her in with the unpopular-in-Alberta Prime Minister Trudeau: "I respect your leadership, but you made a grave mistake with the alliance with Justin Trudeau. You sold Alberta down the river to your ally Justin Trudeau."[27] Kenney was laser-focused on Notley and Notley only had eyes for Kenney.

For them, Mandel and Khan seemed to be merely pieces of furniture on set. Khan at one point tried to grab the spotlight by arguing in favour of a provincial sales tax. "We need a sales tax to stabilize our revenues," said Khan, hoping to spark a debate. "I'm talking about replacing most provincial income tax with an HST (harmonized sales tax)."[28] But the other leaders ignored what is a non-starter in Alberta politics. Other planks in the Liberal platform included electoral reform, easier access to abortions in rural Alberta, and the elimination of personal income tax for most Albertans.[29] All of them were interesting ideas, but largely ignored because they were being offered by a party trailing in fourth place in opinion polls.

Mandel at times seemed to walk in lockstep with Kenney's anti-Ottawa rhetoric. Indeed, the Alberta Party's platform echoed some of the UCP's policies including the need for Alberta to do a better job marketing its energy sector to highlight the industry's environmental record. But Mandel had months before rejected Kenney's war room idea as "juvenile."[30] The Alberta Party platform also included lower corporate taxes, a $1-billion voucher system for day care and dental care for children under twelve.[31]

As a seasoned debater, Notley performed as expected but at times the smile on her face didn't match the venom in her anti-Kenney words. This was not a repeat of the 2015 leaders' debate where Notley clearly emerged the winner and the incumbent, Jim Prentice, the loser.

Kenney, who had likely been preparing for this debate since he first stepped into provincial politics three years previously, emerged unscathed. As the front-runner that was all he needed to do. In the days after the debate, Notley continued to call into question Kenney's character. But it didn't seem to be resonating with voters.

This is not to say that issues of morality, character, compassion weren't important to Albertans. Even though more than a few Albertans were no doubt upset, even frightened, at the thought of a Kenney government—particularly when it appeared he was ready to "out" gay students to their parents[32]—others were conversely fearful of the province's economic future, a dearth of new pipelines, ballooning government debt, and high unemployment. Kenney's simple mantra of "jobs, economy, pipelines" was more attuned to the concerns of voters than Notley's angry warnings over shenanigans in a conservative leadership race two years before.

Why didn't Notley focus more on her own record? That was one of the questions raised by a focus group in Edmonton on 8 April. Organized by the CBC in partnership with Janet Brown Research, ten voters representing a cross section of Albertans by party affiliation, age, and gender, discussed the campaign. Several expressed disappointment that the NDP didn't run a campaign extolling the virtues of its own record. And frustration that Notley hadn't defended her large deficits as a necessary tactic to protect government services, build infrastructure projects, and create jobs. "The NDP's going to lose the election because they really didn't defend why they're running a deficit," said one of the participants. "I thought they would have made an effort to say, you know, 'We're going to start trimming the deficit a little bit or show a path forward,' and they really didn't. There was a path forward, eventually, and it was prudent and the money wasn't being wasted, it was going to be spent prudently."[33]

By focusing so much on Kenney, the NDP was trying to get Albertans to think twice about his ability to be premier. But consequently New Democrats seemed to be afraid to discuss their own record as government. On the surface that was understandable. The province's economic recovery had stalled, unemployment in Edmonton and Calgary was the highest of any major cities outside of Atlantic Canada, and the Trans Mountain pipeline was still not under construction. Kenney had also gained traction by attacking the NDP's CLP, particularly the province's carbon tax. And the provincial debt had hit a record $60 billion under the NDP. It wasn't a record you'd want to shout from the rooftops or wrap around the side of a campaign bus. But perhaps that's exactly what Notley should have done.

In the final week of the campaign, the gap between the UCP and NDP did narrow but not enough to make it a horse race. According to an opinion poll released by ThinkHQ on 9 April, the UCP held a six point lead over the NDP: 46 per cent vs. 40 per cent. The Alberta Party had eight per cent support while the Liberals had two, the Freedom Conservative Party one, and various other parties 3 per cent.

"The 2019 campaign is one of the nastiest ones I can recall, and as the advance polls open, barring a significant shift in campaign momentum in the final days, it looks like we're getting a new government on April 16th," said ThinkHQ president Marc Henry. "The province-wide vote share for the NDP, while closing on the UCP, is very inefficient. Notley's problem is both geography and math; they are running up the score in Edmonton, but trail everywhere else. The (conservative) vote splits that led to 15 NDP seats in Calgary in 2015 just aren't there today."[34]

For Notley, Calgary was the battleground. Thus on Monday 15 April, she donned a hard hat and work boots to tour a pipe fabrication plant in the city for a photo op to help push her own pro-pipeline message to counter Kenney's relentless drumbeat that she was anti-energy and pro-Trudeau. "Through patient and determined action, we have built a durable national consensus on the need for pipelines," said Notley. "A strong and growing majority of Canadians support Alberta pipelines, including in British Columbia. And I intend to keep it that way"[35] (see Jean-Sébastien Rioux's chapter).

For Kenney, the Edmonton region was the battleground but not to win the election. He simply wanted to avoid being shut out of the capital city. Kenney thus spent his last day in Sherwood Park pointing out to a crowd of supporters that 700,000 people had voted in advance polls, three times the number that had voted early in 2015. For him, this was a sign that Albertans wanted a new government: "Just one more sleep, one more day before Albertans have an opportunity to vote for change that gets our province back to work and that gets Alberta back on track."[36]

The following day, election day, proved the opinion polls right. The final tally saw only the UCP and NDP win seats in the legislature. The UCP won sixty-three seats with almost 55 per cent support (a little more than one million votes) while the NDP won twenty-four seats with 33 per cent support (almost 620,000 votes). No other party came close.[37] The Alberta Party's 172,000 votes represented less than 10 per cent of the provincial total and the Liberals, once a major player in Alberta politics, fared even worse with 18,500 votes, or one per cent of the total. Both had been squeezed out of the middle of the political spectrum by the NDP.

The results indicated a lopsided win and geographical split in Alberta for the UCP that dominated Calgary and rural Alberta, but was virtually shut out of Edmonton where the NDP captured every seat but one. The Capital City was an island of NDP orange in an ocean of UCP blue.

Kenney's victory speech on election night glossed over the regional imbalance as he struck a defiant tone aimed at the federal Liberal government. "Today we begin to stand up for ourselves, our jobs and our future," declared Kenney. "Today we Albertans begin to fight back."[38] Kenney had wanted this to be a campaign about the economy, jobs, and pipelines. And he won. Fears over the economy drove the campaign and captured the attention of voters. Not fears over Kenney's socially conservative history, or the intolerant comments from some of his candidates, or an RCMP investigation into the 2017 UCP leadership race.

This was a campaign about who could best kick-start the economy, help create jobs, and get an energy pipeline to the all-important "tidewater." This was a campaign about the anger and frustration of many Albertans who felt the province, still suffering through a recession, had been forgotten or abandoned by the federal government and other parts of the country. Kenney had blamed the NDP's carbon tax for killing jobs, arguing that after four years of incompetence and scheming with her "good friend and ally" Prime Minister Justin Trudeau, Notley had helped destroy Alberta's economy.

These were simplistic and unfair characterizations but, in the midst of an election campaign, politically effective. Kenney had accused the NDP of running an "anger-machine" but he himself was something of a one-man anger juggernaut. Among his promises: enact legislation to "turn off the [oil] taps" to British Columbia to force through a pipeline to the West Coast; hold a provincial referendum to force a change to the federal equalization program; fight the federal carbon tax in court; and begin a constitutional challenge against federal legislation deemed to interfere in Alberta's economic growth. Never mind that constitutional experts said Kenney had little to no hope of succeeding in any of these fights, Albertans just seemed glad he was willing to try. In that, Kenney was channeling the spirit of former-premier Ralph Klein who at one time or another promised to fight the GST, stop same-sex marriage, and withdraw from the equalization program. He didn't do any of those things but conservatives were happy he gave voice to their anger.

Among Kenney's to-do list post-election was a "summer of repeal" where he would hold a legislative session specifically to tear, down, tear up and tear through Notley's legacy. Notley had spent four years planting trees of social justice legislation—and Alberta had just elected a lumberjack. Notley was again relegated to being leader of the official Opposition. However, for the first time in Alberta history the province had an Opposition that was once government, a leader who was once premier, and critics who were once cabinet ministers. "Yes, tonight's vote is not the result we had hoped or worked so hard for," said Notley. "But no matter what our role is in the legislature, we will not rest."[39]

Kenney wasted no time trying to demonstrate how his leadership would bring results for Alberta. Speaking in French during his victory address, Kenney appealed to Quebecers to allow the energy industry to resurrect a proposal to build the Energy East pipeline from Alberta to New Brunswick. The following day, after thanking Kenney for his "elegant gesture" of speaking French, Quebec Premier Francois Legault said "non." "Regarding other oil pipelines, I want to remind him there is no social acceptability for it," said Legault.[40]

Kenney was about to discover that winning the election was the easy part. Governing would prove to be much more difficult.

NOTES

1   Clare Clancy, "'It is a crisis': Alberta premier withdraws support for federal climate plan after Trans Mountain approval quashed," *Edmonton Journal*, 31 August 2018, https://edmontonjournal.com/business/energy/landmark-federal-court-decision-expected-on-trans-mountain-pipeline.

2   *Alberta Hansard*, 18 March 2019, Legislative Assembly of Alberta, 29th Legislature, Fifth Session, 1–5, https://docs.assembly.ab.ca/LADDAR_files/docs/hansards/han/legislature_29/session_5/20190318_1500_01_han.pdf.

3   Emma Graney, "NDP's pre-election throne speech promises to defend against 'American-style health care,'" *Edmonton Journal*, 18 March 2019, https://edmontonjournal.com/news/politics/throne-speech-to-kick-off-final-session-before-alberta-election.

4	Charles Rusnell, "RCMP take Over investigation of United Conservative Party 'irregular financial contribution' allegations," *CBC News*, 15 March 2019, https://www.cbc.ca/news/canada/edmonton/alberta-rcmp-investigation-ucp-financial-contributions-1.5057255.

5	Graham Thomson, "'Them's fighting words': The Alberta election campaign begins," *CBC News*, 19 March 2019, https://www.cbc.ca/news/canada/edmonton/alberta-election-campaign-begins-1.5063686.

6	Drew Anderson, "Rachel Notley and Jason Kenney go head to head as Alberta election called for April 16," *CBC News*, 19 March 2019, https://www.cbc.ca/news/canada/calgary/alberta-election-1.5062451.

7	Slav Kornik, "Alberta Election: Jason Kenney LGBTQ record hot button issue," *Global News*, 21 March 2019, https://globalnews.ca/news/5080076/alberta-election-jason-kenney-lgbtq/.

8	Tyler Dawson, "Alberta election expected to focus on the economy—but NDP hopes to make it all about Jason Kenney," *National Post*, 19 March 2019, https://nationalpost.com/news/politics/alberta-election-2019.

9	*Ibid.*

10	Global/Ipsos Poll, "UCP (52%) Well in Front of NDP (35%) as April 16 Election Called," 19 March 2019, https://www.ipsos.com/en-ca/news-polls/ucp-in-front-of-ndp-leading-to-election.

11	Heide Pearson, "UCP leads NDP as 2019 election campaign underway, Albertans split on best leader: Ipsos poll," *Global News*, 19 March 2019, https://globalnews.ca/news/5069555/ucp-lead-ndp-election-poll-ipsos-march-19/.

12	"UCP candidate steps down after allegations she used white supremacist language," *CTV News*, 19 March 2019, https://edmonton.ctvnews.ca/ucp-candidate-steps-down-after-allegations-she-used-white-supremacist-language-1.4341966.

13	Tyler Dawson, "Alberta election expected to focus on the economy."

14	Michelle Bellefontaine, "UCP candidate Mark Smith under fire for 'homosexual love' comments in 2013 sermon," *CBC News*, 2 April 2019, https://www.cbc.ca/news/canada/edmonton/ucp-mark-smith-drayton-valley-homosexual-1.5081799.

15	*Ibid.*

16	Karen Bartco, "Transcript: Charles Adler's fiery interview with UCP Leader Jason Kenney," *Global News*, 4 April 2019, https://globalnews.ca/news/5129721/alberta-election-charles-adler-jason-kenney-transcript/.

17	*Ibid.*

18	*Ibid.*

19	*Ibid.*

20	"Alberta Strong and Free: United Conservative Party Platform," March 2019, https://albertastrongandfree.ca/wp-content/uploads/2019/04/Alberta-Strong-and-Free-Platform-1.pdf.

21	*Ibid.*

22 Jennifer Ivanov, "Notley unveils Alberta NDP election platform," *Global News*, 31 March 2019, https://globalnews.ca/news/5115957/notley-unveils-alberta-ndp-election-platform/.

23 *Ibid.*

24 Graham Thomson, "In the Alberta leaders debate, nobody scored the knock-out punch," *CBC News*, 4 April 2019, https://www.cbc.ca/news/canada/edmonton/opinion-in-the-alberta-leaders-debate-nobody-scored-the-knock-out-punch-1.5085755.

25 *The Current*, "Albertans are 'yawning' over Jason Kenney, Jeff Callaway controversy, says columnist," *CBC Radio*, 18 March 2019, https://www.cbc.ca/radio/thecurrent/the-current-for-march-18-2019-1.5060777/albertans-are-yawning-over-jason-kenney-jeff-callaway-controversy-says-columnist-1.5060809.

26 *Ibid.*

27 Graham Thomson, "In the Alberta leaders debate."

28 *Ibid.*

29 Alberta Liberal, *The 2019 Election Platform*, https://www.albertaliberal.com/2019_election_platform.

30 Emma Graney, "Kenney's oil war room plan 'juvenile': Alberta Party leader Stephen Mandel," *Edmonton Journal*, 31 December 2018, https://edmontonjournal.com/news/politics/kenneys-oil-war-room-plan-juvenile-alberta-party-leader-stephen-mandel.

31 Emma Graney, "Alberta Election 2019: Here's what the NDP, UCP and other parties promised during the campaign," *Edmonton Journal*, 16 April 2019, https://edmontonjournal.com/news/politics/election-platforms-what-we-know-so-far.

32 Michelle Bellefontaine, "UCP Leader Jason Kenney defends allowing parental notification if child joins GSA," *CBC News*, 26 March 2019, https://www.cbc.ca/news/canada/edmonton/ucp-leader-jason-kenney-defends-allowing-parental-notification-if-child-joins-gsa-1.5072253.

33 Graham Thomson, "Is the NDP's anti-Kenney strategy making the fight more difficult?" *CBC News*, 12 April 2019, https://www.cbc.ca/news/canada/edmonton/alberta-election-rachel-notley-jason-kenney-campaign-strategy-1.5096675.

34 Marc Henry, "Alberta Votes 2019—The Provincial Political Horserace," ThinkHQ Public Affairs, 9 April 2019, https://thinkhq.ca/alberta-votes-2019-the-provincial-political-horserace/.

35 Lauren Krugel and Dean Bennet, "Alberta's Notley talks pipelines, energy on last day of election campaign," *The Canadian Press*, 15 April 2019, https://lethbridgenewsnow.com/2019/04/17/albertas-notley-talks-pipelines-energy-on-last-day-of-election-campaign-2/.

36 Dean Bennet, "Alberta leaders renew attacks on final full day of election campaign," *The Canadian Press*, 15 April 2019 , https://www.winnipegfreepress.com/arts-and-life/life/greenpage/alberta-leaders-renew-attacks-on-final-full-day-of-election-campaign-508609642.html.

37 Elections Alberta, 2019 Provincial General Election Official Results Released, 26 April 2019, https://www.elections.ab.ca/resources/media/news-releases/2019/04/26/2019-provincial-general-election-official-results-released/.

38 Brooklyn Neustaeter, "Jason Kenney's UCP wins majority government in Alberta," *CTV News*, Tuesday, 16 April 2019, https://www.ctvnews.ca/politics/jason-kenney-s-ucp-wins-majority-government-in-alberta-1.4381734.

39 Graham Thomson, "How will Kenney unite Albertans after divisive campaign? For Alberta conservatives, their free-enterprise knight in shining armour has arrived," *CBC News*, 17 April 2019, https://www.cbc.ca/news/canada/edmonton/kenney-campaign-premier-1.5101250.

40 Philip Authier, "Alberta natural gas is welcome—but not oil pipelines, Legault says," *Montreal Gazette*, 17 April 2019, https://montrealgazette.com/news/quebec/alberta-natural-gas-is-welcome-but-not-oil-pipelines-legault-says.

The Alberta 2019 Election Online: A Turn to Two Party Electoral Dominance?

Peter Malachy Ryan and Kate Toogood

This chapter analyzes, from a political communication perspective, how the "new knowledge logic" of algorithmic media technologies,[1] which were available via the Alberta party websites during the 2019 election, were employed by the parties to disseminate the main framing language used in their party platforms. The top five parties in the campaign, as tracked in the mainstream media and polls during the election, are the focus of this analysis (listed here alphabetically): the Alberta Party (AP), Alberta Liberal Party (ALP), Freedom Conservative Party (FCP), New Democratic Party (NDP), and United Conservative Party (UCP). To note, analysis of the FCP is limited because that party did not run a full slate of candidates and could not feasibly form government. Overall, the digital party communication vehicles were assessed for their constructions of idealized voting groups and rhetorical communities to understand the top issues communicated during the election, with the aim of revealing keys to successful campaign strategies online. This paper argues that a turn to two-party dominance is clear from the captured data points, including social media reach, party donations, and third-party support. Further, from a framing theory perspective of strategic communication, it is clear that the NDP-UCP battle was framed as the nurturing parent vs. strict parent, respectively.[2]

Automated digital humanities methods identified the dominant issues that parties developed online and successfully amplified via social media (specifically, Facebook, Instagram, and Twitter in this analysis). With an emphasis on the NDP and UCP campaigns, this paper assesses the effectiveness of the communication strategies employed and how "master brands" were developed to attract and cultivate voters' support.[3]

Two dominant visions of Alberta came to the forefront in the 2019 election (see Figure 2.1a and 2.1b): (1) the Kenney UCP's "jobs, economy, pipelines" nostalgic strict-father vision, and (2) the Notley NDP's "fighting for you" progressive, protective, yet nurturing-parent vision. The 16 April 2019 Alberta election resulted in a majority government, with sixty-three seats for the UCP. The UCP win was built on Kenney's vision for the province, developed over his rapid rise to provincial leadership for the new party formed in 2017 from the remnants of the Progressive Conservatives (PCs) and Wildrose parties. The NDP under Rachel Notley had their seat total cut in half from their 2015 majority government: from forty-eight seats to twenty-four, which is still among the most opposition seats held by non-conservatives in the legislature since 1993, when the Decore Liberals held thirty-two. The AP and ALP both lost their seats, marking the first time since 1993 that only two parties occupied the legislature. It was also the first time for a governing party to lose a majority but not entirely disappear after the election, with the NDP leader and ten cabinet ministers remaining.

The election had the highest voter turnout since 1982 at 64 per cent, up from 57 per cent in 2015. This was the fifth change of government since Alberta had become a province in 1905, and the first time a provincial government had failed to win a second term. In that context, the stage is set for the 2023 election to possibly have Notley and the NDP become the first premier and party to return to government after an election loss. This study presents the online tools and communication strategies that led to this two-party battle of competing visions for Alberta, which will continue to play out until the next provincial election in 2023, and has established a fundamental change from the previous forty-four years of nearly uncontested PC dominance in the province.

Analyzing political communication strategies helps to assess the comparative health of Alberta's democracy. Alberta's democracy is certainly

Figures 2.1a and 2.1b. The 2019 Election Master Brands of the NDP and UCP

Sources: Bill Kaufman, "Notley-Trudeau 'sabotage' of Alberta economy to be answered with constitutional challenge: Kenney," *Calgary Herald*, 21 March 2019, https://calgaryherald.com/news/local-news/notley-promises-2000-more-long-term-care-beds-warns-ucp-is-on-the-road-to-american-style-health-care

Sources: Justin Giovanetti, "Alberta election 2019: NDP seat count cut by more than half as Notley's historic run comes to an end," *Globe and Mail*, 17 April 2019, https://www.theglobeandmail.com/canada/article-alberta-election-2019-ndp-seat-count-cut-by-more-than-half-as-notley

not in decline in terms of the historic level of party donations, at least for the NDP and UCP, and the amount of social media use by both parties and citizens. Notably, the polarization of the social media sphere has benefited the two dominant political parties, though the tone of communication mirrors some of the worst conspiratorial and misinformation tendencies south of the border, exemplified during the Trump presidency leading to the Capitol Riots on 6 January 2021. And while new parties have been created in Alberta (for example, AP, FCP and the Wildrose Independence Party of Alberta [WIPA]) in the hopes of creating a more diverse body politick, money and electoral support have not yet moved toward them; those parties lack visible leaders, candidates with staying power and overall media presence—but they nonetheless contribute to polarization online. Monitoring that polarization is important for gauging the stability of the newly formed UCP under Kenney, and whether the right-wing factions of the party could split again.[4]

Put into context, David Stewart and R. Kenneth Carty's "many political worlds" party-system theory has changed on the prairies with Alberta, Manitoba, and Saskatchewan each having two dominant parties in their legislatures after recent elections.[5] For instance, Manitoba's 2019 election resulted in another conservative majority, with Brian Pallister's PCs winning thirty-six seats, and new leader Wab Kinew's NDPs winning eighteen (the Liberals lost one seat, taking three in total, losing official party status, which requires four seats). Similarly, the 2016 election in Saskatchewan saw conservative Brad Wall lead the Saskatchewan Party to win fifty-one seats, and the NDP ten; while the 2020 election won Wall forty-eight seats, and the NDP thirteen. Given these trends until the end of 2020, Roger Gibbins' earlier insights about the prairies remain informative as regionalism and western alienation fluctuate again in favour of conservative party dominance from Alberta to Manitoba.[6] This two-party dominance dynamic is analyzed in what follows, particularly how social media and policies related to social media have affected the political shift.

The Effects of Social Media Policy Changes: Election Disruptions and Amplifications

Many of the significant changes online during the 2019 Alberta election were documented by researchers in real time.[7] For instance, Jared Wesley partnered with Darkhorse Analytics to monitor Twitter, finding that parties used it to set the agenda of issues being discussed. They documented "a huge spike on March 25 in favour of the NDP on civic rights and education. That spike flowed from the UCP's education platform announcement, which was criticized for its stance on gay-straight alliances (GSAs)."[8] Similarly, Livewire Calgary used the Talkwalker's Free Social Search to study the #abvote hashtag, and others associated with it, for the weeks of 30 March to 5 April, and 6 to 12 April 2019—they likewise identified an agenda-setting use, and the negative sentiment of online discussion, which reflected key disruptions in the race, polarized by the two-dominant parties' supporters and third-party advertisers (TPAs).[9]

"Bots" (fake social media user accounts) and their constructed server-farm amplification of key messages also played a role in the election. Initially, researchers determined that less than 5 per cent of Twitter activity linked with the main parties' communications was due to bot traffic prior to the election writ dropping on 19 March.[10] However, by 13 April, the "Alberta Federation of Labour found that in a five-week period from February to March, nearly one-third of Alberta political tweets were by either bots or humans amplified by bots."[11] These two data points demonstrate an increase in bot traffic as the election proceeded. Both the NDP and UCP used bots for the first time in an Alberta election to text voters, in attempts to assess voter support and gain donations.[12]

Table 2.1 provides a timeline of the main election campaign disruptions to offer context to party scandals and self-inflicted wounds that were amplified by social media.[13]

Scott Pruysers identified how provincial parties with strong alignment to federal parties were better able to communicate professionally during election campaigns due, in part, to shared staff, research, and tools.[14] However, in 2019, the best-funded UCP campaign had a rocky start, in spite of shared federal Conservative Party resources, electoral support for Kenney, and the Alberta PC's historical ties. Early in pre-election

Table 2.1. Alberta 2019 Election Campaign Disruptions—
A Timeline

DATE	ONLINE EVENT OR ISSUE	CAMPAIGN DISRUPTED
9 February 2019	Alberta Party leader Stephen Mandel declared ineligible to run by Elections Alberta because of late paperwork submission (the decision was reversed on 4 March)	AP
24 February 2019	Notley campaigns inside a hospital, breaking election laws	NDP
19 March 2019: Election starts (right after the 18 March Speech from the Throne)		
20 March 2019	Robocalls and text messages from both parties (i.e., virtual door knocking)	NDP and UCP
20 March 2019	UCP Calgary-Mountain View candidate Caylan Ford withdraws from the election because of leaked private Facebook messages	UCP
21 March 2019	20-year-old video of Jason Kenney used to critique his past LGBTQ record	UCP
23 March 2019	"6.9m" road sign modified by two UCP staffers near Kenney speaking to the media	UCP
25 March 2019	UCP Calgary-South East candidate Eva Kiryakos withdraws from the election to avoid being a distraction based on past comments about Muslim refugees and transgender people	UCP
27 March 2019	UCP Edmonton-Gold Bar candidate David Dorward critiqued for statements made in 2016 about transgender people	UCP
2 April 2019	UCP Drayton Valley-Devon candidate Mark Smith's comments advocating the firing of gay teachers critiqued	UCP
12 April 2019	RCMP search business owned by Calgary UCP candidate Peter Singh	UCP

Sources: Data compiled by the authors.

campaigning, Kenney dealt with critiques ranging from having rigged his UCP leadership campaign with a Kamikaze candidate, to stating that "[m]en are better at 'Tactical Politics'" than women—which led to the hashtag "#BetterOffWithRachel" trending on 3 March 2019.[15]

Conversely, very well-run campaigns that do nearly everything right still cannot guarantee a win. In the NDP's case, anger had built up in the province, shifting votes away from the party, and leading to the NDP's negative shadow campaign through the third-party group Press Progress (which eventually became viewed as directly connected to the party). Notley also had a few missteps before the election was called: the $9.87 million cost for the "Keep Alberta Working" advertising campaign and surveys connected with monitoring its success, as well as campaigning in a hospital before the election period, which broke Alberta election laws.

Many Albertans noted the negative tone of the social media campaigns, though it's up for debate whether the sentiment was any different from the previous election. Table 2.1 also excludes at least three more UCP candidate mis-steps, such as robo-calls in Stephen Mandel's riding during the campaign, or the multiple candidates who stepped down because of comments made—all of which demonstrate social media's power to "cancel" political candidates, or hold them to account, depending on the context. Several other "kamikaze candidate" revelations could be added to Table 2.1, to document questions about the UCP leadership campaign. Such instances demonstrate that the UCP's path to victory could potentially have been bigger if the party had better vetted its candidates.

On 13 April 2019, advanced polling ended with Elections Alberta estimating a record 696,000 votes cast, demonstrating a highly engaged electorate. Within this context, it is important to assess the partisan communication strategies and tactics that led to the two competing visions of Alberta.

The Case Study: Analyzing Competing Issue Networks for the Online Campaigns

This content analysis reviews (1) party websites, (2) the top issues that were communicated and the associated issue networks on party apps and platforms, and (3) the partisan social media campaigns. In plain terms, the content-analysis methods employed below include counting the web tools, social media followers, and views or uses of pertinent social media channels for each of the top parties.[16]

1) The New Democratic Party and United Conservative Party Websites

The website content analysis focuses on the two parties that won seats in the legislature: the NDP and the UCP (see Table 2.2). In terms of social

Table 2.2. The New Democratic Party and United Conservative Party Website Splash Pages and Digital Tools

Donation link:	Yes
Newsletter link:	Yes
Issue summary:	Yes
Candidate links:	Yes
Email link:	Yes
Facebook link:	Yes
Twitter link:	Yes
Instagram link:	Yes
YouTube link:	No

Donation link:	Yes
Newsletter link:	Yes
Issue summary:	Yes
Candidate links:	Yes
Email link:	Yes
Facebook link:	Yes
Twitter link:	Yes
Instagram link:	Yes
YouTube link:	No

tools, the 2019 Alberta election websites saw the removal of an official YouTube link and the addition of the first Instagram links on the party websites, as compared to the party websites captured in *Orange Chinook*,[17] which documented the 2015 election as the first to see the political parties reach a professional level of online campaigning. The 2019 websites demonstrated the continuation of professional practices reached in the 2015 election, based on the stable funding for the top two parties. However, the speed at which the UCP ramped up their online presence following the merger of its two predecessors, the PCs and Wildrose party respectively, should be noted.

2) *The Apps and the Party Platform's Top Issues and Associated Issue Networks*

None of the parties began the race using apps for data collection while campaigning door to door, because cellphone and tablet batteries do not last very long when there is still snow on the ground, as was the case in March and early April of 2019. Nonetheless, it was the first Alberta election to reach the same level of market surveillance first achieved in the 2015 federal election with the use of apps and social media combined. For instance, the NDP used two apps (see Figure 2.2): (1) "Forward" was a closed, safe party-supporter community that required users to be invited into it, and (2) "Organizer Canvassing" was used to track voter sentiment at the door. The UCP had a derivative of the federal "C2G" app (or "Conservative to Go") to monitor voter sentiment and issues at the door stop (or if recorded on paper, to be put into the database system at the party headquarters when the app couldn't be used due to weather).

It is important to note that no partisan communication officer or party official would go on the record to confirm that data and information is shared between provincial and federal factions, due to the grey area of political parties using third parties to collect and share voter information; however, off the record, the practice is not just common, but rampant. Voters are unaware of the end-use agreements that allow the party to share voter information with third-party groups, especially via apps used at the door.[18] The UCP and NDP data links with respective federal party networks gave them an advantage over the other parties in the race, as even the ALP third-party access to the federal Liberal database wouldn't have been able to monitor sentiment as well without the same number of volunteers compared to the two dominant parties.

In short, the use of apps by the NDP and UCP allowed for greater voter data tracking, as well as aligning agenda setting with party platforms (i.e., the political manifestos). Local riding representatives were able to try out different messaging at the door, then document if it was useful. If the messaging was effective, it could be amplified online or in the release of the final platform.

Party platforms are a key strategic political communication document for agenda setting during elections.[19] The following content analysis illustrates the links between the NDP and UCP's respective master brands. Figure 2.3 presents a sample of the top forty key words (or "issue units") in the platforms, using common open source concordance lists, visualized using a relational mapping software called RéseauLu.[20] This method focuses on nouns, cutting out some 350 standard "stop words" (i.e., articles,

Figure 2.2. The Three Main Apps in the Campaign

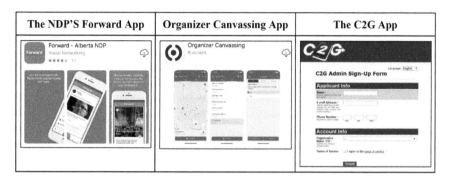

The NDP'S Forward App	Organizer Canvassing App	The C2G App

conjunctions, prepositions, etc.), narrowing in on the top 30 to 40 per cent of repeated words in the document. The method assumes that successfully branded communications are not buried; rather, political parties repeat their top messages. Such repetition is clearly found in the UCP's "jobs, economy, pipelines" slogan, along with other UCP words such as "red tape" and "carbon emissions," which contrasts with the NDP's use of "climate change" (see Figure 2.3).

The two large nodes in Figure 2.3's relational map identify that the UCP and NDP shared the most "issue units" compared with the other parties' platforms (inclusive of the AP and ALP, as the FCP's few links didn't even plot on the map). Using network theory, political analysts and strategists review such maps to understand if the network is homogenous or heterogenous. The central solid-lined sphere identifies the words or issue units that all the parties used in their platforms, homogeneously bringing them together: "Alberta," "Albertans," "care," "education," "government," "industry," "plan," "program," "seniors," "services." However, the points of potential heterogeneity (or difference) among these four platforms are quite small, with the biggest overlap coming between the NDP and UCP, which both focused on "access," communities," "crime," "families," infrastructure," "investment," "jobs," and the two urban battlegrounds of "Calgary" and "Edmonton."

In contrast, the dotted-line spheres in this image identify the party branding and differentiation targets. For example, the UCP did not mention Notley by name or office; they focused on the NDP only as a party,

Figure 2.3. RéseauLu Visualization of the Top 40 Issues Units for Each Party

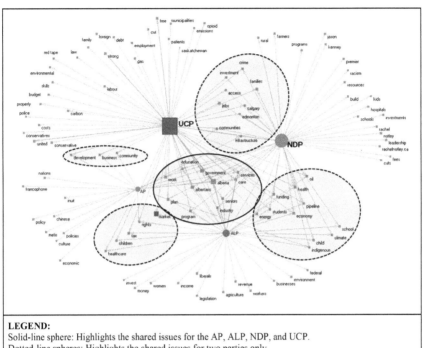

LEGEND:
Solid-line sphere: Highlights the shared issues for the AP, ALP, NDP, and UCP.
Dotted-line spheres: Highlights the shared issues for two parties only.

while the NDP clearly branded "Rachel Notley" as the leader in their platform, and targeted "Jason Kenney." These choices demonstrate the political calculation for the UCP to avoid targeting the well-liked Notley over
the less popular party brand in Alberta, while the NDP chose to target
Kenney's favourability, based on his low poll numbers with undecided
voters, as compared to focusing on the new UCP's developing brand.

Clear branding or differentiation in the AP and ALP top key words
is not found. In political marketing analyses, this arguably means voters
would have had a tougher time knowing what each party was communicating, selling, or offering. This lack of clarity would also affect any circulated media or social media amplifications of those parties' messages.

Importantly, the top issues are not targeted at ethnic, racial, regional
(even rural versus urban voters), or other subject position variations in

terms of creating rhetorical communities to attract voters. Instead, they create two competing visions of Alberta, targeting generic "middle class" nuclear family voters. Such political marketing strategies were used during the federal election in 2015 and 2019, and are now evidently also being employed at the provincial level.

Of note in 2021, the UCP platform did not mention any revision to coal policy, and the document only mentioned "climate change" twice, stating: "The world is grappling with the tension between our need for the carbon-based energy industry and a consensus that its emissions are directly contributing to climate change. The United Conservatives are committed to responsible energy development and that includes action to mitigate greenhouse emissions and reduce their contribution to climate change."[21] "Carbon tax" was mentioned thirty-one times, while "greenhouse gas" emissions were mentioned four times.

In contrast, "climate" was mentioned nine times in the NDP platform, with a focus on the NDP's Climate Leadership Plan, and not a "carbon tax" (no mentions), but a "carbon levy" (one mention). "Greenhouse gas" emissions were mentioned three times. This demonstrates the NDP's strategy to downplay their green initiatives, in favour of focusing on common NDP safe areas like education, health care, and supporting working families. In this way, several pundits identified that the NDP platform avoided running on their economic or energy programs, which some viewed as a strategic error, particularly in hindsight—during the pandemic, Alberta's economy cratered.

3) Partisan Social Media: The Horse Race Online

In the 2019 election, Kenney had a clear lead on social media that was built during his tenure as a federal cabinet minister under Prime Minister Harper (from 2006 to 2015); it is rare to start well ahead of an incumbent premier in terms of social media metrics (see Figure 2.4). Obviously, social media followers do not equal supporters as in polling, but in this instance, the correlated support did hold true for the Kenney UCP win on election day. In the data tracked, Kenney ended up leading in all areas: (1) Facebook "Likes" (131,600 to Notley's 68,674), (2) Facebook "Followers" (133,385 to Notley's 70,359), (3) Twitter followers (172,000 to Notley's 121,000), and (4) Instagram followers (20,500 to Notley's 14,700).

Figure 2.4. The Leaders' Facebook Accounts: Likes

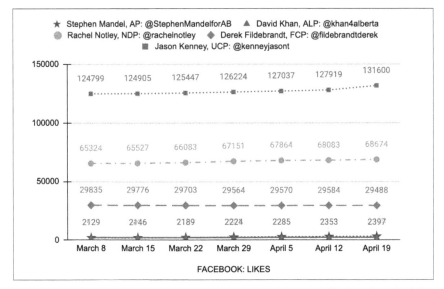

Note: The televised Leaders' debate was 4 April. Stephen Mandel's values here are hidden behind David Kahn's, but are relatively in line. Due to space limitations, some of the lower performing leader and party values are cut off in the tables that follow. The entire data set for the social media content analysis tracked in the following tables is available here: https://docs.google.com/spreadsheets/d/1PvrZKbdr4EIgHOOsd8yqI4c9To-8u-h4P75j8Grh48E/edit?usp=sharing (accessed 1 July 2020).

Figure 2.5. The Parties' Facebook Account: Likes

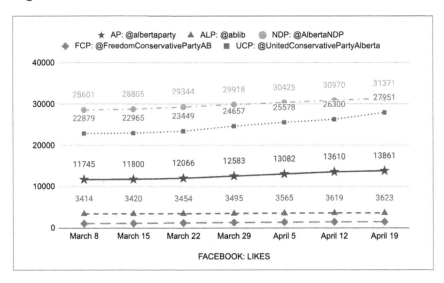

No clear turning points online were evident from this sample, as steady growth for the top two parties was documented throughout the sample (as in Figure 2.4, for example). The televised Leaders' debate was on 4 April 2019, but it did not demonstrate any change in support for the top two parties, which reflects common analyses that most Albertans had decided who they would vote for early in the race. Overall though, the two-party dominance for the NDP and UCP leaders was clear in all social media accounts tracked.

In contrast to the leader accounts, the NDP account led the social media metrics over that of the newly formed UCP, who were starting from behind (see for example, Figure 2.5). In sum, the data trends once again demonstrate the lead of the same two parties online, with the lone exception of the AP's Twitter coming in above the UCP's. Compare the final 19 April metrics for social media accounts at the party level: Facebook "Likes" (the NDP's 31,371 to the UCP's 27,951), "Followers" (the NDP's 31,777 to the UCP's 29,489), Twitter followers (the NDP's 31,900 to the AP's 15,500), and Instagram followers (the NDP's 3,506 to the UCP's 1,623).

Of note here is how the scalability of the 2019 Alberta election's online activity compares with the numbers collected in the three previous Alberta elections.[22] The 2019 scale for rural Alberta is similar to the numbers found in 2008's urban social media numbers (moving from hundreds to thousands of followers online); local urban ridings are at the 2012 election level (in the tens of thousands), but the leaders in 2019 at the provincial levels are reaching numbers that federal leaders achieved in the 2015 election (in the hundreds of thousands). This demonstrates the scalability of social media networks that increase in density and interactions over time. Another finding in these numbers is the clear possibility that the top two parties may have also benefited from constructed "bot" leads, versus constructed losses, in that there were similar gains week after week over the duration of the election in the hundreds of followers.[23]

Analysis and Discussion: Party Election Spending, Third Parties, and Polling

Cournoyer (2019) studied party fundraising and spending accounts for the 2019 election and found UCP and NDP spending was well above any of the other parties. The UCP spent "$4,561,362.10, while raising $3,889,582.70 during the campaign period, ending the campaign with a deficit of $671,779.40."[24] The NDP spent "$5,363,029.30 and raised $3,706,785.66, ending the campaign with a deficit of $1,656,043.64."[25] In a distant third, the AP "raised $206,597 and spent $199,935 during the campaign period."[26]

Beyond party spending totals, Table 2.3 demonstrates the size of TPA groups online, and how this was the first Alberta election where online activity, particularly social media, was a factor in amplifying partisan messages. Alberta Elections reported the total registered spending contributions for TPAs as $1,035,103.17.[27] In November 2016, TPAs in Alberta were required to register separately for election advertising versus political advertising that happened before the election period; the following totals are for the election period ending on 18 April 2019.

In contrast to the official TPA, Table 2.4 presents a list of unregistered third-party groups who also posted messages during the election period, without any consequences for breaking election laws being documented by Alberta Elections. The two types of third-party groups taken together demonstrate a sea change in online activity during a provincial election—Canada's versions of the US "Super PACs." The main concern for Albertans in this context is that the unregistered groups may spread misinformation, and can be problematic for democratic communications, particularly in light of rising conspiracy and hate messaging that has been linked with the Yellow Vest social media groups.

Some groups not listed here also affected the election, such as Alberta Advantage, which didn't operate in 2019, but raised over $1 million in 2017, helping to target the NDP over the carbon tax. Future research into the impacts of TPAs during campaigns could include the role of the mainstream media (MSM) and non-MSM media (such as Breakdown, Press Progress, Rebel Media, the Western Standard, etc.) in amplifying messages and how misinformation can be addressed via platform algorithms and policies. In all cases, third parties can be more extreme in their messaging than political parties, contributing to greater polarization, and their role in 2023's election will have to be monitored, particularly as social media platforms have increased their vetting and policies regarding disinformation and misinformation during the COVID pandemic and subsequent

Table 2.3. Registered Third-Party Advertising Groups (Alberta Elections, 2019)

Alberta Federation of Labour (Messaging: Left leaning): $253,339.89
Facebook Likes: 16,105 | Facebook Followers: 16,078

Alberta Firefighters Association (Messaging: Left leaning): $91,822.52
Facebook Likes: 3,321 | Facebook Followers: 3,371

Alberta Medical Association (Messaging: Left leaning): Not engaged in election event
Facebook Likes: 5,370 | Facebook Followers: 5,479

Alberta Proud: @AlbertaProud.org (Messaging: Right leaning): $165,450.44
Facebook Likes: 174,456 | Facebook Followers: 173,250

Alberta Teachers Association (Messaging: Left leaning): $253,339.89
Tweets: 15.7K | Following: 2,151 | Followers: 24.7K
Facebook Likes: 11,568 | Facebook Followers: 11,904

Shaping Alberta's Future: @shapingalberta (Messaging: Right leaning): $298,000.00
Tweets: 104 | Following: 1,448 | Followers: 1,464
Facebook Likes: 4,210 | Facebook Followers: 4,263

Note: Groups are listed alphabetically. Totals are for the end of the election on 18 April 2019: Alberta Elections, "Third Party Advertisers—Election Alberta," 2019, https://www.elections.ab.ca/political-participants/third-party-advertisers/.

elections. For instance, some TPAs have already turned against Kenney (such as Alberta Blue Skies, not listed in Table 2.3).

About a month out from the 2019 election day, some media polls were identifying that the NDP might be making up ground in Calgary through their door-to-door campaign and grassroots efforts. However, those urban gains were only reflected in the NDP stronghold of Edmonton in the end. In fact, tracking polls demonstrated a similar lead for the UCP from the moment they merged in fall 2017 to election day in April 2019 (see below). Heading into election day, it was clear that the Alberta election had been a two-party race for the entire period, with no possibility of a minority government forming (see Figure 2.6).

Conclusion and Looking Ahead

The Alberta 2019 election was a two-party race in (1) the use of professionally integrated websites, party apps, and databases, (2) targeted platform communications, (3) party fundraising and spending, (4) partisan social

Table 2.4. What about the Unregistered Third-Party Groups' Social Media Numbers?

Albertans against the NDP (Messaging: Right leaning)
Facebook Likes: 49,218 | Facebook Followers: 47,401

Albertans against the UCP (Messaging: Left leaning)
Facebook Likes: 13,078 | Facebook Followers: 14,331

Debunk Inc: @debunkinc (Messaging: Right leaning)
Tweets: 7,301 | Following: 4,360 | Followers: 3,045
Facebook Likes: 26,936 | Facebook Followers: 27,022

Energy Now: @EnergyNow (Messaging: Right leaning)
Tweets: 2,781 | Following: 906 | Followers: 1,737
Facebook Likes: 989 | Facebook Followers: 1,064

Oils Sands Action: @OilsandsAction (Messaging: Right leaning)
Tweets: 3,401 | Following: 574 | Followers: 59.7K
Facebook Likes: 193,416 | Facebook Followers: 191,734

Press Progress (Messaging: Left leaning)
Tweets: 12.8K | Following: 1,783 | Followers: 16.7K
Facebook Likes: 136,107 | Facebook Followers: 134,966

Yellow Vests Alberta Page (Messaging: Right leaning)
@AlbertaForResponsibleGovernment
Facebook Likes: 4,732 | Facebook Followers: 4,833

Yellow Vest: @YellowVestsCA (National group; Messaging: Right leaning)
Tweets: 327 | Following: 774 | Followers: 787

@YellowVestsCanada1 (National group; Messaging: Right leaning)
Facebook Likes: 1,519 | Facebook Followers: 1,567

Yellow Vests Canada Facebook Group (National group; Messaging: Right leaning)
108,569 Members

Note: Groups are listed alphabetically. Totals are for the end of the election on 18 April 2019.

Sources: Data compiled by the authors.

media amplification potential from third parties, (5) the polls, and (6) the final election results. In total, the content analysis of the NDP and UCP's websites and the social media strategy used in the election reinforces a competition between the two parties master brands and visions for the province, as presented in their platforms. That competition is staged to continue in the 2023 election as well.

Figure 2.6. Alberta Election—16 April 2019—CBC Vote Tracker (Aggregated Polls)

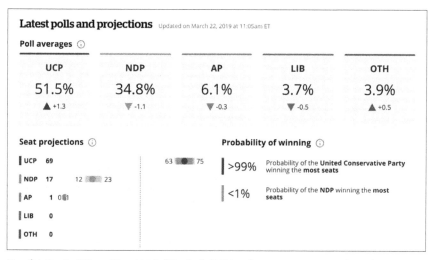

Note: Éric Grenier, "Alberta Votes 2019 Poll Tracker," *CBC News*, https://newsinteractives.cbc.ca/elections/poll-tracker/alberta/ (accessed 22 March 2019).

The issue-networks method identified the top issues communicated during the election, which were amplified via social media groups and TPAs. The method also allows more questions to be raised and explored; for example, which top issue units in the 2019 platforms were missing with the hindsight of the pandemic or other current political issues? Not surprisingly none of the parties used the term "COVID" or "pandemic" in their communications during the election (the virus was first identified in November 2019). However, during the 2019 election, the UCP made a "Health Care Guarantee" to maintain or increase funding. This pledge has since been used to judge the credibility of the UCP's election promises during numerous criticisms of Jason Kenney's handling of the pandemic, including on-going troubled labour negotiations with doctors and nurses and negative voter reaction to some of Kenney's team going on vacation during the travel lockdown at the end of 2020.

At the time of publication, Kenney's UCP have been hammered in the polls for creating new policies not documented in their platform, or policies that went against their original platform promises, such as education and health care cuts, new Alberta Parks policies, a new coal policy, a referendum on equalization, and an Alberta-only pension and police force (that is, no longer using the federal RCMP). These latter trial balloons were not in their original party platform, but emerged via Kenney's Fair Deal Panel after Trudeau's federal re-election win, which, along with communication issues during the COVID pandemic, have led to the Kenney UCP losing credibility and trust from voters. The UCP have gone against their small government brand during the pandemic and possibly permanently damaged their reputation; their new policies might lead to a further loss of support. Current polls show many urban Albertans are feeling more connected to the Canadian government because of the pandemic supports: for example, the Canada Emergency Response Benefit (CERB) and vaccinations. These types of strategic political miscalculations by the Kenney UCP could also lead to further internal party struggles.

By early 2021, Kenney's vision for the province no longer aligned with the realities of the COVID-19 pandemic. The UCP dropped significantly in the polls numbers to second place (36.6 per cent), and members of the party have called for Kenney's resignation to avoid potentially losing the 2023 election to Notley's resurgent NDP, presently first place in the polls at 41.6 per cent.[28] The polls reflect how Notley's caring vision for Alberta attracted voters during the pandemic, with the NDP being presented as a government in waiting and their donations doubling that of the UCP in the first quarter of 2021 ($1,186,245 in donations, while the UCP raised $591,597).[29]

Until the UCP's fall in the polls in 2020, Roger Gibbins' earlier insights about the prairies would have remained informative with regionalism and western alienation fluctuating again in favour of conservative party dominance.[30] However, the competing visions of two-party dominance on the prairies have changed since 2019, with conservative parties struggling to deal with the pandemic and satisfy their bases. In Alberta particularly, WIPA formed in 2020, as a reaction to Trudeau's federal election win, and WIPA gained part of the UCP's support lost during the pandemic, sitting at roughly 12 per cent. This could affect the two-party dynamic for the 2023 election, with vote splitting going to the NDP, like some ridings in 2015, when the Wildrose Party still existed.

Tactically, Kenney's UCP "jobs, economy, pipelines" slogan has been used to target the premier's credibility for a vision that does not match the reality of the times, particularly when US President Biden cancelled the Keystone XL pipeline after the UCP made a billion-dollar gamble on it. Kenney's UCP may also have reached the limit of flirting with Trump-style attack tactics, or of floating trial balloons that attract separatists and far-right votes, when most Albertans are realizing that other provinces have fared better against the COVID pandemic, and that the UCP have frequently ended up adopting the Notley NDP's proposals for dealing with the pandemic, representing a clear vision for a government in waiting. Albertans who have received CERB and other supports from the federal government are now reflecting on Quebec's experiences with separation, possibly realizing the value of the open NDP vision of Alberta's future; Alberta may need more federal help going forward to recover from the pandemic, and the NDP may also be more aligned with the new US Biden administration politically.

Overall, the two competing visions of Alberta's future are rooted in the election platform promises and issues networks documented in this analysis. Time and time again, politicians are held to account over how successfully their visions were achieved over their four-year mandates, and we have watched the battle of two competing visions of Alberta play out in the media and polls ever since the 2019 election. This battle is one that did not exist in Alberta during the PC one-party reign for the forty-four years prior to the 2015 election, and democratic theorists would agree that that battle at least allows a greater diversity of voices in the legislature, supported by two professionalized parties. It is important to note that few Canadian political leaders have recovered from polls as negative as those of Jason Kenney's at the time of writing at roughly 31 per cent; for examples, look no further than minority government electoral comebacks, like Pierre Trudeau's 1980 campaign, which only cracked a 4.23 per cent point swing.

So, the question remains, is the next provincial election becoming Rachel Notley's comeback story as the Official Opposition demonstrates they are a government in waiting? Have Albertans decided that the UCP's 2019 election platform promises are a vision of Alberta that no longer matches the times that we live in, and that Alberta was

"#BetterOffWithRachel" and the NDP's new modern vision of a progressive Alberta? The UCP honeymoon period of electoral support is well past, and their team may have succumbed to a loss of momentum and intellectual capital expended to deal with the pandemic. It will ultimately be up to Albertans to decide which vision for the future they support in 2023.

Notes

The authors would like to acknowledge and thank Duane Bratt for comments and feedback on earlier versions of this chapter presented at the Prairie Political Science Association (PPSA) in 2019, and similarly colleagues who attended the Provincial Politics sessions at the Canadian Political Science Association (CPSA) in June 2021.

NOTES

1   For more on algorithmic media, see Tarleton Gillespie, "The Relevance of Algorithms," *Media Technologies* (Cambridge: MIT Press, 2014), 191–192.

2   See, for more on nurturing and strict parent political frames, George Lakoff, *Don't Think of an Elephant* (White River Junction, VT: Chelsea Green Publishing, 2004; 2014).

3   See, for more on political master brands, Alex Marland, *Brand Command: Canadian Politics and Democracy in the Age of Message Control* (Vancouver: UBC Press, 2015).

4   Duane Bratt and Bruce Foster, "The Dealignment and Realignment of Right-Wing Parties in Canada: The Fragility of a 'Big Tent' Conservative Party" (Canadian Political Science Association Annual Conference, University of British Columbia, Vancouver BC, June 2019), https://www.cpsa-acsp.ca/documents/conference/2019/115.Bratt-Foster.pdf.

5   See, David Stewart and R. Kenneth Carty, "Many Political Worlds? Provincial Parties and Party Systems," *Provinces: Canadian Provincial Politics* 2 (2006): 97–113; David K. Stewart and Anthony Sayers, "Albertans' Conservative Beliefs," in *Conservatism in Canada*, ed. James Farney and David Rayside (Toronto: University of Toronto Press, 2013); and David McGrane, *The New NDP: Moderation, Modernization, and Political Marketing* (Vancouver: UBC Press, 2019).

6   Roger Gibbins, *Prairie Politics & Society: Regionalism in Decline* (Toronto: Butterworth & Co., 1980).

7   See, Alex Hamilton, "Social media paints negative picture of Alberta Election," *Livewire Calgary*, 13 April 2019, https://livewirecalgary.com/2019/04/13/alberta-election-do-tweets-tell-a-tale/ (accessed 1 July 2020); Slav Kornik, "University of Alberta group researching Twitter's impact on Alberta election," *Global News*, 1 April 2019, https://globalnews.ca/news/5118360/university-of-alberta-research-twitter-election/2019 (accessed 1 July 2020); Rachel Ward, "Ping! More political texts expected as election season plods on," *CBC News*, 25 March 2019, https://www.cbc.ca/news/canada/calgary/alberta-election-politics-text-messaging-1.5069643 (accessed 1 July 2020).

8   Kornik, "University of Alberta group researching Twitter's impact."

9   Hamilton, "Social media paints negative picture."

10   See, Global News, "How politicians' marketing strategies could impact the 2019 Alberta election," 23 March 2019, https://globalnews.ca/video/5088667/how-politicians-marketing-strategies-could-impact-the-2019-alberta-election.

11   Hamilton, "Social media paints negative picture."

12   Ward, "Ping! More political texts expected."

13   Peter Malachy Ryan documented similarly how social media was used to amplify disruptions in campaigns during the Alberta 2015 election in "Alberta Politics Online: Digital Retail Politics and Grassroots Growth, 2006–2016," in *Orange Chinook*, eds. D. Bratt, K. Brownsey, R. Sutherland, and D. Taras (Calgary: University of Calgary Press, 2019), 103–144.

14   Scott Pruysers, "Two Political Worlds? Multilevel Campaign Integration in Canadian Constituencies," *Regional & Federal Studies* 25, no. 2 (2015): 165–182.

15   Karen Bartko, "UCP leader Jason Kenney tweet backfires as #BetterOffWithRachel trends," *Global News*, 4 March 2019, https://globalnews.ca/news/5018476/jason-kenney-tweet-betteroffwithrachel-trending/ (accessed 1 July 2020).

16   For those interested, more information about the research methods can be found through Ryerson University's Infoscape Research Lab website and their publications. See, for example, Greg Elmer et al., "Election Bloggers: Methods for Determining Political Influence," *First Monday* 12, no. 4 (2007), http://www.firstmonday.org/issues/issue12_4/elmer/index.html; and Greg Elmer et al., "'Blogs I Read': Partisanship and Party Loyalty in the Canadian Political Blogosphere," *Journal of Information Technology and Politics* 6, no. 2 (2009): 156–165, https://www.tandfonline.com/doi/abs/10.1080/19331680902832582 (accessed 1 July 2020); see also Infoscape Research Lab, "Publications," http://infoscapelab.ca/publications/.

17   See Ryan, "Alberta Politics Online."

18   For the examples of political party app data sharing use and abuse see Christian Paas Lang, "Digital tools power parties' election campaigns but privacy a question," *BNN Bloomberg*, 16 September 2019, https://www.bnnbloomberg.ca/digital-tools-power-parties-election-campaigns-but-privacy-a-question-1.1316744 (accessed 1 July 2020); Alex MacPherson, "Conservatives warn Clarke campaign over 'potential unauthorized use' of internal database," *Star Phoenix*, 4 December 2017, https://thestarphoenix.com/news/local-news/conservatives-warn-clarke-campaign-over-potential-unauthorized-use-of-internal-database (accessed 1 July 2020); Laura Payton, "Conservative campaign database fiasco costs party millions," *CBC News*, 23 October 2013, https://www.cbc.ca/news/politics/conservative-campaign-database-fiasco-costs-party-millions-1.2187603 (accessed 1 July 2020); or see more on CIMS via *The Star*'s archive of the PowerPoint explaining the system here: https://thestar.blogs.com/files/cims.ppt (accessed 1 July 2020); or, see the Constituent Information Management System (CIMS) Replacement Project website from MERX here: https://www.merx.com/ontariopc/solicitations/Constituent-Information-Management-System-CIMS-Replacement-Project/0000163201?language=EN (accessed 1 July 2020).

19   See Anna Esselment, "Designing Campaign Platforms," *Journal of Parliamentary and Political Law* [Special Issue] (2015): 179–192; Marland, *Brand Command*; Alex Marland and Thierry Giasson, *Inside the Campaign: Managing Elections in Canada* (Vancouver: UBC Press), https://www.ubcpress.ca/inside-the-campaign-open-access-edition (accessed 1 July 2020); Peter Malachy Ryan, "The Platform As an Agenda-Setting Document," *Journal of Parliamentary and Political Law* [Special Issue] (2015): 193–214; Ryan, "Alberta Politics Online."

20   For more on the issue networks method, see for example, Noortje Marres, "Net-work Is Format Work: Issue Networks and the Sites of Civil Society Politics," in *Reformatting Politics: Information Technology and Global Civil Society*, eds. Jodi Dean, Jon W. Anderson, and Geert Lovink (New York: Routledge, 2006); Noortje Marres and Richard Rogers, "Recipe for Tracing the Fate of Issues and Their Publics on the Web," in *Making Things Public: Atmospheres of Democracy*, eds. Bruno Latour and Peter Weibel (Cambridge, MA: MIT Press, 2005).

21   United Conservative Party, *Alberta Strong and Free: Getting Albertans Back to Work*, 2019, 33, https://albertastrongandfree.ca/wp-content/uploads/2019/04/Alberta-Strong-and-Free-Platform-1.pdf.

22   Ryan, "Alberta Politics Online."

23   This analysis matches some of the findings in others' work; see for example, Hamilton, "Social media paints negative picture"; Kornik, "University of Alberta group researching Twitter's impact."

24   Dave Cournoyer, "How much Alberta's political parties spent in the 2019 election," *Daveberta.ca*, 27 November 2019, https://daveberta.ca/2019/11/how-much-albertas-political-parties-spent-in-the-2019-election/ (accessed 1 July 2020).

25   Cournoyer, "How much Alberta's political parties spent."

26   Cournoyer, "How much Alberta's political parties spent."

27   Alberta Elections, "Third Party Advertisers," 2019, https://www.elections.ab.ca/political-participants/third-party-advertisers/.

28   Patrick J. Fournier, "Alberta Polls," *338Canada.com*, 20 May 2021, https://338canada.com/alberta/ (accessed 20 May 2020).

29   Michelle Bellefontaine, "Opposition NDP raises twice as much as Alberta's governing UCP during first quarter of 2021," *CBC News*, 23 April 2021, https://www.cbc.ca/news/canada/edmonton/opposition-ndp-raises-twice-as-much-as-alberta-s-governing-ucp-during-first-quarter-of-2021-1.6000154 (accessed 1 July 2020).

30   Gibbins, Prairie Politics & Society.

Standard Error: The Polls in the 2019 Alberta Election and Beyond

Brooks DeCillia

The TV stations' election calls, with their dramatic music and fancy animation declaring a United Conservative Party (UCP) majority government, came quickly after the polls closed on 16 April 2019. It was not even close. The UCP—a party that hadn't even existed two years before election day—captured 55 per cent of the vote, ousting Rachel Notley's New Democratic Party (NDP) after a single term in power. The nascent UCP, a party created when the old Progressive Conservative (PC) Association and the Wildrose Party merged, captured sixty-three of eighty-seven seats in the prairie province's Legislative Assembly. The NDP only captured 33 per cent of the popular vote and twenty-four seats. Yet, you could be excused for thinking the results would be much closer if you only got information about the 2019 campaign from the Alberta news media's reporting of polls. Nine public opinion polls released during the campaign—half the total released during the campaign—suggested a single-digit gap between the NDP and UCP. The news media narrative suggested a much closer race than what voters ultimately decided at the ballot boxes. The coming pages analyze the publicly released polls in the 2019 campaign and critically examine the news media's reporting about them. This chapter also explores the short honeymoon the UCP government had with Alberta voters.

Critiques of public opinion polls are not new. French sociologist Pierre Bourdieu famously declared that "public opinion does not exist" in 1979. In a similar vein, German philosopher Jürgen Habermas charged that polls are used to manufacture public opinion, preventing a deliberative democracy.[1] Scrutiny of polling is not only philosophical, but practical as well. Some high profile misses abroad and at home in the last decade have undermined confidence in the accuracy of polls. Pollsters in the UK underestimated the British public's desire to Brexit and most US pollsters failed to see Donald Trump's narrow path to electoral victory in 2016. Pollsters have produced some spectacularly bad predications in Alberta, too. Notably, during the 2017 municipal election in Calgary, Mainstreet Research, a national public opinion and market research firm, released three polls on behalf of Postmedia, which owns the *Calgary Sun* and *Calgary Herald*, that wrongly forecast that the incumbent—and popular— Calgary Mayor Naheed Nenshi would lose to a relatively unknown challenger. The polls upended the tone and tenure of Calgary's municipal campaign.[2] After the election that Nenshi won handily, Mainstreet Research admitted to "big polling failures."[3] Five years earlier in the 2012 provincial election, many polls were also off the mark, with several surveys during the campaign predicting the upstart Wildrose Party would sweep away the PC government that had ruled Alberta since Peter Lougheed came to power in 1971.[4] While pollsters patted themselves on the back four years later for correctly predicting that a strong *Orange Chinook*, led by the NDP's Rachel Notley, would blow away the formidable PC dynasty,[5] an analysis of the 2019 polls found they were "only marginally better" when compared to polls about other provincial elections around the same time that were labelled "failures" and much worse than the error rate of the polls in the 2015 and 2019 Canadian federal elections.[6]

When it comes to public opinion polls, accuracy can be defined in several ways. Polling should not only be reduced to forecasting the winner in a political campaign. Polls come with caveats, including a margin of error and the assumption that they are a snapshot in time.[7] Accurate polls also correctly gauge the difference between each party's measured level of support and their actual level of support on election day, while not exceeding the polls' stated margin of error. While all the publicly available polls released during the 2019 Alberta provincial election campaign predicted a UCP win, a close examination of all surveys show the polls displayed the "standard" or typical error (pun fully intended) seen historically in Alberta polling—the underestimation of conservative support.

As the number of public polls have grown, so too has the news media's insatiable appetite for public opinion data. In 2019, Alberta's news organizations chewed through the vote preference and leadership approval numbers, spitting out a constant stream of "horserace journalism."[8] While political journalism is obsessed with public opinion data, a recent study suggests journalists are incapable of comprehending the numbers.[9] Dubbing the phenomenon the "Nate Silver Effect," the research questions the news media's traditional role as an independent "gatekeeper," policing the standards and release of polling data. Defenders of political polls argue that the information is invaluable to the public, fuelling a lively democratic debate, and stressing that political parties won't stop polling. If parties have the polling information, the argument goes, so, too, should the public. And polls do matter. They can affect elections. Some research even suggests that voters "jump on the bandwagon," casting their ballots for the party or candidate that pollster predict will win.[10]

Data and Methods

To quantify the extent of the "horserace" news media narrative during the 2019 Alberta provincial election, I conducted a classic content analysis of the reportage of all public polls.[11] An exhaustive corpus of every article in the mainstream news media or on political blogs about opinion polls during the four-week provincial election campaign was compiled. The online news archives Factiva and Infomart and news aggregator Google News were used to compile the comprehensive corpus of sixty-nine articles and posts to evaluate variables, including, among other things, (1) which party was in the lead, (2) if the race was static or dynamic, (3) how the poll was characterized, (4) and if polling methodology was included.[12]

This work's analysis of polling accuracy relies on a list of polls released publicly during the four-week provincial campaign in 2019—19 March to 16 April.[13] There are eighteen polls from a dozen companies in the data set, as detailed in Table 3.1. The polling firms used a range of methods from online panels, interactive voice response (also known as IVR, or robocalling), and traditional random telephone dialling by human interviewers to survey Albertans during the 2019 provincial election. IVR gauged public sentiment by randomly dialling numbers (land and cell phone lines) and eliciting responses to a pre-recorded voice. Online panels, on the other hand, surveyed eligible Alberta voters using their internet-based panels. These online panels usually consist of people who have agreed to complete surveys using the internet.

Recruitment for these online panels varies. Sixty per cent of Leger's panel, for instance, was recruited randomly over the phone. EKOS' methodological description emphasizes that its respondents to online/telephone research panel are "recruited by telephone using random digit dialling and are confirmed by live interviewers."[14] Nanos' random telephone survey of 500 Albertans used a live operator to ask people about their vote intention. Janet Brown Opinion Research/Trend also used random dialling of land lines and cell phones to measure public opinion. Respondents were given a choice of being interviewed by a live telephone operator or completing an online survey later online. Sample sizes in all the 2019 election campaign polls ranged from about five hundred to more than fifteen hundred. Margins of error varied from a high of 4.4 percentage points to a low of 2.7 percentage points.[15] While online surveys are technically convenience samples and not truly random samples, polls conducted through online panels do aim to be representative of the population. In turn, these firms often provide a credibility interval or an equivalent margin of error that *approximates* the range of values if the online panel data were drawn from a truly random probability sample of the same size.

The dataset complied for this research was used to evaluate several considerations, including whether[16]

(1) the poll correctly identifies the winner;

(2) the poll's stated margin of error correctly encapsulates the actual vote for each party;

(3) the poll's stated margin of error correctly encapsulates the actual vote for the NDP and UCP; and

(4) the poll's *total absolute polling error.*[17]

Table 3.1. Polling Summary by Firm

Polling Firm	Release Date	Sample Size (*n*)	Margin of Error +/-	Random	Interview Mode
EKOS Politics	March 31	1015	3.1	Yes[i]	Online Panel[ii]
Research Co.	April 2	600	4	No	Online Panel
Janet Brown Opinion Research / Trend	April 3	900	3.3	Yes	Phone/Online
Leger	April 6	1003	3.1	No	Online Panel
Forum Research Inc.	April 6	1132	3	Yes	IVR
Mainstreet Research	April 8	876	3.3	Yes	IVR
ThinkHQ Public Affairs Inc.	April 9	1139	2.9	No	Online Panel
Ipsos	April 9	800	4	Partially[iii]	Online Panel/Phone
Angus Reid Institute	April 12	807	3.5	No	Online Panel
Innovative Research Group	April 12	500	4.3[iv]	No	Online Panel
Pollara Strategic Insight	April 12	859	3.3	No	Online Panel
Nanos Survey	April 15	500	4.4	Yes	Phone
Leger	April 15	1505	2.5	No	Online Panel
Ipsos	April 15	1202	3.2	Partially	Online Panel/Phone
Pollara Strategic Insight	April 15	898	3.3	No	Online Panel
Mainstreet Research	April 15	1288	2.7	Yes	IVR
Research Co.	April 15	542	4.2	No	Online Panel
Forum Research Inc.	April 16	1140	3	Yes	IVR

Note:

[i] Of note, some of the online panels recruit respondents using random telephone dialing. That is, respondents do not opt themselves into the panel. EKOS, for example, stresses its "panel offers exhaustive coverage of the Canadian population (i.e., internet, phone, cell phone), random recruitment." In fact, most of the polling companies included in this research describe their online panels as representative of the Canadian population.

[ii] This category reports how respondents were interviewed. That is, how the polling firms asked vote intentions during the 2019 campaign. Recruitment for online panels is different—and varied. Some firms, such as EKOS, recruited their internet-based panel using random dialing. Leger reported recruiting 60 per cent of its panel randomly using the phone. Ipsos reported interviewing its respondents "online via the Ipsos I-Say Panel and non-panel sources." Other firms that used online panels to gauge vote intentions during the 2019 provincial election did not detail in their news releases or public-facing documents how their online panels were recruited.

[iii] Ipsos' survey combined a mixture of online interviews and random computer-assisted telephone interviewing (CATI), calling a mix of cell and landlines.

[iv] Innovative Research Group does not report a margin of error, noting that the firm's representative online survey is "not a random probability-based sample." The firm notes: "a margin of error cannot be calculated. Statements about margins of sampling error or population estimates do not apply to most online panels." For comparison purposes, a probability sample of this poll's size would have a margin of error +/- 4.3 percentage points at the 95 per cent confidence interval.

Sources: Table compiled by author.

How the Media Reported on the Polls

Towards the end of the campaign, some news media highlighted public opinion polls with a single digit spread between the UCP and NDP, suggesting the race was tightening.[18] Global News, for example, relying on an Ipsos poll, suggested an eight-point spread between the UCP and NDP, was evidence of a "tightening" race with the "NDP gaining ground" seven days before the UCP crushed the New Democrats.[19] As Figure 3.1 illustrates, the extent to which news media characterized the race as dynamic, in fact, grew at a statistically significant level from zero in the first week of the four-week campaign to 45 per cent in week two, peaking at 76 per cent in week three, before dropping off to 53 per cent in the final week. On election day, for example, the online news source *DailyHive*'s headline read "Mainstreet poll shows UCP and NDP within 2% of each other in YYC."[20] The UCP beat the NDP by 19 percentage points in Calgary in 2019. Only slightly more than a third of the news coverage (36 per cent) mentioned the poll's methodology, including important information such as margin of error, sample size, field dates, etc.

How Accurate Were the Polls?

Table 3.2 outlines, for all eighteen public opinion polls during the 2019 election campaign, how accurate the surveys were in (1) estimating actual support on election day, (2) predicting the correct winner, (3) correctly anticipating each parties' support within its stated margin of error, (4) accurately estimating the correct level of support for the NDP and UCP on election day within the poll's stated margin of error, and (5) getting it right over all (or total absolute error). All the polling firms correctly predicted the UCP would win the election. No polls ever showed the NDP in the lead. The public opinion polls did not, as conventional wisdom holds, become more accurate close to election day. The total absolute error (15.3) for the eight polls taken within a week of the 16 April vote is the same as the total absolute error (15.3) associated with the ten polls conducted earlier in the campaign. Two of the most accurate polls—Forum Research's first poll (3.8 total absolute error) and Janet Brown Opinion Research/Trend[21] (7.3 total absolute error)—came early in the campaign. Forum Research's second campaign poll, with a total absolute error of 9.1, completed its data

Figure 3.1. A "Dynamic" Race by Campaign Week

Source: Brooks DeCillia

collection the day before the 16 April vote. As Table 3.2 details, the total absolute error for all eighteen polls in the 2019 campaign was an average of 15.3.

Only two of the polls—Forum Research's first poll and Janet Brown Opinion Research/Trend—correctly anticipated the level of support for the four main parties within the firm's stated margin of error (criteria two). Most of the polls accurately predict the support for the Alberta Party and the Liberals within their stated margin of error but did not get it right when it comes to the only two parties that had a viable chance at forming government—the UCP and the NDP. Only Forum Research's first poll and Janet Brown Opinion Research/Trend hit the mark when it came to predicting the UCP and NDP's support within their firm's stated margin of error (criteria three). It is particularly notable that all the polls, except Forum Research's first survey, underestimated UCP support. On average, all the public opinion polls during the 2019 Alberta election campaign underestimated the conservative party's support by about seven per cent.

While the total absolute error for all the Alberta election polls in 2019 shrunk from 18.7 points in 2015 to 15.3 points in 2019, all the polls—except for three—produced a total absolute error rate above ten. The total absolute error ranged from a low of 3.8 points in Forum Research's first poll to 22.3 points in both the EKOS and the Research Co. public opinion surveys. As noted above, the total absolute error does not diminish closer to the election. The two most accurate polls—Janet Brown Opinion Research/Trend and Forum Research's first poll—were in the field surveying Alberta voters in the last week of March and first week of April,

Table 3.2. Polling Error in the 2019 Alberta Election Campaign

Polling Firm	Final Field Day	MoE +/-[i]	Party support error (+/- pp)				Criteria 1: Correct Winner	Criteria 2: # of Parties Within MoE	Criteria 3: NDP & UCP Within MoE	Criteria 4: Total Absolute Error
			NDP	UCP	Alberta Party	Liberals				
EKOS Politics	March 26	3.1	9.3	-8.9	-3.1	1	Yes	2	0	22.3
Research Co.	April 1	4	7.3	-9.9	-3.1	2	Yes	2	0	22.3
Janet Brown Opinion Research / Trend	March 30	3.3	1.3	-1.9	-1.1	3	Yes	4	2	7.3
Leger	April 3	3.1	5.3	-7.9	-0.1	3	Yes	2	0	17.2
Forum Research Inc.	April 5	3	-0.7	0.1	-2.1	0	Yes	4	2	3.8
Mainstreet Research	April 5	3.3	5.3	-3.9	-3.1	1	Yes	2	0	13.3
ThinkHQ Public Affairs Inc.	April 6	2.9	7.3	-8.9	-1.1	1	Yes	2	0	18.3
Ipsos	April 8	4	6.3	-7.9	0.9	1	Yes	2	0	16.1
Angus Reid Institute	April 8	3.5	6.3[iii]	-2.9	-3.1	0	Yes	3	1	12.3
Innovative Research Group	April 8	4.3[ii]	-1.7	-10.9	1.9	6	Yes	2	1	20.5
Pollara Strategic Insight	April 10	3.3	5.3	-9.9	-1.1	3	Yes	2	0	19.3
Nanos Survey	April 13	4.4	3.3	-10.9	2.9	2	Yes	3	1	19.1
Leger	April 13	2.5	3.3	-4.9	-1.1	2	Yes	2	0	11.3
Ipsos	April 14	3.2	7.3	-4.9	-2.1	0	Yes	2	0	14.3
Pollara Strategic Insight	April 14	3.3	6.3	-9.9	-1.1	2	Yes	2	0	19.3
Mainstreet Research	April 14	2.7	7.3	-6.9	-1.1	1	Yes	2	0	16.4
Research Co.	April 15	4.2	6.3	-5.9	-0.1	1	Yes	2	0	13.2
Forum Research Inc.	April 15	3	2.3	-3.9	1.9	1	Yes	3	1	9.1
Election results April 16			32.7%	54.9%	9.1%	1%			Average Total Absolute Error	15.3

Note: [i] Representative online panels are not truly random probability samples. Margins of errors are not applicable. Most firms, as reported in this table, offer a margin of error based on a probability sample of a similar size. [ii] Innovative Research Group does not report a margin of error, noting that the firm's representative online survey is "not a random probability-based sample." The firm notes: "a margin of error cannot be calculated. Statements about margins of sampling error or population estimates do not apply to most online panels." For comparison purposes, a probability sample of this poll's size would have a margin of error +/- 4.3 percentage points at the 95 per cent confidence interval. *Sources:* Table compiled by author.

Table 3.3. Average Error in 2019 Alberta Election (by Time, Period) Comparison with Other Canadian Polls

	TIME PERIOD	AVG. TOTAL ERROR
Alberta 2012	**All polls**	**23**
Alberta 2015	**All polls**	**18.7**
Alberta 2019 Election	**All polls**	**15.3**
	Last six polls average	**13.9**
Canada 2015	All polls	6.7
Canada 2019	Final 12 polls	8.5
Canada 2021	Final 15 polls	9.1

Sources: Table compiled by author.

well before the 16 April vote. By means of an example, research evaluating the 2015 Canadian federal election polling concluded that the public polls were fairly accurate, with an average total absolute error of 6.7 points.[22] Four years later, the total absolute error for the final twelve polls in the federal election was 8.5 points.[23] The fifteen polls in the 2021 federal election had a total absolute error of 9.1 points.[24] For comparison, Table 3.3 details the notable total absolute error of public opinion polls in recent federal and provincial elections.[25]

While the total absolute error for all the 2019 Alberta election campaign polls (15.3 points) was better than the 2015 campaign (18.7 points), it is not much better. Additionally, the average error rate in 2019 in Alberta was not much better than the total absolute error (17 points) in the 2013 British Columbia polling debacle that wrongly predicted the Liberals with Christy Clark were tracking to lose to the NDP in an election the governing party won handily. The 2019 Alberta election campaign polls all predicted the right winner, but they did not, for the most part, perform well when it came to estimating the final proportion of votes that both the NDP and UCP earned from voters in the prairie province. Of particular concern, most of the polls did not accurately capture the true extent of the UCP's strong support amongst Alberta voters. Since the UCP's commanding performance on election day in April 2019, however, the polls suggest the governing UCP has lost considerable support amongst Alberta voters.

Jason Kenney and the United Conservative Party's Brief Honeymoon

Jason Kenney was at the height of his popularity on the day that he was sworn in as Alberta's eighteenth premier. His honeymoon, according to the polls, was brief, and ended amidst the global pandemic. Kenney's election win, it is worth stressing again, was impressive. The UCP's 55 per cent of the popular vote bested Ed Stelmach's landslide victory in 2008, where the PCs captured 53 per cent of ballots cast. Even before Kenney became premier, the former federal Conservative cabinet minister was not the most popular political leader in Alberta. Polling data during the 2019 election campaign suggested voters liked NDP leader Rachel Notley (even after she had been premier for four years) more than Kenney, in fact.[26] Kenney's April 2019 election victory glow faded less than a year after his election as Figure 3.2 illustrates. According to survey research conducted by Janet Brown Opinion Research/Trend almost a year after the UCP swept to power, the governing party had dropped twelve points in popular support.[27]

By the spring of 2021—a year into the government's controversial handing of the pandemic—support for the governing UCP had dropped by another ten points, below the NDP.[28] By the time Kenney announced his intention to step down as party leader in May of 2022, polls consistently showed the UCP trailing the NDP in public opinion. Kenney's critics, in fact, frequently used the premier's unpopularity to argue his continued leadership all but assured an NDP victory in the next provincial election expected in May of 2023. Former Wildrose Party leader Brian Jean—arguably, Kenney's biggest critic—returned to politics in the winter of 2022, running successfully for the UCP in the Fort McMurray-Lac La Biche by-election on a "brass knuckles" promise to overthrow Kenney as leader of the UCP.[29] Two months later, Kenney resigned as party leader after receiving a lukewarm endorsement of his leadership from UCP members, telling his party that the bare majority was not "adequate support to continue as leader."[30]

Jason Kenney's approval ratings also dropped significantly from a high of nearly 50 per cent in 2018 to below 20 per cent in the aftermath of his controversial handling of the pandemic in 2021. Figure 3.3[31] illustrates Kenney's drop in voters' estimations and NDP leader Rachel Notley's

Figure 3.2. Vote Choice (United Conservative Party & New Democratic Party), 2018–2022

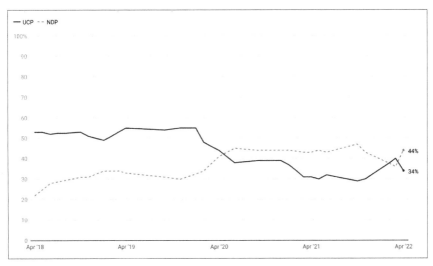

Sources: Janet Brown Opinion Research/Trend Research, created with Datawarpper.

Figure 3.3. Approval of Provincial Leaders, 2018–2022

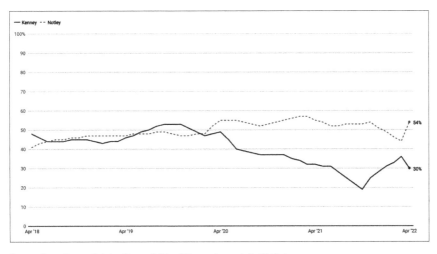

Sources: Janet Brown Opinion Research/Trend Research, created with Datawarpper.

higher favourability since the spring of 2020. By the time Kenney made his surprise announcement to step down as party leader, less than a third of Albertans approved his leadership, while nearly double that (54 per cent) of Albertans approved of opposition leader and former NDP premier Rachel Notley.

Discussion

All the 2019 polls got the winner right. But predicting which party was going to come out on top was hardly a high bar for polls to clear. At best, the 2019 polls were only marginally better than 2015. Importantly, the 2019 election campaign polls persisted in systematically underestimating conservative support in the province of Alberta. Brown and Santos, in their examination of the 2015 polls, highlight how conservative support typically came up short in that campaign's survey. Pollsters, as Brown and Santos suggest, largely "got a pass" for underestimating PC's support because that election ended the party's more than four decades in power.[32] With no single party dominating Alberta politics anymore[33] polling accuracy is increasingly important. More competitive elections—and even a minority government, which Alberta has never had—are possible. Estimating party support is important. Yet, Alberta political surveys traditionally underestimate conservative support in the heartland of Canadian conservatism. It is increasing clear that any read of an Alberta provincial poll should proceed carefully and assume that no poll probably captures the true extent of conservative support in the prairie province.

In Alberta in 2019, neither the interview mode (how people were asked who they planned to vote for) nor the method of coming up with the sample of people (random digit dialing [RDD], online panels) guaranteed that the poll accurately captured voters' intentions. Let's put the three surveys that came close to predicting the UCP's actual vote under the microscope. Forum Research's first poll, which correctly pegged UCP support at 55 per cent, used IVR to ask voters who they planned to vote for in the provincial election. Janet Brown Opinion Research/Trend also came close, predicting UCP support at 53 per cent. Its sample was collected using RDD. Respondents could choose either to share their vote intention with a live telephone interviewer or receive an email to do the survey online. A vast majority (90 per cent) chose to talk with a human. Four days before the

16 April election, the Angus Reid Institute's survey estimated UCP support at 52 per cent. This prediction came from an online survey panel. These three different polls achieved similar results despite using different methods. It is worth emphasizing that most of the polls did not predict the UCP's commanding lead. But underestimating conservative support is not new—and it is not an Alberta anomaly either.

So-called shy Tories or reluctant Republicans perplex pollsters. Surveys around the world have failed to adequately gauge conservative support. At the national level in Canada, polls collectively underestimated Conservative support in Canada's 2019 federal election.[34] In the UK in 2015, most pre-election polls predicted a hung parliament. David Cameron's Conservatives won a majority. In Australia four years later, horse race polls there also underestimated conservative support in that country's federal election.[35] Polls in 2016 and 2020 underestimated support for Donald Trump in the US presidential election. Polling experts have offered a few theories for why polls underestimate conservative voters, including (1) these voters refuse to participate in surveys; (2) conservative voters, fearing retribution for their views, hedge or lie about who they intend to vote for; (3) pollsters do not reach enough conservative-leaning voters (unrepresentative samples); (4) the people who take polls are different than the people who vote; and (5) the voter models used by polling firms are possibly flawed.

On top of not wanting to share how they vote, some experts have hypothesized that these elusive conservative voters simply slip the pollsters' *sampling net*. The thinking is that these voters do not answer or hang up on pollsters, especially when IVR or robocall polls reach them. These voters simply mistrust pollsters. There is, of course, a long history of conservatives casting doubt on public opinion polls. President Richard Nixon often described a "silent majority" that pollsters were not hearing. Post-truth politics accelerated the already declining trust and cynicism that many voters, especially conservative ones, have in institutions.[36] This overarching lack of trust in institutions has also tarnished polls.[37] The mistrust is particularly pronounced amongst Republicans in the US. Donald Trump, after all, frequently challenges the accuracy of polls, calling the ones predicting his loss "fake."[38] There also may be an out-and-out difference between the people who participate in polls and the people who eschew them, resulting in a systematic bias. Robert Putnam in 2001, in fact, found that people who have low levels of trust in people and institutions are less likely to participate in phone surveys.[39] Veteran pollster and Obama presidential campaign advisor David Shor echoes Putnam, noting that people who are more likely to participate in polls in the US are more agreeable, and have higher levels of trust, which, in turn, results in a partisan non-response bias being baked into polls.[40]

Polling leading up to the UK general election in 2015 systematically under-represented conservative supporters.[41] The polling experts who reviewed what went wrong with the UK polls concluded the industry needs to shift its "emphasis away from quantity and towards quality" and to be "more imaginative and proactive" in their efforts to find elusive conservatives.[42] The final report for the British Polling Council and the Market Research Society recommended pollsters work harder to recruit samples that mirror the makeup of the population.[43] American pollster David Shor, on the other hand, is not so sure that traditional survey methods can overcome the partisan non-response that results in undercounting Republican support in the United States. Weighting results against census data, he contends, will not fix the problem. "There used to be a world," he said in a 2020 interview with *Vox*, "where polling involved calling people, applying classical statistical adjustments, and putting most of the emphasis on interpretation."[44] Shor advocates getting more sophisticated by combining polling data with voter files and proprietary first-party data, and using machine learning to interpret the combination of data points. Shor's solution may work in the United States, but in Canada, voter information does not include the party identification or voting history that Shor suggests incorporating into polling analysis.

Some Humility about Polling Results

Polls matter.[45] They *can* shape public discourse, influence campaigns, and motivate parties and caucuses to overthrow their leaders. Voters—especially those looking to vote against an incumbent—sometimes turn to polls to see who or what party has the best chance of winning. Pollsters—and the news media—need to be much more mindful about the potential influence of polls. Transparency about the limits of polls is needed now more than ever, from both the pollsters and the news media that report the data. In the wake of the British polling failure in 2015, Sturgis urged the public—and the news media—to recognize that polls are not perfect. "Even if we move to the most expensive random survey that you can possibly imagine," he told the *Guardian*, "there would still be a chance that you would get it wrong." No pollster, of course, wants to get it wrong. But, after all, the probability theory on which polling rests suggests there is a chance it can happen from time to time. Poll aggregators and election forecasters also need to be interpreted with a critical eye. News organizations and poll aggregators frequently predict the outcome of races, even attaching probabilities to certain outcomes. There is a difference between polls and predictors.

The News Media's Addiction to Polls

Every day, journalists assess the veracity of sources and information. They sort fact from fiction in an ocean of misinformation and disinformation. Journalists seek out the truth, guided by principles such as accuracy, fairness, balance, impartiality, and integrity. Yet, as the evidence presented in this chapter clearly shows, Alberta journalists did not train their usual skepticism on the public opinion polls during the 2019 provincial election campaign. The polls got a pass. A tightening horse race is a better story than UCP cruising to an expected easy victory. A tight race is a better narrative. Considerable evidence from journalism sociology highlights the news media's proclivity to seek out and highlight tension and conflict.[46] It makes for a better story. This bias, arguably, blinded Alberta journalists. Sure, campaigns can matter, but polls consistently—since at least a year ahead of the election—showed the UCP on track to win big.[47] Some research suggests news organizations are incapable of comprehending the data.[48] Perhaps, news executives need to build that expertise into their newsrooms. At a minimum, they need to do a better job of detailing the polls' methodology they report. Maybe, having to think about the margin of error and the probability of incorrect estimations might spark some caution in political journalists' minds. As well, it might help their audiences interpret the results more critically. In addition, journalists need to become more reflexive about Alberta's history of flawed polls.

It is, indeed, remarkable that journalists were so uncritical of the campaign polls in 2019. Alberta journalists had been burned by bad polls in recent elections. Remember, rogue polls in Calgary's municipal election with its "catastrophic polling failure" should have made journalists more skeptical of horse race survey data. *CBC News* in Calgary, of note, conceded it should have been more circumspect of Mainstreet Research's perplexing polling numbers.[49] As well, only seven year earlier, all the polls in the 2012 provincial election pointed towards a Wildrose Party win that never materialized. As this chapter makes clear, Alberta polls consistently underestimate conservative support. Journalists need to incorporate that knowledge into their reporting on polls.

The Unpopular United Conservative Party

Since the spring of 2020, polls have suggested an uncertain future for the UCP. As detailed above, the NDP overtook the governing UCP in public opinion surveys in late 2020. As well, Jason Kenney's personal popularity plummeted alongside his party's precipitous drop in public support. Many long-time political watchers blamed Kenney's controversial handling of the devastating fourth wave of COVID-19. Dubbed the "Kenney effect," analysts suggest Kenney's personal unpopularity even hurt federal Conservative at the ballot box in the 2021 national election. The UCP leader faced down a caucus revolt just days after the federal vote.[50] As Duane Bratt and Bruce Foster have highlighted, "big tent" conservative parties are "fragile," and Canada's political history is filled with right-wing parties splintering and merging.[51] The pandemic exposed real and pronounced divisions in the UCP over how best to handle COVID-19. Duane Bratt argues convincingly that while Kenney's underlying conservative ideology—and its emphasis on personal responsibility, individual freedom, and small government—underlies his controversial response to the pandemic, his worldview is, nevertheless, "out of touch with Alberta values."[52] No matter what his reasons, the response appears to have hurt Kenney and his party politically. In response, the opposition NDP attempted to frame Kenney's handling of the pandemic as politically motivated and not aligned with the public health measures most Albertans support. Unlike the PC dynasty, the UCP faces a single and capable opposition party led by a former premier. In the truest sense of the concept, the opposition NDP are a *government in waiting*. Only four years ago, the New Democrats held power. Alberta politics is decidedly more competitive, and this viable alternative for voters has complicated Kenney's political fortunes. Detractors in his own party, in fact, used Kenney's vulnerability to attack him.

Kenney's biggest threat turned out to be within his party. While the premier managed to stare down caucus critics such as MLAs Todd Loewen and Drew Barnes and fend off a full-fledged caucus revolt in September of 2021, he could not escape the wrath of his party's members. The melodrama associated with the internal skirmishes and infighting also, arguably, tarnished the UCP's image as the no-nonsense, hard-working, pro-business government that would stand up for *everyday* Albertans. Caucus revolts and bruising leadership battles, especially during a crisis-filled global pandemic, likely did not instill confidence in many Albertans' minds. On top of that, the UCP seemingly stumbled from one crisis or gaffe to another. From 2020's Alohagate, where UCP MLAs and staffers jetted off to international Christmas vacation destinations after telling Albertans to hunker down for the holiday, to Premier Kenney's prolonged holiday absence as a fourth wave of COVID-19 surged in August of 2021, the UCP's political communication was often tone deaf. Repairing that damage falls to the party's new leader. It will not be easy.

The governing party faces many challenges. The UCP was largely elected on a promise to get Alberta's economy cooking with oil and gas again. But the province still faces tough economic challenges and volatile forces outside its control.[53] On top of that, health care—with the lingering effects of the pandemic and the political headache of clearing the backlog of delayed medical procedures and cancelled surgeries—will challenge the UCP. The NDP, with its history of being the first North American government to establish universal single-payer medical insurance in Saskatchewan in 1962, tends to own health care as an issue in many voters' minds. The issue could play a big role in the coming 2023 provincial election. What comes next will be fascinating to watch. Gone, it seems, are the days of political dynasties in Alberta, making the need for accurate polls even more important in assessing what is important to Alberta voters and how they feel about the public policy politicians propose. Let's hope during the coming 2023 election campaign pollsters do a better job of capturing a truly representative sample of Albertans, and journalists and consumers of polls approach the numbers with some caution and humility when interpreting them.

NOTES

1   Pierre Bourdieu, "Public Opinion Does Not Exist," in *Communication and Class Struggle 1*, eds. Armand Mattelart and Seth Siegelaub (New York: International General, 1979), 124–130; Jürgen Habermas, *The Structural Transformation of the Public Sphere: An Inquiry into a Category of Bourgeois Society* (Cambridge, MA: MIT Press, 1991).

2   Alyssa Julie, "Mainstreet Research Apologizes for 'Catastrophic Polling Failure' in 2017 Calgary election," *Global News*, 20 October 2017, https://globalnews.ca/news/3816393/mainstreet-research-apologizes-for-catastrophic-polling-failure-in-2017-calgary-election/ (accessed 30 September 2021).

3   Brooks DeCillia, "Mainstreet to release findings of investigation into 'big polling failures' during Calgary election," *CBC News*, 10 December 2017, https://www.cbc.ca/news/canada/calgary/mainstreet-polling-failures-investigation-calgary-election-1.4441063 (accessed 30 September 2021).

4   Polling failures at the provincial level are also notable in the 2013 British Columbia, the 2014 Quebec, and the 2014 Ontario provincial election campaigns.

5   Bruce Cheadle, "Pollsters relieved at getting it right in Alberta's unlikely swing to the left," *Maclean's*, 6 May 2015, https://www.macleans.ca/politics/pollsters-relieved-at-getting-it-right-in-albertas-unlikely-swing-to-the-left/ (accessed 31 August 2021).

6   Janet Brown and John Santos, "Marginally Better: Polling in the 2015 Alberta Election," in *Orange Chinook: Politics in the New Alberta*, eds. Duane Bratt, Keith Brownsey, Richard Sutherland, and David Taras (Calgary: University of Calgary Press, 2019), 79–101.

7   Random surveys often get reported with a 95 per cent confidence interval of an estimated population parameter. This represents the range that would contain the true mean value in the population 95 per cent of the time if that same sample design could be replicated in the population an infinite number of times at the same time. The "margin of error" is technically actually the "margin of sampling error," and only covers error from sampling and no other methodological artefacts like field procedure, question wording, etc.

8   Elizabeth Goodyear-Grant, Antonia Maioni, and Stuart Soroka, "The Role of the Media: A Campaign Saved by a Horserace," *Policy Options* 25 (2004): 86–91; J. Scott Matthews, Mark Pickup, and Fred Cutler, "The Mediated Horserace: Campaign Polls and Poll Reporting," *Canadian Journal of Political Science* 45 (2012): 261–87.

9   Benjamin Toff, "The 'Nate Silver Effect' on Political Journalism: Gatecrashers, Gatekeepers, and Changing Newsroom Practices around Coverage of Public Opinion Polls," *Journalism* 20, no. 7 (2019): 873–889.

10 Jens Olav Dahlgaard, Jonas Hedegaard Hansen, Kasper M. Hansen, and Martin V. Larsen, "How Are Voters Influenced by Opinion Polls? The Effect of Polls on Voting Behavior and Party Sympathy," *World Political Science* 12, no. 2 (2016): 283–300.

11 A classic content analysis is a trusted means of quantify phenomena in news media. It effectively turns words into numbers to draw statistical inferences about the news media. See Klaus Krippendorff, "Content Analysis: An Introduction to Its Methodology," (Thousand Oaks, CA: Sage, 2018) for an overview of the method and its benefits.

12 An independent double-checking produced an intercoder reliability above 80 per cent for all the variables coded in this study, confirming a valid coding process.

13 This study's public opinion dataset (see Tables 3.1, 3.2, and 3.3) was compiled after the 2019 election, using polling information detailed in news releases and mainstream news organizations and "poll aggregators" such as ThreeHundredEight (www. threehundredeight.com) and CBC Poll Tracker (https://newsinteractives.cbc.ca/ elections/poll-tracker/alberta/). This work was done independent of polling firms, the news media, or political bloggers.

14 EKOS, "Rachel Notley Closing Gap on Jason Kenney," 31 March 2019, https://www. ekospolitics.com/index.php/2019/03/rachel-notley-closing-gap-on-jason-kenney/

15 This research uses the reported margin of error of each poll, as reported by the polling firm. It is likely that these margins of errors exclude undecideds and non-voters, meaning the final reported "vote intention" proportions are smaller than the total reported sample size of the poll. Accounting for the smaller sample size would increase the margin of error. As well, it is a common convention for polls to offer one global margin of error for the entire poll. Technically, the margin of error is different for each proportion in a poll.

16 This study does not offer an "index of accuracy" akin to Elizabeth A. Martin, Michael W. Traugott, and Courtney Kennedy, "A Review and Proposal for a New Measure of Poll Accuracy," *Public Opinion Quarterly* 69 (2005): 342–69, which uses similar criteria in quantitative evaluations of polling accuracy.

17 Total absolute error is calculated by summing the absolute differences between each party's level of support in each public poll and the actual vote totals on election day. This measure replicates Brown and Santos, "Marginally Better." See also David Coletto, "Polling and the 2015 Federal Election," in *The Canadian Federal Election of 2015*, ed. Jon H. Pammett and Christopher Dornan (Toronto: Dundurn, 2016), 305–26.

18 The preliminary data from this study was presented as a working paper at the Prairie Political Science Association in 2019. "Alberta's 'Shy Tories': Why Public Polls Underestimate Conservative Voters," with John Santos (presentation, Prairie Political Science Association (PPSA), Banff, AB, 13 September 2019).

19 "Race tightening in Alberta provincial election," *Global News*, 9 April 2019, https:// globalnews.ca/video/5149284/race-tightening-in-alberta-provincial-election/ (accessed 30 September 2021).

20 Chandler Walter, "Mainstreet poll shows UCP and NDP within 2% of each other in YYC," *Daily Hive*, 16 April 2019, https://dailyhive.com/calgary/mainstreet-pollucp-ndp-close-calgary (accessed 30 September 2021).

21 Full disclosure: I have worked with Janet Brown in the past as a journalist on a political research project conducted by CBC News. Brooks DeCillia, "The 'Road Ahead' for Alberta Voters As CBC Surveys Motivations and Polarization in Lead Up to Next Election," *CBC News*, 21 February 2018, https://www.cbc.ca/news/canada/calgary/road-ahead-election-alberta-survey-motivations-1.4544536.

22 Data from: David Coletto and Bryan Breguet, "The Accuracy of Public Polls in Provincial Elections," *Canadian Political Science Review* 9 (2015): 41–54; and David Coletto, "Polling and the 2015 Federal Election," in *The Canadian Federal Election of 2015*, ed. Jon H. Pammett and Christopher Dornan (Toronto: Dundurn, 2016), 305–26.

23   Data from "338Canada Pollster Ratings," 338Canada, last updated 27 September 2021, https://338canada.com/pollster-ratings.htm#ca2019 (accessed 30 September 2021).

24   Data from "338Canada Pollster Ratings."

25   As calculated by Brown and Santos, "Marginally Better"; and Coletto and Breguet, "The Accuracy of Public Polls." Data for 2019 federal election came from "338Canada Pollster Ratings" and was calculated by the author.

26   Janet Brown, "Global Petroleum Show: Provincial Election Survey," Janet Brown Opinion Research, 3 April 2019, http://planetjanet.ca/wp-content/ uploads/2019/04/2019-04-02-NWPA-March-2019-Election-Poll-Report.pdf (accessed 29 September 2021).

27   Janet Brown, "Special Projects," Janet Brown Opinion Research, http://planetjanet.ca/ special-projects/ (accessed 2 June 2022).

28   Janet Brown, "Special Projects."

29   Graham Thompson, "Brain Jean's bylection win sets the stage for showdown with Alberta Premier Jason Kenney," CBC News, 16 March 2022, https://www.cbc.ca/news/ canada/edmonton/brian-jean-s-byelection-win-sets-the-stage-for-showdown-with- alberta-premier-jason-kenney-1.6386455 (access 1 June 2022).

30   Michelle Bellfontaine, "Alberta Premier Jason Kenney resigning as UCP leader despite narrow win in leadership review," CBC News, 17 May 2022, https://www.cbc.ca/news/ canada/edmonton/alberta-premier-jason-kenney-resigning-as-ucp-leader-despite- narrow-win-in-leadership-review-1.6457221 (accessed 29 May 2022).

31   Janet Brown, "Special Projects."

32   Brown and Santos, "Marginally Better," 2019.

33   Anthony M. Sayers and David K. Stewart, "Out of the Blue: Goodbye Tories, Hello Jason Kenney," in Orange Chinook, 399–423.

34   Phillipe J. Fournier, "How polls keep underestimating the Conservative vote: 338Canada," Maclean's, 5 August 2020, https://www.macleans.ca/politics/ ottawa/338canada-how-polls-keep-underestimating-the-conservative-vote/ (accessed 30 September 2021).

35   Ben Westcott, "Australia Election 2019," CNN, 18 May 2019, https://edition.cnn.com/ world/live-news/australia-election-day-2019/index.html (accessed July 22, 2022).

36   For this argument, see Emily Ekins, "Why Did Republicans Outperform the Polls Again? Two Theories," FiveThirtyEight, 2 March 2020, https://fivethirtyeight.com/ features/why-did-republicans-outperform-the-polls-again-two-theories/ (accessed 29 September 2021).

37   Ekins, "Why Did Republicans Outperform."

38   "Survey: Many Americans don't believe polls are accurate," The Hill, 27 December2020, https://thehill.com/hilltv/what-americas-thinking/423023-a-majority-of-americans- are-skeptical-that-public-opinion-polls (accessed 29 September 2021).

39   Richard Putnam, "Social Capital: Measurement and Consequences," Isuma: Canadian Journal of Policy Research 2 (2001): 41–51.

40   For Shor's thoughts, read Dylan Mathews, "One pollster's explanation for why the polls got it wrong," *Vox*, 10 November 2020, https://www.vox.com/policy-and-politics/2020/11/10/21551766/election-polls-results-wrong-david-shor (accessed 29 September 2021).

41   Parts of these recommendations first appeared as commentary in 2019 in Policy Options. See Brooks DeCillia, "The underestimated conservative voter in Alberta polls," *Policy Options*, 25 June 2019, https://policyoptions.irpp.org/magazines/june-2019/underestimated-conservative-voter-alberta-polls/ (accessed 30 September 2021).

42   Tom Clark and Frances Perraudin, "General election opinion poll failure down to not reaching Tory voters," *Guardian*, 19 January 2016, https://www.theguardian.com/politics/2016/jan/19/general-election-opinion-poll-failure-down-to-not-reaching-tory-voters (29 September 2021).

43   Patrick Sturgis et al. "Report of the Inquiry into the 2015 British General Election Opinion Polls," British Polling Council and the Market Research Society, March 2016, https://benjaminlauderdale.net/files/papers/PollingInquiryReport.pdf (accessed 29 September 2021).

44   For Shor's thoughts, read Mathews, "One pollster's explanation."

45   Patricia Moy and Eike Mark Rinke, "Attitudinal and Behavioral Consequences of Published Opinion Polls," in *Opinion Polls and the Media*, eds. Christina Holtz-Bacha, Jesper Strömbäck (London, UK: Palgrave Macmillan, 2012), 225–45.

46   See, for example, Pamela J. Shoemaker and Stephen D. Reese, *Mediating the Message in the 21st Century: A Media Sociology Perspective* (New York: Routledge, 2014).

47   See, for example, Brooks DeCillia, "United Conservative Party on track to win big in Alberta, says poll," *CBC News*, 28 April 2018, https://www.cbc.ca/news/canada/calgary/road-ahead-poll-ucp-win-next-election-1.4636786 (accessed 30 September 2021).

48   Benjamin Toff, "The 'Nate Silver Effect.'" s:

49   Brooks DeCillia, "Mainstreet to release findings of investigation into 'big polling failures' during Calgary election," *CBC News*, 10 December 2017, https://www.cbc.ca/news/canada/calgary/mainstreet-polling-failures-investigation-calgary-election-1.4441063 (accessed 30 September 2021).

50   Drew Anderson and Elise von Scheel, "Jason Kenney survives caucus meeting with leadership review to come," *CBC News*, 21 September 2021, https://www.cbc.ca/news/canada/calgary/jason-kenney-premier-alberta-leadership-review-1.6185362 (accessed 30 September 2021).

51   Duane Bratt and Bruce Foster, "The fragility of a 'big tent' conservative party," *CBC News*, 25 July 2019, https://www.cbc.ca/news/canada/calgary/conservative-party-splitting-merging-western-canada-1.5220417 (accessed 30 September 2021).

52   Duane Bratt, "How Kenney's political ideology is out of touch with Alberta values," *CBC News*, 8 September 2021, https://www.cbc.ca/news/canada/calgary/kenney-political-ideology-1.6167303 (accessed 30 September 2021).

53   David Bell, "Alberta's economic outlook looking up but 'bumpy ride' ahead, says economist," *CBC News*, 19 May 2022, https://www.cbc.ca/news/canada/calgary/alberta-economic-outlook-rob-roach-1.6459790 (accessed 1 June 2022).

III.

Inside the United Conservative Party

4

Divisions among Alberta's "Conservatives"

David K. Stewart and Anthony M. Sayers

As September 2021 drew to a close the United Conservative Party (UCP) of Alberta was anything but. Front page headlines in the *Calgary Herald* blared "UCP knives come out for Kenney" and "Kenney wins battle, but war still on."[1] These and other stories spoke of constituency organizations mobilizing to force a leadership review and of caucus discussions on the same issue. A leadership review was eventually scheduled for the spring of 2022[2] and after one postponement, the outcome was announced on 18 May 2022. Premier Kenney's hopes of surviving such a review were dashed as just over 51.4 per cent (17,638 of 34,298) of the members voting supported the premier and he announced his intention to resign.[3] The Kenney era ended on October 6, 2022, when Danielle Smith captured the leadership of the UCP.

Premier Kenney was in the unenviable position of being unpopular with two different elements of his party. Many on the right of the party were unhappy with the implementation of any kind of vaccine mandate, while others blamed him for taking too long to respond to the emergence of a fourth COVID-19 wave in the late summer of 2021, and, indeed for putting in place policies that might have increased the severity of that wave (see Lisa Young's chapter). There was certainly no debating the fact that Alberta was leading the country in cases and hospitalizations. This despite, or perhaps because of, the declaration that the pandemic was over in the summer. The shuffling of the health minister to a new portfolio was a partial response to the discontent, but the chances of such a move satisfying critics on either side were extremely small.

This disunity in the governing party came just four years after Kenney was easily elected as leader of the new UCP, a party created from the merger of the former Progressive Conservative (PC) and Wildrose parties. This merger was intended to ensure the long-term dominance of the right in Alberta's political system and was based on the assumption that the defeat of the PC government in 2015 was owed largely to divisions on the right, and the Rachel Notley-led New Democratic Party (NDP) government simply a by-product of those divisions.[4]

The attractiveness of that narrative is obvious for both Alberta's right wing and for the assumption that Alberta is the centre of "conservativism" in Canada. This easy analysis ignores the divisions that have existed within Alberta's right-of-centre political parties and the struggles that have taken place on this side of the political spectrum.

This chapter outlines some of those struggles captured in continuity and change in voter support for "conservative" parties in 2015 and 2019[5] as well as the nature of internal divisions on display at the 2020 UCP policy convention.[6] The premier's declining approval ratings were intimately connected to these divisions. The COVID-19 pandemic forced the UCP government to deal with sharply differing opinions within its ranks as to how best to respond to the virus. These divisions greatly complicated the task of governing and of managing the party. With no clear path to resolving differences, ongoing discord diminished the premier's standing as a competent politician, damaged the party's electoral fortunes, encouraging even greater dissent. These factors underpinned the poor result for the premier at the UCP leadership review. As the summer of 2021 drew to a close, the UCP, in stark contrast to their founding myth, trailed its NDP opponent in vote-intention polls and faced the very real prospect of losing power in the next election.[7] As has often been the case in Alberta, and indeed, Canadian politics more broadly, parties faced with such a possibility see a leadership change as providing an opportunity to escape defeat and present a new image.[8]

Before its defeat in 2015, the PCs had controlled the Alberta government since 1971, enjoying the longest continuous reign of a single party in Canadian history. The PCs were able to maintain power in part by dealing with popularity issues through the mechanism of leadership change and a voting process that from 1992–2014 invited all Albertans to vote directly for their next premier through internal party elections. At its apex in 2006, more than 144,000 Albertans availed themselves of this opportunity.

Alberta's parties are very much leadership-dominated institutions, but while this tendency is strong in Alberta it is by no means unique. Writing in the early twentieth century, André Siegfried maintained that "it is of the first importance to the success of a party that it should be led by someone who inspires confidence and whose mere name is a programme in itself. As long as the Conservatives had Macdonald for their leader, they voted for him rather than for the party. So it is with Laurier and the Liberals of to-day. If Laurier disappeared, the Liberals would perhaps find that they had lost the real secret of their victories."[9] Most analyses of Canadian parties suggest that the role of the leader in defining parties is undiminished.

More unique in the Alberta experience was that the election of a new leader was so often successful. In a study of Canadian leadership changes from 1960 to 1992, Stewart and Carty found that a change in the leadership of a governing party was generally followed by an election loss.[10] This is an unsurprising finding given that parties are more likely to change their leader in an environment in which their position in power seems threatened.

In 1992, when Ralph Klein was elected PC leader in the first of the party's "premier primaries," the party was trailing its Liberal opponents in the polls and seemed destined to lose its grip on power. Indeed, Klein himself described the 1993 election victory as the "miracle on the prairie."[11] This miracle undoubtedly helped create an internal dynamic suggesting that unpopularity could be transformed by a new leader.[12] Major Albertan and Canadian parties are not known for consistent policy positions and one of the easiest ways of changing policies is to change the leader. This is a lesson the Alberta centre-right has embraced.

Conservative dominance in Alberta from Klein's election in 1992 through the election of Jim Prentice in 2014 followed a path that has often been missed by causal observers of the province's election results. With the elections of Ralph Klein, Ed Stelmach, Alison Redford, and Jim Prentice, the party changed its leader, but avoided victories for more right-wing candidates within the party. In each case, a more moderate candidate emerged victorious and, until Prentice in 2015, went on to win the provincial election and maintain the Tory dynasty.

These victories were not, however, completely popular within the party. Many felt the openness of the party's leadership process allowed it to be infiltrated by voters who were not truly conservative in their views and prevented the PC party from presenting the more coherent right-wing platform these critics believed Albertans would welcome.[13] These critics wanted a clear shift to the right in party policy.

The perception that the Albertan PCs were not sufficiently conservative can be traced as far back as the Lougheed regime, when in 1982, almost 12 per cent of the vote went to the Western Canada Concept Party. The vagaries of the electoral system, and the popularity of the Lougheed government, resulted in no seats for this contender, but it provides evidence of some dissatisfaction with a government that tried to create a big-tent centrist party.

Klein, for a time, was able to contain such divisions and in 1993 won an election in which there was essentially a two-party competition with no real opposition on the right. Only Liberals and PCs were elected in the 1993 election and together they took almost 85 per cent of the vote.

As the Klein government continued in office and lost its initial focus on spending cuts, dissatisfaction on the right again emerged. In the 2004 election the PC popular vote fell below 50 per cent for the first time since 1993 and the right-wing Alberta Alliance party obtained almost 9 per cent of the popular vote (see Table 4.1). Klein indicated that he would not again lead his party in an election, ushering in an era of unprecedented leadership change in the province.

One of the other factors underlying PC dominance of Alberta was the competition on the centre-left. As Peter McCormick explained, "Alberta does not typically have a governing party, an opposition party, and fragments on the fringes, but a governing party and several opposition fragments."[14] Only in the 2012 election where the PCs pulled off a surprise come-from-behind victory was the combined Liberal-NDP vote below 30 per cent and it appears that the vote was low that year because many former NDP and Liberal voters selected the PCs to keep Wildrose from power. In short, the vote on the centre-left of the Alberta spectrum was never as weak as often assumed and the PCs benefitted from this division.

Table 4.1. Electoral Support in Alberta 1993–2019

Election Year	PC Popular Vote	Other Right Vote	Liberal/NDP Vote	Alberta Party
1993	44.5	Social Credit 2.4	50.7	——
1997	51.2	Social Credit 6.8	41.6	——
2001	61.9	Less than 1%	35.4	——
2004	46.8	Alberta Alliance 8.7	39.6	——
2008	52.7	Wildrose Alliance Less than 1%	34.9	——
2012	44.0	Wildrose 34.3	19.8	1.3
2015	27.8	Wildrose 24.2	44.8	4.2
2019	54.9 (UCP)	Less than 1%	33.7	9.1

Sources: "Historical Results, Summary Tables," Elections Alberta. https://www.elections.ab.ca/elections/election-results/historical-results/ (accessed 6 August 2022).

The election of the UCP in 2019 was based on a popular vote that was actually below the combined centre-right vote in 2008 and 2012 and only 3 per cent points higher than the combined 2015 total.

The centre-right's dominance of Alberta politics this century has not, as was often the case historically, been based on a single leader. Instead, divisions on that side of the political spectrum resulted in almost constant leadership change. Klein was the last PC leader to lead in two successive elections, and he was forced from office earlier than he had wanted by a very tepid leadership review vote in 2006. Ironically, a review vote in which his support actually exceeded that won by Kenney in 2022.

The more right-wing side of the equation was also far from immune from leadership change with new leaders and often new party names on the ballot from 2004 through 2015. For both parties, the incumbent leader left his or her position in a climate of substantial unhappiness with their performance.[15]

In short, the tenure of conservative leaders has been quite brief and most left their position under pressure from their own party. With this history, the challenges faced by Jason Kenney and the divisions on the conservative side do not appear particularly surprising or new. The fact that the UCP will be led by a new leader in the next election is consistent with the dynamics on the right since the end of the Klein regime.

Table 4.2. Centre-Right Political Party Leaders in Elections 2001–2019

Election Year	PC Leader	Other Right-of-Centre Leader
2001	PC Ralph Klein	Less than 1%
2004	PC Ralph Klein	Alliance Randy Thorsteinson
2008	PC Ed Stelmach	Wildrose Alliance Paul Hinman
2012	PC Alison Redford	Wildrose Danielle Smith
2015	PC Jim Prentice	Wildrose Brian Jean
2019	UCP Jason Kenney	Others less than 1%

Sources: Calculated by the authors from Elections Alberta data at https://www.elections.ab.ca/elections/election-results/historical-results/ (accessed 6 August 2022).

Following the 2015 Alberta election the PC party was faced with an existential challenge. The party could continue with its general pattern and contest the next election as a pragmatic big tent party or it could move more to the right and present a more ideological approach. As we argue in *Orange Chinook*[16] the resolution of this dilemma emerged from a leadership election. The party made the decision to hold a leadership convention, rather than a primary, a switch that almost certainly ensured a more ideological electorate and Jason Kenney, a former federal cabinet minister, entered the race with a proposal to unite the right and rid the province of the "accidental" NDP government. Kenney easily won that leadership election, negotiated a merger with the Wildrose party, won that party's initial leadership election, and led the party to victory in the 2019 election.

One way to examine the evolution of conservative parties in Alberta and understand the divisions within conservatism is to compare the attitudes of 2019 UCP voters with the 2015 PC and Wildrose voters. This comparison is based on voter surveys conducted following the two elections that asked largely the same series of attitudinal questions. In *Orange Chinook* we report on the attitudes of party voters in a series of elections and we are not going to recapitulate that discussion here. However, we will point out that PC voters in 2015 were often as close in opinion to the 2015 NDP voters as they were to the 2015 Wildrose voters so the merger was not an inevitable outcome.

Figure 4.1 presents the positions of party voters on a number of scales by presenting the mean location of party votes on a 0–1 spectrum with 0

Figure 4.1. Ideological Scale Means of Party Identifiers, PC or Wildrose 2015, UCP 2019

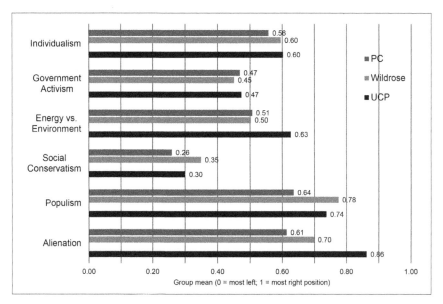

Note: Survey weights applied. (There are no substantive changes from the unweighted results.)

indicating a more leftist position and 1 a more right-wing position. The questions on which the scales are based try to capture key elements of Alberta's political culture by examining attitudes relating to individualism, government activism, prioritizing energy or the environment, social conservatism, populism, and western alienation.[17] We will discuss the positioning on each of these scales in turn. It is also worth keeping in mind that the positioning of PC voters in 2019 is likely to be further to the right than in the past since a large number of 2012 PC voters actually switched to the NDP in 2015.[18]

The first three scales: individualism, support for an activist government, and prioritizing energy rather than the environment show that conservative voters may not be as far to the right as many assume. For individualism, the votes do not go beyond 0.6 on the scale at any point and for government activism, even in 2019, they are almost exactly at the scale's midpoint. Even on energy versus the environment, the voters were at the midpoint in 2015 and the movement to the right in 2019 was likely based on the increased salience of pipelines in the election campaign and Kenney's critique of the NDP government for not getting pipelines built. In 2015 the positioning of Wildrose and PC voters is almost identical on each of these scales and the real movement in 2019 comes on the energy scale where there is a much more pronounced pro-energy position.

The next three scales are more revealing of divisions within conservative politics. Questions relating to social conservatism were limited, focusing on abortion choice and gay and lesbian marriage. Again, the positioning on this scale suggests that conservative voters are far from socially conservative and are essentially in the bottom third. In 2015 we see that Wildrose voters are noticeably more socially conservative than PC voters and the 2019 results indicate that the new party has landed somewhere in the middle—more socially conservative than 2015 PC voters but less socially conservative than 2015 Wildrose voters. Unlike the three previous scales, the position of PC party voters is more moderate than that of Wildrose voters.

The same result can be seen with respect to populism, a concept long argued to be a key component of Alberta politics.[19] In 2015, perhaps unsurprisingly given the campaign of the Prentice PCs, PC voters placed much lower on the populism scale than the Wildrose voters. Losing the populist position from their electoral repertoire is something we believed contributed to the party's defeat in that election. The UCP voters in 2019 were marginally less populist than Wildrose voters in 2015, but farther from the position of 2015 PC voters. Overall, the UCP voters were just below the top quartile for populism.

More dramatic is the positioning relating to western alienation. Like populism, western alienation has long been a key component of Alberta's political culture and provincial governments have often conducted provincial election campaigns as if their major competitor was the federal government, rather than their actual fellow provincial parties.[20] The ability to run against the federal government was critical in the historical success of Alberta governing parties. It is likely significant that when the success of provincial PCs was threatened in 2012 and 2015, the federal government was led by a united Conservative party that held almost every federal seat in the province, making campaigning against them quite difficult. In 2019, Jason Kenney faced no such problem and campaigned as much against the

Figure 4.2. Policy Convention Consensus Scores

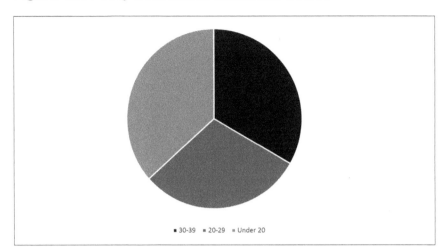

■ 30-39 ■ 20-29 ■ Under 20

Sources: Calculated by authors from United Conservative Party data. See note 6.

federal Liberals as the provincial New Democrats. In this environment it is no surprise that UCP voters were more clearly alienated than either the PC or even Wildrose voters in 2015.

The 2019 UCP voters were somewhat more socially conservative, more pro-energy, and substantially more populist and alienated than the 2015 PC voters. They were also more pro-energy and very much more alienated than the 2015 Wildrose voters. However, they were less socially conservative than Wildrose voters. There were really no differences worth discussing in relation to individualism and government activism either between elections or between the 2015 PC and Wildrose voters.

In an effort to further understand the divisions within Alberta conservatism, we move beyond the views of voters to explore the opinions of activists. In this context we make use of the votes at the UCP policy convention in 2020.

We try here to fit the policy resolutions debated and approved by delegates into the areas we examined with ordinary voters. Instead of focusing as much on the policy (all were approved) we focus on the degree of internal consensus on the various policies. We use a Consensus Index (CI) that measures the nature of division within the party. If there is perfect consensus for or against a policy, everyone takes the same position, the CI is 50. If there is an even 50–50 split, the CI score would be 0. Simply put, the higher the CI score, the more consensus that exists within the party.

Figure 4.2 shows that there is much room for disagreement within the party. None of the 30 policy resolutions generated a CI score of over 40 and the largest number of resolutions generated scores of under 20.

Table 4.3 presents each of the basic policy resolutions debated at the convention using the number provided by the party. We see again that there is a good deal of internal disagreement with a mean CI score of 23.6, just below the midpoint of the range from 0 (where half support and half oppose a motion) to 50 (where everyone either supports or opposes the motion). To get a better sense of the nature of agreement we attempt to position some of the policy resolutions similar to the way we treated voter attitudes, by looking first at policies relating to individualism and government activism.

Given the way the CI measure works, it is a little easier to think in terms of agreement. A high CI score indicates high levels of agreement, and low the obverse. It is these low scores that are of most interest. Low levels of agreement correspond with high levels of division. On these measures we see levels of agreement that range from a low of 2.71 to a high of 36.51. The lowest level of agreement—or highest degrees of disagreement—was with regard to support for privately funded and managed health care, which nearly evenly split the party (CI 2.71). Although it was adopted, 46 per cent of those voting opposed the policy. The highest level of consensus was on equitable transfer and a referendum on equalization (CI 38.93) with government operating within its means and reducing the debt (CI 36.51) the second most agreed upon policy.

Almost two-thirds of the delegates supported ensuring adequate housing and supportive care for seniors (CI 32.04) yet strong majorities supported making Alberta a right-to-work jurisdiction (CI 30.77), not allowing regulations to create a barrier to economic growth (CI 32.04) and contracting out non-essential and ancillary services (CI 31.45). There was a good deal of suspicion directed at teachers' unions, with almost 85 per cent believing that teacher organization should not be involved in collective bargaining (CI 34.16) and around three-quarters calling for the creation of a self-governing regulatory association for Alberta teachers (CI 26.74).

Table 4.3. United Conservative Party Policy Votes 2020 AGM

Policy Question	Yes	No	CI
1. Operate within means and reduce debt	86.51	13.25	36.51
2. Equitable transfer and hold referendum	88.93	10.59	38.93
3. Make Alberta a right-to-work jurisdiction	80.77	18.98	30.77
4. Facilitate private pipeline and infrastructure developments	80.54	18.97	30.54
5. Out of court for non-criminal traffic matters	85.18	14.2	35.18
6. Control spending and reduce size of government	72.55	27.06	22.55
7. Contract out non-essential and ancillary services to private sector	81.15	18.1	31.15
8. Withdraw from Canada Pension Plan (CPP) and start Alberta pension plan	67.13	32.49	17.13
9. Ensure quality of care for elderly, monitor and enforce	82.04	17.21	32.04
10. Collect Alberta taxes directly	64.4	34.57	14.4
11. Support privately funded and managed healthcare option	52.71	46.53	2.71
12. Ensure regulatory environment does not create barriers to growth	81.45	17.66	31.45
13. Balance environmental objectives with need for economic growth	76.3	22.81	26.3
14. Make Alberta global hub for technological innovations	75.74	23.75	25.74
15. Ensure safety of community is priority in consumption sites	78.8	20.69	28.8
16. Create Alberta provincial police	71.1	28.22	21.1
17. Create new vision for K–12 curriculum	62.91	36.96	12.91
18. Remove cap on number of publicly funded surgeries	64.56	35.18	14.56
19. Adopt recall for members of the legislative assembly (MLAs)	71.8	27.83	21.8
20. Work with feds on one-window regulatory approval	80.13	19.35	30.13
21. Develop petroleum reserve and expand storage capacity	60.76	38.58	10.76
22. Ensure publicly funded organizations do not encroach on free enterprise	65.93	33.68	15.93

Table 4.3. (*continued*)

Policy Question	Yes	No	CI
23. Professional teacher organizations can't be involved in collective bargaining	84.16	15.59	34.16
24. Repeal Bill 10 Public Health Emergency Powers Act	78.73	21	28.73
25. Increase investment and oversight of care facilities for seniors	63.66	35.81	13.66
26. Use natural gas resources for growth in petrochemicals	70.57	28.76	20.57
27. Adopt citizen initiated referendums	66.41	32.95	16.41
28. Create self-governing regulatory association for Alberta teachers	76.74	22.75	26.74
29. Prevent municipalities from running budget deficits	68.44	31.17	18.44
30. Support and protect family and small businesses	68.88	30.05	18.88
	73.63267	25.82467	-23.63267

Sources: United Conservative Party. See note 6.

On measures relating to energy and the environment, about one delegate in five always disagreed with the policies approved. Nineteen per cent of the delegates opposed facilitating private sector pipelines and infrastructure and a simplified one-window regulatory approval process. Almost one in four opposed balancing environmental objectives with economic growth, and almost 30 per cent opposed a role for government in encouraging downstream growth in petrochemicals. Disagreement was most intense over the development of strategic petroleum reserves and expanding storage with almost 40 per cent rejecting this position. What is striking is that in an avowedly conservative government majorities were in favour of an enhanced government role in the energy industry.

Perhaps surprisingly there were few policy questions relating to social conservatism. What we do see is a good deal of resistance to a new K–12 curriculum with 37 per cent opposing this development. Populist measures were also a source of some division. Around three delegates in ten opposed the recall of MLAs and citizen initiatives, but only half that number were opposed to placing restrictions on teachers' unions. The latter is a measure that might fit better with individualism. Thirty per cent were also opposed to measures for supporting and protecting family and small businesses.

Finally with respect to western alienation: almost 90 per cent approved calls for a more equitable system of transfers and a referendum on equalization. As well, in relation to measures tied to the decades old idea of a firewall to protect Alberta from the federal government, there was considerable disagreement. Twenty-eight per cent rejected the creation of an Alberta police force, and around one third opposed withdrawing from CPP and launching an Alberta pension plan and collecting Alberta taxes directly.

Overall, the highest levels of consensus came on the idea of a referendum on equalization, operating within means and reducing debt; creating an out-of-court option for non-criminal traffic matters; keeping professional teacher organizations out of bargaining; and ensuring, monitoring, and enforcing quality care for elderly. The lowest consensus levels related to private health care, the development of petroleum reserves, and creating a new vision for a K–12 curriculum.

Although all of the policy resolutions were approved, the actual votes demonstrate considerable differences of opinion within the party and indicate a conservative party that is far from unified.

General surveys relating to the performance of the government since 2019 indicate a good deal of public dissatisfaction with the UCP. For instance, an Angus Reid survey taken in June 2021 revealed that the percentage indicating that the government was doing a good job in handling various policy areas never reached 50 per cent. Just 39 per cent felt the performance was good in handling the environment and climate change, and only a third felt that health care and the response to COVID-19 were positive. These numbers predated the government's self-admitted mismanagement of COVID that summer. Even on issues like energy and government spending less than 30 per cent felt the performance was good.[21] In short there was much unhappiness with the UCP on policy matters.

This dissatisfaction spilled over into evaluations of the premier's performance. Shortly after the election in June of 2019 Kenney's approval rating was over 60 per cent but by February 2020 it had fallen below 50 per cent and did not really recover. In June 2021, fewer than one Albertan in three approved of his performance, and he ranked last out of the ten premiers on this measure.[22] In September 2021, *Calgary Herald* columnist Don Braid suggested that the rating of his performance had fallen even more with a Leger poll suggesting only 23 per cent approved of his handling of the pandemic.[23]

The discussion of divisions within the UCP in this chapter has, to this point, not picked up on issues relating to the COVID-19 crisis, and it is perhaps instructive that there were virtually no policy resolutions directly relating to this at the 2020 policy convention. Protecting seniors and a relatively strong resistance to private health care provide some hints of party divisions on this issue.

The divisions within the UCP relating to COVID-19 were strong and stark and included something of an internal caucus revolt by sixteen MLAs,[24] two MLAs kicked out of caucus for their criticism of pandemic policies,[25] the resignation of the caucus chair,[26] and the removal of the deputy premier from her position shortly after criticizing the premier for a dinner that seemed to violate health rules.[27] As well, Brian Jean, the former Wildrose leader who was runner-up to Kenney in the 2017 leadership election, emerged as a major critic of the premier and successfully sought the UCP nomination for a by-election in 2022. He ran on a platform calling for the premier to step down. His success both in the nomination and in winning the March 2022 by-election helped put even more wind in the sails of the anti-Kenney groups within the party.[28]

Obviously, internal consensus was badly lacking in the government's approach to the pandemic. Polling suggested that the majority of Albertans were supportive of strong measures to manage the pandemic and unhappy with the government's performance. As Kost wrote in early September 2021:

> Seventy-seven per cent of Albertans surveyed said they would either somewhat or strongly support a vaccine passport system requiring proof of vaccination for non-essential services such as bars, restaurants, gyms and festivals. We found that Albertans are not far out of step with Canadians across the country," said Leger vice-president Andrew Enns. Meanwhile, Kenney ranked lower than any other premier in Canada in regard to his handling of the pandemic, according to the same Leger poll. Six-

ty-five per cent of Albertans said they were either somewhat or very dissatisfied with the measures Kenney has put in place to fight COVID-19.[29]

Dissatisfaction with the government was split between those who felt the response had not been strong enough and those who felt the government had gone too far. The problem for the UCP was that most of those who opposed restrictions were generally among those expected to support the party. In essence a good portion of the party's base of supporters were out of step with the views of most Albertans. The challenge for the government was that they could not win re-election without these voters, but sympathy to them might also endanger the prospect of re-election.[30] Public dissatisfaction formed the backdrop for the internal conflict within the party. The premier's attempts to manage the issue led to Kenney providing something of an apology for suggesting in the summer of 2021 that the pandemic was over and the then mayor of Calgary, a city the UCP must win to remain in office, calling the UCP government the most incompetent he had seen.[31]

Attempts to resolve conflict within the party proved unsuccessful. An agreement to hold a leadership review in the early spring of 2022 descended into controversy when the vote was postponed. An in-person vote was scheduled to be held in Red Deer but "That changed to mail-in voting after more than 15,000 people seemed ready to descend on the city."[32] Even the rules surrounding how votes would be cast and ballots delivered generated controversy. Kenney initially indicated that even a modest win would enable him to retain the leadership but, in the end, his support was a little too modest and his resignation announcement removed the danger of complaints about the nature of the review. Complaints that might well have kept issues relating to controversy about the conduct of the 2017 election front and centre.[33]

In 2017 Kenney was elected leader with more than 35,000 votes. In 2022, the overall number of voters in the leadership review was actually lower than just Kenney's 2017 total and his actual support was about half what he had won just five years previously. Many of those who enthusiastically supported him in 2017 were unwilling to vote to keep him in the same position for another election. Indeed, the number supporting

Kenney in 2022 was smaller than the number who supported Brian Jean in his losing leadership run in 2017.[34]

In the aftermath of his disappointing showing in the leadership review, Kenney gave a clear indication that he felt the pandemic issue was critical. As Don Braid explained, "Kenney blamed 'a small but highly motivated, well-organized and very angry group of people who believe that [he] and the government have been promoting a part of some globalist agenda, and vaccines are at the heart of that. [He doesn't] think most of these people have ever before been involved in a mainstream centre-right party and [he] suspect[s] many of them won't be in the future."[35] Braid went on to indicate that Kenney's opponents had a different take on the opposition, with one constituency association president suggesting that the problem related to "'the party being all about Kenney [was that] there wasn't respect paid to the grassroots, there was a very ivory-tower atmosphere where MLAs and even ministers were out of the loop. There is a top-down attitude to government. The fact that his party said "we don't want you," and he's still trying to blame it on those few anti-vaccination people, it doesn't help anybody.'"[36] As the party moves on to seek a new leader, there is not even a clear agreement on what created the opposition to Kenney. The premier's decision to serve as leader until his successor is chosen has also generated some conflict within the party as some, including some in the caucus, would have preferred a more immediate departure.[37]

Throughout this period of turmoil, not surprisingly, polling suggested that the opposition NDP were ahead of the UCP in voter preference. Another indicator of growing NDP strength is their success in fundraising. As Lisa Johnson reported in November of 2021, "The NDP has out-fundraised the UCP in every quarter since the end of 2020. For the first nine months of this year, the NDP brought in just over $4 million compared to the UCP's total of about $2.6 million."[38] All of this relates to the dilemma in which the UCP found itself. The party was essentially created by the efforts of Jason Kenney and his campaign brought them to power. But he and his policies grew increasingly unpopular. The recent history of Alberta conservative parties is clear: when the leader is not in a position to lead them to victory, the leader goes. This is not just an Alberta phenomenon. Writing in 2005 on the personalization of power in political parties, Poguntke and Webb suggest "a shift towards personalized leadership which may be very strong as long as it is successful electorally, but which is likely to be vulnerable in times of impending or actual electoral defeat."[39] The creation of the UCP was in part based on a desire for a more ideological and less pragmatic approach to government. With such preferences, party insiders may be more likely to prioritize particular policy positions to increase electability, although in Alberta there seems to be an assumption that only a fluke can prevent a conservative party from winning elections.

In this context, it was unsurprising that Jason Kenney's leadership of the party was in grave danger. As Carty and Cross have argued elsewhere, "one of the ways in which party members can change party policy is indirect—through a change in personnel. They argue that leadership elections 'represent contests over competing orientations on important social, economic and constitutional issues.'"[40] UCP members can get new policies and perhaps a better hope of re-election with a new leader. Ed Stelmach, Alison Redford, and even Ralph Klein provide evidence that Alberta's governing conservatives see no problem in getting rid of a sitting premier. With a more ideological party, the impetus for change was almost certainly stronger. It remains unclear who will lead the UCP in the next election and somewhat ironically, two of the candidates who may well contest the leadership are former leaders of the Wildrose party who have already lost provincial elections. If they were to prove successful it would seem that the party has decided to shift in a more populist and right-wing direction and ironically, for the first time since Klein, a conservative leader would contest more than one election.

A new leader is not, however, a panacea. As Gary Mason indicates, a new leader will still face challenges:

> [W]hoever wins will have the same problem Mr. Kenney had when he took over: the UCP is an amalgam of two political philosophies, two ideological forces. They are often at odds. To put it another way, the old Wildrose forces often disagree and resent the old Progressive Conservative types. Their interests aren't aligned. They don't like one another. Old war wounds have not healed and may never heal.[41]

Danielle Smith re-entered Alberta politics on October 6, 2022, with a 54 to 46 per cent victory over her main rival, Travis Toews, on the sixth ballot. It is not clear whether the leadership race put the united back in United Conservative, or if Smith is the sort of leader who can boost the party's electoral chances in 2023. Smith's floor crossing from Wildrose to the PCs in 2014 damaged the leadership of Jim Prentice and helped precipitate the collapse of the Tory dynasty. It earned Smith the enmity of members of both parties and led her to move on to work in talk radio. Whether her victory signals the welding together of this coalition into a political force driven by the need to defeat the NDP or a marriage of convenience susceptible to internal dissension is as yet unknown. Untested, too, is her ability to move beyond the narrow focus of her strident leadership campaign to become a successful Premier.

NOTES

1   Don Braid, "UCP knives come out for Kenney," *Calgary Herald*, 22 September 2021, A1; Don Braid, "Kenney wins battle but war still on," *Calgary Herald*, 23 September 2021, A1.

2   Kelly Cryderman, "Jason Kenney avoids non-confidence vote from UCP caucus, agrees to early leadership review," *Globe and Mail*, 22 September 2021, https://www.theglobeandmail.com/canada/alberta/article-jason-kenney-avoids-non-confidence-vote-from-ucp-caucus-agrees-to/ (accessed 24 September 2021).

3   Brittany Gervais, "Kenney stepping down as UCP party leaders after winning only 51% of leadership vote," *Calgary Herald*, 18 May 2022, https://calgaryherald.com/news/politics/kenney-secures-51-of-leadership-vote-steps-down-as-ucp-party-leader (accessed 3 June 2022).

4   Anthony M. Sayers and David K. Stewart, "Out of the Blue; Goodbye Tories, Hello Jason Kenney," in *Orange Chinook: Politics in the New Alberta*, eds. Duane Bratt et al. (Calgary: University of Calgary Press, 2019), 399–423; and Duane Bratt, "Death of a Dynasty: the Tories and the 2015 Election," in *Orange Chinook*, 35–56.

5   Data from Alberta Election Survey of 1500 voters conducted online in the week following each of the 2015 and 2019 provincial elections.

6   Information on the UCP policy resolutions comes from ucpagm.ca voting results (accessed 29 April 2021).

7   "Poll Analysis & Electoral Projections," 338Canada, 338canada.com/alberta/polls.htm (accessed 24 September 2021).

8   David K. Stewart, "Primaries and the Personalization of Party Leadership," in *The Personalization of Democratic Politics and the Challenge for Political Parties*, eds.

William P. Cross, Richard S. Katz, and Scott Pruysers (London: ECPR Press Rowman and Littlefield International, 2018).

9   André Siegfried, *The Race Question in Canada*, (Toronto: McClelland and Stewart, 1966 [1907]).

10   David K. Stewart and R.K. Carty, "Does Changing the Party Leader Provide an Electoral Boost? A Study of Canadian Provincial Parties: 1960–1992," *Canadian Journal of Political Science* 26, no. 2 (1993): 313–330.

11   See David K. Stewart and Keith Archer, *Quasi-Democracy: Parties and Leadership Selection in Alberta* (Vancouver: UBC Press, 2000).

12   *Ibid.*

13   Ted Morton, "Leadership Selection in Alberta, 1992–2011: A Personal Perspective," *Canadian Parliamentary Review* 26, no. 2 (2013): 31–8.

14   Peter McCormick, "Voting Behaviour in Alberta: The Quasi Party System Revisited," *Journal of Canadian Studies* 15, no. 3 (1980): 85–98, 90.

15   See Bratt, "Death of a Dynasty."

16   Sayers and Stewart, "Out of the Blue."

17   The scales are based on answers to a number of questions and converted to a 0–1 scale with 1 indicating the most supportive positions. The individualism scale is based on responses to the following questions: government regulation stifles drive, most unemployed could find jobs, those willing to pay should get medical treatment sooner, a lot of welfare and social programs unnecessary. The activist-government scale is based on responses to the following questions: government should ensure decent living standard, government should ensure adequate housing, government should limit amount of rent increases, government should take over auto insurance. The pro-energy scale is based on responses to the following questions: oil and gas companies have too much say in provincial politics, Alberta should slow pace of oil sands development, tough environmental standards should take precedence over employment, Alberta needs to take firm action to combat global warming, Alberta should increase royalties on natural gas and oil. The social conservatism scale is based on responses to the following questions: abortion is a matter between a woman and her doctor, gays and lesbians should be allowed to marry. The populism scale is based on responses to the following questions: trust ordinary people more than experts, solve problems if government is brought back to grassroots, need government to get things done with less red tape. The western alienation scale is based on responses to the following questions: Alberta is treated unfairly by the federal government; Alberta does not have its fair share of political power in Canada; the economic policies of the federal government seem to help Quebec and Ontario at the expense of Alberta; because parties depend on Quebec and Ontario, Alberta usually gets ignored in national politics.

18   Sayers and Stewart, "Out of the Blue," 412.

19   See for instance Jared J. Wesley, *Code Politics: Campaigns and Cultures on the Canadian Prairies* (Vancouver: UBC Press, 2011).

20   Wesley, *Code Politics*; McCormick, "Voting Behaviour in Alberta"; David K. Stewart and Anthony Sayers, "Albertans' Conservative Beliefs," in *Conservatism in Canada*, eds. James Farney and David Rayside (Toronto: University of Toronto Press, 2013).

21 Angus Reid Institute, "Premiers' Performance," https://angusreid.org/premier-approval-june2021/ (accessed 24 September 2021).

22 *Ibid.*

23 Braid, "Kenney wins battle but war still on," A4.

24 Lisa Johnson, "Quarter of UCP MLAs speak out against Alberta's latest COVID-19 restrictions," *Edmonton Journal*, 7 April 2021, https://edmontonjournal.com/news/politics/fifteen-ucp-mlas-say-kenneys-latest-covid-19-restrictions-move-alberta-backwards (accessed 24 September, 2021). For a more historical analysis see also Duane Bratt and Bruce Foster, "UCP caucus revolt latest in a long history of splintering conservative parties in Alberta," *CBC Opinion*, 13 April 2021 (accessed 24 September 2021).

25 Tyler Dawson, "Two MLAs kicked out of Alberta UCP caucus hours after call for Premier Jason Kenney to resign," *National Post*, 13 May 2021, https://nationalpost.com/news/politics/two-mlas-kicked-out-of-alberta-ucp-caucus-hours-after-calls-made-for-premier-jason-kenney-to-resign (accessed 24 September 2021).

26 Dean Bennett, "UCP caucus chair calls on Kenney to resign," *Calgary Herald*, 13 May 2021. https://calgaryherald.com/pmn/news-pmn/canada-news-pmn/alberta-premier-jason-kenney-faces-call-from-senior-caucus-backbencher-to-resign/wcm/ea98edd4-ec1b-4f33-9d28-96641f5c9a71 (accessed 24 September 2021).

27 Dean Bennett, "Alberta Premier Jason Kenney shuffles cabinet, drops critic Leela Aheer, carves up her ministry," *Globe and Mail*, 9 July 2021, https://www.theglobeandmail.com/canada/article-kenney-shuffles-cabinet-drops-critic-leela-aheer-carves-up-her/ (accessed 24 September 2021).

28 Carrie Tait and Emma Graney, "Alberta Premier Jason Kenney to resign after winning slim majority in UCP leadership review," *Globe and Mail*, 18 May 2022, https://www.theglobeandmail.com/canada/alberta/article-alberta-premier-jason-kenney-announces-resignation-after-poor/ (accessed 30 May 2022).

29 Hannah Kost, "Over 75% of Albertans would support vaccine passport, survey suggests," *CBC News*, 3 September 2021, https://www.cbc.ca/news/canada/calgary/alberta-vaccine-passport-kenney-leger-poll-covid-1.6164353 (accessed 24 September 2021).

30 Excellent discussion of these issues is provided by Graham Thomson, "Not so united conservatives," *CBC News*, 9 April 2021, https://www.cbc.ca/news/canada/edmonton/not-so-united-conservatives-kenney-being-punished-politically-for-doing-the-right-thing-1.5980772; Lisa Young, "Polarization, politics and policy failure: Alberta's response to COVID-19," *CBC Opinion*, 10 April 2021, https://www.cbc.ca/news/canada/calgary/road-ahead-alberta-polarization-covid-lisa-young-1.5981824; Gary Mason, "COVID-19 has exposed Alberta as Canada's other distinct society," *Globe and Mail*, 27 April 2021, https://www.theglobeandmail.com/opinion/article-covid-19-has-exposed-alberta-as-canadas-other-distinct-society/; Chris Nelson, "We are not in this together, we were never in this together," *Calgary Herald*, 6 May 2021, (all accessed 24 September 2021).

31   Michael Franklin, "UCP government 'the most incompetent' he's seen, Calgary's mayor says," *CTV News Calgary*, 16 September 2021, https://calgary.ctvnews.ca/ucp-government-the-most-incompetent-he-s-seen-calgary-s-mayor-says-1.5589053 (accessed 24 September 2021).

32   Don Braid, "Kenney critics blast last-minute change to leadership voting," *Calgary Herald*, 8 April 2022, https://calgaryherald.com/opinion/columnists/braid-kenney-critics-blast-last-minute-change-to-leadership-voting (accessed 2 June 2022).

33   Investigations into the 2017 UCP leadership election were conducted by both Elections Alberta and the RCMP. The issues revolved around identity questions, campaign donations, and the involvement of the Kenney campaign with another candidate's campaign. See Dean Bennett, "Kenney interviewed by RCMP in criminal probe tied to 2017 UCP leadership race," *Canadian Press*, 28 March 2022, https://globalnews.ca/news/8716885/jason-kenney-alberta-rcmp-ucp-leadership-race/ (accessed 3 June 2022).

34   James Wood, "Kenney wins big in UCP leadership race," *Calgary Herald*, 29 October 2017, https://calgaryherald.com/news/politics/kenney-wins-big-in-ucp-leadership-race (accessed 3 June 2022).

35   Don Braid, "UCP erupts again over Kenney's claims about anti-vaxxers," *Calgary Herald*, 1 June 2022, https://calgaryherald.com/opinion/columnists/braid-ucp-erupts-again-over-kenneys-claims-about-anti-vaxxers (accessed 3 June 2022).

36   *Ibid.*

37   Dylan Short, "Jason Kenney to remain as UCP leader until new one can be chosen," *Calgary Herald*, 19 May 2022, https://calgaryherald.com/news/local-news/ucp-mlas-express-mixed-reactions-to-resignation-of-jason-kenney-as-party-leader (accessed 3 June 2020).

38   Lisa Johnson, "Alberta Opposition NDP's fundraising continues to outpace that of governing UCP," *Edmonton Journal*, 1 November 2021, https://edmontonjournal.com/news/politics/alberta-opposition-ndps-fundraising-continues-to-outpace-that-of-governing-ucp (accessed 12 November 2021).

39   Thomas Poguntke and Paul Webb, eds., *The Presidentialization of Politics: A Comparative Study of Modern Democracies* (Oxford: Oxford University Press, 2005), 10.

40   As quoted in David K. Stewart, "Primaries and the Personalization of Party Leadership," in *The Personalization of Democratic Politics*, 92.

41   Gary Mason, "The spectacular fall of Jason Kenney," *Globe and Mail*, 19 May 2022, https://www.theglobeandmail.com/opinion/article-the-spectacular-fall-of-jason-kenney/ (accessed 30 May 2022).

5

Albertans and the Fair Deal

Jared J. Wesley

For generations, many Albertans have longed for a fairer deal in Confederation. The notion that the province and its people contribute more to the rest of Canada than they get in return is engrained in Alberta's political culture.[1] The sentiment predates the oil booms of the late-twentieth century, tracing its roots to the farmers' and Progressive movements decades earlier. The common thread from then to now—western alienation—has taken several forms. These have ranged from calls that the "West Wants In," bolstering Alberta's influence over national decision-making, to the "West Wants Out," manifest most recently in the Wexit movement. In the middle stands calls for the West to be left alone.

Thus, in many ways, the United Conservative Party (UCP)'s push for a "Fair Deal" was nothing new. The party built its successful 2019 provincial election campaign on the notion of "fighting back" to secure better terms for Alberta in Confederation. Aimed squarely at the Government of Canada and oil and gas opponents in British Columbia and Quebec, this edgier form of western alienation underpinned much of the UCP's popular "jobs, economy, pipelines" mantra. In much the same way early Progressives had pushed for lower freight rates and the removal of tariffs on American goods a century ago, the UCP's Fair Deal would involve rolling back newly imposed federal laws that appear to block Alberta's access to tidewater for its bitumen and increasing the province's share of federal transfers. The Fair Deal also aimed to position the new premier as a guardian of Alberta's interests on the national and international stage—a timeworn strategy for boosting the popularity of a government and externalizing its domestic opposition.[2]

The Fair Deal is distinct from other attempts to secure Alberta's future, however. Discussed in this chapter, it is far more provocative and, ultimately, more risky.

This chapter traces the evolution of the Fair Deal concept from its genesis in the "Alberta Agenda" advanced by conservatives in 2001 through the constitutional referendum on equalization twenty years later. This history reveals how populist approaches to western alienation took on a more aggressive tone that is increasingly out of step with public opinion. More concerning, strategic missteps in rolling out the Fair Deal process have placed not just the government's survival, but Alberta's position in Confederation, at greater risk than before the UCP government launched the initiative in 2019. Originally designed to quell separatism and bolster Alberta autonomy, the Fair Deal gamble may end up setting Alberta backwards on both counts. In this sense, the Fair Deal is better considered part of the UCP's failed fight back strategy[3] than as a coherent policy package to reform the terms of Confederation (see chapters from Clark and Rioux for other elements). And as a piece of strategy, it has placed Alberta in a precarious position of making unrealistic demands backed up by unpopular ultimatums. According to our Viewpoint Alberta survey data, the next UCP leader would do well to focus less on building Fair Deal firewalls around the province and more on building bridges with the rest of the country.

Context

The federal election in October 2019 marked a turning point in the Alberta government's approach to federalism and intergovernmental relations. Despite receiving more votes, the Conservative Party of Canada had failed to win more seats than their Liberal opponent. The Conservative performance was buoyed by massive victories in Western Canada—particularly in Alberta, where the party's candidates claimed thirty-three of thirty-four seats and 69 per cent of the popular vote. Including the lone New Democrat, Albertans had sent every one of its MPs to the opposition benches, leaving the province shut out of the Liberal caucus and cabinet.

These losses were compounded by the fact that Prime Minister Justin Trudeau had retained power. Son of the architect of the National Energy

Program, and himself the champion of the carbon tax, coastal tanker ban (Bill C-48), and the so-called no more pipelines law (Bill C-69), Trudeau embodied the Laurentian elitism that animated western alienation for several generations.

To say many Albertans were upset at the election result would be an understatement. Support for separatism suddenly spiked in the province, with up to one-third of the population abandoning the conventional call "the West wants in" for a more radical alternative.[4] The rise of separatist sentiment in the province provided both a risk and an opportunity for the UCP. Fault lines between federalists and separatists within the party's base were threatening to widen, potentially undoing the successes of the provincial "unite the right" movement. On the other hand, with enough animosity toward the federal government and the rest of Canada, the time could be ripe to build a "firewall" around Alberta, strengthening the control of the provincial government and corporate elites over Alberta's economy and society.

Known as the "Alberta Agenda," the so-called firewall measures were designed by Alberta conservatives including Stephen Harper, who proposed them in an open letter to then-Premier Ralph Klein in 2001. At the time, the authors were upset at perceived federal encroachment into areas of provincial responsibility, including the environment (Kyoto Protocol) and firearms (gun registry). They placed these alongside perennial concerns with federal agencies, funding, and programs (e.g., the Canadian Wheat Board, health and social transfers, and Employment Insurance). Their solution involved withdrawing Alberta from national institutions like the Canada Pension Plan (CPP) and Canada Revenue Agency (CRA), and establishing an Alberta Provincial Police Force (APPF) to replace the Royal Canadian Mounted Police (RCMP) (see also King's chapter). These measures would have the dual effect of asserting Alberta's autonomy and sending a message to the rest of Canada that the province was not to be taken for granted. The letter was persuasive enough to prompt Klein to strike a MLA Committee to tour the province listening to Albertans' thoughts about the province's place in Confederation.

Many experts and the public roundly panned the firewall approach, and the Klein government abandoned the measures at the urging of the MLA Committee in their 2004 report. The policy ideas remained alive in conservative policy circles, however, and became the centrepiece of the Kenney government's fight back approach to secure a Fair Deal for Alberta. At least one of the Alberta Agenda authors—Ted Morton—would be cited as advisor to the Kenney government in crafting the Fair Deal mandate. At least one other—Ken Boessenkool—would emerge as one of the harshest critics of some of the tactics employed to secure Alberta's autonomy.

No doubt knowing the relative unpopularity of the firewall measures, the UCP opted not to lead with them as part of their Fair Deal strategy. Instead of focusing on measures that were entirely within the purview of the provincial government, they chose to frontload other elements of the fight back plan. If those proposals were rejected by the rest of Canada, Premier Kenney could then propose the broader Alberta Agenda as a retaliatory response.

Piecing together public remarks from the premier and his allies, the following Fair Deal blueprint emerges. Here is a brief synopsis, followed by a more detailed description of each stage:

1) The government strikes a public panel to offer recommendations on whether to incorporate a series of pre-determined elements of a Fair Deal package. Some of these components would be demands made to the rest of Canada, while others would be used as ultimatums should those demands go unsatisfied.

2) A constitutional referendum on removing equalization from the constitution would be the catalyst to elevate the Fair Deal to the top of the public agenda and obligate other governments to negotiate with Alberta on its terms.

3) Forced to the bargaining table, the federal government and provincial governments would receive Alberta's list of demands. These would include reforms to "discriminatory" federal laws and policies held responsible for landlocking Alberta's oil, plus an enriching of the fiscal stabilization fund. Should the rest of Canada (namely, the federal government) refuse to accede to these demands, Alberta would respond by building a firewall around the province.

This final step appeared to be the ultimate goal of the UCP government. Yet, as discussed later in this chapter, there are heavy risks associated with the previous two stages that put the entire Fair Deal initiative, and Alberta's own autonomy, in jeopardy.

Stage 1: A Panel and Report

Premier Kenney summarized the mood of Albertans within days of the 2019 federal election. "People have a bloody right to be frustrated in this province," he said in a speech just hours after the Trudeau Liberals secured a minority government. "We darn well better get to the bottom of that frustration. And that's what we intend to do."[5]

To do so, Kenney struck a Fair Deal Panel to travel the province listening to Albertans' grievances about their place in Canada and consulting with experts on how best to improve Alberta's standing in Confederation. In his mandate letter to the panel, the premier outlined the context and framed the purpose of its work:

> Albertans have an unprecedented level of frustration with their place in the federation. Five years of economic decline and stagnation have been deepened and prolonged by policies emanating from the federal and some other provincial governments, many of which have sought to landlock Alberta's vast energy resources. This, plus policies that interfere in areas of provincial jurisdiction, are seen by many Albertans as fundamentally unfair, particularly given the province's enormous contribution to the Canadian economy, and to fiscal federalism.

> Recent public opinion surveys suggest that as many as one third of Albertans support the concept of separating from the Canadian federation, and that three quarters of Albertans understand or sympathise with this sentiment. Many Albertans who indicate support for federalism are demanding significant reforms that will allow the province to develop its resources, and play a larger role in the federation, commensurate with the size of its economy and contribution to the rest of Canada.

Our Viewpoint Alberta research aligned with the premier's comments. According to our survey conducted immediately following the 2019 federal election:

- 76 per cent of Albertans felt their province received less than its fair share of federal programs and transfers;

- 75 per cent felt that Alberta was not treated with the respect it deserved in Canada; and

- 70 per cent felt that the federal government treated Alberta worse than other provinces.[6]

When asked which emotion best captured their attitude about Alberta's position in Canada within the next decade, over half (51 per cent) replied "angry." A full 84 per cent felt that "the number of Albertans who are angry about Ottawa's treatment of Alberta is increasing." Most strikingly, 29 per cent of Albertans agreed with the notion that Alberta should "separate from Canada and form an independent country." This was the negatively charged atmosphere in which the Fair Deal Panel conducted its work.

Unlike the MLA Committee on Strengthening Alberta's Role in Confederation established by Ralph Klein in 2004, which included nine elected members of the government caucus, the Fair Deal Panel consisted of three government MLAs and six prominent Albertans. The Fair Deal MLAs were drawn from the populist and libertarian end of the UCP caucus, two of whom would go on, after the panel report was released, to co-author their own "Freedom Alberta" manifesto designed to usurp federal jurisdiction over the province (see Stewart chapter).[7]

The Fair Deal Panel chair had deep, nonpartisan experience in intergovernmental relations, having served as deputy minister at both the provincial and federal levels. Joining her were two sons of former Alberta premiers, a former regional Chief for the Assembly of First Nations, a former provincial Progressive Conservative cabinet minister, and a law professor from the University of Alberta. Coming from diverse backgrounds, all five of these members had close ties to the energy and business sectors in the province. This aligned with the primary mandate of the panel, which was to "look at how best to advance the province's vital economic interests, such as the construction of energy pipelines."

Unlike the 2004 MLA Committee mandate, which gave the investigators relatively free rein to scope and identify possible remedies, the Fair Deal Panel's instructions included developing recommendations related to a series of nine specific policy actions discussed below.

The government tasked the panel with hosting at least seven town hall meetings across Alberta (they held twenty-five), and with allowing all Albertans the opportunity to provide feedback through their MLAs, surveys (over 40,000 responded), and traditional written submissions (over 4,000). The panel was also permitted to conduct its own public opinion research and consult with experts.[8]

In releasing its report in May 2020, the Fair Deal Panel weighed in on the nine initial policy actions included in the mandate letter, along with several others (see Table 5.1). Many of these measures align with those first proposed in the Alberta Agenda and recommendations made in the MLA Committee's Report in 2004. This suggests that the government took into account these earlier initiatives when forming the Fair Deal Panel mandate, and the panel considered them when drafting their final report.

Taken together, these various policies may be grouped under the following approaches:

- autonomist (i.e., withdrawing Alberta from pan-Canadian institutions and/or establishing Alberta-specific institutions);

- bridge-building (i.e., establishing greater influence for Alberta within provincial, federal, or international affairs, or working with other jurisdictions to achieve Alberta's objectives);

- rebalancing (i.e., shifting resources or power within Confederation to Alberta's advantage);

- fighting back (i.e., challenging national institutions or practices to stand up for Alberta); and

- other (i.e., miscellaneous measures to strengthen Alberta).

Not unlike the MLA Committee decades earlier, the Fair Deal Panel rejected a number of prominent policy measures proposed by conservatives

Table 5.1. Elements of the Fair Deal and Earlier Initiatives

	Alberta Agenda (2001)	MLA Report (2004)	Fair Deal Mandate (2020)	Fair Deal Report (2021)	Government Response (2021)
Autonomist Approach					
establishing a provincial revenue agency	✔	✗	✔	✗	?
creating an Alberta Pension Plan	✔	✗	✔	✔*	?
establishing a provincial police force	✔	?	✔	✔	?
appointing a chief firearms officer for Alberta			✔	✔	✔
establishing a formalized provincial constitution			✔	✔	
opting out of federal cost share programs with full compensation		?	✔	✔	
seeking an exchange of tax points for federal health and social transfer cash	✔	✔	✔	✗	✔
supporting Quebec's bid to collect federal and provincial taxes				✔	
Bridge-Building Approach					
reducing internal trade barriers				✔	✔
advancing transportation corridors				✔	✔
working with other jurisdictions to democratize the Senate	✔	✔		✔	✔
working with others re: market-based approaches to environmental protection				✔	✔
seeking Alberta representation in international treaty negotiations			✔	✔	✔
re-establishing an Alberta office in Ottawa				✔	✔
advancing regional strategies for northern development				✔	✔
reforming Employment Insurance		✔			✔

Table 5.1. (continued)

	Alberta Agenda (2001)	MLA Report (2004)	Fair Deal Mandate (2020)	Fair Deal Report (2021)	Government Response (2021)
Rebalancing Approach					
reforming the Fiscal Stabilization Program formula				✔	✔
redistributing seats in the House of Commons				✔	✔
securing more federal government offices and jobs in Western Canada		✔		✔	?
asserting more provincial control over immigration				✔	✔
abolishing residency requirement for federal courts				✔	✔
Fighting Back Approach					
referendum on removing the equalization from the constitution				✔	✔
challenging federal overreach in court		✔		✔	✔
prohibiting use of the federal spending power		✔		✔	✔
resisting federal intrusions into health and social programming		✔		✔	
barring provincial public bodies from agreements with the federal government			✔	✘	✔
Other Approaches					
pursuing market access				✔	✔
diversifying Alberta's economy				✔	✔
using democratic tools to seek Albertans' guidance				✔	✔
affirming Alberta's uniqueness in law and policy				✔	✔

✔ = recommend or support; ✘ = reject; ? = further investigation required; * = only following positive referendum result connected to the governing party. The Fair Deal Report refused to accept two of the four planks in the Alberta Agenda—establishing an Alberta tax collection agency and seeking tax point transfers in lieu of federal health and social transfers—both of which the UCP government had asked them to re-examine. Despite negative public opinion data collected by its own internal polls, the panel nonetheless opted to recommend the establishment of an Alberta provincial police force and Alberta pension plan—neither of which received the support of more than 40 per cent of Albertans polled.[9]

The Government of Alberta responded a month later by indicating which recommendations it supported. These included all of the "bridge-building" measures and all but one of the "rebalancing" proposals. The government committed to investigate other matters further (including three of the four Alberta Agenda policies), and it rejected a few of the Fair Deal Panel's recommendations (including the tax point transfer proposal mentioned above).

The government's agreement with the various bridge-building and re-balancing initiatives aligned well with public opinion. Illustrated in Figure 5.1, those measures were ranked among the most important and most favoured of all of the Fair Deal proposals according to our March 2021 Viewpoint Alberta Survey.[10] Among them, Albertans were very supportive of securing additional federal jobs in the West, something research demonstrates would be of considerable benefit to the region and the federal public service;[11] the Alberta government has committed to exploring this further.

The government's decision not to support firewall measures without further study was also consistent with public sentiment; these were among the least salient and popular Fair Deal measures. None of the four were viewed as being important by the average Viewpoint respondent, and none received a support score of at least five out of ten.

We did not measure Albertans' attitudes about tax points; like the Fair Deal Panel, we found the issue too complex or mundane to measure with public opinion. We did, however, find middling support for the government's signature fight back strategies: challenging the federal government in court and holding a constitutional referendum on equalization. Our attention turns to this latter issue, as it constitutes the second stage in the Government of Alberta's Fair Deal strategy.

Figure 5.1. Fair Deal Measures by Level of Importance and Level of Support, March 2021

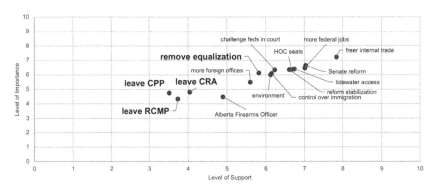

Sources: Viewpoint Survey, March 2021. N=666. Weighted data. Numbers represent mean responses to the question: "For each of the following priorities for [your provincial government], please indicate your level of support for the idea and how important you feel the issue is." Support was measured from 0=completely oppose to 5=neutral to 10=completely support. Importance was measured from 0=entirely unimportant to 5=indifferent to 10=extremely important.

Stage 2: A Constitutional Referendum

Most observers trace the genesis of the UCP's equalization referendum idea to the party's 2019 provincial election campaign platform. In it, the UCP pledged to "hold a referendum on removing equalization from the Constitution Act on 18 October 2021, if substantial progress is not made on construction of a coastal pipeline, and if Trudeau's Bill C-69 is not re-pealed." The threat was aimed squarely at the federal government for drag-ging its feet in constructing the Trans Mountain Pipeline, which Ottawa had purchased from Kinder Morgan in 2019 at a cost of $4.5 billion; and for imposing new health, environmental, and consultative regulations on new infrastructure projects (including pipelines). Later, Premier Kenney would add additional conditions, including reforms to the federal Fiscal Stabilization Fund formula, which he argued had short-changed Alberta billions of dollars by capping the amount the province received as a result of the sudden and dramatic drop in the price of oil. All of these concerns would have been alleviated had the Conservatives won the fall 2019 feder-al election. When they did not, the UCP pushed forward with its plans to hold the equalization referendum.

The formal announcement of the equalization referendum was made in June 2020, as part of the Alberta government's acceptance of the Fair Deal Panel's recommendations. The vote would take place in conjunction with province-wide municipal elections on 18 October 2021. The government released the referendum question on 15 July 2021. It read: "Should Section 36(2) of the Constitution Act, 1982—Parliament and the Government of Canada's commitment to the principle of making equalization payments—be removed from the Constitution?"

Critics were quick to point out that the question failed to match the government's intent. None of the Alberta government's demands had anything to do with the constitution, a point the premier and the flagship "yes" campaign (run by Fairness Alberta) readily conceded. In responding to a *CBC News* story on the absurdity of invoking the constitution as part of the question, a UCP press secretary tweeted "That's not the point of the referendum. It's about creating a political fact in Alberta by asking Albertans a simple, single question and getting it on the official record."[12]

During a Facebook Live session the day before the vote, Premier Kenney outlined the purpose of the referendum as follows:

> The referendum on equalization is a chance for Albertans to say yes to our request for a fair deal in the Canadian federation. Voting yes on this will not end equalization because it is a principle embedded in the Constitution, Section 36, and it could only be amended out of the Constitution with the consent, I believe, of seven provinces representing 50% of the population, plus both houses of the federal parliament, and that's just not going to happen.
>
> Our expectation is not that there will be a constitutional amendment or the end of equalization, but we're using this to get leverage, to basically take a page out of Quebec's playbook in having successfully dominated the political attention of the federation for the last 40 or 50 years.[13]

The decision to pursue a constitutional referendum to spark non-constitutional change has deep roots in Alberta conservative circles. Indeed, like many elements of the Fair Deal, we can trace it to the Alberta Agenda. In the firewall letter, the authors urged Premier Klein to instigate a constitutional amendment regarding Senate Reform. In doing so, they drew on a contested interpretation of the Supreme Court's decision in the Quebec Secession Reference. According to the firewall authors, "Our reading of that decision is that the federal government and other provinces must seriously consider a proposal for constitutional reform endorsed by 'a clear majority on a clear question' in a provincial referendum." They stopped short of arguing that the Secession Reference *obliged* other governments to negotiate. And they did not suggest a constitutional referendum was necessary (although Alberta law requires one before the legislature entertains an amendment). The "yes" side in the equalization referendum took that next leap, however.

On their website, Fairness Alberta described the constitutional obligations that would result from the Alberta referendum:

> This referendum is an opportunity to force negotiations with Ottawa to get Albertans a fairer deal in confederation. . . . In the 1998 Supreme Court reference case concerning Quebec Secession, the Court made clear that a provincial vote supporting any Constitutional change triggered a duty for the Federal government and other provinces to negotiate in good faith. This is why the Referendum question is worded as it is—only a vote in support for Constitutional change compels negotiations. Once negotiations begin, all aspects of fiscal and economic fairness for Albertans can be brought to the table.[14]

Former UCP staffer Bill Bewick headed up the Fairness Alberta campaign. In defence of the government's choice of words, he admitted in an *Edmonton Sun* op-ed:

> It's true the wording for the referendum question asks if you support removing the principle of Equalization from the constitution. Can Alberta unilaterally amend the constitution? Obviously not. Does anyone expect 7 provinces to agree to delete this? Obviously not.

So anyone who tells you this is about actually amending the constitution is completely missing the point. In 1998 the Supreme Court said a province expressing support for constitutional change triggers a duty to negotiate; that's all this vote is about, but that's critically needed right now.[15]

Constitutional experts have challenged the notion that a positive referendum vote would "trigger a duty" or "force negotiations."[16] Even at least one of the architects of the Alberta Agenda is skeptical.[17] Beyond this, however, there are serious doubts as to whether the referendum posed a "clear question," represented a "legitimate attempt" at constitutional reform, and received a "clear majority" of support—three necessary criteria for sparking constitutional negotiations according to the Supreme Court.[18]

Through the referendum question itself, the government asked Albertans to remove equalization from the constitution. At the same time, they insisted the results were never intended to remove equalization from the constitution. This curious contradiction undermines the premier's contention that the referendum was a "legitimate attempt" to spark constitutional change.

These confusing messages did nothing to dispel voters' misconceptions about the referendum. According to our pre-vote Viewpoint Alberta survey, over half (56 per cent) of Albertans thought that a "yes" vote would result in Alberta "withdrawing from the equalization program."[19] This was never a possibility, but it is understandable how voters would gain that impression given the government's positioning of the vote. This creates doubt as to whether Albertans truly understood the question they were being asked.

In the end, "yes" ballots outnumbered "no" ballots in the referendum. While there were regional variations—rural areas voted heavily for yes, while urban areas were less supportive—the results are necessarily tallied on a province-wide level. That over half of Edmontonians who cast ballots voted "no" does not, and should not, matter in interpreting the outcome.

Two things stand out in Elections Alberta's reporting of the results, however. First, the "yes" and "no" percentages were calculated without incorporating the 49,336 declined ballots that were submitted by voters. This amounts to 4 per cent of all ballots cast—substantially higher than in recent provincial elections. We do not know why voters showed up to vote in municipal elections yet chose not to participate in the referendum. But if we count their inaction as some sort of signal, this pushes the "yes" share of the vote down from 62 per cent to 56 per cent of all ballots cast and declined.

Second, Elections Alberta did not report the overall level of turnout. This may be because the referendum was being held in conjunction with municipal elections, and there is no master municipal voters' list with which to calculate a denominator. This leaves us to construct one, the most reliable and conservative of which would be the number of Albertans eligible to vote in the 2019 provincial election (2.82 million). Using that figure, turnout in the referendum was at most 40 per cent.

Taking all votes and rejected ballots into account, the most generous calculation would have one-in-four eligible Albertans turning out to vote "yes" in the constitutional referendum on equalization. This is well below the Kenney government's own threshold for citizens to instigate constitutional amendments through the *Citizen Initiative Act* of 2021, which requires signatures of 20 per cent of voters in each of two-thirds of provincial constituencies. Just like the clarity of the question and the legitimacy of the attempt, the magnitude of popular support flowing from the equalization referendum remained in doubt.

Stage 3: The Negotiations

The day the referendum results were released, Premier Kenney held a press conference to interpret the outcome and lay out the province's next steps:

> Later today I will be tabling a motion in the legislature to ratify these election results and initiate the amendment process. And we fully expect the prime minister to respect the constitutional amendment process and to sit down and negotiate with Alberta in good faith.

> Of course, our focus ultimately, as I say, is a fair deal. A broader reform of the system of fiscal federalism. A retroactive lifting of the fiscal stabilization program cap to recognize the huge adversity Alberta has faced in recent years. The repeal or substan-

tial amendment of the No More Pipelines law, the repeal of the discriminatory tanker ban that targets this province alone. And so much more.[20]

While it is unclear what he meant by "so much more," the premier clearly articulated three demands—all of which require unilateral federal action and none of which involved the constitution. Rather than constitutional negotiations, meeting those demands would require lobbying or the election of a sympathetic Conservative government in Ottawa. They likely wouldn't involve negotiations with any other provincial government.

At the same 26 October 2021 press conference, Premier Kenney was asked about his government's next steps to secure a Fair Deal for Albertans, beyond the constitutional amendment process. Here, the premier reiterated his steadfast commitment to pursuing key elements of the Alberta Agenda, reinforcing the perception that the firewall remains the UCP's ultimate objective.

> Later this week, we will, for example, be releasing the initial study conducted by the Department of Justice and Solicitor General on the costs, benefits, and potential advantages of an Alberta Provincial Police Force. We continue to, at our Treasury Board and Finance ministry, carefully to study the potential benefits of an Alberta Pension Plan, which I think would be enormous given the big demographic advantage—the age advantage—of Alberta for the past 40 or 50 years. We just appointed an Alberta Firearms Officer last month to have more common sense oversight in the application of federal firearms legislation. We upgraded the Alberta Parole Board to have Albertans making common sense decisions over parole applications for provincial inmates. So, of course, we continue to pursue the broader Fair Deal agenda while at the same time expecting the Government of Canada to take this referendum result very seriously.[21]

While the creation of a provincial revenue agency to replace the CRA was not specifically mentioned, these remarks draw clear connections between the Alberta Agenda and the Fair Deal. These were framed as being parallel to his three demands around repealing "discriminatory federal laws" and reforms to fiscal transfer formulas. The implication, however, seemed to be that—if Alberta's demands were not met—they would proceed with plans to build a firewall around the province.

Implications

During the equalization referendum campaign, I penned an opinion piece with one of the original authors of the Alberta Agenda.[22] In it, we urged Albertans to vote "no," warning them of the dangers of engaging in inter-governmental relations at a time when Alberta's hand was so weak. As lead negotiator, Premier Kenney's popularity was abysmally low at the time of the equalization referendum (see DeCillia chapter). In fact, one interpret-ation of the results sees equalization being twice as popular as the premier. Across the table, Alberta would face a Liberal prime minister in a minority government situation dependent upon the support of his Quebec caucus and two federal parties—one with designs on centralizing the federation, the other with bolstering Quebec's influence within it. These are not the type of "winning conditions" that the Quebec playbook prescribes. Nor do they resemble the circumstances under which Alberta achieved signifi-cant gains in the last round of fiscal federalism negotiations in 2006–2010. As a result, Alberta had far more to lose than win in engaging the rest of Canada at the time of writing.

First, by re-opening the constitution, Alberta risks putting its own control over natural resources firmly back on the table. It is naïve to think that only Alberta's demands would be considered during this round of constitutional talks. As the premier, himself, acknowledged, Section 92a was pivotal to Alberta's agreement on the new constitutional order struck in 1982. This control over resources came as part of a series of elaborate trade-offs, however, the most important of which involved enshrining the equalization principle in the constitution. That Alberta would open ne-gotiations by removing Section 36(2) would naturally invite debate over repealing or reducing provincial control over natural resources. Such a tit-for-tat exchange might well end in a stalemate, with the status quo pre-vailing. But it would set an acrimonious tone for the more substantive set of discussions around reforming federal-provincial transfers.

Here, Alberta's potential losses are far more real and significant. The perspective on Alberta's equalization referendum from other parts of Canada would be quite different from Kenney's spin. Canadians outside the province tend to view Alberta as a land of relative prosperity. The Alberta Advantage mantra has made it exceptionally difficult to convince Canadians in other parts of the country that the provincial government is in need of fiscal support. This is especially true in boom times, as returned to Alberta in 2022. Whether valid or not, to many in the rest of Canada, Alberta's worst days are better than their provinces' best. They have also seen Alberta receive more federal pandemic funds, a boost to the fiscal stabilization fund, and sizeable federal investments in the oil and gas industry (including the purchase of a pipeline and orphan well recovery funding). During the pandemic, they saw a province that had to call in the Canadian military and support from other provinces to battle the deadly fourth wave of the pandemic (see Young, chapter twenty). These perceptions will frame their approach to any federal-provincial negotiations.

As will the suggestion that equalization be removed from the constitution and the implied allegation that some provincial governments are not carrying their fair share of the burden for economic development in Canada. This is unlikely to win the Alberta government many provincial allies around the negotiating table.

If Alberta is seeking to further bolster the fiscal stabilization formula or reduce the size of the equalization envelope, this will likely come at the direct expense of other transfers. When the Harper government made the last set of significant reforms to fiscal federalism, they recognized these sorts of trade-offs. To give Alberta what it wanted at the time—namely, shifting health and social transfers to per capita funding, netting Alberta an extra $1 billion per year—the Harper government needed to appease the rest of Canada by enriching equalization.

As was pointed out by Prime Minister Trudeau, then-minister Jason Kenney was part of the Harper government that orchestrated these reforms. The fact that Trudeau has chosen not to re-open them either speaks to the quality of the deal or the unwillingness of the federal government to untie a Gordian knot given other, more pressing, priorities. Among them now: addressing the COVID-19 pandemic and global economic recovery.

Heading back to the negotiating table under these circumstances is immensely risky. Premier Kenney's pursuit of a Fair Deal for Alberta could end up setting the province back in constitutional and fiscal terms. Yet, given the foregoing analysis, that appears to have been part of the gamble from the beginning.

The UCP launched the Fair Deal following the re-election of the Trudeau government in 2019 knowing that the new government would be unwilling to meet any of their three demands. That likelihood became even slimmer when the Liberals secured another term in government in 2021. This suggests that the equalization referendum and three demands are best considered part of the UCP's failed fight back strategy than as legitimate attempts at reforming the constitution or fiscal federalism.

Since the referendum, support for the UCP's firewall approach has plummeted. Depicted in Figures 5.2a and 5.2b, removing equalization from the constitution was the most popular of these firewall initiatives over time; even then, fewer than half of Albertans backed the measure according to our surveys. While support for withdrawing from CPP and creating a provincial tax collection agency increased between August 2020 and April 2022, so did opposition. This indicates a hardening of attitudes against the firewall approach over time.

According to our April 2022 Viewpoint Alberta survey, only 25 per cent of Albertans support withdrawing from CPP to create a provincial pension plan, with even fewer (23 per cent) in favour of creating a new provincial police force. Clear majorities (57 per cent) of Albertans were opposed to both measures. A slightly higher share of the population (28 per cent) would like to see a new provincial tax collection agency to replace the CRA, but 51 per cent are opposed. Support for removing equalization from the constitution rested at 47 per cent in April 2022, with 28 per cent opposed and 25 per cent neutral on the issue.

With Kenney's announced departure from the UCP leadership in 2022, the next UCP leader will have to choose whether or not continue to pursue the Fair Deal strategy. It remains a dangerous political gambit, given the continued unpopularity of the firewall approach and the significant risk it poses to Alberta's autonomy.

Figure 5.2a. Support for Firewall Measures, August 2020 to April 2022

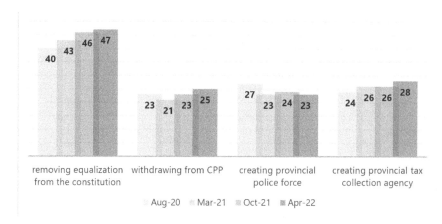

Figure 5.2b. Opposition to Firewall Measures, August 2020 to April 2022

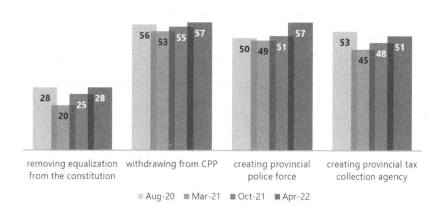

Sources: Viewpoint Surveys. Weighted data. Numbers represent mean responses to the question: "For each of the following priorities for [your provincial government], please indicate your level of support for the idea and how important you feel the issue is." Support was measured from 0=completely oppose to 5=neutral to 10=completely support. "Support" in this figure represents rating from 6 to 10, "neutral" as 5, and "oppose" from 0 to 4.

NOTES

1   Mark Lisac. 2004. Alberta Politics Uncovered: Taking Back our Province. Edmonton: NeWest Press, 2.

2   Jared Wesley. 2019. "Jason Kenney won by portraying himself as the Guardian of Alberta." *The Conversation*. 21 April 2019.

3   Other elements of that fight back approach have seen the Alberta government lose Supreme Court cases over provincial jurisdiction, squander over a billion dollars in investments on the ill-fated Keystone XL pipeline, and generate international embarrassment over the failure of its multi-million dollar energy war room and public inquiry into anti-oil sands funding.

4   Jared Wesley and Clare Buckley. 2020. "Separatism in Alberta." *Viewpoint Alberta*. https://www.commongroundpolitics.ca/separatismab

5   Quoted in: Michelle Bellefontaine. 2019. "Panel will give Albertans chance to share views about Confederation, Kenney says." *CBC News*. https://www.cbc.ca/news/canada/edmonton/alberta-jason-kenney-justin-trudeau-1.5330821

6   Daniel Béland, Loleen Berdahl, Jared Wesley, and Amy Vachon-Chabot. 2020. "Alberta and the Rest of Canada." *Viewpoint Alberta*. https://www.commongroundpolitics.ca/alberta-can

7   One of the three MLAs, Drew Barnes, would go on to be expelled from the UCP caucus for voicing opposition to Premier Kenney's handling of the pandemic. Another Fair Deal Panel MLA, Miranda Rosin, would join Barnes in writing an open letter to Premier Kenney decrying pandemic restrictions. Later in 2021, Barnes and Rosin formed the core of an alliance of MLAs to push a "Freedom Strategy" to usurp federal jurisdiction over Alberta. All of this came after their involvement in the Fair Deal process, which both of them felt fell short of protecting Alberta's interests in Confederation.

8   For full disclosure, the author was invited to deliver a presentation to the Fair Deal Panel and did so in Edmonton on 22 January 2020.

9   The Fair Deal Panel also disagreed with the Government of Alberta's proposal to "more forcefully protect its own powers by requiring that all agreements by municipalities and public agencies with the federal government be pre-approved by Alberta." According to the report, "Most Albertans who responded to the panel were indifferent to this question." Those that did cited the importance of removing red tape and preserving the flow of funds from Ottawa to municipalities for things like infrastructure.

10 Jared Wesley, Loleen Berdahl, and Kirsten Samson. 2021. "Western Alienation in Alberta and Saskatchewan." *Viewpoint Alberta*. https://www.commongroundpolitics.ca/western-alienation

11 Loleen Berdahl. 2021. "The Persistence of Western Alienation." *Centre of Excellence on the Canadian Federation Inaugural Essay Series*. https://centre.irpp.org/research-studies/the-persistence-of-western-alienation/

12 Tweet by Blaise Boehmer (@boehmerB), 8 June 2021, 9:55 AM MT.

13 Jason Kenney. 2021. "Saying YES to a fair deal." Video accessed 11 November 2021: https://fb.watch/952cZgNC1t/

14 Fairness Alberta. 2021. "FAQs." *EqualizationReferendum.ca website.* Accessed 17 October 2021: https://www.equalizationreferendum.ca/faq/. See also Bill Bewick. 2021. "If Albertans vote against equalization, the feds will have a 'duty' to listen. *National Post.* 3 August 2021. https://nationalpost.com/opinion/bill-bewick-if-albertans-vote-against-equalization-the-feds-will-have-a-duty-to-listen

15 Bill Bewick. 2021. "What's at stake with the equalization referendum." *Edmonton Sun.* 14 October 2021. https://edmontonsun.com/opinion/columnists/guest-column-whats-at-stake-with-the-equalization-referendum

16 Eric M. Adams. 2021. "Jason Kenney's equalization referendum is built on a crucial misinterpretation." *The Globe and Mail.* 8 June 2021. https://www.theglobeandmail.com/opinion/article-jason-kenneys-equalization-referendum-is-built-on-a-crucial/

17 Rainer Knopff. 2020. "Refining Alberta's Equalization Gambit." *Fraser Research Bulletin.* https://www.fraserinstitute.org/studies/refining-albertas-equalization-gambit

18 Jared Wesley. 2021. "Why Alberta lacks a mandate to reopen Canada's constitution." *National Post.* 29 October 2021. https://nationalpost.com/pmn/news-pmn/why-alberta-lacks-a-mandate-to-reopen-canadas-constitution

19 Jared Wesley. 2021. "Albertans & Equalization: Divided and Misguided?" *Viewpoint Alberta.* https://www.commongroundpolitics.ca/abequalization

20 YourAlberta. 2021. "Premier Kenney discusses referendum results—October 26, 2021." *YourAlberta YouTube Channel.* https://youtu.be/FdQEd4roOs4

21 *Ibid.*

22 Ken Boessenkool and Jared Wesley. 2021. "Equalization is a good constitutional bargain. Albertans should not vote to scrap it." *CBC News.* 8 October 2021. https://www.cbc.ca/news/canada/calgary/opinion-alberta-equalization-referendum-boessenkool-wesley-1.6201822

6

Policing and Alberta's United Conservative Party Government

Doug King

The election of the United Conservative Party (UCP) on 16 April 2019, ushered in a more divergent, more politicized, governmental stance towards policing in Alberta. The UCP pivoted away from the long standing practice in Canada of elected officials refraining from harsh public criticism of policing—be it municipal, provincial, or federal. The new Alberta government frequently positions itself in opposition to police agencies such as the Royal Canadian Mounted Police (RCMP), the Calgary Police Service, and the Edmonton Police Service. Instead of continued consultation with police stakeholders, the UCP often takes unilateral positions on matters such as rural policing or addressing concerns about the urgency to eliminate racial bias in policing. Also, the provincial government's often shifting and delayed approach to policing the pandemic was seemingly influenced by politics more than the realities facing police agencies and local governments.

While much of the UCP government's approach to policing has been political, it likely has little long-term consequence for public safety in Alberta. The one exception is the government's advocacy to replace the RCMP as Alberta's provincial police service with an as yet ill-defined new Alberta police service.

Policing the Pandemic in Alberta

Keeping track of the different waves of the COVID-19 pandemic and which restrictions were imposed by which level of government is a daunting task. By March 2020, all levels of governments in Canada imposed restrictions on almost all aspects of public life. With the discovery of highly effective vaccines in late December 2020 the roller-coaster of virus waves and associated governmental restrictions began. With the exception of the initial wave of the COVID-19 pandemic, the Alberta government's response to imposing public health restrictions has been typically delayed, without much stakeholder consultation, and often tinged with political purpose (see Lisa Young's chapter on COVID). Most medical experts, municipal governments, local school boards, and businesses were typically ahead of the provincial government in the call for enhanced measures to respond to what soon turned into the next COVID-19 wave. Perhaps the best example of this was when the premier prematurely declared the "best summer ever" on 1 July 2021. This false optimism was soon followed by another cycle of rising COVID-19 hospitalizations and deaths. When provincial restrictions were reimposed, the necessary legislative tools for local authorities to enforce non-compliance to the restrictions were frequently missing.

Voluntary Compliance

It is fair to say that the vast majority of Canadians accepted the importance of voluntarily complying with federal, provincial, and local municipal restrictions from the start of the pandemic. Working from home, masking in public spaces, moving to online learning for all levels of the education system, limiting indoor and outdoor gatherings were all met with a degree of acceptance and compliance by most people. Messaging and leadership in a time of public emergency such as the pandemic must balance conveying the seriousness while guarding against panicking people. By and large, the public messaging from Alberta's chief medical officer Dr. Deena Hinshaw found that delicate balance. However, this cannot be said of the public messaging from Premier Jason Kenney. At various points throughout the pandemic, the premier seemed to discount its seriousness by equating it with "influenza."[1] He further downplayed the seriousness of the virus by suggesting that only the elderly and those with compromised immune systems faced serious illness from COVID-19.[2] Oftentimes, the premier publicly declared that some possible future pandemic restrictions were "off the table" only to soon impose those same restrictions, such vaccine passports (only called a restriction exemption card in Alberta).

The premier's initial response to what became known as "Alohagate" during the second wave of the pandemic in late 2020 and early 2021 and the infamous "sky palace" patio dinner at the end of the third wave in June 2021 also served to erode voluntary compliance. These events sent the unintended message that some in positions of leadership saw limited need for their own voluntary compliance to pandemic restrictions. This had the effect of inspiring others to doing the same—if elected officials were not following the restrictions, why should they?

Lack of Stakeholder Consultation

Under the Province of Alberta's *Public Health Act*, enforcement authority for provincial public health regulations rests with designated Alberta health officials and police officers. Municipal by-law officers, transit security, and provincial fish and wildlife officers are not empowered to enforce provincial health regulations.

Provincial legislation, orders in council, or executive orders are required to temporarily extend pandemic enforcement authority to non-police or to Alberta health officials. Extending authority to municipal non-police peace officers has taken on the appearance of being an afterthought by the UCP government. The chorus of complaints from municipal elected officials and local police agencies was renewed with each new wave of COVID-19. Instead of consulting with local authorities, provincial representatives, including Premier Kenney, frequently downplayed local concerns.

Slow to Respond

It was not until Alberta was well into the third wave of the pandemic that a ministerial order was issued to extend pandemic enforcement authority to municipal community peace officers and to provincial fish and wildlife officers.[3] The March 2021 legislation occurred as public protests grew and non-compliance by some business and churches gained media coverage. But that enhanced authority for non-police peace officers to enforce

COVID-19 restrictions expired with the premier's early July announcement of the "best summer ever."

This pattern of delayed response was again evident as the provincial government announced the reimposition of some pandemic restrictions as the fourth wave of the pandemic raged on. Premier Kenney announced the return to restrictions on 15 September 2021 (in the middle of the fourth wave) with no proactive ministerial order to reimplement the extended enforcement authority for non-police peace officers. Indeed, in a news media story on 17 September 2021, Alberta health spokesperson Tom McMillan suggested that no extended enforcement authority was needed.[4] Not waiting for the justice ministry to extend authority to its municipal by-law and other non-police public safety officers, the city of Calgary imposed very similar restrictions to those mandated by the province to allow municipal officers to enforce the return of the pandemic restrictions.

In the face of increasingly frequent public rallies protesting the provincial government's pandemic restrictions reimposed as the third wave of the pandemic had begun its decline in early May 2021, the minister of justice announced increases in the maximum dollar amount of fines that could be issued for non-compliance to the pandemic restriction.[5] However, local police authorities issued few fines. The lack of consultation by the UCP government was highlighted when Calgary Chief of Police Mark Neufeld identified other factors inhibiting effective enforcement of pandemic restrictions. Chief Neufeld revealed that "our partners at the province" had requested police limit the number of $100 mask bylaw fines so as to "not fill the courts."[6] In the same news interview, the Calgary chief noted that a significant percentage of all tickets issued under the provincial health act had been quashed or withdrawn by Crown prosecutors.

The lack of stakeholder consultation with local municipalities was on display once again as the pandemic's fifth wave was waning in early 2022. The UCP government announced the removal of restrictions related to mask wearing in public indoor spaces, the requirement to show proof of COVID-19 vaccination for certain activities, and restrictions on the size of indoor gatherings. Neither city council in Calgary or Edmonton were consulted by the UCP and both began considering municipal restrictions to replace those being removed provincially. Without consultation, the UCP amended the provincial *Municipal Government Act* in order to require municipalities to obtain provincial authorization for implementing any COVID-19 public health restrictions.[7]

United Conservative Party's Pandemic Response

Several patterns emerge when looking back at the UCP government's responses beginning with the "best summer ever" pronouncement as the third wave of the pandemic waned. The government failed to engage in consultation with various stakeholder groups as to the appropriate response to the newly emerging wave of COVID-19 and became increasingly delayed in responding to subsequent emerging new waves. It declined to extend enforcement authority to enforce pandemic restrictions at the local level. In fact, the UCP took legislative action to limit municipalities from responding to the pandemic. Many in municipal governments and the general population now see the UCP's approach to the pandemic as informed largely by its own political agenda.

Municipal Policing

High profile events in the United States placed a spotlight on excessive use of force by police officers, more often than not against African-Americans. The events south of the border also created political controversy in several cities in Canada. Here in Alberta, controversy was fuelled by confrontational pronouncements by Alberta's then-minister of justice Kaycee Madu who sharply criticized police agencies and city councils for responding to public concerns about police use of force here in Alberta.

#DefundthePolice Movement

The Black Lives Matter movement in the United States is a continuation of the same realities that led to the emergence of community-based policing in the 1960s. Yet, the disproportionate representation of African-Americans in terms of police-stop arrests and criminal convictions persists. The highly publicized shooting of Treyvon Martin in 2013 lead to intense media attention on subsequent fatal police shootings of Michael Brown, Eric Garner, Alton Sterling, Resheda Brooks, Breonna Taylor, Tanisha Anderson, and Dante Wright—to name just a few.[8] It was the murder of African-American George Floyd in May 2020 by Minneapolis police officers that ignited what is now called the "#defundthepolice" movement. In what can only be called callous and cruel actions by the attending police officers, Floyd's death was caused by asphyxia due to neck and back compression as a police officer kneeling on Floyd for nine minutes—despite Floyd's pleads that he could not breathe.[9]

The video of George Floyd's murder triggered the birth of the #defundthepolice movement in both the United States and Canada. The Canadian movement acted on the same underlying issues—persons of colour are more often exposed to excessive use of police force, over-policing through increased vehicle check stops, and "carding," that is, the stopping of a person without reasonable grounds and directing them to produce identification. As municipal police agencies in Alberta responded to the #defundthepolice movement and the underlying issues of systemic racism, Alberta justice minister Kaycee Madu publicly derided the movement. In a November 2020 interview, the minister was quoted as saying "These are a bunch of socialists who would prefer to have a chaotic world"[10] referring to city council members who were considering how to address the #defundthepolice movement.[11] The minister then made the following transparently inaccurate statement: "I do not intend to play politics with law enforcement."

Lack of Stakeholder Consultation

Minister Madu upped the ante by threatening to withhold the annual provincial policing grants to any municipality that redirected any portion of the police budget to address concerns being raised by the #defundthepolice movement.[12] In Calgary, the provincial police grants amount to approximately $30 million in an overall annual police budget of over $450 million. The minister continued his public criticism by saying "I encourage you [Calgary city council] to drop the 'defund' rhetoric and stop pandering to radical activists."[13]

City councils and municipal police commissions in Edmonton and Calgary moved ahead with beginning to address the underlying concerns of systemic racism informing the #defundthepolice movement. It is difficult to see how the plans adopted by the two largest police agencies in Alberta, with the support of their police commissions and chiefs of police, fit minister Madu's "socialist" or "radical" rhetoric. In June 2020, Edmonton city council voted to reallocate $11 million from the annual police budget of $389 million to twenty proposals seeking to address policing reform in the city.[14] In Calgary, city council and the Calgary Police Service contributed approximately $8 million each to establish the Community Safety Investment Framework for a total of $16 million.[15]

Another stark example of the UCP government's pattern of jumping ahead on policing matters without consulting key stakeholders was then-justice minister Madu's mid-July 2021 letter to the federal government calling for the removal of capsaicin spray, or "pepper spray," from the list of prohibited weapons in the Canadian criminal code. This change would allow, according to Minister Madu, "vulnerable people" to protect themselves from "drug-fuelled attacks." The proposal came as a surprise to the Alberta Association of Chiefs of Police (AACP). The AACP found the proposal to decriminalize pepper spray potentially dangerous because it would likely lead to use in other criminal activities, potentially against the very "vulnerable people" the minister was hoping to protect.[16] The overtly political nature of Minister Madu's letter became obvious when he publicly attacked the federal government for rejecting the proposal. Picking a public fight with the government in Ottawa always serves a political purpose for the UCP government.

Rural Policing

Between 1962 and 1993, crime rates in Canada increased at a persistent and sharp pace. The decline in crime rates since 1993 has been equally consistent and sharp. However, the downward trend in crime rates since 1993 and the crime severity index (CSI) ended in 2014 and both indices of crime in Canada have been inching up—about 1 per cent a year.[17] Rural property crime rates in Canada, and in Alberta, showed these same patterns of decades of increase until the mid-1990s, followed by a precipitous decline until the mid 2010s. Still, the inching up of rural crime in the past two decades remains well below the peak seen in the 1990s.

During the tenure of the UCP's first justice minister Doug Schweitzer, a priority was placed on increasing the number of uniformed RCMP officers in those rural areas experiencing the greatest increase in crime. As rural policing in Alberta is provided under contract with the RCMP, the new UCP government worked with the RCMP to transfer additional officers into Alberta. The UCP government committed to increasing RCMP officers in rural Alberta by three hundred plus an additional two hundred support positions.[18] The financial cost associated with any increase in RCMP personnel is under a long-standing cost-sharing contract between the Alberta government (70 per cent) and the Government of Canada (30 per cent).[19] Rural municipalities with populations less than five thousand were not required to pay any portion of the provincial government's contractual obligation. While announcing the increase in RCMP officers, the UCP government unilaterally changed what smaller municipalities paid from 0 per cent to 10 per cent, with an expected increase to 30 per cent of RCMP costs by 2025.[20] This impending financial bill caused alarm in smaller rural municipalities.

The Case of Eddie Maurice

As the newly elected UCP government formed its rural crime strategy, Premier Kenney and then Justice Minister Schweitzer elected to publicly weigh in on the high profile case of Okotoks-area rancher Edouard (Eddie) Maurice who, in February 2018, discharged a rifle in what he said were warning shots at two trespassers on his property.[21] One of the trespassers, Ryan Watson, was struck in the arm by a ricocheting bullet. As outlined in a *CBC News* story, Watson was charged with numerous offences under provincial statute and the Criminal Code of Canada.[22] Maurice was criminally charged with aggravated assault, pointing a loaded firearm, and careless use of a firearm. The fact that Maurice was criminally charged led some in Alberta's more conservative rural circles to question the RCMP's approach to rural law enforcement.

Criminal charges against Maurice were dropped in June 2018. Watson initiated a lawsuit against Maurice in September 2019 claiming he suffered "emotional upset, severe fatigue and insomnia."[23] UCP Premier Jason Kenney used social media to characterize the lawsuit as personal harassment of Maurice and encouraged people to donate to a defence fund for Maurice.[24] Then Justice Minister Schweitzer used *Twitter* to voice apparent support for Maurice despite the fact that the active case fell under his ministry's jurisdiction.[25] Premier Kenney's involvement, as well as Minister Schweitzer's, are best seen as political attempts to influence an ongoing court case. One month after the lawsuit against Maurice was filed, the UCP government announced a five-fold increase in monetary fines for trespassing in the Petty Trespassing Act and added a possible sentence of up to six months of incarceration.[26] The lawsuit against Maurice and his countersuit against Watson were both dropped in January 2020 in light of the new provincial legislation.

Alberta Provincial Police Service

The criticism directed at the RCMP, and the public intervention of both Premier Kenney and then Justice Minister Schweitzer, played into the UCP government's interest in replacing the RCMP with a newly created Alberta provincial police agency. Contract policing in Canada began in response to the financial pressure experienced by Western Canadian provinces during the economic depression in the 1930s.[27] The current Alberta-RCMP contract (renewed under the Stelmach government in 2011) provides for 70 per cent of rural policing costs to be paid by the province and 30 per cent by the federal government.[28] The contract does not require the province to contribute to the costs of recruiting, training, outfitting, equipping, and housing the officers. Individual municipalities can also enter into a separate contract with the RCMP for municipal policing services at no cost to the provincial government.

Replacing the RCMP in Alberta was first raised in the 2001 "Alberta firewall" open letter to then Premier Ralph Klein. The letter was penned by notable provincial conservative advocates such as future Prime Minister Stephen Harper and several University of Calgary academics.[29] The idea was again promoted in the May 2020 final report of the UCP government's Fair Deal Panel. Oddly, the recommendation to remove the RCMP appears not to be supported by the panel's own survey and public forums. Only 35 per cent of those participating in the panel's "public opinion research" supported an Alberta provincial police service either "a lot or somewhat."[30] Further, an Alberta provincial police service ranked fourteenth out of the fifteen ways to "help Alberta improve its place in the federation" outlined in the final report.[31] The modest support for replacing the RCMP is echoed in a survey commissioned by the National Police Federation (NPF) in mid-2021. The NPF is the sole bargaining agent for the over 20,000 frontline RCMP officers in Canada and abroad. The NFP survey indicated over 80 per cent of Albertans who are currently served by the RCMP are satisfied with the policing services they receive.[32]

The logistics and increased financial commitment needed to implement an Alberta provincial police service are daunting. The Government of Canada's current share of the cost of the RCMP as Alberta's provincial police agency is estimated to be approximately $160–$170 million.[33] Besides having to absorb the cost of officers' salaries and benefits, the Province of Alberta would need to absorb the costs of recruiting and ongoing officer training, establishing capacity for provincial police major crimes investigations, developing and implementing a promotion process, and budgeting for ongoing capital costs (e.g., buildings and equipment) associated with a decentralized police agency. Replacing the 3,500 RCMP officers in 115 Alberta detachments in over three hundred municipalities and twenty-one First Nations communities in the province would be challenging and obviously cost Albertans more.[34]

In August 2020, the Honourable Kaycee Madu replaced Minster Schweitzer as the minister of justice and solicitor general. PricewaterhouseCoopers (PwC) was commissioned in October 2020 for $2 million to research the transition to a provincial police agency.[35] With his appointment as justice minister, Mr. Madu adopted a more public and vocal role related to replacing the RCMP. Some of Minister Madu's 9 October 2020, comments to the *Calgary Sun* questioned the professionalism of the RCMP: "At the end of the day it is important that an Alberta provincial police service that is absolutely loyal to the province and responsive to the needs of our people right here,"[36] Minister Madu is quoted as saying. He is also quoted as saying that the RCMP is "not in tune with the culture and traditions of our communities" and not accountable to the people of Alberta.[37]

The PwC's *APPS Transition Study Final Report* was released on 29 October 2021.[38] The 100-page report (about 50 per cent comprises photos) was prepared with minimal stakeholder consultation. The report lays out two possible models of police deployment that would have annual costs of between $735 to $758 million.[39] According to the report, the proposed operating costs of an Alberta agency would be approximately $25 million to $50 million less than the current costs of $783 million associated with the RCMP plus the Alberta sheriffs.[40] However, the federal government's contribution of approximately $160–$170 million to current provincial policing costs in Alberta is not included in the report and not accounted for in the $783 million estimate of current costs. Alberta taxpayers would have to absorb the federal share should the province opt to remove the RCMP and institute a new Alberta police service. To be clear, this added cost to Alberta taxpayers would be a minimum of $1.6 billion over a ten-year period.

The PwC transition report also indicates that there would be an estimated $366 to $371 million in transition costs spread over six years.[41] The report proposes no additional facilities would be needed to train the new Alberta provincial police service. Instead, it is suggested that existing training facilities run by municipal police agencies in Alberta could assume the training of the new provincial police agency. This suggestion came without much consultation with Alberta's two largest municipal police agencies and seems challenging, given the ongoing in-service and recruit training that currently takes place in municipal policing facilities throughout the province. The UCP government has attempted to minimize the fiscal impact of a move to an Alberta provincial police service by suggesting that no additional tax burden would be placed on Albertans. This begs the question—where would the money come from?

Lack of Stakeholder Consultation

The lack of stakeholder consultation in constructing the transition report was evident in the criticism following the release of the PwC report. The Treaty 8 First Nations and the Treaty 6 First Nations have indicated their lack of support for replacing the RCMP.[42] Mayors from several communities (e.g., Red Deer, Edson, and Okotoks) currently served by the RCMP have expressed their lack of support for the proposed new Alberta provincial agency.[43] In March 2022, the representatives of more than three hundred Alberta municipalities, rural and urban, passed a resolution opposing the provincial policing models presented in the PwC report.[44] The resolution passed with 80.9 per cent support. The Rural Municipalities of Alberta (RMA) also passed a resolution indicating its lack of support for the removal of the RCMP. The resolution passed by a margin of 67 per cent to 33 per cent. Moving forward with replacing the RCMP with an Alberta provincial police service has only tepid support within the UCP membership, little support among First Nations and municipalities currently policed by the RCMP, and little support among the general population.

Alberta taxpayers would have to absorb the added costs of both the transition away from the RCMP and the added costs of an Alberta-owned provincial police service. The UCP government has yet to make a convincing case that replacing the RCMP will benefit Albertans.

The Removal of Kaycee Madu as Justice Minister

In mid-January of 2022, the CBC reported that Justice Minister Madu had been ticketed under the provincial *Motor Vehicle Act* for distracted driving while driving through an Edmonton school zone. The ticket had been issued on 10 March 2021—almost one year before the CBC published its story. While receiving a traffic-related ticket may have been the source of minor embarrassment, Minister Madu's response to the ticket became a much larger concern. According to news sources, and later confirmed in retired Alberta Court of Queen's Justice C. Adele Kent's report on the matter,[45] Minister Madu had called Edmonton's chief of police, Dale McFee, within a few hours of receiving the ticket. In a conversation Chief McFee later characterized as "jumbled," Minister Madu raised concerns about racial profiling and that he had been targeted because of his involvement in ongoing matters related to the Lethbridge police service. The minister's demeanour during the call was characterized as "frustrated," "concerned," and "worked up." Minister Madu quietly paid the $300 fine for distracted driving a week after his call to Chief McFee.

When reports of Minister Madu's ticket and subsequent contact with the Edmonton chief of police made the news media almost a year after taking place, Premier Kenney acknowledged having passing knowledge about the ticket around the time it was issued. Only after the news reports did the premier asked Minister Madu to temporarily step aside from the justice portfolio while an independent third-party investigation was conducted. Minister Madu remained in cabinet with undefined responsibilities during the course of the investigation. Retired Court of Queen's Bench Justice C. Adele Kent was appointed, on 22 January 2022, to conduct the investigation. Madam Justice Kent's report was released to the public on 25 February 2022. After interviewing all relevant individuals, Justice Kent arrived at three conclusions.[46] First, Minister Madu's call to the chief of police did not result in a successful attempt to interfere with the administration of justice. Second, Justice Kent concluded that calling the chief of police was outside the ethical standards expected of public officials and was an attempt to interfere with the administration of justice. Third, the justice concludes at an informed "reasonable person" would come away with the perception that Minister Madu had interfered with the administration of justice. These findings are remarkable, especially given that Minister Madu was, at the time of the call, the chief law enforcement officer in the province. In response to Justice Kent's conclusions, Premier Kenny removed Minister Madu as minister of justice on 25 February 2022. However, he was not removed from cabinet but rather appointed minister of labour and immigration. This is hard to reconcile with the serious findings of ethical misconduct in Justice Kent's report.

What remains uncertain is exactly what information Premier Kenny had about Minister Madu's actions in the months immediately following the minister's call to the chief of police. To put it bluntly, was Premier Kenny's call for an independent third-party investigation prompted by the fact that the news media reported the story rather than Minister Madu's actions? Former Health Minister Tyler Shandro, who had moved into the labour portfolio in September 2021, became the new justice minister. The fact that Minister Shandro, a lawyer, was under ethical investigation by the Alberta Law Society did not seem to factor into his move into the justice portfolio.

Unfinished Business

The tumultuous nineteen-month tenure of Minister Madu in the justice portfolio concluded with many key issues and initiatives ongoing. The most pressing is the UCP's advocacy to replace the RCMP as Alberta's provincial police agency with a new Alberta provincial police service. Interestingly, in a passing comment regarding rural municipalities' opposition, Justice Minister Shandro seemed to backtrack somewhat from the position taken by former Justice Minister Madu. In committing to more discussion about replacing the RCMP, Minister Shandro stated, "We have not made any decision, but we are going to work with those municipal leaders to make sure we are addressing the gaps that we are seeing now."[47] In response to the support the municipalities have expressed for the RCMP, Minister Shandro said, "That's support that is shared by government, by me—our RCMP officers do great work."

Conclusion

Since its 2019 election, two recuring themes in how the UCP government approaches serious policing concerns are obvious. The first recuring theme in the UCP government's approach has been to publicly frame important aspects of policing in overtly political ways. Then Justice Minister Madu's over-the-top comments about local governments and police agencies charged with addressing the #defundthepolice calls to action were overtly political and not helpful. When Premier Kenney and then Justice Minister Schweitzer publicly expressed support for an Okotoks-area rancher who faced criminal charges, it seemed intended to reinforce their own political support. Delays in implementing pandemic restrictions until the province was already at the peak of yet another COVID-19 wave seemed calculated to avoid the political consequences the UCP government would take from its base if it had acted sooner. Retaining former Justice Minister Madu in cabinet in the face of Justice Kent's damning report seems to be based on the fact that Minister Madu is the only elected UCP representative from Edmonton. However, having done so may have consequences for both Minister Madu and the UCP in the next election. Politicising policing and justice are very problematic. It builds scepticism in a system that relies upon public trust and confidence. The political neutrality of the administration of justice is the necessary cornerstone upon which that public trust and confidence is built.

The second theme, and potentially the more damaging, is the government's failure to consult with key stakeholders—including police agencies, local governments, and Albertans directly impacted by government initiatives and plans. This was seen throughout the pandemic when the UCP government delayed implementing pandemic restrictions to help curb the serious public health risk. The lack of consultation was also obvious when the minister of justice publicly attacked police agencies and city councils over plans to address public concerns associated with the #defundthepolice movement.

The ramifications of the UCP's lack of stakeholder consultation related to its pandemic restrictions or the #defundthepolice initiatives are likely to have limited future consequences. However, pressing ahead with the removal of the RCMP as Alberta's provincial police agency based on very limited stakeholder consultation is perilous. The vast majority of municipalities are currently policed by the RCMP, and Albertans who live in those municipalities object to the removal of the RCMP. The framework for the proposed Alberta police service outlined in the PwC report does not provide any indication on how a new Alberta police service would provide better, let alone the same, level of policing. One thing is certain, the removal of the RCMP would add hundreds of millions of dollars of added costs to Alberta taxpayers each year with very uncertain benefit.

NOTES

1   Mel Wood, "Jason Kenney keeps calling COVID-19 'Influenza,'" *HuffPost Canada*, 29 May 2020, https://www.huffpost.com/archive/ca/entry/jason-kenney-influenza-COVID-19_ca_5ed16a02c5b67cf3bf0528a7 (accessed 11 May 2022).

2   Stephanie Thomas, "Concerns arise over premier's 'influenza' comments, focus on seniors' death," *CTV News Calgary*, last modified 29 May 2020, https://calgary.ctvnews.ca/concern-arises-over-premier-s-influenza-comments-focus-on-seniors-death-1.4959251 (accessed 11 May 2022).

3   Jason Herring, "Authority to enforce COVID-19 restrictions renewed for peace officers," *Calgary Herald*, 5 March 2021, https://calgaryherald.com/news/local-news/authority-to-enforce-COVID-19-restrictions-renewed-for-peace-officers/ (accessed 11 May 2022).

4   Dylan Short, "Nenshi calls on province to give city power to enforce COVID-19 restrictions," *Calgary Herald*, 17 September 2021, https://calgaryherald.com/news/local-news/nenshi-calls-on-province-to-give-city-power-to-enforce-COVID-19-restrictions (accessed 11 May 2022).

5   "Alberta doubles fines, brings in new enforcement protocols for COVID-19 rule breakers," *CBC News Edmonton*, last modified 5 May 2021, https://www.cbc.ca/news/canada/edmonton/alberta-doubles-fines-brings-in-new-enforcement-protocol-for-COVID-19-rule-breakers-1.6015710 (accessed 11 May 2022).

6   "Calgary police chief says challenges facing public health tickets in court 'frustrating' after dozens withdrawn," *CTV News Calgary*, last modified 4 May 2021, https://calgary.ctvnews.ca/calgary-police-chief-says-challenges-facing-public-health-tickets-in-court-frustrating-after-dozens-withdrawn-1.5414410#:~:text=withdrawn%20%7C%2-0CTV%20News (accessed 11 May 2022).

7   Emily Mertz, "Alberta municipalities will need province's OK for face mask or COVID-19 vaccine passport bylaws," *Global News*, last modified 8 March 2022, https://globalnews.ca/news/8667463/alberta-government-legislation-face-mask-vaccine-passport-covid/ (accessed 11 May 2022).

8   Nicole Dungca, "A dozen high profile encounters that have galvanized protests nationwide," *Washington Post*, 8 June 2020, https://www.washingtonpost.com/investigations/a-dozen-high-profile-fatal-encounters-that-have-galvanized-protests-nationwide/2020/06/08/4fdbfc9c-a72f-11ea-b473-04905b1af82b_story.html (accessed 11 May 2022).

9   Dungca, "A dozen high profile encounters."

10   Rick Bell, "Bell: Madu squares off with the Nenshi-led council on cop defunding," *Calgary Sun*, 13 November 2020, https://calgarysun.com/opinion/columnists/bell-madu-squares-off-with-nenshi-led-council-on-cop-defunding (accessed 11 May 2022).

11   Bell, "Bell: Madu squares off."

12   Tyler Dawson, "Alberta justice minister warns Edmonton and Calgary not to comply with calls to 'defund the police,'" *National Post*, 10 September 2020, (accessed 11 May 2022).

13   Jordan Kanygin and Mark Vallani, "Calgary councillor calls out justice minister over 'lack of judgement' in police funding criticism," *CTV News Calgary*, last modified 18 November 2020, https://calgary.ctvnews.ca/calgary-councillor-calls-out-justice-minister-over-lack-of-judgement-in-police-funding-criticism-1.5193981 (accessed 11 May 2022).

14   Emily Mertz, "Alberta hires PwC to look at transition from RCMP to provincial police force," *Global News Calgary*, last modified 2 October 2020, https://globalnews.ca/news/7384137/alberta-provincial-police-rcmp-pwc-canada-study/ (accessed 11 May 2022).

15   Madeline Smith, "Calgary police, city unveil details of $16M to reform crisis response," *Calgary Herald*. 3 June 2021, https://calgaryherald.com/news/local-news/calgary-police-city-unveil-details-of-16m-to-reform-crisis-response (accessed 11 May 2022).

16   Rick Bell, "Bell: Madu blasts Trudeau over liberal no to pepper spray," *Calgary Sun*, 5 August 2021, https://calgarysun.com/opinion/columnists/bell-madu-blasts-trudeau-over-liberal-no-to-pepper-spray (accessed 11 May 2022).

17   Statistics Canada, *Police-Reported Crime Statistics in Canada, 2020* (Ottawa: Government of Canada, 27 July 2022), https://www150.statcan.gc.ca/n1/pub/85-002-x/2021001/article/00013-eng.htm (accessed 11 May 2022).

18   "Protecting Property Owners," Government of Alberta, 3 January 2022, https://www.alberta.ca/protecting-property-owners.aspx (accessed 11 May 2022).

19   "Alberta and Canada sign new 20-year contract for RCMP," Government of Alberta, 19 August 2011, https://www.alberta.ca/release.cfm?xID=31119E29C72B8-94D2-0888-764FC9E45F4B9CA3 (accessed 11 May 2022).

20   Barb Glen, "Alberta introduces measures against rural crime," *Western Producer*, 14 November 2019. https://www.producer.com/news/alberta-introduces-measures-against-rural-crime/ (accessed 11 May 2022).

21   Amy Tucker, "'I stood up for . . . my rights against criminals on my property': Lawsuit dropped against landowner," *CBC News Calgary*, last modified 17 January 2020, https://www.cbc.ca/news/canada/calgary/edouard-maurice-landowner-trespasser-lawsuit-ryan-watson-alberta-1.5429322 (accessed 11 May 2022).

22   Tucker, "I stood up."

23   Rick Bell, "Bell: Kenney called Eddie Maurice lawsuit harassment," *Calgary Sun*, 25 September 2019, https://calgarysun.com/opinion/columnists/bell-kenney-calls-eddie-maurice-lawsuit-harassment (accessed 11 May 2022).

24   Bell, "Bell: Kenny called Eddie Maurice."

25   Jeremey Wakefield, "Justice minister faces criticism for comments on active cases," *Edmonton Journal*, 1 November 2019, https://edmontonjournal.com/news/local-news/justice-minister-faces-criticism-for-comments-on-active-cases (accessed 11 May 2022).

26   "Protecting Property Owners."

27   Colin Campbell, John Cater, and Nahanni Pollard, *Canadian Policing (Second Edition)* (Toronto: Oxford University Press, 2021), 12.

28   "Alberta and Canada sign."

29   "Original letter, an open letter to Ralph Klein," AlbertaPolitics.ca, accessed 23 January 2022, https://albertapolitics.ca/wp-content/uploads/firewall.pdf (accessed 11 May 2022).

30   Fair Deal Panel, *Report to Government*, 31 May 2021, https://open.alberta.ca/dataset/d8933f27-5f81-4cbb-97c1-f56b45b09a74/resource/d5836820-d81f-4042-b24e-b04e012f4cde/download/fair-deal-panel-report-to-government-may-2020.pdf (accessed 11 May 2022).

31   Fair Deal Panel, *Report to Government*, 65.

32   "With a provincial police service, Albertans will pay more for less," National Police Federation, 15 September 2021, https://www.keepalbertarcmp.ca/ (accessed 11 May 2022).

33   "With a provincial police service," 3.

34   "With a provincial police service," 1.

35   Mertz, "Alberta hires PwC."

36   Rick Bell, "Bell: Dump the RCMP. Is it Alberta's one-finger salute to Trudeau?" *Calgary Sun*, 9 October 2020, https://calgarysun.com/opinion/columnists/bell-dump-the-rcmp-is-it-albertas-one-finger-salute-to-trudeau (accessed 11 May 2022).

37   Bell, "Bell: Dump the RCMP."

38   PricewaterhouseCoopers, *APPS Transition Study: Final* Report, last modified 29 October 2021, https://open.alberta.ca/publications/apps-transition-study-final-report (accessed 11 May 2022).

39   PricewaterhouseCoopers, *APPS Transition Study*, 77.

40   PricewaterhouseCoopers, *APPS Transition Study*, 78.

41   PricewaterhouseCoopers, *APPS Transition Study*, 18.

42   Shari Narine, "Treaty 8 rejects provincial police service contemplated by Alberta," *CTV News Edmonton*, last modified 20 October 2021, https://edmonton.ctvnews.ca/treaty-8-rejects-provincial-police-service-contemplated-by-alberta-1.5644948 (accessed 11 May 2022); Kerry McAthey, "'Very sporadic': Treaty Six First Nations says consultation on provincial police force fell short," *CTV News Edmonton*, last modified 2 November 2021, https://edmonton.ctvnews.ca/very-sporadic-treaty-six-first-nations-says-consultations-on-provincial-police-force-fell-short-1.5649845 (accessed 11 May 2022).

43   Adam Lachacz, "They're not listening: Alberta mayors and First Nations caution against provincial police force," *CTV News Edmonton*, last modified 30 October 2021, https://edmonton.ctvnews.ca/they-re-not-listening-alberta-mayors-and-first-nations-caution-against-provincial-police-force-1.5645648 (accessed 11 May 2022).

44 "Your police—your future: Listening to Albertans," National Police Federation, 27 April 2022, https://npf-fpn.com/news-item/keep-alberta-rcmp-engagement-tour-confirms-strong-support-for-rcmp-reveals-resistance-to-high-transition-cost-and-concern-over-justice-system/ (accessed 11 May 2022).

45 C. Adele Kent, "Report on the Investigation of a Phone Call, March 10, 2021 from the Honourable Kaycee Madu, Q.C. to Chief Dale McFee, Chief, Edmonton Police Service," 15 February 2022, https://www.alberta.ca/external/news/kent-report-final.pdf (accessed 11 May 2022).

46 Kent, "Report of the Investigation of a Phone Call."

47 Christina Max, "ABMunicipalities leaders reject provincial police force models," *Wetaskiwin Times*, 16 March 2022, https://www.wetaskiwintimes.com/news/abmunicipalities-leaders-reject-provincial-police-force-models (accessed 11 May 2022).

7

Playing the Populist Victim: Women, Gender, Representation, and the United Conservative Party

Melanee Thomas[1]

Introduction

Alberta is rarely seen as a place where one would expect to see gender equality or feminist politics. It is instead stereotyped as a bastion of conservative thought, wherein the prototypical Albertan is perceived to be a rural cowboy or an oil and gas roughneck: always a man and often white, conservative, and devoutly Christian (Banack 2016; Wesley 2021a). Despite being one of the most diverse, urban places in Canada (Statistics Canada 2021), Albertans who do not fit these mostly masculine stereotypes are at best seen as an odd fit; at worst, they are erased from the province's identity and key constituencies. In this context, the idea that Alberta's provincial government and the conservative parties that form it are somewhat cool to women and gender equality is well founded (Harder 2003).

The 2015 provincial election and subsequent New Democratic Party (NDP) government seemed to upset this narrative. The premier, Rachel Notley, had consistently raised issues relating to gender, equality, and diversity in the legislature since her first election in 2008 (Thomas 2019a), fielded a gender-balanced slate of candidates for the first time in Canadian history (Thomas 2019b), and appointed parity cabinets throughout the duration of her government. Several NDP MLAs were the first to use gender-neutral pronouns in the legislature, and the substantive discussion of, and policy developments relating to gender and equity issues skyrocketed compared to previous governments (Thomas 2019a).

With the election of the United Conservative Party (UCP) in 2019, some may have been tempted to conclude that women, gender, and equity issues were simply moved off the government's agenda, or that the party was simply silent on, or quietly hostile to these issues (see Harder 2003). I argue that only characterizing the UCP's relationship with gender this way is a mistake. Instead, like many conservative and populist parties, gender in general and masculinity in particular are both central to the party, and strongly structure its policy priorities and general approach to representation. This does not mean, however, that gender outside of men and masculinity, or women are well represented by the UCP government. The UCP fails to meet the most basic thresholds of adequate gendered representation now expected from political parties and elected representatives. Instead, like other populist conservative parties, their chosen representations of women and gender issues are posed and Janus-faced (see Akkerman 2015; Celis and Childs 2020), with carefully crafted victim narratives designed to represent a different constituency or ideology than women or a multifaceted understanding of gender (see Gordon 2021).

I build this argument in three stages. First, I outline how the UCP can be understood in a gendered political context. Though it is a new political party, the UCP reflects larger trends relating to gender and party politics. Second, I outline and empirically assess the UCP's performance in four areas of political representation relating to women and gender: descriptive, substantive, symbolic, and affective. Of these, affective representation is particularly interesting, because if can be particularly important for conservative parties. A part of new understandings of feminist democratic representation, affective representation focusses on process and unlike earlier iterations of feminist examinations of representation, it explicitly aims to take conservative advocacy for women and gender issues seriously (Celis and Childs 2020). Despite this opportunity, the UCP fails worst at affective representation. I conclude by outlining potential changes the UCP could enact to better represent women and gender.

Situating the United Conservative Party in the Gender and Politics Literature

Given its recent formation in 2017, it may be tempting to see the UCP as a blank slate with respect to gender, equity, representation, and politics. Yet, the UCP does not exist in a vacuum. Contextualizing the UCP in a larger gender and politics context helps explain its approaches to women and gender, particularly with respect to when and how women merit representation as a group, or when equity-related policies are forwarded on women's behalf. Here I address three: stereotypes and status threat, issue ownership, and ambidextrous positioning with respect to gender (Gordon 2021) in populist political parties.

Stereotypes and Status Threat

In general, politics is strongly structured by gender, because politics exists within a larger society that operates on long-standing gendered norms and stereotypes. Because of this, gender stereotypes are relevant for politics. Stereotypes are shared beliefs about someone's attributes and behavior based on their group membership (Bauer 2013). Often rigid and blunt, stereotypes can be positive, negative, or neutral, and address ideas about character, competence, appearance, and skills. For example, women are stereotyped as kind, supportive, and warm; as pretty and petite; as imaginative and creative; and as gullible, subordinate, and nagging. In contrast, men are stereotyped as competitive and courageous; as strong and muscular; as analytical and good with numbers; and as arrogant and egotistical. Because many of the stereotypes associated with men are also linked to leadership (Eagly and Karau 2002), men in politics are more likely to be described as driven and leaders (Schneider and Bos 2014, 255), as they benefit from overlapping stereotype profiles.

Many gender stereotypes stem from social roles—that is, the different family, social, and occupational roles taken on predominantly by women and men (Schneider and Bos 2019, 175; Kerevel and Atkeson 2015, 733). Women are stereotyped as caring and mothering, even if they are not mothers or carers themselves, because women are far more likely than men to occupy caring roles. This includes providing care for children, family, and friends (Statistics Canada 2018), or being more likely be employed in caregiving occupations (Moyser 2017). Stereotypes generated from these social roles are often abstractions, and when an individual from a stereotyped group appears to be incongruent with them, they may be sanctioned. These sanctions for role incongruity extend to politics, as the stereotypes associated with being a "good" woman and a "good" politician do not overlap. Instead, women politicians are seen as "deviant" women who do not possess typically feminine traits, yet who cannot quite conform to the positive traits desired of politicians. They become cold rather than emotional (*feminine)* and calculating rather than assertive (*masculine, politician*, see Schneider and Bos 2014; 2019).

Stereotypes based on social roles are certainly malleable over time, especially as women and men move into different roles. However, instead of transforming the gendered social expectations of those roles, it is expected that women who move into more traditionally masculine roles or fields will become more like men (Diekman and Eagly 2000). This suggests that stereotypes about men predominate the "ideal" image many have in their minds, particularly when it comes to venues where men predominate, like politics. It also implies that more traditional stereotypes about women are not necessarily displaced as women take on "newer" roles.

Gender stereotypes are relevant for analyzing and understanding the UCP for several reasons. First, as noted above, the stereotypical image of the prototypical Albertan is almost always highly masculinized and often conservative. This suggests that many in Alberta may expect that their elected representatives will also be masculinized conservatives. Second, the competitive and zero-sum nature of politics means that for some men, losing to women in a neutral, non-political context makes them more likely to subscribe to sexist views and to prefer men's leadership in politics (Mansell et al. 2021). For Albertans in the lead up to the 2019 election, this sense of loss was driven, in part, by two things: a left-leaning party in government and the ongoing bust in the oil and gas industry. Both were framed as a loss of an established order, with a degree of entitlement informing part of the desire to have the old order back (see Gerson 2019). Importantly, the oil and gas bust was popularly framed as primarily about men's losses (Unwin 2016) and used to argue by some conservatives that greater equity in politics (e.g., gender-based budgeting) was an explicit attack on Alberta's men (Dawson 2018).

Much of the UCP's rhetoric plays into this narrative, especially with respect to its defence of oil and gas as a waning industry (see Bratt, Clark, and Rioux in this volume). Part of this defence can be reasonably characterized as sense of grief for the loss of benefits and goods that previously existed under boom times. Though this sense of grief is certainly not restricted to men, the politicization of it has, in other areas, been located with men when it is accompanied by a sense of entitlement to, or a perception that those benefits have been unreasonably snatched away (see Kimmel 2017). Similarly, conservatism tends to surge in response to nostalgia for the stability of the past, and this reasonably characterizes many Albertans who long for the return of a booming fossil fuel industry. This nostalgia may be accompanied by a sense of threat and corresponding defensive response if it is perceived to be accompanied by greater social and political equity—the sense is that their loss is someone else's gain.

For example, despite popular narratives, support for Donald Trump's presidency in the United States was not driven by (often explicitly stated) economic anxiety, but rather perceived threats to dominant groups' status (e.g., white Americans, men) in relation to equity-deserving groups including women, visible and racialized minorities, and 2SLGBTQA+ folks (Mutz 2018). This is one reason why Trump's accusation that Clinton was "playing the woman card" resonated: it was most persuasive amongst voters who perceive that any equitable advances for women come predominantly at men's expense and/or that women overplay things like sexual harassment to inappropriately sanction men (Cassese and Holman 2018).

This parallels parts of the UCP's 2019 campaign. The party refused to drop Mark Smith, the UCP's candidate in Drayton Valley-Devon, despite him making explicitly homophobic statements as late as 2015, including likening sexual diversity to pedophilia and arguing that schools should be permitted to fire teachers simply for their sexual orientation. In response, many voters claimed to have supported him because the economy, specifically as it relates to oil and gas, was more important to them (Maimann 2019). Given the content of Smith's statements, it is difficult to interpret this as solely about the economy. Instead, as is the case with Trump in the United States, the speed with which some dismissed others' constitutionally guaranteed right to freedom from the explicit discrimination evident in Smith's comments, suggests the NDP's explicit support of women, gender, sexual diversity, and equity (Thomas 2019a) may have constituted a threat to some voters, and their defensive reaction to that threat made the UCP an appealing alternative.

Issue Ownership

I can understand skeptical readers dismissing the possibility that much of the UCP's rhetoric and support is driven by sexist, racist, or homophobic reactions to group hierarchies being potentially eroded by the NDP government or the oil and gas bust. In that context, it is worth observing that a standard feature of electoral politics—issue ownership—is also highly gendered. The idea of issue ownership is uncontroversial: political parties are ascribed ownership of an issue based on stereotypes and, at times, past performance. Once a party "owns" an issue, they are assumed to have a greater degree of competence on that issue than do other parties. Conservative parties in North America "own" the economy as an issue, while left-leaning parties "own" issues relating to social programs, such as health care and education (Bélanger and Meguid 2008; Winter 2010).

Importantly, the role of stereotypes in issue ownership is key, because gender and gendered issues structure how voters perceive parties. This, in turn, helps build the association between a party and issues required to form issue ownership (Winter 2010). For the UCP, the actions of other conservative parties in Canada would reasonably inform the stereotypical issues a party like the UCP would own. For example, previous Progressive Conservative (PC) governments in Alberta had a long-standing track record of ambivalence and hostility towards women's advocacy (Harder 2003). At the federal level, the Reform Party explicitly argued there are "no women's issues" in hopes of rejecting equity-based group politics (Thomas 2017). Reform, the Canadian Alliance, and the merged Conservative Party of Canada all addressed gendered issues such as childcare only through tax credits (*ibid.*). Thus, the process that helps associate the economy with parties such as the UCP is decidedly not gender neutral, nor is the simple campaign slogan "jobs, jobs, jobs." When the "jobs" in question are primarily in industries such as oil and gas, while public sector jobs (held predominantly by women) are identified for cuts to positions and pay (Bennett 2020), it shows how the economy, as used by the UCP, is gendered and primarily, for them, about men.

Ambidextrous Populist Gender Positioning

Like issue ownership, populist political parties are not readily seen as gendered, at least on the surface. Certainly, populism has been a feature of Alberta's politics for decades (Sayers and Stewart 2019) where various political parties argued they best protected regular people from victimization and abuse from "elites" (Gordon 2021). Key to these arguments is the construction of the victim, as evidenced by both conservative and progressive populist narratives. On one hand, more progressive populist appeals focus on rights, linking systemic racism, sexism, and class into systems of oppression that victimize equity-deserving groups (*ibid.*). In contrast, more conservative populist arguments in Canada construct different victims as part of their rhetoric, such as children, taxpayers, and perhaps most relevant for the UCP, the West, particularly with respect to how Western provinces, including Alberta, are "victimized" by the federal government (*ibid.*). Because populist arguments are a flexible tool, there is considerable disagreement about which pairings of victim and oppressor, regular people and elites are most important (*ibid.*, 45). This disagreement is often gendered, shedding light on how a political party understands when, why, and how gender becomes a relevant concept or when women as a group merit advocacy and policy attention.

The clearest statement of this is Gordon's (2021) examination of populist rhetoric in arguments advocating for tough-on-crime legislation (Bill C-10) and legislation in response to Supreme Court decisions invalidating Canada's prostitution laws (Bill C-36). Both bills were introduced by the Conservative Party of Canada while in government under Stephen Harper's leadership. On one hand, the populist rhetoric around Bill C-10 focused on being tough on crime for the sake of those victimized by someone else's criminal actions. In this, gender is virtually absent: only one speech from a conservative member of parliament addressing Bill C-10 mentioned gender at all, and most of the arguments failed to address how crime and violence are connected to systemic sexism or racism. On the other hand, though, the rhetoric around Bill C-36 was profoundly gendered, as "women and gender were at the very centre of many of the most frequent arguments" in support of the bill (*ibid.*, 51).

The reasons behind this ambidextrous use of gender as a populist rhetorical device are key for understanding the UCP. Gordon argues that "conservative actors in Canada selectively centre issues and sources of gender inequality, while conspicuously avoiding them in other contexts" (53). This dichotomy may reflect a strategic use of previously successful strategies, where a party knows it does not "need" to address gender to achieve its goals on one hand, while trying to explore new strategies to mitigate critique or expand support on the other. This sometimes means borrowing "political concepts and language from its progressive and liberal opponents to make its conservative case" (*ibid.*, 55). Whether this borrowing is sincere is crucial for assessing how well populist parties represent women and gender. Assessing the quality of that representation is where we now turn.

Finding Gender in Political Representation in Alberta under the United Conservative Party

Political representation typically involves five things: someone who is being represented; someone who is doing the representing; the thing or things that are being represented; a context where the representation takes place; and the things that are left out or excluded (Dovi 2009). In Alberta, by design, this means that voters in a district are represented by their MLA in the legislature. The key thing being represented is usually geography (e.g., the district itself) or party, given strong norms of party discipline. This potentially leaves out a whole host of things that could and, perhaps, should be represented. How, then, can gender's representation (or lack thereof) be credibly assessed in this context?

Feminist scholars have developed useful tools for conceptualizing representation that allows gendered representation to be assessed in several ways. Most are based on Hannah Pitkin's (1967) classic statement of representation, focusing on descriptive, substantive, and symbolic representation. To this, I add a fourth conceptualization of representation called affective representation (Celis and Childs 2020). Each is defined and discussed below.

Descriptive Representation

Descriptive representation focusses on describing the gender composition and balance of a legislature, on the assumption that women's presence will help ensure women's perspectives and experiences are brought forward into policymaking (Mansbridge 1999). However, even Pitkin herself was skeptical of descriptive representation insofar as it simply described a legislature's composition and not its activity. Similarly, it is too easy to describe legislatures along a gender binary, only looking at women and men, without examining other relevant features of representatives' identities (Celis and Childs 2020). This renders descriptive representation a preliminary, blunt, but necessary step in assessing how gender is represented in any given political context.

Here, I present two measures of descriptive representation: nominated candidates for election and cabinet appointments. Both measures directly address how a party leader in particular views gender and how it should be represented. Candidates capture who is available to be elected to a party's caucus. Patterns of gender bias are commonly found across political parties in Canada, as parties consistently nominate women in districts they are less likely to win (Thomas and Bodet 2013). It is clear, however, that if a party leader wants to ensure their candidates are balanced across genders, they will direct their party organizers to do so (Thomas 2017; 2019b). As leader, it is reasonable to assume that Jason Kenney knows this, as he promised as much at the outset of his campaign to lead the UCP (CBC News 2018). Similarly, as premier or prime minister, party leaders in government in Canada determine the structure of government through their cabinet. Thus, not only are the demographics of cabinet ministers important, but so too are the portfolios they are responsible for (Annesley, Beckwith, and Franceschet 2019).

Both measures of descriptive representation show that representing women is not a priority for the UCP; instead, the representational focus is on men. This is perhaps unsurprising, given how the UCP is best contextualized within gender and politics outlined above. With respect to candidates, while they only make up 36 per cent of the Canadian population (Ouellet, Shiab, and Gilchrist 2021), white men were 54 per cent of the UCP's candidates in 2019. In contrast, white men were only 34 per cent of NDP candidates that same year. Women overall comprised only 30 per cent of the UCP's candidates (compared to 53 per cent of the NDP's). Both parties nominated about the same proportion of visible and racialized minority candidates (7 per cent for the NDP and 8 per cent for the UCP), but because the UCP nominated so few women overall, racialized women are a larger proportion of the UCP's women candidates overall (27 per cent compared to the NDP's 15 per cent). To date, it is not yet known how many candidates, if any, identified outside the gender binary.[2]

Cabinet appointments are similar. Here, I only focus on the twenty-three individuals appointed to the original UCP cabinet, or added in a subsequent shuffle; as a result, associate ministers are excluded from this analysis. Like candidates, 52 per cent of UCP cabinet ministers are white men. Similarly, white women comprise 22 per cent of the UCP's candidates and cabinet ministers. Visible and racialized minority women and men are present at the same rate (13 per cent each). Notably, very few women serve in a high profile, powerful cabinet ministry. Those who do are white (e.g., LaGrange in Education, Savage in Energy).

How does this match with Kenney's commitment to recruit more women and diverse candidates? Some may look at this record and argue it is good enough. Women are certainly present at levels thought to create a critical mass, typically understood as 30 per cent; however, it is important to note that this argument is based on a faulty reading of the literature (see Childs and Krook 2008). Others may argue that unless a legislature is a true microcosm of the population it is supposed to represent, then descriptive representation has not been achieved. Given how candid most party leaders are when they achieve gender parity amongst their candidates or in cabinet, it may be worthwhile asking leaders who choose not to ensure their candidates and ministers better match the population they are supposed to represent why this is less of a priority for them.

Substantive Representation

Substantive representation addresses the shortcomings of descriptive representation by focussing more on action, asking who is "acting for" women with respect to policies, issues, inside the legislature itself. Scholars typically identify key issues important to women and then assess how well a legislature addresses them, if at all. While substantive representation avoids the inactive pitfalls of descriptive representation, this definition creates its own challenges. Typically, researchers are choosing the issues that "best" capture women's "interests" in a top down manner (Celis and Childs 2020). These issues typically focus on policies that are known to disproportionately affect women with respect to the welfare state (e.g., health care, education, children, and childcare). In so doing, these analyses can miss issues of particular importance to diverse groups of women who, based on their communities may be more interested in issues and policies that, on the surface, do not necessarily look like traditional "women's issues" (Celis and Childs 2020). With that caveat in mind, I focus my analysis on women's substantive representation under the UCP in three areas: how women and gender are discussed in party platforms; the frequency, context, and content of when women and gender are raised in legislative debates; and the position of the Status of Women Ministry in cabinet.

The first two analyses—party platforms and legislative debates via *Hansard*—were conducted similarly. Simple keyword searches are used to assess the presence of the following key terms: gender, women, men, feminine, masculine, caregiving, caregiver, childcare, and diversity. This kind of analysis has been used in the past to assess how well women premiers substantively represented women during their time in government (Bashevkin 2019); given that, it seems an appropriate standard to hold other provincial governments, such as the UCP's, to as well.

Substantively, gender was not discussed much in the UCP platform in 2019. Women were mentioned a total of nine times, with men mentioned four times. What is perhaps more notable is where the platform is silent: equity, diversity, and gender are not at all present. In contrast, while the NDP platform mentioned women fewer times (four total), it also mentioned gender (N=4), equity (N=2), and diversity (N=4). The largest difference between the two platforms is with respect to mentions of childcare (NDP=20, UCP=0), as this reflects the importance of the NDP's $25/day childcare plan to their 2019 platform. None of the other search terms appeared in either party's platform.

Hansard data shows some striking similarities between how the UCP and the old PCs and Wildrose substantively discuss women and gender. Past analyses show that PC MLAs disproportionately used "women" to refer to "men and women in uniform" during legislative statements (Thomas 2019a). While this is still the case, UCP MLAs have expanded their use of "men and women" to refer to men and women as Albertans (e.g., "men and women across Alberta," "men and women who built Alberta") or more specifically as workers in oil and gas (e.g., "men and women of the oil patch," "men and women in the industry"). Beyond this, women UCP MLAs are more likely to mention "women" in *Hansard*, often with explicit reference to issues emerging from Status of Women, and both UCP and NDP MLAs use terms like "gender-based violence" in reference to Clare's Law (discussed below as part of the analysis of affective representation). Overall, though, if the bulk of UCP MLAs' use of the term "women" is part of the rhetorical devices noted above, it does not meet the requirements for substantive representation as presented in the academic literature.

In contrast, NDP MLAs use "women" substantively differently in legislative debate in several ways. First, NDP MLAs are as much as three times more likely to mention the word "women," because they are more likely to mention women as part of substantive debate addressing women's equality, sexism, and misogyny, and women's under-representation in politics. However, NDP MLAs are more likely to mention "women" when addressing other issues, including housing, workforce participation, and the COVID-19 pandemic. NDP MLAs are also disproportionately likely to use terms like "gender," particularly with respect to calls for gender-based policy analysis. The overwhelming majority of content about the affordability and accessibility of childcare, elder care, caregiving benefits, and caregiver abuse also come from NDP MLAs. Finally, only NDP MLAs used terms like "feminine" and "masculine" in *Hansard*; most of these interventions addressed Bill 8 (Education Amendment Act) to draw attention to how negative remarks about gender identity expression (e.g., not feminine or masculine enough) affected students. Though this analysis could certainly be pushed further, it shows how MLAs can, in fact, use the language of women and gender to raise substantive issues.

Finally, the UCP's approach to the Status of Women Ministry is similar to its use of language in *Hansard*: it is closer to practice under previous PC governments, rather than a continuation of the substantive representation that occurred through the ministry under the Notley government. While the federal and other provincial governments have long-standing units dedicated to the status of women, Alberta was the first to create a full department with its own deputy minister in 2015 (Ontario followed in 2017; see Thomas 2019a). After 2019, Status of Women is no longer a standalone ministry, but was instead merged into the Ministry of Culture, Multiculturalism and Status of Women, with a deputy minister primarily responsible for Culture. Thus, the importance and position of the Status of Women Ministry in Alberta was meaningfully eroded following the 2019 election.

How the Ministry of Culture, Multiculturalism, and Status of Women addresses women in their annual reporting (Government of Alberta 2020) strongly reflects Gordon's (2021) ambidextrous construction of the victim in conservative populist parties outlined above. On one hand, the annual report focuses on two pieces of legislation—the *Disclosure to Protect Against Domestic Violence* (Clare's Law) and the *Protecting Survivors of Human Trafficking Act*—focus on women as victims. The report highlights how the government of Alberta proclaimed a day for the Zero Tolerance for Female Genital Mutilation/Cutting. Certainly, these issues are important, but it is telling how absent women are from other government priorities and policy discussions when they cannot be so easily framed as victims. This is also clear in the Status of Women's annual report, as women and the economy are mentioned only to highlight a continued investment in a program designed to support women who wish to pursue training and work in the skilled trades. Further details, including budgetary allocations are not provided there, suggesting that for the most part, women are conspicuously absent from larger policies and narratives about the economy and economy recovery. Childcare is not mentioned at all, and children are primarily discussed in contrast to adults with respect to participation in sport. This is a striking example of Gordon's argument that "conservative actors in Canada selectively centre issues and sources of gender inequality, while conspicuously avoiding them in other contexts" (53). It appears that, for the UCP, unless women can be framed as a particular kind of victim, they are conspicuously excluded from many substantive policy discussions and rationales. This, in turn, seriously hampers the substantive representation of women in Alberta.

Symbolic Representation

Symbolic representation holds great potential to help show how well women are represented. Common representative symbols include flags, anthems, and landmarks to "stand for" a nation or a country. The presence of women in a legislature can be used as an example of how equal women and men are in politics, but other symbols are also useful, too (Celis and Childs 2020). For example, a standout role model can symbolize women's presence in politics, as can media coverage and framings of women "doing" politics. Other theorizations of symbolic representation ask who is, and is not, symbolically represented, as well as asking what symbols evoke for the represented (Lombardo and Meier 2014, in Celis and Childs 2020, 76–77).

One of the most potent symbols of women in Alberta politics pre-dates the UCP's election in 2019. Arguably, the violence directed at Rachel Notley as Alberta's premier communicates much symbolically to Alberta's women about their place in politics here (see Thomas 2019a). Similarly, the assertion that the 2015 election result produced an "accidental" government could be interpreted as a symbolic denigration of an election result that brought a woman to the premier's office in the least common way: first through a general election (see Thomas 2018). There are few women in the UCP caucus who stand as symbols for women in politics, in part because so few of them are sufficiently high profile to be commonly identified as a potential symbol for even conservative women in politics.[3] Beyond this, the UCP routinely uses a series of symbols, including (blue) half-tonne trucks, and worksites commonly associated with oil and gas or construction. All of these are stereotypically masculine symbols connected to social role theory and the corresponding stereotypes highlighted earlier in this chapter. None of these symbols used by the UCP are designed to symbolize women in particular, and while it is certainly plausible that these symbols may resonate with some women—specifically, women who see symbols as benefitting their husbands and, thus, the "family unit"—it is also likely that many women find these symbols exclusionary and off-putting.

Across the most common measures of women's representation in politics, then—descriptive, substantive, and symbolic—the UCP fares poorly. It is not unreasonable to conclude that the UCP's representation of women is mediocre at best, and non-existent at worst. But this leaves space for a new measure of representation that purports to make more serious space for conservative claims to be representing women: affective representation (Celis and Childs 2020).

Affective Representation

Affective representation is the core idea of Celis and Childs' book, *Feminist Democratic Representation*. The problem they address is that for many, "women are not explicitly considered to be a group to which decision makers should be accountable" (2020, 29). Instead of focusing on the content of representation and how it relates to women, Celis and Childs instead focus on the *process*, asking who stands for and acts for differently *affected* groups of women. Here, they look specifically for group advocacy and account giving. Group advocacy allows for differently affected groups of women to advocate for what they need. Account giving requires representatives to return to those who advocated for their groups and give an account of what they did with that advocacy. This could include how it was included in a policy or piece of legislation, or it could address why the information provided through that advocacy was ultimately not used.

To be feminist, affective representation rests on three principles: inclusiveness, responsiveness, and egalitarianism.[4] Inclusiveness addresses the extent to which women's heterogeneous views are present in representation. Responsiveness asks if women, in all their diversity, broadly agree with what is being done in their name. And egalitarianism requires that all voices must be part of the processes where claims are received, considered, and deliberated, and then rejected or accepted. It requires a great deal of open and fairmindedness, both on the part of those providing group advocacy, and by elected representatives, particularly with their account giving back to those most affected by a policy.

Certainly, this argument is not without critique, as some have argued this conceptualization means that virtually anything could constitute women's representation. For Celis and Childs, this is what renders affective representation feminist: it avoids universalizing women's experiences and instead explicitly addresses differences across women. It expects those differences to be seriously considered and deliberated, and honestly reported as part of the policy process. It makes space across ideological divisions, in part because the process as they outline it should not be tied to any one ideological perspective or view.

In sum, the process of affective representation requires sincere advocacy by representatives from affected groups, serious deliberation from elected representatives, honest accounting from elected representatives back to affected groups, and then judgement or endorsement of elected representatives' work by affected groups.

To assess the extent to which this is happening in Alberta, I examined the processes through which members of the public can engage in advocacy and consultation directly to the provincial government via the Government of Alberta's website (2021a). This ability to offer advocacy is a necessary, but insufficient condition for affective representation to take place. The results are a bit grim. At the time of writing, women are not included as a category for public engagement. Diversity and inclusion is included as a category, but the one engagement listed was an initiative of the previous NDP government and concluded in 2019. There, other necessary conditions for affective representation appear to be in place, including a report back to affected communities about what representatives heard and what action they took based on that advocacy, an outline of actions taken in response to information given in advocacy, and a solicitation for further feedback (Government of Alberta 2019).

Unfortunately, this process does not appear to be the current norm under the UCP. Instead, a keyword search for "women" brought up a single consultation: a working group on Missing and Murdered Indigenous Women and Girls (MMIWG). There is no public engagement, but rather a working group of five members of the public (Government of Alberta 2021b). As members of the public, the advisory group has no institutional power, and thus has no ability to enforce or implement their recommendations to the government. This is clear in the working group's mandate: it would only meet Celis and Childs' requirements for affective representation if it could be plausibly argued that the working group alone were sufficient to act as affected representatives. While I do not deny that it is plausible a working group could possibly fulfill this role for some narrowly defined policies, for an issue as grave and important as MMIWG, the absence of options for affected representatives to be involved in advocacy and accountability beyond the working group suggests this process does not meet the requirements for meaningful affective representation. This is not to say the working group cannot or is not doing good work; on the contrary, I would contend the work of the working group is necessary and important, but it alone cannot be sufficient to meet these representational requirements.

Two interconnected examples show how, instead of engaging in affective representation, the UCP poses as representing women while actually presenting victim narratives that characterize populist conservative parties. First, in October 2021, the minister of jobs, economy and innovation in Alberta, Doug Schweitzer, explicitly stated, "A lot of women came back in the workforce as the school year began because a lot of women *took time off during COVID*. It disproportionately impacted women and we saw a lot of women return to the workforce looking for jobs in September" (May 2021, emphasis added).

Many reacted critically to this statement, as women's exit from the workforce due to COVID was driven by childcare centre and school closures, leaving parents scrambling given the obvious incompatibility between caring for children full time while simultaneously trying to work. This affected women's employment more than men's, a pattern candidly observed in several media reports, but also by banks (Desjardins and Freestone 2021), and consulting firms such as McKinsey & Company (2021) and PriceWaterhouseCoopers (2021). Yet, when members of the public, including me, observed that they expected the minister of jobs to be more attuned to these gendered effects of COVID, the minister reacted on social media by presenting himself as the victim of an unfounded attack, because he had previously acknowledged that some of COVID-19's economic effects were gendered (Schweitzer 2021). Some members of the public rejected this, instead asking for greater focus on what the UCP government was going to do with respect to COVID-19's gendered economic effects, specifically citing the UCP's budget and their reluctance to sign a childcare deal with the federal government (Bergstrom 2021). The minister's response was to block many who were critical, leading some to ask the minister explicitly how he thought his victim narrative contributed to affective representation (Wesley 2021b).

The second example relates to the childcare funding deal signed between the provincial and federal governments. For the UCP, securing federal funding for childcare as offered by the federal government could have been used as an opportunity for the premier to reinforce his minister's claim that the UCP genuinely understands the gendered effects of the COVID-19 pandemic. That announcement could have been an ideal time to communicate how the UCP understands the economic benefits childcare investments produce, as these disproportionately come from mothers' participation in the labour force (Alexander et al. 2017). Instead, the announcement was characterized by the premier's repeated references to a common victim narrative from the UCP: that Alberta routinely gets an unfair deal from the federal government compared to other provinces (Leavitt 2021). This victim narrative appears so central to the UCP that it could not be displaced, even when presented with an easy opportunity to offer gender-based representation.

Celis and Childs clearly argue that affective representation, when done well, should increase trust in government. Thus, a third indicator to suggest this form of representation is not occurring under the UCP is a low level of trust in government, as evidenced by consistently high levels of disapproval for government action and performance. While the requirements for meeting affective representation are steep, the transparency, open-mindedness, fairness, and accountability required to achieve this type of representation are arguably not yet present. If they were, it may go some way to addressing the systematic unpopularity experienced by the UCP throughout much of their time in office, especially in 2020–21.

Predicting a Path Forward

From its inception through its first term in government, the UCP fails to meet the most basic thresholds of adequate gender representation now expected from political parties and elected representatives. The party's performance with respect to descriptive representation is mediocre, as a third of its nominated candidates in 2019 were women, even though this threshold lags considerably behind its primary competitor in Alberta (the NDP). Arguably, the UCP performs most poorly with respect to affective representation, in no small part to reluctance to engage in sincere public engagement, or receive and digest candid public feedback. This approach renders affective representation effectively impossible. Instead, the best way to understand how the UCP approaches women and gender rests with

Janus-faced, ambidextrous populist parties, where they use gender and progressive language when it helps craft a useful victim narrative, and otherwise ignore or refuse to sincerely address gendered issues or policies that differently affect women.

Ironically, affective representation was developed, in part, to sincerely address how well conservative parties represent women and gender. While genuine affective representation would be an admirable goal for any political party because it is based on process and transparency, it is especially important for conservative parties who otherwise may be keen to avoid more conventional feminist representative actions. Thus, while it is plausible the UCP may continue to perform with mediocrity on some measures of women's representation (e.g., descriptive representation), their past performance on more substantive and affective forms of representation suggest that women and gender will continue to be poorly represented by the party, if represented at all.

NOTES

1   I would like to thank Saaka Sulemana for his excellent work as an RA for this project.

2   Federally, nine candidates nominated for the 2019 election identified as non-binary (Johnston et al. 2021). Increasing numbers of non-binary candidates should be expected, as gender identities beyond "woman" and "man" become more commonly accepted.

3   For example, none have the profile of Calgary Nose Hill Member of Parliament, Michelle Rempel Garner.

4   This argument is particularly well developed in Chapters 3 and 4 of Celis and Childs (2020).

REFERENCES

Alberta Hansard. 21 May 2019–4 December 2019, "The 30th Legislature, First Session." Province of Alberta. https://docs.assembly.ab.ca/LADDAR_files/docs/hansards/cpl/legislature_30/session_1/20190521_1330_01_cpl.pdf

Alberta Hansard. 25 February 2020–7 December 2021, "The 30th Legislature, Second Session." Province of Alberta. https://docs.assembly.ab.ca/LADDAR_files/docs/hansards/cpl/legislature_30/session_2/20200225_1500_01_cpl.pdf

Alexander, Craig, Kip Beckman, Alicia Macdonald, Cory Renner, and Matthew Stewart. 2017. "Ready for Life: A Socio-Economic Analysis of Early Childhood Education and Care." *Conference Board of Canada*, 26 October 2017. https://www. conferenceboard.ca/e-library/abstract.aspx?did=9231.

Annesley, Clare, Karen Beckwith, and Susan Franceschet. 2019. *Cabinets, Ministers, and Gender.* Oxford: Oxford University Press.

Akkerman, Tjitske. 2015. "Gender and the Radical Right in Western Europe: A Comparative Analysis of Policy Agendas." *Patterns of Prejudice* 49(1–2): 37–60.

Banack, Clark. 2016. *God's Province: Evangelical Christianity, Political Thought, and Conservatism in Alberta.* Montreal & Kingston: McGill-Queen's University Press.

Bashevkin, Sylvia, ed. 2019. *Doing Politics Differently? Women Premiers in Canada's Provinces and Territories.* Vancouver: UBC Press.

Bauer, Nichole. 2013. "Rethinking stereotype reliance: Understanding the connection between female candidates and gender stereotypes." *Politics and the Life Sciences* 32(1): 22–42.

Bélanger, Éric and Bonnie Meguid. 2008. "Issue salience, issue ownership, and issue-based vote choice." *Electoral Studies* 27(3): 477–491.

Bennett, Dean. 2020. "Alberta's UCP government wants 24,000 public sector workers to take pay cut." *Global News.* 7 February 2020. https://globalnews.ca/news/6523530/ albertas-ucp-government-wants-24000-public-sector-workers-to-take-pay-cut/

Bergstrom, Heidi (@heidibergstrom). 2021. "Ok so if you understand that the pandemic is disproportionately affecting women then I would expect a bit more focus on that. Women were barely seen in your budget video and we're still waiting on a deal for affordable child care with the federal government." Twitter, 13 October 2021. https://twitter.com/heidibergstrom/status/1448480746272747524.

Cassese, Erin and Mirya Holman. 2018. "Playing the Woman Card: Ambivalent Sexism in the 2016 U.S. Presidential Race." *Political Psychology* 40(1): 55–74.

CBC News. 2018. "Will face of UCP caucus change, given diverse slate of nomination hopefuls?" *CBC News*, 13 August 2018. https://www.cbc.ca/news/canada/ edmonton/jason-kenney-ucp-diversify-1.4783508.

Celis, Karent and Sarah Childs. 2020. *Feminist Democratic Representation.* Oxford: Oxford University Press.

Childs, Sarah and Mona Lena Krook. 2008. "Critical Mass Theory and Women's Political Representation." *Political Studies* 56(3): 725–736.

Dawson, Tyler. 2018. "What you need to know about Trudeau's comments on 'gender impacts' and construction worders." *National Post*, 5 December 2018. https:// nationalpost.com/news/canada/heres-what-you-need-to-know-about-the- controversy-over-trudeaus-comments-about-gender-impacts-and-construction- workers.

Desjardins, Dawn and Carrie Freestone. 2021. "COVID Further Clouded the Outlook for Canadian Women at Risk of Disruption." *Royal Bank of Canada*, 4 March 2021. https://thoughtleadership.rbc.com/covid-further-clouded-the-outlook- for-canadian-women-at-risk-of-disruption/?utm_medium=referral&utm_ source=media&utm campaign=special+report.

Diekman, Amanda B. and Alice H. Eagly. 2000. "Stereotypes as Dynamic Constructs: Women and Men of the Past, Present, and Future." *Personality and Social Psychology Bulletin* 26(10): 1171–1188.

Dovi, Suzanne. 2009. "Political Representation." *Stanford Encyclopedia of Philosophy.* https://plato.stanford.edu/entries/political-representation/.

Eagly, Alice H. and Steven J. Karau. 2002. "Role Congruity Theory of Prejudice Toward Female Leaders." *Psychological Review* 109(3): 573–598.

Gerson, Jennifer. 2019. "Governing this province should be an honour, not an inheritance." *CBC News*, 22 March 2019. https://www.cbc.ca/news/canada/calgary/alberta-election-campaign-ndp-united-conservative-party-1.5066997.

Gordon, Kelly. 2021. "Mobilizing Victimhood: Situating the Victim in Canadian Conservatism." *Canadian Journal of Political Science* 54: 41–59.

Government of Alberta. 2019. "Fostering an inclusive Alberta engagement: Gathered input on the government's next steps to combat racism." https://www.alberta.ca/inclusive-alberta.aspx.

Government of Alberta. 2020. *Annual Report: Culture, Multiculturalism and Status of Women, 2019–2020*. https://open.alberta.ca/dataset/4a9716c2-e826-4bdd-bcdd-8aefd8e9fc12/resource/2b1ec7aa-ec4a-40ef-8ef7-66f209c1052a/download/cmsw-annual-report-2019-2020.pdf.

Government of Alberta. 2021a. "Search public engagements: Find out how government is involving Albertans in making decisions, and how you can participate." https://www.alberta.ca/search-public-engagements.aspx?status=All&topic=All&opportunity=All&keyword=Clare&archived=yes.

Government of Alberta. 2021b. "Alberta Joint Working Group on MMIWG: Providing input on government's action plan to address the Calls for Justice of the National Inquiry of Missing and Murdered Indigenous women and girls (MMIWG)." https://www.alberta.ca/alberta-joint-working-group-on-mmiwg.aspx.

Harder, Lois. 2003. *State of Struggle: Feminism and Politics in Alberta*. Edmonton: University of Alberta Press.

Kerevel, Yann P. and Lonna Rae Atkeson. 2015. "Reducing Stereotypes of Female Political Leaders in Mexico." *Political Research Quarterly* 68(4): 732–744.

Kimmel, Michael. 2017. *Angry White Men: American Masculinity at the End of an Era*. New York: Bold Type Books.

Leavitt, Kieran. 2021. "Justin Trudeau and Jason Kenney trade shots at testy child-care announcement." *Toronto Star*, 15 November 2021. https://www.thestar.com/news/canada/2021/11/15/justin-trudeau-and-jason-kenney-trade-shots-at-testy-child-care-announcement.html.

Maimann, Kevin. 2019. "Homophobic comments failed to fell UCP's Mark Smith. What does that say about the Alberta election?" *Toronto Star*, 17 April 2019. https://www.thestar.com/edmonton/2019/04/17/what-this-riding-says-about-the-alberta-election-as-homophobic-comments-fail-to-fell-ucps-mark-smith.html.

Mansbridge, Jane. 1999. "Should Blacks Represent Blacks and Women Represent Women? A Contingent 'Yes.'" *The Journal of Politics* 61(3): 628–657.

Mansell, Jordan, Allison Harell, Melanee Thomas, and Tania Gosselin. 2021. "Competitive Loss, Gendered Backlash and Sexism in Politics." *Political Behavior.* https://doi.org/10.1007/s11109-021-09724-8.

May, Connor. 2021. "Minister of jobs in Alberta is excited about how much progress the province is making." *Discover Airdrie*, 12 October 2021. https://www.discoverairdrie.com/local/minister-of-jobs-in-alberta-is-excited-about-how-much-progress-the-province-is-making.

McKinsey & Company. 2021. "Seven charts that show COVID-19's impact on women's employment." 8 March 2021. https://www.mckinsey.com/featured-insights/diversity-and-inclusion/seven-charts-that-show-covid-19s-impact-on-womens-employment.

Moyser, Melissa. 2017. "Women and Paid Work." *Women in Canada: A Gender-based Statistical Report.* https://www150.statcan.gc.ca/n1/pub/89-503-x/2015001/article/14694-eng.htm.

Mutz, Diana C. 2018. "Status threat, not economic hardship, explains the 2016 presidential vote." *Proceedings of the National Academy of Sciences of the United States of America* 115(19): E4330–E4339.

Ouellet, Valérie, Naël Shiab, and Sylvène Gilchrist. 2021. "White men make up a third of Canada's population but a majority of MPs—here's why." *CBC Radio Canada*, 26 August 2021. https://ici.radio-canada.ca/info/2021/elections-federales/minorites-visibles-diversite-autochtones-racises-candidats-politique/en.

Pitkin, Hannah. 1967. *The Concept of Representation.* Chicago: University of Chicago Press.

PriceWaterhouseCooper. 2021. "COVID-19 is reversing the important gains made over the last decade for women in the workforce." *PwC Women in Work Index.* https://www.pwc.com/gx/en/news-room/press-releases/2021/women-in-work-index-2021.html.

Sayers, Anthony and David K. Stewart. 2019. "Out of the Blue: Goodbye Tories, Hello Jason Kenney." In *Orange Chinook: Politics in the New Alberta*, eds. Duane Bratt, Keith Brownsey, Richard Sutherland, and David Taras, 399–423. Calgary: University of Calgary Press.

Schneider Monica C. and Angela L. Bos. 2014. "Measuring Stereotypes of Female Politicians." *Political Psychology* 35(2): 245–266.

Schneider, Monica C. and Angela L. Bos. 2019. "The Application of Social Role Theory to the Study of Gender in Politics." *Political Psychology* 40(S1): 179–213. DOI: https://doi.org/10.1111/pops.12573

Schweitzer, Doug. 2021. @doug_schweitzer. 13 October 2021. "You can't leave out the very next sentence . . . 'It disproportionately impacted women and we saw a lot of women return to the workforce looking for jobs in September.' #BeBetter." *Twitter.* https://twitter.com/doug_schweitzer/status/1448466576445902855.

Statistics Canada. 2018. "Time use: Total work burden, unpaid work, and leisure." *Statistics Canada: The Daily.* https://www150.statcan.gc.ca/n1/daily-quotidien/180730/dq180730a-eng.htm.

Statistics Canada, 2021. "Calgary [Census metropolitan area], Alberta and Alberta [Province]." *Census Profile, 2016 Census.* https://www12.statcan.gc.ca/census-recensement/2016/dp-pd/prof/details/page.cfm?Lang=E&Geo1=CMACA&Code1=825&Geo2=PR&Code2=48&Data=Count&SearchText=calgary&SearchType=Begins&SearchPR=01&B1=All&TABID=1.

Thomas, Melanee. 2017. "Equality of Opportunity but Not Result: Women and Federal Conservatives in Canada." *The Blueprint.* Toronto: University of Toronto Press.

Thomas, Melanee. 2018. "In Crisis of Decline? Selecting Women to Lead Provincial Parties in Government." *Canadian Journal of Political Science* 51(2) 379–403.

Thomas, Melanee. 2019a. "Governing as if Women Mattered: Rachel Notley as Alberta Premier." In *Doing Politics Differently? Women Premiers in Canada's Provinces and Territories*, ed. Sylvia Bashevkin. Vancouver: UBC Press.

Thomas, Melanee. 2019b. "Ready for Rachel: The Alberta NDP's 2015 Campaign." In *Orange Chinook: Politics in the New Alberta*, 57–77.

Thomas, Melanee and Marc André Bodet. 2013. "Sacrificial lambs, women candidates, and district competitiveness in Canada." *Electoral Studies* 32(1): 153–166.

Unwin, Jack. 2016. "How the Sputtering Oil and Gas Industry Is Destroying Men." *Vice*, 26 April 2016. https://www.vice.com/en/article/xdm48a/boomtown-bust-how-the-sputtering-oil-and-gas-industry-is-destroying-men.

Wesley 2021a. "Who do Albertans think they are?" *CBC Opinion*, 25 October 2021. https://www.cbc.ca/news/opinion/opinion-who-do-albertans-think-they-are-municipal-election-results-1.6221407.

Wesley, Jared (@DrJaredWesley). 2021b. "I'm trying my best to have something good come from this. Clarity on @doug_schweitzer's approach to blocking might help us all understand how it leads to 'a better dialogue on complicated issues.' Here's my letter to the Minister. #ableg #abpoli." Twitter, 15 October 2021. https://twitter.com/DrJaredWesley/status/1449116351096709120.

Winter, Nicholas J.G. 2010. "Masculine Republicans and Feminine Democrats: Gender and Americans' Explicit and Implicit Images of the Political Parties." *Political Behavior* 32: 587–618.

8

Kenney's Ride: Albertan Neo-Liberal Myths and the Symbology of a Blue Dodge Ram

Chaseten Remillard and Tyler Nagel

> If you like it up loud and you're hillbilly proud
> Throw your hands up now, let me hear you shout
> Truck yeah
>
> Tim McGraw, "Truck Yeah"[1]

Introduction

A pickup truck invokes themes of power. You can tow house-sized travel trailers, livestock, other vehicles, and building materials. A truck portrays independence: you're your own man—and yes, a truck is gendered.[2] As the preponderance of advertising and country songs emphasize, pickup trucks are semiotically a man's vehicle,[3] even though the gender balance in pickup truck ownership is approaching equality.[4]

A pickup truck is unstoppable. You don't get stuck—in the oilfield or your back lane. A pickup truck is quintessentially a blue-collar symbol of "git'er'done" and pragmatism.[5] Of course, the pricing of pickup trucks far exceeds most other types of passenger vehicles, and many of the owner's practical budgets, but the value proposition of the pickup truck is emphasized through ad campaigns that draw on the themes of freedom, individualism, and chauvinism. A famous pickup truck television ad starts with the words "America is still the land of rugged individualism" before cutting to Bob Seger's "Like a Rock," all the while accompanied by images of hard-working men, cowboys, and dirt roads. A "coal-rolling" truck is a political statement against climate science, or at least a willful blind eye towards it.[6] In other words, a truck is not simply a truck; a truck is a powerful cultural artifact of visual communication, a discursive moment through which myths of masculinity, independence, resource extraction, and settler culture assemble, are reaffirmed, and embodied.

Jason Kenney chose a truck early in his rise to power in Alberta. In fact, it was a signature object from the start. Following the 2015 election victory of the New Democratic Party (NDP) (led by Rachel Notley) against a conservative movement fractured into the Wildrose Party and the Progressive Conservative (PC) Party, there was a general recognition among conservatives of the need to "unite the right"—to effectively challenge Notley in the 2019 Alberta election. In August 2016, Jason Kenney took up the challenge of merging the two parties, and launched the "Unite Alberta Truck Tour," visiting all eighty-seven Alberta constituencies over the following months in a blue Dodge 1500 pickup truck.[7] Ultimately, he was successful—merging the PCs and the Wildrose Party to form the United Conservative Party (UCP).

The blue Dodge Ram rolled out again for the 2019 Alberta election. Using the same truck with new decals, Kenney crisscrossed the province with powerful messages of "jobs, economy, and pipelines"[8] for a province in the midst of an oil downturn. Mostly eschewing a campaign bus, he used the vehicle to arrive at campaign stops, sometimes jumping out to greet crowds while the truck was still rolling.[9] The truck led him to victory—he literally rolled to victory in it, driving right inside UCP headquarters for his election night victory speech. A photo of him that night—leaning out of the window, waving as the truck drives through the crowd inside the Calgary convention centre, became emblematic of the decisive UCP election in 2019.[10] Since the 2019 victory, the truck has made periodic appearances—for example, rolling out for events following the June 2021 "Open for Summer" announcement during the COVID-19 crisis and even becoming Kenney's Twitter profile picture.[11] The truck again went into hiding as pandemic deaths surged in September 2021, expunged even from the premier's Twitter profile picture.

We propose that when Kenney began his "Truck Tour" in August 2016, his vehicle of choice—a blue Dodge Ram 1500—functioned to mobilize a powerful set of existent cultural and societal repertoires. In entering the truck, Kenney literally entered (and metaphorically took the wheel of) a symbology that neatly aligned with a host of neo-liberal populist myths of what Alberta is and who Albertans are. The image of Kenney and his truck aligned his own personal political brand with the well-trodden symbology of the pickup truck, and brought together powerful myths of Alberta exceptionalism, sovereignty, anti-elitism, and populist homogeneity.

At the same time, the symbology of the truck, as is the case for all cultural artifacts, is somewhat of an inside game. You need to believe in unlimited resource extraction and consumption, normative notions of cisgender heterosexual masculinity, settler culture, rugged individualism, and rural (or so-called redneck) homogeneity and chauvinism to see the truck as a positive assemblage of these myths. Otherwise, as some critics pointed out, and many people intuitively feel, the truck is a symbol of an antiquated, troubled (and troubling) reliance on old thinking about resource management, exclusionary and pugilist politics, and conservative (non-liberal) populist values and politics.

In short, the truck (as a form of visual communication, as a symbol, as a cultural artifact) is rich, nuanced, and contradictory. On the one hand, the truck is a dog-whistle symbol, communicating (without explicitly saying) that the neo-liberal populist Albertan myths are on the road again and that a new masculine sheriff is in town and at the wheel. On the other, the truck also mobilizes, meaningfully and implicitly, a spectrum of Albertan values that resist and challenge that same version of Albertan identity. As such, the truck functions to enable us to discuss the Janus-faced political landscape of Alberta: one that looks back towards a mythic past when driving a truck down a rural dusty road to an oil rig was uncomplicatedly celebrated, and one that looks forward to an Alberta less reliant on oil, and more urban, inclusive, federalist, and cosmopolitan.

In what follows, we offer a "reading" of Kenney's pickup as a cultural artifact and a form of visual communication. We look to understand how the truck aligns with the political culture of the UCP brand of neo-liberal populism and the version of Alberta it wants to represent. Ultimately, we claim that although drivers may come and go (Kenney in particular), the myths that the blue truck mobilize (and the social repertoires these myths rely on) are much more difficult to dislodge. In other words, the blue truck—like Stephen King's Plymouth *Christine*—has a life of its own.

Alberta and Neo-Liberalist Populism

Kenney's truck arrived on the political scene with both bravado and pugilism. "I figured," Kenney stated, "my Dodge Ram would do the job better than a Prius."[12] During his "Truck Tour," Kenney promised to visit all eighty-seven electoral districts and sign up "tens of thousands" of grassroots Albertans.[13] Kenney's tour, his words, and his choice of vehicle all align with a particularly recognizable form of Albertan neo-liberalist populism.

Populism as a political movement, as defined by Mudde,[14] "considers society to be ultimately separated into two homogenous and antagonistic groups, 'the pure people' versus 'the corrupt elite,' and which argues that politics should be an expression of the volonte generale (general will) of the people."[15] As such, Mudde continues, populism is antithetical to both elitism and pluralism. Elitism because the elite is the enemy of the people, by definition, and pluralism because pluralism decenters the assumed homogeneous nature of the "pure people," or questions the very existence of homogeneity with concepts such as positionality. At its core, therefore, populism is fundamentally bellicose, as it is premised on the need to combat the oppositional forces of elitism and pluralism and their respective definitions of political ideology and policy. Moreover, the battle that populism wages is much less about observational differences in policy and practice, and more about the perceived irreducible difference between populist, elitist, and pluralist political positions. As Mudde concludes, in populism "there are only friends and foes."[16]

In 2016, Kenney found himself in just such a precarious environment. Kenney's path to power was beset on all sides. To the right, he found himself contesting the fractured base, and he vowed to bring homogeneity back to conservatives: to create a unified conservative party. To the left, if he was successful, he needed to confront the new pluralism and perceived elitism of the urban, liberal, and environmentalist NDP. Kenney proposed an explicit platform that promised both unity and confrontation. He also signaled a return to an Alberta of populist lore: prosperous, maverick, masculine, and rooted in settler culture. To help him create and maintain this neo-liberal populist myth of Alberta, he stepped into a blue Dodge Ram. Kenney's truck should not be considered inherently meaningful, therefore, but be understood as an assemblage of meanings from, and an agent to give voiced meaning to, different cultural and social tropes that support a particular set of myths about what Alberta is and who Albertans are.

Kenney's Truck and Myth of Albertan Exceptionalism

In the neo-liberal populist myth of Alberta exceptionalism, Alberta is a maverick province, populated by (an ironically homogenous group of) mavericks. Alberta has a long history as a province with notions of its own. Excepting the province of Quebec, few provinces have expressed a desire to diverge with the other provinces as much as Alberta has. Because of the obvious distinctiveness of its economy (based on oil), its physical remoteness to other population centres in Canada, and its social conservative values, Alberta often finds itself proudly differing with other provinces. Alberta as the "maverick" province of confederation has become a trope, culminating, among other things, in permanent exhibit at the Glenbow Museum—*Mavericks: An Incorrigible History of Alberta*.[17] In this myth of exceptionalism, Alberta is also a land populated by mavericks: people who thrive through personal enterprise more than social endeavour. While the early cowboy and homesteader history of the province is rife with left-wing politics (including the formation of public health care, pro-labour legislation, and social credit theory), this ended with the premiership of Ernest Manning, and a (seemingly permanent) shift in ideology toward conservative.[18]

The early left-leaning political days are now largely unknown, replaced with a perception of a conservative cowboy ideology that claims a lineage straight back to the first white settlers (see Roger Epp's chapter). Now, the images of the lone cowboy on the range, of the little house on the prairie, of the intrepid North-West Mounted Policeman at the whiskey forts, easily manifest themselves in many cultural icons, but none so relevant than that of a pickup truck. From the Tim McGraw country song "Truck Yeah" to images of trucks dominating untamed wilderness, the pickup truck is an easy symbol of personal freedom and masculine individualism.[19] The maverick identity of a province forging its own road despite the judgement and direction of others is typified by the visual artifact. As a visual symbol, the truck provides utility, reliability, functionality, and ultimately, independence. As Hirschman writes, "The rugged individualist seeks equipment that is or at least appears to be rugged, solid, and dependable, just as he is. . . ."[20] Or as *Petersen's 4-Wheel & Off-Road* magazine puts it: "something about the raw lines of the truck just screams that it is a truck. They evoke the days when trucks were actually trucks and had the aerodynamics of a barn door, got the gas mileage of a tank, and had the drivetrain of a semi-truck."[21] According to the myth of exceptionalism, Alberta and Albertans are as unapologetic as these trucks, defiant and unique in their capacity.

A pickup truck removes limits and invokes pioneering homesteader themes. A pickup truck is emancipation from cramped public transit, offering instead the open road. A truck invokes themes of abundance. No longer do overflowing trunks pose a problem; a truck answers the question of how to bring home IKEA purchases or lumber or the bacon. A truck is a necessary tool (and logical consequence) of natural resource extraction. You both need and generate abundance when you drive a truck. Indeed, the myth of Alberta exceptionalism is imbued with an independence derived from the prosperity of natural resource extraction. This too combines with the populist myth that Alberta and Albertans support themselves within confederation and individually (through private enterprise, oil and cattle). This mythical veneration of private enterprise and resource extraction fosters an inherent antagonism toward those who rely on the government for support and has galvanized resentment in Alberta towards provinces that need support—typified by the resentment toward recipients of equalization payments like Quebec and politics (and politicians) that are viewed as "socialist" (Notley's NDP, Trudeau's Liberals). When Kenney drives his truck, he sends a message that Alberta is resource(full), unique in its capability and prosperity.

Kenney's Truck and the Myth of Albertan Sovereignty

Popular sovereignty is an important myth of Albertan populism—governance that leaves "the power to the people."[22] In this populist myth, Alberta is a non-elite province, not just an outsider, but actively shut out of the halls of power in the East. The feeling of western impotence in shaping national discourse resulted in the 1980's proposals for a US-style "Triple E Senate" (elected, effective, and equal), which would have given equal geographic representation (and inequal per-capita representation) to the Canadian provinces.[23] "The West's demand for equality among the provinces precludes acceptance of any provision that creates a hierarchy of provinces."[24] In essence, the populists of Alberta demand a greater per-capita influence in the senate than other, more populous provinces would receive.

Justifications for demands of greater power often relate to Alberta's financial contributions to the rest of the country. Misperceptions of federal equalization as a literal transfer that Alberta sends to Ottawa each year,[25] and the oil industry contributing to the overall prosperity of Canada are used to justify demands for a bigger say at the table[26] (see Jared Wesley's chapter). Growing popular support for proposals to reform Canadian political institutions, such as the Senate and the equalization formula, endorsed by conservative politicians including Preston Manning, Ralph Klein, and Jason Kenney, belie a profound dissatisfaction in the voice Alberta has in the context of other populations and provinces in Canada. Conservative governments of the past and present seem all too keen to stoke these fires of resentment, in the full knowledge that revisions to the constitution are unlikely to occur.

Takach describes the Alberta legend—"rugged individualists, carving out a living and a future from dust."[27] With this identity of individualism and labour comes expectations of autonomy. The populist myth of Alberta demands a greater sovereignty over their natural resources, economy, and control over federal institutions. Such values enmesh with the symbology of a truck, an iconic vehicle providing mobility and motricity to its owner. The truck is not the public transit of confederation, it is an icon for personal sovereignty, an empowerment to choose one's own destination and route, pavement or not, with the ability to take as much cargo as you'd like along for the ride. The personal sovereignty manifested in the desire for a pickup truck is a proxy for the desire of a greater say in Confederation. As such, the myth of Albertan sovereignty finds voice in a call for non-federalist alliances and pro-oil stances. To that end, Kenney's promise that his "Dodge Ram would do the job better than a Prius"[28] speaks simultaneously in opposition to a politics of social inclusion, federal allegiance, and environmental stewardship. Kenney's truck distinctly counters a perceived left-wing environmentalism associated with Prius ownership, since a Prius is a "visible marker of moral commitment and ecopiety."[29] Kenney's truck reaffirms and undercuts a perceived environmentalist smugness and elitism and reaffirms the capacity of Alberta to go it alone.

Similarly, within the symbolic system of Alberta public culture, Kenney in his truck will accomplish what Rachel Notley and Justin Trudeau (implied drivers of said Prius) would (or did) fail to accomplish. He'll reaffirm Albertan sovereignty where they couldn't or won't. Furthermore, Kenney's truck claims the primacy of a resource-based economy as a central engine of Albertan sovereignty. In contrast to a Prius, a Dodge Ram is clearly a less environmental vehicle (see Duane Bratt's chapter).

The truck also signals a shift in gendered leadership. A pickup truck is more expressly a masculine symbol and plays into Kenney's political antagonism against both Trudeau and Notley. As Lezotte argues: "of all the vehicles produced for the American automotive market, perhaps none is more strongly associated with masculinity than the full-size pickup."[30] Pickup advertisements routinely emphasize the gendered expectation of truck ownership, although "women are the fastest growing segment of pickup truck buyers they have been notably absent in truck advertising."[31] Conversely, "the Prius may technically fulfill the needs of much of an individual's heavy work, or even every day lifestyle, but it does not fulfill the accompanying need: being masculine."[32] Kenney's truck, therefore, reaffirms a mythic need for masculine, non-environmentalist rule within Alberta, in contrast to both Rachel Notley and the self-professed feminist leadership of Justin Trudeau[33] and their green policies.

Kenney's Truck and the Myth of Grassroots Albertans

Alberta populism perceives itself as a non-elite within a non-elite. First, Alberta defines itself as non-elite within confederation. Historic perceptions of anti-western behaviour—typified as "The West verses the Rest"[34] have been fuelled by a perceived exploitation of the western provinces as a frontier for the metropolitan east—an application of Canadian historian Careless' metropolis-hinterland theory.[35] These concerns by Albertans— of "The East" viewing Alberta as nothing more than a hinterland—have provided a lens through which to view many federal (and federalist) initiatives as fuel for western alienation. The literal binary in "The West verses the Rest" has the effect of dividing Canada into the virtuous Alberta, and the antagonistic "Rest of Canada." Indeed, this divide fuels an entire vernacular for the relationship, including the "Wild West,"[36] "Maverick Alberta,"[37] and even slogans such as the infamous "Let the Eastern bastards freeze in the dark."

The second elite/non-elite division occurs within the borders of Alberta. Drawing on popular perceptions of the maverick, the conservative Albertan ideal is inherently anti-elitist. Those Albertans in fields such as public service, academia, and education are certainly perceived as antagonistic elites, but a stamp of approval is given to some that would be perceived as elite in other contexts: "Alberta oil executive? One of us. Quebec-raised Prime Minister (named Trudeau!)? Definitely one of them."[38] In this way, the uniquely Albertan perception of elitism has less to do with material wealth and access to power than it has to do with perceptions of Eastern imperialism and those that support it verses the energy industry and those that oppose it. Kenney himself draws directly on anti-elite sentiment. Speaking in a truck stop diner in Calgary in 2016, during the Notley NDP government, he said "There are a number of Albertans who are off the radar screen for the elites, and they are going through serious adversity right now. They are decent, dignified hard-working people who feel totally disoriented about what's going on and they feel like the government is working against them, not for them."[39]

The blue truck serves as a rallying call to the Albertan version of anti-elitism. The truck serves up motifs of the west, of individualism and independence, of fossil fuel consumption and resource exploitation. It inherently supports the fossil fuel industry, and inherently rejects ideas of climate change initiatives of the prior Alberta NDP government and the federal Liberals. The blue truck is a symbol for the binary division of elites and non-elites: a shorthand way of expressing anti-elitist sentiments.

Kenney's Truck and the Myth of Populist Homogeneity

Homogeneity's role in populism is somewhat under debate. While viewed as intrinsic by Mudde,[40] some scholars believe the role of homogeneity is overstated—that populism is not necessarily linked to anti-pluralism, but rather is linked to a sense of unity *in* the populist group.[41] Other scholars view homogeneity as peripheral to the core of populism, but commonly encountered.[42] Regardless, homogeneity can be antecedent to populism as well as a result of it. In Alberta, views of the "mavericks" are often homogenous and hegemonic: the white rancher, the male oilman, the middle-aged cisgendered labourer. One of the most influential depictions of Alberta's history is the Glenbow Museum's exhibit. Although some of the Glenbow museum's van Herk-guided *Mavericks: An Incorrigible History of Alberta* exhibit features some "mavericks" that are not hegemons (for example, black rancher John Ware and women's rights activist Henrietta Muir Edwards) the list of featured mavericks speaks to the preponderance of white, cisgendered men in non-elite roles.[43] This extends to a homogeneity in the image of a model disenfranchised westerner: a rural, white, hardworking, cisgendered Albertan-born conservative, espousing traditional conservative social values. In short, a match for the traditional image of a pickup truck owner.[44]

Owning a pickup truck is "as Albertan as being rat-free and not having a sales tax"[45]—a claim borne out by the official Statistics Canada numbers on new vehicle sales. Alberta outpaces the Canadian average on truck sales: 86 per cent of new vehicles sold in Alberta are classified as trucks.* In Quebec, trucks account for only 68 per cent of new vehicle sales.[46] Pickup truck ownership is linked to a provincial identity—and

---

* Statistics Canada divides new vehicle sales into two categories: "passenger cars" and "trucks." Trucks include minivans, sport-utility vehicles, light and heavy trucks, vans and buses.

represents a near-universal homogeneity among Albertans. Startlingly, Kenney's choice of a campaign vehicle representing nearly nine out of ten new vehicle purchases resonates with more Alberta voters than being staunchly against a provincial sales tax (opposed by 73 per cent of Albertans in 2018 and by 57 per cent in 2020).[47] It's difficult to contemplate a characteristic more Albertans share than their taste in vehicles.

Kenney's Truck: The Dangers of an Autonomous Vehicle

Anthropologist Alfred Gell proposes that artifacts have agency—that they are created by humans who intend to change the world, rather than just comment upon it.[48] However, Gell contends, artifacts may have an agency of their own, capable of effects that differ from the intentions of the human creator. A structuralist approach to meaning making, as we've invoked in our reading of Kenney's blue truck, assumes that the significance of any one cultural object is beyond the object itself, and certainly beyond the creator of the object. The discourse, the social and cultural repertoires that inform the meaning of any artifact flood into the object to fill it with meaning. As such, the power of the truck is beyond any one driver. No driver can fully control the symbology of the truck. The myths of neo-liberal populist Alberta and the social and cultural repertoires that inform the meaning of pickup trucks more generally exist with or without Kenney at the wheel.

The truck, if taken as totemic of conservative populist myths, has a surprisingly robust and stable set of meanings that do not adapt well to changing political realities. By taking on the truck, Kenney entered a preformed set of constraints that limited his ability to govern effectively—especially in an increasingly complex political environment. Ultimately, Kenney was elected (at least partially) on the depth of the neo-liberal populist myths that enriched the symbology of the blue truck. But the "blue truck" approach is not always the most expedient nor most effective remedy for Alberta's political challenges.

While Kenney and the truck were physically and idealistically one during his run for the leadership and the subsequent 2019 election that took the UCP to power, cracks began to emerge between the blue truck and Kenney. In a series of policy reversals, the UCP government has diverged several times from the "true blue" conservative values manifested in the truck.

One of the first reversals was a policy on removing dozens of parks from the provincial park system, reverting some to Crown land, and allowing others to be operated by private partners. The policy was ultimately stymied by widespread outcry.[49] On Crown land in Alberta, off-road driving is generally allowed—in provincial parks, not so much. The initiative to convert these lands to ideal habitat for blue trucks was defeated.

Another major policy reversal was on coal mining. A large-scale mining project, promoted by an Australian mining company, was the standard-bearer for a larger policy that would have allowed coal mining in the eastern slopes of the Albertan Rocky Mountains. Coal mining and jobs—linked strongly to blue truck ideology—seemed to be a policy that would resonate with Kenney's conservative base. But the predictable opposition from the left-leaning environmental lobby was unexpectedly joined by small town councils and ranchers, concerned about pollution and destruction of a landscape that their livelihood depended upon.[50] Kenney misread his base: blue truck drivers love the eastern slopes as they are (see Roger Epp's chapter).

The COVID-19 pandemic has been the most polarizing reversal of all. Throughout the pandemic, Kenney has been slow to implement restrictions and fast to rescind them. These policies, seemingly an effort to maintain the support of his right-leaning base, have no doubt resulted in the deaths of some Albertans who would have survived under more protective policies. Kenney justified this course of action under two auspices: the economic costs of lockdowns, and personal freedoms infringed by public health measures. When restrictions finally were imposed, there was hesitation in enforcing them, culminating in a series of high-profile evangelical Christian clergy and small business owners flouting the rules. As the death toll mounted and the hospitals filled, an untenable situation developed between the government and the scofflaws, culminating in a series of high-profile arrests that galvanized the right wing against Kenney.[51] Paradoxically, attempts to deliver policy that would resonate with these right-wingers resulted in delays in implementing restrictions in the second, third, and fourth waves, and ultimately led to the need for much harsher restrictions than were required in more moderate and left-ist provinces. Weekly anti-restriction protests, predominately attended by right-wing, anti-vaccine, anti-maskers continue, seemingly regardless of the policy that the government adopts.

In each of these reversals (parks, coal, and COVID-19), Kenney had to get out of the truck, attend to business, and try to get back into the truck again. Each time this maneuver was performed, the social licence for Kenney's use of the blue truck diminished.

While the blue truck imagery propelled Kenney to power, the same imagery has made it difficult for him to shift to the centre of the political spectrum. Although Kenney's policy reversals have indicated some attempts to shift left, he does so at the peril of alienating right-wing elements of the party he "united" on his truck tours. And given his intentionally linked identity to the blue truck motif, Kenney had a difficult task in endearing himself to centrist moderates. Adopting a symbol of masculinity, of purposeful antagonism, and of the oil sector left an indelible mark that limits his ability to shift his base to more moderate supporters. At the beginning of his decline and in the midst of the anti-restriction caucus insurrection, Kenney realized the limitations of his chosen symbology, allegedly saying he wanted a "new base."[52] Further challenging Kenney was a growing segment of Albertans that no longer identify with the blue truck ideology. Those Albertans don't believe in the neo-liberal populist myths of Alberta, and instead see the truck as worn, outdated, troubled, and antiquated.

With each policy reversal, Kenney eroded his licence to drive the blue truck and represent the conservative base symbolized by it. The blue truck, with an agency of its own, continues down the road with or without Kenney, in the form of anti-vaccine protests, anti-masking, pro-oil sands development, anti-union sentiment, in the form of conservative social values, and in a vehement distaste for "Eastern" values. Increasingly Kenney appeared to be left behind by the blue truck, standing by the side of the road, his driver's licence revoked, as the Dodge minivans of the centre and the Priuses of the left pass him by.

One of the least obvious details in the historic blue truck entrance to the 16 April 2019 Calgary UCP election night headquarters is perhaps the most important of all: Kenney was not driving the truck that evening. In the iconic photograph of him waving from the truck, Kenney is seated in the passenger seat of the blue truck that carried him to victory. He was not behind the wheel. It's unclear who was driving the truck that night (perhaps the truck drove itself), but it certainly wasn't Kenney. And it's not clear that he has been in the driver's seat since.

Conclusion

Convenient to populists is to adopt symbols that easily mobilize a host of cultural myths, in the case of Albertan neo-liberal populism, a symbol that communicated exceptionalism, sovereignty, grassroots masculine rule, and demographic homogeneity. As Kenney said, his Dodge Ram did the job better. In this sense, we argue that his blue truck was a perfect assemblage of pre-existing neo-liberal populist myths of Alberta, and as a symbol, it became central to his leadership campaign and election win.

A symbol is always ambiguous and dangerous. While a symbol can communicate more succinctly than words, its meaning predates its contemporary usage. No one person can control the meaning of a symbol, especially one as rich and nuanced as a blue pickup truck. Instead, the symbol may shape future discourse in an unpredictable way, connecting current actions to scenarios of the past and providing unanticipated lenses through which to view current events. As Jason Kenney discovered, this connection can be both constraining and difficult to sever. The symbol of the truck is bigger than Kenney, and it will continue down the road with or without him.

NOTES

1   Tim McGraw, "Tim McGraw—Truck Yeah," YouTube video, 3:40, 17 September 2012, https://www.youtube.com/watch?v=rf7GfUORHtw (accessed 28 September 2021).

2   Chris Lezotte, "A Woman and Her Truck: Pickups, the Woman Driver, and Cowgirl Feminism." *European Journal of American Culture* 38, no. 2 (1 June 2019): 135–53, https://doi.org/10.1386/ejac.38.2.135_1 (accessed 25 September 2021).

3   Lachlan B. Barber, "Automobility and Masculinities between Home and Work: Trucks as the 'New Normal' in Newfoundland and Labrador," *Gender, Place & Culture* 26, no. 2 (4 April 2019): 251–71. https://doi.org/10.1080/0966369X.2018.1552926 (accessed 29 September 2021).

4   Ford, "The Great American Truck Survey," https://media.ford.com/content/dam/fordmedia/North%20America/US/2020/06/22/The-Great-American-Truck-Survey-2020.pdf (accessed 29 September 2021).

5   Elizabeth C. Hirschman, "Men, Dogs, Guns, and Cars—The Semiotics of Rugged Individualism," *Journal of Advertising* 32, no. 1 (2003): 9–22. https://doi.org/10.1080/00913367.2003.10601001 (accessed 29 September 2021).

6   Sarah McFarland Taylor, "'I Can't! It's a Prius': Purity, Piety, Pollution Porn, and Coal Rolling," in *Ecopiety*, by Sarah McFarland Taylor (New York: New York University Press, 2019), 68–90, https://doi.org/10.18574/nyu/9781479810765.003.0004 (accessed 28 September 2021).

7   Rob Drinkwater, "Jason Kenney Launches 'Unite Alberta Truck Tour,'" *Global News*, 1 August 2016. https://globalnews.ca/news/2859411/jason-kenney-launches-unite-alberta-truck-tour/ (accessed 30 September 2021).

8   Jason Kenney (@jkenney), "Jobs, economy and pipelines are what mattter most to Albertans. And that's what the UCP will stand up for. Each and every day. #abstrongandfree #ableg," Twitter, 18 March 2019, 5:52 p.m., https://twitter.com/jkenney/status/1107791835043225602 (accessed 30 September 2021).

9   Stuart Thomson, "On the Road with Jason Kenney and Laureen Harper as the Alberta Election Enters Its Final Leg," *National Post*, 12 April 2019, https://nationalpost.com/news/politics/on-the-road-with-jason-kenney-and-laureen-harper-as-the-alberta-election-enters-its-final-leg (accessed 30 September 2021).

10 Michael Fraiman, "If Jason Kenney's Truck Could Run in an Alberta Election, It Just Might Win," *Macleans.ca* (blog), 18 April 2019, https://www.macleans.ca/politics/if-jason-kenneys-truck-could-run-in-an-alberta-election-it-just-might-win/ (accessed 30 September 2021).

11 Alex Boyd, "Why Does Jason Kenney Love This Pickup Truck so Much?" *Toronto Star*, 26 July 2021, https://www.thestar.com/news/canada/2021/07/26/why-does-jason-kenney-love-this-pickup-truck-so-much.html (accessed 30 September 2021).

12 Paige Parsons, "Jason Kenney Launches 'Truck Tour' to Unite Alberta's Right and Stop Another 'Catastrophic' NDP Win," *Edmonton Journal*, 1 August 2016, https://edmontonjournal.com/news/politics/jason-kenney-launches-truck-tour-to-unite-albertas-right-and-stop-another-catastrophic-ndp-win (accessed 29 September 2021).

13 *Ibid.*

14 Cas Mudde, "The Populist Zeitgeist," *Government and Opposition* 39, no. 4 (2004): 541–63, https://doi.org/10.1111/j.1477-7053.2004.00135.x (accessed 29 September 2021).

15 *Ibid*, 544.

16 *Ibid*, 544.

17 Glenbow Museum, "Mavericks: An Incorrigible History of Alberta," https://www.glenbow.org/mavericks/ (accessed 29 September 2021).

18 Jen Gerson, "The Great Myth of Alberta Conservatism," *Walrus*, 4 February 2019, https://thewalrus.ca/the-great-myth-of-alberta-conservatism/ (accessed 30 September 2021).

19 Barber, "Automobility and Masculinities."

20   Hirschman, "Men, Dogs, Guns, and Cars."

21   Craig Perronne, "Old School, New Tricks," *4-Wheel & Off-Road*, August 2000, 109.

22   Anne Schulz et al., "Measuring Populist Attitudes on Three Dimensions," *International Journal of Public Opinion Research* 30, no. 2 (Summer 2018): 316–26, https://doi.org/10.1093/ijpor/edw037 (accessed 28 September 2021).

23   David C. Docherty, "The Canadian Senate: Chamber of Sober Reflection or Loony Cousin Best Not Talked About," *The Journal of Legislative Studies* 8, no. 3 (2002): 27–48, https://doi.org/10.1080/714003922 (accessed 30 September 2021).

24   Michael Lusztig, "Federalism and Institutional Design: The Perils and Politics of a Triple-E Senate in Canada," *Publius* 25, no. 1 (Winter 1995): 35–50.

25   Kevin Maimann, "Is Alberta Really Getting Shafted on Equalization Payments? We Talked to an Expert," *Toronto Star*, 24 June 2018, https://www.thestar.com/edmonton/2018/06/24/is-alberta-really-getting-shafted-on-equalization-payments-we-talked-to-an-expert.html (accessed 30 September 2021).

26   Ted Morton, "Equality or Asymmetry? Alberta at the Crossroads," School of Policy Studies—Asymmetry Series, Queen's University, https://www.queensu.ca/iigr/sites/webpublish.queensu.ca.iigrwww/files/files/WorkingPapers/asymmetricfederalism/Morton2005.pdf (accessed 29 September 2021).

27   Geo Takach, *Will the Real Alberta Please Stand Up?* 1st ed (Edmonton: University of Alberta Press, 2010), 154.

28   Parsons, "Jason Kenney Launches 'Truck Tour.'"

29   Taylor, "'I Can't! It's a Prius.'"

30   Lezotte, "A Woman and Her Truck."

31   *Ibid.*

32   Heather Champeau, "Driving Force: An Exploration of Texan Prius Drivers," (master's thesis, University of Texas at Arlington, 2010), https://rc.library.uta.edu/uta-ir/handle/10106/5146 (accessed 30 September 2021).

33   "Trudeau: 'I'll Keep Saying I'm a Feminist,'" *BBC News*, 17 March 2016. https://www.bbc.com/news/av/world-us-canada-35836279 (accessed 30 September 2021).

34   Mary Janigan, *Let the Eastern Bastards Freeze in the Dark: The West Versus the Rest Since Confederation*, (Toronto: Knopf Canada, 2012).

35   J.M.S. Careless, *Frontier and Metropolis: Regions, Cities, and Identities in Canada before 1914* (Toronto: University of Toronto Press, 1989).

36   Daniella Roschinski, "'Wild' vs 'Mild' West: A Binary or Symbiotic Unit? The Complexity of the Mythic West Re-Imagined from a Canadian Perspective, 1970–1914," (master's thesis, University of Saskatchewan, 2002), https://harvest.usask.ca/handle/10388/7008 (accessed 28 September 2021).

37   Aritha Van Herk, *Audacious and Adamant: The Story of Maverick Alberta* (Toronto: Key Porter Books, 2007).

38 Drew Anderson, "(Mis)Truths and Consequences in Alberta," *CBC News*, 22 March 2021, https://www.cbc.ca/news/canada/calgary/mistruths-alberta-government-gaslighting-1.5957396 (accessed 29 September 2021).

39 Justin Giovanetti, "Jason Kenney Channels Populism—but Not Donald Trump—in Alberta," *Globe and Mail*, 29 December 2016, https://www.theglobeandmail.com/news/national/jason-kenney-channels-populism-but-not-donald-trump-in-alberta/article33453019/ (accessed 29 September 2021).

40 Mudde, "The Populist Zeitgeist."

41 Giorgos Katsambekis, "Constructing 'the People' of Populism: A Critique of the Ideational Approach from a Discursive Perspective," *Journal of Political Ideologies* 27, no. 1 (November 2020), https://doi.org/10.1080/13569317.2020.1844372 (accessed 28 September 2021).

42 Jane Mansbridge and Stephen Macedo, "Populism and Democratic Theory," *Annual Review of Law and Social Science* 15, no. 1 (2019): 59–77, https://doi.org/10.1146/annurev-lawsocsci-101518-042843 (accessed 28 September 2021).

43 Glenbow Museum, "Mavericks Biographies," 2 August 2019, https://web.archive.org/web/20190802160909/https://www.glenbow.org/mavericks/english/bioindex.html (accessed 28 September 2021).

44 Lezotte, "A Woman and Her Truck."

45 Justin Archer, "Is the Pickup Truck Alberta's Unofficial-Official Vehicle?" *CBC News*, 6 November 2017, https://www.cbc.ca/news/canada/edmonton/alberta-truck-debate-edmonton-am-1.4389105 (accessed 28 September 2021).

46 Statistics Canada, "New Motor Vehicle Sales, by Type of Vehicle," 29 September 2021, https://doi.org/10.25318/2010000201-eng (accessed 29 September 2021).

47 Bryan Labby, "Albertans Warming to Idea of a Provincial Sales Tax, According to Poll," *CBC News*, 12 June 2020, https://www.cbc.ca/news/canada/calgary/alberta-pst-opinion-poll-favour-oppose-1.5603707 (accessed 28 September 2021).

48 Alfred Gell, *Art and Agency: An Anthropological Theory*, illustrated ed. (Oxford; New York: Clarendon Press, 1998).

49 Andrew Jeffrey, "Alberta Government Won't Close or Delist Provincial Parks," *CBC News*, 23 December 2020, https://www.cbc.ca/news/canada/edmonton/alberta-government-won-t-close-or-delist-provincial-parks-1.5852504 (accessed 30 September 2021).

50 Jill Croteau, "Southern Alberta Ranchers Weigh In on Coal Mining after Corb Lund, Paul Brandt Speak Out," *Global News*, 14 January 2021, https://globalnews.ca/news/7577558/southern-alberta-ranchers-coal-mining-corb-lund/ (accessed 30 September 2021).

51 Sarah Rieger, "Calgary Pastor Arrested after Breaking Pandemic Gathering Rules for Months," *CBC News*, 16 May 2021, https://www.cbc.ca/news/canada/calgary/tim-stephens-fairview-baptist-church-arrest-1.6029078 (accessed 30 September 2021).

52 Dave Naylor, "Kenney Tells UCP Caucus: 'I Want a New Base,'" *Western Standard*, 4 May 2021, https://www.westernstandard.news/news/exclusive-kenney-tells-ucp-caucus-i-want-a-new-base/article_a4b63b7f-ea23-5b54-99df-7fe3f36a1fdf.html (accessed 25 May 2022).

IV.
Oil and Gas Policies

9

Alberta's Climate Policy: Public Kenney versus Private Kenney

Duane Bratt

Introduction

On 5 May 2015, Rachel Notley and the New Democratic Party (NDP) shocked Albertans and Canadians by winning the Alberta election and ending the forty-four year Progressive Conservative (PC) dynasty. The surprising NDP victory led to high expectations that fundamental change in many aspects of Alberta's political and economic life would ensue, in particular, how the oil and gas dependent province would recognize the need to address fully the issue of climate change. Half a year later that is what happened. In November 2015, Premier Rachel Notley announced Alberta's Climate Leadership Plan (CLP). It was the most ambitious plan for reducing greenhouse gas (GHG) emissions seen in Canada. It brought together the key stakeholders (industry, environmentalists, and Indigenous leaders) and would heavily influence the federal government led by Justin Trudeau. Yet by the summer of 2019, the centrepiece of the CLP—the economy-wide carbon tax—was in tatters. The United Conservative Party (UCP) led by Jason Kenney campaigned on repealing the CLP (ending the carbon tax was Bill 1). After it won a majority government in April 2019, it announced that it would start to dismantle the CLP, beginning with the carbon tax (formally repealed on 5 June). However, on closer examination, the Kenney government has actually maintained much of the CLP and, in some cases, even strengthened it. Explaining the Kenney government's climate policy is the purpose of this chapter.

Measuring rhetoric versus reality is a common political science tool. However, this tool is stood on its head when we analyze Alberta's climate policy under the Kenney government. With the notable exception of the economy-wide carbon tax, the Kenney government maintained or enhanced Alberta's CLP that was introduced by the previous NDP government. In addition, despite the strong anti-Trudeau rhetoric, the Kenney government has worked together with Ottawa on several key climate initiatives. The contradiction between Alberta's climate rhetoric and its reality can be explained by examining the Public Jason Kenney versus the Private Jason Kenney. Public Kenney is what is emphasized in speeches, press conferences, advertising, and high-profile announcements. Private Kenney is what is de-emphasized behind the scenes with bureaucrats, industry, cabinet officials, and relations with other governments.

This chapter is divided into six parts. Part one is a methodological statement. Part two briefly describes the background and history of Alberta and climate change. Part three examines the CLP that was introduced by the Notley government in 2015. Part four examines the Public Kenney as it relates to climate policy. Part five examines the Private Kenney as it relates to climate policy. Part six offers a brief conclusion.

Methodology

This chapter updates, expands, and modifies an earlier study that I did for the University of Ottawa's Positive Energy program.[1] It relies on the official documents from both Alberta's NDP and UCP governments. Public opinion survey data was also utilized. These documents were supplemented by important secondary material from books, academic articles, and news pieces. This study also includes fourteen elite semi-structured interviews from the architects, participants, and observers of the creation of the CLP as well as its dismantlement. In most cases, these interviews were conducted on the record, but some subjects requested anonymity for all or some of their comments.[2]

Background

Alberta is the oil and gas capital of Canada. Since the famous Leduc strike of 1947, and especially after the oil shocks of the early 1970s, Alberta has been a major economic engine of Canada with the largest per capita income in the country. However, the extraction of oil and gas, combined with a heavy reliance on coal-generated electricity, meant that Alberta had the highest levels of GHG emissions in Canada. In 2013, Alberta's GHG emissions were 267 Mt and were projected to grow to 297 Mt in 2020 and 320 Mt in 2030.[3] Alberta accounted for 37 per cent of Canada's GHG emissions with less than 10 per cent of the population. Moreover, per capita emissions were "five times higher in Alberta than Ontario, Quebec, or British Columbia."[4]

Given its reliance on oil and gas, and a realization that it was the country's largest GHG emitter, it is not surprising that there has also been a long history of the Alberta government being skeptical of climate change. World leaders had first agreed to set GHG emission targets at the Rio Summit in 1992 (which created the United Nations Framework Convention on Climate Change), through the Kyoto Protocol in 1997, which established legally binding commitments on developed countries to reduce GHG emissions. Under the Kyoto Protocol, Canada was required to reduce its 1990 GHG emissions by 6 per cent by 2010. Canada ratified the Kyoto Protocol in 2002.[5] The Alberta government staunchly opposed the Kyoto Protocol. Premier Ralph Klein dismissed climate change as being caused by "dinosaur farts."[6] Klein went further and threatened a constitutional challenge over the Kyoto Protocol, advocating instead a "made in Alberta" approach to climate change.

The Alberta government tried to reframe the issue of climate change by focusing on the "carbon intensity" of emissions as opposed to "total" emissions. As Ian Urquhart would later show, Alberta was effective in reducing its carbon intensity from 1.14 (millions of tonnes of GHG emitted/ GDP in millions) in 2000 to 0.85 by 2014. However, the total GHG emissions rose from 232 million tonnes in 2000 to 274 in 2014.[7] The reason why GHG emissions kept rising in Alberta was that the growth in oil and gas production outpaced reductions in GHG emissions intensity. Nevertheless, pressure within Alberta, the rest of Canada, and internationally, continued to try to get Alberta to tackle seriously its emissions. In 2007, Premier Ed Stelmach introduced the Specified Gas Emitters Regulations (SGER) with a $15 a tonne carbon tax for large emitters.[8] SGER established benchmarks for each large emitter to reduce their carbon intensity by 12 per cent. However, SGER also included a large swath of exemptions and offsets that limited its effectiveness. As a result, the Ecofiscal Commission concluded that SGER compliance was only $1.14 a tonne, and not $15 a tonne, in 2012.[9]

Notley's Climate Leadership Plan

The NDP did not campaign in 2015 on a plan to address climate change. Instead, the NDP focused on health care, education, PC corruption, and highlighted leader Rachel Notley.[10] Its party platform did mention that "we will take leadership on the issue of climate change," but there were no specifics outside of a pledge to "phase out coal-fired generation" and introduce "an energy efficiency strategy and a renewable energy strategy."[11] There was no mention of a carbon tax.

Yet soon after winning the 2015 election, the NDP decided to quickly address climate change. Notley appointed Shannon Phillips, one of the NDP's star candidates from Lethbridge, as minister of environment and parks. Appointing a powerful minister to the environment portfolio was a clear signal that the NDP would seriously engage with the challenge of climate change. The Climate Change Advisory Panel was formed in June 2015, chaired by University of Alberta energy economist Andrew Leach, with the aim of reviewing "Alberta's existing climate change policies, engaging with Albertans, and providing the Minister of Environment and Parks with advice on a comprehensive set of policy measures to reduce Alberta's greenhouse gas emissions."[12] The Leach Panel recommended the creation of a framework that would provide the foundation of a lower carbon economy, especially the introduction of a broad-based carbon tax. The Leach Panel's framework was largely adopted by the Notley government when it released its Alberta CLP.

On 22 November 2015, a large press conference was held when the Alberta CLP was announced. Standing on stage with Premier Notley were Minister Phillips and Panel Chair Andrew Leach, but they were joined by industry leaders (Canadian Natural [CNRL]'s Murray Edwards,

Suncor's Steve Williams, Cenovus' Brian Ferguson, and Shell's Lorraine Mitchelmore), environmentalists (Pembina Institute's Ed Whittingham, Environmental Defence's Tim Gray, Équiterre's Steven Guilbeault, Stand Earth's Karen Mahon), and Indigenous leaders (Treaty 6 Grand Chief Tony Alexis). The range and power of the individuals on stage created a media sensation. Particularly when Murray Edwards appeared on stage.[13] Edwards, who founded CNRL and built it into one of the biggest companies in Canada, is a major player in the oil patch. In addition, he was not previously seen as particularly progressive on climate change issues. According to Whittingham, who also attended the Paris climate conference of 2015, "attendees marvelled at the composition of the stage given the level of conflict that existed around Alberta's oil sands."[14]

There were several components to the CLP.[15] Many of the measures had already occurred in other jurisdictions, i.e., an economy-wide carbon tax in British Columbia and a coal phaseout in Ontario. Nevertheless, having multiple items all being included at once was revolutionary, especially for Alberta, given its prior history on climate change. It was clear that the Notley government wanted something "big and bold." As Ed Whittingham explained, "we were surprised by the breadth and depth of the CLP. The NDP had inherited a "climate pariah" and wanted to change the channel.[16]

The most significant aspect of the CLP was an economy-wide price on carbon. As the Leach Panel stated, "putting a price on emissions leverages the power of markets to deploy both technologies and behavioral changes to reduce emissions over time. Carbon pricing is the most flexible and least-costly way to reduce emissions."[17] The carbon tax would start at $20 per tonne in 2017 and rise to $30 per tonne in 2018. It would apply to gasoline (6.73 cents a litre), diesel (8.03 cents a litre), natural gas ($1.517 a gigajoule), and propane (4.6 cents a litre) with exceptions for farm fuels, flights outside of Alberta, biofuels, and fuels for export. Small oil and gas producers were also given an exemption from the carbon tax until 2023. This had been a goal of many in the oil and gas industry who had argued against an increase in the SGER. If the principle was "polluter pays" than the carbon tax should not be applied solely to producers, but also to consumers.[18] In fact, the SGER would eventually be replaced in 2018 by the carbon tax.

The second part of the CLP was phasing out coal-fired electricity by 2030. Alberta was the most coal-dependent province in Canada with coal supplying 55 per cent of Alberta's electricity in 2014.[19] Already federal regulations brought in by the Harper government would see the phased retirement of Alberta's oldest coal plants, but the CLP called for shutting down the remaining six facilities. Some of this coal generation would be replaced by Alberta's plentiful supply of natural gas that already supplied over 30 per cent of Alberta's electricity. However, the government set a target that 50–75 per cent of retired coal generation would be replaced by renewables. In fact, a target of 30 per cent of all electricity generation from renewable sources by 2030 was set.[20]

The third aspect was to establish a 100 Mt emissions limit on the oil sands. This was not part of the Leach Panel but was the key part of the negotiations between the large oil sands CEOs and the environmental non-governmental organizations (ENGOs) that had begun under PC government led by Jim Prentice and had continued through the initial Notley years. The oil sands represented 22 per cent of all of Alberta's total GHG emissions in 2013 and was projected to rise to 35 per cent by 2030.[21] The purpose of the cap was to either slow the development of the oil sands or force "oil sands operators to develop technology that significantly reduces carbon emissions."[22] A cap of 100 Mt, as Urquhart pointed out, would allow oil sands emissions "to increase by a stunning 52 percent from the 65.6 megatonnes of greenhouse gases" that were emitted in 2014.[23] However, as Dave Collyer, former CEO of the Canadian Association of Petroleum Producers (CAPP), pointed out, "it was a cap on emissions, not on production growth (this was very important). If industry could continue to reduce its intensity through technology and other initiatives, it would allow the sector to continue to grow. . . . It was a demonstrable limit, which was hugely symbolic. But focused on emissions not on growth of the industry."[24]

The fourth aspect was reducing methane emissions. The Leach Panel's discussion document noted "[m]ethane is over 20 times more potent in global warming potential, over a 100-year period, than carbon dioxide."[25] Methane comes from cow manure (22 per cent of emissions) and landfills (6 per cent), but the largest amount of emissions is through venting and flaring from the oil and gas sector (70 per cent).[26] The CLP put a target of reducing methane emissions 45 per cent from 2014 levels by 2025.[27] The carbon tax, industry expertise, and regulatory measures would be used to reduce methane emissions.[28]

There were several goals of the CLP. As Notley stated, "responding to climate change is about doing what's right for future generations of Albertans—protecting our jobs, health and the environment. It will help us access new markets for our energy products, and diversify our economy with renewable energy and energy efficiency technology. Alberta is showing leadership on one of the world's biggest problems, and doing our part."[29] The first was to reduce Alberta's GHG emissions that, as previously stated, were the highest in Canada. The second was to help Alberta diversify to a greener economy. The proceeds of the carbon tax would be used, in part, for investments in renewable energy technology. The third was to encourage conservation with an energy efficiency program. The fourth was to gain public acceptance for pipelines. Pipelines are essential for Alberta, a landlocked province, to get market access for its oil and gas. A fifth goal, and related to public acceptance for pipelines, was to change the reputation of Alberta's oil and gas sector. Alberta's oil and gas sector had become an international "pariah."[30]

There was opposition to most aspects of the CLP. For example, the town of Hanna—home of a major coal plant—strongly opposed the coal phaseout. However, the biggest backlash was to the carbon tax. Brian Jean, leader of the Wildrose Party and leader of the Official Opposition, argued that the NDP was in bed with "big oil" and pointed out that the NDP did not campaign on a carbon tax.[31] Jean called it the "tax on everything" and argued that it hurt families and the economy.

There was also a significant split in Alberta's oil and gas sector. The largest companies, such as the ones that joined Notley on stage in announcing the CLP, operate around the world. They realized that they needed to reduce their carbon footprint and rehabilitate Alberta's energy reputation around the world. For them, a carbon tax made total business sense. However, medium and small companies who only operated in Alberta spoke out strongly against the carbon tax. This was despite the fact that the smaller companies were exempted from the carbon tax until 2023.[32] As Taft noted, "these companies were tuned to the finer, short-term details of costs and markets. The carbon tax was an added cost they did not want. It was also a symbol of unwanted government intervention and a harbinger of more threats to the fossil fuel industry."[33] These smaller companies were also politically influential because they represented the traditional donor base of the Wildrose Party.

While there were many reasons for the merger of the PC and Wildrose Parties,[34] their shared hatred of the CLP was one of the more important ones. For example, 92 per cent of UCP supporters wanted to eliminate the carbon tax.[35] The NDP's 2015 election victory had been due, in part, to the vote split between the two conservative parties. The NDP had 40.6 per cent of the popular vote in 2015, and the combined PC and Wildrose share was 52 per cent. Once the UCP was formed, it was going to be very tough for the NDP to get re-elected.

The promise to repeal the CLP was front and centre in the UCP's 2019 election campaign. It was part of Jason Kenney's "fight back" strategy on behalf of Alberta's oil and gas sector. At a large energy conference in October 2018, Kenney provided the details of his fight back strategy:

- repealing the carbon tax;
- creating a $30 million government funded "war room" to defend Alberta's oil and gas sector from perceived lies and misrepresentation;
- creating a legal defence fund for pro-energy litigation from Indigenous groups;
- investigating ENGOs for violations of their charitable status;
- boycotting companies who criticized Alberta's oil and gas sector;
- using "turn off the taps" legislation against British Columbia if it blocked pipelines;
- holding a referendum on the federal equalization program if Québec (a major recipient of equalization) blocked pipelines; and
- defeating the Trudeau government to prevent the federal carbon tax backstop from kicking in.[36]

When the UCP released its party platform for the 2019 election, it also emphasized the fight back strategy. It promised, "Bill 1 of a United Conservative government will be the Carbon Tax Repeal Act. At $1.4 billion, this will be the largest tax cut in Alberta's history. We will stop the NDP's planned 67% increase to the carbon tax, and sue the Trudeau government if it tries to impose a carbon tax on Alberta."[37] On 16 April 2019 the UCP won a majority government with sixty-three of eighty-seven seats and 54.9 per cent of the vote. They quickly went to work repealing the CLP. A spring session of the legislature was held and Bill 1 was passed and given royal assent on 5 June 2019; Albertans immediately stopped paying the carbon tax.

On 23 October 2018, Trudeau announced the details of the federal backstop.[38] The federal backstop would apply to provinces, such as Saskatchewan, who refused to adopt a price on carbon, and it would apply to provinces, such as Ontario and Alberta, who had eliminated their price on carbon. Approximately 90 per cent of the proceeds of the federal carbon tax would be rebated back to individuals through the income tax system. A group of recently elected conservative premiers led by Kenney that also included Scott Moe (Saskatchewan), Doug Ford (Ontario), Brian Pallister (Manitoba), and Blaine Higgs (New Brunswick) all opposed the federal backstop and many of the climate change initiatives of the Trudeau government. This led them to sue Ottawa over its federal carbon tax backstop.[39] These suits failed when, in March 2021 in a six to three decision, the Canadian Supreme Court ruled that the federal government has the unilateral ability to address climate change through the ability to impose a national carbon tax.[40]

Public Kenney

The Kenney government never repealed the other aspects of the CLP: the coal phaseout, the oil sands emissions cap, and the methane emissions reductions plan (although part of reducing methane emissions was through the carbon tax). In the case of the coal phaseout, many of the facilities were already being retrofitted to handle natural gas, so there was going to be no reversal. In addition, the NDP had created a compensation program for coal companies and their workers. "The Coal Workforce Transition Program provides financial assistance for re-employment, retirement, relocation and education as workers prepare to start new jobs or retire." The CLP anticipated completing the coal phaseout by 2030, but this has been accelerated by the Kenney government and is expected to be completed by 2023; seven years ahead of schedule. The Kenney government has also maintained both the 100 Mt emissions cap on the oil sands and the methane reduction target.

More remarkably, the Kenney government introduced the Technology Innovation and Emissions Reduction (TIER) regulations in October 2019. TIER is a price on carbon for high emitters similar to the old SGER. However, unlike SGER, it was initially priced at $30 a tonne (as opposed to the previously planned $20 a tonne) beginning on 1 January 2020. This meant that it was likely stringent enough to prevent the federal backstop from kicking in, and in fact, that is exactly what happened. In December 2019, Ottawa agreed that TIER met the federal standard. TIER, which was in the UCP election platform, is an acknowledgement that the Kenney government supports carbon taxes, but on companies, not individuals. This is not as effective as an economy-wide carbon tax, but easier to manage politically.

The gap between Kenney's harsh rhetoric towards the CLP and the reality that almost the entire program has either been maintained or strengthened can only be explained by the contradictions between Public Kenney and Private Kenney. The Public Kenney can be seen in the development, promotion, and implementation of the fight back strategy. As promised, the Kenney government quickly repealed the economy-wide carbon tax. Then, when the federal carbon backstop kicked in, Jason Kenney actively campaigned against Trudeau's re-election in 2019 and joined the, ultimately unsuccessful, lawsuits by Saskatchewan and Ontario against the constitutionality of the federal carbon backstop.

A second component of the fight back strategy was the creation of a war room to defend Alberta's oil and gas sector. The war room was established with the formal name of the Canadian Energy Centre (CEC) and an annual budget of $30 million. However, it has been constantly mired in embarrassing scandals due to maintaining internal secrecy, plagiarizing its initial logo, bullying the small *Medicine Hat News* into publishing an op-ed, criticizing the *New York Times*, attacking the fictional cartoon movie *Bigfoot's Family*, and ineffectual advertising campaigns (see Brad Clark's chapter). Even the Allan Inquiry (discussed below) was highly critical of the CEC, writing that it "has come under almost universal criticism."[41]

Third, was the formation of the *Public Inquiry into Anti-Alberta Energy Campaigns*, led by the forensic accountant Steve Allan, in July 2019. The purpose of the Allan Inquiry was to investigate foreign-funded efforts to undermine Alberta's oil and gas industry. However, the Allan Inquiry, like the war room, has been beset by problems and controversies. Originally scheduled to be released on 30 October 2020 with a budget of $2.5 million, it went through several delays and eventually cost $3.5 million. The fundamental problem with the Allan Inquiry was that it was not really a public inquiry, which would involve a search for the truth through interviews, research, and public hearings. Instead, the Kenney government pre-determined the answer: Americans financed Canadian ENGOs in order to landlock Alberta oil. The Allan Inquiry was created to find evidence for the pre-determined result. Procedurally, it lacked fairness by refusing to hold public hearings, commissioning reports from climate change deniers, and giving tight timelines for ENGOs to respond to the draft report. The Allan Inquiry was presented to the government in July 2021 and publicly released on October 21, 2021.[42] Neither Steve Allan nor Kenney were at the press conference, but Energy Minister Sonya Savage believed that the government was vindicated and that ENGOs had engaged in coordinated efforts to try and derail the oil sands to "hurt" Albertans. Savage admitted that ENGOs did nothing illegal, but she maintained that it was wrong. "I think the majority of Albertans would say it was wrong, and they want to know how it happened, who was involved, and how they can make sure it doesn't happen to the energy resources of the future."[43] However, the report actually exonerated ENGOs. Allan could not "trace with precision the quantum of foreign funding applied to anti-Alberta energy campaigns" (p.13). In addition, he noted that "while anti-Alberta energy campaigns may have played a role in the cancellation of some oil and gas developments, I am not in a position to find that these campaigns alone caused project delays or cancellations" (p.14). Most importantly, Allan emphasized that "in no way does participating in an anti-Alberta energy campaign indicate that an organization has acted in a manner that is illegal, improper, or otherwise impugnable, nor does it mean the organization is 'against Alberta' in some manner" (p.16).

Fourth, a referendum to remove equalization from the Canadian constitution was held, in conjunction with Alberta's municipal elections, on 18 October 2021 (see Jared Wesley's chapter). This was also a major campaign promise of the UCP in 2019. The question stated, "Should Section 36(2) of the Constitution Act, 1982—Parliament and the government of Canada's commitment to the principle of making equalization payments—be removed from the constitution?" This passed with 61.7 per cent, but with only 37.8 per cent of eligible Albertans voting. In addition, Kenney explained that the referendum was more about giving him leverage to negotiate on pipelines or other oil and gas federal pieces of legislation, and sending a message to Ottawa and Quebec, than it was about equalization. For example, the motion that was introduced in the Alberta Legislature (a requirement to initiate constitutional negotiations) lists the following schedule: "(d) direct the Government of Alberta to take all necessary steps to secure a fair deal for Alberta in the Canadian federation, including the reform of federal transfer programs, the defence of provincial powers in the Constitution, and the right to pursue responsible development of our natural resources."[44] This is much broader than the narrow question about removing Section 36(2) from the Constitution that was in the referendum. Yet, despite the results of the referendum, the Kenney government took few steps in the following months to try and put equalization on the national agenda.

Fifth was the "turn off the taps" legislation designed to stop the flow of oil and natural gas to British Columbia. It was originally passed, but never proclaimed into law, by the NDP in 2018 at the height of the battle between Alberta and British Columbia over the Trans Mountain pipeline. When the UCP formed government, it quickly proclaimed it into law. However, the Kenney government has never used it, although as Environment Minister Jason Nixon noted, "[t]his is like a fire extinguisher, having it on the shelf ready to go. Hopefully, we never need it, but we need to have it in place."[45]

There were three other acts that were never part of the original fight back strategy, but clearly fit with its spirit. In March 2020, just after COVID-19 began, the Alberta government purchased a stake in the Keystone XL (KXL) pipeline project (see Jean-Sébastien Rioux's chapter). It paid TC Energy $1.5 billion with another $6 billion in loan guarantees. This was designed to spur on construction and to give the oil sector a confidence boost. However, it backfired when newly elected US President Joe Biden, on his first day of office, signed an executive order revoking KXL's permits. In June 2020, Bill 1—the Critical Infrastructure Defence Act—was passed. This was in response to rail and road blockades across Alberta and the rest of Canada in solidarity with the Wet'suwet'en hereditary chiefs that erupted in February–March 2020, who were protesting the construction of a natural gas pipeline in northern British Columbia. Finally, Kenney and other members of his cabinet decided not to attend the COP26 climate summit in Scotland in early November 2021. Kenney explained that he would not attend a "gabfest" and instead "expressed great concern" about Canada's "ever-changing [emissions] targets."[46]

A second part of the Public Kenney was the harsh anti-Trudeau rhetoric. Kenney campaigned against Trudeau in the 2019 federal election, not only in Alberta, but also, in an unprecedented move for a sitting Premier, in Ontario and Manitoba. Following Trudeau's election victory, albeit with no seats in Alberta (the Liberals had won four in 2015). Kenney created the Fair Deal Panel (see Wesley chapter) that would hold public hearings around the province investigating the idea of, among other things, an Alberta Revenue Agency, Alberta Pension Plan, and an Alberta Police Force to replace the Canadian Revenue Agency, Canadian Pension Plan, and the Royal Canadian Mounted Police. It was designed to assert Alberta's authority in areas of provincial jurisdiction. As of May 2022, the Kenney government has accepted all of the recommendations of the Fair Deal Panel but has not taken steps to act on any of them (with the exception of the referendum on equalization).[47] When Biden cancelled KXL, Kenney also lashed out at Trudeau for failing to stand up for Alberta against the new US President. He also demanded that Trudeau apply economic sanctions against the US (which was ignored by Trudeau).

In March 2022, the Trudeau government released its long awaited emissions reduction strategy. It set a target of reducing emissions of 40 per cent below 2005 levels by 2030 and net-zero emissions by 2050.[48] In response, Alberta's Environment Minister Jason Nixon wrote an incendiary op-ed attacking the emissions reduction strategy, maintaining that it was "insane" and designed to "destroy Alberta's economy."[49] Despite the fact that no oil and gas production cut was included in the strategy, instead it was an emissions cap. Which, as discussed above, already existed in the oil sands as part of the compromise between leading oil company CEOs and environmental leaders (including current federal Environment Minister Steven Guilbeault). In contrast to the harsh rhetoric from the Kenney government, Alberta energy industry leaders were cautiously optimistic that they could work with the federal government on reducing emissions intensity. According to the Oil Sands Pathways to Net Zero Alliance, which represents the large oil sands producers, stated that "while we recognize the federal government's ambition to drive even faster results, the Pathways Alliance has been clear that the interim goals set for our industry must be flexible, realistic and achievable."[50]

The Public Kenney has also spent years attacking, in very strong terms, two pieces of federal legislation adopted by the Trudeau government: Bill C-69 and Bill C-48. Bill C-69 involved substantial changes to Canada's energy regulatory framework, but Kenney nicknamed it "the no more pipelines bill." In September 2019, the Kenney government filed a reference with the Alberta Court of Appeal on the constitutionality of the Impact Assessment Act (Bill C-69). The court, in a four to one decision, found that Bill C-69 intruded too far into provincial jurisdiction.[51] This was a rare win for the Kenney government's fight back strategy, but it was a limited win. First, the reference decision is being appealed to the Canadian Supreme Court, which previously upheld the constitutionality of the federal carbon tax. Second, even the Alberta Court of Appeal recognized that the federal government would continue to have jurisdiction over matters crossing provincial boundaries, such as an inter-provincial pipeline. Bill C-48 codified an existing moratorium on tanker traffic along the northern coast of British Columbia. Not only would this effectively prevent a future pipeline such as Northern Gateway, but there was also no equivalent tanker ban on the Atlantic coast or the St. Lawrence River. So, from the perspective of Public Kenney, this was a direct targeting of landlocked Alberta oil. Following the September 2021 federal election, Trudeau announced his new cabinet, which included former Greenpeace and Équiterre member Steven Guilbeault as the new environment minister. Kenney called the appointment "very problematic," and warned that Guilbeault could kill "hundreds of thousands of jobs" in resource-producing parts of Canada. Kenney stated that Guilbeault's "own personal background and track record on these issues suggests somebody who is more of an absolutist than a pragmatist."[52]

Private Kenney

When we examine Private Kenney, there is a realization that the Alberta government has actually accomplished a lot on the climate file. This can be seen most evidently with the CLP. The coal phaseout has been accelerated, the oil sands emissions cap and methane reduction program has been maintained. Even with the carbon tax, despite the anti-carbon tax rhetoric, cancelling the provincial carbon tax, and fighting the federal backstop in court, Albertans continue to pay the carbon tax. In addition, the Kenney government introduced, via TIER, an industry-wide carbon tax for the oil sands.

The Private Kenney is much more aware of the problem of climate change than Public Kenney. Andrew Leach, the architect of Notley's CLP, maintained, "to his credit, Kenney could have run and won as a climate change denier, but he chose not to do so. In fact, he has an emissions reduction strategy; it is just weaker than the CLP. Kenney is more of a centrist on climate change than he gets credit for."[53] In a February 2020 speech at the Woodrow Wilson Centre, a major think tank in Washington, Kenney acknowledged that "[o]ver the next decades as we go through the energy transition, we all know that there will be a continued demand for crude. It is preferable that the last barrel in that transition period comes from a stable, reliable liberal democracy with among the highest environmental, human-rights and labour standards on earth."[54] In a follow-up interview, Kenney said "I have a firm grasp of the obvious. There is no reasonable person that can deny that in the decades to come we will see a gradual shift from hydrocarbon-based energy to other forms of energy."[55] It is notable that Kenney emphasized an energy transition to a US audience of policy-makers, industry professionals, and investors; not in Alberta or Canada. This was echoed in a high profile hearing in front of US senators in Washington on 17 May 2022 (one day before he announced his intent to resign after receiving a slim majority in the UCP leadership review), when Kenney avoided criticising the federal carbon tax instead deferring to Canadian Natural Resources Minister Jonathan Wilkinson. The

Public Kenney does not acknowledge an energy transition, but the Private Kenney is preparing for one.

In contrast to the harsh rhetoric towards the Trudeau government by the Public Kenney, the Private Kenney is working quietly behind the scenes on a number of climate initiatives with them, for example, the carbon capture utilization storage strategy (CCUS). "CCUS is a suite of technologies that capture CO_2 from facilities, including industrial or power applications, or directly from the atmosphere. Once the CO_2 is captured, it is then compressed and transported to be permanently stored in geological formations underground (e.g. saline aquifers, oil reservoirs), or used to create products such as concrete and low-carbon synthetic fuels. CCUS technologies can deliver 'negative emissions' by removing CO_2 from the air (direct-air-capture) or from biomass-based energy and storing the CO_2."[56] Carbon capture and storage will not only reduce emissions, but adding utilization means creating economic opportunities through the use of the captured CO_2. A federal-provincial working group on CCUS was created in March 2021. Savage praised the cooperation between the federal and provincial government on CCUS: "The ingenuity of Alberta's energy sector combined with our geological capacity to store carbon and the federal government's commitment to invest in CCUS is a winning combination for Alberta."[57] Kenney wants Ottawa to put $30 billion over ten years towards CCUS in Alberta. He also acknowledged that we've "had a lot of good discussions with senior people in the federal government recognizing they need something like this to have any hope, realistically, of achieving their emissions targets."[58] The April 2022 federal budget included a large tax credit for industry investment into CCUS. The tax credit is 60 per cent for equipment in a direct carbon capture project, 50 per cent if emissions come from an industrial facility, and 37.5 per cent for equipment to transport and store carbon dioxide. It is estimated that these supports could cost the federal treasury over $1.5 billion annually.[59] The Private Kenney can have constructive discussions with Ottawa, but the Public Kenney is combative towards Ottawa.

A second area of cooperation is with small modular reactors (SMRs). SMRs are smaller than traditional nuclear power plants, producing less than 300 MW of electricity. Modular refers to standardized construction at off-site factories, with the units shipped by rail and trucked to sites.

SMRs are expected to be safer and more economic than traditional re-actors. Natural Resources Canada (NRCan) has identified three major areas where SMRs could be deployed: in remote communities (primarily in northern Canada), for use in heavy industry (e.g., mining), and for re-placing coal-generation in smaller provinces (e.g., Saskatchewan and New Brunswick).[60] At the provincial level, Ontario, Saskatchewan, and New Brunswick signed a memorandum of understanding (MOU) on SMRs in December 2019.[61] Alberta announced its intention to join the MOU on 7 August 2020[62] and officially signed the document at a virtual press con-ference on 14 April 2021.[63] A year later, in March 2022, all four provinces (including Alberta) released a strategic plan.[64]

SMRs illustrate federal-provincial cooperation in the often highly contested area of energy-environmental policy (e.g., interprovincial oil pipelines, carbon taxes, etc.). For example, governments typically jealously guard their constitutional jurisdiction and political interests over energy and the environment. The fact that SMRs reveal cooperation between a Liberal federal government and four conservative provincial governments is important. In addition, Ontario, Saskatchewan, and Alberta unsuccess-fully sued Ottawa over the federal carbon tax that, like SMRs, is designed to reduce GHG emissions in the energy sector.

While Saskatchewan and Ontario have disagreements with the Trudeau government, the antagonism is strongest in Alberta with Public Kenney. This explains why Private Kenney, in the official Alberta gov-ernment press releases surrounding the SMR announcement, the August 2020 video starring Kenney and Savage, and the April 2021 press confer-ence with the four premiers, emphasized working with the other prov-inces and never once mentioned the federal government. This was despite the fact that the MOU explicitly states the commitments of the provinces:

- To work co-operatively to positively influence the federal government to provide a clear unambiguous statement that nuclear energy is a clean technology and is required as part of the climate change solution;

- To work co-operatively to positively influence the federal government to provide support for SMRs identified in the Canadian SMR Roadmap. . . .

- To work co-operatively to positively influence the federal government to make changes as necessary to facilitate the introduction of SMRs.[65]

Moreover, the federal government, which has the constitutional authority over nuclear energy and whose financial investments will be critical, is the key actor in the development and deployment of SMRs.

Conclusion

In evaluating the UCP government's climate policy, two things stand out. First, Notley's CLP has had significant policy resilience. Policy resilience "is a concept that focuses on understanding the ability of systems, organizations, policies, and individuals to persist over time against 'external' shocks (without, however, identifying the specific reasons for or causes of this ability)."[66] In other words, a policy is resilient when there is strong opposition to its creation, a major political party actively campaigns against it in a subsequent election, that party wins the election in large part to its opposition to the specific policy, but once in office is either unwilling or unable to change substantively the policy. For example, think of the introduction of the Goods and Services Tax in Canada in 1991 or the Affordable Care Act in the United States in 2010. Both were strongly opposed by the Liberals and Republicans, but neither of them abolished the policy when they subsequently took office. The CLP meets that definition. The conservative parties (Wildrose and PCs) in Alberta strongly opposed the CLP when it was announced. The UCP, after the party merger, kept up the fight during the 2019 provincial election. Once in office, the UCP quickly moved to repeal the carbon tax, but by 1 January 2020 the federal carbon tax backstop had kicked in. More notably, the newly elected UCP government did not alter the other aspects of the CLP (coal phaseout, emissions cap on the oil sands, methane reduction). In fact, the introduction of the TIER policy was the UCP's carbon tax on high emitters in the oil sands signalling that even the UCP supported some of the goals of the NDP's CLP.

Second, there is great contradiction between what the UCP government has said about climate policy versus what it has done. Interestingly, the reality of climate policy has been more effective than the rhetoric of the UCP towards climate policy. Usually, governments over promise and under deliver, but on the issue of climate, the Kenney government has done the reverse. This contradiction can be explained by the difference between Public Kenney and Private Kenney. The Public Kenney promotes Alberta's oil and gas sector, threatens any of its critics, and attacks the Trudeau government. However, the Private Kenney has taken a number of initiatives aimed at reducing Alberta's GHG emissions and works collaboratively behind the scenes with the Trudeau government. It is a fascinating political story. It is a good news story regarding climate, but something that the Kenney government refuses to publicly admit to. With a UCP leadership race underway to replace Kenney as party leader and premier, it will be interesting to see if his successor will illustrate this same dichotomy of public opposition to efforts to reduce GHG emissions and private support that recognizes the reality of climate change.

Acknowledgements

I would like to thank Dave Collyer, Jeremy Rayner, Janet Brown, and Monica Gattinger for their comments on earlier drafts of this study.

NOTES

1   Duane Bratt, "Addressing Polarization: What Works? The Alberta Climate Leadership Plan," Positive Energy at the University of Ottawa (March 2020). Available at https://www.uottawa.ca/positive-energy/sites/www.uottawa.ca.positive-energy/files/adressing_polarization_-_what_works_-_clp_website.pdf

2   This project has ethics approval. Mount Royal University, Human Research Ethics Board, Application Number 101937 (8 October 2019).

3   Alberta, *Climate Leadership—Discussion Document* (August 2015), 14–15.

4   Kevin Taft, "The Politics of Alberta's Carbon Tax," in Duane Bratt, Keith Brownsey, Richard Sutherland, and David Taras, eds., *Orange Chinook: Politics in the New Alberta* (University of Calgary Press: Calgary, 2019), 173.

5   The Harper government formally pulled out of the Kyoto Protocol in 2011.

6   Canadian Press, "Creeps, bums and a foot in mouth," *MacLean's* (29 March 2013).

7   Ian Urquhart, *Costly Fix: Power, Politics, and Nature in the Tar Sands* (University of Toronto Press: Toronto, 2018), 244.

8   Alberta Environment, *Frequently asked questions for baseline emissions intensity applications and compliance reporting* (2008). Accessed at http://environment.gov.ab.ca/info/library/7932.pdf

9   Canada's Ecofiscal Commission, *The Way Forward: A Practical Approach to Reducing Canada's Greenhouse Gas Emissions* (April 2015), 36.

10   Melanee Thomas, "Ready for Rachel: The Alberta NDP's 2015 Campaign," in Bratt, Brownsey, Sutherland, and Taras, eds., *Orange Chinook*, 57–77.

11   Alberta's NDP, *Election Platform 2015* (2015), 18.

12   Alberta, *Climate Leadership—Report to the Minister* (20 November 2015), 96.

13   All interview subjects commented on the importance of Murray Edwards endorsing the CLP.

14   Ed Whittingham, "Pipeline expansion is the right move," *Globe and Mail* (19 June 2019).

15   Alberta, "Climate Leadership Plan," *Press Release* (22 November 2015). Accessed at https://www.alberta.ca/release.cfm?xID=38885E74F7B63-A62D-D1D2-E7BCF6A98D616C09 on 6 July 2019.

16   Interview with Ed Whittingham.

17   Alberta, *Climate Leadership—Report to the Minister*, 5.

18   Confidential interviews with oil & gas executives.

19   Alberta, *Climate Leadership—Discussion Document*, 27.

20   Alberta, *Climate Leadership—Report to the Minister*, 6.

21   Alberta, *Climate Leadership—Discussion Document*, 20.

22   Gillian Steward, "Betting on Bitumen: Lougheed, Klein, and Notley," in Bratt, Brownsey, Sutherland, and Taras, eds., *Orange Chinook*, 159.

23   Urquhart, *Costly Fix*, 282.

24   Interview with Dave Collyer.

25   Alberta, *Climate Leadership—Discussion Document*, 24.

26   Alberta, *Climate Leadership—Report to the Minister*, 7.

27   Alberta, "Climate Leadership Plan."

28   Confidential interviews with oil & gas executives.

29   Alberta, "Climate Leadership Plan."

30   Sydney Sharpe and Don Braid, *Notley Nation: How Alberta's Political Upheaval Swept the Country* (Dundurn: Toronto, 2016), 128.

31   Alberta Legislature, *Hansard* (7 June 2016), 1552.

32   A senior oil & gas executive complained that many of the smaller companies did not even know about the exemption.

33   Taft, "The Politics of Alberta's Carbon Tax," 179.

34   Anthony M. Sayers and David K. Stewart, "Out of the Blue: Goodbye Tories, Hello Jason Kenney," in Bratt, Brownsey, Sutherland, and Taras, eds., *Orange Chinook*, 399–423.

35   CBC, *Road Ahead Survey* (April 2018).

36   Duane Bratt, "How Jason Kenney's plan to 'fight back' helps and hurts him," *CBC News* (October 25, 2018). Accessed at https://www.cbc.ca/news/canada/calgary/road-ahead-duane-bratt-jason-kenney-war-room-opinion-1.4878953 on 25 October 2018.

37   UCP, *Getting Alberta Back to Work* (April 2019), 12.

38   Justin Trudeau, "Government of Canada fighting climate change with a price on pollution," 23 October 2018. Etobicoke, Ontario. Accessed at https://pm.gc.ca/en/news/news-releases/2018/10/23/government-canada-fighting-climate-change-price-pollution on 17 September 2019.

39   The Saskatchewan and Ontario Court of Appeals upheld the federal carbon tax, but the Alberta Court of Appeal ruled that the federal carbon tax was unconstitutional.

40   Supreme Court of Canada, "References re Greenhouse Gas Pollution Pricing Act," Case in Brief (25 March 2021). https://www.scc-csc.ca/case-dossier/cb/2021/38663-38781-39116-eng.aspx

41   J. Stephens Allan, *Report of the Public Inquiry into Anti-Alberta Energy Campaigns* (Government of Alberta, 30 July 2021), 649. https://open.alberta.ca/dataset/3176fd2d-670b-4c4a-b8a7-07383ae43743/resource/a814cae3-8dd2-4c9c-baf1-cf9cd364d2cb/download/energy-report-public-inquiry-anti-alberta-energy-campaigns-2021.pdf

42   Allan, *Report of the Public Inquiry into Anti-Alberta Energy Campaigns.*

43   Lisa Johnson, "No evidence of wrongdoing found in Allan inquiry report into 'Anti-Alberta' campaigns," *Edmonton Journal* (22 October 2021).

44   Alberta, *Hansard* (26 October 2021), 2.

45   Canadian Press, "Alberta revives turn-off-taps resources bill that sparked legal row with B.C.," *CBC News* (25 May 2021).

46   Chris Varcoe, "UCP not going to COP26 'gabfest,' promises new climate plan," *Calgary Herald* (26 October 2021).

47   Fair Deal Panel, *Report to Government* (May 2020). https://open.alberta.ca/dataset/d8933f27-5f81-4cbb-97c1-f56b45b09a74/resource/d5836820-d81f-4042-b24e-b04e012f4cde/download/fair-deal-panel-report-to-government-may-2020.pdf

48   Environment and Climate Change Canada, *2030 Emissions Reduction Plan: Canada's Next Steps for Clean Air and a Strong Economy* (2022). Available at https://www.canada.ca/content/dam/eccc/documents/pdf/climate-change/erp/Canada-2030-Emissions-Reduction-Plan-eng.pdf

49   Jason Nixon, "Alberta won't accept a climate plan that destroys its economy," *Edmonton Journal* (2 April 2022).

50   Kyle Bakx, "In new emissions plan, Ottawa gives oilpatch a pass—for now," *CBC News* (30 March 2022). https://www.cbc.ca/news/business/bakx-emissions-reductions-plan-oilpatch-1.6401297

51   Alberta Court of Appeal, "Reference re Impact Assessment Act, 2022 ABCA 165 (10 May 2022). https://www.albertacourts.ca/docs/default-source/ca/reference-re-impact-assessment-act-2022-abca-165.pdf?sfvrsn=8eeea683_5

52   Geoffrey Morgan, "'Heads exploding' in oilpatch, Alberta over appointment of former activist," *Calgary Herald* (27 October 2021).

53 Interview with Andrew Leach.

54 Don Braid, "In public shift, Kenney says Alberta has to go green over time," *Calgary Herald* (10 February 2020).

55 Braid, "In public shift."

56 Natural Resources Canada, "Carbon capture, utilization and storage strategy" (7 September 2021). https://www.nrcan.gc.ca/climate-change/canadas-green-future/carbon-capture-utilization-and-storage-strategy/23721

57 Graham Thomson, "Kenney's carbon capture conundrum: How do you fight Ottawa while also begging for money?" *CBC News* (12 March 2021).

58 Hannah Kost, "Alberta asks federal government to commit $30B to advance carbon capture technologies," *CBC News* (8 March 2021). https://www.cbc.ca/news/canada/calgary/ucp-federal-government-30-billion-carbon-capture-1.5941518

59 Kyle Bakx, "With a windfall from Ottawa comes great climate expectations for the oilpatch," *CBC News* (8 April 2022). https://www.cbc.ca/news/business/bakx-federal-budget-2022-ccs-ccus-1.6412524

60 Natural Resources Canada, *A Call to Action: A Canadian Roadmap for Small Modular Reactors* (November 2018). Available at https://smrroadmap.ca/wp-content/uploads/2018/11/SMRroadmap_EN_nov6_Web-1.pdf?x64773

61 New Brunswick, Ontario, Saskatchewan, *Collaboration Memorandum of Understanding* (1 December 2019). Available at https://news.ontario.ca/assets/files/20210430/eecbe8cbb264cd80f7d6bf96a672ef05.pdf

62 Jason Kenney, "Alberta signing on to support Small Modular Reactors" (7 August 2020). Available at https://www.facebook.com/kenneyjasont/videos/alberta-signing-on-to-support-small-modular-reactors/2392607921043337/

63 Alberta, "Alberta signs small modular nuclear reactor MOU," *News Release* (14 April 2021). Available at https://www.alberta.ca/release.cfm?xID=779532BE17742-9A86-61A0-8EE237BE8A6450E0

64 Ontario, New Brunswick, Alberta, Saskatchewan, *A Strategic Plan for the Deployment of Small Modular Reactors* (29 March 2022). Available at https://open.alberta.ca/publications/a-strategic-plan-for-the-deployment-of-small-modular-reactors

65 New Brunswick, Ontario, Saskatchewan, *Collaboration Memorandum of Understanding*, 2.

66 Giliberto Capano and Jun Jie Woo, "Resilience and robustness in policy design: a critical appraisal," *Policy Sciences* 50 (5 January 2017), 7. DOI: 10.1007/s11077-016-9273-x

Jason Kenney, Energy, and Pipelines in the 2019 Alberta Election: A Study in Hubris

Jean-Sébastien Rioux

Introduction

Between 1970 and 2015, for almost two generations but with one notable exception in the mid-1980s resulting from Pierre E. Trudeau's National Energy Program, Alberta has been a high-growth province, welcoming people, capital, and technologies largely linked to the development of the oil sands. Alberta's population grew from 1.6 million in 1971 to 4.4 million in 2021, mirroring the growth of its oil production, which averaged just over 1 million barrels per day in 1970 to about 4 million in 2021.[1] These fortunes have enabled Alberta to become a perennial "have" province since the 1960s, and thus a positive contributor to Canada's equalization payments, reflecting higher incomes linked to the economic value of the energy sector.

Those good times, however, have been declining since the global oil price collapse of 2014–2015, locking Alberta into a seemingly interminable recession that still endures: while the unemployment rate in 2013 averaged about 4.5 per cent, it reached an unimaginable rate of 15.8 per cent in June 2020, when Calgary made the national headlines as having the highest unemployment rate in Canada.[2] To be sure, this Canadian record was set during the global COVID-19 pandemic, but prior to that the unemployment rate did reach 9 per cent in 2016, still among the highest of any Canadian metropolitan area.[3]

It was thus during this long-term recession that Jason Kenney, who had been a federal member of parliament since 1997, decided to leave his seat in the House of Commons in September 2016 to seek the leadership of the Alberta Progressive Conservative (PC) Party, which he succeeded in achieving in March 2017. He then set his sights on uniting the PCs and the Wildrose Party, which happened in July 2017; he became the United Conservative Party (UCP)'s first leader in October of that year, then won his seat in the Legislative Assembly in a December 2017 by-election in the constituency of Calgary-Lougheed. His political acumen, tireless backroom work, and infamous blue Ford F-150 pickup truck were a testament to his determination, with a healthy balance of political capital thanks to having served with distinction in the Stephen Harper federal conservative cabinet. And while his ascension to become the leader of the united conservative movement in Alberta did not come without controversies—which are detailed in other chapters of this book—there was always a sense of inevitability to his goal of merging and leading the two centre-right parties in Alberta.

His election to the Legislative Assembly of Alberta in December 2017 afforded him the higher profile of leader of the opposition during the height of the energy policy crises faced by the Rachel Notley New Democratic Party (NDP) government, and about fifteen months to gather his forces to win the next provincial election, held in April 2019.

Relentlessly, the campaign focussed on the perceived shortcomings of the NDP government on the energy file: low oil prices, lack of pipeline take-away capacity, a growing flight of valuable capital away from Alberta's energy sector, and a growing environmental and activist-investor climate that hammered on the most valuable commodity produced in Canada: oil. Alberta faced anti-oil and anti-pipeline provinces to its west in British Columbia, and to the east in Québec—not to mention Prime Minister Justin Trudeau, whose cabinet had cancelled the Northern Gateway pipeline project in November 2016 and enacted Bill C-69 in June 2019—titled "The Modernization of the National Energy Board and Canadian Environmental Assessment Agency"—but which conservatives across Canada would label the "no more pipelines act."

Jason Kenney's promise to Alberta's electorate went along these lines: elect me, and I can fix this. Elect me, and I can speak to my fellow premiers across the country and stand toe-to-toe with Justin Trudeau. Elect me and I will go to New York and Washington to speak to the Wall Street investors, policymakers, and lobbyists; they will listen to me. I can bring them around and we'll get our energy industry back on track. I'll get Alberta open for business again.[4]

These promises worked to get him and the UCP elected to form government with 54.8 per cent of the popular vote and sixty-three of the eighty-seven seats in the Legislative Assembly, but were predicated on the notion that the Notley NDP government had done nothing to help stave off the threats to Alberta's energy sector, and that the NDP was somehow responsible for consistently lower oil prices for Alberta crude oil, for the lack of pipeline capacity, etc. (see Graham Thomson's chapter). Merriam-Webster defines *hubris* as "exaggerated pride or self-confidence," while the Cambridge online dictionary defines it as "a way of talking or behaving that is too proud."[5] While perhaps a difficult concept to use as a theoretical framework and with which one can deduce and test hypotheses, in this chapter I use *hubris* as an analytical framework to highlight the gap between rhetoric and action that characterizes the Kenney-led UCP government.[6]

Hubris in Politics and Decision-Making

While "hubris" is not a utilized (or even a developed) theoretical framework in political science, the concept has been used in academic literature to provide a basis to analyze decision-making in the context of what political science and public policy literature would call complex and even "wicked problems." Among the most difficult public policy dilemmas, complex or wicked problems are "characterized by conflicting values and perspectives, uncertainties about complex causal relationships, and debate about the impacts of policy options."[7] For example, Sovacool and Cooper analyze four of the largest energy "megaprojects" ever developed in Asia to understand why these massive undertakings all went well over budget, over timeline, and generally failed to meet their intended expectations. The authors point out that studying these megaprojects is worthy because of the massive investments required, "their failures have greater relative impacts on markets . . . [and] also produces greater opportunity costs."[8] Moreover, scholars are forced "to not view megaprojects as a 'black box'" and to focus on the accountabilities for their failure.[9] They find that, despite multiple examples of failures, cost and time overruns, project proponents keep pushing for more megaprojects for a few reasons, such as the "seduction of standardization"[10] and the "allure of modernism."[11] In other words, the previous project proponents failed because they had inferior designs, technologies, or project managers. The hubris of proposing more megaprojects is that this time, this project won't fail like the previous ones did because we know what to do and what to avoid. But megaprojects never get better because of the hubris displayed each time a new proposal is created.

The well-known Canadian trade negotiator Michael Hart wrote about hubris in the context of global climate change policy (which, incidentally, is often used as a prime example of a wicked problem due to all the complexities involved). Hart's thesis is that the endogenous (anthropomorphic) and exogenous (geophysical, solar) causes of climate change are extremely complex, and the possible solutions are even more so because of the nature of State sovereignty, macro and micro-economic levers and impact, global trade, etc. Therefore, anyone or any organization proposing a clear set of policy responses to impact climate change amounts to hubris.[12]

One final example to illustrate the concept of *hubris* in public policy is drawn from the field of international development studies. Writing about the disproportionate role of International Organizations (IOs) in shaping domestic policies in many African countries, Professor Desmond Odugu describes the "intellectual hubris of ascribing IOs with objectivity and neutrality" in designing public policies, because they are by their nature founded on the neoliberal ideologies of the prevailing notions of "development" found in donor States.[13] In his analysis, it is hubris to think that adopting public policies say, on education or social welfare, developed in the IO headquarters of New York, Paris, or Geneva will be relevant and transferable to Sub-Saharan Africa.

It would be difficult in many specific cases to separate true hubris from the normal exuberance and excitement of a political rally; politicians are as good as any Hollywood comedian in warming up a crowd or convincing them to take time out of their day to cast a ballot. But perhaps we can infer—particularly in consideration of the aforementioned Sovacool and Cooper study of energy megaprojects—that repetitive failures, supported by lofty rhetoric, can point to that direction. Whether the policy issues of the day revolve around energy policy or the province's COVID-19 response, hubris and groupthink are as damaging as bad data and information in developing policy.

The Global Energy Collapse of 2015 and the Alberta New Democratic Party's Response

The Alberta NDP electoral victory happened during a serious economic downturn linked to a crash of commodities prices, mostly of oil and gas.[14] Successive Alberta governments have relied heavily on non-renewable resource revenues—i.e., royalties, fees, and taxes linked to oil and gas production—to the tune of up to 30 per cent of its budgetary expenditures; the 2014–2016 downturn was calamitous for provincial revenues. In 2016, "real per capita resource revenues collapsed to a level not seen since the 1950s."[15] In addition to the global factors causing the collapse of oil and gas prices,[16] the long-term prospects for further energy and pipeline development projects in Alberta and Canada were, by 2015, in serious decline. Detailed in chapters by Gillian Steward and Deborah Yedlin in *Orange Chinook: Politics in the New Alberta*, the public's appetite for drilling more oil and building more pipelines had already been waning due to a confluence of events.[17] An increasingly challenging social environment for the energy sector began in July 2006 when the Ralph Klein government decided to shine a spotlight on Alberta's burgeoning oil sands by displaying giant bitumen hauling trucks on the National Mall in Washington, DC, as part of Alberta's exhibit at the Smithsonian Folklife Festival.[18] Two experienced energy reporters, Jason Fekete and Chris Varcoe, wrote that the "stunt backfired" and "the truck unexpectedly became a powerful symbol and prime target for a U.S. environmental movement searching for a focal point for its next campaign."[19]

In quick succession after the oil sands were elevated into the public (and environmental groups') spotlight, several disasters struck and ensured that oil became synonymous with risk and danger. In April 2008 an estimated 1,600 ducks became disoriented during a spring storm and landed on a tailings pond, killing them. Two years later, in April 2010, the BP Deepwater Horizon offshore platform exploded and created the largest oil spill in history. That same year, an Enbridge-owned pipeline failed in the Kalamazoo River in Michigan and in July 2013, a train carrying light crude oil derailed and exploded in downtown Lac Mégantic, Québec, killing forty-seven people and destroying half of the town.

These disasters happened in the context of several major pipeline projects under development at the same time, and the desire to develop *more* of Alberta's oil sands were also tied to building the needed take-away capacity—all while the environmental movement was gaining momentum thanks to burgeoning social media.[20] Caught in these crosshairs were the TransCanada Keystone XL project, proposed in 2010 and ultimately aborted in 2021; TransCanada's Energy East pipeline project, proposed in 2013 and abandoned in 2017; Imperial Oil's Mackenzie Valley Gas Pipeline project, first proposed in the 1970s and also abandoned in 2017; Enbridge's Northern Gateway pipeline project, proposed in 2002 and killed by a federal cabinet decision in 2017; and the Kinder Morgan Trans Mountain Expansion pipeline project, first proposed in 2012 and may actually be completed in the next few years. It should be noted that during all these tumultuous events that directly affected Alberta's—and therefore Canada's—economic potential, the federal government under Stephen Harper was largely uninvolved and perhaps even unhelpful in resolving some of the issues that were actually under federal purview.[21]

As Rachel Notley's government came to power, all these issues were happening in real time, and faced with the greatest threat to Alberta's economic future in decades, she became "the unlikely advocate for Alberta's energy development."[22] Notley went to work immediately to strike a "grand bargain" that would hopefully demonstrate to the other Canadian provinces that Alberta was serious about reducing its environmental and carbon footprint, in exchange with more positive engagement over pipelines. Aware that a key UN climate conference (COP-21) was soon to be held in Paris in December 2015 and hoping to have something to show to other jurisdictions, the investor community, and perhaps even some climate groups, her government produced the Climate Leadership Plan in November, right before the COP-21 meeting. In it was a hard cap on oil sands emissions of 100 Mt; it introduced a levy, or tax, on oil and gas consumption; it accelerated the phaseout of coal-fired electrical plants; and it developed new programs and funding to lower individual, household, and industrial emissions (see Duane Bratt's chapter). These initiatives were meant to coordinate with the newly elected federal liberal government's environment policies and to "soften opposition by opponents in other provinces to proposed new oil pipelines."[23] Moreover, Notley outright embraced the energy sector by proposing several policies to diversify Alberta's energy markets and embracing pipeline construction in the May 2016 Throne Speech.[24]

Finally, another crisis hit during the fall of 2018: as oil prices recovered around the world (except in Alberta due to our lack of pipeline takeaway capacity), some key US refineries had to shut down during a severe hurricane season on the Gulf Coast. These events caused a massive differential between the price of US West Texas Intermediate (WTI) crude oil and Alberta's Western Canada Select (WCS) crude, where Alberta oil was selling at a 70 per cent discount. The Notley NDP government responded by appointing three "special envoys" to study the issue and report their recommendations directly to her.[25] The panel eventually proposed, and the NDP government acted upon its recommendation, curtailing production to reduce the glut of oil, and leasing 4,400 rail cars to transport 120,000 barrels per day of crude.

At the same time, the relatively new NDP government in British Columbia, made possible by a deal with three Green Party MLAs to ensure that the NDP had one more seat than the long-governing Liberals, began litigating and legislating against the Trans Mountain Expansion project (TMX), which would have been the single outlet for Alberta crude oil outside the US. The legal and regulatory environment became so fraught that Kinder Morgan, the TMX proponent, announced that it was seriously considering abandoning the pipeline project. In a last-ditch effort to save Canada's investment climate, the Trudeau government negotiated the purchase of the Kinder Morgan assets for US$4.5 billion and vowed to see the project completed.[26]

All the events described above created a climate in which oil prices (and thus, revenue for the province) were perennially low due to mostly exogenous factors; the necessary infrastructure to access global markets (e.g., pipelines) were stalled, thus exacerbating the longer-term impacts of low oil prices; and the broader societal environment to address the first two were going against the province's and the energy sector's interests. By 2019, an estimated US$30 billion in foreign capital had left Alberta, as companies divested assets in the province.[27] Thus was the energy policy climate as the 2019 provincial elections were being contested. One thing seems obvious, however, upon recounting the events of 2015–2019: there is no evidence that Premier Notley did "nothing" to counter the unfortunate series of events. To the contrary, Notley consulted a broad range of stakeholders at every decision point and convened expert panels to solicit advice.[28]

The 2019 Election: Only the United Conservative Party Can Revive Alberta's Energy Sector

Jason Kenney saw many of these issues transpire firsthand as leader of Her Majesty's Loyal Opposition in the Legislative Assembly of Alberta. The situation for oil, gas, and pipelines was dire, and politically, he had two easy scapegoats around which to mount a strong electoral challenge: first, Premier Rachel Notley as his main "villain," and second, Prime Minister Justin Trudeau, son of the man who imposed the despised National Energy Program in 1980, which many Albertans were still cursing nearly forty years later.

Justin Trudeau's policies on energy and environment at times seemed purposeful, and at others seemed random and spiteful. In his initial prime ministerial campaign in 2015, he had taken aim at the venerable National Energy Board as having lost the trust of the people. His government introduced Bill C-69 in February 2018, titled "An Act to enact the Impact Assessment Act and the Canadian Energy Regulator Act, to amend the Navigation Protection Act and to make consequential amendments to other Acts." It eventually replaced the National Energy Board with the Canadian Energy Regulator, and the Canadian Environmental Assessment Agency with the Impact Assessment Agency of Canada. The changes to the existing way of assessing major projects were so massive that Jason Kenney and other pro-energy opponents would dub the bill the "No More Pipelines Act."[29]

Indeed, Justin Trudeau seemed somewhat schizophrenic when it came to his support of pipelines: his government strongly stated that the

TMX was in Canada's national interest by purchasing it; yet his support for other pipelines was nonexistent—his cabinet delivered the fatal blow to the Northern Gateway pipeline project in 2016 by declaring that it was not in Canada's national interest to approve it. This was in addition to his government's Bill C-48, the Oil Tanker Moratorium Act banning oil tanker traffic from the northern tip of Vancouver Island to the Alaska border, thus ensuring that no pipeline can be built around Kitimat or Prince Rupert. Bill C-69 and the new, retroactively applied criteria for assessing the proposed Energy East pipelines was one reason why TC Energy abandoned the proposed project to carry Alberta (and Bakken) oil across Canada, to the Irving refinery in New Brunswick—another reason being Quebec's strong opposition to it.

On 19 March 2019, Premier Notley called the election to be held on 16 April. Riding the issues described above, Jason Kenney "made his first official campaign appearance at an Edmonton-area energy services company where he accused Notley of pandering to Prime Minister Justin Trudeau and driving the province to 'economic stagnation.'"[30] His slogans were "Alberta strong & free" and "getting Alberta back to work" as the unemployment rate still hovered around 7 per cent in Alberta.[31]

The UCP election platform was a staggering 114 pages in length. It listed three priorities, which are discussed in other chapters, but which all wrapped around the energy sector: "getting Albertans back to work," "making life better for Albertans," and "standing up for Alberta."[32] More specifically, it contained measures such as promises to

- repeal the carbon tax (pp. 17–18 of the UCP platform);

- create jobs in oil and gas (pp. 30–33);

- get pipelines built, including several items to fight Bill C-69 (p. 94);

- stand up to foreign influences—including a $30 million war room (pp. 95–97); and

- unusually specific "to-do" items like "[f]ire Ed Whittingham from his position at the Alberta Energy Regulator" (p. 97).

Jason Kenney relentlessly campaigned on these issues, with the ubiquitous UCP campaign slogan of "jobs, economy, pipelines"; unsurprisingly given the moribund state of Alberta's economy in the spring of 2019, the UCP won.

In his victory speech on the night of 16 April 2019, and true to his pipeline agenda, he not only thanked electors and laid out his electoral commitments, but also included a section aimed directly at Quebec Premier François Legault and Quebeckers in general, in which he spoke in French and repeated many key points in English. In some of the French passages that he did not repeat in English, he talks about the natural alliance between Quebec and Alberta, of his admiration for Premier Legault, and about the tough economic times Albertans are experiencing because there are no outlets for our crude oil. Of the passages that he spoke in both languages, he touched on the core of his message that if Quebec is to keep receiving equalization payments, it behooves the province to support the Western Canadian industry that is chiefly responsible for generating the wealth that keeps the dollars flowing:

And now I would like to speak directly to our friends in Quebec.

We need pipelines for the prosperity of all Canadians, including Quebeckers!

The decision we need to make is not difficult: must we favour Alberta's oil, which is produced at the highest standards of environmental and social responsibility? Or must we choose oil from the United States and foreign dictatorships?

If Quebec and other provinces want to accept massive fiscal transfers generated in Alberta, then please help us develop our resources and get them to global markets! It's a win-win!

Let us work together to strengthen our shared prosperity in the Canadian federation![33]

It is worth recalling that although Legault had been elected Premier of Quebec only six months previously in October 2018, he had been a Member of the National Assembly as a *Parti Québécois* MNA and cabinet minister for eleven years, from 1998 to 2009. Then, after a brief departure from politics he co-founded the *Coalition Avenir Québec* (CAQ) in 2011, and he was re-elected to the National Assembly in 2012 as leader of the CAQ and second opposition leader. The point is that he was a savvy and long-serving politician, minister, and party leader with over seventeen years of elected experience by that point.

So it was that Premier Legault did not flatter that easily, and when reporters asked for his reaction to Premier Kenney's speech the next day he responded that while he congratulated him on his victory, all political parties in Quebec oppose any new oil pipeline: "[w]hat I am saying is there is no social acceptability for a new oil pipeline in Quebec," thus putting the notion of reviving Energy East to rest.[34]

That *contretemps* aside, once his cabinet was named and work in the Legislature resumed, Kenney launched his "summer of repeal," where many programs and policies enacted by the previous Notley government were overturned and/or replaced. Indeed, Bill 1 of the new 30th Legislature was titled "An Act to Repeal the Carbon Tax ($)"—with the dollar sign indeed on the actual title of the Bill and introduced by Premier Kenney himself. The title was even somewhat misleading because Bill 1 did more than simply repeal the carbon tax; in only one section consisting of seventeen words, it said, "The Climate Leadership Act is repealed immediately at the beginning of the day on May 30, 2019."[35] This was to be expected since he had campaigned on it, but nevertheless came as a shock to many corporations that had been working to implement all the provisions of the Climate Leadership Act (and likely violated energy analyst Peter Tertzakian's "First Rule for attracting investors," which is "Create Policy Certainty").[36]

Continuing the UCP's "summer of repeal" were Bill 2, An Act to Make Alberta Open for Business; Bill 3, Job Creation Tax Cut (Alberta Corporate Tax Amendment) Act; and Bill 4, styled the Red Tape Reduction Act. Significantly, Bill 3 cut the corporate tax rate from 12 per cent to 11 per cent and eventually to 8 per cent in 2022; yet, despite the electoral rhetoric about creating jobs, supported by an actual corporate tax cut, global majors were still exiting Alberta in 2019 and early 2020. And the "summer of repeal" would not be complete without the "fighting back" strategy, so in June 2019 Kenney announced that he would soon launch an energy war room to counter misinformation related to oil and gas—which led to the incorporation of the Canadian Energy Centre Limited in December 2019 (see Brad Clark's chapter).

In spite of all this "fighting back" and "restoring the Alberta Advantage," in October 2019 the Norwegian Sovereign Wealth Fund announced that it was divesting its shares in the largest oil sands operators in Alberta (Cenovus, Suncor, Imperial Oil, and Husky); in February 2020, Teck Resources announced it was withdrawing its application to build the $20 billion Frontier oil sands project; a few months later in July 2020, French energy giant Total announced it was writing off $9.3-billion worth of oil sands assets in Alberta; later that same month, Deutsche Bank announced it would henceforth ban financing of oil sands operations. Jason Kenney's policies were not having the intended effect at all, and then a global pandemic only made matters worse for him—not only on the health policy front—but on the energy front as well.

Kenney, COVID, and KXL

By mid-March 2020 the global COVID-19 pandemic had reached Alberta and it was now our turn to begin society-wide lockdown measures (see Lisa Young, chapter twenty). Domestic and international air travel restrictions, border closures, and stay-at-home measures, while not stopping the spread of the virus, certainly stopped vehicular, air, and rail travel, not to mention cruise ships and holiday travel. This caused an unseen-before drop in oil prices due to an estimated 90 per cent drop in demand: by April 2020 oil prices even dropped into *negative* territory for a few days when WTI traded at (-)$37 per barrel, meaning that "producers were paying buyers to take their product."[37] Indeed, during the month of April 2020, WCS averaged only $3.50 per barrel,[38] placing a huge strain on revenues but more importantly, further demonstrating Alberta's continued lack of take-away capacity as the glut of oil simply filled all reservoirs with nowhere to go.

Ironically, the UCP government was now in a very similar position to that of the Notley government less than two years previously, in 2018, when a North American glut of oil caused prices to drop and caused the NDP government to stand the expert advisory panel that ultimately recommended the curtailment and crude-by-rail actions described previously: it had to do something to help the energy sector in this unprecedented situation. So Kenney's government—like Trudeau before him—decided to purchase (part of) a pipeline.

Prime Minister Trudeau's government had taken a significant—yet calculated risk—when it purchased Kinder Morgan's Trans Mountain pipeline and related assets in May 2019 for US$4.5 billion, not to mention the actual construction costs. It was a calculated risk because the federal government had many of the necessary levers to—in Roger Fisher and William Ury's famous phrase—"get to yes" on a decision to construct.[39] The federal government "owns" the Crown-Indigenous relationship, for example, as well as the purse strings and legal authority over things like marine spill response. Therefore, if it did a good job on meeting the needs of various stakeholders, its investment would likely pay off and its plan, after all, was to hold on to the investment until it could find another suitable commercial buyer for the project and assets.[40] Premier Jason Kenney's reaction to the federal purchase of the Trans Mountain Expansion project was "cautious," and he was quoted as saying he wouldn't celebrate "until shovels are in the ground and the project . . . is built."[41]

Then, just a few months after the federal cabinet did give its final approval for the construction to begin in the summer of 2019, the US federal election cycle kicked in when Democratic Party hopefuls began announcing their candidacies in the summer and fall of 2019. Over the next few months, Senator Joe Biden locked up enough Democratic state primaries and caucuses by May 2020 to secure the nomination, and indeed was officially selected by the democrats at their August nomination convention to face Donald J. Trump in the November 2020 election.[42] Senator Biden had been Barack Obama's vice-president for all of Obama's eight years as US president and therefore had a front row seat to Obama's opposition to the Keystone XL pipeline, which was still embroiled in judicial contestations in Nebraska and even in a US District Court in Montana, and therefore not yet formally approved for completion. Biden had also reiterated his opposition to Keystone XL during the campaign.

It was in this context that on 31 March 2020, Premier Jason Kenney announced it was investing $1.5 billion to "cover planned construction costs through the end of the year," with an additional $6 billion loan guarantee, stating that the "investment in Keystone XL is a bold move to re-take control of our province's economic destiny and put it firmly back in the hands of the owners of our natural resources, the people of Alberta."[43] To be sure, this Kenney government investment was on-brand with the 2019 platform of "economy, jobs and pipelines," but also somewhat incomprehensible because he seemed to be betting either that the legal issues would be resolved, and President Trump would approve it in the next six months, or squarely betting that Trump would win the November 2020 election. Even more incomprehensibly, Kenney stated a few months later that his government made that decision because he "doesn't trust Prime Minister Justin Trudeau to stick with the completion of the Trans Mountain pipeline Ottawa bought in 2018," and that "the federal Liberals want to destroy Canada's oil and gas sector . . . I was not prepared to put all of our eggs in the basket of the Justin Trudeau-owned pipeline."[44]

The logic of Kenney's position is unusual: he did not "trust" the federal prime minister to follow through on resolving the legal issues and constructing a pipeline situated entirely in Canada, where the feds hold most levers to make it happen, yet his counter-move was to invest even more money—comparatively speaking on a per capita basis—to own a stake in a pipeline in which the provincial government had almost no legal power to influence because most of it was across an international border—and where a very consequential election was to be held mere months later. Alberta held none of the levers to influence the legal and regulatory processes or outcomes. Was that hubris-level confidence on display?[45]

Perhaps so, because Jason Kenney seemed convinced that he could achieve a feat that neither Jim Prentice nor Rachel Notley provincially, nor Stephen Harper or Justin Trudeau federally, had been able to accomplish: to convince American governors, legislators, and others of the importance of the Keystone XL pipeline. Like other Alberta premiers before him, Kenney had

> [a]ppealed to pro-pipeline American governors and unions for help, tried to get as much of the pipeline constructed as possible before the Nov. 3 presidential election, and vowed to use every legal means to protect the investment . . . Alberta's government also recently approved more than $1 million to hire influential

Capitol Hill lobbyists and communication experts to help win support in Washington for the pipeline and other trade interests south of the border.[46]

These tactics have been used by Alberta premiers before. Jim Prentice details in *Triple Crown: Winning Canada's Energy Future* his trip to Washington and New York to speak to politicians and investors, and the efforts deployed by Alberta's and Canada's representatives in Washington on the pipeline files.[47] Premier Notley travelled to Washington and New York to deliver the same messages. But in Jason Kenney's worldview, perhaps *his* plan would have a higher chance of success.

What eventually happened is known: Joe Biden won the November 2020 presidential election and was sworn in at noon on 20 January 2021. That very afternoon on his first day in office, he revoked the permit and effectively killed the project. Premier Kenney reacted by saying that the decision was a "gut punch to the Alberta and Canadian economies" and an "insult" to the cross-border relationship, and called on the federal government to consider retaliatory measures.[48] He also noted that as a part-owner of the pipeline, Alberta would have a seat at the courthouse to defend their interests under the Canada-US-Mexico Trade Agreement; these steps were not to become necessary, as TC Energy formally terminated the Keystone XL project in June 2021, leaving Albertans on the hook for $1.3 billion.[49]

The End of Hubris?

As I mentioned towards the beginning of the chapter, a "hubris hypothesis" is difficult to operationalize and measure, in part because "energizing the base" and "hubris" could look alike during a campaign. Perhaps one defining characteristic of hubris might be the *inability* or *unwillingness* to change course even in the face of contrary evidence.

Another related concept might be groupthink, which Irving Janis defined as a psychological drive for consensus that suppresses dissent and minimizes any systematic appraisal of alternative choices in decision-making settings.[50] *Calgary Sun* columnist Rick Bell has written that Premier Kenney does not consult widely, and often calls him "Professor Kenney" because of his "know-it-all" attitude.[51]

Whatever scholarly analysis may eventually emerge from a "hubris hypothesis," we can tentatively and likely correctly assert that Jason Kenney has, to date, failed to deliver the results he campaigned on the energy, jobs, and pipelines fronts: oil prices are still well below WTI average,[52] unemployment is still stubbornly high at 7.9 per cent,[53] investments have declined by $50 billion in 2020 in spite of his corporate tax cuts,[54] and no new pipelines have been approved or built—except for the one owned by the Canadian government. To be sure, the global COVID-19 pandemic caused the drop in oil demand and prices, but no one cut Rachel Notley much slack when other global forces were at play in the oil price collapse of 2018, and she was forced to take unprecedented action as well.

But to add insult to injury in Jason Kenney's platform and further contrast his rhetoric with events happening "on the ground," two news items dropped in October 2021 that further undermined Kenney's pro-pipeline stance and constant messaging of the "Alberta Advantage." On 1 October 2021, the Canadian Energy Pipeline Association (CEPA), which is the industry association for Canada's gas and liquid pipeline owners and operators, announced that after almost thirty years of advocacy and representation, it was ceasing operations on 31 December 2021. The short news release cites "recent changes to CEPA's membership which makes it no longer feasible to carry on operations and effectively execute CEPA's mandate in the future."[55] Indeed, three of the largest association members had left the organization since 2019—Enbridge, Pembina, and TC Energy—but one reason discussed by experts is simply that there were no new energy pipelines being proposed or planned in Canada by anyone, so an industry-wide advocacy mandate was now moot.[56]

Another negative news item that recently came out is that for the second year in a row, there was a net *outmigration* from Alberta to other provinces. In other words, Alberta is losing more people to other provinces than are coming into Alberta, particularly in the crucial youth demographic, raising concerns that "a brain drain has begun."[57] Alberta's overall population has still grown by just over 20,000 people due to immigration and natural population replacement, but the Alberta Advantage no longer seems attractive to the eighteen-to-twenty-four-year-old demographic.

In conclusion, no one knows when—or even whether—the global economy will revert to a pre-pandemic "normal" with respect to demand for oil and gas. But we can confidently predict that the Trans Mountain Expansion pipeline will likely be the last major piece of linear energy infrastructure to be built in Canada, and we can predict that most countries and even global corporations are moving to a lower carbon future. Whether Jason Kenney's psychological make up tends to hubris, exuberance, or a victim of groupthink, the best way out of the current doldrums is to "be more like Rachel" and consult more broadly with stakeholders. listen to differing voices, look beyond hydrocarbons to fuel Alberta's economy, and embrace the opportunities coming from outside traditional resource sectors.

NOTES

1   See Alberta Economic Dashboard, "Net Migration, 1946–2021," https://economicdashboard.alberta.ca/NetMigration and "Oil Production," https://economicdashboard.alberta.ca/OilProduction (both accessed 28 September 2021).

2   Melissa Gilligan and Caley Ramsay, "Calgary's unemployment rate the highest in Canada for second straight month," *Global News*, 7 September 2020, https://globalnews.ca/news/7316107/calgary-edmonton-alberta-unempyment-rate-august-2020/ (accessed 29 September 2021).

3   See Alberta Economic Dashboard, "Unemployment Rate," https://economicdashboard.alberta.ca/Unemployment (accessed 28 September 2021).

4   National Post, "Jason Kenney's prepared victory speech in full after UCP wins majority in Alberta election," 17 April 2019, https://nationalpost.com/news/canada/read-jason-kenneys-prepared-victory-speech-in-full-after-ucp-wins-majority-in-alberta-election (accessed 29 September 2021).

5   Merriam-Webster Dictionary, "Hubris," https://www.merriam-webster.com/dictionary/hubris; and Cambridge Dictionary Online, "Hubris," https://dictionary.cambridge.org/dictionary/english/hubris (both accessed 16 September 2021).

6   Although beyond the scope of this chapter, the concept of hubris may also explain some of Premier Kenney's actions during the global COVID-19 pandemic. Two examples come to mind: first is the now-infamous "Open for Summer" announcement in June 2021 that was purportedly based on Kenney's confidence in one British epidemiological model he was shown; and a second example of this excess of confidence is his aide Matt Wolf's June 2021 Tweet saying, "The pandemic is ending. Accept it," (see https://twitter.com/mattwolfab/status/1400182922427043840?lang=en).

7   Brian Head, "Understanding 'wicked' policy problems," *Policy Options/Options Politiques*, 9 January 2018, https://policyoptions.irpp.org/magazines/january-2018/understanding-wicked-policy-problems/ (accessed 16 September 2021).

8   Benjamin Sovacool and Christopher J. Cooper, *The Governance of Energy Megaprojects: Politics, Hubris and Energy Security* (Northampton, MA: Edward Elgar, 2013), 4.

9   *Ibid.*

10 Sovacool and Cooper, *The Governance of Energy Megaprojects*, 20.

11 Sovacool and Cooper, *The Governance of Energy Megaprojects*, 22.

12 Michael Hart, *Hubris: The Troubling Science, Economics, and Politics of Climate Change* (Ottawa, ON: Compleat Desktops Publishing, 2015.)

13 Desmond Ikenna Odugu, "International Corporate Politics and the Hubris of Development Discourses," in *Indigenous Discourses on Knowledge and Development in Africa*, eds. Edward Shizha and Ali A. Abdi (New York: Routledge, 2015), 156.

14 John Gibson, "Alberta recession one of the most severe ever, TD Economics report finds," *CBC News*, 19 July 2016, https://www.cbc.ca/news/canada/calgary/td-economics-report-alberta-recession-gdp-forecast-1.3684056 (accessed 24 September 2021).

15 Ron Kneebone and Jennifer Zwicker, "Fiscal Constraints on the Orange Chinook," in *Orange Chinook: Politics in the New Alberta*, ed. Duane Bratt, Keith Brownsey, Richard Sutherland, and David Taras (Calgary: University of Calgary Press), 232.

16 Prentice and Rioux discuss some of these causes in chapter 2 of their book. In summary, the refinement of hydraulic fracturing and deep horizontal drilling techniques enabled the US to unexpectedly double its oil and gas production between 2008 and 2015, creating a glut in global markets, thus lowering prices and decreasing imports. Russia and OPEC collaborated to increase their production to undercut American domestic investments and prices plunged further. Alberta was caught in the middle, with no option to access oil customers outside the US due to lack of crude oil export capacity and our reliance on that single customer. See Jim Prentice and Jean-Sébastien Rioux, *Triple Crown: Winning Canada's Energy Future* (Toronto: HarperCollins, 2017).

17 Duane Bratt, Keith Brownsey, Richard Sutherland and David Taras, eds., *Orange Chinook: Politics in the New Alberta* (Calgary: University of Calgary Press, 2019).

18 See Gordon Kent, "Big trucks, dead ducks put Alberta's oilsands under environmental scrutiny," *Calgary Herald*, 28 September 2017, https://calgaryherald.com/business/energy/big-trucks-and-dead-ducks-put-albertas-oilsands-in-the-environmental-spotlight (accessed 27 September 2021); and Deborah Yedlin, "Notley: The Accidental Pipeline Advocate," in Bratt et al., *Orange Chinook*, 191–206.)

19 Jason Fekete and Chris Varcoe, "How an Alberta PR stunt backfired in the U.S., sparking a decade of oilsands opposition," *National Post*, 25 July 2016, https://nationalpost.com/news/canada/a-decade-of-bitumen-battles-how-10-years-of-fighting-over-oilsands-affects-energy-environment-debate-today (accessed 19 September 2021).

20 Yedlin, "Notley."

21 See Prentice and Rioux, *Triple Crown*, and Yedlin, "Notley."

22 Yedlin, "Notley," 206.

23 Gillian Steward, "Betting on Bitumen: Lougheed, Klein and Notley," in Bratt et al., *Orange Chinook*, 160.

24   The Honourable Lois E. Mitchell, CM, AOE, LLD, *Alberta Throne Speech*, 8 May 2016, https://www.poltext.org/sites/poltext.org/files/discoursV2/Alberta/AB_DT_2016_29_02.txt (accessed 26 September 2021).

25   The CBC reported that on 19 November 2018, WCS crude oil closed at US$17.43 a barrel, while WTI closed at US$57.02 (CBC News, "Notley appoints 3 envoys to find solutions to oil-price differential," https://www.cbc.ca/news/canada/edmonton/notley-announcement-oil-differential-1.4911499 (accessed 28 September 2021).

26   Steward, "Betting on Bitumen."

27   Kevin Orland, "US$30-billion oilsands exodus marches on," *Calgary Herald*, 26 August 2019: NP6.

28   Steward, "Betting on Bitumen," 161.

29   Josh K. Elliott, "Why critics fear Bill C-69 will be a 'pipeline killer,'" *Global News*, 21 June 2019, https://globalnews.ca/news/5416659/what-is-bill-c69-pipelines/ (accessed 29 September 2021).

30   Canadian Press, "Leaders set sights on each other as Alberta election called for April 16," 19 March 2019, https://www.ctvnews.ca/canada/leaders-set-sights-on-each-other-as-alberta-election-called-for-april-16-1.4342401 (accessed 28 September 2021).

31   Alberta Economic Dashboard, "Unemployment Rate," https://economicdashboard.alberta.ca/Unemployment (accessed 28 September 2021).

32   United Conservative Party, *Alberta Strong & Free: Getting Alberta Back to Work* (2019 electoral platform), https://albertastrongandfree.ca/getting-alberta-back-to-work/ (accessed 29 September 2021).

33   National Post, "Jason Kenney's prepared victory speech."

34   Jacques Boissinot, "Legault congratulates Kenney but says Quebec won't accept a new oil pipeline," *Globe and Mail*, 17 April 2019, https://www.theglobeandmail.com/canada/article-legault-congratulates-kenney-but-says-quebec-wont-accept-a-new-oil-2/ (accessed 16 September 2021.)

35   Legislative Assembly of Alberta, 2019 Bill 1. First Session, 30th Legislature, 68 Elizabeth II, https://docs.assembly.ab.ca/LADDAR_files/docs/bills/bill/legislature_30/session_1/20190521_bill-001.pdf.

36   Peter Tertzakian, "What is 'green energy' anyway? For investors, fifty shades of green really means fifty shades of risk," *Calgary Herald*, 16 June 2021: A16.

37   Allison Bench, "Oil prices are in the negative: COVID-19 rules to stay home played a huge part," *Global News*, 20 April 2020, https://globalnews.ca/news/6844391/coronavirus-oil-prices-stay-home-rules/ (accessed 26 September 2021).

38   Alberta Economic Dashboard, "Oil Prices," https://economicdashboard.alberta.ca/OilPrice (accessed 28 September 2021).

39   Roger Fisher and William Ury, *Getting to Yes: Negotiating Agreement Without Giving In* (New York: Penguin Books, 1991.)

40   Kathleen Harris, "Liberals to buy Trans Mountain pipeline for $4.5B to ensure expansion is built," *CBC News*, 29 May 2018, https://www.cbc.ca/news/politics/liberals-trans-mountain-pipeline-kinder-morgan-1.4681911 (accessed 29 September 2021).

41   Dean Bennett, "Jason Kenney gives cautious praise for federal Trans Mountain approval, says Trudeau needs to do more," *National Post*, 18 June 2019, https:// nationalpost.com/news/politics/take-two-alberta-lauds-federal-re-approval-of-trans-mountain-pipeline-project (accessed 29 September 2021).

42   Scott Detrow, "Biden Formally Clinches Democratic Nomination, While Gaining Steam Against Trump," *NPR*, 5 June 2020, https://www.npr.org/2020/06/05/869553801/ biden-formally-secures-democratic-nomination-while-gaining-steam-against-trump (accessed 29 September 2021).

43   Nicole Gibillini, "Kenney aims to 're-take control' by investing US$1.1B in Keystone XL," *BNN Bloomberg News*, 31 March 2020, https://www.bnnbloomberg.ca/alberta-investing-us-1-1-billion-in-keystone-xl-pipeline-1.1415107 (accessed 29 September 2021).

44   Emma Graney, "Keystone pipeline investment a hedge against Trudeau 'political risk,' Kenney says," *Globe and Mail Report on Business*, 13 November 2020, https://www. theglobeandmail.com/business/article-keystone-pipeline-investment-a-hedge-against-trudeau-political-risk/ (accessed 26 September 2021).

45   In the same article cited previously, journalist Emma Graney writes that in an interview with conservative podcaster Corey Morgan, "Mr. Kenney also took a swipe at Michigan's Governor, Gretchen Whitmer, and its Attorney-General, Dana Nessel, calling them 'brain dead' over the state's legal challenge in the summer to try and decommission the Enbridge Inc. Line 5 oil pipeline . . . 'I mean, how brain dead do you have to be to try to shut off your largest source of energy?' [Kenney said]" (*ibid.*).

46   Kyle Baxx, "Why Kenney is having a rougher ride than Trudeau with his pipeline purchase," *CBC News*, 19 January 2021, https://www.cbc.ca/news/business/trans-mountain-keystone-pipeline-trudeau-kenney-1.5877983 (accessed 26 September 2021).

47   Prentice and Rioux, *Triple Crown*.

48   Robert Tuttle, "Jason Kenney calls Biden's Keystone XL cancellation an 'insult' as he urges retaliation," *BNN Bloomberg News*, 21 January 2021, https://financialpost.com/ commodities/energy/bidens-keystone-insult-sees-alberta-leader-urging-retaliation (accessed 4 October 2021).

49   See TC Energy, "TC Energy confirms termination of Keystone XL Pipeline Project," news release, 9 June 2021, https://www.tcenergy.com/announcements/2021-06-09-tc-energy-confirms-termination-of-keystone-xl-pipeline-project/ (accessed 17 July 2021); Reuters, "TC Energy abandons Keystone XL pipeline," *Calgary Herald*, 10 June 2021: B1; CBC News, "Keystone XL is dead, and Albertans are on the hook for $1.3B," 9 June 2021, https://www.cbc.ca/news/canada/calgary/keystone-xl-termination-1.6059683 (accessed 17 July 2021); and Lisa Johnson, "KXL project officially dies with Albertans owing $1.3B," *Calgary Herald*, 10 June 2021: A2.

50   Irving Janis, *Victims of Groupthink: A Psychological Study of Foreign-Policy Decisions and Fiascoes* (Boston: Houghton Mifflin, 1972).

51   See as an example: Rick Bell, "Premier Kenney, get your act together!" *Calgary Sun*, 28 January 2021, https://calgarysun.com/opinion/columnists/bell-premier-kenney-get-your-act-together (accessed 4 October 2021).

52   On 30 September 2021, WCS closed at US$63.41 while WTI was at US$75.03, for a differential price of $11.62, an 18 per cent discount.

53   Alberta Economic Dashboard, "Unemployment Rate."

54   Alberta Economic Dashboard, "Investment," https://economicdashboard.alberta.ca/Investment (accessed 4 October 2021).

55   Canadian Energy Pipeline Association, "CEPA comments on its future," CEPA website, 1 October 2021, https://cepa.com/en/cepa-comments-on-its-future/ (accessed 7 October 2021).

56   Emma Graney, "Canadian Energy Pipeline Association to cease operations by Dec. 31," *Globe and Mail*, 1 October 2021, https://www.theglobeandmail.com/business/article-canadian-energy-pipeline-association-to-cease-operations-by-dec-31/ (accessed 4 October 2021).

57   Chris Varcoe, "Young Albertans leaving now for greener pastures," *Calgary Herald*, 2 October 2021, A4.

11

Just *Our* Facts: The Energy War Room's Adventures in Branded Content

Brad Clark

Introduction

Much was said about the United Conservative Party's (UCP) proposed "Energy War Room" in advance of its actual launch, but—with the benefit of hindsight—its origins and true purpose were best summed up in a news release, quoting Energy Minister Sonya Savage:

> Thanks in a large part to the research of Vivian Krause, we know that the foreign-funded "Tar Sands" campaign has links to bills C-69 and C-48 [the modernization of the National Energy Board and Canadian Environmental Assessment Agency Act, and the Oil Tanker Moratorium Act], which are detrimental to the interests of Alberta's responsible energy sector. Our Energy War Room will be a platform to amplify what has been uncovered by research from Ms. Krause, and other industry stakeholders who have been on the front lines of the effort to combat the misinformation about Alberta.[1]

Krause, a writer and researcher, not a journalist, as described by then Premier Jason Kenney, has circulated an argument that US-funded environmental activism has selectively targeted the Alberta oil patch in an effort to landlock bitumen from the oilsands, all to the benefit of US producers.[2] The Anti-Energy Campaigns Inquiry was also established to investigate Krause's claims. Her argument has been taken up by politicians and many in Alberta's energy sector looking for someone to blame as pipeline projects have run into opposition at home and abroad. It is the foundation of the UCP's energy policy and fundamental to the "Standing Up for Alberta" campaign slogan from the 2019 election, despite independent reporting that substantially challenges the Krause conspiracy.[3] Even the final report by the Anti-Energy Campaigns Inquiry undermined Krause's assertions, with commissioner Steve Allan finding no wrongdoing: "no individual or organization, in my view, has done anything illegal. Indeed, they have exercised their rights of free speech."[4]

However, the UCP government makes no apologies for pushing back hard against dissent, whether it comes from health experts, municipal leaders, or environmentalists. The nascent conservative party endeavoured to defend the oil patch on its own terms by directing public funds ($30 million annually) to establish what would officially be called the Canadian Energy Centre (CEC), "an 'Energy War Room' to respond in real time to the lies and myths told about Alberta's energy industry through paid, earned, and social media."[5] Yet since its launch in late 2019, the CEC has become best known for its frequent missteps and belligerent tone, its credibility as the arbiter of lies and myths frequently shredded. Perhaps the deepest cut of all comes from the Anti-Energy Report and Allan who notes the war room has been met with "almost universal criticism" and piled on by assailing its lack of "independence, openness, transparency and accountability."[6] This chapter traces the CEC's brief but fraught history, and analyzes the content it has produced and disseminated through its website and social media. Its political mandate to fight perceived "misinformation" targets not just "anti-energy" environmental activists, but any person or group who does not share the most optimistic view on the future of fossil fuel. From its outset, the CEC has sought to take on the air of credibility associated with institutions associated with informational rigour, namely journalism and academic research. While its content follows the conventions of news reports or scholarly papers, the analysis here shows that in practice, war-room content is highly selective in the voices and perspectives it incorporates, narrowly amplifying themes consistent with UCP rhetoric, and attacking, discounting, or excluding legitimate points of view. History has shown that political branding initiatives such as this, which seek to assume an air of authority, are met with derision and struggle to achieve legitimacy.

The First Eighteen Months: A Shaky Start Dogged by Controversies

The UCP campaigned hard on the notion that then Premier Rachel Notley's New Democratic Party (NDP), and Prime Minister Justin Trudeau's Liberal government, had abandoned Alberta's prosperous energy industry by capitulating to radical socialists and environmentalists (see Graham Thompson's chapter). While federal and provincial environmental standards were tightened, Trudeau's government secured the future of the Trans Mountain (TMX) pipeline expansion by buying it for $4.5 billion (see Jean-Sébastien Rioux's chapter).

At the same time, Notley was a tireless promoter and defender of Alberta's energy interests. She won the support of oilsands chief executives for her government's climate initiatives; she abandoned Trudeau's carbon tax provisions in the wake of the federal appeal court overturning TMX approval; and she launched a $31 million nation-wide promotional campaign, "Keep Canada Working," aimed at winning support for TMX, a move which drew condemnation from the Green Party and environmental groups. The advertising blitz consisted of television, radio, print, and online spots making the case that the pipeline project would create jobs and boost the Canadian economy, and specifically targeted opposition from the NDP minority government in British Columbia.[7] Public opinion polling by Angus Reid at the time showed the campaign had "moved the dial," according to Notley, to the point where 6 in 10 Canadians, and 53 per cent of British Columbians, believed "lack of new oil pipeline capacity is a national crisis."[8] Her defence of the industry and its workers was as ardent as Jason Kenney's. However, low commodity prices, a shale oil boom in Texas, and newfound energy independence in the Unites States, left the industry in an extended price slump, and allowed the UCP to masterfully demonize Notley's energy bona fides.

Of course, Notley and the NDP claimed the top spot in the UCP's list of the unholy, those who had seemingly condemned Alberta's once thriving energy sector to a purgatory of climate change responsibility, divestment, and limited access to foreign markets. The UCP would exorcise the Greta Thunbergs, Justin Trudeaus, or HSBC Holdings (one of several European banks declining to finance oilsands projects) of the world by "standing up" to them. The UCP included plans to boycott institutional investors divesting from the Alberta oil patch, noting that "the investment community needs to be made aware that foreign oil regimes have horrible records when it comes to the environment, human rights, labour, the treatment of women, and democratic norms."[9] They also offered support to "pro-development First Nations" litigating their rights to be consulted on energy projects, as well as companies "willing to challenge the campaign of defamation by anti-Alberta special interests," essentially engaging the courts with what are known as strategic lawsuits against public participation (SLAPP), an unethical (and illegal in some jurisdictions) corporate strategy to silence critics.

The notion of challenging the public discourse critical of resource development was not entirely new to conservative governments in Alberta. When Ed Stelmach was premier, his government set up a website known as "For the Record" which published counter-narratives "usually over media reporting about the oilsands and climate issues."[10] As with the proposed war room, its mandate was to "dispel myths and to provide more 'balance'" to energy discussions, or as Stelmach's press secretary, Tom Olsen, stated at the time, "It's not a forum to argue philosophy and spin . . . It's about factual information."[11] That same language, and that same Tom Olsen, would become integral parts of the CEC, eleven years later. It is worth acknowledging that *Calgary Herald* writer Chris Varcoe observed that For the Record "didn't last very long, nor was it particularly effective."[12]

References to journalistic terms such as balance, facts, and spin would also frame much of the language in the development of the CEC in the months after the UCP's election victory. Claudia Cattaneo, a retired, long-time columnist on energy issues for the *Financial Post*, was hired to develop the CEC. However, she did not stay on to lead the initiative as chief executive officer, and that position went to Olsen, another former journalist, who had also run unsuccessfully as a UCP candidate. A news release on the day of the CEC's launch in December of 2019, reiterated the mandate and operational structure that had been discussed in the media for months. The war room would be comprised of three units working "together to tell Canada's energy story:"

> A rapid response unit to issue swift responses to misinformation about Canadian oil and natural gas. A pro-active energy literacy unit that creates original content to elevate the general understanding of Canada's energy sector and help the country take control of its energy story. A data and research unit that centralizes and analyses data targeting investors, researchers, and policy makers.[13]

From the very beginning, the CEC's website and social media have assumed many of the conventions of journalism. Articles on the website have bylines and headlines; editorial copy is supported by photos and infographics; some articles are distinguished as "commentary," a distinction news organizations use to separate fulsome reporting from opinion, columns, and op-eds. However, the veneer of a professional organization committed to informational integrity eroded in short order. In his first piece for the website, Olsen mistakenly called the war room a "crown corporation." Following the journalistic protocol, a "correction" was added to the story, explaining that the CEC is in fact, "a provincial government corporation," an early blow in what would develop into a long list of shots to the war room's credibility. Despite Olsen's assurances that the CEC would provide "a fact-based narrative," the website's terms of use, as pointed out by Postmedia columnist Don Braid, initially included this statement: "We do not warrant the accuracy, completeness or usefulness of this information. Any reliance you place on such information is strictly at your own risk."[14] As Braid observed, "Most big commercial and organization websites publish general terms of use, but it's unique for any agency to call BS on itself."[15]

Then the CEC drew condemnation and a rebuke from the Canadian Association of Journalists (CAJ) when it was confirmed that its writers had been identifying themselves as reporters when contacting sources. CAJ president Karyn Pugliese said journalists must operate at arms' length from government, and for CEC staff to "blur the lines between truth and messaging" was wrong: "Don't pretend that you're doing journalism, because you're not. When the government hires its own PR firm, that's fine. But when you pretend that PR firm is journalism, that's positively Orwellian."[16] A chef in Vancouver featured in a CEC article extolling the benefits of cooking with natural gas said he was furious the writer he spoke to never explained the agency's connection to the provincial government and the UCP.[17]

While the backlash against the CEC's methods unfolded, it also very quickly ran into trouble over its logo, being accused of plagiarism—not once—but twice. The war room's initial design was an exact replica of the symbol used by US-based Progress Software. Olsen acknowledged it was a mistake and laid the blame on the Calgary marketing agency that produced the logo.[18] However, when a second design was revealed days later, another US software company, ATK Technologies Inc., pointed out it was very similar to theirs, prompting a warning from the company that "[w]e have already consulted our legal team, and our legal team is on top of it."[19] A Vancouver company apparently could not resist and developed a spoof CEC logo-generator, churning out exact depictions of some of the most famous corporate symbols around (MacDonald's, Nike, Twitter, NASA) with the caption "Canadian Energy Centre" and a rationale. For example, Apple's familiar icon, as a CEC logo, is explained as representing "the importance of Nature Stewardship working in harmony with Commerce."[20]

The logo fiasco drew attention to another storm swirling around the war room: its organizational status as a provincial government corporation, living outside the usual accountability and access-to-information provisions. Corporate oversight falls on the CEC's board of three directors, made up of Savage, Environment Minister Jason Nixon, and the then Justice Minister, Doug Schweitzer. Opposition politicians and journalists wanted to know the cost of developing multiple logos and any expenses incurred to scrub them from CEC documents but had no access to those details. Tom Olsen was asked why the war room was structured to avoid the transparency required of other government agencies, and stated that he supported the approach, "essentially FOIP [Freedom of Information and Protection of Privacy] allows people who want you to fail to look at your playbook.... The media will hold us to account.... It made no sense to allow our strategy to be seen in real time by people who want us to fail."[21] However, less than a year into its mandate, the CEC would come under fire from the provincial auditor-general, Doug Wylie, over concerns for $1.3 million in single-source contracts.[22] Savage's press secretary stated in an email that "the Board of Directors [Savage, Nixon, and Schweitzer] of the Canadian Energy Centre are committed to ensuring that fiscal reporting is comprehensive and transparent." However, when even the Allan inquiry dedicated space in its final report to the CEC calling its structure and reputation "seriously compromised," Olsen and Savage both had to defend its existence, with Olsen stating the war room had "overcome its growing pains" and "hit its stride."[23]

Two months after launching the CEC, Olsen and his staff, were again issuing apologies. When *The New York Times* ran an article detailing the flight of international investment from the oilsands, the CEC Twitter account posted a series of tweets questioning the newspaper's credibility, accusing it of bias, and oddly, given the topic, pointed out *The Times* had been "called out for anti-Semitism countless times."[24] When the war room retweeted a post laden with inaccurate data on emissions from a proposed oilsands project, and University of Alberta economist Andrew Leach pointed it out, the CEC account responded with "Whoops. That was done in error. I was givener [*sic*] this morning and got a little carried away. Sorry about that."[25]

However, the UCP continuously defended the war room, and blamed the energy apostates who inspired the CEC in the first place. Savage asserted the war room was under attack by the very "environmental activists and green left" whom she accused of killing the Northern Gateway pipeline project and promoting harmful environmental legislation.[26] "I spent 13 years working in the oil and gas sector, and I saw that kind of organized campaign unfold," she told reporters, "it was always going to be targeted."[27] Nonetheless, the "green left" was joined by critics who could only be described as stalwart supporters of the energy industry, and the UCP. *Edmonton Sun* columnist Lorne Gunter called the CEC "amateur hour" and warned that "its incompetence reflects badly on both Kenney and our leading industry."[28] A column in the industry publication *BOE Report* began by summing up the CEC era as "months lost in the advocacy wilderness" and urged war room staff to "go wait quietly in the cigar lounge with all the others from whom we expect more."[29] Kenney acknowledged there had been some missteps by the CEC, but when pressed on the sheer volume of gaffes Kenney replied, "Talk to me a year from now about the efficacy of the Canadian Energy Centre."[30] Almost exactly a year later, at a time when the CEC had seen its budget reduced in response to COVID, the war room would be garnering its biggest headlines yet, aiming its rapid response team at a children's animated film.

When *Bigfoot Family* was released on Netflix, a sequel to *Son of Bigfoot*, the CEC unleashed one of its most high-profile campaigns to date. The film tells the story of a Sasquatch, his human son, a racoon, and a bear trying to stop an evil company, Xtrakt, from destroying a pristine wildlife preserve in a bid to extract oil. The story takes place in Alaska, not Canada. Xtrakt's drilling plan involves using bombs, a fictional storyline in today's world, but based in fact: in the late 1950s, Alberta's Social Credit government considered using a nuclear blast to extract oilsands bitumen in a plan named "Project Cauldron."[31] When a parent complained about the film, the CEC sprang into action, setting up an online petition and letter-writing campaign calling on Netflix to set the record straight, noting that the cartoon "inaccurately portrays the oil and gas industry" and "ignores the industry's commitment to environmental stewardship."[32]

The story was picked up in national and international media, including *The Guardian*, the *Daily Mail*, and *The Irish Sun*. The war room's efforts were lauded by UCP and federal conservative politicians, and by some columnists, such as David Staples in *The Edmonton Journal*. Olsen did media interviews defending the campaign. But once again there was also a good deal of ridicule, even from usually supportive pundits, in both mainstream and industry media. An Australian industry publication offered some cheeky comments on the controversy: "*Energy News* can't recall any recent example of Australia's petroleum association attacking children's films, but we did dig up an old Andrew Bolt [a controversial political commentator] column that suggested *Finding Nemo*'s pernicious influence on promoting vegetarianism in children."[33] The article included a subhead that read, "HOW do you annoy a Canadian? Make an animated children's film targeting the US oil and gas industry, apparently."[34] A parody petition was also created, referencing Kenney's unpopular plan to develop coal on the east slopes of the Rockies, urging Netflix to "make Bigfoot Family 2: Kenney's Coal Mine Boondoggle."[35]

It remains unclear exactly what the CEC was trying to accomplish, but in the end, the controversy seems to have created so much awareness around *Bigfoot Family* that it became one of the top streamed movies in Canada, and the film's director, Ben Stassen, thanked the Alberta government for the "silly" campaign against it: "It's just entertainment. It has nothing to do with Alberta. Why they felt targeted by the film, that I do not know."[36]

Given its history, the war room seems to inspire a reaction almost anytime it is mentioned. When news of a plan to have the CEC lead a campaign on environment, social, and governance (ESG) standards in Alberta, even industry insiders wondered if the war room's reputation undermined its chances of success. Well-known Calgary-based energy economist Peter Tertzakian pointed out the need for "trust-building," and the CEC's challenges on that front, because "they have never established trust with the public, so the public doesn't believe it. Nor do environmental groups. Nor do people outside of Alberta."[37] For an organization established to dispel myths and lies that statement should have amounted to an existential crisis, but the CEC continues to enjoy the support of the UCP and create content. A closer look at the body of work emanating from the war room illustrates the ways it frames information about the energy sector and the stories it tells, as well as the issues, voices, and points of view it dutifully excludes or attacks.

Canadian Energy Centre Media Content

The war room's digital media is anchored by its website, canadianenergycentre.ca. Content is divided into sections: Environment, Economy, Community, and Research, then further broken down into subsections under headings of Indigenous, Innovation, Natural Gas, Oil Sands, Renewables, Jobs, LNG, Pipelines, Collaboration, and People. Content can appear in multiple subsections. Despite the "Renewables" section, the CEC's focus is firmly on oil and gas development, and discussions of alternative sources are almost always in support of conventional extraction. Research has its own subcategories of Columns, Economic and Financial Data, ESG, First Nations, and Global Comparisons. Adhering to a digital news site format, some articles are labelled as columns or commentary. There are research-based "Fact Sheets" and a regular feature titled "Matter of Fact," which follows the format of fact-checking from the perspective of the staff at the CEC. These articles generally target "recent commentary" or specific reports from the media or other sources that the war room claims "misrepresent" or "mislead" the truth about the energy industry, such as this example from 12 February 2020, "A Matter of Fact: *New York Times* article on oil sands divestment misleading."

Most of the content is text-based, including French-language versions of a few articles, though there are some video and audio items as well. The audio typically features interviews with the CEC's executive director of research, Mark Milke, being interviewed by a sympathetic host, in most cases, Danielle Smith, at the time former Wildrose Party leader, on Global News Radio 770 CHQR. The articles, videos, and audio that appear on the CEC website are promoted and circulated—sometimes in re-versioned forms—on its social media accounts. Eighteen months after its launch, the CEC's Facebook site had almost fifty-six thousand followers and seems to be its most popular platform. Videos posted on Facebook have generally garnered the most interaction; for example, one titled "A Message for Jane Fonda" garnered over 310 thousand views. The war room also has a YouTube channel; however, it does not seem to get nearly as much attention with only 161 subscribers and much fewer views than Facebook. The CEC's Twitter account has just under 7,200 followers. For comparison, a parody account, Canadian Energy Centre War Room @AbWarRoom, is followed by 5,824.

Since much of the content associated with the CEC's digital operations originates on its website, for the purposes of this chapter, a content analysis was used to throw into relief the core messages war room staff seek to share. Classic content analysis combined with the use of text-mining software was deployed to examine all the articles posted at canadianenergycentre.ca through its first eighteen months of operation. This did not include any audio content or video content, though typically those items were often connected to specific research reports. Text mining software Wordstat 9 helped identify keywords and phrases to further facilitate the deduction of categories and themes and address some of the subjectivity associated with content analysis methods. Table 11.1 provides a snapshot

Table 11.1. Themes in the Canadian Energy Centre's Website Content

Themes	Associated Keywords/ Phrases	Headline and Subhead Examples
1. The energy sector provides Canada with high levels of employment, income, and taxes, and boosts the economy.	Jobs; Indirect; GDP; Direct; Impact; Output; Wages; Impacts; Responsible; Services; Broad; Significant; Economic; Canadian Economy; Canadian Oil; Canadian Oil and Gas Sector; Interprovincial Trade; Goods and Services Produced	Commentary: A healthy Canadian energy industry means jobs, revenue and opportunity *"The energy sector is not just about numbers. It's about people and families and the benefits that accrue to all Canadians."* A Matter of Fact: Mythbusting on Keystone XL Crucial pipeline project brings the promise of jobs and prosperity for thousands in Canada and the United States
2. Indigenous Peoples support energy development and are benefiting from it.	Indigenous Communities; Support; Development; First Nations; Benefits; Indigenous; Projects; Pipeline; Reserve; British Columbia; Coastal Gaslink; Trans Mountain; Indigenous Owned	Twenty B.C. First Nations and pipeline prosperity *Coastal GasLink project will provide employment and revenue for Indigenous partners* First Nations communities increasingly see oil and gas projects as pathways to prosperity *"To say that we are all against development is ludicrous. We're in favour of prosperity"*
3. Global demand for oil will increase, it is not in decline, and Canada should take advantage of that.	Greenhouse Gas Emissions; Vaclav Smil; Complete Elimination of Fossil Carbon; Ignores Fundamental Physical Realities; Global Energy Supply; Foreign Oil Imports	Russia firing up massive oil project to meet growing global demand as Canada sits on the sidelines IEA's "fantasy island" net-zero pathway risks oil supply shortfall, price spike: BMO *"We believe it is highly unlikely that oil demand will decline meaningfully over the next decade"*

Table 11.1. *(continued)*

Themes	Associated Keywords/ Phrases	Headline and Subhead Examples
4. Climate change policies will kill jobs and economic growth.	Climate; Change; Environment; Greenhouse; Policies; Emissions; Exercise in Wishful Thinking; Emissions in Canada; Energy Transitions; Greenhouse Gas Emissions Intensity	Green pivot would rob Canada's Indigenous communities of opportunity: B.C. MLA Clean Fuel Standard threatens Canadian jobs: Report *"Canada should not be going it alone, especially given its minimal impact on global GHG emissions"*
5. Canadian energy is better for the world than fuels produced in "not free countries."	Russian; Autocracies; Tyrannies; Germany; Dependent; Democracies; Russia; Opposition; Saudi Arabia; Freedom Rankings; Partly Free Countries; Degree of Freedom; Producing Countries; Territory Ratings and Statuses; Global Freedom Scores	Dependency on tyranny oil and gas in the G20 democracies *Five democratic G20 nations rely heavily on oil imports deemed to be "Not Free"* Commentary: Tyranny oil should be in the same category as blood diamonds *Attacks on Canadian energy sector ensure oppressive regimes will continue to thrive from oil and gas exports*
6. Lack of pipelines and LNG infrastructure are resulting in missed opportunities, and a need for Canadian energy imports, while other countries take advantage of the global market.	Flow; Crude; Decades; Security; Critical; Transport; Canada; Trillion; Energy; Billion; Pipelines; Energy Products; Petroleum Products; Refined Petroleum; Energy Trade; Natural Gas Development; Pipeline Ukraine; Tyranny Natural; Pricing Dispute; Russian Natural; Tyranny Oil; Alexei Navalny; German Chancellor Angela Merkel; Pipeline Transportation	Commentary: Weak oil and gas investment still plagues Canada *While oil and gas investment has grown substantially in other parts of the world, Canada has failed to keep pace* Commentary: The natural gas export boom—for Canada's competitors Canada's potential to join in the global export surge was hobbled by activists, politicians and red tape
7. Divestment, de-insuring of oilsands projects and companies is hypocritical.	Worldwide; Zurich; Swiss; Axa; Million; China; Billion; Insurance Coverage; Insurance Premiums Written; Billion in China; Russia; Tyranny Oil; Autocracies	Open letter to NY pension fund: Divesting from oil sands doesn't support ESG goals Divestment in Canadian oil and gas compared with their investments in "Not Free" countries

Table 11.1. (*continued*)

Themes	Associated Keywords/ Phrases	Headline and Subhead Examples
8. Energy workers are good, hardworking, intelligent, and ethical people.	Canadians; Albertans; Jobs; Wages; Responsible; Energy Sector; Indigenous Communities; Employment Income; Small Businesses	From pipeline protester to Indigenous energy advisor: The fresh and innovative perspective of Kaella-Marie Earle
		A co-op education placement with Enbridge Gas changed her mind on the role energy can play
		Looking to the future is the job description for transplanted Newfoundlander
		Deidre Norman leading the way on innovation and next generation technologies for energy sector
9. The energy industry is environmentally responsible, minimizes impact, innovates, and develops alternative sources.	Intensity; GHG; Emissions; Decline; Combustion; Falling; Reduction; Emissions Intensity; Environment; Environmental Protection; Environmental Spending; Alberta Spent; Oil and Gas Sector Spent	Commentary: Who spends the most on the environment? Oil and gas firms—and Alberta
		10 environmental successes achieved by Canada's oil and gas industry *Characterizations by opponents that the sector is a laggard are incorrect*
10. Pipelines are safe.		Canada's oil and gas pipelines far safer than competitors *2019 government, industry data shows low spills compared to Russia and U.S.*
		Line 5 shutdown threatens thousands of jobs in Canada, U.S.
		Planned replacement tunnel expected to create jobs and provide safety certainty

Sources: The author.

of the findings, and a breakdown of the ten themes identified in the CEC content, the associated keywords and phrases, and the headlines and subheads from stories that fall under each identified theme.

The first theme is reflected in the detailed statistics compiled by CEC staff to demonstrate the energy sector's contribution to the Canadian economy. The assertion is made often and with conviction. The second theme is represented in stories that counter the narrative of Indigenous opposition to resource development. Typical stories bear headlines such as "Calgary 'Indigeneer' shaping the future of Canadian Energy" or "Indigenous-owned pipeline and construction company sees explosive growth." In the third theme identified in the analysis, CEC staff argue the demand for oil is *not* going to decline in the coming years. In ten separate articles in the research section, either in the text or endnotes, the same expert, Vaclav Smil, is referenced, and on nine occasions the same quotation (in whole or in part) from one of his papers appears: "Designing hypothetical roadmaps outlining complete elimination of fossil carbon from the global energy supply by 2050 is nothing but an exercise in wishful thinking that ignores fundamental physical realities."[38]

While war room content recognizes climate change as an issue, a fourth theme emerges on the threat of climate change measures to prosperity (see Duane Bratt's chapter on an evaluation of the Kenney government's climate policies). It manifests in articles critical of carbon taxes, the incorporation of alternative sources of energy, and international conventions to reduce greenhouse gas emissions. Theme 5 takes the form of the argument made by *Rebel News* founder Ezra Levant in his book *Ethical Oil: The Case for Canada's Oilsands* that the environmental and financial cost of developing synthetic crude ought to be balanced against the human rights records of totalitarian oil producers. The CEC features its own "Tyranny Index" to assess "worldwide oil and natural gas production and market share over four decades for countries in three categories: nations (or territories) that are Free, Partly Free, or Not Free."[39] "Not Free" countries are producing more and more energy, the report asserts. The sixth theme makes the case that Canada is missing out on economic opportunities due to a lack of pipelines and LNG infrastructure, while other countries—including the Not Free nations from the tyranny index—are taking advantage of global demand. The argument is frequently made in CEC content that Canadian natural gas could displace more GHG-intensive fuels in other parts of the world, if it could only get to market.

The seventh theme also has ties to Levant's ethical oil argument, whereby the CEC argues that the divestment and de-insuring of oilsands development is ill-informed, disingenuous, and an exercise in hypocrisy. Companies that cut ties with Alberta's bitumen producers come under fire for business ties to Not Free countries. And if there was any doubt about who the victims of divestment are, an eighth theme emerges in articles that characterize energy workers as down-to-earth, nature-loving, and honest folks who come from a variety of backgrounds. A number of these feature-style reports focus on Indigenous Peoples.

A ninth theme coming out of the analysis challenges the perception of the oil and gas industry as "dirty" by repeatedly offering evidence to the contrary. A recurring argument is the idea that the *intensity* of greenhouse gases from oilsands production is dropping. However, the reduction frequently cited is actually a ratio to GDP. In the sample period for the content analysis, there appears to be no reference to total greenhouse gas emissions or the fact that they have increased.[40] The last theme, pipelines are safe, appears in abundant coverage on the CEC website. When the state of Michigan sought to shut down Enbridge's Line 5, which carries oil and natural gas liquids from western Canada through the Straits of Mackinac between Lakes Michigan and Huron, the CEC published stories contending the pipeline had never leaked in its sixty-eight years of existence. However, contrary to the CEC articles, Line 5 has leaked dozens of times, and has "violated safety standards," according to court documents filed by the state of Michigan.[41]

Outside the thematic analysis, there are other observations of note that emerge from examination of CEC content. While journalistic conventions are followed throughout much of the website, research articles, fact sheets, and briefs take on elements associated with the rigour required by academic publications. This includes detailed references, endnotes, and appendices, all of which provide fulsome support for the analyses and arguments published. There are also allusions to peer review in notes at the bottom of the research items, such as this one: "The authors and the Canadian Energy Centre would like to thank and acknowledge the assistance of Philip Cross in reviewing the data and research for this Fact

Sheet." Cross is a former chief economic analyst at Statistics Canada, worked for the Macdonald-Laurier Institute, a columnist for the *National Post*, and a senior fellow at the Fraser Institute,[42] where Milke also worked as a researcher. In the majority of Fact Sheets, Cross is the only person credited for review, though sometimes there are one or two "anonymous reviewers" or one of a handful of other individuals. Cross also appears on the website as the author of an article headlined "Guest commentary: A response from Philip Cross to a CBC story; 'Clearly, Canada's energy sector is extremely important to Canada's economic well-being.'"

Peer review in academia is founded on notions of independence and impartiality. Typically, authors and reviewers are anonymous to each other to ensure an unbiased, critical appraisal. There can be no circumstance where a reputable publisher would ask the same reviewer to evaluate the same authors almost two dozen times in the span of eighteen months; nor with someone with whom you might have had a previous research relationship. In another clear break from conventional peer review, University of Calgary economist Jack Mintz receives thanks for reviewing a CEC fact sheet that extensively references his own research and arguments.[43] Mintz too, is associated with the Fraser Institute and a frequent contributor to the *Financial Post*, sits on the corporate board of Imperial Oil, and is a UCP appointee to the board of Alberta Health Services and the Premier's Economic Recovery Council (as chair). Mintz's economic analysis on reducing corporate taxes as a catalyst for job creation has been often cited by UCP officials to justify their cuts to the corporate rate early in their mandate.[44] In addition to his consistent fiscal, free-market conservatism, Mintz's flirtation with Alberta separatism, and his assertion that "'diversity' makes countries weaker—not stronger,"[45] align with the social conservatives in the UCP ranks. His views on the economics and politics of energy are clear, and he and his work are featured in several CEC articles.

On the whole, war room content pursues a narrow range of discourse, so resolutely pro-oil and gas in its outlook that there is no room for the slightest nod to dissent. Activists, motivated by an increasingly dire climate crisis, are one-dimensional villains bent on "the death of one of Canada's largest, best-paying industries which benefits everyone from First Nations to blue-collar workers to government coffers."[46] Throughout CEC copy, the word activist is routinely qualified with "anti-oil," "anti-oil and gas," "anti-reality," or "anti-energy"; activists have "hobbled" or "hamstrung" energy exports and production. United Nations or International Energy Agency discussions on fossil fuel reduction scenarios are dismissed in their entirety. A story on wood bison "thriving" on a reclaimed oilsands site, thanks to a partnership between the Fort McKay Nation and Syncrude, only quotes a Syncrude executive, no one from the First Nation, no biologists, and no wildlife officials.[47] While the representation of Indigenous Peoples is positive, it is narrowly focused on those who support energy development, ignoring legitimate opposition, the concerns of First Nations peoples impacted by resource projects and climate change, or those living on unceded territory. The analysis of CEC content here underscores the limited range of facts the war room is willing to accept and disseminate, and an overt bias against the perspectives it dismisses as "anti-reality," myths, or "fantasy island."

Discussion

The CEC's key themes are not only in lockstep with the UCP's "standing up for Alberta" campaign platform, they promote and reinforce the Kenney government's energy policies, uncritically. The UCP backed TC Energy's Keystone XL project with a $1.3 billion stake and loan guarantees; the CEC followed the lead with articles detailing the economic benefits of the pipeline and attacking its opponents and US president Joe Biden. Both Kenney and Savage frequently reference tyranny oil and have compared crude imports from countries such as Saudi Arabia or Venezuela to blood diamonds, a theme picked up in a CEC commentary,[48] a notion that seems to have garnered little traction outside Alberta. UCP policy announcements find space on the CEC website too, as when the Alberta Indigenous Opportunities Corporation was launched and went into operation, and the CEC provided coverage. Whether it is attacking divestment, asserting the long-term growth and viability of the energy sector, or burnishing the industry's record on the environment, the CEC and UCP are synchronized in their messaging.

This was always going to be the case, given the barriers to access to information erected by the UCP, and the background of the CEC's two most prominent employees. Olsen's ties to the party include a failed bid as a UCP candidate and working for former Premier Stelmach. Milke is a well-known conservative and author, and on his personal website he is described as "the lead architect of the United Conservative Party election platform and principal policy advisor to UCP leader Jason Kenney."[49] The website also promotes his book *Ralph vs. Rachel: A Tale of Two Alberta Premiers* with an article titled "Why did Ralph Klein succeed where Rachel Notley failed?"[50]

The CEC invites others to republish its material, "unaltered . . . with attribution to Canadian Energy Centre Ltd." and many like-minded publications do so. These include both news and energy-focused websites such as Resource World Magazine, Troy Media, Todayville (out of Red Deer), Nanaimo, BC-based Business Examiner, and the Post Millennial, a news outlet with ties to the federal conservatives and the UCP.[51] Postmedia sites and newspapers have published a lot of UCP material, mostly commentaries and analysis by Milke and CEC chief research analyst Lennie Kaplan. After the UCP election victory in the spring of 2019, Postmedia hired Kenney's former chief of staff and campaign manager, Nick Koolsbergen, to lobby the UCP to consider the company as a potential source of content for the war room.[52] No deal was ever struck, but the *Financial Post* continues to publish CEC pieces.

As with so many UCP policy decisions, from pandemic measures to betting on Keystone to the review of the K–12 curricula, the CEC was established on questionable ideological assumptions. The Krause work cited by Savage has not stood up to scrutiny, not even from the Kenney government's own investigation. As Andrew Nikiforuk pointed out shortly after the CEC's launch, the five environmental groups targeting the oilsands sat down with four executives from bitumen producers and agreed to a plan to "to limit emissions as opposed to production, which, rightly or wrongly, largely derailed the campaign."[53] Similarly, the assumption that the energy sector struggles to have its message heard, despite the communications budgets at multi-billion-dollar energy corporations, and well-resourced industry associations, is contradicted by research. Studies have repeatedly shown that at the intersection of energy development and the environment, the reporting is "particularly susceptible to corporate influence."[54] A recent Canadian analysis of 173 newspaper articles about the five biggest oil companies found that just nine featured an interview with an environmentalist.[55]

Canadian governments have often acted on the temptation to create their own press narrative by embracing the concept of news-styled agencies for communication. Ed Stelmach's "For the Record" initiative, referenced earlier in this chapter, is one such example, as is Ontario Premier Doug Ford's Ontario News Now (ONN). The similarities between ONN and the war room are striking. ONN operates outside access-to-information provisions as it is funded by Progressive Conservative caucus services and falls outside disclosure legislation.[56] As with the CEC, the presentation is consistent with journalistic conventions, "raising concerns about whether the government is purposefully trying to blur the lines between partisan messaging and journalism."[57] Stephen Harper's Conservatives rolled out a video service called "24 Seven" that promoted his government's policies but also ran into controversy, as when it broadcast the faces of Canadian special forces soldiers during a prime minister's visit to Kuwait and Iraq.[58] 24 Seven, ONN, and the CEC all share the dubious honour of drawing heavy criticism from the Canadian Taxpayers Federation, an organization once led by Jason Kenney.

Marland, Lewis, and Flanagan point out that governments will use "controllable media to get unfiltered brand messages to target audiences" and specifically reference Harper's 24 Seven approach, which they also note, "bordered on propaganda."[59] To protect the political brand, they write, "government departments operate 'detect and correct' activities to push back against misinformation and to spin a more favorable slant."[60] While the strategy "reduces the potential for misinformation or a blunder rocketing across social media," it comes at a cost, accentuating "politicization of governance and simplification of information."[61]

Alberta's energy war room can best be understood as an exercise in political branding, regardless of the veneer of informational rigour. Its content is perfectly in line with UCP rhetoric, whether the subject is climate change, corporate taxes, or pipelines. Its body of work is a consistent, one-sided, pro-oil-and-gas perspective highlighting the Kenney government's policies, legislation, and actions, attacking anyone not fully on board with the next big oil and gas boom, whether they are "anti-energy" activists, the news media, academics, or the producers of children's cartoons. As an entity operating as a so-called energy centre, it really is more of a "war room."

1   Government of Alberta, "First steps in establishing Energy War Room," *Alberta Government News* (7 June 2019). Accessed at https://www.alberta.ca/release.cfm?xID=6402004FF0FF3-99E9-EBE8-BBFCA6912BD8CCC4 on 6 June 2021.

2   Vivian Krause, "Vivian Krause: The cash pipeline opposing Canadian oil pipelines," *Financial Post* (3 October 2016). Accessed at https://financialpost.com/opinion/vivian-krause-the-cash-pipeline-opposing-canadian-oil-pipelines on 6 June 2021.

3   See Sandy Garossino, "A data-based dismantling of Jason Kenney's foreign-funding conspiracy theory," *National Observer* (3 October 2019). Accessed at https://www.nationalobserver.com/2019/10/03/analysis/data-based-dismantling-jason-kenneys-foreign-funding-conspiracy-theory on 8 June 2021; Markham Hislop, "Vivian Krause's shoddy research exposed. Has Kenney bought a very large barrel of snake oil?" *EnergiMedia* (7 October 2019). Accessed at https://energi.media/markham-on-energy/vivian-krauses-shoddy-research-exposed-has-kenney-bought-a-very-large-barrel-of-snake-oil/ on 8 June 2021.

4   J. Stephens Allan, "Report of the Public Inquiry into Anti-Alberta Energy Campaigns," *Public Inquiry into Anti-Alberta Energy Campaigns* (30 July 2021), 596. Accessed at https://open.alberta.ca/dataset/3176fd2d-670b-4c4a-b8a7-07383ae43743/resource/a814cae3-8dd2-4c9c-baf1-cf9cd364d2cb/download/energy-report-public-inquiry-anti-alberta-energy-campaigns-2021.pdf on 29 September 2021.

5   United Conservative Party, "United Conservatives Strong & Free Getting Alberta Back to Work," *United Conservative Party* (1 April 2019), 96–97. Accessed at https://albertastrongandfree.ca/wp-content/uploads/2019/04/Alberta-Strong-and-Free-Platform-1.pdf on 6 June 2021.

6   Allan, "Report of the Public Inquiry into Anti-Alberta Energy Campaigns," 649.

7   Adam MacVicar, "'This is B.C. vs. Canada': Alberta has spent $23M on Keep Canada Working campaign," *Global News* (24 January 2019). Accessed at https://globalnews.ca/news/4884829/keep-canada-working-campaign-trans-mountain/ on 3 May 2021.

8   Lindsay Morey, "Alberta spends millions to inform Canadians about TMX," *Sherwood Park News* (22 January 2019). Accessed at https://www.sherwoodparknews.com/news/local-news/alberta-spends-millions-to-inform-canadians-about-tmx on 8 June 2021.

9   United Conservative Party, "United Conservatives Strong & Free Getting Alberta Back to Work," 96.

10 Chris Varcoe, "Varcoe: What's old is new again in Alberta's energy war room," *Calgary Herald* (11 October 2019). Accessed at https://calgaryherald.com/opinion/columnists/varcoe-on-energy-war-room on 12 June 2021.

11 Varcoe, "What's old is new again in Alberta's energy war room."

12 Varcoe, "What's old is new again in Alberta's energy war room."

13 Canadian Energy Centre, "Canadian Energy Centre launches with mandate to promote Canadian energy," *Globe Newswire* (11 December 2019). Accessed at https://www.globenewswire.com/news-release/2019/12/11/1959469/0/en/Canadian-Energy-Centre-launches-with-mandate-to-promote-Canadian-energy.html on 10 June 2021.

14   Don Braid, "Braid: UCP admits war room 'hasn't been clear sailing'; NDP says it should be scuttled," *Calgary Herald* (6 January 2020). Accessed at https://calgaryherald.com/opinion/columnists/braid-ucp-acknowledges-troubled-launch-of-war-room on 15 June 2021.

15   Braid, "UCP admits war room 'hasn't been clear sailing.'"

16   Bob Weber, "Journalist group protests Alberta war room's use of term reporters," *Calgary Herald* (24 December 2019). Accessed at https://calgaryherald.com/pmn/news-pmn/canada-news-pmn/journalist-group-protests-alberta-war-rooms-use-of-term-reporters/wcm/08286d76-dba9-4de4-88d8-82a512545be0/ on 25 May 2021.

17   James Keller, "Vancouver chef featured in article by Alberta 'energy war room' furious he wasn't told of links to government," *Globe and Mail* (25 December 2019). Accessed at https://www.theglobeandmail.com/canada/alberta/article-vancouver-chef-featured-in-article-by-alberta-energy-war-room/ on 25 May 2021.

18   Jordan Omstead, "Alberta energy 'war room' discovers its logo was lifted from American software company," *CBC News* (19 December 2019). Accessed at https://www.cbc.ca/news/canada/edmonton/alberta-energy-war-room-discovers-its-logo-was-lifted-from-american-software-company-1.5403077 on 5 June 2021.

19   Bill Kaufman, "Second logo for Alberta's energy war room comes under fire from U.S. tech firm," *Calgary Herald* (27 December 2019). Accessed at https://calgaryherald.com/news/local-news/alberta-governments-war-room-possibly-runs-afoul-over-second-logo on 1 June 2021.

20   Goat—a Design Agency, "Energy War Room Logo Creator" (30 December 2019). Accessed at https://energywarroomlogogenerator.com/ on 11 May 2021.

21   Dallas Flexhaug, "Extended: Sitting down with the CEO of Alberta's 'war room,'" *Global News* (17 December 2019). Accessed at https://globalnews.ca/video/6303594/extended-sitting-down-with-the-ceo-of-albertas-war-room on 25 April 2021.

22   Amanda Stephenson, "Energy 'war room' criticized by auditor general for single-source contracts," *a* (5 November 2020). Accessed at https://edmontonsun.com/business/local-business/energy-war-room-criticized-by-auditor-general-for-single-source-contracts on 29 October 2021.

23   Lisa Johnson, "Allan inquiry's report triggers war of words with Alberta's energy war room," *Edmonton Journal* (October 22, 2021). Accessed at https://edmontonjournal.com/news/politics/allan-inquirys-report-triggers-war-of-words-with-albertas-energy-war-room on 29 October 2021.

24   Canadian Press, "Alberta energy 'war room' chief apologizes for tweets attacking New York Times," *CBC News* (12 February 2020). Accessed at https://www.cbc.ca/news/canada/calgary/alberta-energy-war-room-tom-olsen-jason-kenney-energy-1.5461950 on 25 May 2021.

25   Brodie Thomas, "Canadian Energy Centre head apologizes for tone of tweets," *Calgary Herald* (12 February 2020). Accessed at https://calgaryherald.com/news/local-news/canadian-energy-centre-really-givener-on-twitter on 28 April 2021).

26   Amanda Stephenson, "War room under attack by organized activists and 'green left': Savage," *Calgary Herald* (19 February 2020). Accessed at https://calgaryherald.com/news/local-news/war-room-under-attack-by-organized-activists-savage on 2 May 2021.

27   Stephenson, "War room under attack by organized activists and 'green left': Savage."

28   Lorne Gunter, "GUNTER: Focus on social media spats at Alberta's 'war room' reflects badly on premier," *Edmonton Sun* (14 February 2020). Accessed at https://edmontonsun.com/opinion/columnists/gunter-focus-on-social-media-spats-at-albertas-war-room-reflects-badly-on-premier on 3 May 2021.

29   Terry Etam, "Column: Everyone paying attention now? THAT's what a swing producer can do," *BOE Report* (9 March 2020). Accessed at https://boereport.com/2020/03/09/column-everyone-paying-attention-now-thats-what-a-swing-producer-can-do/ on 7 June 2021.

30   Kirby Bourne, "Premier Jason Kenney defends Alberta's 'war room' on 630 CHED amid opposition," *Global News* (March 4, 2020). Accessed at https://globalnews.ca/news/6629544/jason-kenney-war-room-630-ched/ on 7 June 2021.

31   Mack Lamoureux, "The Bizarre Story of the Time a Canadian Province Tried to Nuke Itself," *Vice* (15 December 2015). Accessed at https://www.vice.com/en/article/avyqbp/the-bizarre-story-of-that-one-time-alberta-tried-to-nuke-itself on June 9 on 9 June 2021.

32   Support Canadian Energy, "Tell the Truth Netflix!" *Support Canadian Energy* (13 March 2021). Accessed at https://www.supportcanadianenergy.ca/tell_the_truth_netflix on 9 June 2021.

33   Energy News Bulletin, "Canadian oil association attacks children's film," *Energy News Bulletin* (22 March 2021). Accessed at https://www.energynewsbulletin.net/on-the-record/news/1406919/canadian-oil-association-attacks-children%E2%80%99s-film%C2%A0 on 9 June 2021.

34   Energy News Bulletin, "Canadian oil association attacks children's film."

35   change.org, "Ask Netflix to make Bigfoot Family 2: Kenney's Coal Mine Boondoggle," *change.org* (17 March 2021). Accessed at https://www.change.org/p/netflix-produce-bigfoot-family-2-coal-mine-boondoggle-for-netflix on 9 June 2021.

36   Fahkiha Baig, "Director of 'Bigfoot' movie thanks Alberta energy centre for controversy," *Toronto Sun* (28 March 2021). Accessed at https://torontosun.com/entertainment/movies/this-is-ludicrous-director-of-bigfoot-movie-thanks-alberta-energy-centre-for-controversy on 9 June 2021.

37   Emma Graney, "Concerns raised about Alberta energy war room's history as it prepares to lead ESG campaign," *Globe and Mail* (24 March 2021). Accessed at https://www.theglobeandmail.com/business/article-concerns-raised-about-alberta-energy-war-rooms-history-as-it-prepares/ on 11 May 2021.

38   Mark Milke and Lenny Kaplan, "Commentary: Canadian oil and gas fueled $493 billion in revenue for governments since 2000," *Canadian Energy Centre* (12 November 2020). Accessed at https://www.canadianenergycentre.ca/commentary-canadian-oil-and-gas-fueled-493-billion-in-revenue-for-governments-since-2000/ on 20 June 2021.

39   Mark Milke and Lenny Kaplan, "The tyranny index for oil and gas," *Canadian Energy Centre* (19 May 2020). Accessed at https://www.canadianenergycentre.ca/the-tyranny-index-for-oil-and-gas/ on 20 June 2021.

40   Government of Canada, "Canadian Sustainability Indicators: Greenhouse gas emissions," *Environment and Climate Change Canada* (2021). Accessed at https://

www.canada.ca/content/dam/eccc/documents/pdf/cesindicators/ghg-emissions/2021/
greenhouse-gas-emissions-en.pdf 5 August 2021.

41 Samantha Beattie, "Line 5 pipeline between U.S. and Canada could cause 'devastating
damage' to Great Lakes, say environmentalists," *CBC News* (3 August 2021). Accessed at
https://www.cbc.ca/news/canada/toronto/line-five-environment-great-lakes-1.6120882
on 5 August 2021.

42 Fraser Institute, "Philip Cross," *Fraser Institute* (23 April 2021). Accessed at https://
www.fraserinstitute.org/content/philip-cross on 6 August 2021.

43 Lennie Kaplan and Mark Milke, "Analyzing claims about oil and gas
subsidies," *Canadian Energy Centre* (27 April 2021). Accessed at https://www.
canadianenergycentre.ca/analyzing-claims-about-oil-and-gas-subsidies/ on 6 August
2021.

44 Lisa Johnson, "NDP calls on UCP government to release fiscal analysis of corporate tax
cut," *Edmonton Journal* (3 November 2020). Accessed at https://edmontonjournal.com/
news/politics/ndp-calls-on-ucp-government-to-release-fiscal-analysis-of-corporate-
tax-cut on 6 August 2021.

45 Jack Mintz, "Jack Mintz: Actually, evidence shows 'diversity' makes countries weaker—
not stronger," *Financial Post* (29 August 2018). Accessed at https://financialpost.com/
opinion/jack-mintz-actually-evidence-shows-diversity-makes-countries-weaker-not-
stronger on 8 August 2021.

46 Mark Mike and Lennie Kaplan, "Commentary: Don't kill off Canada's oil and
gas sector," *Canadian Energy Centre* (9 April 2021). Accessed at https://www.
canadianenergycentre.ca/column-dont-kill-off-canadas-oil-and-gas-sector/ on 8
August 2021.

47 CEC Staff, "Energy sector can lead Canada's economic recovery," *Canadian Energy
Centre* (23 July 2020). Accessed at https://www.canadianenergycentre.ca/energy-sector-
can-lead-canadas-economic-recovery/ on 8 August 2021.

48 Mark Milke, "Commentary: Tyranny oil should be in the same category as blood
diamonds," *Canadian Energy Centre* (26 May 2020). Accessed at https://www.
canadianenergycentre.ca/commentary-tyranny-oil-should-be-in-the-same-category-
as-blood-diamonds/ on 8 August 2021.

49 Mark Milke, "Author, columnist, contrarian," *markmilke.com*. Accessed at https://
markmilke.com/about on 10 August 2021.

50 Mark Milke, "Author, columnist, contrarian."

51 Jeff Yates and Kaleigh Rogers, "Canadian news site The Post Millennial blurs line
between journalism and conservative 'pamphleteering,'" *CBC News* (27 June 2019).
Accessed at https://www.cbc.ca/news/politics/the-post-millennial-journalism-
conservative-advocacy-1.5191593 on 6 August 2021.

52 Michelle Bellefontaine, "Postmedia hires former Kenney chief of staff to lobby on
'energy war room,'" *CBC News* (17 May 2019). Accessed at https://www.cbc.ca/news/
canada/edmonton/postmedia-hires-lobbyist-alberta-government-war-room-1.5140631
on 6 August 2021.

53 Andrew Nikiforuk, "The Silly, Scary Truth about Alberta's New Ministry of Truth," *The Tyee* (1 January 2020). Accessed at https://thetyee.ca/Opinion/2020/01/01/Alberta-Jason-Kenney-Candian-Energy-Centre/ on 14 August 2021.

54 Ellen Moore, *Journalism, Politics, and the Dakota Access Pipeline* (Routledge: New York, 2019), 46.

55 Sean Holman, "Op-ed: Canada's oil giants deserve tougher coverage," *Columbia Journalism Review* (3 September 2020). Accessed at https://www.cjr.org/covering_climate_now/canada-oil-production-demand-climate-crisis.php on 21 August 2021.

56 Laura Stone, "'A propaganda machine': How Doug Ford's government skirts media with Ontario News Now," *The Globe and Mail* (15 May 2019). Accessed at https://www.theglobeandmail.com/canada/article-a-propaganda-machine-how-ford-government-skirts-media-with-ontario/ on 21 Augsut 2021.

57 Laura Stone, "'A propaganda machine.'"

58 Canadian Press, "Poilievre ads on YouTube: Innovative or a new low?" *Maclean's* (15 May 2015). Accessed at https://www.macleans.ca/politics/poilievre-ads-on-youtube-innovative-or-a-new-low/ on 27 August 2021.

59 Alex Marland, J.P. Lewis, and Tom Flanagan, "Governance in the Age of Digital Media and Branding," *Governance: An International Journal of Policy, Administration, and Institutions* 30, no.1 (2017): 132.

60 Alex Marland, J.P. Lewis, and Tom Flanagan, "Governance in the Age of Digital Media and Branding," 133.

61 Alex Marland, J.P. Lewis, and Tom Flanagan, "Governance in the Age of Digital Media and Branding," 125.

V.
Alberta's Fiscal Situation

12

The Long Slide towards Fiscal Reckoning: Managing Alberta's Finances in an Age of Decline

Trevor Tombe

Introduction

In an early April 2020 televised address, Alberta's Premier Jason Kenney delivered grim news about the COVID-19 pandemic. It was not only a health crisis, but an economic and fiscal one as well. "[Albertans] will face a great fiscal reckoning in the future," he warned.[1] But while the significant disruptions from the pandemic accelerated many of the fiscal pressures facing Alberta, it was by no means the cause. In a very real but underappreciated sense, Alberta has been managing a steady fiscal decline for over four decades. Successive governments have responded to this in different ways, though none—including the new United Conservative Party (UCP) government—have fully come to grips with the scale of the challenge. Despite recent increases in global oil and gas prices—leading to historically high levels of resource revenues for the province in 2022—Alberta's long slide towards fiscal reckoning continues. And fiscal, economic, and political constraints to substantive reforms mounted during the UCP's term and will continue to pressure future Alberta governments.

Managing public finances is never easy, of course, though it is especially difficult in Alberta. Large and unexpected swings in revenues create short-term challenges that would be difficult in the best of times.

But steadily and consistently declining revenues in recent decades creates increasingly binding constraints on the government's range of action. Alberta's heavy reliance on revenues from natural resources—primarily natural gas and oil sales—is behind both its recent short-term challenges and its future long-term ones. And while not a new development, managing Alberta's dependence on resource revenues is more difficult for the current government than past ones. Significant economic disruptions, a rapidly aging population, a shrinking gap between Alberta and other provinces, and a political atmosphere averse to thoughtful compromise all make fiscal policy more difficult. Despite this, Alberta's still notable economic strength, and the potential for strong future growth, provides options. In this chapter, I explore the nature of Alberta's fiscal decline, analyse its prospects going forward, and identify how the new UCP government has managed provincial finances. In short, the challenges are significant, but there are several options to address them. An important legacy of the UCP first few years in office, however, may be in having made these challenges more difficult to overcome.

Before unpacking the fiscal challenges that Alberta faces, a broad overview of its budget and recent political developments is necessary. As with other Canadian provinces, the bulk of program expenditures are accounted for by a few core functions: health care, education, and social services. Combined, these activities account for approximately three-quarters of total program expenditures in the province—which is a similar pattern observed elsewhere. Other areas, such as agriculture, environment, infrastructure, justice, transportation, and so on, are all critical but relatively insubstantial for the overall budget. This high degree of expenditure concentration is important to appreciate because any move to restrain spending growth or reduce spending outright will unavoidably affect health care and educational services. It also means changes in demand for these services—primarily through demographic changes—will have large implications for Alberta's fiscal future.

On the revenue side, Alberta differs in several important ways from other provinces. First, taxation funds a uniquely small share of public services. In the 2019/20 fiscal year, before the pandemic hit, tax revenues were just over $19 billion—equivalent to approximately one-third of total government spending. By contrast, Canadian provincial governments, on the whole, fund slightly more than half of total spending using tax revenues. Alberta's lower taxation revenues, due in part—though not exclusively—to its lack of a general sales tax, are (typically) made up for by far larger than average amounts of investment income and natural resource revenues. The former is from over $21 billion in savings within the Alberta Heritage Fund plus related endowments. The latter is primarily from royalties on oil and gas production, especially bitumen in recent years. This dependence is the central fiscal policy challenge for Alberta both in the short-term and the long. Overall, as I will show, roughly one-quarter of total revenues to the Alberta government needs to come from natural resource revenues to balance the budget.

Unfortunately for the government, disappointing oil prices since 2014, however, have made that impossible. It is also the proximate cause of recent political turmoil and of the UCP's eventual rise. From an average of nearly $100 per barrel (USD WTI) between 2011 and mid-2014, oil prices fell to less than $50 per barrel by January 2015 and to $30 per barrel by early 2016. Although many prior governments ran modest budget deficits, this decline in price dramatically increased provincial borrowing. "We are at a turning point in our province," said former Alberta Premier Jim Prentice in a televised address on March 24, 2015. "We need to get our program expenditures off the energy revenue rollercoaster and make our revenues more secure," he continued.[2] Alberta's budget that year (tabled, though never passed) detailed a comprehensive plan to ease reliance on resource revenues through a combination of real per capita expenditure reductions, meaningful tax increases, and gradually saving an increasingly large portion of natural resource revenues. But this plan was not to be. The Prentice government was defeated in an historic election in 2015 that brought the New Democratic Party (NDP), led by Rachel Notley, to power.

Instead of continuing the reform of Alberta's fiscal policy, the new government quickly opted to shelve Prentice's plan and continue the same general fiscal and economic strategy of previous Progressive Conservative (PC) governments in the years prior to the 2014 oil price decline. That is, they opted growth spending in line with population and prices while making only modest changes in tax rates and structures. Their hope was the same as past PC governments: rebounding oil prices and production would spare the government from making difficult budget decisions.

These hopes had regularly been dashed in the past, but it remained a central pillar of the NDP's longer-term fiscal plans. Their "Path to Balance" in early 2019, for example, which was released shortly before the election campaign that year, was based almost entirely on rising oil prices and resource revenues. It required nearly $12 billion in natural resource revenues to balance by 2024.[3] But this too was not to be and the NDP were defeated at the polls—at least partially due to public concerns over rising deficits.

Following their election in April 2019, the UCP under Jason Kenney introduced their first comprehensive fiscal plan in late October that year. Unlike previous governments who largely held the line, their plan centred on shrinking the size of government. In the year prior to their election, total operating expenses of the Government of Alberta exceeded $48.4 billion, but by 2022/23 the UCP planned to reduce this to $47.1 billion.[4] While a modest aggregate reduction of only 2.7 per cent, the real level of spending per person is substantially lower. The budget projected population growth of 7.5 per cent by 2023, for example, and overall price inflation of nearly 8 per cent over that same time. For operating expenses to merely keep pace with population and inflation, an increase of over 16 per cent would therefore be required. And relative to the NDP fiscal plan for 2022/23, I estimate operating expenses were actually lowered by $7 billion or nearly 13 per cent that year. This is large. Excluding health, education, and child and social services, total government operating expenditures in all other areas of government, for comparison, was less than $9.3 billion in 2018/19.

On the revenue side of the UCP fiscal plan, while there were modest increases in some areas, the government's overall plan was to reduce or eliminate taxes. It lowered the corporate tax rate from 12 per cent to 8 per cent (phased gradually over time) and eliminated one of Alberta's two carbon taxes (the one on retail fuel that individuals see) (see Duane Bratt's chapter). Along with other developments, the UCP plan projected total revenue by 2022/23 at $57.5 billion, or approximately $6 billion (9.4 per cent) less than the NDP fiscal plan for that year. Taken together, the UCP fiscal policy represents a meaningful reduction in the size and scope of the provincial government and was therefore a clear departure from previous governments. Looking beyond 2022/23, however, current fiscal policy falls short of addressing the gap between government revenues and expenditures and, more importantly, is ill-prepared to address longer-term challenges. These challenges pre-date COVID, but the economic and fiscal disruptions from the pandemic added significantly to them.

The Effect of COVID-19 on Alberta Finances

The pandemic took a fiscal toll on all provincial governments, though costs to Alberta were particularly large (see also Lisa Young's chapter). Economic disruptions from the pandemic, including significant employment losses and business closures, meant provincial revenues from a variety of sources fell sharply. In addition, rising direct program expenditure within health care and for individual and business income supports added to the deficit. The original fiscal plan in Budget 2019 targeted a deficit of $5.9 billion for fiscal year 2020/21. The actual deficit for the year came in at $17 billion.[5] For additional context, I illustrate the past half century of Alberta surpluses and deficits in Figure 12.1, adjusted for inflation and population growth over time. Though the borrowing through the pandemic was high, so too were the years leading up to, for reasons discussed earlier. But at approximately $3,800 per Albertan, I estimate the 2020/21 deficit—though smaller than some feared early in the pandemic—was the largest in Alberta's history.

The full fiscal implications of the pandemic are not yet known, but recent Government of Alberta budgets provide a good first look.[6] Total income tax revenues, from individuals and corporations, were $2.9 billion lower in 2020/21 than was previously projected in Budget 2019 for that same fiscal year. Other tax revenues sources also declined significantly, notably gasoline taxes as fuel purchases during the early months of the pandemic were very low, and revenues from gaming and lottery activities fell in half, from a planned $1.4 billion to $774 million. Finally, as this chapter will explore in greater detail later, Alberta's reliance on revenues from natural resources also posed a challenge. Global oil prices declined precipitously during the pandemic, and therefore natural resource revenues to Alberta fell as well—by nearly $2.3 billion. Overall, excluding federal transfers, total revenues fell by nearly $8.6 billion due to pandemic-related disruptions. Cushioning this decline, however, were sharp increases in federal transfers. Total transfers to provincial and territorial governments in Canada rose in 2020 to its highest level since 1867, as a

Figure 12.1. Alberta Government Budget Balances, 1965/66 to 2024/25 (F)

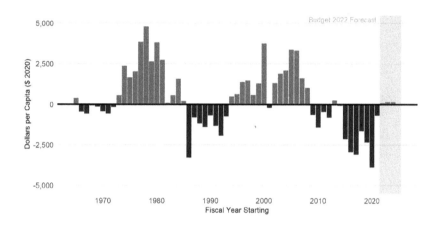

Sources: Own calculations from Finances of the Nation "Government Revenue and Expenditure" dataset, accessed 4 May 2022, and projections for 2022/23 onwards from Alberta's Budget 2022 (Government of Alberta, Fiscal Plan: Moving Forward (Alberta Treasury Board and Finance: Edmonton, 2022). Available at https://open. alberta.ca/publications/budget-2022).

share of the overall economy.[7] For Alberta, this meant a boost of roughly $1.4 billion in 2020/21.

Pandemic-related expenditures were also significant. In 2020/21, total operating expenditures related to COVID-19 and certain economic recovery initiatives approached $4.1 billion. Much of this was increases in health expenditures, which reached nearly $1.1 billion (see Gillian Steward's chapter). Other significant costs included support to municipal governments ($621 million), to schools ($248 million), to children and social services ($229 million), and more. Higher expenditures continued through to 2021/22 but are currently forecast to decline to $2.8 billion, and further to less than $500 million by 2023/24.

Disruptions to Alberta's broader economy compound these fiscal challenges. But as is evident in Figure 12.1, the shock of COVID-19 occurred following years of prior challenges. Indeed, it is difficult to overstate the scale of the shock that started in 2014. Between 2014 and 2016, I estimate the province's nominal GDP per capita fell by roughly one-fifth—larger

Figure 12.2. Government Revenues as a Share of GDP, 1970/71 to 2020/21

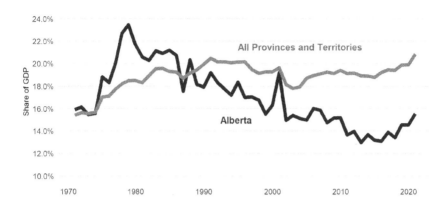

Note: The increase in 2020/21 total revenues as a share of GDP is largely due to contracting economic activity that year due to the COVID-19 pandemic.

Sources: Own calculations from Finances of the Nation "Government Revenue and Expenditure" dataset. Accessed 4 May 2022.

than the contraction due to COVID-19—and roughly corresponds to how much lower total incomes are in the province. The recovery from this decline was also slower than many hoped for, and sharply interrupted by the pandemic. Only by 2024 does the government project that Alberta's overall economy will return to pre-pandemic levels. This is an historically significant period of economic decline. Using long-run provincial economic data, I find only three other periods compare.[8] First, following the First World War, Alberta's per capita level of economic activity contracted by approximately 30 per cent and remained relatively flat for many years through the droughts and agricultural challenges of the 1920s. Second, the Great Depression hit all regions hard, to be sure, but it hit Alberta and other agriculturally oriented regions hardest. By 1933, I estimate Alberta's real GDP per economy was roughly half what it was in 1929. And it only gradually recovered from there. Finally, the 1986 oil price drop was the most recent comparable period with Alberta's economy contracting by roughly one-fifth per capita and remaining there for nearly a decade until growth resumed in the late 1990s. But unlike this most recent comparable contraction, Alberta faces a confluence of mounting fiscal pressures and far less room to maneuver, despite recent increases in resource revenues helping balance the provincial books in 2022.

Alberta's Long Fiscal Decline

Declining natural resource revenues has been the central short-term challenge facing several successive Alberta governments. Recent increases due to rising global oil and gas prices, especially following the Russian invasion of Ukraine, are helpful to ease these challenges but this is a temporary reprieve from longer-term challenges.

The scale of Alberta's long fiscal decline is not broadly appreciated and one Alberta has not yet come to grips with. Over the past forty years, total government revenues as a share of the province's overall economy declined by nearly ten percentage points. And this is entirely accounted for by falling natural resource revenues, as displayed in Figure 12.2. In 1979, when government revenues were highest at roughly 24 per cent of GDP, natural resource revenues alone were 12 per cent—or half of the province's total. By 2019, total government revenues declined to 14.5 per cent of GDP and natural resource revenues to less than two. More precisely, total revenues declined roughly ten percentage points over this period and natural resource revenues declined slightly more. Meanwhile, other provincial and territorial governments in Canada gradually increased their revenues from approximately 15 per cent to 20 per cent between 1970 and 1990, remaining relatively stable thereafter. Alberta's experience is markedly different and the entire story of the province's fiscal challenge over these decades is one of declining revenues from oil and gas. This is the fundamental fiscal challenge facing Alberta, and one that appears increasingly difficult for successive governments to confront. Recent increases in natural resource revenues in 2021, which may potentially increase in subsequent years, does not fundamentally change this picture. In 2021/22, for example, Budget 2022 projects natural resource revenues in excess of $13 billion—but this is less than 3.7 per cent of GDP. Higher than recent years, but a small increase relative to the province's long-run decline.

Historically, Alberta governments responded to this long slide in different ways. At first, there was considerable space in Alberta's budget to absorb the revenue decline through shrinking surpluses, gradually de-clining shares of natural resource revenues that were saved in the Alberta Heritage Savings Trust Fund and using income from that fund towards government operations. In 1982/83, for example, a portion of income from the fund was shifted into general government revenue.[9] And one year later, the share of resource revenues saved was cut in half. During moments of sharp and unexpected declines in revenue, however, more dramatic chan-ges were required.

Consider the large decline in natural resource revenues in 1986, when resource revenue declined from over $4.9 billion to $1.9 billion. In re-sponse, Budget 1987 featured a mix of tax increases and expenditure cuts to achieve what they hoped would be a balanced budget by 1990/91. The strategy was "a three-pronged attack on the deficit," said Finance Minister Johnston during the budget address, but one whose actions "will be fair and those Albertans in need will be protected."[10] First, the government undertook a detailed review of expenditures to reduce spending but in a manner to "have the least possible adverse effect on Albertans." Health, education, and social services were largely spared but other program ex-penditure areas declined by an overall average of 25 per cent by 1988/89 compared to 1985/86. Second, contributions to the Heritage Fund were ended, which boosted resource revenues available for the general budget. Finally, there were tax increases—substantial ones. The government in-creased the province's basic income tax by 7 per cent,[11] introduced an 8 per cent surtax on high-income individuals, levied a new one percentage point flat tax on all incomes, increased tobacco taxes by one dollar per pack, increased liquor markups, introduced a 5 per cent tax on hotel rooms, in-creased gasoline taxes by 5 cents per litre, increased the corporate income tax from 10 to 15 per cent, and more. These were large increases. Relative to total taxation revenues, I estimate these increases are equivalent to ap-proximately $7 billion per year today.

This mixed approach of both expenditure reductions and revenue in-creases were deliberately chosen by Premier Getty's government. They had the luxury of large revenue and expenditure side options to fill the hole left by falling resource revenues. The subsequent government under Premier Klein, however, had different priorities and when additional fiscal actions were necessary following the recession of the early 1990s, the government

Figure 12.3. Real Per Capita Provincial Program Spending, 1965/66 to 2024/25 (F)

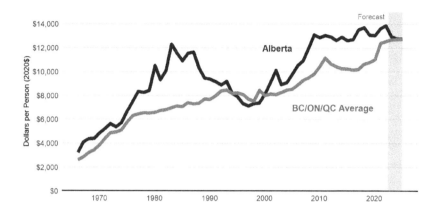

Sources: Own calculations from Finances of the Nation "Government Revenue and Expenditure" dataset, accessed 4 May 2022, and projections for 2022/23 onwards from various provincial government budgets.

Figure 12.4. Resource Revenues Required to Balance Alberta's Budget (As a Share of Total Revenue)

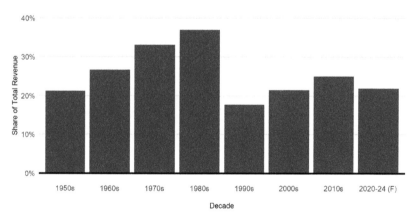

Sources: Own calculations from Boothe, Kneebone and Wilkins, and the Government of Alberta's Budget 2022. Recent years are presented on a fiscal plan basis. (Paul Boothe, *The Growth of Government Spending in Alberta* [Canadian Tax Foundation: Toronto, 1995]; Ronald Kneebone and Margarita Wilkins, "Canadian Provincial Government Budget Data, 1980/81 to 2013/14," Canadian Public Policy [2016] 42 [1], 1–19. Updated February 2021.)

more aggressively pursued program-spending reductions. Specifically, the government lowered program-expenditures by roughly the equivalent of $3,000 per person today. I illustrate this in Figure 12.3. Combined with significant and rising natural resource revenues later in Premier Klein's mandate, the government was able to avoid deep reforms to the province's fiscal policy to eliminate its dependence on natural resource revenues. Today, a similar focus on expenditure restraint is sufficient to overcome Alberta's short-term fiscal challenges only due to rising natural resource revenues from high global oil prices. In future years, absent continued increases in resource revenues, spending restraint alone may prove insufficient. And with Alberta nearly aligned with other large provinces in Canada, the scope for such restraint may also be less than it has been historically.

Challenges Facing the UCP's Fiscal Policy

Despite recent increases in resource revenues, Alberta's long slide towards a fiscal reckoning may soon be unavoidable. Managing this will be more difficult for governments today than it has been in the past. The scale of the provincial government's dependence on resource revenues remains high, the scope for program-expenditure reductions is limited, economic disruptions make raising revenue more difficult, and long-term spending pressures from an aging population and a coming bulge in the number of post-secondary-age students must be accommodated. I unpack in detail each of these and explore how they may challenge the UCP's approach to fiscal policy.

First, the provincial government's dependence on natural resource revenues is as high as ever. Since the 1990s, when our reliance on resource revenues was lowest—due to large spending reductions by the former PC government under Premier Klein just discussed—our reliance has steadily increased. Since 2010, for example, the government has required one-quarter of all revenues to come from natural resources to balance its books. Though not near its historic highs, this is significant. I display this measure in Figure 12.4, projected forward using the latest fiscal forecasts from Budget 2022. The short-term risks that come with funding public services with a volatile revenue source will therefore remain. More challenging, though, are the long-term risks of falling oil and gas revenues as the global energy transition accelerates. Serious efforts to get off the "energy revenue rollercoaster," as Premier Prentice put it, were abandoned by the former NDP government and current UCP government alike. They instead largely hoped for rebounding oil prices and production to spur not only economic recovery but also patch the government's fiscal holes. Since 2021, this strategy has paid off for the government, but historically high resource revenues may provide only temporary relief as longer-term pressures mount.

Reducing Alberta's dependence requires lower spending growth, higher revenues, or some combination of the two. Relying on only one side of the budget or the other requires infeasibly large changes. For perspective, by 2023, a general sales tax harmonized with the GST would need to be approximately fourteen percentage points—far beyond rates found elsewhere in Canada. Alternatively, existing tax rates would need to rise by two-thirds across the board. On the expenditure side, the entire combined budgets of the Ministries of Education and Advanced Education would need to be eliminated. And if health, education, and social services were protected, cutting every single dollar of spending in all other areas of government operations would fall short of what's needed. In short, gradual moves on both the revenue and the spending side of the budget would be required to address Alberta's fiscal challenges. Something on the order of achieving spending parity with other large provinces, growing with population and inflation thereafter, and phasing in a broad sales tax of approximately 5 per cent could eliminate Alberta's reliance on resource revenues fully sometime in the 2030s.

High resource revenues are, of course, a boon that governments have difficulty resisting when they happen—as they are now. Following Alberta's Budget 2022, released in late February 2022, for example, the originally projected deficit for 2021/22 fell from $18.2 billion projected in Budget 2021 to just $3.2 billion in Budget 2022.[12] A massive decline largely accounted for by natural resource revenues rising to over $13 billion for the year. Future fiscal years have also improved, with modest surpluses projected in Budget 2022 for 2022/23 onwards. High resource revenues, however, merely paper over the underlying fiscal risk that the provincial budget is exposed to. And over the longer run, global climate polities and the gradually accelerating energy transition will eventually—and permanently—eliminate these revenues as a meaningful contributor to Alberta finances. But by saving resource revenues today, a physical asset whose value may not last can be transformed into a financial one that can be maintained in perpetuity. To date, however, successive governments have resisted even contemplating any policy like what former Premier Prentice put forward in 2015.

The second challenge facing the UCP directly constrains their preferred policy option. In stark contrast to previous Alberta governments, the scope for expenditure reductions is significantly narrower today. As illustrated in Figure 12.3, the government's previous ability to engage in this significant spending reduction was substantial. The gap between Alberta average spending and other major provinces, for example, was over $6,000 per person in the early 1980s. The expenditure reductions during Premier Getty and Klein's early years shrank this gap, though it increased again from 2000 onwards. Today, the gap between Alberta program spending and those same provinces is smaller. And the UCP's fiscal plan enacted in Budget 2019 and re-committed to in subsequent budgets will bring average spending in Alberta in line with other large provinces by 2022/23. Despite that, a large deficit would remain were it not for increases in resource revenues because taxation revenues are far below levels found elsewhere. Today, Alberta maintains the second lowest average rate of income taxation, the lowest rate of gasoline taxes, does not have a payroll tax, health care levies, nor—most importantly—does it levy a general sales tax. The only province with lower income taxes is British Columbia, but it can do so because of provincial carbon tax revenues, general sales taxes, and health care premiums. The ability of the UCP to enact greater expenditure reductions than currently planned may therefore be limited.

The composition of spending today is also more constraining than in the past. Past governments had greater scope for spending restraint outside of core areas of health care, education, and social services. In 1985, for example, only slightly more than half of total program spending was in those areas. Today, that share has increased to three-quarters—driven largely by increases within health care. Looking forward, expenditure pressures on provincial governments will be incredible. Significant public sector compensation restraint may be unavoidable. This isn't a new development. The previous NDP government, for example, pursued public sector compensation freezes in its negotiations. The UCP, in contrast, originally pushed for wage rollbacks on the order of 3–5 per cent. Importantly, a wage freeze is an effective real reduction in compensation as inflation erodes the purchasing power of each dollar earned. With inflation averaging around 2 per cent per year, the NDP and UCP approaches to public sector compensation are not materially different over a multi-year horizon. They differ primarily in the speed of implementing public sector compensation reductions, but also in their public communications on the issue.

The UCP consistently opts for combative and adversarial language, which is a marked departure from prior governments. In a fiscal update in November 2020, for example, the government wrote that the public sector "does not create jobs or generate wealth,"[13] despite the significant role played by many to improve lives and livelihoods during the pandemic. And, to highlight another example, the Alberta finance minister accused the United Nurses of Alberta of engaging in a "a shameful effort to take advantage of a health crisis" during negotiations.[14] This polarizing rhetoric may complicate future negotiations. To be sure, the additional fiscal room provided by boosted resource revenues allowed the government to agree to modest nominal wage increases for several public sector unions. This helped avoid significant labour disruptions in the year prior to the provincial election. Historically high inflation, however, which reached 6.7 per cent in March 2022, effectively makes a 1 per cent nominal increase equivalent in real terms to what a 3 per cent nominal rollback would have meant if inflation remained near at its normal level. If higher rates of inflation continue, negotiations could become especially challenging once again in the coming years.

These are but short-term considerations; the longer-term ones are even more daunting. Canada's population is growing older. By 2050, Statistics Canada's medium-case projection anticipates approximately one in four Canadians will be age sixty-five or older. This is significantly above the one in six today and double the one in eight who were above sixty-five in 2000. By 2050, there may be as many individuals over the age of 80, as a share of the population, as there were those over sixty-five in 2000. While Alberta is currently the youngest province by a wide margin, and will continue to be in these scenarios, it will not be spared the pressure on government budgets. This population aging will pressure public finances through rising health care costs and declining rates of economic growth.

The direct effects on health expenditures can be quantified in a straightforward way. The Canadian Institute for Health Information estimates that the average person aged sixty-five and over accounts for approximately $15,000 per year in provincial government health care spending and those over age eighty account for nearly twice that—at over $27,000 per year.[15] Younger individuals in their twenties and thirties, meanwhile, barely account for more than $3,000. As the share of the province's population among older age groups increases, health spending will almost surely rise. Combined with the typically faster pace of price increases for health care equipment and supplies than the overall rate of economy-wide inflation, rising health costs will be the most important source of increased government expenditure pressures for years to come. In previous research, I estimated that by 2050, rising health care spending will account for half of the total increase in government spending.[16] And overall spending on health will rise from just over one-third of total program expenditures in 2019 to nearly 45 per cent. For context, that increased share is equivalent to nearly $9 billion per year in additional health care expenditures today. Alberta is not yet ready for this, to say nothing of the full long-term implications of COVID-19 on the health system.

Budget pressures from an aging population go beyond health care expenditures. As more individuals retire and exit the labour force, total taxable incomes will naturally decline. If historic norms for labour force participation hold, I estimate Alberta's aging population implies approximately 0.3 percentage points slower economic growth over the next two decades. And since slower economic growth tends to lower household taxable incomes, government revenue growth will be correspondingly slow. Indeed, this revenue pressure may be greater in Alberta than elsewhere. Tax payments by elderly individuals, after all, tend to be accounted for mainly by property taxes and sales taxes.[17] Alberta has the former but lacks the latter.

Health care is not the only source of expenditure pressure facing Alberta soon. At the younger end of the age distribution, the population of individuals in typical post-secondary education age groups is set to rise significantly as well—starting as soon as 2024. Currently, there are approximately 380,000 Albertans between the ages of eighteen and twenty-four. The Government of Alberta projects this to remain relatively flat for the next couple years.[18] But between 2024 and 2034, the population growth of this age group may exceed the province's total growth rate by a half point per year—resulting in an increase of nearly 30 per cent by 2034 or over 100,000 persons. And in their high-growth scenario—one that presumably the government believes its economic recovery and growth policies would stimulate—this population increases by nearly 150,000. Not all will seek university or college admissions, to be sure, but fully 60 per cent of Albertans historically enroll in a post-secondary institution or registered apprenticeship program within six years of entering grade 10.[19] If this transition rate holds, there may be 60,000 to 90,000 more persons looking for space at already heavily constrained institutions in Alberta. Recent choices by the government to constrain university and college budgets will make it difficult to accommodate this growth, which may open the door to younger Albertans leaving the province to access space elsewhere.

With such expenditure pressures mounting in several areas, tax increases will be increasingly difficult for governments to avoid. Luckily, a strong economy also allows Alberta's government to raise more revenues than identical tax rates would elsewhere. Economic pressures, however, make raising revenues more difficult than it was for past governments in Alberta. As discussed earlier in the chapter, Alberta's economy contracted significantly from late 2014 onwards as global oil prices collapsed. By January 2020, for example, average weekly earnings were no higher than five years earlier. Adjusting for inflation, they were over 10 per cent lower. Business incomes also declined significantly. And with lower incomes and corporate profits comes lower taxation revenues. Each point of corporate income tax, for example, raised over $500 million in 2014 but less than half that in 2021. Too appreciate the scale of this decline, I plot the per capita value of both corporate profits and total labour compensation in Figure 12.5. Both account for most income earned by Albertans, and—more importantly for government finances—are the largest tax bases in the province. As is evident in the figure, both have significantly declined since their peaks in 2014. Corporate profits, or more precisely corporate net operating surpluses, fell in half from nearly $20,000 per capita (in 2020 dollars) in 2014 to about $10,000 per capita five year later and to less than

Figure 12.1a. Real Corporate Profits and Labour Compensation per Capita

(a) Corporate Profits

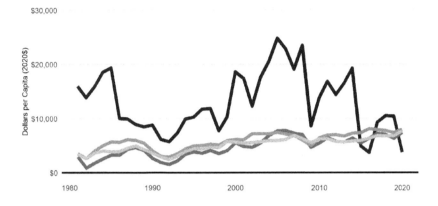

(b) Labour Compensation

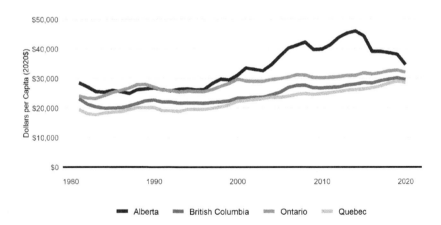

Note: Corporate profits here reflects net operating surpluses of corporate entities within the provincial economic accounts. This approximates, though differs from, accounting definitions of profit.

Sources: Authors' calculations from Statistics Canada data tables 36-10-0221-01, 17-10-0005-01, and 18-10-0005-01.

$4,000 in 2020. Total labour compensation has also declined in recent years, from $46,100 per capita in 2014 (in 2020 dollars) to $38,100 by 2019 and to less than $34,600 by 2020. Despite recent increases in oil prices—which has dramatically increased corporate profits—the general pattern that Alberta has converged to, which is something closer to normal levels of economic activity in Canada, may continue. If it does, this will dampen the government's ability to raises revenues through taxation.

Of course, two positives must not be neglected. First, though it has experienced a significant reduction, Alberta remains above where the other three large provinces in Canada are. Total labour compensation, for example, has declined by 25 per cent since 2014, but it remains approximately 8 per cent above Ontario levels and 20 per cent above Quebec's. This is also evident in Figure 12.5. Second, and more importantly, Alberta's large ups and downs appear firmly anchored by a nearly identical trend in rate of growth compared to other provinces. Long time-series data on provincial economic conditions are rare in Canada, but we do have nearly a century of data on household disposable incomes. This is the after-tax income that households have available to purchase goods and services or to save for the future. Between 2015 and 2019, average real disposable incomes fell 12 per cent. This is very large.

Indeed, that four-year decline is larger than at any point since 1929 through 1933. Despite such a large decline, Alberta remains a leader in Canada. And over the ninety-three years between 1926 and 2019, where Statistics Canada data on real household disposable income per can be compiled, the average growth over time in Alberta is like other regions, despite Alberta's far higher degree of volatility. On average, growth in real disposable incomes is 2 per cent nationally and 2 per cent in Alberta. If this historic average growth continues, then following Alberta transition to a level of income closer to the average—though still above most—it would take approximately six years to cover the drop experienced in the previous recession. Of course, COVID changes this picture, but does so for all. And given emergency response measures from the federal government, disposable incomes increased in 2020 and the post-COVID recovery has, so far, been robust. That complicating factor aside, by the sheer force of normal economic growth, Alberta households may see their living standards exceed their pre-recession peak by the latter half of the decade—continuing to improve thereafter. Sharp declines since 2014 do not imply the province's best days are behind it.

Conclusion

These fiscal hurdles are not insurmountable. Despite the large decline in Alberta's economy recently, it remains strong relative to other provinces. Average wages are higher than elsewhere, overall employment is a higher share of its population, and corporate profits remain robust. The need for fiscal adjustment stems from a ratcheting down in the overall level, though to one that remains enviable to other provinces. The UCP government did respond to recent fiscal shortfalls modestly but did so focused on the expenditure side of the budget and with moves that will likely prove insufficient. Worse, the combative political rhetoric of Premier Kenney specifically—and the UCP government generally—may constrain the government and complicate efforts to adapt provincial policies to Alberta's new fiscal and economic reality. Worse, the government's claims that much of Alberta's economic weakness is caused by hostile federal policies may also distract from necessary fiscal reforms that the province itself can adopt. Simply put, polarized political rhetoric may pay short-term dividends but at the cost of delaying action on, and therefore exacerbating, Alberta's long-term challenges.

Fiscal policy reforms will be increasingly necessary to ease Alberta off its resource revenue dependence and to accommodate pressures from an aging population. Several reasonable options are available thanks to Alberta's still enviable (though diminished) economic advantages, but none are easily adopted. Lower program spending and higher taxes impose real costs on Alberta's families and businesses. Public acceptance of difficult choices is necessary and requires clear, honest leadership. The fiscal realities facing Alberta make an all-of-budget approach unavoidable. By focusing heavily on the spending side of the budget, the UCP government delayed a broader and longer-term conversation about how Alberta recovers from the pandemic in a sustainable way.

Alberta is and has been on a long slide towards a fiscal reckoning. The only questions that now remains is how disruptive and divisive that reckoning will be.

NOTES

1   Jason Kenney, "Protecting Lives and Livelihoods: Premier Kenney Address," Government of Alberta (7 April 2020). Available at https://www.alberta.ca/release.cfm?xID=7003168647E46-E91D-4945-E9517ABC712B807E.

2   *Edmonton Journal*, "Jim Prentice Televised Address: Budget," video, 2:14, 16 February 2018. Available at https://www.youtube.com/watch?v=hZHDfdzfz7I.

3   Government of Alberta, *2018–19 Third Quarter Fiscal Update and Economic Statement* (Alberta Treasury Board and Finance: Edmonton, 2019), 36.

4   Government of Alberta, *Budget 2019: A Plan for Jobs and the Economy* (Alberta Treasury Board and Finance: Edmonton, 2019). Available at https://open.alberta.ca/dataset/budget-2019-a-plan-for-jobs-and-the-economy.

5   Government of Alberta, *Fiscal Plan: Moving Forward* (Alberta Treasury Board and Finance: Edmonton, 2022). Available at https://open.alberta.ca/publications/budget-2022.

6   *Ibid.*

7   Based on data from Trevor Tombe, "Final and Unalterable—But Up for Negotiation: Federal-Provincial Transfers in Canada," *Canadian Tax Journal* (2018) 66 (4), 871–917.

8   Analysis based on Statistics Canada, "Table 36-10-0229-01, Long-run Provincial and Territorial Data." Available at https://doi.org/10.25318/3610022901-eng.

9   Government of Alberta, *Alberta Heritage Savings Trust Fund Annual Report 2020–21* (2021). Available at https://open.alberta.ca/publications/0702-9721.

10   *Alberta Hansard*, 21st Legislature, Second Session, 20 March 1987, at 247.

11   At this time, provincial income taxes were levied on federal income taxes paid rather than taxable income earned. Alberta's tax-on-tax rate was increased from 43.5 per cent of the basic federal tax to 46.5 per cent. On average, this would result in a 7 per cent increase in provincial income taxes owing.

12   Government of Alberta, *Fiscal Plan: Moving Forward* (Alberta Treasury Board and Finance: Edmonton, 2022). Available at https://open.alberta.ca/publications/budget-2022.

13   Government of Alberta, *2020–21 Mid-year Fiscal Update and Economic Statement* (Alberta Treasury Board and Finance: Edmonton, 2020). Available at https://open.alberta.ca/publications/6042188.

14   Phil Heidenreich, "Alberta Finance Minister Accuses Nurses' Union of Trying to 'Take Advantage of a Health Crisis,'" *Global News* (8 October 2020). Available at https://globalnews.ca/news/7387670/alberta-finance-minister-nurses-union-ahs-negotiations-pandemic/.

15   Canadian Institute for Health Information, *National Health Expenditure Database, 2020* (2020), Table O.2. Accessed 13 July 2021. Available at https://www.cihi.ca/en/national-health-expenditure-trends.

16   Trevor Tombe, "Provincial Debt Sustainability in Canada: Demographics, Federal Transfers, and COVID-19," *Canadian Tax Journal* (2020) 68 (4), 1083–1122.

17   Daria Crisan, Kenneth McKenzie, and Jack Mintz, "The Distribution of Income and Taxes/Transfers in Canada: A Cohort Analysis," *The School of Public Policy Research Papers* (2015) 8 (5), 1–36.

18   Government of Alberta, *Alberta Population Projections, 2021–2046—Alberta and Census Divisions—Data Tables* (2021). Available at https://open.alberta.ca/opendata/ alberta-population-projections-2021-2046-alberta-census-divisions-data-tables.

19   Government of Alberta, *High School to Post-Secondary Transition Rate by Post-Secondary Service Region* (2021). Accessed 3 August 2021. Available at https://open. alberta.ca/opendata/high-school-to-post-secondary-rate-by-post-secondary-service-region.

Always More Than It Seems: Rural Alberta and the Politics of Decline

Roger Epp

Arrivals and Departures

The Road Home might have been the last of the glossy, coffee-table-size books, supported with public money, to emphasize the point that Alberta was no cultural backwater. Published in 1992, with copies distributed to every high school and municipal library, it featured evocative new writing and striking photographic portraits. It reads now like an artefact from a more optimistic time. Despite its title and, for that matter, its cover photograph of a rancher and a dog in silhouette, the book celebrated the new Alberta: sophisticated, multicultural, Indigenous—"the world in a nutshell," as the introduction put it, and nothing like the stereotypes that presumably still lingered in other parts of the country and some corners of this province.[1] The new Alberta was a place of arrival, a place with prospects. It told stories of people arrived from around the world. They had come, almost all of them, to Calgary and Edmonton. Give or take a funny-dark rumination on hunters and hunting season in Peace River country and Sid Marty's poem about the gamble of buying a little house for a lifetime, tucked into a hillside at the foot of the Livingstone Range, *The Road Home* was a very urban register of Alberta as a place of arrival. Rural, when it appeared, was a place of return: a drive out to the fall turkey supper in Tofield. Or else lament: the sale of a family farm, the kind of place where a farmer, when they were still called that, "walked between buildings with a meadowlark on his lips."[2]

The question of whether Alberta is on the brink of decline is, in an important sense, about arrivals and departures. By that measure, there is no single trajectory. The reality is that much of what we call rural Alberta has been in decline for a generation, maybe two, living in the second-hand lustre of a prosperous, young, resource-based province, one of the most urban in Canada; its statistical markers have been increasingly out of step but mostly hidden in aggregate figures. In rural places, people have lived on the defensive for a long time. They have worried about community futures, jobs, and Main Streets. They have worried about whether their own young people, enough of them, will stay home or return home with education enough to be a nurse in the local hospital or a teacher in the school, and about keeping that hospital or school open at all. This might not be every rural place—not the ones near the mountains or a major city, or the ones that get the Wal-Mart as economies concentrate into region-al centres. But it is many of them. The 2021 national census registered another round of population loss in some communities, even as Alberta grew by another 200,000 people. In recent years, century-old villages like Granum and New Norway have voted themselves out of existence. Battle River School Division framed its 2020–21 strategic plan around a 30 per cent drop in student numbers over the past quarter-century (more than 40 per cent in Flagstaff County), an average bus ride of ninety-seven minutes per day, and most of its eleven high schools across east-central Alberta having fewer than seventy-five students.[3]

This chapter considers the decline question through a rural lens. It comes with an important caveat: a skepticism that there is a coherent, sin-gle place called rural Alberta, much less the one so often invoked to de-scribe the cultural heartland of the province or one side of a simple, polar-ized politics or vaccination compliance ledger.[4] The word rural can serve both as a synonym for backward and as an oppositional identity marker. There are no clear lines marking where it begins or ends. Sometimes in policy and in public discourse rural is a residual category that contains everything outside of the metropolitan regions of Calgary and Edmonton. But Red Deer, with more than 100,000 people, is not rural, not even close by any of Statistics Canada's measures. Grande Prairie, Airdrie, and Camrose are not rural—not "really rural," as people say—though you might be able to see it from there.

In Alberta, rural is agrarian, northern-boreal, industrial, Indigenous, acreage-residential, and mountain playground. It is never hermetically sealed. Rural people know their way around cities. They regularly move back and forth, to shop, visit family, work, see a doctor, or watch a hockey game, though the same is far less likely to be true of those who live in cities. In the end, what defines rural Alberta in 2023 might be some combination of the everyday experience of distance, the likelihood of a gravel road, and a poor internet connection. In that case, rural is not so much a solid-line demarcation as a shading out from the centre towards the perimeter of the province. Typically, that shading also reflects older populations—First Nations communities are a marked exception—as well as significantly lower per-capita incomes, poorer health outcomes, and higher levels of dependency on government transfers, including pensions. The provincial government has tracked those disparities at least twice: once, in a "resource package" compiled for internal purposes in 2002; then, a decade later, in a commissioned study, which concluded that economic growth in rural Alberta had "decelerated noticeably," despite years of post-Klein reinvestment, and that income levels remained "well below" those in cities.[5]

The words rural and decline share a material, measurable quality, but they are each more than that: they sometimes show themselves as anxiety, fatalism, anger. They suggest the temptation of a politics of nostalgia—of better times remembered, lost, or taken. There is, as colleagues have suggested, reason to think about rural Alberta through narratives imported from the United States: a "politics of resentment" for places that are "left behind."[6] Those themes certainly resonate in rural speech; they have been mobilized politically to effect. In this chapter, however, I want to challenge the sufficiency of that reading in light of two considerations. One is that the Kenney government has demonstrated that its strongest interest in rural Alberta lies in resource extraction, not communities. The other is that rural places, at least some of them, drained of any sense of their exceptional place in the provincial mythos, are where we might look for signs of adaptation, not just decline.

Where to Start

The story of decline—a rapid descent into unfamiliar hardship—depends on where and when you start. The settler-colonial countryside is layered with the story-arcs of decline. The first is an Indigenous one. From the early 1870s, when smallpox had already ravaged populations, it took less than a generation. Indigenous leaders—offended by the sale of Rupert's Land, as if it belonged to anyone, and anxious for the future—petitioned for treaty, a way to share the land, and for the tools of an agrarian transition that mostly never arrived. The Dominion of Canada used the hardship of disease and famine to force First Nations to take up reserves and submit to its authority, including an Indian Act.[7] Waves of homestead settlers followed the surveyors. The first church-run residential schools opened in the 1880s. Eventually, there would be more of them in Alberta than anywhere else in Canada. The story still haunts the province. In summer 2021, the prospect that ground-penetrating radar would confirm unmarked graves of children at residential school sites prompted the United Conservative Party (UCP) government to announce an $8-million grant program to support documentation, site-work, and commemoration—this while its controversial curriculum review equivocated about whether and how to teach that history in Alberta schools.

At the same time, decline was not disappearance. Populations began to rebound in the 1920s. Indigenous peoples reasserted themselves politically, in the League of Indians of Canada, which drew 1,500 people to its national meeting at Samson reserve,[8] and the Indian Association of Alberta, which met for the first time at Wabamun in 1939, when it was essentially illegal to do so.[9] In 1969, a decade of parent agitation at Blue Quills residential school near St. Paul became a three-week sit-in, resulting in the first Indigenous-administered school in Canada.[10] That same year, when Pierre Trudeau's federal government proposed in a White Paper to eliminate the Indian Act, Indian status, and historic treaties on principle—Canadians should be treated equally and individually under the law—it was the Indian Association of Alberta and its young president, Harold Cardinal, from Sucker Creek, that led the national response. The Red Paper articulated a fundamentally different set of principles based on treaties and inherent rights; it forced Trudeau to acknowledge the prejudices of his liberalism.[11]

Against that first story-arc, the perverse paradox of the homestead era was a relatively egalitarian distribution of land that gave rise to one of the most creative political-economic movements in Canadian history.[12] A century ago, the United Farmers of Alberta (UFA) swept into office as part of a broader agrarian political sweep across North America. Theirs was a reluctant government, divided over whether it could achieve its purposes through the ballot box and parliamentary institutions; it was elected without a leader—a strange, telling populism. But it had strength in numbers. UFA locals drew on the same organizational energy that built cooperatives of all kinds, notably the Wheat Pool in 1923; cooperation was liberty, the higher law. Actual farming, though, was as hard as governing a cash-strapped province. If there was a golden age of rural Alberta, it was over soon enough. Its decline was captured visually in Henry Glyde's 1941 painting, "The Exodus," in which a ragged procession of men and women climbs to an indistinct city under an orange-brown sky.[13] Within a generation, the agrarian countryside had become a place of departure more than arrival, beginning with climate refugees from the dustbowl of the Palliser Triangle. It was more mechanized and dependent on bank credit. The 1951 census showed, for the first time, that most Albertans lived in cities and towns. Farming was no longer their primary occupation. Edmonton and Calgary were booming, helped by oil discoveries at Leduc and Redwater. The urban-rural gap was as basic as paved roads, indoor plumbing, and electrical appliances,[14] but it was also psychological: prosperity and power—the future—had been relocated. For the provincial government, the most important economic relationships now lay with industry and American capital. Oil leases were its primary source of revenue. Oil had first call on the land.

The political management of this shift has had an enduring impact on Alberta politics. First, it meant a rhetorical veneration of the pioneer, removed from a history of smallholder radicalism or an imposed settler-colonialism—but re-enacted in the 1955 Diamond Jubilee[15] and annually in the Calgary Stampede. This veneration fed a powerful sense of heartland exceptionalism increasingly at odds with actual rural life or the choices people made to leave. Second, from the 1950s until the early 1990s, governments used the resources that rolled into the provincial treasury to secure rural political support.[16] They built roads, consolidated schools, and hospitals. Sometimes the explicit purpose was to shrink the gap between rural and urban standards of living: electrification in one generation, natural gas in the next. Other times it was to sustain profitability and generational succession in agriculture: a fleet of grain cars, a West Coast port, an irrigation dam, a farm lender. This patron-client relationship ensured that some of the benefits of oil-and-gas prosperity were redistributed to those who often lived closest to the extraction and shipping of those resources. It came with the disciplining fear of electing an opposition member; it co-opted municipalities; and then it stopped. As one researcher concludes, the failure of "rural development" has been its success: to ensure acceptance—no other choice—for an economy that extracts resources and wealth from the countryside.[17]

Rural Consciousness and Its Limits

DON'T PULL THE
PLUG ON PUBLIC
HEALTH CARE

United Nurses sign, posted on a farmyard,
outside of St. Paul

WILL TRADE
RACISTS
FOR
REFUGEES

T-shirt, draped over a chair, in Daysland

"Alberta's best country music"

Windspeaker radio, CJWE-FM, broadcasting
on ten frequencies in English, Cree,
Nakoda, Dene, and Blackfoot

Rural Alberta, according to an important ethnographic study published in 2020, ought to be regarded as a social identity, a kind of "consciousness"—"a sense that rural citizens understand themselves to be both fundamentally different from urbanites and often ignored by urban-focussed decision makers."[18] The study, an attempt to understand how people think, not just what they think, or how they vote, involved coffee-shop political conversations in sixteen communities. It concluded that its subjects considered themselves as rural, as "ordinary people," and as Albertans, perhaps the real Albertans. As such, they were alienated and angry. While they represented a "moral code" of "hard work, self-reliance and equal treatment," their experience was that governments neglected people like them and routinely violated the code in favour of "cultural minorities, newcomers, and Indigenous peoples."[19]

The conversations were conducted in the months before and after the election that brought the UCP to office. They record no mention of Jason Kenney, only an admiration for US President Donald Trump. For that matter, they record only a passing mention of Rachel Notley, whose New Democratic Party (NDP) government had generated a firestorm of protest in the countryside early in its term by introducing a bill to bring farm workers under the jurisdiction of provincial labour law. In the overheated rhetoric of the time, the bill was taken up as an attack on the family farm, even an entire way of life, and proof that the NDP did not understand rural Alberta. What the NDP did represent was a post-rural politics. It did not give the homestead pioneer pride of place. It broke with the politics of rural exceptionalism. It had limited rural instincts. Though it spoke in terms of families, communities, and workers, it did not foreground rural in the way it presented Alberta or in the kind of economy it proposed to build.[20]

From inside the consciousness attributed to rural coffee-shop patrons, this would have been tantamount to hostile indifference. Like all identity politics, this one seems focussed on respect and recognition—it wants to be heard—rather than on the details of policy. It echoes the localism of the old agrarian populism as well as its insistence on the dignity of the "plain common people." But it asks far less in return. It does not build things. Its politics require a champion or patron: someone who speaks the same "common-sense" language, accords rural people an important rhetorical place, and shields them from one-size-fits-all bureaucratic impositions from Edmonton. Its populism is highly individuated around work and personal responsibility. It borrows from elsewhere, as populism increasingly does, drawing symbols, language, and clothing (MAGA hats, yellow vests, and Confederate flags) from a worldwide web. Indeed, it might sound something like the "lost cause" discourse that has resurfaced so powerfully out of the American South.[21] That discourse, too, is about loss, respect, and heritage. It is a matter of co-creation, involving its subjects and powerful political interests over time. It is both malleable and portable. As one historian writes, it became a national bulwark against "racial, political, and industrial disorder" and "a model of masculine devotion and courage." The coffee-shop participants, as the study acknowledges, were disproportionately male and older. Judging from the talk about minorities, newcomers, and Indigenous peoples, they were also white and straight; they were insiders, those who know who belongs in the rural and who does not.

Two observations are in order here. First, the study's construction of social identity refers to rural Alberta as if it were both uniform, since themes recur across locations, and timeless, that is, without a history. The voices in those conversations and their sensitivity to any hint of urban condescension are familiar enough. But the rural consciousness characterized in the study is far from static and uncontested. It is not the discourse, not exactly, of nurses and other health care workers whose rural hospitals, emergency wards, and jobs have been under threat since 2019—shielded only partly and temporarily by the realities of a pandemic. It is not the discourse of rural school boards, almost all of them, that declined to pilot the provincial government's controversial draft K–6 social studies curriculum.[22] It is not the discourse of those who have worked to make their communities places of welcome rather than departure for 2SLGBTQA+ residents: students and teachers who have built gay-straight alliances into the fabric of rural high schools, and activists who have raised pride flags in unlikely places. Rural consciousness is not the discourse of those who intend that their communities serve as places of arrival for refugees and immigrants, like the increasing numbers of Filipinos settled in places like Lac La Biche. Rural Alberta is always more than it seems.

Second, the UCP's pitch to rural voters in the 2019 election campaign mapped closely onto the study's construction of identity and grievance.

The campaign was light on policy: commitments to funding equity for rural schools, action on rural crime, and incentives to attract entrepreneurial immigrants (the right kind) to smaller communities—not even the perennial all-party pledge to improve broadband service.[23] But the party got identity politics. It understood, it said, how keeping "farms and ranches sustainable is vital to the fabric of Alberta's history and culture." The most prominent photograph inside its lengthy platform document, subtitled "Getting Alberta back to work," besides the one with the ubiquitous blue campaign truck parked alongside grain bins, featured a young rancher, sitting on a round bale with a child, staring into wide-open space. Freedom. Family. Hard work. That photograph appeared beside the priority commitment to repeal the NDP's Bill 6 and replace it with the Farm Freedom and Safety Act, once it had "listen[ed] to farmers, ranchers, and agriculture workers that the NDP ignored."[24] When the promised legislation appeared in the UCP's first six months, it did not gut the principle of workplace insurance in agriculture, which farm organizations actually supported, so much as exempt small operations and introduce an element of public-or-private choice for larger ones.

The UCP government, however, soon encountered the limits of the grievance language of rural consciousness. The issue was Grassy Mountain, the open-pit metallurgical coal project proposed for a legacy mining area north of Crowsnest Pass. In May 2020, without public consultation, the government rescinded a four-decade policy that, in varying degrees, protected the Eastern Slopes of the Rockies from coal development. The change authorized the Alberta Energy Regulator to issue approvals on a case-by-case basis. It delighted major Australian mining companies; six proposed mines were already in the queue. Months later, the government invited and granted more than 150 exploration leases covering almost half a million acres, including land around the headwaters of the Oldman River. The policy shift prompted immediate alarm in the area, where groups like the Livingstone Range Landowners, comprised primarily of ranch families, have been active for years on conservation issues. But the opposition only gained a wider public traction in early 2021, as prominent Albertans like singer Corb Lund—"a great musician who hates politics but loves the mountains"[25]—went public with concerns, and as regional municipalities, environmental organizations, landowners, and several

First Nations began to coalesce against the project. Legal fights loomed. While his energy minister cancelled some of the new coal leases, Premier Kenney went on the offensive. On talk-radio, he defended the decision to rescind a "dead letter" policy; he gave assurances about the "exhaustive environmental review" that awaited any mine project; and, not least, he played the urban-rural card: "There's thousands of Alberta families who put food on the table because of the mining industry. *I don't think those of us who live in the city should look down on those folks.*"[26] The premier's intervention did not divide the opposition or bring ranchers and council-lors into line. The government, in retreat, appointed a five-person commit-tee—including a representative from the Livingstone Range group but not from any environmental organization—to hold public consultations and make recommendations on coal policy. When the joint federal-provincial review panel concluded in June 2021 that the Grassy Mountain project was not in the public interest, the Kenney government simply said that the review process had worked. One journalist added: "But it was Albertans who rallied and did that alone, without their government."[27]

The story of Grassy Mountain is far from over. The policy review committee's report was released in 2022. Using the language of "halt," but also "pause," for "advanced projects," it recommended that regional and sub-regional land use plans, involving Indigenous communities, be completed first in order to rebuild public trust and provide "investment certainty"; it did not rule out future mining.[28] The mayor of High River reported after a meeting with the premier that Kenney remained an "un-apologetic supporter of coal."[29] Nonetheless, the story suggests a very dif-ferent rural consciousness, one that is more about land and water than identity and recognition. Likewise, it suggests that the UCP government's rural policy interests under Kenney were focussed on resource extraction: mining in the mountains; logging in old-growth, caribou-habitat forest near Willmore Wilderness Park; new oil and gas leases on native grass-lands in the south. Given its primary focus on the oil and gas industry, including pipelines, in the face of a prolonged downturn, it introduced measures to reduce or suspend tax assessments for energy producers, over the strong objections of the provincial organization, Rural Municipalities of Alberta. Counties and municipal districts—who were owed an esti-mated $250 million in unpaid industry taxes at the end of 2021—were left to absorb a significant loss in revenue, in effect, a transfer of wealth from the countryside.[30] At the same time, they were dealing at close range with the massive environmental liability of 73,500 abandoned and 97,000 inactive well-sites in places from which the industry had already exited—a liability long in the making, but intensified as prices dropped.[31] That was the downward legacy of oil and gas in the countryside. If the government's direct investment in the Keystone XL pipeline gave a temporary benefit to towns like Oyen, at least until construction was halted by decisions made by a new US administration, it had already chosen not to intervene when Battle River School Division closed the school in Hardisty, the originating terminal, due to low enrollment. Even if resources flowed south, that would not translate into more of the kinds of steady local jobs that supported families.

If the UCP government viewed rural Alberta through a resource extraction lens, the same could be said for how it viewed Indigenous peoples. Notably, it created the Alberta Indigenous Opportunities Corporation with an initial billion-dollar allocation to provide access to credit and "support Indigenous-led investment in energy, mining, and forestry projects."[32] It also created a legal defence fund to "help groups with Indigenous membership defend their right to economic prosperity."[33] In early 2020, the premier gave a major speech to the Indian Resource Council's national conference in Calgary in which he accused "urban green left militants" of "misappropriating the voice and the cause of Indigenous people" and the federal government of suffocating new energy projects that promised economic development for communities.[34] Alberta oil, in effect, was not only ethical oil in a world where dictators and human rights abusers were going to keep producing it; it had also become reconciliation oil. The message was amplified by the government's energy "war-room" and the Canadian Association of Petroleum Producers.[35] A government that had been deeply suspicious of the idea of social licence as an argument for a carbon tax embraced it vis-à-vis Indigenous peoples. Better shield than barricade.

In pre-pandemic times, getting resources out of the ground and shipped to market was the biggest file on the premier's desk. Teck Resources had withdrawn the Frontier oilsands project just south of Wood Buffalo National Park from review, having signed benefit agreements with Indigenous governments in the region. The Trans Mountain pipeline expansion had run aground on the federal government's failure to meet the test of consultation with affected Indigenous communities along the route. The Coastal GasLink pipeline in British Columbia faced blockades in traditional Wet'suwet'en territory and solidarity blockades in Alberta, including the CN line through Enoch First Nation. The government's first response had been the Critical Infrastructure Defence Act, Bill 1, which limited protest around pipelines, oil and gas production sites, refineries, mines, utilities, highways, and railways. The premier said at the time the bill was about "lawlessness" and Albertans "getting to work and putting food on the table."[36] The Opportunities Corporation was the positive invitation to Indigenous peoples to be industry partners. The logic was no secret: "The more deeply vested First Nations are in the resource industry, the more overall aboriginal support there will be for projects like pipelines."[37]

The message evidently had some appeal. Already in 2016, the Mikisew Cree and Fort McKay First Nations had bought an equity stake in Suncor's new tank farm, payable on opening. The Athabasca Tribal Council announced its ownership interest in the Trans Mountain Pipeline. Leaders like Alan Adam, Chief of the Athabasca Chipewyan First Nation and a prominent critic of the industry's impact, had come around. Better to sign a deal and get some of the benefits.[38] That still left Indigenous communities deeply divided about resource development, as they were about coal, in the case of the Piikani, the Stoney Nakoda, and the Grassy Mountain mine; or the case of Ermineskin and Whitefish Lake First Nations, which have benefit agreements riding on Coalspur Mines' proposed expansion near Hinton and sided with the company against federal review.[39] In this sense, their division and ambivalence over large-scale resource extraction mirrored that of other rural communities with what seem limited options for economic development and jobs. If anything, they had more public leverage and access to capital. But the economic and environmental stakes of investing in oil sands and pipelines were higher too: was this good money after bad? As it was, some of the province's abandoned and inactive conventional wells could be found on reserves further south.

In the case of rural municipalities, there were fewer carrots in the UCP government's approach. On the issues of taxation and unpaid taxes, it sided with oil and gas producers. At the fall 2020 conference of Rural

Municipalities of Alberta (RMA), the premier told delegates that they needed to do more to reduce red tape in order to attract economic investment.[40] It was their problem. Soon after, his government introduced an online tool so that Albertans could compare tax rates and expenditures across communities. If rural municipalities had once been the linchpin in the patron-client relationship, they now felt, as one county councillor put it, "under attack."[41] Or, as a reeve said, after the province changed the municipal funding formula for policing: "How come we don't have that strong rural voice that we thought we were going to have?"[42] About the same time, the government announced major cuts to Alberta Agriculture and Forestry positions and facilities around the province.[43]

The political emergence of rural municipal leaders from a culture of deference did not begin with the UCP government. To some extent, it has tracked the province's declining fiscal ability to reward and punish. It was visible in 2016 when the NDP deputy premier was booed at the RMA fall convention during her remarks on climate policy. That political emergence might sometimes sound like straight-up rural resentment. But it has also taken the form of polished media campaigns and policy briefs on issues like taxation through the RMA; legal action on Grassy Mountain; practical regional collaborations with First Nations governments; a public defence of hospitals, obstetrics, and emergency wards as doctors began to leave rural communities after the provincial government tore up the existing fee schedule. Historically, that kind of oppositional advocacy has been rare enough. Add to it the considerable efforts from rural municipalities to shift towards alternative energy sources in their own operations—that is, to treat oil and gas as tools, and not the only ones, rather than as identity. From Raymond and Carmangay in the south, to Smoky Lake and Big Lakes County, municipalities have installed large photovoltaic systems towards net-zero emissions. In that sense, the transitional energy economy might be a local one. (In Fort Chipewyan, too, Mikisew Cree First Nation, Athabasca Chipewyan First Nation, and the Fort Chipewyan Métis Association have worked with ATCO Utilities on a solar project that will displace an estimated 800,000 litres of diesel each year.) The mayor of Oyen, meanwhile, sounded more stoic than outraged at the impact of the Keystone XL cancellation. Construction was mostly complete, he said,

COVID has had more impact on the local economy, and wind and solar might have better long-run potential.[44]

Indeed, large-scale private solar developments—attracted by plenty of sun, a deregulated energy market, and advance contracts with companies as big as Amazon—had begun to pop up on tracts throughout southern Alberta, leaving municipalities scrambling to put policy tools like reclamation bonds in place and balance the concerns of neighbours. The new energy economy needed land and capital perhaps more than it did people. So did schemes for bitcoin mining, powered by abandoned gas wells, and a racetrack resort for middle-aged men. And so did a global market for land itself that, according to a 2021 report,[45] had pushed prices in Alberta increasingly out of reach of local people and livelihoods—a reality that might work for those ready to sell, but that will certainly result in the transfer of more wealth out of rural places to lenders, investors, and heirs. Unregulated land prices make a community-supporting food-and-fibre economy elusive, especially at greater distances from urban markets. What the countryside is for, for whom, and who decides, is still the issue.

Conclusion

In October 2021, past the midway mark in the UCP government's term, one of two MLAs elected under that banner but expelled after calling publicly for Kenney's resignation, circulated a five-page discussion paper, asking whether there was "a better way to protect rural voters from opportunistic politicians who abandon rural policies in pursuit of urban voters."[46] The paper defined rural in the most expansive terms: everything outside of Calgary and Edmonton. That was precisely the political divide—strong echoes of the language of rural consciousness. The paper accused the UCP of a "sharp left turn" away from the "rural values" that got it elected. The solution, it suggested, was a new Rural Voice party that would "embrace the idea of Alberta exceptionalism," grassroots democracy, and "economic and social freedom." Heavily sprinkled with the word rural, it said strikingly little about actual rural communities, including Indigenous ones, only that they all wanted limited government and a "resource-driven economy." It might still strike a chord, especially in the post-Kenney period, though the electoral map is no longer in its favour. At about the same time, however, Corb Lund re-recorded his conservation anthem, "This is

My Prairie," with help from a number of well-known country singers, plus the Cree-Dene musician Sherryl Sewepagaham, who contributed a verse in Cree. The last message on the video is this: "We stand in solidarity with urban and rural Albertans, ranchers and First Nations communities, in strongly opposing coal mining in the heart of our Rocky Mountains."[47] Sid Marty, the poet, had already made his own prosaic statement in a much-circulated article in *Canadian Cowboy Country* magazine.[48] Rural Alberta is always more than it seems.

Decline is not disappearance. It is not fate. It is not acquiescence. It is not a future without choices to make, and, if the experience of rural Alberta has anything to teach, those choices, while not open-ended, become more meaningful when the easy money and the mythology of the exception are gone, and when the authority to make them has to be reclaimed. This future is certainly not as simple as resource development or not. But adaptation in the face of decline does mean letting go of a deep investment in a particular story, one that positions rural as the real Alberta and thinks only in terms of restoration to a rightful place. Instead, it calls for a clear-eyed realism and a wariness of would-be patrons. The departure of people, especially young people, remains the reality of rural places. The UCP government has not reversed that experience. Apart from an implied visual campaign commitment to bring back outdoor jobs for men dressed in denim, it made no such promise. Moreover, at the end of its term in office, rural places in Alberta—north, south, and central, inside and outside the corridor, Indigenous and not—continue to face significant challenges. Climate change impacts, direct and observable, will intensify.[49] COVID will continue to mean the digitization and ownership concentration of economies away from small-town main streets. In health terms, recovery, when it comes, will require an unlikely investment in rural rehabilitation professionals, doctors, and nurses to deal with the virus' long-term effects as well as the backlog of elective surgeries. Distance and connectivity will matter even more. If the policy response to a post-oil reckoning in public finances is simply to shrink, the provincial state will recede further from a meaningful service, infrastructure, and regulatory presence in the countryside. The temptation to double down on resource extraction—as plunder, not transition—will invite hard choices and, in places, oppositional vigilance. In all of these ways, the potential story-arc of a province in decline will matter to rural people. One more thing: they will surely be caught in its politics of blame and resentment, for which people might already be primed, if the coffee-shop conversations are any indication; but they will also have reason to resist the idea that Ottawa is the sole author of their misfortune—or that a different UCP premier-champion, steeped in "rural values," will turn back the clock in their favour.

Acknowledgement

In writing this chapter, I have benefited from conversations and research materials developed in collaboration with Stacey Haugen, and from exchanges with Clark Banack, Ken Eshpeter, and the editors of this volume.

NOTES

1   Fred Stenson, ed., *The Road Home: New Stories from Alberta Writers* (Edmonton: Reidmore Books, 1992), p. xi.

2   Gordon Pengilly, *They Don't Call Them Farmers Anymore*, quoted in Stenson, *The Road Home*, p. 105.

3   Battle River School Division, Board of Trustees, *Strategic Plan 2020–2021*. Copy in possession of the author.

4   I first made this argument in "The End of Exceptionalism: Post-rural Politics in Alberta," in Duane Bratt, et al, eds., *Orange Chinook: Politics in the New Alberta* (Calgary: University of Calgary Press, 2019): 293–315.

5   Government of Alberta, Economic Development, Business Information and Research, "Regional Disparities in Alberta: Resource Package," 4 March 2002; Conference Board of Canada, "Alberta's Rural Communities: Their Economic Contribution to Alberta and Canada," March 2012.

6   See Clark Banack, "Ethnography and Political Opinion: Identity, Alienation and Anti-establishmentarianism in Rural Alberta," *Canadian Journal of Political Science* 54 (2021): 1–22; Clark Banack, "Rural Resentment: No Party Is Looking Out for Rural Albertans," *Alberta Views*, 1 June 2021, 26–32. See also the work of the Common Ground project, including Jared Wesley's *Research Brief*, "Who Is 'Average Joe' Albertan?" 10 March 2021, https://drive.google.com/file/d/1M-hayplW0IiB8BzD2_bIKZBzd5zzULA5/view.

7   See, e.g., James Daschuk, *Clearing the Plains* (Regina: University of Regina Press, 2013); Sheldon Krasowski, *No Surrender: The Land Remains Indigenous* (Regina: University of Regina Press, 2019); Sharon H. Venne, "Understanding Treaty 6: An Indigenous Perspective," in Michael Asch, ed., *Aboriginal and Treaty Rights in Canada* (Vancouver: UBC Press, 2002); Hugh Dempsey, "1870: A Year of Violence and Change," and Sarah Carter and Walter Hildebrandt, "'A Better Life with Honour,'" both in Michael

Payne, Donald Wetherell, and Catherine Cavanaugh, eds., *Alberta Formed Alberta Transformed* (Edmonton: University of Alberta Press; Calgary: University of Calgary Press, 2006).

8 Donald B. Smith, *Seen But Not Seen: Influential Canadians and the First Nations from the 1840s to Today* (Toronto: University of Toronto Press, 2021), 137–144.

9 Laurie Meijer Drees, *Indian Association of Alberta: A History of Political Action* (Vancouver: UBC Press, 2002).

10 Tarisa Dawn Little, "Setting a Precedent: The Power of Public Protest at Blue Quills Residential School, 1970," in Leon Crane Bear, Larry Hannant, and Karyssa Robin Patton, eds., *Bucking Conservatism: Alternative Stories of Alberta from the '60s and '70s*, 33–52 (Edmonton: Athabasca University Press, 2021).

11 Leon Crane Bear, "Indian Status as the Foundation of Justice," in *Bucking Conservatism*, 15–32.

12 The best account is still David Laycock, *Populism and Democratic Thought on the Canadian Prairies* (Toronto: University of Toronto Press, 1990), especially ch. 3.

13 H.G. Glyde, "The Exodus," Collection of the Alberta Foundation for the Arts, http://alberta.emuseum.com/objects/1401/the-exodus?ctx=2254ad5c-269f-4eee-b420-0e8c56ebf906&idx=3.

14 Doug Owram, "Oil's Magic Wand," in *Alberta Formed Alberta Transformed*, 575–77.

15 Frances Swyripa, "1955: Celebrating Together, Celebrating Apart," in *Alberta Formed Alberta Transformed*, 596–602.

16 Roger Epp, "1996: Two Albertas—Rural and Urban Trajectories," in *Alberta Formed Alberta Transformed*, 726–46.

17 Lars Hallstrom, "Rural Governmentality in Alberta: A Case Study of Neoliberalism in Rural Canada," *Revue Gouvernance* 15 (2018): 27–49.

18 Banack, "Ethnography," 3.

19 *Ibid.*, 12, 15–17, *passim.*

20 See Epp, "The End of Exceptionalism."

21 David Blight, *Race and Reunion: The Civil War in American Memory* (Boston: Belknap Press, 2001), 266.

22 The board of Palliser School Division, for example, cited "underrepresentation of First Nations, Metis and Inuit perspectives as well as the limited alignment to the Truth and Reconciliation Commission findings and Calls to Action," and "concerns with how the curriculum deals with ethnic diversity and racism." Stephen Tipper, "Palliser schools will not pilot province's draft K–6 curriculum," *Vulcan Advocate*, May 5, 2021.

23 In summer 2021, the Alberta government announced a $150-million contribution towards a federal-provincial initiative to improve rural broadband access. The national initiative was launched in late 2020.

24 United Conservative Party, *Alberta Strong and Free: Getting Albertans Back to Work* (2019), quotations at pp. 15, 27, https://albertastrongandfree.ca/wp-content/uploads/2019/04/Alberta-Strong-and-Free-Platform-1.pdf.

25 Andrew Nikiforuk, "Who Saved Alberta's Mountaintops and Precious Clean Water? Albertans," *The Tyee*, 18 June 2021, https://thetyee.ca/Analysis/2021/06/18/Alberta-Mountaintops-Precious-Clean-Water-Saved-Albertans/. See also Amanda Stephenson, "Five questions about Alberta's new coal policy, under fire from critics," *Calgary Herald*, 21 January 2021; Chris Arsenault, "Canadian country music star Corb Lund spurs unlikely coalition against coal," *Globe and Mail*, 19 July 2021; and Bob Weber, "More southern Alberta communities voice concern over province's decision to drop coal policy," *Globe and Mail*, 27 January 2021.

26 Bob Weber, "Kenney defends Alberta government's coal mining decision, says old policy was obsolete," *Globe and Mail*, 3 February 2021. My emphasis.

27 Nikiforuk, "Who Saved Alberta's Mountaintops." As of writing, the federal and provincial denials were the subject of separate appeals by Benga Mining as well as two First Nations whose governments had signed benefit agreements with the company.

28 *Final Report: Recommendations for the Management of Coal Resources in Alberta*, Report of the Coal Policy Committee to the Alberta Government, December 2021, 7.

29 Bob Weber, "Alberta mayor fears Rocky Mountain coal-mining concerns will be ignored after meeting with Jason Kenney," *Globe and Mail*, 27 January 2022, https://www.theglobeandmail.com/canada/article-alberta-mayor-fears-rocky-mountain-coal-mining-concerns-will-be/.

30 Rural Municipalities of Alberta, "Municipal Taxation and Assessment," Position Statement (2020), at https://rmalberta.com/wp-content/uploads/2021/01/Municipal-Taxation-and-Assessment-Position-Statements.pdf. The estimate of unpaid taxes comes from the RMA.

31 Alberta Energy, "Oil and gas liabilities management," https://www.alberta.ca/oil-and-gas-liabilities-management.aspx. For a critical analysis of the provincial government's efforts to accelerate cleanup during the pandemic, using federal money, see Megan Egler, "Not Well Spent: A Review of $1-Billion Federal Funding to Clean Up Alberta's Inactive Oil and Gas Wells" (Edmonton: Parkland Institute, 2021).

32 Government of Alberta, Alberta Indigenous Opportunities Corporation, website, https://www.theaioc.com/.

33 Government of Alberta, Litigation Fund, website, https://www.alberta.ca/litigation-fund.aspx.

34 Jason Kenney, "The path to First Nations prosperity," Government of Alberta News, 29 April 2020, https://www.alberta.ca/release.cfm?xID=70206D1D9E834-C21C-53E3-F6B72F0E6CCD2244.

35 Mark Milke and Lennie Kaplan, "How the energy sector impacts Indigenous incomes, employment and prosperity," *Research Brief: Canada's Oil Sands and Local First Nations* (Calgary: Canadian Energy Centre, March 2020). CAPP's webpage on Indigenous Relations makes a direct connection to the TRC, https://www.capp.ca/explore/indigenous-relations/.

36 Jason Kenney, quoted in Alberta Government, News, "Protecting infrastructure from illegal activity," 25 February 2020, https://www.alberta.ca/release.cfm?xID=68684ECA2E9B2-C992-9251-78C0AE348BC7A61F.

37 Jason Kenney, quoted in Justin Giovannetti, "Alberta Indigenous Opportunities allocated $1-billion by Kenney government," *Globe and Mail*, 27 January 2020.

38 Adam told a reporter: "I don't want to do this. I didn't want to make this decision but I had no choice. I had to make sure my nation was protected, and that our people are going to benefit from it for the future." Shawn McCarthy, "First Nation chief who opposed oil sands signs deal with Teck sharing benefits of bitumen expansion," *Globe and Mail*, 23 September 2018.

39 Bob Weber, "Environment minister restores federal assessment of Alberta coal mine," *CBC News*, 1 October 2021, https://www.cbc.ca/news/canada/edmonton/hinton-alberta-coal-mine-assessment-1.6196590.

40 Lisa Johnson, "Kenney urges rural municipalities to do more to attract investment," *Edmonton Journal*, 5 November 2020.

41 The story quoting a councillor from the County of Newell, in response to the premier's speech at the RMA conference, appeared in the *Brooks Bulletin* online—I read it—and it was taken down almost immediately.

42 Quoted in Paige Parsons, "New funding proposal for policing angers rural municipalities," *CBC News*, 10 October 2019, https://www.cbc.ca/news/canada/edmonton/rural-policing-funding-alberta-1.5315674.

43 Ryan Dahlman, "UCP job cuts in ag research deal major blow to Lethbridge, Brooks and Alberta's future," *Medicine Hat News*, 24 October 2020.

44 Lisa Johnson, "'We're pretty resilient': COVID-19 a bigger blow to Oyen, Hardisty than killing Keystone XL pipeline expansion: Mayors," *Edmonton Journal*, 20 June 2021.

45 Katherine Aske, *Finance in the fields: Investors, lenders, farmers, and the future of farmland in Alberta* (Edmonton: Parkland Institute, 2022).

46 Drew Barnes, "Making Room for a Rural Voice: A Discussion Paper," unpublished paper, 2021.

47 Corb Lund, "Corb Lund x Terri Clark x Brett Kissel—This is My Prairie (Official Music Video)," video, 4:24, 19 October 2021, https://www.youtube.com/watch?v=X_h354W4d2M.

48 Sid Marty, "You Can't Rebuild a Mountain," *Canadian Cowboy Country*, April/May 2021, https://issuu.com/tanneryoung.com/docs/ccc2102_issuu/s/12100142.

49 Kelly Vodden and Ashlee Cunsolo, "Rural and Remote Communities," in Fiona Warren and Nicole Lulham, eds., *Canada in a Changing Climate: National Issues Report* (Ottawa: Government of Canada, 2021), ch. 3; Jennifer Henderson, "Alberta's rural communities will deeply feel the effects of climate change, new study says," *Globe and Mail*, 23 July 2021.

Cultural Industries Under the United Conservative Party

Richard Sutherland

It may seem that in the policy world of Alberta, the word culture has not been conspicuously present, unless accompanied by "agri" as a prefix. When it is mentioned, it often seems perfunctory, without any of the passion and commitment that accompanies discussion of oil and gas, or beef. The Fair Deal Panel's call to affirm Alberta's cultural (alongside its political and economic) uniqueness is a case in point.[1] There is no elaboration in the report of what this cultural uniqueness amounts to, although there is plenty of discussion of the ways in which the province is economically and politically distinct. Likewise, the Arts Professionals Recognition Act, announced by Culture Minister Ron Orr in October 2021, which claims to "promote greater economic security, freedom of expression and professional recognition for Alberta's artists,"[2] seems largely symbolic with no commitment to spending in these areas (the United Conservative Party [UCP] has reduced arts funding by $3 million during its time in office). In fact, Alberta was amongst the first provinces to develop generous funding programs for the arts, dating back to the early years of the Lougheed government in the 1970s. But the (generally comparatively good) support for the arts in this province has tended to position them as an accoutrement, rather than a driver, of prosperity—nice to have but not necessary. Amongst other things, this chapter looks at how this discourse has shifted in recent years, not only under Rachel Notley's New Democratic Party (NDP), but at least as much under the current UCP government, as each has turned to culture, more specifically cultural industries, as a possible site for economic diversification. The timing of this shift in policy towards a more favourable view of the cultural industries' economic potential is strongly related to a prolonged downturn in Alberta's economy, primarily in the energy sector, as well as, more recently, the considerable impact of the pandemic on employment. In particular, the sharp increase in film production in 2020–2021 offered Kenney's UCP government one of very few bright spots on the economic front during its first two years in office.

As is not infrequently observed, Alberta's engagement with economic diversification rises and falls in inverse proportion to the price of oil and gas. When energy prices are low, the benefits of a more diverse economy become obvious; when they are high, diversification seems unnecessary. Of course, low energy prices also impact provincial government revenues (see Trevor Tombe's analysis in this book), hampering the government's ability to mobilize policies that would assist with the process. Not surprisingly, calls for economic diversification in Alberta have intensified over the last several years, due to the prolonged downturn in the energy sector. The economic impact of the pandemic has only increased the sense of urgency, and even as oil and gas prices have rebounded almost to 2014 levels, there is the sense that this may not bring employment back to the levels previously enjoyed. Much of the diversification pursued by Alberta's provincial governments over the years has not been so much away from oil and gas, but within it, finding new ways to add value and employment, building on the strengths of the sector. Other attempts at diversification, such as transportation or the telecommunications industry have a mixed track record, and in a province where conservative views often prevail, government attempts at "picking winners" have been frequently criticized.[3] Ralph Klein's government was lauded for reversing many of the attempts of his predecessors, Peter Lougheed and Don Getty along these lines, stating that the Alberta government should not be in the "business of business."

Such thinking, along with the prosperity that the energy industry has usually meant for the province have stymied attempts at diversification beyond the energy sector, and it is hard to imagine a set of industries more distantly removed from oil and gas than the cultural industries (which include sectors such as film and television production, music industries, publishing, and digital media). The Lougheed government was a pioneer in provincial arts policy, but this did not result in any coherent strategy for cultural industries. While grants for some of these industries were available, many of these were drawn from the same programs as arts funding, and these were not industrially focused. Seemingly, the economic potential of these sectors may not have been as pressing a concern for a government overseeing a thriving energy-based economy. Nonetheless, as this chapter shows, cultural industries have gradually attracted more attention from provincial governments as calls for diversification intensify. Two sectors in particular form the focus for this chapter—film and television production and video game development. Not only have they attracted notice for their potential to contribute to economic growth and employment, but they are also the two cultural industries that have seen significant policy developments under the UCP government, even if, in one case, that is simply a case of repealing the previous NDP policies.

Alberta's Recovery Plan, released in June 2020 offers some insight into where cultural industries fit in the UCP's vision for the Alberta economy.[4] Cultural industries and technology featured in the Diversifying section. If the order of topics is any indication, diversification was hardly at the top of the government's agenda, which emphasized more general economic measures, such as low corporate taxes and investment in infrastructure. Even within the Diversifying section, pride of place was given to the energy sector, followed by agriculture and forestry, and tourism. Culture was fourth on the list. Film and television production was certainly prominent within that category, but much of what was discussed here was aspirational, with little reference to concrete measures, beyond the tax credit. To the extent that video game production (or interactive digital media [IDM] as it is referred to in the report) featured at all in the government's plans, it was as a brief mention in the Technology category that followed Culture in the document. This reflects how the two sectors have fared under the UCP with film and television production enjoying at least some success in economic and policy terms, whereas government aspirations and policy directions for IDM remain unfulfilled.

Film and Television Production in Canada and Alberta

We hear a lot about the big Hollywood productions that have been shot in Alberta—*Legends of the Fall*, *Brokeback Mountain*, or *The Revenant* among others. These are all examples of "runaway" productions, or more formally, Foreign Service and Location Productions (FSLs), and, in fact, most of the film and television production activity in Canada is made up of such productions, shot on location here. Vancouver, in particular, has acquired the label of "Hollywood North," as a result of its burgeoning film and television industry since the 1970s. Toronto has also become a leading centre for such productions. Canada offers many attractions in this regard, among them skilled, experienced crews, and varied and accessible locations (not far from the US) that can stand in for other (usually American) places. Film commissions and offices, operating at the municipal and provincial level, promote these advantages as they try to recruit Hollywood studios to film in their cities or provinces. But, of course, economic considerations are central to Canada's viability as a location for film production for Hollywood. A favourable exchange rate is useful, but the major policy tool of governments in this regard has been incentives in the form of grants or, more often, tax breaks, which are more appealing to international producers. The federal government has offered such incentives since the 1970s,[5] and many provinces have also provided generous tax breaks along the same lines. The scope and extent of these incentives vary, but generally they are fully refundable, and they apply to spending on production (that is the actual filming of the project) within the particular jurisdiction. To be clear, the discussion in the chapter focuses on FSL productions, rather than on Canadian productions. While these policies can be used for Canadian made film and television, the largest uptake in these tax credits is from FSLs, and the discussion in Alberta has focused mainly on the presence of these kinds of productions in the province.

Alberta was amongst the first provinces to develop a policy for film production, establishing the Alberta Motion Picture Development Corporation in 1982. By 1994, government contributions amounted to $1.8 million, generating $18 million of direct production expenditures in the province.[6] However, all of this was dismantled early in the Klein

Table 14.1. Total Volume of Film and Television Production, Alberta and Canada

($millions)	2010/11	2011/12	2012/13	2013/14	2014/15	2015/16	2016/17	2017/18	2018/19	2019/20	Share of Total 2019/20
Alberta	148	167	155	274	254	231	246	226	254	220	2%
Canada	5560	5963	5830	5962	7092	6831	8352	8866	9425	9322	100%

Sources: Canadian Media Producers Association, 2020 Profile: Economic Report on the Screen-based Media Production Industry in Canada, p. 12.

Table 14.2. Volume of Foreign Location and Service Production, Alberta and Canada

($millions)	2010/11	2011/12	2012/13	2013/14	2014/15	2015/16	2016/17	2017/18	2018/19	2019/20	Share of Total 2019/20
Alberta	4	13	4	88	92	34	54	31	86	0	0%
Canada	1874	1687	1740	1826	2600	2644	3779	4707	4858	5248	100%

Sources: Canadian Media Producers Association, 2020 Profile: Economic Report on the Screen-based Media Production Industry in Canada, p. 64.

era, just as other provinces were introducing or increasing incentives. The Alberta Film Development Program, introduced in 1998 under the administration of the Alberta Foundation for the Arts (AFA), offered grants reimbursing 20 per cent of production expenditures in the province. The inclusion of the program under AFA positioned film in terms of arts rather than in terms of industry. More recently, the creation of Alberta Film under Alberta Economic Development may have signalled a renewed awareness of the economic potential of film production but did not come with any notable increase in support. The exception to this trend was Ralph Klein's 2005 decision to provide $5.5 million in funding for *Passchendaele*, a film shot near Calgary, produced by and starring Canadian actor Paul Gross and about Canadian troops fighting in the eponymous First World War battle.[7]

Generally, however, Alberta support for the sector remained low, relative to other provinces in Canada. Subsequent Progressive Conservative governments did little to improve Alberta's policies for attracting productions. Another ingredient that has helped to consolidate the success of Vancouver and Toronto has been creating the necessary infrastructure, such as studio facilities. Alberta's investment in this area has been low, and subject to cutbacks, again suggesting a limited commitment to supporting the sector. In 2009, the provincial government announced that it was planning to build the Alberta Creative Hub in Calgary. But in 2013, it backed out on its funding commitment to provide $13.2 million of the $32 million total.[8] The scaled-back project eventually did go ahead, with the Alberta government contributing $5 million of $22.8 million. It was the City of Calgary that played a much larger role in the project, contributing $10 million in funding, alongside a further $6.8 million from Calgary Economic Development, which took over the studio in 2018, two years after it opened.[9]

In some respects, the 2019 provincial election was a watershed moment for the film and television sector in Alberta. For the first time, all the major parties contesting the election included policy for the sector in their platforms. The incumbent NDP government had revised the province's film policy in 2017, replacing the Alberta Production Grant with the Screen-Based Production Grant, increasing both the funding cap on individual projects from $5 million to $7.5 million and the overall annual funding from $30 million to $45 million.[10] In the 2019 campaign, the Alberta Party promised to substantially enhance incentives to the sector with a tax credit of up to 65 per cent for eligible salaries, and 35 per cent for eligible expenses within the province.[11] This announcement was matched by the provincial Liberals. Shortly after this, the UCP likewise announced that it would replace the current program with a tax credit. The NDP was vague in its promises for the future, simply announcing that it would "work with the film and television industry to determine the right policy levers."[12]

The First Year: Freezes, Cuts, and Delays

The UCP government's victory signalled that Alberta's film and television policy would change again for the second time in two years. The change to a tax credit was certainly in line with industry demands, but the UCP's new policies did not get off to a promising start. No changes were announced until the fall. The uncertainty itself was problematic, as producers planning projects had no clear idea about how and when the government would proceed, leading some to move projects elsewhere.[13] The government's announcement in September that it was suspending the Screen-Based Production Grant, claiming that it had been mismanaged and was oversubscribed, did little to help matters. There was no word on a replacement, and the lack of any clarity on how a tax credit would be structured or when it would be introduced caused considerable distress in the province's film sector.

The October 2019 provincial budget officially cancelled the program, announcing a tax credit as a replacement. The value of the tax credit was less than the grant had been—22 per cent of eligible expenditures as opposed to 30 per cent, although the project cap of $10 million was an increase on the previous $7.5 million.[14] However, the biggest issue was the overall cap on funding. The UCP announced that there would be a limit of $15 million for the entire program in 2020–2021, down from $45 million. This would rise to $30 million the next year and reach $45 million in 2022–2023. These amounts meant that incentives would be limited to $90 million over the next three years, in contrast to other provinces, which had no such cap. All in all, the UCP's policies seemed set to shrink rather than grow film production in the province for the next several years. As

Calgary Economic Development's film, television, and creative industries commissioner Luke Azevedo pointed out, Alberta's position as a location was already far behind that of British Columbia, Ontario, and Quebec, and Manitoba was threatening to overtake Alberta for fourth place.[15] Figures from the Canadian Media Producers Association show that Manitoba did, in fact, overtake Alberta in 2019–2020, with $242 million in total production volume, as compared to $220 million in Alberta.[16] There were no foreign service or location projects in Alberta that year, down from eighty-six in 2018–2019.[17] While there was a sharp decline in British Columbia's number of projects and spending during that year, the province still saw 2,800 projects filmed on location there, and 30 per cent of Canada's total production spending, whereas Alberta's film industry appeared to be in danger of disappearing altogether.

Early into the new year, the government began to outline the details of the new tax credit. In January, these were finally announced, consisting of two streams. One offered a tax credit of 22 per cent on eligible production expenditures in the province by producers not based in Alberta. The other stream offered Alberta-based productions a tax credit of 30 per cent.[18] In February, the government budget for 2021–2022 raised overall funding for the coming year to $22 million.[19] While this was certainly an improvement, it still left Alberta's incentives well behind those of other jurisdictions. The new tax credit seemed underwhelming as a policy intended to grow the sector, and the local production sector continued to express its concerns that the caps on spending would see Alberta lose out to other provinces (see Table 14.2).[20] On top of this, the pandemic resulted in border controls and quarantine measures that discouraged many productions from locating in Canada. Later in the year, there was hope that Alberta would benefit from the Calgary International Airport's selection by the federal government to pilot a program allowing travellers with negative tests for COVID to quarantine for two days rather than two weeks.[21] It was hoped this would strengthen Alberta's advantage as a viable location for production, but this advantage did not last very long, as the pilot was discontinued in early 2020. Moreover, as cases rose in Alberta, tighter restrictions on social distancing were introduced in early December.

The Turnaround: Out of COVID

All in all, 2020 saw a significant drop in Alberta's production numbers, particularly for foreign productions. However, as the year wore on, it appeared that the Alberta government was actively pursuing ways to enhance the province's appeal as a filming location, speaking with large producers in Hollywood, including streaming platforms such as Netflix.[22] The UCP also appears to have listened to the voices of organized labour in the sector, including locals of the International Association of Theatrical Stage Employees (IATSE), and ACTRA, a notable exception in a government that has not enjoyed good relations with labour overall (see Lori Williams' chapter on labour relations under the UCP). Already in January 2021, the coming year looked extremely promising for film production in the province, with Damian Petti, president of IATSE local 212 suggesting that it could be the biggest year ever for the province.[23] Petti pointed to a number of factors, including high COVID rates in Los Angeles, a favourable exchange rate, as well as federal and provincial tax incentives. He said he hoped that the industry would do $400 million in production in 2021.[24]

On 26 March 2021, Jobs and Economic Development Minister Doug Schweitzer announced that the government was dropping the $10 million cap on individual projects, while also announcing a $19 million increase in the tax credit program to $52 million for the coming year. Indeed, 2021 turned out as Petti and Schweitzer hoped and saw a tremendous increase in the number and value of productions taking place in Alberta. As of July, production spending in the province was projected to be $482 million for the year,[25] well in excess of the previous high of $274 million in 2013–2014.[26] One production alone, the HBO television series "The Last of Us" (a drama based on a video game set in a post-apocalyptic United States scoured by a pandemic), accounted for over $200 million in spending in the province.[27] Dropping the cap in per project funding was clearly instrumental for this production to go ahead in Alberta, as a $10 million maximum tax credit was much less than the production might have got in other jurisdictions. While this level of production may not be sustained every year, Alberta still appears to be better positioned than previously to compete with other provinces for a share of foreign service location spending. In a sign of improving times, the City of Calgary was able to announce in June 2021 that, thanks to new investment, it was divesting its share of the Calgary Film Centre it had bailed out in 2018.[28]

The conspicuous rise in film production in the province has been one of the few bright spots in the government's efforts at diversifying the economy. The film production tax credit represents a positive change in policy during the UCP's time in office, and it appears to have provided a more attractive climate for international productions. However, the UCP cannot take all the credit for this increase. The global film and television production industry has also experienced considerable growth over the past two years. Even in a year beset by delays and cancellations due to COVID, the global industry grew by over 16 per cent.[29] And while Canada's overall production numbers fell slightly in 2020, the value of FSLs still grew by 8 per cent that year (off the average annual growth rate of 11.3 per cent over the past decade).[30] At the time of writing, 2021 was equally notable for increased activity across the country, supported by strict COVID testing protocols on sets, government-backed insurance, and government policies allowing for foreign principals to continue to work in Canada.[31]

Still, Alberta's 2021 growth in the sector remained extraordinary, bouncing back from the nadir of 2019–2020. There are a number of ways to assess the UCP government's track record here. The best that might be said is that the UCP showed itself willing to listen to voices from the industry both within and outside of the province, to recognize the opportunities for growth, and to adjust its policies to take advantage of these. On the other hand, the sharp drop-off in film and television activity in the province in 2019–2020, compared to other provinces, suggests that it was a wasted year for the sector, a result of the incoming government's hasty termination of the NDP's incentives, delays in implementing a tax credit to replace them, and inadequate funding of the tax credit in its initial formulation. Nonetheless, from an inconspicuous start in 2019, the government can now boast that Alberta's film and television production sector is larger and more prosperous than it has ever been, one of the very few industries of any kind in the province for which this claim could be made. Minister Schweitzer continued to tout the success of the government's tax incentives to the point of suggesting that the government will lift the $50 million dollar cap on funding for 2022 year, should it be necessary.[32] This was confirmed in the 2022 provincial budget, which set aside $71 million for the program in 2022, as part of an increase of $81 million over three years.[33]

Interactive Digital Media in Canada and Alberta

Alberta, and in particular Edmonton as the location of Bioware, have some history of participation in video game production, producing titles such as *Mass Effect* and *Dragon Age*. However, Alberta's overall share of the industry remains very small, accounting for 4 per cent of total expenditure in the sector and employing 1,300 (a distant fourth place amongst provinces).[34] The video gaming or IDM sector has become one of the largest cultural industries globally, experiencing tremendous growth in recent years. Global revenues for the industry in 2021 were US$176 billion, 21 per cent higher than in 2019.[35] Canada's industry saw similar growth over that time, with revenues estimated at US$3.4 billion.[36] These kinds of figures have generated a good deal of interest in the sector on the part of several Canadian provinces and municipalities, and a number of them have developed incentives and programs to attract and develop the industry in their locales such that by 2009, Canada had emerged as the third largest site worldwide for employment in the sector,[37] primarily in British Columbia, Ontario, and Quebec.

Alberta's relatively small industry notwithstanding, municipal governments in both Calgary and Edmonton, as well as the previous NDP provincial government, have demonstrated interest in growing the sector. Calgary Economic Development commissioned Nordicity Group to develop a strategy for "nurturing Calgary's . . . emerging video games development and immersive media industries.[38] Edmonton Global (and previously Edmonton Economic Development Corporation) have a long history of support for the sector. Under the NDP, Alberta introduced a targeted tax incentive for IDM in 2018, replacing an earlier grant-based pilot program from 2017.[39] The tax incentive, the first of its kind in Alberta, offered a 25 per cent refundable tax credit for labour costs associated with the production of IDM products.[40] This was relatively low compared to similar incentives offered by other provinces, but was well above that for British Columbia (17.5 per cent).[41]

Initially, the trajectory of policy for video games was very similar to that for film and television production. In its 2019 budget the UCP removed the targeted tax incentives developed under the NDP, including the Interactive Digital Media Tax Credit. Instead, the government suggested that its more general lowering of corporate tax rates would help all businesses, by creating a more favourable economic climate. However, as a number of parties observed, small start-ups did not generally benefit from a wholesale reduction in corporate taxes.[42] The reaction from the industry was similar to the dismay of the film and television production sector, but here there was even less reason for optimism, as there was nothing yet proposed to take the place of the incentive. Instead, in December 2019 the government set up an advisory council, the Innovation Capital Working Group to propose what policies could be used to grow the technology sector in the province. The report from the group was expected for the end of February 2020, but it was pushed back to the spring. In the meantime, the 2020 provincial budget offered nothing to the sector, with Economic Development Minister Tanya Fir repeating its position that the tax cuts announced in 2019, along with a reduction in red tape would provide benefits to the sector without having to pick "winners and losers."[43] The treatment of the sector contrasted sharply with that received by the oil and gas sector, particularly the establishment of the Canadian Energy Center (the "war room"—see Brad Clark's chapter) with a $30 million annual budget.[44]

The Innovation Capital Working Group finally released the report in May 2020. It noted that Alberta was the only Canadian province that offered no tax incentive support to technology entrepreneurs, and as a result Alberta was missing out on new investment in this sector.[45] The report also called for fourteen measures aimed at the technology sector. Video gaming was not singled out in the report, which was more focused on other areas of the technology sector, especially Scientific Research and Development. In July 2020 the provincial government responded to some of the recommendations, with the Innovation Employment Grant for small and medium enterprises, as well as adding $175 million to Alberta Enterprise Corp. to help with the process of accessing venture capital.[46] As the government announced these measures, Minister Fir said "Maybe there was a bit of time between ending the [NDP] programs and introducing ours, but we wanted to take the time to do it right."[47] But more time would continue to elapse. The 2021 provincial budget saw increases to this funding, but there was still nothing specific for the video gaming sector.

In contrast to film and television policy, there has been no sign of the UCP government changing course from its initial round of cutbacks. As noted above, Alberta's video gaming sector remains disproportionately small within Canada. The province has been able to point to growth in the number of technology companies in Alberta over the past few years, with annual growth of 27 per cent in the number of firms. However, most of this growth seems to have occurred before 2020,[48] and both the NDP opposition, and many in the technology sector have suggested that this growth could have been much greater had Alberta continued to offer tax incentives. Calgary Economic Development's report likewise suggested that the lack of any incentive programs at the provincial level represented a major stumbling block to building an electronic gaming industry in the city.[49] In November 2021, Fir's replacement in the portfolio, Doug Schweitzer, was apparently still in listening mode as he responded to continued calls for the government to take action.[50] However, the 2022 provincial budget offered no targeted programs or incentives for the sector.[51]

Comparisons: Low Hanging Fruit versus Playing the Long Game

The contrast in the government's treatment of the two sectors is perhaps down to more than the vagaries of provincial politics. For a start, the voices advocating for the film and television production sector have been stronger than those for IDM, which has had some disruptions in sector representation.[52] Moreover, while both sectors have focused on tax incentives as their policy instrument of choice, there are some important differences between these sectors in terms of risk, as well as how the foregone tax revenues can be recovered by the province. One of the key characteristics of most cultural markets is the relative uncertainty in demand for any given product. In fact, most of the films, television shows, recordings, or video games produced fail to make back their costs. This, however, is not a problem where tax incentives for film and television production are concerned. The benefit to the province is seen relatively quickly as the spending on any given production occurs over a relatively short period of time, to be replaced by new projects. Regardless of whether or not the film or television series is ultimately successful, the spending has already taken place in the province. By the government's own estimate, every $1 in tax credits creates $4 in spending in the province.[53] In this regard, tax incentives in this sector are relatively risk-free. From this perspective it becomes easier to see why the provincial government would reverse course and remove many of the initial constraints it had placed on the program; the only question is why it took them so long to realize this.

Video game production is structured somewhat differently. Production timelines are often much longer, and tax breaks and grants are not project-based but are targeted at firms with an ongoing presence in the province. Nurturing a video game production must target locally based firms or branches, whose viability depends on achieving success in a very competitive and uncertain market. This requires much more of a long-term commitment with much less certainty of benefits to the provincial economy. Spending on labour still takes place, but the profits that would sustain a firm and contribute to provincial taxes may be a long time coming, if they come at all. Bearing this in mind, government contributions to this sector may carry more risk, notwithstanding the overall growth of the sector, and developing a viable policy becomes more difficult. That said, prior to introducing its Interactive Digital Media Tax Credit, the NDP had already engaged in extensive consultations and study, all of which counted for very little with the incoming UCP government.

In fact, the need to dismantle the previous government's legacy (or at least appear to do so) seems to be one of the forces driving UCP policy in both sectors, amongst many others (see Duane Bratt's chapter on climate policy, as well as Graham Thomson's chapter on the 2019 campaign and its aftermath). The termination of the programs for both film and television production and IDM in the October 2019 budget was in this sense a continuation of the "Summer of Repeal" that reversed many of the NDP's signature policies—the carbon tax, minimum wage increase, and agricultural labour reform. This may also help to explain the way in which the trajectory of policies for both sectors diverged after the budget. With the film and television production tax credit, the UCP had already articulated an alternative to the NDP's Screen-Based Production Grant. Reversing the reduction in funding and project caps of the initial policy did not have to mean reinstating NDP policy, the UCP could continue to claim that a tax credit was substantively different from, and even an improvement on, a grant. No such alternative was in place for the Interactive Digital Media Tax Credit and there have been no targeted measures for the sector. Introducing the tax incentives that the industry appears to want would amount to admitting that the NDP was, after all, on the right track. Whether or not this precludes the incentives ever being reinstated, is far from certain, but the sector might be justified in viewing the delay as simply a needlessly missed opportunity.

Conclusion

There is another development that is common to both film and television production and IDM in the province, but perhaps one that sees more continuity between the UCP and the NDP, where digital media fell under the purview of Economic Development Minister Deron Bilous. The UCP government has extended this, choosing to frame policies for film production in terms of economic development rather than culture as well. It is the economic development ministers, Tanya Fir and her successor Doug Schweitzer that have been the voice of government for these policies throughout the UCP's time in office. This suggests that the government is now viewing these particular sectors in terms of their economic potential rather than as culture, a process which has been slowly taking shape over successive governments. Film and television production and, to some extent, digital media appear to have carved out a status that stands apart from the arts, although other cultural industries such as music or publishing have yet to make that transition, there is now the acknowledgement that some cultural industries are indeed industries. In this respect at least, Alberta has fallen more into line with other governments in Canada, both provincial and federal.

These industries are not going to displace oil and gas (or indeed any of Alberta's leading industries) as the main contributor to the province's economy any time soon. They remain relatively minor players. At \$482 million, the spending brought by film and television production in 2021, would amount to less than 0.16 per cent of GDP as it was calculated for 2020.[54] The 9,000 jobs this activity represented is likewise small, at less than 0.4 per cent of total employment in the province.[55] The digital media sector's numbers are even more insignificant. Although the UCP have been keen to tout the jobs and spending that the film sector brings, its importance to them is still more symbolic (even if it is couched in economic terms). The UCP government's focus on the province's energy sector is clear both in the amount of attention and spending it attracts (see Duane Bratt's, Jean-Sébastien Rioux's, and Brad Clark's chapters). Given that, it is not surprising that the Alberta government's commitment to cultural industries will likely remain limited. However, the disproportionately large symbolic value of these industries means that governments will likely continue to highlight them.

NOTES

1   Alberta, *Fair Deal Panel Report to Government* (June 2020), 49.

2   Alberta. Upholding arts as a profession. https://www.alberta.ca/upholding-the-value-of-artists-to-alberta.aspx

3   Ted Morton and Meredith McDonald, "The Siren Song of economic diversification: Alberta's legacy of loss," *University of Calgary, The School of Public Policy SPP Research Papers* 8, 13 (March 2015).

4   Alberta, *Alberta's Recovery Plan* (June 2020), 20–28.

5   Serra Tinic, *On Location: Canada's Television Industry in a Global Market* (University of Toronto Press: Toronto, 2005), ix.

6   David Whitson, Karen Wall and Donna (Cardinal) Gannon, "Alberta: From Rags to Riches to Roulette," in *Cultural Policy: Origins, Evolution and Implementation in Canada's Provinces and Territories*," Diane Saint-Pierre and Monica Gattinger, eds, 439–480 (University of Ottawa Press: Ottawa, 2021), 459.

7   Alberta, Alberta's military history to come alive via Passchendaele film (8 November 2005).

8   Eric Volmers, "Film studio for Calgary," *Edmonton Journal* (5 February 2014).

9   "City to divest from Calgary Film Centre as industry sees more activity," *CBC News* (4 June 2021). Accessed at https://www.cbc.ca/news/canada/calgary/city-calgary-divest-film-centre-1.6054082 on November 9, 2021.

10 Eric Volmers, "Alberta film and TV production now on election platforms of political parties," *Calgary Herald* (4 April 2019.)

11 *Ibid.*

12 *Ibid.*

13 Joel Dryden, "Alberta losing out on film production, union says," *CBC News* (13 September 2019). Accessed at https://www.cbc.ca/news/canada/calgary/calgary-film-industry-production-grants-alberta-1.5282031, 25 May 2021.

14 Jon Roe, "Alberta's film industry worried it has lost competitive edge in latest provincial budget," *Calgary Herald* (25 October 2019).

15   *Ibid.*

16   Canadian Media Producers Association, *Profile 2020*, 12.

17   *Ibid.*, 64.

18   Alberta, Film and Television Tax Credit (2021), https://www.alberta.ca/film-television-tax-credit.aspx.

19   *Ibid.*

20   Crystal Laderas, "Film industry wants tax credit caps lifted" *CityNews, Edmonton* (3 March 2020). Accessed at https://edmonton.citynews.ca/2020/03/03/film-industry-wants-tax-credit-caps-lifted/ on May 25, 2021.

21   Elise von Scheel. "Alberta pursues cinema giants in effort to brand province as film hub," *CBC News* (20 November 2020). Accessed at https://www.cbc.ca/news/canada/calgary/alberta-pursuing-cinema-giants-to-brand-province-as-film-hub-1.5806035 on 25 May 2021.

22   *Ibid.*

23   "Lights, camera, action in Alberta: Film industry readies for booming year," *CBC News* (22 January 2021). Accessed at https://www.cbc.ca/news/canada/calgary/alberta-film-industry-booming-1.5884089 on 25 May 2021.

24   *Ibid.*

25   *Ibid.*

26   Canadian Media Producers Association, 12.

27   Elise von Scheel, "Recent film, TV projects bringing $482M to Alberta's economy," *CBC News* (31 July 2021). Accessed at https://www.cbc.ca/news/canada/calgary/alberta-film-spending-1.6124746 on 27 September 2021.

28   "City to divest from Calgary Film Centre."

29   Chris Evans, "Global film and TV production spend rose by 16% in 2020, despite COVID," Kemps Film TV Video (28 June 2021).

30   Canadian Media Producers Association, 13.

31   Brad Wheeler, "In a pandemic, why is film and TV production in Canada the picture of health," *Globe and Mail* (29 May 2021), 8.

32   Kelly Cryderman, "Ghostbusters: Afterlife puts focus on Alberta film industry's role in province's economic diversification plans," *Globe and Mail* (12 November 2021).

33   Josh Aldrich, "Alberta Budget 2022 puts emphasis on filling skilled labour void," *Calgary Herald* (24 February 2022). Accessed at https://calgaryherald.com/news/alberta-budget-2022-focusses-on-business 11 May 2022.

34   Entertainment Software Association of Canada, *The Canadian Video Game Industry 2021* (9 November 2021).

35   *Ibid.*

36   *Ibid.*

37 Greig de Peuter, "Video Games Production: Level Up," in *Cultural Industries.ca*, Ira Wagman and Peter Urquhart, eds, 72–93 (James Lorimer and Company: Toronto, 2012), 85.

38 Nordicity, *Calgary's Video Games and Immersive Technology Strategy: Final Report* (May 2020), 3.

39 Travis McEwan, "'Ready to explode': Alberta video game developer wants tax break for high-tech industry," *CBC News* (1 March 2017). Accessed at https://www.cbc.ca/news/canada/edmonton/ready-to-explode-alberta-video-game-developer-wants-tax-break-for-high-tech-industry-1.4005894 on 27 September 2021.

40 Alberta, *Interactive Digital Media Tax Credit (IDMTC) Program Guidelines* (January 2019), 4.

41 Nordicity, 13–14.

42 Stefanie Marotta, "Alberta launches new R&D incentives for innovation, tech a year after cuts," *Globe and Mail* (24 July 2020).

43 David Bell, "Gaming and tech ecosystem shows potential as Alberta drops tax credits, adds panel," *CBC News* (27 February 2020). Accessed at https://www.cbc.ca/news/canada/calgary/tech-for-tomorrow-homestretch-1.5478559 on 25 May 2021.

44 *Ibid.*

45 Alberta, *Innovation Capital Working Group Report* (May 2020), 44.

46 Marotta, "Alberta launches new R&D incentives."

47 *Ibid.*

48 "Number of Alberta tech companies has more than doubled since 2018," *CBC News* (22 April 2021). Accessed at https://www.cbc.ca/news/canada/calgary/tech-companies-alberta-doubles-1.5998124 on April 22, 2021.

49 Nordicity, 13.

50 Bill Kaufmann, "Alberta losing out on investment in the video game industry, says tech sector," *Edmonton Journal* (9 November 2021).

51 Stephen David Cook, "Alberta video game developers say industry is being left behind in province," *CBC News* (1 March 2022). Accessed at https://www.cbc.ca/news/canada/edmonton/alberta-video-game-developers-say-industry-is-being-left-behind-in-province-1.6367800 on 11 May 2022.

52 Nordicity, 37.

53 Alberta, *Lifting the curtain on blockbuster supports for film* (26 March 2021). Accessed at https://www.alberta.ca/release.cfm?xID=778135B52DB3E-D51D-71D4-78E198FBCDCCDF1B on 9 November 2021.

54 Alberta, *Gross Domestic Product* (October 2021). Accessed at https://economicdashboard.alberta.ca/grossdomesticproduct on 9 November 2021.

55 Alberta, *Labour Force Statistics* (October 2021). Accessed at https://open.alberta.ca/dataset/4f027606-b2d9-46d8-85e2-ccf73b9a1f06/resource/26eef4d5-6a00-43ec-a058-02b135e1dfb7/download/lbr-lfs-package-2021-10.pdf on 9 November 2021.

VI.
Health Care, Education, and Public Sector Policies

15

Bitter Battles: The United Conservative Party's War on Health Care Workers

Gillian Steward

There was a time in Alberta when its political leaders and scientifically minded bright lights aimed to make the province a hub of medical research and clinical practice that would rank with the best in the world. Not just the best in Canada, the best in the world: a "Houston of the North," which could one day rival the University of Texas' renowned medical centre, according to *Maclean's Magazine*.[1]

It was March 1979, the Alberta treasury was awash in money thanks to OPEC pushing the price of oil sky high, and Peter Lougheed was running for re-election after having served as premier for eight years. Among his election promises was a $300 million endowment for the Alberta Heritage Foundation for Medical Research.

After Lougheed and the Progressive Conservatives (PCs) handily won (seventy-four out of seventy-nine seats) that election, Lougheed fulfilled his promise to support biomedical and health research at Alberta universities, affiliated institutions, and other medical and technology-related institutions.

With operating funds of up to $80 million a year over the next thirty years, the program lured hundreds of talented doctors to the province, enabling many to conduct research while they worked as clinicians, emergency room doctors, or other specialists.[2] In 2009, Globe and Mail health columnist Andre Picard was so impressed that he declared Alberta's health care system the best and most innovative system in Canada. He cited strong alliances between university researchers and health care regions as a key factor.[3]

By 2021, Alberta's ambition to become a medical mecca had not only stalled, it was in reverse gear. Alberta's health minister, Tyler Shandro, was openly fighting with the Alberta Medical Association (AMA) and individual physicians. After fifteen months of relentless work by the province's unionized nurses during the pandemic, Alberta's finance minister, Travis Toews, told them the government was looking for a 3 per cent wage cut. After decades of Alberta attracting doctors and other health care workers, the tide turned and they started leaving. Family doctors left their practices. Specialists in rural areas closed their clinics. New hospitalists were hard to find. Nurses resigned or retired. Beds in emergency departments and ICUs were closed due to lack of staff. If the Lougheed era had ushered in the hope of many made-in-Alberta medical miracles, Jason Kenney and the United Conservative Party (UCP) seemed just as keen to usher it out.

Election Prescriptions and Their Side Effects

During the March/April 2019 election campaign Jason Kenney, leader of the newly minted UCP, assured Albertans that "a universal, comprehensive health-care system is a core part of UCP policy." To further emphasize the point, the section on health care in the official party platform was labelled as the "Health Care Guarantee" and pledged to maintain or increase government funding for the province's public health care system.

Despite Albertans' traditional conservative leanings formed over decades and manifested in successful political parties from Social Credit to the UCP, there is strong support in Alberta for publicly funded health care insurance as first introduced in Saskatchewan by the Co-operative Commonwealth Federation (CCF) government and later established across Canada by a Liberal government through the Canada Health Act. Even in Alberta, a political party that advocates for a two-tier system in which people can pay to get faster access or superior treatment can find itself in trouble. Ralph Klein was a popular premier but after he blew up a Calgary hospital, closed hundreds of beds in other hospitals, and promised to establish private clinics that would permit overnight stays for complicated surgeries such as hip replacements, he found himself the target of province-wide protest rallies. A watered-down version of the Klein plan for private hospitals took effect in 2001, but since it didn't appear either investors or the government were eager to move forward with new facilities, opposition melted away. In 2006, Klein made one last attempt to further a private health agenda with what he called the "Third Way." It would have expanded the role of private insurance companies in health care, increased user fees, and reviewed services to determine if some should be delisted from coverage by public health insurance (this would of course spur private insurance companies to offer coverage for a fee). Once again Albertans mobilized against Klein's plans. In the end, Klein and his health care strategies became so unpopular even among PCs that he was eventually replaced as party leader and left the premier's office. His successor, Ed Stelmach, quietly ditched the Third Way.

While Kenney publicly pledged support for public health care during the 2019 election campaign, he also made it clear that a UCP government would undertake a thorough review of Alberta Health Services (AHS), which manages and staffs the hospitals, laboratory services, ambulance services, long term care facilities, and other entities that are included in the province's public health care system. And it is that extensive review, conducted by Ernst & Young, an international private sector business consultancy, combined with the report of the Blue Ribbon Panel on Alberta's Finances whose members were appointed by the UCP, that reveal the UCP's real intentions for public health care.

The Blue Ribbon Panel was the first to come up with prescriptions for reducing the Alberta government's spending, spending that had left it with sizeable budget deficits and debt due mainly to a severe drop in the price of oil. Since the panel was mandated to devise ways to balance the budget without raising taxes it focused on cutting budgets for the government's big spenders—health, education, and post-secondary education (see Charles Webber's and Lisa Young's chapters on the latter two sectors). The biggest of all was health care, which in 2018/19 cost $20.4 billion, 42 per cent of the province's operating budget.[4] The panel then focused on how this compared to health care spending in other provinces and found that even though Alberta's health indicators were lower, its per capita spending was higher. The panel also emphasized that while doctors, nurses, and health care workers in Alberta were generally paid more than in other provinces those costs could be cut if the government replaced them with lower paid workers such as nurse practitioners or licensed practical nurses. It also suggested that contracting out some hospital services would save money. No one on the panel had management or frontline experience in health care—its focus was supposed to be strictly financial. But that didn't deter the panel from stating early in the report: "it is time to dig deeper, explore new approaches and alternatives for delivering public services. . . ."[5] It then recommended that day surgery and other procedures now undertaken in hospitals "could be delivered in private or not-for-profit facilities."[6]

The Blue Ribbon Panel also set its sights on the contracts drawn up between the AMA and the Alberta government, which establish fees paid to physicians for everything from office consultations by general practitioners to complicated heart surgeries. The panel recommended limiting the increasing cost of physician services by providing incentives for physicians to move to alternative payment plans (which usually refers to salaries rather than fee for service). If the contract with the AMA couldn't be renegotiated in the government's favour, the panel suggested the government should consider its "legislative options."[7]

The panel's recommendations would undoubtedly impact the people providing the services and the people receiving them but that wasn't its first priority. It was focused only on money and how the government could spend less of it on health care. But these recommendations could only be implemented by changing health care legislation and policies. And indeed as events unfolded on the health care front over the next two years, it became clear that the Blue Ribbon Panel on Alberta's Finances had in fact created a blue print that the UCP government would eagerly use to engineer sweeping policy changes to public health care.

After the panel's recommendations were released, the government moved quickly to enact some of them. Two months later, on 28 October 2019, the UCP government introduced Bill 21—The Fiscal Sustainability Act. It boldly stated that the government could terminate any contract, now or in the future, with the AMA. It also set out terms for limiting the number of physicians who could practice in Alberta. The bill became law in early December and three months later, as COVID-19 was making its first appearances in Canada, Health Minister Tyler Shandro did indeed tear up the AMA contract even as negotiations were proceeding. By this time the government had also let it be known that it was going to lay off between 4,000 and 5,000 unionized health care workers. The Blue Ribbon Panel had provided the expert seal of approval that the government had sought and it wasted no time using that expert advice as cover for controversial decisions.

The UCP government also had another set of experts at work scrutinizing AHS, which manages and operates the province's public health care system. The ($2 million) Ernst & Young investigation of AHS also focused on how much health care workers were costing the system. It pointed out that AHS is Alberta's largest employer with just over 102,000 employees of which 91.3 per cent are unionized: "Employee compensation makes up the largest independent driver of AHS' cost base, with salary and benefit expenses representing approximately 54.3 per cent of AHS' total expenses. When including the employees of AHS' contracted health service providers and other contracted services (including Covenant Health), the percentage would be approximately 70 per cent of total expenses."[8] The Ernst & Young report also went into specific detail about the comparatively high cost of overtime, sick pay, and part-time employment for nurses and pointed out that the United Nurses of Alberta (UNA) collective agreement contained provisions that were not part of agreements in other provinces.

AHS does not negotiate fee schedules with the province's physicians (that is the responsibility of the health ministry) but the Ernst & Young report recommended lower fees for physicians, such as radiologists, who provide services to the province's hospitals. It also recommended that AHS not pay its share of salary increases awarded by universities to academic researchers who also provide clinical services in hospitals. Like the Blue Ribbon Panel, the Ernst & Young report not only focused on the cost of health care workers but also went to great lengths to point out that some of this cost could be reduced if AHS made greater use of alternative delivery of services, such as non-hospital surgical facilities or private clinics. But in neither the Blue Ribbon report nor the Ernst & Young report is there any explanation of how this would save money. No examples of successful models were provided either.

Both the government-commissioned reports came to basically the same conclusions: since the largest percentage of the provincial health care budget goes to paying the people who work in the public health care system, most of whom belong to a union or in the case of physicians the AMA, minimizing the influence of the unions and the AMA on salaries would lead to reduced costs for the government (see also Lori Williams' chapter). One of the ways to minimize the influence of unions and the AMA, these reports suggest, is to provide workplaces where health care workers wouldn't have to negotiate their salaries through a union or the AMA but directly with the minister or with the owners of these facilities. The new work places would be stand-alone surgical clinics for both day surgery and more complicated surgeries that required overnight stays, such as hip and knee replacements—two of the most common procedures in Canada, with more than 138,000 surgeries a year and estimated in-patient costs of over $1.4 billion annually. Laboratories, laundry services, food and housekeeping services could also be contracted out and managed by private investors. Alberta Health would provide funding for the services these corporations provide. But neither the Blue Ribbon or the Ernst & Young reports provide any guidelines for transparency of bidding for contracts, the contracts themselves, or the regulatory framework that would be necessary to ensure sufficient public oversight of government spending in concert with high standards of patient care. Nevertheless, both reviews claimed such an approach would result in reduced government spending on health care even though nowhere in either report is this claim backed up with hard data. It is simply asserted as a positive outcome of contracting out surgical and auxiliary services. Health Minister Tyler Shandro took up these claims and often referred to these reports as the blue prints for an improved public health care system that would cost the government less money and provide faster access for patients on surgical waiting lists.

In summary, these government-commissioned reports concluded that health spending is the largest chunk of the government budget, and growing, therefore it must not only be brought under control but also reduced. Since the largest chunk of AHS' budget is people (mostly women), who must be paid, and since 91.3 per cent of them belong to a union, worker collaboration must be broken if salaries, and therefore costs, are to be reduced. The unions targeted are UNA, which accounts for 28 per cent of AHS employees and 32 per cent of AHS salaries and benefits expenses;

the Health Sciences Association of Alberta (HSAA), which includes pharmacists, physical therapists, paramedics, dialysis technicians, respiratory therapists, psychologists, and public health inspectors and accounts for 19 per cent of AHS employees and 23 per cent of AHS salaries and benefits expenses; Alberta Union of Provincial Employees (AUPE), which represents licensed practical nurses and health care aides, who make up 15 per cent of AHS' workforce and account for 10 per cent of salaries and benefits; AUPE's General Support Services (GSS), which includes administrative support, human resources technicians, food service workers, financial analysts, pharmacy assistants, electricians, maintenance workers and information-technology analysts and accounts for 27 per cent of AHS' workforce and 19 per cent of salaries and benefit expenses; the Professional Association of Resident Physicians of Alberta (PARA), which accounts for 2 per cent of the workforce and 2 per cent of salary and benefits expenses. Managers and senior leaders account for 3 per cent of the AHS workforce and 6 per cent of salary and benefits expenses.[9] From the point of view of the UCP government that's why contracting out to third-party, non-unionized employers is so attractive when it comes to reducing the cost of AHS employees. And that's why breaking the power of the AMA—which according to the 2020 Funding Framework costs the government $4.5 billion a year or 25 per cent of the health care budget—as the only negotiator for medical doctors became so important.

Six months after Ernst & Young completed its report, Alberta Health awarded the company a $986,500 contract to establish a Health Contracting Secretariat.[10]

The United Conservative Party Move Forward Despite the Pandemic

The UCP didn't really need those reports to justify their health care decisions. It had already made plans, as was evidenced by Kenney's announcement on 30 November 2019 (before the Ernst & Young report was even completed) that the government would lay off between 4,000 and 5,000 health care workers. Alberta's first presumptive case of COVID-19 was discovered three months later and the scramble to contain and treat the deadly virus began in earnest. Obviously, it was not a good time to be laying off health care workers. But as we shall see, despite the disruption cause by the pandemic, a public health emergency that served to highlight the importance of a strong, coordinated public health care system, the UCP not only still wanted to cut down the number of people who work in the system but took many steps to do so.

Health Minister Tyler Shandro tore up the government's contract with the AMA on 20 February 2020 while negotiations for a new contract were ongoing. The government then imposed its own Funding Framework on AMA members. COVID-19 cases had already been reported in Ontario and British Columbia and infection was likely to spread across the country. A week later the Kenney government tabled its 2019/2020 budget in which it allotted $400 million to be spent on contracting out surgeries to private surgical facilities and $100 million for public sector operating rooms. The government also committed to doubling the number of contracted-out surgeries over three years—from 15 per cent to 30 per cent of total surgeries province-wide, a significant shift of surgeries from the public sector, and a very significant amount of public funding flowing to the private surgical sector. When Health Minister Shandro tore up the contract with the AMA, he already knew that the government would be contracting more private clinics to provide surgical services. Three weeks later when it was clear that COVID-19 cases were on the rise in Alberta, Shandro announced a partnership with Telus, Canada's second largest telecom company, to provide an app for homebound people needing to get in touch with a doctor. But it was soon discovered that the Telus docs were getting paid more per virtual visit than doctors in Alberta who were seeing patients in their offices or bypassing the Telus app and virtually consulting with their patients using whatever technology was available to them in their clinics. The fees were adjusted after Alberta doctors loudly complained. But the government never revealed what kind of fees or benefit Telus got from the arrangement.

Meanwhile there were other steps in the works that would make privatization of health care much easier. In July 2020 after most public health restrictions had been lifted following the first wave of the pandemic, the government introduced Bill 30—The Health Statutes Amendments Act— legislation intended to speed up the process by which owners/investors of private surgical clinics could receive permits for their proposals. It also gave the minister the power to enter into contracts with corporations in addition to groups of physicians such as ophthalmologists who wanted to contract for a specified number of cataract surgeries to be covered by public health insurance.

The bill detailed significant changes in how physician remuneration is structured in Canada—by allowing physicians working in the public health care system to be paid via corporate structures and not directly by government. The proposed section 20.1(1) grants new power to "a person" to directly "submit a claim" to the public plan. These new "persons" according to the bill "do not include an individual or a professional corporation" but refers to private corporations or non-profit societies. The legislation gave the health minister the power to contract with corporations, and for corporations to directly bill the public plan for services provided by physicians who may be employed or subcontracted by the corporation.

Premier Kenney told the legislature Bill 30 "would make it easier for chartered surgical facilities to work with us and AHS to provide publicly funded surgeries to people who need them. [. . .] The proposed amendments here in Bill 30 would reduce barriers and administrative burdens so that new chartered surgical facilities can more easily open, reducing surgical wait times for cataracts among other surgeries. Now, of course, strong oversight of these facilities would be maintained, and the College of Physicians and Surgeons of Alberta (CPSA) would continue to accredit these facilities to ensure that they provide safe, quality procedures. The current process for chartered surgical facilities to open and contract with AHS can take as much as two years."[11]

All of this assumed there was not much operating room capacity in Alberta's hospitals so additional capacity was needed. And demand was indeed exacerbated when non-urgent surgeries had to be put on hold as patients infected with COVID-19 filled hospital beds and required a large share of hospital resources. But even the Ernst & Young report found there was more operating room capacity in the province's hospitals than the 90 per cent capacity that AHS had claimed: "Our assessment indicates that operational OR capacity was utilized 71 per cent of the time across AHS in 2018/2019 indicating an additional 18,713 slates to be undertaken."[12]

The Doctors Rebel

A few days after the introduction of Bill 30 (10 July 2020), the AMA released a survey of its members that revealed almost nine-in-ten physicians (87 per cent) would be making changes to their medical practices as a result of Health Minister Tyler Shandro's Funding Framework for physicians. Of this group, 49 per cent had made plans or were considering looking for work in another province (this represents 42 per cent of all Alberta doctors). One-third (34 per cent) of physicians who would be changing their practices said they may leave the profession or retire early, with other alternatives being mulled including changing how they offer services/withdrawing services from AHS facilities (48 per cent), reducing their hours (43 per cent), or laying off staff (34 per cent).[13]

Minister Shandro followed up by threatening to disclose individual physicians' annual billings. He also sent a letter to the College of Physician and Surgeons of Alberta, the medical profession's regulatory body, directing it to change its standards of practice for physicians by 20 July in an attempt to stop the province's doctors from leaving their practices en masse due to an ongoing dispute over pay.[14]

The AMA had not been consulted about Bill 30 and roundly criticized the government for introducing it at a time when physicians were pre-occupied with responding to the pandemic. In its response to the government AMA officials wrote (12 July): "the most concerning aspect of Bill 30 is that these changes are being sought at a time when the health system, and physicians' fundamental relationship with it, appears to be getting dismantled through a series of government-led impositions (e.g., those affecting Practitioner IDs, Bill 21, termination of our Agreement, the Physician Funding Framework, Medical Staff Bylaws, limited access to community infrastructure stabilization supports during the pandemic, reducing and removing AMA's administration of the MLR, etc.). Understanding this perspective held by pretty much every physician in this province is important as we go through some of our specific concerns with respect to Bill 30."[15]

While the AMA was alarmed about the bill's content and asking for further clarification, it's safe to say that most Albertans were too distracted by the ups and downs of the pandemic and summer vacations to pay much attention to what was going on in the legislature. The bill was passed by the legislature at the end of July 2020, three weeks after it had been introduced. But Health Minister Shandro didn't even wait for the bill to receive final approval before he issued a request for proposals from orthopedic surgery clinics for knee and hip replacement surgery.

Less than a month later Deena Hinshaw, Alberta's chief medical officer of health, was once again sounding the alarm about rising COVID-19 case numbers. It was the beginning of the second wave of the pandemic in Alberta that would eventually see hospitals and ICUs fill up with patients infected by COVID-19 while physicians and other health care workers struggled to look after them.

In early October, Dr. Christine Molnar's term as AMA president ended. In a letter to members she wrote that the organization "had never faced so many fundamental challenges in so many areas at one time." She then issued a warning about what the next two years might hold: "Government policies and decisions have impacted our livelihoods, our families, our practices and our ability to fulfill our duty to our patients. We are experiencing this in the midst of an unprecedented, global health crisis with COVID-19. To that heavy burden, add threat and pressure from a government that is moving to reshape our health care system without the meaningful advice of organized medicine or patients."[16]

Later that month at the UCP's annual general meeting in Calgary, a narrow majority of delegates voted in favour of establishing a two-tier health care system where patients could pay a user fee for services. The motion was put forward by the Calgary Varsity constituency. The MLA for that constituency, Jason Copping, was appointed health minister about a year later.

It was still pre-vaccine days as physicians toiled from October 2020 through Christmas, New Year's, and into January to treat the victims of the second wave of COVID-19. Yet the AMA and the government were still negotiating a new contract to replace the one that had been scrapped by Health Minister Shandro in February of 2020. A tentative agreement was eventually voted on in March 2021 but it was turned down by 53 per cent of the membership. In the comments section of the AMA's website several doctors said they would never vote for a contract until Bill 21 was rescinded. That's the legislation that allows the health minister to terminate any contract with the AMA now or in the future.

By March the second wave had waned and Health Minister Shandro announced that because there was such a backlog of surgeries (36,000) put on hold because of the pandemic the Alberta government would fund non-hospital clinics to perform the surgeries so patients would not have to wait so long. The funding would cover 55,000 surgeries. It seemed that the pandemic had given the government the immediate rationale that it needed to promote private clinics as a better alternative to in-hospital surgery. Patients would pay with their Alberta Health Care Insurance for a procedure but given the arrangement was made in such haste there wasn't any information about how much this would eventually cost the government in added fees and administrative costs. And since the government had passed Bill 30—The Health Statutes Amendment Act—the year before how many of these clinics would be owned and operated by corporations rather than by individual doctors or professional associations of doctors? It was clear that the UCP government had no intention of abandoning its plans for the health care system even though the pandemic had disrupted normal operations and health care workers were being stretched beyond their capacity.

At the end of April the UCP took another step on its path to privatizations. K-Bro Linen Inc. announced that it had been named the successful bidder for the Request for Proposals put out by AHS in October 2020. They became the sole providers of laundry services for AHS across the province. Although K-Bro had already been providing two-thirds of AHS laundry services particularly in Calgary and Edmonton, the new contracts would include rural hospitals and health facilities. According to the Friends of Medicare, in Medicine Hat where approximately 1.2 million kilograms of laundry is processed every year at the Medicine Hat Regional Hospital (MHRH), contract changes impacted surrounding communities such as the Brooks, Bassano, and Bow Island hospitals; seniors' residences in Medicine Hat; home care; and the residential detoxification centre, and would mean the loss of at least 250 jobs in the MHRH alone. Most of those workers would have been members of AUPE.

As the health ministry advanced its agenda for privatizing health care as recommended in both the Blue Ribbon report and the Ernst & Young review of AHS, Alberta entered the third wave of the pandemic. During this wave Alberta recorded more active cases than anywhere else in Canada. At one point it had the highest rate of COVID-19 cases in North America. Despite this, at the end of May, Premier Kenney announced that if hospitalizations continued to decline and the vaccination rate increased all public health restrictions would be lifted on 1 July. And that is indeed what happened, with Kenney declaring "the best summer ever" and encouraging everyone to attend the Calgary Stampede.

Five days later Finance Minister Travis Toews announced that AHS would be asking for a 3 per cent wage cut as part of ongoing labour negotiations with the UNA, AHS' largest union whose members had worked tirelessly to care for Albertans during the three waves of the pandemic. Toews praised nurses for all they had done but said Alberta needed to get is finances back on track. Despite the harrowing pandemic experiences for health care workers, patients, and Albertans at large, the UCP was obviously determined to stick to its agenda of bringing unionized health care workers and doctors represented by the AMA to heel.

But not all doctors accepted the UCP's tactics. When Chief Medical Officer Deena Hinshaw announced in late July that the province would be moving to the endemic stage of the pandemic and would therefore drop testing, contact tracing, and isolation for people infected with COVID-19, Dr. Joe Vipond of Calgary mobilized daily protests in front of the government's southern Alberta headquarters, Calgary's McDougall Centre. Over fourteen days thousands of people attended and by mid-August the government backed off its plans for the endemic stage.

As case counts and hospitalizations made it clear Alberta was in a fourth wave of the pandemic, Dr. Vipond expanded his group of medical and epidemiology experts and organized YouTube broadcasts to inform Albertans about what the latest statistics indicated about the growth of the Delta variation of the virus and what needed to happen if the province was to avoid the worst scenarios.

United Conservative Party Loses Face at the Bargaining Table

In 2020, the Alberta government had instructed AHS to seek large pay cuts and rollbacks in contract language for the UNA, AHS' largest union. But on 7 September 2021, AHS tabled a new proposal that represented significant progress in negotiations even though it still included several serious rollbacks, including a proposal that would amount to an immediate 2 per cent pay cut for UNA members and another that would take away important scheduling protections for nurses. "But this was far from the government's original position, brought to the table by AHS," David Harrigan, UNA's director of labour relations told the union's annual general meeting in October 2021.

Harrigan also said that UNA has always had channels of communication with Alberta governments during negotiations, noting this was true with premiers Ralph Klein, Ed Stelmach, Alison Redford, Jim Prentice, and Rachel Notley. However, he added, Premier Jason Kenney's UCP barely acknowledges the existence of UNA. "They don't like us, they don't like you, they don't like public sector employees, and they don't like the fact that employees can form unions," he said.

Nevertheless, Harrigan continued, the government in its directions to AHS clearly recognized that UNA meant business when the union accepted AHS' essential services proposals and asked the Labour Relations Board to appoint a mediator. In December 2021 the mediator issued his report in which he recommended a 4.25 per cent wage increase over four years and a one-time lump sum payment of 1 per cent for 2021 in recognition of nurses' contribution during the pandemic. The UNA members voted to accept the deal, which made Alberta nurses the highest paid in Canada. There would no wage rollback as the UCP government had pledged.

As of May 2022, the AMA had yet to sign a new contract with the government. At the end of December 2021, Dr. Michelle Warren, the AMA president, reported that a survey completed by 1,300 members pinpointed fair compensation and a new master agreement as the two top concerns. Dr. Paul Boucher, the former AMA president, had cited the same sorts of concerns a year earlier: an insufficient budget increase that takes into account a population increase but leaves physicians with less compensation;

the need for a transparent and fair process when it comes to determining physician compensation; and the need for a dispute resolution mechanism that involves third parties. Boucher also said that the most recent survey of physicians "indicates a lack of confidence in the overall management of the system and the significant challenges physicians face in meeting the demands being placed on them. Compared to our last member survey the situation today is worse." During the worst years of the pandemic, physicians had worked without a negotiated contract with the government.

Needless to say, that left many physicians—family doctors, general practitioners, and specialists—disgruntled at the way they had been treated during the worst health crisis the province had ever endured. Data compiled by the CPSA in March 2022 clearly showed that while Alberta had once been considered an attractive place to practice, doctors weren't moving here or staying here as much as they used to. According to the CPSA, almost twice as many doctors left Alberta (140) compared to 2017 (75). The number of doctors who voluntarily dropped their registration also doubled; from 79 in 2017 to 158. Taking into account all reasons for deregistering, Alberta lost 568 doctors. On the other side of the ledger there were 613 new registrants in 2021. But the net increase of 45 doctors was significantly lower than in 2017 when a total of 328 were added to the province's medical community.[17] The drop in the number of physicians while Alberta's population was still growing reverberated to family doctors who found they could not keep up with demand. The number of Alberta family doctors accepting new patients through an online portal dropped by half—from 907 to 446—between May 2020 and January of 2022, according to data provided by the Primary Care Networks.[18] Specialists were also seeking greener pastures. In March 2022, twenty-four doctors publicly expressed concern over cancer treatment because of the departure of radiation oncologists, including the Director of Medical Physics at the Tom Baker Cancer Centre in Calgary, due to insufficient renumeration and heavy workload. Rural areas were hit hardest by the exodus of doctors because it had been difficult to recruit them for those areas in the first place. AHS was concerned enough that it was monitoring the situation closely and categorizing rural communities as high, medium, or low risk of physicians withdrawing their services. An AHS document obtained by the New Democratic Party Official Opposition through Freedom of

Information laws and made public in June 2020 stated that "legal and emergency measures may be enacted if deemed necessary for the health and safety of Albertans."

In late October 2021 two public opinion polls made it clear that a majority of Albertans had given UCP health care policies a failing or barely passing grade. In a survey conducted by Think HQ of 1,116 Albertans, 70 per cent—said the province's health-care system had gotten worse over the last two years, and nearly half of those—42 per cent—said it is "a lot worse." Only 5 per cent believed health care had improved. Think HQ president Marc Henry told *CTV News*: "We've done this survey going back to the Redford government (2011–2014). This is one where it is different because we are dealing with a pandemic, but the level and intensity of dissatisfaction with the performance of the government is actually quite astounding. . . . That's why we made a point of saying, 'Ok, well, is this because it's something they did? Or is it because of, you know, it's tough dealing with COVID?' People are not letting them off the hook in terms of excusing their performance on this because of COVID."

A poll conducted in early October 2021 of 600 random online members of the Angus Reid Institute forum found that only one in five Albertans believed the government was doing a good job of handling health care. Institute president Shachi Kurl told CBC that that proportion has dropped substantially since just before the global pandemic hit. "Exactly two years ago, we were at a place where 60 per cent saw the provincial government doing a good job. That dropped to 36 per cent this time last year, and now it's down to 20 per cent," she said. "What we are seeing is a really significant downward trend." By early April 2022 the UCP appeared to have found a scapegoat for all the discontent with health care: Dr. Verna Yiu, AHS President and CEO, was fired even though she had led the organization through the worst of the pandemic. She had been publicly criticized by some UCP MLAs for failing to increase ICU capacity during infection peaks and for issuing a vaccine mandate for all AHS employees. No one in government publicly refuted those accusations.

Two and half years had passed since the election campaign when Jason Kenney and the UCP assured Albertans that "a universal, comprehensive health-care system is a core part of UCP policy." The official party platform was labelled as the "Health Care Guarantee" and pledged to maintain or increase government funding for the province's public health care system. Obviously, the UCP government did not anticipate that it would spend the first half of its mandate dealing with a pandemic that would hospitalize thousands and take the lives of just over 4,500 Albertans by the end of May 2022. Nevertheless, it's clear that the UCP had an agenda for public health care that wasn't fully revealed in their campaign platform. In fact, looking back on the events of the past two and half years it is easy to see that the UCP intended to weaken the collective associations of health care workers, including physicians and surgeons, so that they would have less power when it came to negotiating their salaries, benefits, and fees. It is also easy to see in hindsight that UCP had plans to dismantle the public health care system as we know it and make it more entrepreneurial, turn it into business opportunities for investors and health care corporations staking their future on a steady supply of money from the public purse.

For the most part their campaign against doctors, nurses, and other health care workers backfired. The UCP campaign didn't turn Albertans against them because they cost too much money, it made the public more sympathetic to health care workers especially in light of the pressure they were under due to the pandemic. The government backed down in negotiations with the UNA, and as of June 2022 had yet to finalize a contract with the AMA. The UCP have lost so much public support for their performance on the health care file that it's doubtful trust will soon be regained, particularly if expert and skilled health care practitioners leave the province or those outside Alberta don't see it as a place to advance their careers. As for the UCP push to privatize some surgical services; that might succeed because the pandemic created such a backlog of surgeries that it will need to be attended to and the UCP can say they have the perfect solution for people desperate for those surgeries.

But the UCP has changed the health care climate in Alberta and it is going to take a long time to recover. Alberta is no longer a province where the government aspires to create a medical mecca that attracts physicians and researchers from all over the world. Those days are over.

NOTES

1   Skene, W. (1979, March 26). Playing the ace in a high-stakes brain game. *Maclean's Magazine.*

2   Zwicker, J., & Emery H. (2015, August). How is funding medical research better for patients? Valuing the impact of Alberta's health research. University of Calgary School of Public Policy.

3   Picard, A. (2009, June 11). The future of Medicare is in his hands. *Globe and Mail*, L4.

4   Blue Ribbon Panel on Alberta's Finances. (2019, August). *Government of Alberta*, 2. https://open.alberta.ca/dataset/081ba74d-95c8-43ab-9097-cef17a9fb59c/ resource/257f040a-2645-49e7-b40b-462e4b5c059c/download/blue-ribbon-panel-report.pdf

5   Blue Ribbon Panel on Alberta's Finances (2019, August). *Government of Alberta*, 4. https://open.alberta.ca/dataset/081ba74d-95c8-43ab-9097-cef17a9fb59c/ resource/257f040a-2645-49e7-b40b-462e4b5c059c/download/blue-ribbon-panel-report.pdf

6   Blue Ribbon Panel on Alberta's Finances (2019, August). *Government of Alberta*, 6. https://open.alberta.ca/dataset/081ba74d-95c8-43ab-9097-cef17a9fb59c/ resource/257f040a-2645-49e7-b40b-462e4b5c059c/download/blue-ribbon-panel-report.pdf

7   Blue Ribbon Panel on Alberta's Finances (2019, August). *Government of Alberta*, 7. https://open.alberta.ca/dataset/081ba74d-95c8-43ab-9097-cef17a9fb59c/ resource/257f040a-2645-49e7-b40b-462e4b5c059c/download/blue-ribbon-panel-report.pdf

8   Ernst & Young. (2019). *Alberta health services performance review.* Alberta Health Services, 25.

9   Ernst & Young. (2019). *Alberta health services performance review.* Alberta Health Services, 26.

10 Alberta Purchasing Connection. (2020). *Opportunity Notice.* https://vendor. purchasingconnection.ca/OpportunityAwards.aspx?Guid=370efa55-05c7-f35e-1174-39c2ed480000&

11 Alberta Legislative Assembly, *Hansard*, 30th Leg, 2nd Sess, Day 40 (7 July 2020) at 1783 (Hon. J. Kenney).

12 Ernst & Young. (2019). *Alberta health services performance review.* Alberta Health Services, 8.

13 Alberta Medical Association. (2020, July 10). Looming physician exodus from Alberta caused by failed provincial funding framework. https://www.albertadoctors.org/8196. aspx

14 Rusnell, C. (2020, July 15). Shandro directs doctors regulatory college to stop doctors leaving province en masse. *CBC News.* https://www.cbc.ca/news/canada/edmonton/ shandro-directs-doctors-regulatory-college-to-stop-doctors-from-leaving-practices-en-masse-1.5650940

15 Huston, J. (2020, July 12). *Letter to Alberta health from AMA*. https://www.albertadoctors.org/Media%202020%20PLs/2020-07-09-ama-ltr-bill-30-hcp-act.pdf

16 Molnar, C. (2020, October 6). Final thoughts on a tumultuous year. *AMA President's Letter*. https://www.albertadoctors.org/services/media-publications/presidents-letter/pl-archive/final-thoughts-on-a-tumultuous-year

17 College of Physicians and Surgeons Alberta (March 2020). *Changes in Physician Workforce*. https://cpsa.ca/wp-content/uploads/2022/01/Changes-in-physician-workforce-2021-2017.pdf

18 Lee, J. (2022, April 27). Concerns grow as more and more Albertans can't find a family doctor. *CBC News*. https://www.cbc.ca/news/canada/calgary/fewer-family-doctors-accepting-new-patients-1.6432767

Education and the United Conservative Party of Alberta

Charles F. Webber

The discourse among educational stakeholders in Alberta since the 2019 provincial election has reflected the wide variety of views that Albertans held about the form and function of schools. Much of the debate focused on power and control; the Alberta Teachers' Association (ATA) and the United Conservative Party (UCP) competed for dominance in decisions about curricular revision, external student assessment, and teacher discipline, while both claimed to speak in the best interests of Alberta students and on behalf of Albertans (see also Lori Williams' chapter on labour and the UCP government). The two organizations entrenched their disagreement about the rights of parents to select their children's schools. Parents, members of various faiths, opposition parties, and academics contributed their often-conflicting opinions about whether charter and independent schools should continue to exist or, if they do, if they should receive any government funding. All stakeholders voiced strong opinions about the operation of gay-straight alliances in schools, whether prayer had a place in nondenominational schools, and when elementary students should learn what details about the lives of First Nations children in residential schools. Financial matters also featured prominently in post 2019 educational discussions, including teachers' salary levels and administration of the Alberta Teachers' Retirement Fund. However, by far the most disruptive issue for school and community members was the impact of COVID-19.

It is in this turbulent educational milieu that the UCP developed policies and implemented practices affecting the over 730,000[1] Alberta students attending Early Childhood Services (ECS) through grade 12. The following account explores the bifurcated perspectives evident among stakeholders in relation to many important educational issues in recent years. It considers the historical and recent relationship between the ATA and the UCP government. The development of a controversial draft K–6 elementary curriculum is summarized, followed by an overview of how pandemic factors disrupted schooling for all Albertans. A concluding section will highlight the drivers of educational change in Alberta and speculate about the future of Alberta school communities. First though, a brief explanation—necessary for contextualizing the rest of this report—will share the origins of the provincial education system and the features that distinguish education in Alberta from other Canadian provinces and territories.

A Brief Contextual Description

International visitors are always curious about why the Alberta government funds Catholic and nondenominational schools separately, but equally, yet describes them both as "public education." When visitors learn that some but not all Canadian provinces fund both Catholic and nondenominational schools, depending upon decisions made when each province joined the Canadian Confederation, the next question usually relates to the absence of a federal education office that most other nations have. The answer is that Section 93 of the British North America Act of 1867, subsequently renamed the Constitution Act 1867,[2] assigns responsibility for education to each province, except for the education of First Nations children, armed forces personnel, and federal prison inmates. The Constitution Act 1982 affirmed these arrangements.

So, when Alberta became a Canadian province in 1905[3] it gained control of education within its borders subject to guaranteeing the rights of Catholics and Protestants to operate separate school systems. As a result, Catholic and Protestant schools[4] continue to be parts of the fully funded public education system.

Overall, the structure and governance of the Alberta school system reflects the cultural, religious, and linguistic legacies of two of Canada's founding cultures—the French and the English. The First Nations of Canada constituted a third founding culture, but the education of First Nations children followed a very different trajectory. The Constitution Acts of 1867 and 1982 assigned responsibility for First Nations to the federal government, which led to the establishment of residential schools that First Nations children were required to attend. Residential schools operated in Canada from the late 1800s to the mid-1990s.[5] Albertans of all races and religions continue to grieve the emotional trauma caused by separating generations of First Nations children from their families. In addition, the legacy of residential schools includes many reports of physical and sexual abuse of students by those who were entrusted to teach and care for them.

In the late twentieth century and more recently, the federal government began to share greater control of education with local education authorities in First Nations communities and in alignment with Treaties 6, 7, and 8[6] between the Canadian government, i.e., the Crown, and First Nations in Alberta. Thus, reserve schools operate under the local jurisdiction of Chief and Council while retaining close association with the Alberta department of education in terms of curriculum and teachers' credentials. The complex arrangements for education in Alberta manifest the influence of English and French colonization, legislation from the nineteenth and twentieth centuries, Catholic and Protestant religions, the history of residential schools, and the *Truth and Reconciliation Commission of Canada: Calls to Action.*[7]

Legislation that was passed by successive conservative governments led Alberta to develop an education system that is relatively unique within Canada. Alberta has the highest degree of school choice in Canada.[8] Parents can elect to send their children to a wide array of schools organized according to academic focus, sports, arts, gender, religion, language, learning challenges and strengths, and more. Parents also may choose to homeschool their children or to pay tuition fees—in addition to their school taxes—to enroll them in private schools that serve their cultural and academic interests. Even greater choice is provided through charter schools that are required to offer the Alberta Program of Studies[9] in ways that attract students with interests in, for example, gifted education, gender-specific schooling, and back-to-the-basics teaching and learning.

Bifurcated Educational Perspectives

The political right in Alberta has dominated educational policy setting since 1935 when the Social Credit Party of Alberta replaced the previous Liberal government. As part of a general endorsement of school choice, Alberta became the only Canadian province to establish and operate charter schools,[10] a form of public school with freedom to offer unique programming intended to enhance student learning in innovative ways. Independent schools and homeschooling also feature as central elements of school choice.

The ATA has long opposed charter[11] and private schools[12] and declined to recognize charter schools as public schools. It publicly opposed the 2020 Choice in Education Act[13] that removed the cap on the number of charter schools permitted in Alberta and allowed charter school applications to go directly to the minister of education, bypassing the previous requirement for applications to first go to the local school board. Perhaps contradictorily, it claimed that the Act eroded public education and, concurrently, it observed that public schools, i.e., Catholic and nondenominational school districts, already contained a variety of school types from which parents and students could choose.[14]

Standardized testing was institutionalized by past Alberta legislatures in the form of provincial achievement tests administered at grades 3, 6, and 9, and diploma exams for grade 12 courses.[15] The former were not designed to affect learners' grades but, rather, intended to gather data that would inform instructional improvement, curriculum revisions, staffing needs, professional development programming, resource allocation, and more. Grade 12 diploma exams were expected to inform summative evaluations and serve a gatekeeping function for post-secondary institutions and employers.

The New Democratic Party (NDP) government that was elected in 2015 modified the grade 3 provincial achievement test so that it was administered at the beginning of the school year, not at the end. The name was changed to student learning assessments. Relatedly, the weighting of grade 12 diploma exams was reduced from 50 per cent to 30 per cent of students' final grades. Both of these moves reflected the views of the ATA that sees external examinations[16] as an infringement on teacher professionalism and autonomy. After their election in 2019, the UCP government mused publicly about the possibility of reversing the format of grade 3 assessments and increasing the weighting of grade 12 diploma exam marks, but the changes did not emerge as priorities and to date have been left undone. However, the COVID-19 pandemic caused Education Minister Adriana LaGrange to make grade 12 diploma exams optional during the 2020–21 school year but to require them for 2021–22, but with a temporary weighting of 10 per cent of students' final grades. The exams will return to a 30 per cent weighting effective September 2022.[17]

Opposing views about pedagogy were highlighted in 2020 discussions of curriculum reform in Alberta, when Education Minister Adriana LaGrange stated her government's opposition to inquiry-based or discovery learning.[18] Rather, she said that literacy and numeracy would form the foundation of a new K–6 curriculum. Her statement was viewed positively by representatives of some school districts but criticized by the teachers' union, which subsequently panned the entire proposed K–6 curriculum.

Stark contrasts in views about school choice, assessment, curricular decisions, and accountability elicited emotional online exchanges and too often vitriolic social media postings. The tension-filled communications occurred in the context of a UCP government that began to govern a few months prior to a global pandemic, which led to the near collapse of the Alberta health care system, intermittent workplace and school closures, and extensive job losses. Thus, conflicted and heated dialogue was exacerbated by the unprecedented social disruption caused by COVID-19. Indeed, the CBC experimented with turning off the comments sections on its online news sites[19] because of the severe abuse directed toward journalists and other viewers.

Government and the Alberta Teachers' Association

There was a time when the ATA arguably perceived its working relationship with the conservative government of the day as much closer, or at least more amicable, than the one that they currently have with the UCP government. For instance, Halvar Jonson,[20] a former president of the ATA, was elected in 1982 in Ponoka, Alberta, as a Progressive Conservative (PC) member of the legislative assembly and subsequently served for over three years as minister of education during the Klein Revolution. Jonson's relationship with the teachers' union went through times of tension, but he was described by a former executive staff member of the union as ". . . the best minister we could have had at a very difficult time."

Frank Bruseker[21] was another former president of the ATA who also served as a provincial member of the legislative assembly. Following two terms as a Liberal opposition member, Bruseker served three terms as leader of the teachers' union. Like Jonson, Bruseker moved with apparent ease between government and the union. In fact, in 2019, Bruseker received honorary membership in the ATA, its highest recognition for service.

Given the current fractious context of Alberta politics, it is difficult to imagine the current president of the union, Jason Schilling, moving into a legislator role with a political party other than the NDP. Moreover, it is unlikely that the current minister of education, Adriana LaGrange, will be honoured or described fondly decades from now by a senior teachers' union staff member. In May 2021, approximately 99 per cent of the nearly 450 members of the Annual Representative Assembly, the policy making arm of the ATA, passed a motion of non-confidence in the education minister.[22] The members of the assembly represent the over 46,000[23] certificated full and part-time teachers who are members of the ATA.

The motion of non-confidence was the culmination of a series of disagreements between the teachers' union and the provincial government, the most prominent of which was the draft K–6 curriculum.[24] The motion was accompanied by claims that the curriculum development process did not involve teachers sufficiently. There was dissatisfaction with the scope and sequence of the curriculum, particularly the social studies component, described by various teacher and university faculty member reviewers as loaded with too much Eurocentric content for young learners but, concurrently, inadequate coverage of francophone, First Nations, and Métis cultural knowledge and perspectives.

Other disputed issues include the government's decision in 2019 to move the administration of the Alberta Teachers' Retirement Fund to the government-owned Alberta Investment Management Corporation. The ATA initiated a court challenge that was dropped in the fall of 2021 after an agreement[25] was reached to permit the Alberta Teachers' Retirement

Fund board to retain control of pension fund investment strategies. Another controversial issue was the decrease in funding for the equivalent of approximately 1,800 education assistants and classroom aides, the result of lower-than-anticipated enrolments at the early childhood level and the increase in parents electing to educate their children at home rather than send them to school during the COVID-19 pandemic.[26]

The Teaching Profession Act[27] combined the functions of the ATA as a union and a professional association. That is, the association was entrusted with negotiating working conditions for its members while also fostering improvements to the profession and disciplining members who are found to have contravened the Code of Professional Conduct.[28] Different opinions about appropriate disciplinary action emerged in a 2019 case of a teacher who inappropriately touched elementary students over a period of four years. The ATA recommended suspensions of the teacher's certificate for two years, but Minister LaGrange permanently revoked the teaching certificate and vowed to review recent cases of teacher misconduct.[29] The response from the association was to suggest the minister was seeking to discredit the organization. This example highlights the challenges associated with the dual union-professional association function of the ATA, a tension that contributed to the separation of those roles in Ontario and British Columbia and the establishment of the Ontario College of Teachers[30] and the Teacher Regulation Branch[31] (previously the British Columbia College of Teachers[32]).

The Alberta education minister's concerns about teacher professional discipline led to a government proposal in late 2021 to remove responsibility for teacher discipline from the ATA.[33] The association responded by charging the provincial government with politicizing teacher discipline, de-professionalizing teachers, and fostering an adversarial culture in education.[34] Nonetheless, Education Minister LaGrange observed that she perceived it to be a conflict of interest for the teachers' union to be responsible for defending its members while concurrently disciplining them for unprofessional conduct. She also stated that Alberta is the only Canadian province or territory where the teachers' union is responsible for disciplining its members and proposed that teacher discipline be the mandate of an independent commissioner.[35] The government's proposal calls for the commissioner to make decisions, potentially recommend penalties, forward complaints to mediation, or have concerns heard by a panel of teachers and community members, with decisions posted online. The proposed change is scheduled to come into effect in January 2023.[36]

Draft K–6 School Curriculum

The proposed elementary school curriculum elicited an unabated storm of controversy when it was introduced in the spring of 2021. Politicized from the start, it was preceded by suggestions that the former NDP government wanted to reinforce inquiry-based discovery learning and teaching, which needed to be corrected by the UCP government. An Alberta government website[37] states that the new curriculum will deliver essential knowledge to students in the areas of literacy, numeracy, citizenship, and practical skills.

Criticism of the draft curriculum began with opposition statements[38] that the draft curriculum failed to adequately include the First Nations experiences related to residential schools. Further, the curriculum was deemed to be Eurocentric and age inappropriate with its inclusion of content about ancient Rome and China. The ATA observed[39] that the curriculum does not reflect current theory and research about teaching and learning. The ATA shared the finding of its poll of 900 Albertans[40] that just over half of respondents believed the curriculum would not provide students with the knowledge and skills they need. Other criticisms included statements that the draft curriculum does not facilitate inclusion and acceptance of 2SLGBTQA+ students.[41]

A group stating that it is sponsored by the Association of Alberta Deans of Education[42] responded to the draft curriculum by inviting and sharing reviews from individuals with expertise in curriculum and child development. Its website, titled Alberta Curriculum Analysis,[43] stated that it is designed to share nonpartisan and expert advice on the draft curriculum. Members of the steering committee and contributors to the site represent primarily teachers and teacher educators from Alberta universities.

Virtually all the subject areas in the draft curriculum received a host of negative reviews on the Alberta Curriculum Analysis site. The English language arts curriculum area received some positive comments but even this subject was criticized by most reviewers. The social studies content in the draft curriculum was a flashpoint for extremely negative reviews. It was said to perpetuate patriarchal stereotypes within Canadian society and to reinforce white privilege. Other descriptions stated that the social studies curriculum failed to incorporate First Nation, Métis, and Inuit perspectives; presented Christianity as a dominant world view; and inadequately facilitated research and inquiry skills.

The dialogue about the draft K–6 curriculum was turbulent, unrelenting, and divisive. Most Alberta school boards chose not to participate in piloting the draft K–6 curriculum during the 2021–2022 school year.[44] Following the October 2021 municipal election, the school board members of the province's two largest public school boards in Edmonton[45] and Calgary[46] voiced their united opposition to the proposed curriculum. Nonetheless, the UCP government mandated in April 2022 that the new programs in K–6 English language arts, mathematics, and physical education and wellness would begin in September 2022.[47] The government also expects that the remainder of the K–6 draft curriculum, including social studies, would be piloted in September 2023 and implemented fully by September 2024.

The ATA cautioned[48] its members against participating in working groups charged with developing new curricula for the secondary grades. The Alberta NDP stated that they would reverse[49] the implementation of the draft K–6 curriculum if they won the next election and would follow that by the launch of a new public consultation process about curriculum changes.

Pandemic Factors

Underpinning the disruptive politics of education since March 2020 was the COVID-19 pandemic. School staff members were frontline workers and, although many expressed concerns about transmissibility of the virus to students and colleagues, virtually all school workers navigated the intermittent opening and closures by going to school when asked. They shifted from in-school to online teaching and learning, sometimes on a few hours' notice. It was observed by one school superintendent that the pandemic caused school community members—teachers, students, and parents—to coalesce around the care and education of students in unprecedented circumstances.[50]

The work of school community members occurred in a context of uncertainty. Masking initially was thought to be unnecessary but that changed as the pandemic gained momentum, so teachers and all students, except those in early childhood classrooms, shifted to wearing masks. Parents and teachers watched elementary students struggle to keep masks covering their mouths and noses, with frequent lapses throughout the school day. Handwashing and use of hand sanitizer quickly became routine but so did more frequent bouts of anxiety among students who were afraid of getting sick and, in the case of high school students, worried about admission to post-secondary studies.

Teachers and school administrators followed government and school board directives to rearrange life in schools.[51] For example, they organized class cohorts designed to reduce widespread transmission of COVID-19. They monitored the isolation of individual students who tested positive for the virus. They shifted entire classrooms from gathering in school to meeting online for up to two weeks whenever someone in the class qualified as a close contact, although that requirement relaxed as the pandemic progressed. Parents were unable to enter schools and had to wait outside to collect their children. School staff were advised to increase ventilation whenever possible, although most schools were built with closed heating and ventilation systems and with windows that do not open or perhaps have no windows at all.

The periods of uncertainty and conflicting advice led some parents to keep their children at home even when schools were open. Homeschooling in Alberta increased dramatically[52] and there is the possibility that homeschooling will continue even as pandemic restrictions ease. Parents who opted to teach their children at home found they had to take on the role and the work associated with being a teacher. They also had to grapple with computer access and bandwidth issues[53] when one or more children were studying at home and parents were doing their work online. Adequate workspace also factored into accommodating study and work at home. In rural and marginalized communities all these considerations emerged as equity issues.

Educators and parents worried about the impact of provincially mandated lockdowns and restricted access to schools. The possibility of learning loss[54] was real for isolating students, particularly those with limited access to online learning. Limited or no participation in school and community sports and arts activities affected major parts of many students' lives. These circumstances meant greatly reduced social interaction and missed opportunities to mark learning milestones. Although in-person high school graduations throughout Alberta are planned for 2022, graduation ceremonies in 2020 and 2021 were missed or reduced to parking lot gatherings where drive-by waves substituted for walking across a school stage to receive a parchment.[55] A recent study[56] of student wellness found that approximately three-quarters of students between the ages of twelve and eighteen feel that they are adjusting to the regular educational changes associated with the pandemic. However, female students aged fifteen to eighteen felt more stress than males and younger students (see also Lisa Young's chapter on COVID-19).

What Is Ahead?

The politics of education are not distinct from the larger contested Alberta political landscape. A return to pre-pandemic teaching and learning is unlikely. Polarized views of what schooling should be—traditional learning versus inquiry-based learning—have been expressed so strongly within school communities, by provincial politicians, and in the media that the politics of education are likely to continue to divide into the near future.

There is the distinct possibility that, if a new program of studies is perceived implementable by enough Albertans, more parents than ever will seek forms of schooling for their children that align with their views on traditional versus inquiry-based learning. The draft K–6 curriculum has been disappointing to those who have responded quickly and vociferously: some parents certainly but also teachers, the ATA, the Official Opposition, and some university teacher educators. However, the views of other Albertans are represented in the draft K–6 curriculum, including wariness and unclear understandings of inquiry-based learning, discovery learning, and constructivism.

That means alternative schools within districts may expand and thrive, and the numbers and types of charter schools will increase, particularly considering the recent addition of $25 million over three years to support charter school expansions.[57] Parents may seek the purpose-driven independent schools that currently exist and the ones that may form in response to parents' and learners' perceived need for schools that address specific learning interests. The current UCP government supports school choice—evidenced in the Choice in Education Act, 2020—and the magnitude and popularity of school choice among Albertans suggests that subsequent governments are unlikely to remove or reduce existing forms of school choice.

The relationship between the UCP government and the ATA will continue to be challenging. An institutional memory will linger of how teachers perceived the curriculum redevelopment process, the proposed shift in responsibility for teacher discipline, and of how they were not considered priority frontline workers when vaccines became available. Pre-pandemic discussions by the government of budget cuts and management of teachers' pension funds may challenge future collective bargaining. However, even a change in government may not remove larger budgetary concerns about funding education and other government services in an Alberta economy shifting from oil and gas production to other sectors, so collective bargaining and school funding are unlikely to diminish in significance.

Diversity in Alberta will continue to grow. Calgary Economic Development reports[58] that the city's population represents 240 ethnic origins and is third in the proportion of visible minorities in Canadian cities. As diversity increases so does the need to recognize and adapt to differences in culturally relevant schools. In particular, the Alberta *Teaching Quality Standard*[59] foci on inclusive school environments and on teachers' knowledge of First Nations, Métis, and Inuit cultures suggests that these will continue to influence the politics of education. School names will continue to be challenged and to change as increasing awareness of the legacies of school namesakes lead school officials and community members to strive to balance intercultural understanding with recognition of our past. School prayer in nondenominational schools has been processed and at least partially resolved in some school settings but may remain a contested feature in others. Catholic schools have largely found ways to accommodate gay-straight alliances, however uncomfortably, but they will grapple with their historical association with residential schools and growing public awareness of their church's involvement in separating First Nations children from their families, child abuse, and unmarked graves. Pope Francis' April 2022 apology to Indigenous Canadians for the Roman Catholic Church's involvement in residential schools[60] and his scheduled visit to Alberta in July 2022[61] may address Albertans' concerns to some extent while also underscoring the severe intergenerational harm caused by residential schools.

Despite the difficult pedagogical, cultural, and financial issues facing the Alberta school system, it can build on the provincial history of educational success. Various reports[62] describe its education system as one of the top systems internationally. Students who are new Canadians generally perform well and, compared to other nations, differences in how Alberta students achieve relative to socioeconomic stratification are relatively low. There is a strong and well-established educational architecture that includes a common program of studies, however contested, plus opportunities for community voice, school choice, and information technology access. There also is a plethora of formal and informal organizations that represent student, educator, and community member interests. Perhaps most important, annual satisfaction surveys indicate that students, teachers, school trustees, and parents express extremely high satisfaction levels with the quality of teaching and learning in Alberta schools.

Drivers of Change

Premier Jason Kenney's announcement on 18 May 2022 that he would step down as leader of the UCP[63] introduced yet more uncertainty to the future of schooling in Alberta. His decision launched declarations by several prominent current and past members of the legislative assembly that they planned to seek the leadership of the UCP. The leadership campaign may well foreshadow a revised set of provincial goals for Alberta students, parents, and educators, either as the mandate of a UCP government re-elected in 2023 or of an NDP government that could be returned to power after a four-year hiatus.

Whatever the outcome of the 2023 provincial election, Albertans can anticipate that educational policies and a provincial mandated program of studies, accompanied by some form of external accountability framework, almost certainly will continue to elicit diverse opinions from community stakeholders, as they have throughout Alberta's history. The challenging nature of educational decision-making will continue to be influenced by several factors, ranging from the COVID-19 pandemic to the economy to social justice issues and technological innovations.

The pandemic of 2020 until the present disrupted schooling in ways not seen since the 1918 flu epidemic. Both viruses circulated suddenly and unexpectedly. The 2020 COVID-19 pandemic led to social and economic disruption that continues. Alberta Health Services suggested that the virus may shift from a pandemic to become endemic,[64] with a lower transmission rate as more Albertans twelve and older are vaccinated and as vaccines for children under twelve are accessed.[65] However, Albertans are slower than the rest of Canada to become fully vaccinated and their vaccine hesitancy[66] may affect how many young children receive the vaccine now available for them,[67] with a direct impact on the frequency and size of COVID-19 outbreaks in schools. We can anticipate that current and future provincial governments and school boards will struggle with vaccine hesitancy and with resistance to vaccine mandates for children. It is also possible that other viruses will emerge to continue to impact the health and safety of students and staff.

Gay-straight alliances[68] in schools were implemented fully throughout Alberta, including in Catholic schools and in some alternative schools where policy makers and educators struggled with the juxtaposition of the mandate for the peer support networks and their religious or cultural beliefs. However, the work to make schools safe and welcoming for 2SLGBTQA+ students will continue as young people identify, for example, as gay, queer, or trans gender.

The *Truth and Reconciliation Commission of Canada: Calls to Action* will drive educational policies and practices in band-operated schools, even though they are not governed by the provincial government, and in all schools: public, Catholic, charter, and independent. In particular, the *Call to Action* to reduce the differences between education funding for First Nations children on and off reserves will demand attention. The Alberta *Teaching Quality Standard* requires teacher educators in provincial universities to ensure that their graduates understand the social and educational implications of treaties and residential schools. This is a positive step in attending to the educational challenges and opportunities for First Nations, Métis, and Inuit students but ongoing achievement gaps between Indigenous youth and the general population of provincial students will need continued attention. Although Alberta schools enjoy broad support from students and community members, Indigenous students in band-operated schools and in urban schools have not achieved academic-ally to the levels of other students.

Alberta has relied on oil and gas for its prosperity and funding for public services like education. There are exceptions in rural and remote communities, but most Alberta schools are well equipped with technology and internet access in support of teaching and learning. However, the large drop in oil prices in 2019–2020 was accompanied by job losses and deficit provincial budgets (see Trevor Tombe's chapter on Alberta's fiscal situation). Although oil prices increased in 2021 and soared in the first half of 2022, due in part to Russia's invasion of Ukraine, it is reasonable to anticipate ongoing fluctuations in provincial oil and gas royalties, even if the Trans Mountain pipeline[69] is completed and new markets for natural resources are accessible. Opposition to pipelines and to the burning of fossil fuels is likely to continue so the future of Alberta's natural resource industries is uncertain and, correspondingly, historically high levels of funding for schools may be increasingly difficult to maintain. Similarly, the salaries[70] of Alberta educators are high compared to those in other Canadian provinces so collective bargaining may be challenging with the current UCP government but also future provincial governments.

Conclusion

Alberta has a diverse population, so wide-ranging opinions about education should be expected. The provincial education system is an artifact of a complex history that is replete with strong cultural, economic, and colonial dimensions that Albertans still are processing. Current forms of school structures and curricula are the result of past governments and citizens seeking to accommodate differences in how Albertans wish to educate their children. The draft K–6 curriculum that currently is the centre of heated debate eventually will emerge during the mandate of the current or a future provincial government in a form that will continue to be debated and revised to reflect changing learner needs.

The ATA continues to offer professional development to its members and to sponsor theoretical, empirical, and politicized perspectives on teaching and learning, while also exhibiting an increasing presence as a union. The strong unionized representation is evident in the recent campaign[71] launched by the ATA to lobby for public support against the UCP government. Objections are directed toward what the association perceives as funding cuts, large class sizes, and an inappropriate K–6 curriculum. Basically, ATA is renewing and expanding its mandate as a union.

The UCP has governed, and educators have fulfilled their duties during a challenging time in Alberta's history. Perhaps the turbulent political landscape would have formed without the intensity wrought by the COVID-19 pandemic. Nonetheless, the difficult issues facing Alberta's school system will continue to demand the attention of Albertans for some time, no matter which political party forms government after the next election in 2023.

NOTES

1   Government of Alberta, *Student Population Statistics*, 2021, https://www.alberta.ca/student-population-statistics.aspx

2   Government of Canada, *Consolidation of Constitution Acts, 1867 to 1982*, https://laws-lois.justice.gc.ca/eng/Const/index.html

3   Government of Canada, *The Alberta Act, 1905*, https://www.justice.gc.ca/eng/rp-pr/csj-sjc/constitution/lawreg-loireg/p1t121.html

4   Alberta Education, *Alberta Schools and Authorities*, 2021, https://education.alberta.ca/alberta-education/school-authority-index/everyone/alberta-schools/

5   Government of Alberta, *Residential School Research and Recognition*, 2021, https://www.alberta.ca/residential-school-research-and-recognition.aspx

6   Alberta Regional Professional Development Consortium, *Alberta Treaties 6, 7, 8*, https://empoweringthespirit.ca/wp-content/uploads/2017/05/Alberta-Treaties-678-1.pdf

7   Truth and Reconciliation Commission of Canada, *Truth and Reconciliation Commission of Canada: Calls to Action*, 2015, https://www.irsss.ca/downloads/trc-calls-to-action.pdf

8   Lynn Bosetti, Deani Van Pelt, and Derek J. Allison, "The Changing Landscape of School Choice in Canada: From Pluralism to Parental Preference?" *Education Policy Analysis Archives* 25, no. 38 (2017): 12. http://dx.doi.org/10.14507/epaa.25.2685

9   Government of Alberta, *Programs of Study*, https://www.alberta.ca/programs-of-study.aspx

10 Government of Alberta, *Charter Schools*, 2021, https://www.alberta.ca/charter-schools.aspx

11 Alberta Teachers' Association, *School Choice: Charter Schools, Private School and Vouchers*, https://www.teachers.ab.ca/News%20Room/Issues/Pages/School-Choice.aspx

12 Alberta Teachers' Association, *Province Increases Private School Funding: Government Sneaking Privatization in the Back Door, Warns ATA*, 2008, https://www.teachers.ab.ca/News%20Room/ata%20news/Volume%2043/Number%201/In%20the%20News/Pages/Province%20increases%20private%20school%20funding.aspx

13   Legislative Assembly of Alberta, *Bill 15: Choice in Education Act, 2020*, https://www. assembly.ab.ca/assembly-business/bills/bill?billinfoid=11845&from=bills

14   Eva Ferguson, "Choice in Education Act Raises Concerns of Eroding Public System," *Calgary Herald*, 28 May 2020, https://calgaryherald.com/news/choice-in-education-act-raises-concerns-of-eroding-public-system

15   Government of Alberta, *K to 12 Provincial Assessment*, 2021, https://www.alberta.ca/k-12-provincial-assessment.aspx

16   Alberta Teachers' Association, *A Note about Standardized Testing*, 2019, https://www. teachers.ab.ca/News%20Room/The%20Learning%20Team/Vol22/Number-4/Pages/A-note-about-standardized-testing.aspx

17   Government of Alberta, *Diploma Exams—Overview*, 2022, https://www.alberta.ca/ diploma-exams-overview.aspx#jumplinks-2

18   Morgan Black, "Alberta Government New School Curriculum Focused on 'Evidence, Numeracy & Literacy': LaGrange," *Global News*, 6 August 2020, https://globalnews.ca/ news/7254886/alberta-government-curriculum-review/

19   Brodie Fenlon, "Why CBC Is Turning Off Facebook Comments on New Posts for a Month," *CBC News*, 15 June 2021, https://www.cbc.ca/news/editor-blog-facebook-comments-1.6064804

20   Karen Virag, "Halvar Jonson—Best Possible Education Minister at a Very Difficult Time," *ATA Magazine*, 10 December 2012, https://www.teachers.ab.ca/News%20Room/ ata%20magazine/Volume-93/Number-2/Pages/Halvar-Jonson.aspx

21   Frank Bruseker, "From the President—A New School Year and a New President," *ATA Magazine*, 2003, https://www.teachers.ab.ca/News%20Room/ata%20magazine/ Volume%2084/Number%201/Pages/From%20the%20President.aspx

22   Stephen David Cook, "Teachers Assembly Votes Non-Confidence in Alberta Education Minister," *CBC News*, 23 May 2021, https://www.cbc.ca/news/canada/edmonton/non-confidence-alberta-teachers-1.6038125

23   Alberta Teachers' Association, *Association Structure and Organization*, 2021, https:// www.teachers.ab.ca/SiteCollectionDocuments/ATA/About/Governance/ATA%20 Structure%20and%20Organization%20Chart%20IM-2.pdf

24   Government of Alberta, *Draft K–6 Curriculum*.

25   Sarah Rieger, "Alberta Teachers Association Reaches Pension Agreement with AIMCo, Ending Lawsuit against Province," *CBC News*, 8 September 2021, https://www.cbc.ca/ news/canada/calgary/ata-aimco-pension-agreement-1.6168921

26   Lauren Boothby, "Alberta Budget 2021: Province Says It Won't 'Penalize' School Boards for Lower Enrolment, But Nearly 2,000 Jobs Lost to Pandemic Won't Return," *Edmonton Journal*, 26 February 2021, https://edmontonjournal.com/news/politics/ alberta-budget-2021-province-will-not-penalize-school-boards-amid-covid-19-enrolment-drop

27   Alberta Queen's Printer, *Teaching Profession Act: Revised Statutes of Alberta 2000*, Chapter T-2, 2020, https://www.qp.alberta.ca/documents/Acts/T02.pdf

28   Alberta Teachers' Association, *Code of Professional Conduct*, 2018, https://www. teachers.ab.ca/SiteCollectionDocuments/ATA/Publications/Teachers-as-Professionals/ IM-4E%20Code%20of%20Professional%20Conduct.pdf

29   Sammy Hudes, "Education Minister Orders Permanent Ban for Teacher Accused of Touching Students, Overruling Union Decision," *Calgary Herald*, 20 December 2019, https://calgaryherald.com/news/politics/education-minister-orders-permanent-ban-for-teacher-accused-of-touching-students-overruling-inappropriate-union-decision

30   See *Ontario College of Teachers*, https://www.oct.ca/

31   See *British Columbia Ministry of Education*, https://teacherregulation.gov.bc.ca/Index. aspx

32   See "B.C. Ends Teachers' Control of Disciplinary College," *CBC News*, 26 October 2011, https://www.cbc.ca/news/canada/british-columbia/b-c-ends-teachers-control-of-disciplinary-college-1.1028673

33   Janet French, "Alberta Teachers' Association to Lose Disciplinary Role, Province Announces," *CBC News*, 9 December 2021, https://www.cbc.ca/news/canada/ edmonton/alberta-teachers-association-discipline-1.6279621

34   Madeline Smith, "ATA Says UCP's Teacher Discipline Changes Would 'Politicize' Process," *Edmonton Journal*, 6 April 2022, https://edmontonjournal.com/news/local-news/ata-says-ucps-teacher-discipline-changes-would-politicize-process

35   Dean Bennett, "Alberta Proposing That an Independent Commissioner Discipline Teachers," *Global News*, 31 March 2022, https://globalnews.ca/news/8726333/alberta-teachers-discipline-ata/

36   Government of Alberta, *Bill 15: The Education (Reforming Teacher Profession Discipline) Amendment Act*, 2022, https://docs.assembly.ab.ca/LADDAR_files/docs/ bills/bill/legislature_30/session_3/20220222_bill-015.pdf

37   Government of Alberta, *Draft K–6 Curriculum*, 2021, https://www.alberta.ca/ curriculum.aspx

38   Dean Bennett, "Alberta's Proposed K–6 School Curriculum Focuses on Basics, Practical Skills," *Global News*, 29 March 2021, https://globalnews.ca/news/7726173/alberta-proposed-k-6-curriculum-basic-skills/

39   Lucie Edwardson, "'A Failure': Teachers Overwhelmingly Oppose K–6 Draft Curriculum, ATA Reports," *CBC News*, 29 September 2021, https://www.cbc.ca/news/ canada/calgary/a-failure-teachers-overwhelmingly-oppose-k-6-draft-curriculum-ata-reports-1.6193547?__vfz=medium%3Dsharebar

40   Alberta Teachers' Association, *Fewer Than One-In-Five Albertans Support Draft Curriculum*, 5 October 2021, https://www.teachers.ab.ca/News%20Room/NewsReleases/ Pages/Fewer-Than-One-in-Five-Albertans-Support-Draft-Curriculum.aspx

41   Kristopher Wells, "Opinion: Seeing Who Is Reflected in Alberta's School Curriculum," *Edmonton Journal*, 13 August 2021, https://edmontonjournal.com/opinion/columnists/ opinion-seeing-who-is-reflected-in-albertas-school-curriculum

42   *Association of Alberta Deans of Education*, https://www.ualberta.ca/education/media-library/faculty/documents/about-us/aade-curriculum-statement-.pdf

43   *Alberta Curriculum Analysis*, 2021, https://alberta-curriculum-analysis.ca/

44 Eva Ferguson, "Opposition to K–6 Curriculum Draft Grows as 11,723 Parents Sign Petition," *Calgary Herald*, 29 April 2021, https://calgaryherald.com/news/local-news/opposition-to-k-6-curriculum-draft-grows-as-11723-parents-sign-petition

45 Lauren Boothby, "'Rocky Roads Ahead' All of Edmonton's New Public School Trustees Have Vowed to Oppose Alberta's K–6 Draft Curriculum," *Edmonton Journal*, 20 October 2021, https://edmontonjournal.com/news/local-news/rocky-roads-ahead-as-nearly-all-of-edmontons-new-public-school-trustees-vow-to-fight-alberta-on-k-6-draft-curriculum

46 Mark Villani, "Newly-Elected Calgary Board of Education Trustees United against Alberta's Draft Curriculum," *CTV News*, 20 October 2021, https://calgary.ctvnews.ca/newly-elected-calgary-board-of-education-trustees-united-against-alberta-s-draft-curriculum-1.5631481

47 Government of Alberta, *Three Subjects of New Curriculum Ready for Classrooms*, 2022, https://www.alberta.ca/release.cfm?xID=82345661B5300-CB57-0922-7DEF28F231D359B0

48 Alberta Teachers' Association, *Teachers Should Exercise Extreme Caution Before Volunteering for Curriculum Work*, 16 June 2021, https://www.teachers.ab.ca/News%20Room/Issues/Pages/Teachers-Should-Exercise-Extreme-Caution-Before-Volunteering-for-Curriculum-Work.aspx

49 Quinn Campbell, "NDP Says New Alberta Curriculum Will Be Tossed If Elected in 2023," *Global News*, 6 April 2021, https://globalnews.ca/news/7741996/alberta-ndp-new-curriculum/

50 Cappy Smart School, "Year-End Message from the Chief Superintendent," 11 August 2021, https://school.cbe.ab.ca/school/CappySmart/about-us/news-centre/_layouts/15/ci/post.aspx?oaid=4fa077d6-0734-4a9e-aac4-b7164d99c969&oact=20001

51 Government of Alberta, *Staying Safe and Healthy This School Year*, 2021, accessed 25 May 2022 at https://www.alberta.ca/k-12-learning-during-covid-19.aspx

52 Lucie Edwardson, "Home School Enrolment Nearly Doubles in Alberta," *CBC News*, 26 January 2021, https://www.cbc.ca/news/canada/calgary/home-schooling-enrolment-alberta-education-covid-children-students-1.5887496

53 Jennifer Henderson, "Poor Internet Makes Online Education Impossible in Rural Alberta," *CTV News*, 23 September 2020, https://edmonton.ctvnews.ca/poor-internet-makes-online-education-impossible-in-rural-alberta-1.5116340

54 University of Calgary, *How Addressing Our Young Kids' COVID-19 Learning Loss Is a Matter of Child's Play*, 20 September 2021, https://ucalgary.ca/news/how-addressing-our-young-kids-covid-19-learning-loss-matter-childs-play

55 Wallis Snowdon, "No Slow Dances: High Schools Find New Ways to Mark Graduation During Pandemic," *CBC News*, 11 June 2021, https://www.cbc.ca/news/canada/edmonton/alberta-high-school-graduation-covid-1.6060575

56 Kelly Dean Schwartz et al., "COVID-19 and Student Well-Being: Stress and Mental Health During Return-to-School," *Canadian Journal of School Psychology* 26, no. 2 (2021), https://doi.org/10.1177/08295735211001653

57   Eva Ferguson, "UCP Announces Additional $25 Million to Support Charter Schools," *Calgary Herald*, 16 March 2022, https://calgaryherald.com/news/politics/ucp-announces-additional-25-million-to-support-charter-schools

58   Calgary Economic Development, *Demographics: Ethnic Origin*, 2016, https://www.calgaryeconomicdevelopment.com/insights/demographics/

59   Alberta Education, *Teaching Quality Standard*, 2018, https://open.alberta.ca/dataset/4596e0e5-bcad-4e93-a1fb-dad8e2b800d6/resource/75e96af5-8fad-4807-b99a-f12e26d15d9f/download/edc-alberta-education-teaching-quality-standard-2018-01-17.pdf

60   Elisabetta Povoledo and Ian Austen, "'I Feel Shame': Pope Apologizes to Indigenous People of Canada," *New York Times*, 1 April 2022, https://www.nytimes.com/2022/04/01/world/europe/pope-apology-indigenous-people-canada.html

61   Matthew Black, "Pope Francis to Visit Edmonton in July," *Edmonton Journal*, 13 May 2022, https://edmontonjournal.com/news/local-news/pope-francis-to-visit-edmonton-in-july

62   Conference Board of Canada, *Education and Skills*, 2014, https://www.conferenceboard.ca/hcp/provincial/education.aspx?AspxAutoDetectCookieSupport=1; Sean Coughlan, "How Canada Became an Education Superpower," *BBC News*, 2 August 2017, https://www.bbc.com/news/business-40708421; David Staples, "Alberta's Education System Earns Top Marks in Science, Reading," *Edmonton Journal*, 6 December 2016, https://edmontonjournal.com/opinion/columnists/david-staples-albertas-education-system-earns-top-marks-in-science-reading

63   Dean Bennett, "Controversy, COVID-19, and the Oil Crash: A Look Back at Jason Kenney's Rise and Fall," *CBC News*, 19 May 2022, https://www.cbc.ca/news/canada/edmonton/jason-kenney-resignation-ucp-alberta-1.6459124

64   Government of Alberta, "Shifting from Pandemic to Endemic," *COVID-19 Information*, 2021, https://www.alberta.ca/assets/documents/health-covid-19-pandemic-to-endemic.pdf

65   Government of Alberta, *COVID-19 Vaccines and Records*, 2021, https://www.alberta.ca/covid19-vaccine.aspx

66   Jennifer Henderson, "Rural Mayors Battle Fourth Wave, Vaccine Hesitancy," *CTV News Edmonton*, 24 September 2021, https://edmonton.ctvnews.ca/rural-mayors-battle-fourth-wave-vaccine-hesitancy-1.5599958

67   Alberta Health Services, *COVID-19 Immunization for Children Under 12*, 2022, https://www.albertahealthservices.ca/topics/page17746.aspx

68   Government of Alberta, *Gay-Straight Alliances*, 2021, https://www.alberta.ca/gay-straight-alliances.aspx

69   *Trans Mountain*, 2021, https://www.transmountain.com/

70   Dean Bennett, "Alberta Finance Minister Says No Money Available for Teacher Salary Increases," *Global News*, 3 March 2020, https://globalnews.ca/news/6626420/alberta-budget-teachers-school-boards-bill-5/

71   Hamdi Issawi, "Alberta Parents, Teachers Launch Ad Campaign Against Draft Curriculum, Class Sizes and Cuts," *Edmonton Journal*, 12 October 2021, https://edmontonjournal.com/news/local-news/alberta-teachers-and-parents-unite-to-launch-new-campaign-for-public-education

17

Riding the Roller Coaster: Post-Secondary Education in Alberta under Kenney

Lisa Young

Alberta's colleges and universities have for decades been passengers on a funding rollercoaster, enjoying generous funding when times are good, and then hanging on while funding plunges in the harder times. Elected on its platform of "jobs, economy, pipelines," the Kenney government's approach to post-secondary education predictably focused on the role of colleges and universities in developing the labour force, with a heavy emphasis on the value of skilled trades. Paying homage to the Klein government's sharp reductions to provincial government expenditures in the early 1990s, the United Conservative Party (UCP) government's first budget singled out post-secondary education for a series of drastic cuts to operating budgets over the following three years, with a notion that colleges and universities could compensate by raising tuition, recruiting more international students, and reducing or holding constant employee compensation. By 2022, the roller coaster hit the bottom of the track, with a final set of cuts to operating grants being partially offset by funding for new seats and some infrastructure priorities.

But this latest chapter of the ongoing roller coaster ride takes place against a different backdrop. As other chapters in this volume suggest, Alberta is facing a moment of transition from a period of remarkable wealth generated through fossil fuel extraction to a more uncertain future. Young

Albertans have for several decades been less likely than their counterparts in many other provinces to participate in post-secondary education. Despite this, Alberta's population is as well educated as that of other provinces. This feat has been achieved through migration of educated people from other provinces and elsewhere in the world. Now that the relatively high-paying jobs that were available to those without post-secondary education are in question, the matter of participation in higher education has become a pressing issue. Compounding this, as Tombe shows in Chapter 13, the province is expected to have a significant increase in post-secondary-age population in the coming years. If the province were to increase its participation rate to the national average and prepare to accommodate population growth, it would require an estimated *90,000 additional seats by 2025*.[1] The 2022 budget included funding for 7,000 additional seats.

In undertaking a system review, the Kenney government availed itself of awareness of these issues, and some advice about what should be done to address them. There is no evidence that the government plans to act on the pressing issues of reforming its student aid system, incentivizing institutions to enrol first-generation students, or funding new seats for the projected population growth. This is a missed opportunity that will compound many of the pressures that are contributing to out-migration and social strife.

The government's efforts to influence the internal workings of post-secondary institutions were periodically successful. The critical tool for this influence is the government's power of appointment of the majority of board members, and the board chair, at all publicly funded post-secondary institutions. The initial instance was the edict that all post-secondaries should adopt policy protecting free speech on campus, which was successful. During the 2021/22 academic year, the government tried, with varying degrees of success, to dictate the institutions' internal COVID-19 policies. And in 2022, the government issued directives to Athabasca University that it abandon its decision to become a virtual institution with a very limited footprint in the town of Athabasca.

The period from 2019 to 2022 was a difficult one in Alberta's post-secondary sector. The substantial cuts to operating budgets would have been difficult to manage under the best of circumstances. But the COVID-19 pandemic ensured that the circumstances were anything but ideal. The sector was thrown into crisis in the Spring of 2020, forcing a year-long experiment in offering instruction online. The 2021/22 academic year offered only a partial return to normal, with conflicts between government, administrations, faculty, staff, and students on how best to manage the ongoing risks and uncertainty. Border closures and online instruction significantly reduced international student enrolments, affecting the institutions' ability to cope with cuts to their operating expenditures. The sector experienced its first faculty strikes, including a lengthy and bitter strike at the University of Lethbridge.

This chapter offers an overview of the Alberta post-secondary system, an analysis of the UCP platform, and traces the key actions of the government in this sector. Its focus is on the post-secondary system's educational mission, not the research and commercialization elements of the system, which warrant their own analysis.

The Alberta Post-Secondary Education System

Over the past fifty years, the Government of Alberta has invested heavily in its post-secondary education system. The full system, as of 2022, is comprised of four comprehensive universities, three undergraduate universities, two polytechnics, eleven comprehensive community colleges, one arts and culture university, and five private institutions receiving some public funding. Figure 17.1 provides an overview of the sector, with columns showing the number of institutions in each category, and the line showing the number of students enrolled in each type of institution in 2020.

Like other Western Canadian provinces, Alberta struggles with the challenge of a relatively small population spread across a large geographic area. Comparing the number of institutions relative to the population, however, it does not stand out from other provinces. Figure 17.2 shows that Alberta is quite similar to Ontario in terms of the population per college and per large research university. (Research universities are identified through their membership in the "U15" all of which are research intensive and have medical schools attached to them). British Columbia's system is more "efficient" as it has only one U15 institution (UBC) serving the entire province, but it also has several large comprehensive universities—where Alberta has Lethbridge and Athabasca Universities, British Columbia has

Figure 17.1. The Post-Secondary Sector: Institutions & Enrolment

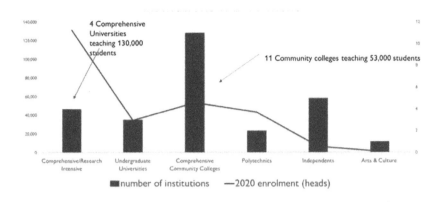

Sources: Data compiled by author.

University of Victoria, Simon Fraser, and University of Northern British Columbia.

According to Alex Usher, Canada's leading expert on post-secondary education policy,

> Alberta certainly does spend a lot on post-secondary education on a per student basis.... And what Alberta has been buying with that are, I would argue, three things. First, two public universities that are in the top-200 in the world by most reckonings, which is pretty impressive for a jurisdiction of fewer than five million people. Second, in NAIT and SAIT it has bought two polytechnics which are, again I would argue, among the best and most-industry focussed non-university higher education institutions in the world. And third, it has bought a system of regional colleges which provide access to high quality programs in relatively sparsely-populated areas. None of these things are cheap.[2]

Compared to many of their Canadian counterparts, these institutions have enjoyed generous public funding. In 2018/19, Alberta ranked third

Figure 17.2. Institutional Density, Selected Provinces

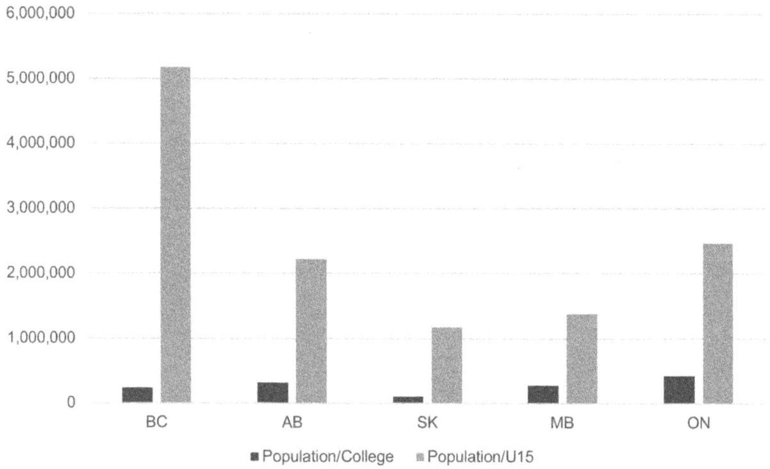

Sources: Author's calculation from Statistics Canada Population data, membership data for U15 and Colleges Canada.

(after Newfoundland and Saskatchewan) in its expenditures per full-time equivalent post-secondary student.[3] As will be discussed in detail below, Alberta post-secondary institutions have relied more heavily on transfers from the provincial government than have their counterparts in several other provinces, notably Ontario and British Columbia. As a proportion of the province's GDP, however, Alberta's spending is relatively low: in 2017/18, transfers to institutions for operating expenses comprised 0.7 per cent of the province's GDP. This was similar to British Columbia (0.8 per cent) and Ontario (0.7 per cent) but substantially lower than all other provinces.[4]

Alberta lags the other large provinces substantially in terms of participation in post-secondary education. Looking at the participation of 20–24-year-olds in post-secondary education in 2018, there was a ten percentage point gap between Quebec and Ontario on one hand, and New Brunswick, Alberta, and Saskatchewan on the other.[5] Women's

Figure 17.3. Participation Rate: Colleges, 18–24-Year-Olds

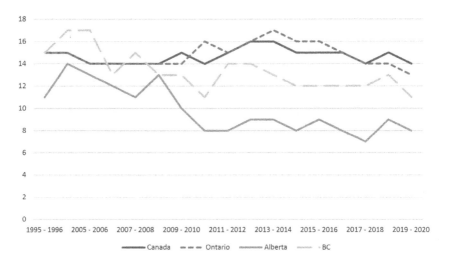

Sources: Calculated from Statistics Canada. Table 37-10-0103-01 (formerly CANSIM 477-0099). Release date: 19 March 2021.

Figure 17.4. Participation Rate: Universities, 18–24-Year-Olds

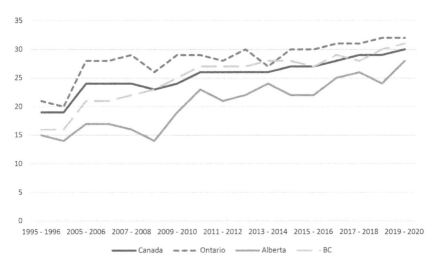

Sources: Calculated from Statistics Canada. Table 37-10-0103-01 (formerly CANSIM 477-0099). Release date: 19 March 2021.

participation and completion rates are higher than men's resulting in gender gaps in attainment close to 20 percentage points in some provinces (notably Saskatchewan, Alberta, and British Columbia).[6] Figures 17.3 and 17.4 show the participation rate of the 18–24 age group in college and university education from 1995 to 2019 in Alberta and selected provinces. They show that the university participation rate is increasing, but still lags that in Ontario and British Columbia, and the college participation rate is stagnant and falls below that in the two comparator provinces.

The Alberta post-secondary system is governed by the Post-Secondary Learning Act (PSLA), which establishes the governance structure for these public institutions. The PSLA sets out a Six Sector Model for post-secondary education, setting out clear mandates for each sector. The intention is to keep institutions "in their lane," focusing on delivery of particular types of credentials. This means, for example, that institutions in the "baccalaureate and applied studies" sector could offer undergraduate degrees, but not graduate.

All public institutions are governed by boards, with the province appointing the majority of board members. The combination of heavy reliance on provincial funding and majority control by provincial appointees has given the provincial government significant influence over the institutions within the system.

Under the Notley government from 2015 to 2019, the post-secondary sector had enjoyed a period of relative stability. Appointments to post-secondary education boards were made for the most part through a process of application by interested members of the public, generating board membership that was more diverse than under prior governments. In the name of affordability for students, tuition was frozen and operating grants backfilled the amount that tuition increases would have provided. Despite rhetoric about access and affordability, the Notley government did not alter the student aid system, which offers assistance predominantly in the form of loans, not grants.

The Notley government also oversaw a process of modernization of labour relations in the post-secondary sector. The *PSLA* had designated faculty and graduate student associations as bargaining agents without access to the province's Labour Relations Board. In effect, this prevented unionization of either group and established compulsory binding arbitration when negotiations were unsuccessful.[7] The Supreme Court's 2015 decision in *Saskatchewan Federation of Labour* found that workers have a Charter-protected right to strike, necessitating amendments to the *PSLA*. This means that faculty and graduate student associations at Alberta post-secondaries are now effectively unions with the right to strike. Throughout its term, the Notley government pursued wage constraint in the post-secondary sector, effectively mandating settlements of 0 per cent increases throughout the mandate, with allowance for wage re-openers in the final year of collective agreements, many of which came due in 2019.

The United Conservative Party and Post-Secondary Education

A core pledge in the UCP's 2019 platform promised that "Post-Secondary Education will be supported as critical both to Alberta's future economy and to a vibrant Alberta."[8] At first glance, this was good news for the post-secondary sector. The platform commitment recognized post-secondary education both as important to the development of a skilled labour force, but also as contributing to economic diversification and prosperity through research. Given what was to come once the party was elected, it is worth noting that the platform was silent both on the question of funding for the sector and on issues like the post-secondary participation rate in the province.

The ideological orientation of the governing party can be an important factor shaping post-secondary education policy. Scanning the North American horizon, conservative politicians have in recent years stressed three key themes with respect to post-secondary education: an emphasis on labour-market outcomes, a preference for trades and colleges over universities, and a concern about freedom of speech on campus. Each of these themes was well represented in the 2019 UCP platform.[9]

A central preoccupation of conservative parties with respect to post-secondary education policy relates to labour market outcomes: does education result in graduates finding related employment? Axelrod et al. observe that conservative governments may be motivated to "increase the integration of post-secondary education into the market economy" citing the Harris conservatives in Ontario as an example.[10] This conception of post-secondary education as having vocational training as its core purpose resonates with Canadian conservatives (and others) and is reflected in policy frameworks that use labour market outcomes of graduates as a key indicator of success. In this vein, the UCP platform committed to "Measure labour market outcomes of post-secondary programs to identify the correlation between provincial subsidies and economic returns for taxpayers."[11]

Canadian conservative parties have also become vocal advocates of "the trades" and apprenticeship education, portraying this practically oriented education as more desirable than university studies. One might argue that this is related to the focus on labour-market outcomes, although the evidence does not support the claim.[12] Arguably, the focus on the value of vocational education is intended at least in part to appeal to conservative parties' populist bases, which are less likely to have attained tertiary education and who are untrusting of "elite" institutions or the individuals that animate them.

The UCP platform devoted two pages to a discussion of vocational education and the trades, leading with the statement that "Apprenticeship learning has every bit as much value as academic learning, and skilled trades have every bit as much value, merit, and worth as a university degree."[13]

Influenced by the American "culture wars," Canadian conservative parties have increasingly adopted a Republican critique of universities as dominated by "woke" liberal academics who stifle free speech. Although the evidence supporting this critique is weak,[14] conservative politicians in both the United States and Canada have accepted it and sought to address the problem through their regulatory authority over public institutions. Following the lead of the Ontario conservatives, the UCP platform committed to "Require all universities and colleges to develop, post, and comply with free speech policies that conform to the University of Chicago Statement on Principles of Free Expression."[15]

The other commitment in the platform was to "Encourage efforts by Alberta universities and colleges to attract more qualified foreign students. (Alberta post-secondary institutions are well below the national average, and leaders in the information technology sector report that their principal challenge is a shortage of labour with relevant skills)."[16]

Other platform planks related to finding ways to leverage the expertise of international students in the labour force, so the platform represents an authentic desire to increase international student enrolments as a means of bringing talented individuals to the province. While it would be cynical to dismiss the desire to increase international students only for generating additional revenue for institutions, institutions in other jurisdictions have filled funding gaps through recruitment of international students whose tuition dollars subsidize institutional operations and supplement provincial operating grants.

After taking office in the Spring of 2019, the UCP held off on tabling a budget, choosing instead to appoint a "blue ribbon" panel to report on the province's finances. It was chaired by former Saskatchewan finance minister Janice MacKinnon, who led a program of significant cuts and restructuring during her time in office. While waiting for the MacKinnon report, the government terminated the appointments of board chairs and board members for most of the major post-secondary institutions and replaced them with their own appointees. Notably, most had significant corporate executive experience. Among the key responsibilities of institutional boards are approval of budgets and negotiation mandates for collective agreements. Given the government's planned (but as yet unannounced) funding reductions and plans for reductions in public-sector compensation, these changes to the composition of the board were essential.

The political purpose of the MacKinnon report was to establish a case for reducing government expenditures in several key areas, including health care, K–12 education, and post-secondary education. Released with considerable fanfare, it made the case that Alberta had a "spending problem" and not a revenue problem: deep cuts to the public sector would solve the province's fiscal woes (see also Gillian Steward's chapter on health care).

The MacKinnon report made this scathing observation about the post-secondary system:

> There does not appear to be an overall direction for Alberta's postsecondary system. The current funding structure doesn't link funding to the achievement of specific goals or priorities for the province such as ensuring the required skills for the current and future labour market, expanding research and technology

commercialization, or achieving broader societal and economic goals. There also continues to be extensive overlap and duplication among post-secondary institutions, each operating with their own boards of governors and with what appears to be only limited collaboration.[17]

Grounded in this critique of the system as unfocused and inefficiently structured, the blue-ribbon panel went on to recommend that the government should "Consult with post-secondary stakeholders to set an overall future direction and goals for the post-secondary system along with appropriate governance models" (Recommendation 7) and also assess the financial viability of its post-secondary institutions (Recommendation 9).[18]

The report also took aim at the revenue mix for post-secondary institutions, recommending that the government move them away from their heavy reliance on provincial operating grants in favour of reliance on tuition revenues, thereby achieving a revenue mix closer to that of British Columbia or Ontario.[19] These recommendations set the agenda for the newly appointed minister of advanced education, Demetrios Nicolaides, who undertook a system review, oversaw significant changes to institutional operating grants, and took a directive role toward institutions on a number of matters important to the government.

The System Review

Having received the advice that the post-secondary system lacked purpose and direction, the government undertook a review of the post-secondary system. It awarded the contract to the consulting firm McKinsey for $3.5 million to consult with stakeholders and make recommendations. The report McKinsey produced was entitled *Alberta 2030: Building Skills for Jobs (10-Year Strategy for Post-Secondary Education)*[20] and released in April of 2021.

As the title suggests, the report adopted the UCP focus on post-secondary education as tightly linked to labour market outcomes, rather than any of the other societal benefits that might result from higher learning. It did not endorse the party's emphasis on trades and apprenticeship, opting instead to cite research that predicts that jobs of the future will require higher cognitive skills, social and emotional skills, and technological competence.[21] It did, however, include several recommendations focused on increasing enrolments in the trades and supporting apprentices.

In some respects, it appears the consultants were convinced by the arguments presented by the stakeholders they consulted—institutional administrators, student organizations, and faculty associations. Rather than recommending closure or amalgamation of colleges, for instance, it recommended a strategic council to advise the minister and system-co-ordinating councils in two sectors (university and college). Most re-markably, it recommended that consideration be given to changing the composition of boards of governors to reduce provincial influence and increase institutional autonomy.

Rather than a blueprint for profound change in the system, the re-port's recommendations generally kept it on roughly the track it was on, identifying opportunities for improvements in various areas. Its boldest "flagship" recommendation was to make Alberta the first province to of-fer access to work-integrated learning to all students. It did not lay the groundwork for the provincial government to restructure the system (such as single boards for all institutions in a sector), which some had imagined would be the result of a system review. And although it prioritized student experience, it did not recommend any goals or even significant initiatives focused on addressing Alberta's lagging participation rate.

In 2021, the government amended the *PSLA* to implement some of the recommendations from the funding review. Most notably, it gave the minister authority to establish the Minister's Advisory Council on Higher Education and Skills (MACHES), to advise on strategic goals and direc-tion for post-secondary education in Alberta, and on metrics for measur-ing the performance of public post-secondary and independent academic institutions in Alberta.[22]

The Revenue Mix and Institutional Funding

The MacKinnon report observed that Alberta universities rely more heav-ily on government grants, and less heavily on tuition revenue, than their counterparts in Ontario and British Columbia. Quebec universities rely even more heavily on government grants than Alberta institutions, but the panel did not consider Quebec an appropriate comparator. Accordingly, it recommended that the government work "to achieve a revenue mix comparable to that in British Columbia and Ontario, including less reliance on government grants, more funding from tuition and alternative revenue sources, and more entrepreneurial approaches to how programs are financed and delivered. This includes lifting the current freeze on tuition fees."[23]

Ontario's approach to university funding was radically transformed in the late 1990s. As part of its "Common Sense Revolution," the Harris government cut operating grants to Ontario universities and colleges by over 15 per cent in a single year. At the same time, it permitted institutions to raise tuition by 10 per cent for most students, and by more for those in professional or graduate programs.[24] These changes combined to produce the funding mix that has Ontario institutions more reliant on tuition dollars than government grants.

But the Harris government did not invent this policy trajectory. In fact, it was emulating policy changes that had taken place a few years earlier in Alberta. In 1993, the Klein government introduced an austerity budget that significantly cut transfers to the post-secondary sector—by 21 per cent over three years.[25] In the years that followed, institutions could bid for a share of "performance envelopes" allocated according to "key performance indicators," which included enrolment, graduate employment rate, graduate satisfaction, administrative expenditures, and enterprise revenue. Institutions made up the difference in part with tuition increases: Hauserman and Stick report that between 1990/91 and 2000/01, tuition fees in Alberta rose 209 per cent, compared to a national average of 126 per cent.[26]

Post-secondary funding in Alberta over the past forty years is best compared to a roller coaster. When governments were flush with energy revenue, cash flowed to the province's post-secondary institutions, and residents were reassured that tuition fees would remain stable. But when resource royalties went down or governments wished to demonstrate their fiscal conservatism, post-secondary budgets were slashed and tuition rates allowed to rise.

The election of the Kenney government and the recommendations of the MacKinnon report sent government funding for the post-secondary sector plummeting, just as it had three decades earlier. The Kenney government's 2019 budget (introduced in October of that year) imposed a mid-year cut of 7 per cent to institutions' operating grants. The magnitude of the cuts varied from no cuts to private faith-based institutions that received some government support, to 6.9 per cent for the two largest universities, to a high of 7.9 per cent for MacEwan University. Institutions that held larger financial reserves were penalized more heavily.

Less than five months later, the February 2020 budget set out multi-year cuts that once again differentiated among institutions, this time based on an assessment of their costs relative to those of peer institutions elsewhere in the country. The government did not publicly release the specific adjustments to operating grants by institution, so they were unavailable until CBC journalist Janet French obtained them through a Freedom of Information request.[27] The data for select institutions is presented in Figure 17.5. The largest cuts, in both absolute and proportional terms, was to the flagship University of Alberta, which was cut by 9 per cent for 2020/21 and 11 per cent for 2021/22. Both Keyano College (cut by 10 per cent in 20/21 and 6 per cent in 21/22) and Grand Prairie Regional College (cut by 9 and 6 per cent) suffered substantial proportional cuts as well. The 2022 budget set out another round of cuts for the 2022/23 fiscal year, but did announce some targeted reinvestments and funding for 7000 new seats in areas of high labour-market demand.

These cuts have prompted significant restructuring across all Alberta post-secondary institutions, but particularly those that have experienced the largest proportional cuts. Hundreds of staff positions have been abolished. While it is generally very difficult to lay off faculty members, those who retire are often not being replaced. The large universities are complex financial undertakings, and it is difficult to determine the differential impacts of the government cuts versus efforts to reallocate resources among units within the institution. Certainly, the desired shift to the funding mix of the institutions has occurred. Looking at the University of Alberta's financial statements, the ratio of Government of Alberta funding to tuition and student fees was 2.84:1 in 2018, and 2.01:1 in 2021.[28] This is a significant restructuring of revenue in a short period of time.

Under the best possible circumstances, reducing the budgets of post-secondary institutions by this amount would place significant stress on the institutions. And, of course, the 2019/20, 2020/21 and 2021/22 academic years were anything but the best possible circumstances. In addition

Figure 17.5. Operating Grants to Selected Post-Secondary Institutions

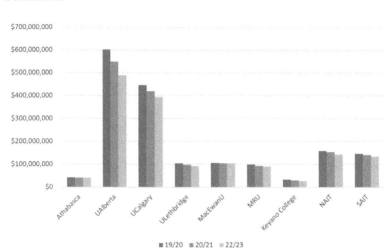

$700,000,000
$600,000,000
$500,000,000
$400,000,000
$300,000,000
$200,000,000
$100,000,000
$0

Athabasca UAlberta UCalgary ULethbridge MacEwanU MRU Keyano College NAIT SAIT

■ 19/20 ■ 20/21 ■ 22/23

Sources: Calculated from data in Janet French, "Some Alberta post-secondary institutions left relatively unscathed while U of A funds slashed, new data shows," *CBC*, 28 June 2021, https://www.cbc.ca/news/canada/edmonton/some-alberta-post-secondary-institutions-left-relatively-unscathed-while-u-of-a-funds-slashed-new-data-shows-1.6081029.

to forcing universities to pivot to online instruction, the pandemic posed significant challenges for international students who could not travel. A Statistics Canada analysis projected revenue losses of anywhere from 2 per cent to 8 per cent for post-secondary institutions in Canadian provinces.[29] In this analysis, Alberta fared relatively well because of its low reliance on international students. In effect, however, one of the key tools for replacing government operating grants became more difficult for Alberta post-secondaries. Most institutions have responded to the cuts by increasing tuition fees by the maximum permitted 7 per cent each year. While this can replace some of the government funding that has been cut, most will find themselves worse off than they were when the Kenney government was elected.

Performance-Based Funding

Just as the Klein government's cuts to the sector had been accompanied by a performance-based funding scheme, so too were the Kenney government's. Unlike the Klein approach, which created an envelope for restoring funding, the 2020 plan put up to 40 per cent of institutions' core funding at risk if targets were not met.[30] In announcing the framework, the government indicated that performance measures would be established in consultation with institutions and other stakeholders, but would include measures such as "graduate employment rate, median graduate income, graduate skills and competencies, work-integrated learning opportunities, administrative expense ratio, sponsored research revenue, enrolment (including potential targets for domestic students, international students and under-represented learners)."[31]

This kind of approach to post-secondary education funding can range from almost meaningless to high impact, depending on the metrics selected. A government that wants to proclaim that it has imposed accountability on institutions can establish a set of metrics that institutions would almost certainly meet. Alternatively, a government that wanted to reduce funding to institutions, reallocate among institutions, and/or push institutions to achieve particular outcomes could use such a system to accomplish its goals.

We will never know what the Kenney government's original intentions were, as the COVID-19 pandemic interrupted their implementation. The initial plan was to put agreements with institutions in place as of 1 April 2020. When the pandemic forced post-secondaries to pivot to online instruction in March of that year, the ministry postponed implementation until 2021. In March of 2021, the ministry announced that agreements with institutions on metrics would be for a single year, for 2021/22, with only one target (participation in work-integrated learning) and only 5 per cent of operating grants at risk.[32] This limited plan replaced the government's original intention to put in place three-year agreements with 15 per cent at risk in year 1, ramping up to 40 per cent in year 3.[33]

Affordability, Access, and Participation

Alberta has long reported a relatively low participation rate in post-secondary education, particularly among young men. This reflects the reality that the energy sector offered lucrative wages for its workers with little or no formal education. Even if the oil and gas sector was to continue producing significant product for export from the province, technological changes have reduced the labour needs of the industry.[34] Alberta has, for some time, matched other provinces in the educational attainment of its population. However, it has done so through inter-provincial migration, as individuals with post-secondary education have migrated to the province either from elsewhere in Canada, or elsewhere in the world. To the extent that these well-educated newcomers prosper, there are risks of economic anxiety and resentment on the part of long-time Albertans.

Much depends on the province's ability to increase post-secondary participation among young people, particularly men. And, as Tombe's chapter shows, it will be essential that this occur while also coping with an expansion of seats in the province's post-secondary institutions. According to a brief from the Council of Post-Secondary Presidents of Alberta, by 2025 the province would need 90,000 additional seats to accommodate population growth and an increased participation rate.

While the *Building Skills for Jobs* report had relatively little of substance to say about these twin challenges, the "Analysis and Stakeholder Input" PowerPoint presentation that accompanied it offers a clear-headed analysis of the challenges and recommends required actions. It offers this observation: "COVID-19 and the collapse of the oil market is driving the worst recession in the past century, generating enrolment uncertainty, accelerating financial pressures and shifting demand for skills, delivery models and research models."[35]

One of the key barriers to improving access and thus participation rates in post-secondary education has to do with affordability and student assistance. Alberta aims to increase participation in post-secondary education while simultaneously increasing its costs through tuition increases. Institutions have been permitted to increase tuition by 7 per cent each year over three years, to replace government operating grants to institutions and achieve a revenue mix closer to that of Ontario.

Accompanying the decision to reduce operating grants and allow institutions to increase tuition were several measures that affected students' and graduates' finances. The 2019 budget removed education and tuition tax credits, which previously could yield up to $1600 each year for full-time students. It also changed the interest rate for student loans from prime to prime plus 1 per cent.[36] Estimates associated with the 2022 budget show the budgeted amount for student aid increasing from $55 million in 2021 to $60 million in 2022, and the student loan amounts increasing from $731 million in 2021 to $980 million in 2022. This indicates that the government plans to maintain its reliance on loans over aid in providing student assistance in the new higher-tuition environment.[37]

Since the government is pursuing the Ontario model, it is important to look more closely at that model in its entirety. Undergraduate tuition in Ontario for 2020/21, as reported by Statistics Canada, was $7938 (the fourth highest in the country). Alberta's tuition for the same year was reported as $6567. Despite this higher tuition rate, Ontario's post-secondary education participation rate is the highest in the country. It is tempting to conclude that higher tuition would not be a barrier to increasing post-secondary education. However, this conclusion would be incorrect.

Ford et al. find that "Relative to other provinces (excluding Quebec), Ontario is the only province to see improvements in attendance rates in both university and non-university postsecondary education for students with any level of family income in the past 20 years. . . . Ontario experienced the highest postsecondary attendance among those with lowest income and the second-lowest income elasticity of postsecondary attendance in 2015. . . . [T]hrough successive policy changes, Ontario appears to have created one of the more favourable environments in Canada for supporting the postsecondary education of its high school graduates from lower-income families."[38] Most significant of these policy changes was a massive increase in grant-based student aid in 2016.[39]

Two aspects of the funding made available for student assistance in Alberta work against the objective of increasing student access: Alberta has historically delivered a substantial proportion of its student assistance dollars through merit-based scholarships, notably the Rutherford Scholarship available to all high school graduates who achieve grade cutoffs. In addition, the student aid system relies on loans (rather than grants) to a greater extent than many other provinces.[40] Consequently, the financial barriers to students with lower incomes is greater.

In recognition of this, the consultants charged with the system review recommended that the province "double non-repayable needs-based aid and innovate financial aid offerings" to ensure that post-secondary education is inclusive and affordable.[41] The estimated cost of this initiative was between $5 and $18 million dollars in year 1, $13 and $33 million in year 2, and $17 and$26 million in year 3. The report also notes that "the amount of incremental investment may be $0 if merit-based aid is converted." This is effectively a suggestion that the beloved Rutherford Scholarship be converted to needs-based student aid. The increase to student aid budgeted in the 2022 estimates is consistent with the lower end of the proposed new investment in year 1. It remains to be seen whether there will be larger investments in subsequent years.

Governance

Post-secondary institutions are nominally independent of the provincial government, but in practical terms are established by the *PSLA*, able to offer only those credentials approved by the province, and heavily reliant on government funding. Their internal governing body is a board of governors, with a majority of its members appointed by the provincial government. (Academic matters are governed by general faculties councils or academic councils.) With operating funds allocated (and cut) without a transparent formula, and institutions competing with one another for provincial infrastructure funding, the administrations of post-secondary institutions enjoy relatively little autonomy from government, should it wish to impose itself.

The Kenney government has imposed itself on a number of issues. The first was to "ask" all post-secondaries to fulfil the UCP platform promise that all institutions would comply with the Chicago principles regarding free speech no later than December of 2019. All did so with relatively little resistance.

While there is no available documentary evidence that the provincial government was issuing guidelines for post-secondary institutions' collective bargaining, those bargaining units that have disclosed the first offers they received from their board of governors reveal remarkable similarities. There were media reports that the opening position from the Universities of Alberta and Lethbridge involved retroactive pay cuts (requiring employees to pay back some salary from the prior year); there were similar reports for non-academic staff at the Universities of Alberta and Calgary. The 2021/22 academic year saw the first faculty strikes in Alberta's history, with the faculty associations of the privately run Concordia University of Edmonton striking for 12 days, and the University of Lethbridge Faculty

Association striking for 40 days in February and March of 2022. Strikes were narrowly averted at the University of Alberta and Mount Royal University around the same time.

There is also significant circumstantial evidence that the provincial government pushed post-secondary institutions to forgo various measures intended to reduce the spread of COVID-19 on campus during the 2021/22 academic year. In August of 2021, with many classes set to return to in-person delivery, but COVID numbers increasing dramatically (see Chapter 21), there were calls from faculty, staff, and some students' associations for post-secondaries to impose more rigorous COVID restrictions on campus, including vaccination and mask mandates. Administrations resisted until, on August 17, the Universities of Alberta, Calgary, and Lethbridge issued a joint announcement that they would require either vaccination or regular COVID testing for everyone on their campuses, and that they would require masking in public places.[42] It is unusual for post-secondary institutions to make joint announcements about what would normally be understood as an internal matter, so it appears that the joint announcement was intended to insulate the institutions from repercussions. Once the three larger institutions made this move, many smaller ones followed suit.

In February of 2022, when the province was ordering school boards to drop mask mandates and contemplating legislation to prevent municipalities from maintaining their mandates, the minister of advanced education wrote a public letter to the board chairs for all post-secondaries stating that it was his "expectation" that they would align their internal COVID policies with those of the provincial government (which was dropping all restrictions by March 1, as the premier prepared to face a leadership review).[43] For institutions that had started the term promising students and faculty that vaccination and mask mandates would remain in place through the term, this edict was difficult to follow. Nevertheless, the University of Alberta and many smaller institutions followed the order, while the Universities of Calgary and Lethbridge ignored it.

Also in the Spring of 2022, the Kenney government became closely involved in the internal strategic direction of Athabasca University. A newly appointed president had announced to faculty and staff that the institution, which provides online instruction only, would become a "fully virtual" institution with less presence in the town of Athabasca. This prompted an outcry from the Town Council, concerned about the economic impact of losing well-paid university employees. In response, the minister issued a statement requiring the university to develop a plan for ongoing operation based in the town.[44] When the university's administration did not capitulate, the province removed the board chair and replaced her with an appointee with close ties to the governing party.[45]

All of these incursions and directives from government might seem minor when taken in isolation, but examined as a pattern they indicate a fairly limited autonomy for post-secondary institutions in Alberta. The antipathy between the government and the faculty and staff working in the institutions is significant, and places university administrators in difficult positions. Over time, this kind of relationship shapes the morale, ethos, and productivity of post-secondary institutions.

Conclusion

The coming years do not look bright for post-secondary education in Alberta. Demoralized by budget cuts and government rhetoric, exhausted and in disarray after coping with three academic years destabilized by COVID, Alberta's post-secondary institutions will need to rise to the challenges of finding financial stability, responding to the government's ongoing initiatives around performance-based funding, and working with government to pursue its objectives around improving participation rates and accommodating the wave of potential new students in coming years. They will likely do this against the backdrop of ongoing labour strife and low morale.

Like the Harris government in Ontario, the Kenney government will be able to claim that it has fundamentally changed the funding mix of its post-secondary institutions. But the singular focus on this objective, combined with the timing of COVID, means that the province and its post-secondary sector will not be well positioned to undertake the kind of substantial enrolment growth and improvements to participation rates that would position the province for the economic transitions that lie ahead.

NOTES

1   Council of Post-Secondary Presidents of Alberta, *Post-Secondary Education Position Paper*, 2019, https://coppoa.ca/wp-content/uploads/2019/01/PSE-Position-Paper.pdf.

2   Alex Usher, "That Alberta Budget," *One Thought* (blog), Higher Education Strategy Associates, October 25, 2019, https://higheredstrategy.com/that-alberta-budget/

3   Alex Usher, *The State of Post-Secondary Education in Canada* (Toronto: Higher Education Strategy Associates, 2020), 41.

4   Canadian Association of University Teachers, *Almanac*, https://www.caut.ca/resources/almanac/2-canada-provinces, accessed October 3, 2021.

5   Statistics Canada, *Education Indicators in Canada: An International Perspective 2018* (Ottawa: Queen's Printer, 2018), https://www150.statcan.gc.ca/n1/en/pub/81-604-x/81-604-x2018001-eng.pdf?st=vXT0UyMN.

6   *Ibid.*

7   Alberta, "Post-Secondary Learning Act Consultations: What We Heard," https://www.alberta.ca/assets/documents/labour-essential-services-psla-what-we-heard.pdf. Accessed October 1 2021.

8   United Conservative Party, *Alberta Strong and Free: Getting Alberta Back to Work*, 2019, 48, https://www.poltext.org/sites/poltext.org/files/plateformesV2/Alberta/AB_PL_2019_UCP.pdf.

9   The platform also promised to "Reduce provincial red tape and mandates on universities and colleges, freeing them to innovate and compete more and comply with bureaucratic mandates less." This sparked joy in the hearts of academic administrators who had struggled through the Ministry of Advanced Education's templates for degree approval. In October of 2021, the Ministry of Advanced Education announced significant changes to the credential approval process.

10   P. Axelrod et al. "People, Processes, and Policy-Making in Canadian Post-secondary Education, 1990–2000," *Higher Education Policy* 24 (2011): 143–166, https://doi.org/10.1057/hep.2010.29.

11   United Conservative Party, *Alberta Strong and Free*, 61.

12   Two years post-graduation, the median income of university graduates is $6000 higher than college graduates; the differential increases over time. See Statistics Canada, "Labour Market Outcomes for College and University Graduates: Interactive Tool," last modified 3 November 2021, https://www150.statcan.gc.ca/n1/pub/71-607-x/71-607-x2019031-eng.htm. Employment rates for college and university graduates are similar, although there are meaningful differences across disciplines and by gender. See Alana Reid et al., *Labour Market Outcomes of Postsecondary Graduates, Class of 2015* (Ottawa: Statistics Canada, 2020), https://www150.statcan.gc.ca/n1/pub/81-595-m/81-595-m2020002-eng.htm.

13   United Conservative Party, *Alberta Strong and Free*.

14   Sean M. Kammer, "The 'Intellectual Diversity' Crisis That Isn't: Liberal Faculties, Conservative Victims, and the Cynical Effort to Undermine Higher Education for Political Gain," *Quinnipiac Law Review* (QLR) 39, no. 2 (2021): 149–224.

15   United Conservative Party, *Alberta Strong and Free*, 61.

16   *Ibid.*

17   *Ibid*, 42.

18   *Ibid*, 42–3.

19   Blue Ribbon Panel on Alberta's Finances, *Report and Recommendations*, August 2019, 42, https://open.alberta.ca/publications/report-and-recommendations-blue-ribbon-panel-on-alberta-s-finances.

20   Alberta Advanced Education, *Alberta 2030: Building Skills for Jobs* (Edmonton: Treasury Board, 2021).

21   *Ibid*, 8.

22   Alberta, *Modernizing Post-Secondary Education*, https://www.alberta.ca/modernizing-post-secondary-education.aspx#jumplinks-3. At time of writing, appointments had not yet been made to the board.

23   Blue Ribbon Panel, *Report and Recommendations*, 42. Accessed 26 April 2022.

24   Glen A. Jones, "Ontario Higher Education Reform, 1995–2003: From Modest Modifications to Policy Reform," *Canadian Journal of Higher Education* 34, no. 3 (2004): 41.

25   Calvin P. Hauserman and Sheldon L. Stick, "The History of Post-Secondary Finance in Alberta—An Analysis," *Canadian Journal of Educational Administration and Policy* 42 (2005): 1–25.

26   *Ibid*, 20.

27   Janet French, "Some Alberta post-secondary institutions left relatively unscathed while U of A funds slashed, new data shows," *CBC*, 28 June 2021, https://www.cbc.ca/news/canada/edmonton/some-alberta-post-secondary-institutions-left-relatively-unscathed-while-u-of-a-funds-slashed-new-data-shows-1.6081029.

28   University of Alberta, "Annual Financial Statements," 2018 and 2021, https://www.ualberta.ca/university-services-finance/reports/annual-financial-statements.html. Accessed 25 April 2022.

29   Christopher Matias, Andrija Popovic, and André Lebel, *Projected Financial Impact of the COVID-19 Pandemic on Canadian Universities for the 2020/21 Academic Year* (Ottawa: Statistics Canada, 2021), https://www150.statcan.gc.ca/n1/pub/81-595-m/81-595-m2021002-eng.htm.

30   Usher, *The State of Post-secondary Education*, 43.

31   Alberta, "Transforming Post-Secondary Funding," 20 January 2020, https://www.alberta.ca/release.cfm?xID=67447A51C2BC1-CBF8-78E9-C6759CE8A736486C.

32   Janet French, "Pandemic Prompts Alberta Government to Pare Back Post-Secondary Funding Model Changes," *CBC*, 21 March 2021, https://www.cbc.ca/news/canada/edmonton/pandemic-prompts-alberta-government-to-pare-back-post-secondary-funding-model-changes-1.5957497.

33   *Ibid.*

34   Lance Mortlock, "Rethinking the Oil and Gas Workforce in 2040," Ernst & Young, 8 August 2020, https://www.ey.com/en_ca/oil-gas/rethinking-the-oil-and-gas-workforce-in-2040.

35   Alberta Advanced Education, *Analysis and Stakeholder Input* (Edmonton: Treasury Board, 2021), 7.

36   Alberta, *Budget 2019: Fiscal Plan, A Plan for Jobs and the Economy 2019–23* (Edmonton: Treasury Board, 2019), https://open.alberta.ca/dataset/3d732c88-68b0-4328-9e52-5d3273527204/resource/2b82a075-f8c2-4586-a2d8-3ce8528a24e1/download/budget-2019-fiscal-plan-2019-23.pdf.

37   Alberta, *2022–23 Government Estimates: General Revenue Fund* (Edmonton: Treasury Board, 2022), 25, https://open.alberta.ca/dataset/65514c30-e9f9-4951-9bae-7134edbe293c/resource/efa42333-29d4-4f0e-a45d-3713bcd8194e/download/budget-2022-estimates-government-2022-23.pdf.

38   Reuben Ford, Taylor Shek-wai Hui, and Cam Nguyen, *Postsecondary Participation and Household Income* (Toronto: Higher Education Quality Council of Ontario, 2019), 7, https://heqco.ca/pub/postsecondary-participation-and-household-income/.

39   Alex Usher, "New Student Aid Data," *One Thought* (blog), Higher Education Strategy Associates, 2 September 2020. https://higheredstrategy.com/new-student-aid-data/.

40   *Ibid.*

41   Alberta Advanced Education, *Analysis and Stakeholder Input*, 40.

42   Madeleine Cummings, "3 Alberta universities announce mandatory masking, rapid testing for back to school," *CBC*, 17 August 2021, https://www.cbc.ca/news/canada/edmonton/3-alberta-universities-change-back-to-school-plans-pandemic-1.6144026.

43   Demetrios Nicolaides, "Letter to Board Chairs," Twitter, 9 February 2022, https://twitter.com/demetriosnAB/status/1491549863426895877/photo/1.

44   Michelle Bellefontaine, "Minister pushes back against Athabasca University president's defence of virtual campus," *CBC*, April 13, 2022. https://www.cbc.ca/news/canada/edmonton/minister-pushes-back-against-athabasca-university-president-s-defence-of-virtual-campus-1.6417933.

45   Jennie Russell and Charles Rusnell, "Inside Kenney's University Power Play," *The Tyee*, 26 May 2022, https://thetyee.ca/News/2022/05/26/Letter-Reveals-Kenney-Power-Play-Athabasca-University/#:~:text=Oil%20exec%20Nancy%20Laird%20served,time%20conservative%20supporter%20and%20candidate.

18

Labour in the Time of COVID

Lori Williams

Jason Kenney's approach to unions and professional associations reverberated through virtually every aspect of his government, shaping relations with doctors, nurses, frontline health care workers, teachers, prosecutors, professors, and public sector workers. He was motivated in part by a mistaken image of Alberta's essential character. He returned to Alberta on a mission to unite the right and restore conservatism to its perceived former status. As this chapter will trace, there has long been a dissonance between Alberta's conservative reputation and reality, and that gap widened in the years Kenney spent in Ottawa. Many Alberta governments have spoken the language of conservatism, casting a critical eye at socialist ideas and organized labour. However, the reality of Alberta's political culture is more nuanced and complex, presenting challenges for Kenney's vision that he did not anticipate, and that he ultimately failed to effectively manage.

Alberta's Reputation

Alberta's individualistic, self-reliant, innovative, entrepreneurial, and conservative brand is often referenced to suggest a less supportive climate for organized workers. Premiers from Ernest Manning to Peter Lougheed, Ralph Klein, Jason Kenney and even Rachel Notley have championed Albertans' resilience, initiative, and innovative spirit.[1] A 2019 New Democratic Party (NDP) government ad evoked these qualities: "When the going gets tough, Albertans don't back down. We roll up our sleeves and . . . do it ourselves."[2]

Prior to Notley's NDP government coming to power in 2015, this image was often invoked in support of conservative values. Anti-socialist rhetoric was common. In 1944, Ernest Manning campaigned against socialism, and as Alberta's prosperity grew following the 1947 Leduc oil discovery, he increasingly championed the innovation, risk-taking, self-reliance, and enterprise that Alberta has become known for.[3] Peter Lougheed brought his Progressive Conservative (PC) party to power in 1971 with a fresh vision, evoking Alberta's entrepreneurial spirit: "We stand for free enterprise—not socialism. We stand for social reform and individual rights—not big government control."[4] Ralph Klein, despite a history as a card-carrying Liberal, used accusations of socialism to dismiss policies and critics. He denounced the Canadian Wheat Board as "goofy, Liberal, (and) socialist,"[5] and responded to criticism as "typical socialist claptrap."[6] He popularized the mantra of the "Alberta Advantage," a combination of low taxes, an attractive business environment, and high-quality government services, using it to justify cuts to civil service jobs, health care, and education.

The boom-bust cycles of Alberta's economy, dominated by oil, gas, and mining, have had a significant impact on attitudes to organized workers, particularly those paid by the government. During economic downturns Alberta governments look for cost savings from those who are reliant on the public purse. Governments have repeatedly, and successfully, argued that public sector workers need to defer raises or accept pay reductions using rhetoric like "share the pain" or "do your part" to help during tough economic times.[7] Public support for unions may be affected by unemployed or underemployed Albertans who have little sympathy for workers asking for pay increases, thinking that they should be grateful to have jobs or simply find better paying work.[8] However, as this chapter traces, support for those earning government incomes surged as the crucial services they provided, especially during the pandemic, grew more visible.

Reality

Albertans' self-image may include values consistent with conservatism, e.g., independence, self-reliance, and innovation, however it is not particularly ideological. Over 86 per cent of Albertans self-identify as centre (26.7 per cent), centre-left (24.3 per cent), or centre-right (35.3 per cent).[9] Polls consistently show that Albertans' opinions on a range of policy and social issues do not significantly diverge from those of other Canadians. More than 80 per cent of Albertans support same-sex marriage, medical assistance in dying, and a woman's right to make decisions about abortion.[10] Alberta's political culture is diverse, and while there are widely shared views, like suspicion of central Canada, it not a conservative monolith. The reality is more nuanced.

Many point to over eight decades of conservative governments (Social Credit, PC, and United Conservative Party [UCP])[11] as evidence of conservative dominance in Alberta politics. However, a review of the practices and policies of those governments reveals a more complex history. Alberta's innovative spirit has been expressed in conservative *and* progressive ways. Alberta's first governments, led by Liberals (1905–1921), and the United Farmers Association (UFA: 1921–1935), were centrist or populist. Albertans were the first in the British Empire to elect women to a legislature in 1917; Louise McKinney and Lieutenant Roberta McAdams. And in 1921 Irene Parlby (UFA) was the first female to be appointed a cabinet minister in Alberta, and the second in the British Empire.[12] The Cooperative Commonwealth Federation (CCF), precursor to today's NDP, held its founding convention in Calgary in 1932.[13] Naheed Nenshi was the first Muslim elected mayor of a major city in North America in 2010. The NDP came to power under Rachel Notley in 2015, and continues to enjoy strong voter support as a credible government in waiting.[14]

And while several Alberta premiers have championed free markets, explicitly rejecting socialism, in practice their governments have been much more interventionist and less opposed to organized workers than their rhetoric suggests. While they campaigned from the right, in many ways they governed from the left.

Manning invested generously in education and social programs and issued resource dividend cheques to all Albertans.[15] Lougheed established Alberta's first bill of rights, and invested in the oil industry, economic diversification, rural telephones, parks, universities, and the arts. He established the Alberta Energy Company and Syncrude to develop Alberta's oil sands, purchased Pacific Western Airlines, and dramatically raised energy royalties by almost 50 per cent, establishing the Heritage Savings Trust Fund with some of the resulting revenues. His government supported economic growth through agencies like Vencap, a venture capital fund to launch Alberta's petrochemical industry and promote economic diversification, the Alberta Housing Corporation to help manage housing prices, and subsidized mortgages when interest rates peaked. He also established Alberta's first income support program for disabled people unable to work, now known as Assured Income for the Severely Handicapped (AISH).[16] In developing the oil sands, Lougheed discerned that alliances with organized labour were critical to success and agreed to award Syncrude pipeline contracts to a unionized bidder in exchange for no strikes or lockouts.[17] Lougheed established the right to binding arbitration for public sector workers in exchange for suspending the right to strike[18] and established new legislation to protect workers, the Occupational Health and Safety Act.[19]

Klein's conservative rhetoric diverged considerably from reality. His aggressive public opposition to unions dissipated in the face of united opposition. Despite famously declaring he would not "blink" in response to organized worker protests, scarcely two years after embarking on his deficit slashing agenda, a growing wildcat strike by health care workers forced Klein to retreat, reversing planned cuts to health care spending.[20] He pronounced that the Alberta government was "no longer in the business of being in business," yet awarded the oil industry $314 million in subsidies, tax, and royalty breaks, and issued $4 billion to offset the cost of his deregulation of electricity.[21] Fiscal conservatism gave way to record spending, ballooning by 60 per cent between 1997 and 2001, and rising to historic highs in the 2005 budget.[22] Alberta's opposition to "big government" has not meant less government. Alberta's spending per capita has often ranked higher than other governments in Canada.[23] Natural resource riches have enabled generous social programs while maintaining low taxes.

Alberta's unionization rate is the lowest in Canada, but not by much. Statistics Canada figures from 1997 to 2020 show Alberta below other provinces, but only 1.4 per cent below Ontario in 2020, and at most 4 per cent below Ontario in 1997.[24] By contrast to provinces like British Columbia and Ontario, the dominant industries in Alberta are not unionized. Most unionized workers are in the public sector, and while the gender-earnings gap is larger in Alberta than in any other province, that gap is smaller for women belonging to unions.[25] Those working in lucrative oil industry jobs may see no need to organize, and its high levels of remuneration set a competitive standard for other sectors. Six-figure salaries can be earned by workers who have not yet completed high school, forcing employers outside the oil patch to offer higher compensation. Farm and ranch operations are often family-run small businesses that employ temporary seasonal workers, many brought into Canada under a program which was considerably expanded under Kenney as a minister in Stephen Harper's cabinet—the Temporary Foreign Workers program.

Organized worker negotiations in Alberta have historically tended to fly under the radar, with most of the action taking place in private, through arbitration or in the courts. Governments and workers may resist public disclosure to avoid losing bargaining clout. Stalled negotiations tend to go to arbitration or lead to court action. One factor contributing to this pattern is that Alberta public sector workers had a legislated right to binding arbitration in place of the right to strike from 1977 until 2015, when the Supreme Court established a constitutionally recognized right to strike, or to binding arbitration for essential workers.[26]

Nevertheless strikes, including wildcat strikes, have forced resolution of disputes more frequently than one might expect in Alberta.[27] Broad coalitions of organized labour and the general public have emerged in response to controversial initiatives of even popular Alberta governments. One of the issues that has generated coordinated opposition is health care. A wildcat strike launched on 14 November 1994 by sixty Canadian Union of Public Employees (CUPE) laundry workers ballooned over ten days to about 2,500 workers, with hundreds of additional health care workers joining work-to-rule and other job actions. The growing union and public opposition forced Ralph Klein's retreat from proposed health care cuts. Similarly, the united efforts of public supporters, health care workers, nurses, doctors, and Friends of Medicare have repeatedly resisted threats to public health care, notably attempts at privatization.[28] Jason Kenny underestimated this potential.

Orange Chinook to Blue Storm

RACHEL NOTLEY

When Rachel Notley ascended to the premiership of Alberta, she brought to the bargaining table significant credibility as a labour lawyer and community advocate. While a student at Osgoode Hall Law School she studied in their poverty law program with Parkdale Community Legal Services. She articled with an Edmonton labour lawyer, advocated for injured workers through the Alberta Union of Provincial Employees (AUPE),[29] and worked in the British Columbia attorney general's office, "earning a reputation as a persuasive advocate, able to find common ground between adversaries."[30]

As premier, Notley partnered across a range of industries and interests, recognizing the importance of building trust, particularly among those who were tentative about her government. Rather than prioritizing business and industry she balanced them with other interests. Notley included a variety of stakeholders in review panels and committees to develop energy policy, including Indigenous Albertans, environmental groups, academic advisors, and citizens.[31] Her first budget committed to avoid public sector layoffs and projected 20,000 "new infrastructure-based jobs" over two years.[32] This set a tone of mutual respect and openness, which was reinforced by hiring a former AUPE staff negotiator as the government's "chief adviser on negotiations."[33] Facing budgetary challenges, she set an example by freezing the salaries of cabinet ministers, MLAs, political staff, and non-unionized workers at government agencies boards and commissions.[34] This helped her secure agreements to defer wage increases with a number of groups, including the Alberta Teachers' Association (ATA), United Nurses of Alberta (UNA), AUPE, and Health Sciences Association of Alberta (HSAA) in exchange for reopening negotiations and commitment to binding arbitration in year three of contracts.[35]

Notley's government amended Alberta's Labour Code and Employment Standards Code, modernizing some laws that had not been changed since the 1970s. The changes protected parental leaves, overtime pay, and vacation time. It also made it easier to form unions, established first contract binding arbitration, provided remedies for unfair labour practices, and established automatic dues payments in unionized workplaces.[36] Despite initial concerns that an NDP government might institute dramatic revisions, the changes were seen as moderate. This was partly because the mandate letter sought ideological balance, including recommendations that had been made under previous conservative governments, and also because the expert chosen to draft the legislative changes, Andrew Simms, was widely respected as balanced and fair.[37]

The Notley government also extended to farm and ranch workers the protection of occupational health and safety and workers compensation coverage. Bill 6, the Enhanced Protection for Farm and Ranch Workers Act, sought to align Alberta with worker protections in the rest of the country, but was communicated poorly, triggering protests and petitions. Notley apologized for not being clear that the changes would only apply to paid farm and ranch workers, making amendments that were endorsed by farm leaders as an improvement over the private liability coverage they had previously relied on. Nevertheless, the rift between rural Alberta and the NDP government endured.[38]

Notley's approach to legislation and negotiation was pragmatic. She was able to pivot in response to public critiques, moderating campaign commitments in order to balance the demands of business, workers, and others as seen in her phased approach to minimum wage increases, changes to labour laws, and modification of Bill 6. She built trust among government-paid workers in exchange for delayed increases backed by binding arbitration. Her personal popularity and support consistently exceeds that of her party. However, despite relatively stable support, economic challenges and the reunification of conservative supporters under Jason Kenney's UCP relegated her to Official Opposition in the 2019 election.

JASON KENNEY

Jason Kenney returned to Alberta on a mission to unite the right, defeat what he called an "accidental" NDP government, and restore conservatism to what he saw as its rightful place. His was an ambitious, and aggressive agenda detailed in a 114-page election platform. In a dramatic change of tone from the Notley government, he quickly embarked on what he called the summer of repeal. Citing the largest mandate in Alberta history, Kenney almost immediately depleted trust, breaking arbitration agreements in June 2019, and betraying election promises not to cut frontline health care jobs with plans to contract out nearly 11,000 health care positions. While it is true that his government won more votes than any in Alberta's history, it ranks far from the top in percentage of the popular vote or seats in the legislature. Kenney's personal popularity never approached that of Lougheed or Klein, and even before the election tracked lower than his party's. Nevertheless, he persistently focused on his mandate and his plan, repeating a mantra of "promises made, promises kept," apparently unable to pivot in response to challenges, particularly the unprecedented ordeal of COVID-19 (as detailed in Lisa Young's chapter on COVID's impact).

Kenney's "War on Labour"

Several of Kenney's reforms centred on reducing spending on government services, health care, and education, including compensation of doctors, nurses, teachers, and public service workers. Beyond monetary restraint, several legislative changes affected things like the autonomy and protections of these same groups, described by critics as a "war on workers."[39]

As argued above, Alberta has never been as ideologically conservative as Jason Kenney envisioned, and in many ways his agenda appeared tailored to a distorted image of the province he left in the 1990s. His record in Harper's cabinet foreshadowed his approach to workers, including the temporary foreign worker program criticized for perpetuating poor working conditions, low wages, and vulnerability to unscrupulous employers, and the Canada Job Grant ostensibly meant to provide training to unemployed workers, but which mostly subsidized employer training costs.

Decreasing Worker Power

Kenney's first two legislative initiatives limited protests (Bill 1)[40] and the power of workers (see Table 18.1). Billed as a law to "Make Alberta Open for Business," Bill 2 decreased overtime pay provisions, made it more difficult for workers to join unions, and reduced the minimum wage for students under eighteen. Two other laws transformed the Labour Relations Code, the Employment Standards Code, the Occupational Health and Safety Act and Workers Compensation Act. Despite recent Supreme Court of Canada decisions, Bill 32, Restoring Balance in Alberta's Workplaces Act, and Bill 47, Ensuring Safety and Cutting Red Tape Act, raised the bar for joining unions and collecting union dues, and restricted picketing, requiring labour relations board permission before engaging in secondary picketing. These laws imposed restrictions on what decisions could be made by arbitrators, and made it easier for the labour board to overturn those decisions. It became easier to lay off workers, giving employers

Table 18.1. New United Conservative Party Legislation Summary

Bill 1	Critical Infrastructure Defence Act June 2019	Limited protests in places deemed essential infrastructure
Bill 2	An Act to Make Alberta Open for Business June 2019	Reduced youth minimum wage, limited overtime pay, and made it harder for workers to join unions
Bill 9	Public Sector Wage Arbitration Deferral Act* June 2019	Revoked contractual commitments to binding arbitration
Bill 21	Ensuring Fiscal Sustainability Act* Introduced 28 October 2019	Empowered government to determine wage settlements and the length of contracts, reversed the ban on replacement workers for essential services, enabled gov't to tell docs where they could practice, and made changes to the master agreement with physicians
Bill 22	Reform of Agencies Boards and Commissions and Government Enterprises Act* November 2019	Transferred control of teachers' retirement fund to AIMCo
Bill 30	Health Statutes Amendment Act July 2020	Allowed government to publish physicians' compensation received from the province
Bill 32	Restoring Balance in Alberta's Workplaces Act July 2020	Amended Labour Relations Code and Employment Standards Code
Bill 47	Ensuring Safety and Cutting Red Tape Act Introduced November 2020	Changes to Occupational Health and Safety Act and Workers Compensation Act
	*= court challenge	

greater power over them.[41] The changes limited when workers could refuse to work in hazardous conditions and removed employers' obligation to reinstate injured workers. It became more difficult to claim workers' compensation coverage for psychological injuries.[42]

Fight with Organized Workers

The Kenney government's argument for fiscal restraint included controlling labour costs. However, this stood in stark contrast to government spending on business, pledging to cut corporate taxes by $4.5 billion over four years, and investing $1.3 billion in the failed Keystone XL pipeline.

Within a month of being elected premier, Kenney introduced legislation (Bill 9) revoking a contractual commitment to arbitration for 65,000 AUPE workers employed by Alberta Health Services (AHS) or the provincial government. The law affected arbitration agreements with later deadlines for 160,000 additional workers and foreshadowed the eventual breach of the government's master agreement with doctors.

Bill 9 delayed arbitration hearings until the end of October, anticipating the release of the MacKinnon Report's recommendations on curtailing government spending. This report recommended reductions in public sector compensation, and if necessary, imposing back-to-work legislation and using the notwithstanding clause if the courts found such a law unconstitutional.

The NDP launched a filibuster against Bill 9 in the legislature, and Kenney allegedly handed out earplugs so his caucus would not have to listen to the concerns raised by the opposition. A rather hypocritical response from a premier who had promised greater respect and consultation with Albertans. The law was challenged by several groups in the courts and generated a series of pickets during lunch breaks and after work. When arbitration was permitted to proceed in October, the government escalated from demanding a wage freeze to a reduction of 2 to 5 per cent.[43]

The UCP's first budget was delivered on 24 October 2019, followed by legislation signalling sweeping reductions to the power of government-paid workers. The Ensuring Fiscal Sustainability Act (Bill 21) empowered government to determine wage settlements and the length of contracts, removed a ban on replacement workers for essential services, and authorized the government to make changes to the master agreement with physicians and assign where they could practice.

Control over the ATA's pension, the Alberta Teacher's Retirement Fund (ATRF), was diminished in November 2019 under the Reform of Agencies Boards and Commissions and Government Enterprises Act (Bill 22). This law transferred management of the ATRF to Alberta Investment Management Corporation (AIMCo) to save on management fees but required negotiating an agreement to transfer the funds. When negotiations stalled in the fall of 2020, a ministerial order was issued to effect the transfer, allowing AIMCo to veto ATRF investment instructions and to act as arbiter in the event of any disagreements. This imposition, combined with the controversy over AIMCo's $2.1 billion loss in 2020 prompted a court challenge by the ATA.[44]

The relationship with teachers was further soured when the government imposed curriculum changes (see Charles Webber's chapter on education). Failure to adequately consult on these changes generated widespread criticism from educational experts, Indigenous leaders, cultural groups, parents, school boards, and community members. The draft curriculum was slammed for its coverage of race, Indigenous history and colonialism, and ridiculed for including passages apparently plagiarized from, among other sources, Wikipedia. Despite these concerns, the government proceeded with a voluntary pilot of the curriculum, planning to implement it fully in September 2022. Fifty-seven of Alberta's sixty-one school boards, including three of the province's largest four boards, declined to pilot the curriculum.[45] Having campaigned on a "grass roots guarantee" to consult with Albertans, such decisions compounded questions about arrogance and competence that were ultimately catastrophic for Kenney's leadership.

Losing Battle

The government's negotiation strategy with unions and professional associations began to appear uncompromising and needlessly punitive, perhaps most dramatically characterized by the government's relationship with Alberta doctors (see also Gillian Steward's chapter on health care). Negotiations between Alberta's physicians and the health minister, Tyler Shandro, to balance the government's fiscal agenda with patient care stalled in February 2020. The government unilaterally ended the master agreement with physicians and imposed new fee rules to take effect in April 2020. The Alberta Medical Association (AMA) warned that the imposition would negatively impact patient care, increase hospitalizations, and be disastrous for some rural and family practices. Then head of the AMA, Dr. Christine Molnar, went public, noting the substantial financial concessions that had been offered by the AMA, explaining how they had been preparing to deliver another offer when the agreement was "torn up," and describing the government's move as "an attack on physicians."[46] The AMA also launched a court challenge. The government's tactics were seen as problematic even before COVID-19 swelled support for health care workers. The government likely meant to strengthen its negotiating power; however, by breaking a contract before it expired, during ongoing negotiations, the government materially debilitated trust. This would have implications for future negotiations with doctors and other groups. The government's approach was described as "draconian" and unprecedented. Concerns were raised about aggravating shortages of rural physicians and undermining the quality of health care.[47] Don Braid warned that "doctors—and soon . . . nurses—will pay for this now. If service erodes, the government will pay later."[48] Health care policy experts questioned the antagonistic approach, warning that effective policy changes cannot be accomplished without the cooperation of those required to implement them. Strategists noted that physicians are usually the easiest group to negotiate with and that the precedent set would make negotiations with other health care groups more difficult.[49]

The wisdom of the government's strategy became even more questionable when the COVID-19 pandemic hit. By the end of March, expressions of appreciation for health care workers proliferated. There were nightly demonstrations of gratitude for workers risking their lives to save those of others. Signs expressing support for health care workers emerged on lawns that had displayed UCP signs during the 2019 election. Amid this celebration of health care workers, Tyler Shandro made headlines for verbally attacking a physician in his neighbourhood who had questioned whether the health minister and his wife were in a conflict of interest. When another critic sent an email raising similar concerns, Shandro responded that any further emails would "be referred to protective services." This prompted the first in a series of demands for the resignation or removal of the health minister.[50]

A number of physicians, many in rural communities, indicated that they planned to withdraw their services from hospitals, prompting a June 2020 government letter asking the College of Physicians and Surgeons for rules to prevent groups of doctors from quitting. In July the Health Statutes Amendment Act was introduced, allowing the government to publish how much doctors are paid. Physicians countered that the government figures were misleading, since they did not reflect the costs of running a practice with employees, medical equipment, etc. At the end of July, an AMA referendum signalled that 98 per cent of members "don't have confidence in

Health Minister Tyler Shandro." Nevertheless, the premier continued to support Shandro, while expressing a willingness to meet with the AMA. This tone-deaf endorsement continued through the fourth wave of the pandemic, and by the time Shandro was finally replaced in September 2021, it was too little, too late.[51]

Things appeared to improve in February 2021 when a tentative agreement was reached between the AMA and the government. Strangely, Shandro claimed in a committee hearing that there had been no fight with the AMA, prompting journalists to recall the litany of disputes initiated by the government. In the year that had elapsed between scrapping the master agreement and the tentative deal, the government had attacked critics and attempted to undermine support for physicians, by accusing them of only being interested in money, by passing a law to publish their compensation, and by trying to "dilute the AMA's power by setting specialties against each other."[52] So, few were surprised when the majority of doctors voted against the tentative agreement at the end of March. The most frequently cited reason for rejecting the agreement was that it allowed too much discretion for the health minister and lacked the protection of binding arbitration. The majority of doctors, despite their desire to have an agreement, did not trust a government that had failed to honour previous agreements. This came at a very bad time for the government, polling lower than health care workers or the NDP (39.1 per cent compared with 29.8 per cent for the UCP), and facing negotiations with radiologists, nurses, other health care workers, teachers, and public service workers.[53]

The issue of trust reverberated among other health care workers as well. In October 2020 the UNA, representing over 30,000 nurses, rejected AHS' proposal to postpone bargaining until 31 March 2021. Finance Minister Travis Toews claimed that they were demanding "indefinite job security (in) a shameful effort to take advantage of a health crisis." The UNA publicly countered that Toews' comments were misleading, and that they would have agreed to the postponement had the government been willing to extend the existing agreement not to impose layoffs until a new collective agreement had been reached. Their spokesperson added that he "needs to tone down the rhetoric and stop insulting the group of workers who are keeping the health-care system running through this crisis. . . . The belligerent tone of the minister's statement is extremely unhelpful under the circumstances when we should all be pulling together for the good of Albertans." When Toews countered that the HSAA had agreed to postpone negotiations, the HSAA issued a statement exposing the government's divisive tactics as "clearly meant to be inflammatory and to cause division and polarization amongst Albertans. . . . This is not what Albertans want." The HSAA expressed hope that the government would "learn to become more respectful of the process as we move forward."[54] Attempts to divide and conquer had now failed with doctors and two other health care unions.

Within days of this dust up with the UNA, the government announced plans to cut up to 11,000 frontline health care positions in order to save $600 million. This, combined with revelations of the government's refusal to protect 750 nursing jobs, violated Kenney's campaign promise not to cut frontline health care workers. This further eroded trust. The government claimed the jobs would not be lost, but rather outsourced to private companies. The workers in question worked in laboratories and provided laundry and food services. These cuts targeted particularly vulnerable, marginalized workers, mostly women and newcomers.[55] The claim was criticized by the AMA, UNA, public sector unions, and medicare advocates. Health care policy expert Steven Lewis said the government's "bellicose public behaviour toward doctors and unions will make it nearly impossible to successfully implement the changes, which require collaboration with staff. The irony is that the government is right about many of the problems in the system; it just has no clue about change management."[56] Targeting health care workers in the middle of a pandemic seemed particularly tone-deaf. Similar cost-saving policies forcing low-paid, part-time workers to work at multiple long-term care facilities had worsened the spread of COVID-19. These cuts risked replicating this hazard in additional health care facilities.

Thirteen days later, on 26 October 2020, those workers launched a wildcat strike at twenty-seven locations across Alberta. The government called an emergency meeting of the Labour Relations Board which declared the strike illegal and Toews warned that the responsible parties would be "held accountable."[57] AUPE said the strike was a grassroots reaction to protect Albertans against the impact of UCP policies during a pandemic, and that the union had not ordered the strike. Punishments were imposed within three months. On 23 February 2021, AUPE reported that grievances had been filed by almost 800 workers who received letters of reprimand, and twenty-seven workers who had been suspended from work for up to five days. AHS also filed a labour relations board action against AUPE. These actions were unprecedented. The numbers for this single day of protest were equivalent to what would normally occur over two years. This was apparently meant to send a message to other workers. The scale of reaction surprised labour scholars, who noted that the volume of grievances could create an unanticipated burden on the government due to the time and expense involved in processing them. It also risked further deterioration in relations with these and other groups.[58]

Increased attention was focused on the risks faced by essential workers in grocery stores, meat-packing plants, and those providing social supports to keep government and society functioning.[59] Government and businesses established temporary measures to compensate such workers. Some grocery stores increased wages for frontline workers, however this didn't last through later waves that saw case counts, and concomitant risks, soar. The Alberta government created the Critical Worker Benefit offering a one-time $1,200 payment available to 380,000 frontline workers. This also covered frontline retail workers and food processing workers, such as those working in meat packing plants. Eligible workers included nurses, respiratory therapists, orderlies, and patient services providers, and some of the workers whose jobs were scheduled to be contracted out, including food service, housekeeping, and maintenance workers. Social services workers, included those providing services for disability, child development, family and youth counselling, crisis intervention home supports, and seniors' lodges were also included. In education, the eligible workers included teacher assistants, bus drivers, and cleaning and maintenance workers making $25 an hour or less. "Critical retail workers" included those employed in grocery stores, pharmacies, and gas stations, and private health providers such as dental assistants and massage therapists.[60] However, temporary or one-time payments were insufficient to convey respect for workers facing workplace safety issues or job losses. Public statements of appreciation rang hollow for those whose work and careers had been negatively impacted by other laws and tactics.

Promise vs Practice

While Kenney began with a strong mandate, he squandered significant political capital by needlessly engaging in disrespectful, adversarial relations with stakeholder groups, often adding insult to injury. The contrast to his promises of improved consultation and respect left many feeling betrayed by his hypocrisy. The impact was magnified by the government's management of the COVID-19 pandemic, decimating government approval and intensifying support for the frontline workers it had targeted. Kenney's preoccupation with his 114-page plan seemed to impair his ability to pivot when other issues preoccupied Albertans. His propensity to list off accomplishments when facing criticism fell flat. As COVID-19 case numbers peaked to the highest in the country, Kenney faced plummeting polls and a caucus revolt, yet he repeatedly, and even after announcing his resignation, touted his accomplishments and fulfilled promises. A particularly illustrative incident occurred when photos were released of Kenney violating his own health regulations on the terrace of the infamous "Sky Palace." After a week of attacking critics and denying that any rules had been broken, he held a news conference on the equalization referendum, trying to shift the focus to "promises made, promises kept." Eventually reporters' challenges forced an acknowledgment of what he had been repudiating for a week, and a reluctant apology. This revealed three problems. Firstly, it showed a persistent pattern of attacking people raising legitimate issues. Secondly, none of the "promises kept" addressed his failures to respond to pressing concerns like the escalating health care crisis. Thirdly, this expanded the growing list of incidents where UCP MLAs or staffers flouted rules that other Albertans were expected to follow.

Misrepresentations of worker and professional groups by the premier, his staff and cabinet ministers detracted from real issues and undermined the government's credibility. The cumulative effect of the government's antagonistic, disrespectful relations with workers diminished trust, increased desperation, and promoted solidarity and support across worker groups and the general public. This was particularly true for those providing health care services, but extended to educators, critical public service providers, and even prosecutors.

Concerns about the education system began in December 2019 with Education Minister Adriana LaGrange's autocratic response to the Calgary Board of Education's claim that government cuts would cost 300 teaching jobs. She ordered an audit of its books and threatened to fire the entire board despite finding no evidence of "reckless" spending or fiscal mismanagement.[61] Concerns resonated beyond teachers and school boards to parents and the public. Frustrations proliferated around controversial curriculum changes, changing policies for school openings, protections for students and teachers, predictability for working parents, and vaccinations for frontline education workers. By May 2021, exasperated teachers delivered a vote of non-confidence in the education minister and rejected the draft curriculum.[62]

The government's response to such criticisms failed to address genuine concerns. In question period Jason Kenney dismissed the ATA non-confidence vote, saying that the "government is accountable to Albertans . . . not to a union that spent $2 million trying to re-elect the NDP in the last election." ATA president Jason Schilling demanded a retraction, since the ATA did not and could not have done so without violating election laws, and advocated for education, not parties or candidates.[63] The premier's remark was neither accurate, nor effective at addressing widely shared concerns.

Similar concerns emerged in the Kenney government's approach to post-secondary education (PSE). The funding and independence of post-secondary institutions were dramatically altered (as detailed in Lisa Young's chapter on PSE) and this loss of independence extended to faculty associations and boards. Negotiations between boards and faculty associations were constrained by government directives mandating what boards could offer, raising questions about fairness and compliance with Charter protections of meaningful and productive collective bargaining.[64]

The Kenney government's persistent attacks on critics as socialists, as supporters of unions or the NDP, or as enemies of Alberta did nothing to inspire confidence in the government or its policies. As criticism escalated around Kenney's leadership, he impugned the questioners, accusing them of "Alberta bashing," engaging in "drive-by smears" of Alberta, or of asking questions that sound more like an NDP speech.[65] Such responses suggested he did not see union members as true Albertans, or recognize that their leaders had also been democratically elected. When health leaders and journalists raised questions about rising fourth wave case counts, Kenney and government officials accused them of fear mongering and not wanting the pandemic to end.[66] His retorts conflated questions about his record as attacks on Alberta.

Such tactics, combined with the premier's inability to recognize warning signs or respond to emerging issues, profoundly compromised confidence in his capacity as leader. This resulted in challenges on multiple fronts. Kenney's mismanagement of the health care system in the fourth wave of the pandemic precipitated slumping polls, projections that the NDP could win sixty of Alberta's eighty-seven legislative seats, and six consecutive quarters in which the NDP more than doubled the funds raised by the UCP.[67] Repeated calls for a leadership review or outright resignation came from within his own caucus, a UCP board member, constituency associations, former leadership rivals, and a litany of critics, many of whom had once been supporters.[68] As confidence in Kenney's leadership collapsed,[69] Albertans turned to health care experts and workers for reliable information and credible responses. Frontline health care workers reported overburdened hospitals and workers for weeks while Kenney vacationed in an undisclosed location in August 2021. AHS announced mandatory overtime and vacation cancellations for health care workers as hospital and ICU capacity was expanded to 169 per cent of their baseline.[70] Just before the 20 September federal election the UNA, HSAA, AUPE, and CUPE issued an open letter pressing Kenney to request military support for Alberta's overwhelmed hospitals.[71] But Kenney waited until *after* the federal election to send a letter to Bill Blair, minister of public safety and emergency preparedness. On the same day Kenney replaced his beleaguered health minister. These delays added to concerns that politics was taking priority over health.

In the face of all this uncertainty, with COVID deaths exceeding the combined totals of Ontario, Quebec, and Saskatchewan,[72] the embattled premier who had invoked Ralph Klein's promise not to "blink," reversed demands for AUPE concessions in October 2021. The government's original calls for a 4 per cent decrease in salary, reduced overtime, and benefits were dropped in a mediated settlement offering increases of 1.25 per cent and 1.5–2 per cent in January and September 2023. The finance minister struck a more respectful tone than in previous press releases, and AUPE president Guy Smith reported that the government had made concessions in negotiations with other worker groups.[73] The government's choice to attack workers that were making sacrifices to help patients, students, and citizens reliant on their services backfired. If such demands were simply a negotiating tactic to strengthen the government's bargaining position, they proved counterproductive, stoking anger and shrivelling confidence in the premier and his government. And the unintended consequence was to strengthen support and appreciation for organized workers and professionals protecting health care, education, and government services.

The Long Goodbye

The more conciliatory approach to worker negotiations did not last. By December 2021, calls for a leadership review came to a head, forcing the UCP executive to move a planned leadership review from the autumn to an in-person vote on 9 April 2022, and then to a mail-in ballot with results to be announced 18 May 2022. Some wondered if the prospect of an early review might prompt Kenney to listen to some of his critics, adopt a shift in tone, and campaign to win back disgruntled voters. Government coffers overflowing with oil revenues enabled him to crisscross the province promising better economic fortunes, however, polls reflected sustained dissatisfaction with his leadership.[74] A comprehensive survey measuring public opinion spanning the mail-in ballot period (8 April to 4 May) revealed that almost 60 per cent of Albertans, and over 56 per cent of UCP identifiers, wanted Kenney removed as leader. Only 21 per cent thought he should continue.[75] The promise of prosperity was not enough to outweigh the anger against a persistent pattern of arrogant, insular leadership and imposition of top-down policies.

That pattern continued as the leadership review approached. In March, Crown prosecutors, whose repeated pleas for adequate funding had fallen on deaf ears, faced the prospect of over 3,000 criminal cases being dismissed for exceeding time limits. In desperation, they threatened to strike. The initial government response was to deny that any criminal cases were in jeopardy,[76] and the government repudiated the prosecutors' union-like strike threat. Then Tyler Shandro, now justice minister, backtracked, agreeing to negotiate. However, the prospect of serious criminals evading justice, particularly in rural Alberta, further undermined Kenney's leadership, since many already-angry voters were also upset about failures to curtail crime.

Apparently confident of a win, Kenney reverted to confrontation, including against health care workers. The conciliatory negotiations of the previous autumn evaporated. In March, with COVID death counts reaching new highs and shortages of health care workers, the government offered an 8 to 11 per cent pay *cut* to HSAA workers, including respiratory specialists, hailed as life-savers throughout the pandemic.[77] With UCP voters about to mail in their leadership review ballots in early April, AHS CEO and president Dr. Verna Yiu was fired with a year remaining in her contract—widely seen as paving the way for privatization. In April and May, concerns about the health care system grew as a procession of health care crises made headlines. These included repeated transfers of surgical patients from Red Deer to other hospitals due to chronic shortages, and photographs of parents and their children in a line up extending outside a children's hospital emergency entrance. AHS announced an end to a program funding insulin pumps, and public backlash forced a pause. However, in a town hall "consultation," patients complained that they were not listened to. Kenney held a press conference announcing plans to open beds at Rockyview Hospital, however his pledge was undercut by revelations that two dozen surgeries at that same hospital had to be postponed due to staff shortages.[78]

Kenney reaped 51.4 per cent support in the leadership review, and announced his plans to resign on 18 May. The result surprised Kenney and his inner circle, but few outside this insular group. The demise of Alberta's previous conservative dynasty was attributed to arrogance, hypocrisy, and entitlement—particular liabilities for conservative governments. These qualities can manifest in failure to respect or effectively respond to the voices, needs, and sacrifices of citizens. For a populist leader, such shortcomings are crippling. In his campaign to unite the right and become UCP leader, Kenney repeatedly decried the arrogance that defeated Alberta's PC dynasty. "We had leaders telling people what to think, rather than listening to them in humility. We must not repeat the mistake of that arrogance, we must have an approach of humility and servant leadership that empowers the grassroots members to decide the policy direction of this new party."[79] Haunting words for a leader who betrayed promises, failed to recognize or respond to unanticipated problems, and increasingly was seen as fighting against, rather than for Albertans. His tenacious grip on power fed suspicions that Kenney prioritized his own political fortunes over the health and concerns of Albertans.[80]

A more respectful, consultative, and inclusive approach could have helped Jason Kenney govern more effectively. Had he engaged questions and input from more Albertans, including workers and elected leaders of the unions and professional associations discussed, he might have consolidated support. He apparently misread Alberta, and support for the workers needed to facilitate its governance. Ultimately, he was unable to adapt to the new Alberta he encountered, or chart a course correction.

NOTES

1   Sydney Sharpe and Don Braid, *Notley Nation* (Toronto: Dundern, 2016), 42; Doreen Barrie, *The Other Alberta: Decoding a Political Enigma* (Regina: Canadian Plains Research Center, 2006), 116–7.

2   Jason Markusoff, "Rachel Notley fought like hell for Alberta, but the province isn't about to thank her," *Maclean's*, 11 March 2019 https://www.macleans.ca/politics/rachel-notley-fought-like-hell-for-alberta-but-the-province-isnt-about-to-thank-her/ (accessed 29 May 2021).

3   Barrie, *The Other Alberta*, xii, 115; Jen Gerson, "The Great Myth of Alberta Conservatism," *Walrus*, 4 February 2019, https://thewalrus.ca/the-great-myth-of-alberta-conservatism/ (accessed 5 June 2020).

4   Barrie, *The Other Alberta*, 77. The anti-socialist language was used to target his electoral rivals, the CCF.

5   Ken MacQueen, "King Ralph's parting shots," *Maclean's*, 29 March 2013, https://www.macleans.ca/news/canada/king-ralphs-parting-shots/ (accessed 21 May 2021).

6   Bill Kaufmann, "Remembering Ralph," *Edmonton Sun*, 29 March 2013, https://edmontonsun.com/2013/03/29/remembering-ralph (accessed 21 May 2021). "He doesn't seem to take criticism very well," said Martin of Klein . . . Retorted Klein: "It's typical socialist claptrap and I'm surprised it came from a gentleman like Mr. Martin."

7   Alvin Finkel, *Working People in Alberta: A History* (Edmonton: Athabasca University Press, 2012), ch. 8, https://read.aupress.ca/read/working-people-in-alberta/section/80778f1b-aae0-414e-b45c-57924d227713 (accessed 31 May 2021).

8   A striking union worker described such attitudes: "We've got these oil workers coming in and saying, 'Well, go get a job. Why are you out here on the picket line? If you only make $7 or $8 an hour, why don't you go work somewhere else?'" Finkel, *Working People in Alberta*, ch. 8.

9   Jared Wesley, "Albertans Want and Expect Kenney to Lose Leadership Review," *Common Ground*, 16 May 2022, https://www.commongroundpolitics.ca/kenneyreview (accessed 18 May 2022)

10 Gerson, "The Great Myth of Alberta Conservatism."

11 The Social Credit party governed from 1935–1971, the PC Party from 1971–2015, and the UCP from 2019 to time of writing.

12 Sydney Sharpe, *The Gilded Ghetto* (Toronto: Harper Collins, 1994), 71–2.

13 Sharpe and Braid, *Notley Nation*, 87.

14 Polls in spring 2021 placed the NDP ten points ahead of the UCP, and by the autumn this lead had grown to 23 per cent. Philippe J. Fournier, "Will Jason Kenney sink the UCP experiment?: 338Canada," *Maclean's*, 24 October 2021, https://www.macleans.ca/politics/338canada-will-jason-kenney-sink-the-ucp-experiment/ (accessed 1 November 2021).

15 Barrie, *The Other Alberta*, xii, 115; Gerson, "The Great Myth of Alberta Conservatism."

16 Sheila Pratt, "Peter Lougheed leaves lasting economic and political legacy for Alberta," *Edmonton Journal*, 12 September 2012, https://edmontonjournal.com/news/politics/peter-lougheed-leaves-lasting-economic-and-political-legacy-for-alberta (accessed 6 June 2021).

17 Gillian Steward, "Betting on Bitumen: Lougheed, Klein, and Notley," in *Orange Chinook: Politics in the New Alberta*, eds. Duane Bratt, Keith Brownsey, Richard Sutherland and David Taras (Calgary: University of Calgary Press, 2019), 151.

18 The Public Service Employee Relations Act 1977. Postmedia News, "Landmark court ruling pushes Alberta to review Lougheed-era ban on civil service strikes," *National Post*, 3 March 2015, https://nationalpost.com/news/canada/premier-jim-prentice-must-decide-which-alberta-civil-servants-will-regain-right-to-strike (accessed 17 June 2021); Guy Smith, "*Shameful abuse of rights and government power,*" *ATA News*, Volume 48 2013–4, no. 10 (28 January 2014), https://www.teachers.ab.ca/News%20Room/ata%20news/Volume-48-2013-14/Number-10/Pages/Viewpoints.aspx (accessed 17 June 2021).

19 Alvin Finkel, "More than Wages; What unions have achieved for all Albertans," *Alberta Views*, 1 May 2012 https://albertaviews.ca/more-than-wages/ (accessed 23 May 2021). The OHSA entitled workers to know about occupational health hazards, to joint management & worker health and safety committees to reduce safety risks, and to refuse unsafe work.

20 Brian Bergman and John Howse, "Ralph Klein blinks," *Maclean's*, 4 December 1995, https://archive.macleans.ca/article/1995/12/4/ralph-klein-blinks (accessed 6 June 2021).

21 Barrie, *The Other Alberta*, 78.

22 Doreen Barrie, "Ralph Klein, 1992–," in *Alberta Premiers of the Twentieth Century*, ed. Bradford J. Rennie (Regina: Canadian Plains Research Centre, 2004) 266, Barrie, *The Other Alberta*, 78.

23 Barrie, *The Other Alberta*, 115.

24 Statistics Canada, "Union Status by Geography; Table: 14-10-0129-01," https://www150.statcan.gc.ca/t1/tbl1/en/tv.action?pid=1410012901 (accessed 28 May 2021). Alberta's union participation rate ranges from 24.4 to 25.9 per cent, Ontario's ranges from

26.2–29.9. The gap between Alberta and other provinces is the largest when compared with Quebec, which has the highest union participation rate.

25   AFL, "The Union Advantage for Women in Alberta," https://d3n8a8pro7vhmx. cloudfront.net/afl/pages/690/attachments/original/1331222461/2012-10-Backgrounder%20IWD.pdf?1331222461 (accessed 22 November 2021), see also https:// www.parklandinstitute.ca/on_the_job.

26   Established in *Saskatchewan Federation of Labour v. Saskatchewan* 2015 SCC 4. The change was first introduced by Jim Prentice. Postmedia News, "Landmark court ruling."

27   Wildcat strikes have occurred six times since 1994, in most cases forcing government concessions. Bob Barnetson, "Kenney's War on Workers; Contracts broken, wages cut and unions undermined," *Alberta Views*, 1 January 2020, https://albertaviews.ca/ kenneys-war-workers/ (accessed 21 May 2021).

28   This has involved the coordination of the UN A and the HSAA, the Alberta Federation of Labour, and Friends of Medicare. Finkel, *Working People in Alberta*, ch. 8.

29   Sharpe and Braid, *Notley Nation*, 95.

30   Lori Williams, "A League of Their Own: Alberta's Women Party Leaders," in *Orange Chinook*, 332.

31   Gillian Steward, "Betting on Bitumen: Lougheed, Klein, and Notley," 161. The panels included the Climate Change Policy Review Panel, the Royalty Review Advisory Panel, the Energy Efficiency Advisory Panel, and the Energy Diversification Advisory Committee.

32   Graham White, "What's Past is Prologue: Ontario 1990 and Alberta 2015," in *Orange Chinook*, 388.

33   Harry Vandervlist, "The Year of Bargaining Diplomatically; Public-sector negotiations in the Notley era," *Alberta Views*, 1 May 2018, https://albertaviews.ca/year-bargaining-diplomatically/ (accessed 7 June 2021). The negotiator was Kevin Davediuk.

34   Michelle Bellefontaine, "Salary freeze announced at Alberta's agencies boards and commissions," *CBC News*, 24 March 2016, https://www.cbc.ca/news/canada/edmonton/ salary-freeze-announced-at-alberta-s-agencies-boards-and-commissions-1.3506673 (accessed 29 March 2016).

35   This commitment was thwarted after the UCP came to power in May 2019. Michelle Bellefontaine, "Bill to delay wage arbitration for Alberta nurses, teachers, government workers coming Thursday," *CBC News*, 12 June 2019 https://www.cbc.ca/news/canada/ edmonton/alberta-wage-arbitration-delay-1.5172949 (accessed 7 June 2021). Some of the collective agreements committed to negotiations with a provision for an arbitration hearing if a settlement could not be reached in in June 2019.

36   Bill 17, The Fair and Family Friendly Workplaces Act. Dave Cournoyer, "NDP finally introduce their Labour Law modernization bill," *Daveberta*, 25 May 2017, https:// daveberta.ca/2017/05/alberta-ndp-labour-law-bill-17/ (accessed 7 June 2021).

37   Critics from the right and the left judged the changes as limited and balanced. Lorne Gunter, "Notley NDP should tread carefully with labour review," *Edmonton Sun*, 20 April 2017, https://edmontonsun.com/2017/04/20/gunter-notley-ndp-should-tread-carefully-with-labour-review (accessed 7 June 2021); David J. Climenhaga, "Celebrating

a different kind of Labour Day in Alberta," Rabble.ca (blog), 4 September 2017, https://rabble.ca/blogs/bloggers/alberta-diary/2017/09/celebrating-different-kind-labour-day-alberta-one-something (accessed 7 June 2021).

38   Roger Epp, "The End of Exceptionalism: Post-rural Politics in Alberta," in *Orange Chinook*, 293–5.

39   Barnetson, "Kenney's War on Workers."

40   Bill 1, The Critical Infrastructure Defence Act, limited protests in places deemed essential infrastructure. The law was meant to target protest against pipelines, but raised concerns it could be used to suppress opposition on other issues.

41   Jason Foster, "Alberta's Bill 32 is a Seismic Break in Labour and Employment Law," *Canadian Law of Work Forum*, 10 July 2020, https://lawofwork.ca/albertas-bill-32-is-a-seismic-break-in-labour-and-employment-law/ (accessed 21 May 2021).

42   Lisa Johnson, "Alberta introduces labour legislation that reverses several worker protections put in place by NDP," *Edmonton Journal*, 5 November 2020, https://edmontonjournal.com/news/politics/alberta-introduces-labour-legislation-that-reverses-several-worker-protections-put-in-place-by-ndp (accessed May 21, 2021).

43   CBC News, "Union's bid to appeal Alberta's wage arbitration bill rejected by Supreme Court," 12 March 2020, https://www.cbc.ca/news/canada/edmonton/aupe-bill-9-wage-arbitration-talks-alberta-appeal-supreme-court-1.5495058 (accessed 21 May 2021); Barnetson, "Kenney's War on Workers."

44   Janet French, "Alberta Teachers' Association, principal sue government over pension order: New law will require Alberta Teachers' Retirement Fund to use AIMCo as investment manager," *CBC News*, 13 March 2021, https://www.cbc.ca/news/canada/edmonton/alberta-teachers-association-principal-sue-government-over-pension-order-1.5948456 (accessed 23 May 2021).

45   Virginia Wright, "Calgary separate school district latest board to opt-out of Alberta's draft curriculum pilot," *CTV News*, 29 April 2021, https://calgary.ctvnews.ca/calgary-separate-school-district-latest-board-to-opt-out-of-alberta-s-draft-curriculum-pilot-1.5407296 (accessed 19 June 2021); "57 School Boards Refusing to Pilot Curriculum," *Students Deserve Better*, https://www.studentsdeservebetter.ca/ (accessed 19 June 2021); Pamela Fieber, "CBE will not test drive controversial new Alberta curriculum this fall," *CBC News*, 10 April 2021, https://www.cbc.ca/news/canada/calgary/calgary-board-of-education-will-not-participate-alberta-curriculum-1.5982490 (accessed 7 June 2021).

46   *CBC/Canadian Press*, "Alberta ends master agreement with doctors, new rules to be in place April 1," 20 February 2020, https://www.cbc.ca/news/canada/calgary/alberta-government-doctors-pay-ama-agreement-1.5470352 (accessed 20 May 2021).

47   Jason Markusoff, "Jason Kenney is sinking. How it all went wrong for him," *Maclean's*, 1 November 2021, https://www.macleans.ca/longforms/jason-kenney-is-sinking-how-it-all-went-wrong-for-him/?utm_source=OneSignal&utm_medium=WebNotifications&utm_campaign=MME_WN&utm_term=01-Nov-2021&utm_content=Kenney_the_sinking_man (accessed 1 November 2021).

48   Don Braid, "UCP cancels doctor pay contract, imposes radical change," *Calgary Herald*,
     20 Feb 2020, https://calgaryherald.com/opinion/columnists/braid-ucp-cancels-doctor-
     pay-contract-imposes-radical-change (accessed 20 May 2021).

49   Ashley Joannou, "How the Alberta doctors' contract dispute could impact the UCP
     government now and in the 2023 election," *Edmonton Journal*, 2 April 2021, https://
     edmontonjournal.com/news/politics/alberta-doctors-dispute-ucp-kenney (accessed
     May 21, 2021).

50   Sammy Hudes, "Kenney rejects NDP's calls to fire health minister over confrontation
     with doctor," *Calgary Herald*, 27 March 2020, https://calgaryherald.com/news/politics/
     bizarre-reckless-and-frankly-intimidating-ndp-calls-on-premier-to-fire-shandro-
     from-health-portfolio (accessed 20 May 2021).

51   Ashley Joannou, "Nearly 98 per cent of Alberta doctors who voted in AMA referendum
     said they don't have confidence in Shandro," *Calgary Herald*, 29 July 2020, https://
     calgaryherald.com/news/politics/nearly-98-per-cent-of-alberta-doctors-who-voted-in-
     ama-referendum-said-they-dont-have-confidence-in-shandro/wcm/14c40630-bf44-
     47db-ac63-b4991bc8d8f8/amp/ (accessed 20 May 2021).

52   Don Braid, "Fight with doctors? Never happened, says health minister," *Calgary Herald*,
     9 March 2021, https://calgaryherald.com/opinion/columnists/braid-fight-with-doctors-
     never-happened-says-health-minister (accessed 20 May 2021), Joannou, "Nearly 98 per
     cent of Alberta doctors."

53   Ashley Joannou, "How the Alberta doctors' contract dispute could impact the UCP
     government."

54   Phil Heidenreich, "Alberta finance minister accuses nurses' union of trying to 'take
     advantage of a health crisis,'" *Global News*, 8 October 2020, https://globalnews.ca/
     news/7387670/alberta-finance-minister-nurses-union-ahs-negotiations-pandemic/
     (accessed 24 May 2021).

55   The Current, "Alberta health-care workers 'drawing the line' on further privatization:
     union leader," *CBC Radio*, 2 November 2020, https://www.cbc.ca/radio/thecurrent/the-
     current-for-nov-2-2020-1.5786016/alberta-health-care-workers-drawing-the-line-on-
     further-privatization-union-leader-1.5786378 (accessed 21 November 2021).

56   Jennie Russell & Charles Rusnell, "Alberta Health Services to lay off up to 11,000 staff,
     mostly through outsourcing," *CBC News*, 13 October 2020, https://www.cbc.ca/news/
     canada/edmonton/alberta-health-services-job-cuts-tyler-shandro-1.5760155 (accessed
     20 May 2021).

57   Bill Kaufmann, "Hospital workers walk out in protest across province prompting
     surgery postponements, threats of discipline," *Calgary Herald*, 26 October 2020, https://
     calgaryherald.com/news/local-news/hospital-workers-walk-out-in-calgary-across-
     province-to-protest-ucp-policies (accessed 27 Oct 2020 & 20 May 2021).

58   Janet French, "AHS sanctioned hundreds of workers after wildcat strike," *CBC News*, 23
     February 2021, https://www.cbc.ca/news/canada/edmonton/ahs-sanctioned-hundreds-
     of-workers-after-wildcat-strike-1.5924007 (accessed 20 May 2021).

59   Michael Franklin, "'Contempt for workers': Union says Alberta's public service
     employees victimized by proposed cuts," *CTV News*, 7 November 2020, https://calgary.
     ctvnews.ca/contempt-for-workers-union-says-alberta-s-public-service-employees-
     victimized-by-proposed-cuts-1.5179248 (accessed 21 May 2021).

60   David Opinko, "Kenney announces $1,200 payments for 'critical workers' in Alberta," *Lethbridge News Now*, 10 February 2021, https://lethbridgenewsnow.com/2021/02/10/kenney-announces-1200-payments-for-critical-workers-in-alberta/ (accessed 21 May 2021).

61   Drew Anderson, "LaGrange threatens to fire CBE trustees despite no evidence of 'reckless' spending in audit," *CBC News*, 10 April 2021, https://www.cbc.ca/news/canada/calgary/cbe-calgary-board-of-education-schools-audit-1.5577794 (accessed 7 June 2021).

62   Stephen David Cook, "Teachers assembly votes non-confidence in Alberta education minister," *CBC News*, 23 May 2021, https://www.cbc.ca/news/canada/edmonton/non-confidence-alberta-teachers-1.6038125 (accessed 23 May 2021).

63   *Alberta Hansard*, 25 May 2021, 4837, Legislative Assembly of Alberta, https://docs.assembly.ab.ca/LADDAR_files/docs/hansards/han/legislature_30/session_2/20210525_1330_01_han.pdf; Alberta Teachers' Association, "Jason Kenney Fact Check," 27 May 2021, https://www.teachers.ab.ca/News%20Room/NewsReleases/Pages/Jason-Kenney-Fact-Check.aspx (accessed 3 June 2021).

64   CBC News, "Manitoba government must pay U of M union $19.3M for interfering in 2016 contract negotiations: judge," 24 February 2022, https://www.cbc.ca/news/canada/manitoba/university-manitoba-union-wins-legal-decision-1.6362857 (accessed 17 May 2022).

65   Dean Bennett, "Kenney rejects criticism he waited on new COVID rules, calls it 'Alberta bashing,'" *Calgary Herald*, 9 December 2020, https://calgaryherald.com/news/kenney-rejects-criticism-he-waited-on-new-covid-rules-calls-it-alberta-bashing (accessed 5 June 2021). In an interview with radio host Shaye Ganam the premier boasted about Alberta's pandemic response the previous spring. When Ganam respectfully pointed out that the successes of months past did not address the current problems ranking Alberta among the worst provinces, Kenney responded "I don't accept the Alberta bashing that is going on here." When asked by Postmedia reporter Sammy Hudes if he acknowledged responsibility for his handling of the second wave he replied "That sounds more like an NDP speech than a media question, Sammy. . . . You have just joined folks who are doing drive-by smears of Alberta."

66   Robson Fletcher (@CBCFletch), "June & July: Experts warning of a 4th wave in Alberta and the journalists who report on their warnings are repeatedly attacked by top government officials," Twitter, 9 September 2021, 4:17 p.m., https://twitter.com/cbcfletch/status/1436091495249965087 (accessed 9 September 2021).

67   Philippe J. Fournier, "Will Jason Kenney sink the UCP experiment?," Elections Alberta Quarterly Reports by Party, https://efpublic.elections.ab.ca/efEventQ.cfm?MID=FE_Q_2021_P&OFSFID=30&YEAR=2021 (accessed 1 November 2021); Gillian Steward, "Rachel Notley and the NDP have Alberta conservatives on the defensive," *Toronto Star*, 2 May 2022, https://www.thestar.com/opinion/contributors/2022/05/02/rachel-notley-and-the-ndp-have-alberta-conservatives-on-the-defensive.html (accessed 5 May 2022).

68   UCP board member Joel Mullan called for Kenney's resignation after the federal election. Just prior to the UCP AGM in November 2021, twenty-two constituency associations signed a letter demanding an early leadership review. Brian Jean, who lost the UCP leadership to Kenney, announced he was running for the UCP nomination in

a by-election, openly calling for Kenney's resignation. UCP senior policy advisor/press secretary Blaise Boehmer quit and took to social media to decry Kenney's autocratic leadership style. Columnist Rick Bell who once supported Kenney had become one of his harshest critics.

69   Kenney dropped to 20 per cent support in October 2021 (https://angusreid.org/provincial-spotlight-health-care-economy/ (accessed Oct 27/21)) and "twice as many Alberta voters were satisfied with the federal Liberals than with the UCP," see Fournier, "Will Jason Kenney sink the UCP experiment?:

70   Charles Rusnell, "Alberta Health Services invokes emergency work rules for nurses as COVID hospitalizations rise," *CBC News*, 20 August 2021, https://www.cbc.ca/news/canada/edmonton/alberta-nurses-emergency-work-rules-1.6148537 (accessed 19 November 2021). The expansion to 169 per cent was reached around 18 September (see Brittany Gervais below).

71   Brittany Gervais, "Alberta health care unions call on Kenney to request immediate military aid," *Calgary Herald*, 18 September 2021, https://calgaryherald.com/news/local-news/alberta-healthcare-unions-call-on-kenney-to-request-immediate-military-aid (accessed 19 September 2021). Together these unions represented over 100,000 health care workers. Kenney, as a former federal cabinet minister, knew Blair could have responded before the election, and Blair had offered help just before election day, but Kenney claimed the request could not be made earlier because the government was in caretaker mode.

72   Markusoff, "Jason Kenney is sinking."

73   Tricia Kindleman, "AUPE, provincial government reach tentative deal," *CBC News*, 13 October 2021, https://www.cbc.ca/news/canada/edmonton/aupe-provincial-government-reach-tentative-deal-1.6209444 (accessed 16 October 2021).

74   Andrew Parkin, "Forget Ottawa—Albertans growing alienated from their own leaders, too," *CBC News*, 16 May 2022, https://www.cbc.ca/news/canada/calgary/opinion-alberta-western-alienation-survey-1.6453154 (accessed 17 May 2022).

75   Wesley, "Albertans Want and Expect Kenney to Lose Leadership Review."

76   Meghan Grant, "Justice Minister Tyler Shandro says no criminal cases at risk over delay—but there are thousands," *CBC News*, 11 March 2022, https://www.cbc.ca/news/canada/calgary/justice-minister-tyler-shandro-jordan-cases-alberta-1.6382170 (accessed 26 April 2022).

77   Ashley Joannou, "AHS proposing significant pay cuts for social workers as part of contract negotiations," *Edmonton Journal*, 14 March 2022, https://edmontonjournal.com/news/local-news/ahs-proposing-pay-cuts-for-social-workers (accessed 15 May 2022).

78   Jennifer Lee, "Staffing shortages worsen as patients transferred out of Red Deer for surgery," *CBC News*, 10 May 2022, https://www.cbc.ca/news/canada/calgary/staffing-shortages-patients-transferred-red-deer-hospital-1.6447849; Kylee Pederson, "Changes to insulin pump therapy program has some Albertans with diabetes worried," *CBC News*, 4 May 2022, https://www.cbc.ca/news/canada/calgary/changes-alberta-insulin-pump-therapy-program-1.6440668; Michelle Bellefontaine, "Insulin pump town hall only a first step in consultation, health minister says," *CBC News*, 26 May 2022, https://www.cbc.ca/news/canada/edmonton/alberta-health-diabetic-insulin-pump-program-copping-1.6466074; Jennifer Lee, "Concerns grow as ER wait times at Alberta's pediatric

hospitals balloon," *CBC News*, 6 May 2022, https://www.cbc.ca/news/canada/calgary/er-wait-times-alberta-childrens-hospital-1.6443892; Dylan Short, "Operations cancelled at Rockyview hospital due to staff illnesses and absences," *Calgary Herald*, 14 May 2022, https://calgaryherald.com/news/local-news/operations-cancelled-at-rockyview-hospital-due-to-staff-illnesses-and-absences (all accessed 26 May 2022).

79   David Climenhaga, "Rest in Peace, 'Grassroots Guarantee'—Jason Kenney's Famous Promise is Gone With the Wind," *Alberta Politics*, 15 November 2021, https://albertapolitics.ca/2021/11/rest-in-peace-grassroots-guarantee-jason-kenneys-famous-promise-is-gone-with-the-wind/ (accessed 20 November 2021).

80   This perception was reflected in a 26 May 2022 ThinkHQ poll; two-thirds of Albertans thought Kenney would do almost anything to keep the leadership: Rick Bell, "Kenney soon out, UCP bouncing back without a new leader," *Calgary Sun*, 26 May 2022, https://calgarysun.com/opinion/columnists/bell-kenney-soon-out-ucp-bouncing-back-without-a-new-leader (accessed 26 May 2022).

VII.
COVID in Alberta and Ontario

19

Comparing the Kenney and Ford Governments

Jonathan Malloy

Two provincial conservative political regimes were elected to power within a year of each other in 2018–2019: Jason Kenney's United Conservative Party (UCP) government in Alberta, and Doug Ford's Progressive Conservative (PC) government in Ontario. Both elections represented a clear swing away from more interventionist governments of the left, and the new premiers were clearly bent on a course correction for their province. Both premiers were also relative newcomers to the provincial political scene, as Kenney had built his reputation in federal politics and Ford at the municipal level. They also oversaw parties in evolution. Kenney led a party that had recently united from two separate parties. Ford had very recently taken over his party and swung it in significantly different directions than his predecessor.

But much is also different. This chapter draws out similarities and differences between the Ford and Kenney governments to better understand the distinctive characteristics of the latter. We see very different leadership styles and governing philosophies, which were particularly evident in the reactions to COVID-19 (see Lisa Young's chapter), as well as increasingly divergent paths of successful re-election for Ford and political demise for Kenney. Yet there are also similarities in general policy directions and visions for the provincial state. Examining the two regimes, we see how each reflects the distinctive political culture and environment of their respective provinces.

The chapter begins with the political contexts of each province and their contrasting political cultures and histories. It then gives a high-level overview of the two governments prior to the onset of the COVID pandemic. We then focus specifically on each premier and government's response to the pandemic. The chapter concludes with an overall analysis of the two governments and leaders, and their increasingly divergent political paths.

Ontario and Alberta Compared

While "political culture" can be an imprecise concept, there is little doubt that Alberta and Ontario have contrasting political systems, histories, and recurring values. Albertan politics have long had a populist streak, with recurring periods of confrontation with federal authorities and a sense of alienation from the political, economic, and social structures of central or "Eastern" Canada. In contrast, Ontario politics have been identified as managerialist and fundamentally moderate by nature.[1] While not without its own confrontation with federal authorities historically, including recent disputes over fiscal arrangements and transfers, disputes are more technical and intergovernmental. There is no broader sense of alienation among the general Ontario population comparable to Alberta.

The provincial party systems are also different. While the two provinces happen to hold records for the longest unbroken party regimes in Canadian politics (forty-four years for the Alberta PCs and forty-two years for the Ontario PCs), the similarities stop there. The Ontario party system is remarkably durable. Until the election of a Green MPP in 2018, the Ontario Legislative Assembly had had the same three parties since 1955.[2] The Alberta system is more fluid, with Social Credit dominating the province from 1935–1971 but then disappearing, and the rise of the Wildrose Party in the 2000s leading to a newly constituted UCP.

Alberta governments are also more dominant. The province has never had a minority government (Ontario has had four since 1975) and opposition parties at times have been reduced to a bare presence. In contrast, Ontario opposition parties have always remained robust, and all three parties held power in a remarkable rotation between 1985 and 1995. Since 1995 the Liberals and PCs have alternated in power while the New Democratic Party (NDP) remains a robust force, vaulting to second place in the legislature in 2018 and retaining that status in 2022. The current Alberta dynamic with two well-matched and experienced government and opposition parties facing each other is new to the province, while Ontario is accustomed to a strong three-way dynamic.

The two conservative parties are also different. The Alberta UCP are a recent construction from the longstanding PCs and the Wildrose Party, which arose largely as a right-wing reaction to what was seen as excessive centrism in the PCs. Jason Kenney's entry into Alberta politics was predicated on bringing the warring parties back together, which he did. But fault lines remained between ideologues and moderates, and became increasingly evident during the COVID pandemic and challenges to Kenney's leadership.

In contrast, the Ontario PCs are an ideologically lurching yet perennially unified group. The party has cycled through the "bland" Bill Davis, the "Common Sense Revolution" of Mike Harris, the distinctive moderation of John Tory (leader from 2004 to 2009), and the more hard-edged Tim Hudak (2009–2014). The party's most recent leader before Ford was Patrick Brown. Brown strongly identified himself with Bill Davis and his moderate legacy, and built a centrist platform in the runup to the 2018 election, embracing climate taxation for example. But Brown's removal in early 2018 due to sexual harassment allegations triggered a leadership race won by Ford, over two more moderate candidates, Christine Elliott and Caroline Mulroney, and a social conservative, Tanya Granic Allen. Ford discarded much of Brown's platform and yet oversaw a unified party to victory. And as we will see, while there has been dissent in the PC caucus, it is not indicative of broader fault lines. In short, despite leading "conservative" parties, Kenney and Ford oversaw very different parties amid historically different party systems and political cultures.

Ford and Kenney—Origins and Political Philosophies

While all provincial premiers tend to dominate their cabinets and governments, Kenney and Ford are particularly outsized personalities that monopolized attention and overshadowed the rest of their teams. It is important to examine each leader at a personal level to gain clues to their styles and philosophies of governing, which we can then link to their policies and especially their response to COVID-19.

Jason Kenney has spent his entire adult life in politics and political advocacy, briefly as a political staffer, later in the Canadian Taxpayers Federation, and then nineteen years as an MP and eventual cabinet minister, before switching to Alberta politics. Kenney has arguably never really laid out his political philosophy in any extended fashion, though others, especially his opponents, have conjectured at length. But Kenney is widely associated with having acute political and ideological antennae and a strategic mindset that bridges ideology and pragmatism. His reputation for outreach as a federal minister to ethnic and racial communities has become almost apocryphal, and for a long time was key to the Kenney image as a strategic politician. His move to provincial politics with the express goal of reunifying the two warring parties can also be seen as evidence of a careful and strategic approach to politics.

Doug Ford has a more complicated background. His chief job before politics was working in the family business, Deco Labels, a small Toronto manufacturer. His father and the founder of the business, Doug Ford Sr., served briefly as a backbench MP in the Harris conservatives in the 1990s. Most importantly, his brother Rob Ford was a Toronto municipal councillor first elected in 2000, becoming mayor in 2010 for a single stormy term. Doug Ford Jr. did not run for office until 2010, when he took over his brother's municipal seat. He served a single term and then unsuccessfully ran for mayor himself in 2014, in place of his terminally ill brother. (The seat was then held by a nephew, Michael Ford, who was himself elected to the legislature in 2022 as a member of his uncle's caucus, perpetuating the image of a family political machine.)

Surprisingly, Doug Ford has laid out his political philosophy, at least in a rudimentary way, in the book *Ford Nation*, written in his voice but presenting a single Ford family approach to politics.[3] A key recurring concept in *Ford Nation* is "customer service." Ford repeatedly refers to this as the core of the Ford family approach to politics. While starting with the general delivery of public services, Ford frames this as a larger approach anchored on personal contact: "Return every single phone call or, better yet, show up at the caller's door."[4] The tendency of both Rob and Doug Ford to give out their personal phone numbers and to take and return individual citizen calls is well documented, along with indeed showing up unexpectedly at their homes. More than just a personal quirk, this fundamentally reflects the Ford view of politics as retail and individual, and a possible inability to think in broader systemic terms. This is quite different from the strategic mindset attributed to Jason Kenney. And while Ford repeatedly expresses support for "business," this is based more on his own self-identified background and retail approach to politics, rather than an ideological commitment to market forces or small government and libertarian values. This is key to understanding his response to COVID-19 and how it differed from Kenney.

On the other hand, one commonality with Ford and Kenney is their chronic positioning against an external enemy. Another recurring phrase in *Ford Nation* is disdain for "downtown [Toronto] elites," and establishment "lefties" that the Fords positioned themselves against. This is not unlike Kenney's positioning against central Canada and Ottawa.

Ford has been compared to Donald Trump and other disruptive politicians because of his amateurism and impulsiveness. But he does not display the same level of disdain and contempt for government and experts, at least not publicly. Nor is Ford narcissistic by the standards of modern politicians, though he attracted ridicule for pursuing a customized van at government expense.[5] Rather, Ford projects a sense of paternalism—an image of an authentic, well-meaning, even humble, leader who wants to do his best for the province. This taps into a longstanding tradition of paternalistic leadership in Ontario politics, reminiscent of not only Bill Davis but also Dalton McGuinty, known for his "Premier Dad" image and phrase "it may not be popular, but it's the right thing to do."[6] Ford occasionally brings his family into the public spotlight, and of course acts as the patriarch of the "Ford family" political force.[7]

In contrast, Jason Kenney struggles to project personal authenticity. A life narrative shaped entirely by politics has left him with a combative and single-minded image. His adoption of the "blue truck" to campaign through the province was seen as contrived (see Chase Remillard and Tyler Nagel's chapter) and not a natural fit with his personality and character. Kenney does fit with an Alberta history of strong, distinctive premiers. But Kenney lacks the paternalism of Ernest Manning and Peter Lougheed, nor the man-of-the-people style of Ralph Klein (who shares many characteristics with Doug Ford). Rather, Kenney appears solely as a political animal, driven by ideology and strategy.

Overall then, while Kenney has a long political record associated with a strategic mindset that balances ideology and pragmatism, Ford has a more eclectic record, anchored in his family narrative and more impulsive than consistently ideological in a conventional sense. This is important for analyzing their governments and especially their responses to COVID-19.

Governments before March 2020

The Kenney government came to power with a clear agenda. While explored more fully elsewhere throughout this book, we can identify two overarching strategies. The first was a rollback of many of the initiatives of the Notley NDP government, which the UCP saw as unnecessarily costly and/or interventionist, in favour of more small-government and market-based policies. The second was a determined assault to advance Alberta's interests externally, including a more confrontational approach to Ottawa and the targeting of pipeline opponents. These priorities were both consistent with the long-time views of Kenney and his party. They also clearly tapped into longstanding patterns in Alberta politics, particularly confrontation with the federal government.

The Ford government was more erratic. One of Ford's first moves was to downsize Toronto city council, an unexpected and seemingly revengeful action; he also instituted an immediate freeze on government hiring and restrictions on small expenditures.[8] Yet these were more impulsive than indicative of a clear governing strategy. On a larger scale, Ford cancelled the Wynne government's cap-and-trade program and other green energy programs, along with a basic income pilot project and planned minimum-wage increases, and instituted "free speech" policy requirements for universities. He also capped public sector wage increases at 1 per cent.[9] But the government showed a wavering commitment to confrontation. After announcing in-year cuts to municipalities, these were reversed,[10] as was a controversial change to autism programming. While the government certainly made significant cuts, they were not always as consistent or as deep as some anticipated.[11] In education, a slow-burning series of rotating teacher strikes dragged out, suggesting the government was determined to meet its objectives yet not prepared to provoke a full-scale walkout. The government also brought in performance-based funding for the university sector but showed a tepid commitment to serious change in post-secondary education, quite different from the major cuts and interventions in Alberta.

The competence of the Ford government was also unclear. The Harris government of the 1990s was noted for its exceptionally strong understanding of government and its successful harnessing of the bureaucracy to pursue its strategic goals.[12] In contrast, the Ford government regularly went off-message on strange tangents, such as the customized van. Much of the initial chaos was attributed to the premier's first principal secretary Dean French, who was widely accused of personalized and erratic decisions.[13] However, responsibility ultimately lies with Doug Ford and his idiosyncratic ways of operating.

One of the most high-profile examples of this erraticism was Ford's nomination of Ron Taverner to serve as the new commissioner of the Ontario Provincial Police (OPP).[14] While there were good arguments for bringing in outside leadership to the OPP, Taverner was a seventy-two-year-old district superintendent within the Toronto police force, showing no obvious distinction to head the provincial police force. He was, however, a long-time acquaintance of Ford, overseeing the district of Etobicoke where the Ford family is based. The Taverner nomination was eventually withdrawn but not before the government spent considerable political capital on it.

Overall then the Ford government was ideological but inconsistent. There was limited sense of an overall cohesive strategy, or a disciplined commitment to follow through on major items regardless of political opposition and difficulties. When the government did dig in its heels, it was on erratic and sometimes minor items. While the Kenney government also has its share of policy retreats and dubious appointments and initiatives, it stands, for better or worse, as a much more disciplined and consistent operation compared to Ford in Ontario.

Jason Kenney also faced a clearer legislative opposition in the Alberta NDP, led by former premier Rachel Notley. The straightforward polarization, and Notley's experience and enduring popularity, gave clarity to Alberta's legislative and partisan struggles. In contrast, the multipolar Ontario party system became even more complicated when Doug Ford came to power, nearly obliterating the Liberals to 7 seats in the 124 seat legislative assembly and driving their leader Kathleen Wynne to political retirement, while the NDP under Andrea Horvath unusually formed the Official Opposition with forty seats. Ford thus faced a divided opposition— one party profoundly weakened, and the other relatively inexperienced— and it was in the PC's long-term strategic interest to keep it fractured.

The two leaders and governments also had very different relationships with the federal government, each consistent with historic provincial patterns. Jason Kenney came to power explicitly promoting an aggressive stance against the federal Liberal government and central Canada in general. Kenney's Alberta-first stance promoted pipelines and targeted equalization programs. This is of course consistent with Alberta's longstanding combative relationship with Ottawa. In contrast, while Ontario has been more assertive in the twenty-first century on issues of fiscal federalism, its overall relationship with the federal government has long been pragmatic, with issues being more technical than combatively political.

Doug Ford in fact had a curious relationship with the federal Liberal government. In the fall 2019 federal election Prime Minister Justin Trudeau regularly attacked Ford and his cuts as an example of what a federal Conservative government would do. Yet Ford did not directly respond and remained on the sidelines of the election. Following the Liberal minority win, Ford issued a conciliatory statement congratulating Trudeau and pledging to work with the renewed government.[15] Later Ford did get into political combat with the federal Liberals at the height of issues around procuring sufficient COVID vaccines[16] but even this dissipated by the 2021 federal election in which Ford reportedly instructed his party to not get involved[17] and in turn Trudeau did not attack Ford. Overall, the patterns in each province are not surprising—combative in Alberta, pragmatic in Ontario—and both are highly consistent with the longstanding relationships each province has with the federal government.

A final pre-COVID comparative aspect is the direct relationship between the two premiers. Initially, Ford and Kenney appeared close both ideologically and personally, as part of a larger group of conservative men premiers coming to power, including Manitoba's Brian Pallister and Saskatchewan's Scott Moe. While their personalities and backgrounds had little in common, both Kenney and Ford embodied traditional masculine values of aggressiveness and confrontation. Kenney reportedly referred early on to a "bromance" between the two and hailed Ford's early cancellation of the Wynne government's cap-and-trade approach to carbon taxation.[18] However, over time the relationship grew more pragmatic. It probably did not serve either politician to be too closely associated with the other, given the conflicting national priorities of their provinces. The arrival of the COVID-19 pandemic then forced both to concentrate on local priorities. And despite similar pandemic responses at times, they did not seek a common front.

To conclude this section, the pre-COVID Ford and Kenney governments were ideologically on the same track, but operated differently. Some of these differences are attributable to each leader's distinct philosophy of governing. Others followed logically from the different historic patterns and specific political and economic contexts of the two provinces.

COVID Responses

This background is essential for examining each premier and government's response to the COVID-19 pandemic—by far the dominant issue for both governments. At the height of the pandemic in late 2020 and early 2021, both were seen as among the weakest responses to the pandemic in Canada. But in Alberta, there was a significant polarization of public opinion on COVID-related measures, and a major rebellion within the UCP and Kenney's political base. In Ontario, opinion was less polarized and political rebellion more marginal. And in both cases, the premier's personal style of governing was key to the pandemic response.

Given its complexity and ongoing nature at the time of writing, I will not get into a detailed examination of either province's COVID responses, and in any event the Alberta response is covered more fully elsewhere in this book. But we can take a high-level view and identify the different motivations and dynamics behind each province's, and each premier's, response.

In Ontario, Doug Ford's initial reactions swung widely. As late as 12 March 2020, two days after the global pandemic had been declared, Ford urged families to relax and "go on vacation."[19] Yet later that day the province suspended schools until April. In the next weeks, Ford was a model of patrician leadership in the style of Bill Davis, largely supporting and deferring to expert authorities on public health measures. When a small group of protestors appeared on the Ontario Legislature lawn, Ford memorably dismissed them as a "bunch of yahoos"—a significant phrasing for someone occasionally accused of yahoo status himself.[20] On the other hand, the more substantive provincial response was weak. Most importantly, retroactive studies have found significant and deadly failings in the provincial long-term care system.[21] The government was better at overall communication of health restrictions, led by Ford in daily press conferences, than the tougher work of systemic responses to major underlying vulnerabilities.

As the second wave built in the fall of 2020, contrasts were made between the Kenney and Ford responses; the former as ideological and the latter as pragmatic. The *Globe and Mail* remarked: "The country's two leading provincial conservative figures have taken drastically different approaches to COVID-19."[22] The difference was most noticeable in style. Both spoke about making difficult decisions, but Kenney framed the difficulties as ideological, while Ford's concerns were more pragmatic, especially about the disruption to businesses.

In line with his background, Doug Ford was clearly uncomfortable restricting commercial activity and forcing businesses to close, and he expressed this often. In October 2020 he said, announcing new and continuing restrictions:

> I can't stress enough . . . how difficult, how painful it was to make this decision. . . . [If] I put my business hat on I'd switch those things open in a heartbeat but I can't. I have to listen to the health experts. It's proven, it works, and that's how we've been able to move forward this whole time. I'm a business person. I don't want to close these down but health trumps my personal belief of doing something.[23]

Digging deeper, the reality is more complicated, though again consistent with Ford's philosophy of governing. Indeed, evidence suggests that "business" rather than either ideology or public health science determined the increasingly complex restrictions and exemptions in the province. Examining the provincial lobbyist registry, the *Toronto Star* found clear links between business lobbying and exemptions in the provincial restrictions.[24]

But absent from Ford's rhetoric were references to larger abstract ideas of personal freedom or individual choice. Ford did not express the same sort of discomfort about mask mandates, social distancing, or other general public health measures. He did not pour his heart out in the same way about school closings as he did with businesses. He was in fact more likely to take a patrician attitude, as he did in the early days of the pandemic, telling "folks" (a common Ford phrase) that necessary measures had to be taken for the public good and urging their compliance.

In contrast, Jason Kenney tweeted on 13 October 2020: "We're not going to enforce our way out of COVID. Alberta's approach is to focus on the broader health of society—physical, mental, social, and economic—by encouraging personal responsibility, rather than micro-managing people's lives."[25] There was a clear and unmistakable difference between the two leaders, corresponding broadly to both their own political philosophies and the political contexts of their provinces. Ford was reactive and paternalistic, while Kenney expressed more overall reluctance and only grudging assent to restrictions.

Contrast is found even in how both leaders violated their own COVID restrictions. In May 2020, Ford admitted his own family had broken social distancing rules by gathering together for Mother's Day.[26] In contrast, Kenney apologized in June 2021 for the infamous "Sky Palace" dinner in which he and several ministers and staff were photographed eating together in violation of restrictions, all in professional dress. The Sky Palace dinner did further damage to Kenney's image, while Ford's Mother's Day actions probably reinforced his own family paternalistic brand and Ford's projection of flawed but well-meaning authenticity. There is also a contrast in how the leaders dealt with ministers who travelled internationally over the 2020 winter holidays despite strong advice to avoid foreign travel. Ontario Finance Minister Rod Phillips resigned after a holiday trip, with Ford calling the trip "unacceptable" (though Ford had learned about the trip while it was in progress, and Phillips was later reinstated to cabinet in June).[27] In contrast, a much larger contingent of UCP cabinet ministers and MLAs were found to have travelled over the holidays, and Kenney was slow to take responsibility and impose disciplinary measures in what became known as the "Alohagate" affair.[28]

Partisan and Political Environments

The two leaders also faced different partisan environments. In Alberta, Kenney faced strong opposition to the pandemic response within his own caucus and the UCP grassroots. This led to an April 2021 public letter signed by seventeen UCP MLAs condemning pandemic restrictions. Even while being criticized by much of the province for not sufficiently responding to the pandemic, Kenney faced very clear challenges from the right to the restrictions he did introduce. The insurrection continued to grow, especially with the return of former rival Brian Jean to the legislature in March 2022 expressly as a challenger to Kenney's leadership.

Doug Ford did not face the same scale of challenges. Two backbench MPPs, Belinda Karahalios and Roman Baber, were expelled from caucus in July 2020 and January 2021 for opposing pandemic restrictions. A third, Rick Nicholls, was expelled in August 2021 for refusing to be vaccinated, and a fourth, Lindsey Park, resigned from the PC caucus in October 2021 also over her vaccination status. A fifth outspoken anti-restrictions MPP, Randy Hillier, had already been expelled from the Tory caucus before the pandemic. While Karahalios co-founded a new party, the New Blue Party, and Nicholls affiliated himself with the minor Ontario Party, this opposition was far more individualistic and eclectic than the organized dissent found in the UCP. It did not constitute a serious threat to Ford's grip on the durable Ontario PC party. More generally, while there were many reports of serious and prolonged discussions in the Ford cabinet over COVID responses, leaks and public dissent were limited and there was no strong sense of an ideological fault line within the cabinet nor the larger caucus.

This reflected larger public opinion in the province. While comparable data at the provincial level is somewhat limited, Ontarians clearly were more generally supportive of pandemic measures than Albertans. For example, a January 2021 poll[29] found that 75 per cent of Ontarians supported the closing of most retail stores and restriction to pick up only, compared to 47 per cent of Albertans (though British Columbia was even lower at 46 per cent). Religious institutions were a special flashpoint for Albertans, given the historically close intertwining of religion and Alberta politics; 83 per cent of Ontarians supported the closing of places of worship compared to 62 per cent of Albertans. An Edmonton church, GraceLife Church, refused to comply with restrictions and became a rallying point garnering national attention. While some Ontario churches also refused to comply, their impact was more isolated. A May 2021 poll[30] comparing vaccine acceptance found that 73 per cent of Ontarians had taken the vaccine or would as soon as they could—above the national average of 71 per cent—while only 61 per cent of Albertans said the same. Interestingly, outright opposition was not as different—9 per cent of Albertans said they would never get the shot compared to 6 per cent of Ontarians (and 10 per cent of residents in Saskatchewan and Manitoba)—but hesitancy was much higher in Alberta. (See below for actual rates of vaccination in each province.)

Jason Kenney thus led both a divided party and a province where a significant portion of the population was skeptical of COVID-19 measures. Regardless of his own views—which may themselves have contributed to and reinforced some of the skepticism—Kenney did face a volatile situation, most importantly within his own party. In contrast, Doug Ford had a much more free hand politically. While there was likely more skepticism expressed privately within PC circles, his party remained fundamentally united publicly, with malcontents quickly marginalized. And Ontario public opinion was more solidly in favour of restrictions. We must also take into account the differing economic and fiscal climates of the two provinces. The Albertan economy and deficit were already weak and concerning even before the pandemic struck, fuelling further worries about the impact of business restrictions and closures. In contrast, while the Ontario economy was also at risk, it lacked the same worry of being pushed over the brink by pandemic restrictions.

The greater political freedom allowed Ford's idiosyncratic approach to flourish in the pandemic. At times, the Ford government *exceeded* recommended measures. This was particularly evident in April 2021, when new province-wide measures were introduced to combat the third wave. Among the many measures, the government announced that police would have the power to randomly stop pedestrians and drivers to ask why they were out of their homes. This alarmed many, and at least twenty-three police services, including Toronto, Ottawa, and Hamilton, announced they would not conduct random stops. The measures were quickly withdrawn and Ford said "we got it wrong. We made a mistake."[31] Yet it is hard to imagine Jason Kenney ever pursuing such a strong infringement of civil liberties. A smaller but high-profile reversal at the same time was on playgrounds. The new measures shut down playgrounds, despite expert consensus that they were low risk; after an outcry from parents, playgrounds were reopened. According to one analysis, the overreach was motivated by a desire for Ford to look sufficiently proactive after a tepid response earlier in February[32]—thus motivated by image rather than ideological reasons.

Perhaps the all-time illustration of Doug Ford's unique style of policy-making occurred in May 2021. The Ontario government announced that schools would stay closed for the remainder of the school year—but outdoor graduation ceremonies would still be held. School boards and principals questioned the practicality of the latter. Upon closer inquiry, Ford revealed that the outdoor graduation idea had come through a letter from a young boy named Arthur. In true Ford style, he had then visited Arthur's house, unannounced, to discuss the idea further.[33]

Ford also showed emotion and apologized for errors, sometimes tearing up, in a way quite different from the stoic and combative Kenney. After withdrawing the police powers above, Ford said: ". . . as premier, as I said right from the beginning, the buck stops with me. Again, I'm sorry and I apologize to each and every one of you."[34] Such contriteness is typical for Ford, who at least *appears* to wear his heart on his sleeve, as did his brother Rob. Ford also appears impulsive and overly eager in his actions, such as early in the pandemic when he personally drove his own truck to pick up a donation of masks.[35] As in all things Ford, personal engagement and "customer service" are at the heart of his philosophy of governance, different from the more ideological and supposedly strategic Kenney.

Still, the two leaders shared one thing in common in mid-2021: low popularity. Ford's popularity initially soared at the start of the pandemic, jumping from 31 per cent in March 2020 to 69 per cent in April.[36] It slowly declined but was still at 50 per cent in March 2021. In contrast, Kenney had no initial peak at the beginning of COVID, and went from 47 per cent in March 2020 to 39 per cent in March 2021. Both then dropped dramatically, so that by June they were two of the lowest ranking premiers in popularity in Canada (along with Manitoba's Brian Pallister). Ford's June approval rating was 35 per cent and Kenney's 31 per cent; in comparison, other conservative premiers were much higher, such as Quebec's Francois Legault at 66 per cent and Saskatchewan's Scott Moe at 61 per cent.

But as the pandemic continued, the two provinces, and their leaders' political fortunes, began to diverge further. While Alberta dropped most restrictions in early July and Kenney proclaimed "the best summer ever," Ontario retained key restrictions, especially mask requirements. Most Ontario businesses, especially retail stores, were reopened and were able to operate with some normalcy. This likely relieved Ford of his chief concern, as unlike Kenney, he never expressed much discomfort with restrictions on principle, but only their direct economic effects. On the other hand, both premiers resisted vaccine passports despite their adoption in other provinces, though Ford reversed his position in late August.

By fall 2021, the public health situation was vastly different in the two provinces. On 24 September 2021, Ontario's COVID rates were half that of Alberta's, with 6,500 cases per 100,000 in Alberta compared to 3,949 in Ontario.[37] Even more, hospitalizations were drastically different, with 1,061 in Alberta, far higher than any other province, compared to only 308 in much more populous Ontario. Vaccination rates also differed at 72 per cent for eligible Albertans compared to 79 per cent for Ontario, though most other provinces had crested 80 per cent.[38] The disastrous situation in Alberta led to Kenney's dramatic 15 September announcement reimposing heavy restrictions and adopting vaccine passports, along with an admission that the "best summer ever" had been a disaster. In contrast, Doug Ford's Ontario retained a relatively steady course.

By early 2022, the two leaders and governments were on vastly different political paths. Ford and the Ontario PCs grew steadily in the polls while the opposition parties struggled for traction, leading to a smashing PC re-election victory in June 2022 with an increased seat count. In contrast, the UCP were anything but united, with the disastrous spiral of challenges to Kenney's leadership leading to his May 2022 decision to step down as leader in favour of a replacement.

Conclusion

There is much more that can be said about both the Kenney and Ford governments. However, in this final section, we will consider how they ultimately compare. The beginning of this chapter noted the similarities in how Doug Ford and Jason Kenney came to power, within a year of each other. They also both oversaw conservative governments generally pursuing reductions in the scope and size of the public sector. Yet they led two quite different provinces, and this chapter has outlined their very different personalities, governing styles, and approaches to COVID-19. They also experienced very different political fates. Ultimately, which prevails—the similarities or the differences? And what does this comparison ultimately tell us about Jason Kenney and his government, the focus of this book?

Jason Kenney and Doug Ford are very different personalities. But they ultimately share common views, especially a skepticism of traditional government and intellectual elites. They both favour, at least in principle, a broad rollback of the public sector and scope of government. For Kenney this is based on libertarian individualism and a belief in market forces. For Ford it is a more instinctive sense of "business" unencumbered by government regulation. They also rely on constructing and emphasizing external threats. As premier, Kenney emphasized external enemies of Alberta, especially in central Canada. While Toronto resident Doug Ford himself nominally fits in that category, Ford has long positioned himself against his own political enemies of Toronto's "downtown elites."

The two leaders operate in different contexts. Kenney fit with Alberta's historic political traditions of strong leaders and populist politics, at least until his stunning demise. Despite his sometimes amateurish and impulsive style, Ford ultimately fits with Ontario's tradition of pragmatism and "managing government." Kenney operated in a volatile environment with both a polarized legislature and significant internal dissent within his own ranks. Ford enjoyed a more multipolar environment without sustained opposition, and led a party that has always been highly adaptable and continued to follow him throughout the pandemic with little (public) dissent.

But while their styles and political context differ considerably, the substantive outputs of the Ford and Kenney governments are not as dissimilar. Both cut back the public sector, in a clear commitment to restraint and smaller government. They valorize the private sector, and show little interest in cultivating other types of elite opinion or support. Kenney's government made more drastic cuts, but also dealt with a more difficult fiscal and economic environment for much of its term. Both governments followed erratic approaches to managing the pandemic, failing to act particularly on systemic problems and issues, though as time went on, the provinces had increasingly different strategies.

What we ultimately see in any comparison is that both Jason Kenney and his government are fundamentally an Alberta phenomenon, in the same way that Doug Ford and his government are of Ontario. Each led parties rooted in their provincial political traditions, and governed distinct and contrasting populations. Jason Kenney is a more disciplined political thinker than Doug Ford, who is an unusual figure in Canadian politics by any standard. But both are fundamentally leaders of the political right, and each pursued their policy and ideological agendas in ways that suited their province.

NOTES

1   Sid Noel, "The Ontario Political Culture: An Interpretation," in *The Government and Politics of Ontario*, ed. Graham White, 5th ed. (Toronto: University of Toronto Press, 1997).

2   While two of the MPPs who broke from the Ford PCs over pandemic issues affiliated themselves with small parties for the remainder of their time in the legislature, they failed to be re-elected in 2022 under their new party labels.

3   Doug Ford and Rob Ford, Ford Nation: Two Brothers, One Vision-The True Story of the People's Mayor (Toronto: Harper Collins, 2016).

4   Ford and Ford, *Ford Nation*, 7.

5   Mike Crawley, "Doug Ford's van customization has $50K price tag, documents show," *CBC News*, 25·February 2019.

6   Anna Esselment, "An Inside Look at the Liberals in Power," *The Politics of Ontario*, ed. Cheryl Collier and Jonathan Malloy (Toronto: University of Toronto Press, 2017).

7   The visibility of Ford's family and especially his four daughters seems to have diminished since his daughter Krista Ford Haynes became outspoken against COVID-19 vaccines. See Mike Crawley, "Doug Ford acknowledges division in his family over COVID-19 rules," *CBC News*, 15 February 2022.

8   Justin Giovannetti, "Ontario's Doug Ford orders hiring freeze for public servants," *Globe and Mail*, 18 June 2018.

9   Canadian Press, "Ontario government passes bill to cap public sector wage increases at 1 per cent," 8 November 2019.

10 Jeff Gray and Laura Stone, "Ontario Premier Doug Ford cancelling retroactive cuts to municipalities," *Globe and Mail*, 27 May 2019.

11 Laura Stone and Jeff Gray, "Ontario government plans to balance budget in five years, with deficit now at $11.7-billion," *Globe and Mail*, 11 April 2019.

12 David R. Cameron and Graham White, *Cycling into Saigon: The Conservative Transition in Ontario* (Toronto: University of Toronto Press, 1999).

13 CBC News (2019a), "Doug Ford's chief of staff resigns following patronage controversy," 21 June 2019.

14 CBC News (2019b), "Ron Taverner, friend of Doug Ford, withdraws from consideration for OPP commissioner," 6 March 2019.

15 Travis Dhanraj, "Canada election: Did Doug Ford laying low work for Andrew Scheer?" *Global News*, 22 October 2019.

16 Joan Bryden, "Trudeau pushes back against Premier Ford's criticism of federal vaccine procurement," *Canadian Press*, 31 March 2021.

17 Robert Benzie, "Doug Ford was Justin Trudeau's punching bag in 2019. For this campaign, insiders say, the leaders will keep the peace," *Toronto Star*, 16 August 2021.

18 Kieran Leavitt and Alex Boyd, "Jason Kenney and Doug Ford's bad bromance: Why the premiers' close friendship seems to be cooling," *Toronto Star*, 9 February 2020.

19 Jacquie Miller, "Coronavirus: Premier Doug Ford's advice for travel on March break no longer applies," *Ottawa Citizen*, 13 March 2020.

20 Ryan Rocca, "'Bunch of yahoos': Doug Ford blasts Toronto protest against coronavirus-related restrictions," *Global News*, 25 April 2020.

21 Nicole Thompson and Shawn Jeffords, "Ontario had no plan to address pandemic or protect residents in long-term care, final commission report says," *Canadian Press*, 30 April 2021.

22 Laura Stone and Jeff Keller, "In Alberta and Ontario, two conservative premiers take very different approaches to COVID-19," *Globe and Mail*, 30 October 2020.

23 Stone and Keller, "In Alberta and Ontario."

24 Richard Warnica and Andrew Bailey, "Several of Doug Ford's key pandemic decisions were swayed by business interests, Star analysis suggests," *Toronto Star*, 15 July 2021.

25 https://twitter.com/jkenney/status/1316030172148064261?s=20.

26 Shanifa Nasser, "Doug Ford admits daughters visited his home on the weekend, contrary to Ontario's COVID-19 rules," *CBC News*, 11 May 2020.

27 Chris Herhalt, "Rod Phillips Resigns as Ontario Finance Minister Following Secret Pandemic Getaway," *CTV News*, 31 December 2020, https://toronto.ctvnews.ca/rod-phillips-resigns-as-ontario-finance-minister-following-secret-pandemic-getaway-1.5249471.

28 "Editorial: Albertans Won't Forget Aloha-gate," *Edmonton Journal*, 4 January 2021.

29 Maru Blue, "Support for Pandemic Lockdown Rules," 9 January 2021, https://www.marugroup.net/polling.

30 Abacus Data, "Vaccine Acceptance is on the Rise," 15 May 2021, https://abacusdata.ca/vaccine-acceptance-on-the-rise/.

31 Kerrisa Wilson, "'We got it wrong:' Ford says about COVID-19 police powers to arbitrarily stop people," *CP24 News*, 22 April 2021.

32   Mike Crawley, "The inside story of Doug Ford's COVID-19 climbdowns," *CBC News*, 22 April 2021.

33   Jacquie Miller, "Who is Arthur? How a boy from Etobicoke helped the Ontario premier with education policy," *Ottawa Citizen*, 3 June 2021.

34   Wilson, "We Got it Wrong."

35   Valerie Dittrich, "COVID-19: Premier Doug Ford seen personally picking up mask donation from dental office," *National Post*, 31 March 2020.

36   Angus Reid Institute, Premiers' Performance: Ford and Kenney's popularity & political fortunes bear brunt of pandemic management, 9 June 2021.

37   Globe and Mail, "COVID-19 By the Numbers," accessed 26 September 2021 at globeandmail.com.

38   Government of Canada. Government of Canada National Vaccination Coverage, accessed 26 September 2021 at https://health-infobase.canada.ca/covid-19/vaccination-coverage/.

20

"With Comorbidities": The Politics of COVID-19 and the Kenney Government

Lisa Young

The COVID-19 pandemic ended Jason Kenney's political career.

Kenney entered the pandemic with political "comorbidities"—factors that would make it more difficult to survive the political challenge the pandemic represented. His United Conservative Party (UCP) was a product of a merger that had not fully gelled, even when it won a huge majority government. In his first year in office he was unable to deliver on his promise of "jobs, economy, pipelines." His inexperienced government fumbled some of its first attempts to tackle health care spending, most notably starting a highly visible fight with doctors by cancelling their contract.

As the waves of infection rolled across the province, the Kenney government was torn between two contradictory imperatives. On one hand, many MLAs and party supporters favoured a minimal response, taking some steps to protect "the vulnerable" but otherwise allowing Albertans to chart their own course and exercise personal responsibility. The deep strain of populism in Alberta's political culture, characterized by distrust of scientific expertise and government, contributed to this sentiment. On the other hand, many voices—including doctors, epidemiologists, and other experts—demanded government interventions to reduce the spread of infection. The consequence of ignoring these calls included not only a mounting death toll, but also the prospect of overwhelming the province's health care system, forcing doctors to implement triage protocols determining which patients would receive treatment and which would be left to die.

Caught between these imperatives, Kenney and his government alternated between inaction and action, sometimes dismissing measures as ineffective or inappropriate only days before enacting them. This policy response is best characterized largely as a failure. As of May 2022, Alberta Health Services reported over 4,300 Albertans had died of COVID. This is likely an underestimate; using the parameters for Alberta from a study published in *The Lancet*, we can estimate total deaths as of May 2022 of over 6,000.[1] Alberta's reported death rate was lower than that of Quebec, Saskatchewan, and Manitoba, but higher than all other provinces.[2] Alberta's rate of cases exceeded the rest of Canada's in the second through fourth waves; this will have implications for the prevalence of Long COVID in the population (see Figure 20.1). Alberta's vaccination rates are the lowest of any province (see Figure 20.3). At least 15,000 surgeries were postponed. On the positive side of the ledger, Alberta's approach kept schools open more than other provinces outside the Atlantic bubble[3] and relatively weak public health restrictions allowed businesses to remain open.

Just as evident as this policy failure was a political failure that culminated in Kenney's resignation as party leader. The government's approach to COVID satisfied neither those who wanted minimal government intervention nor those demanding a robust response. Confidence in the ability of the government to manage the pandemic declined precipitously, as did the premier's approval rating, from a high of 61 per cent in 2019 to only 11 per cent in the fall of 2021. Backbench MLAs publicly criticized the government's approach to COVID and tried to hold a vote of non-confidence in their leader, setting in motion the leadership review process that resulted in Kenney's resignation in May 2022.

Alberta's failed pandemic response is in large measure a product of the internal turmoil of the Kenney government. Caucus unrest made the government hesitant to act, contributing to delays and unwise public health decisions. These delays and failures to act added to the contentiousness of the pandemic response, eroding public confidence in the provincial government's ability to manage the crisis. The premier found himself defending the government's inaction to reporters at COVID briefings, and then justifying taking any action at all to enraged citizens who joined his Facebook Live events. Each wave of the virus further weakened the Kenney government politically, culminating in his resignation. And, as Kenney's grasp on power became weaker, so too did the province's pandemic response, resulting in preventable deaths from the virus.

The First Wave (March–May 2020)

On 11 March 2020, the World Health Organization declared COVID-19 a global pandemic, Italy declared a national lockdown, and Alberta reported its first confirmed cases of COVID. The Alberta Chief Medical Officer of Health (CMOH), Dr. Deena Hinshaw, issued her first orders, banning large gatherings and meetings with international participants. By Friday, there were numerous closures and cancellations, and the next week the premier declared a state of emergency and Dr. Hinshaw ordered schools, post-secondaries, and child-care facilities closed. Like the rest of Canada, the province was "locked down."

Dr. Hinshaw was to become the public face of the government's response to the COVID pandemic. The CMOH is a role occupied by a medical doctor who serves as a key advisor to government during a public health emergency. The Alberta Public Health Act authorizes government to act on the advice of a CMOH during an emergency, and assigns significant authority to the CMOH, who issues public health orders. Although the Act is somewhat unclear on how independently the CMOH can exercise their authority, Hinshaw maintained throughout the pandemic that her role was to advise government, which would decide.[4]

Within government, the body responsible for making decisions about health restrictions once an emergency was declared was the Emergency Management Cabinet Committee. Chaired by the premier, the committee included the ministers of transportation, finance, environment, Indigenous relations, community and social services, justice, education and children's services, as well as one government MLA.

While the CMOH advises cabinet, issues public health orders, and keeps the public informed, Alberta Health Services (AHS), the province-wide health system, shouldered responsibility for organizing all testing, providing care to individuals infected with COVID-19, coordinating the eventual vaccination campaign, and enforcing the CMOH's orders.

Essential to a public health approach to infectious disease is the practice of "test, trace and isolate." Testing establishes prevalence and allows public health officials to trace the source of infection and alert those who might be infected. A positive test triggers mandatory isolation to limit spread of infection. In pandemics, public health officials supplement this approach with "non-pharmaceutical interventions" designed to reduce the likelihood of transmission. These include restricting the numbers of people who can gather, closing schools, workplaces and borders, and requiring people to "shelter in place" in their homes. With limited capacity to test for COVID at the outset of the pandemic, and seeing it ravage the health care system in Italy, Alberta and many other jurisdictions turned quickly to measures designed to limit the ability of the virus to spread.

Weeks into the lockdown, with world oil prices plummeting and public anxiety about COVID high, the premier made a public address from the Cabinet Room, comparing the situation to the Spanish Flu, the Great Depression, and the Great War. Facing the interlinked challenges of COVID and the economy, Kenney employed rhetoric common to Alberta populists, calling on Albertans to be like the "buffalo [and] herd closely together and face the storm head on, coming out of it strong and united."[5] The address established what would become a consistent pattern in his public statements, rebutting the notion that the province should do less or let the virus run its course. In this instance, he indicated that inaction could result in up to 32,000 deaths and collapse of the health care system.

Although the government response was tinged with a sense of crisis, Alberta's first-wave restrictions were somewhat less stringent than those in many other provinces. Schools were closed and those who could work from home were expected to do so, but the provincial government identified many businesses as "essential workplaces" permitted to stay open; these included most of the energy sector, construction sites, and the agricultural sector. Several outbreaks were associated with meat processing facilities.[6] An outbreak at a Cargill plant in High River resulted in over 1,500 COVID infections (950 of them among Cargill workers) and 3 deaths. Workers at the plant were predominantly recent immigrants, establishing the pattern of COVID having disproportionate impact on racialized workers.

Despite less stringent restrictions, Alberta's overall death toll from COVID during the first wave of the pandemic was relatively low (see

Figure 20.1).[7] Alberta avoided the carnage that occurred in long-term care facilities in Quebec and Ontario. Restrictions on visitors to long-term care homes and limits on the practice of employing staff across multiple facilities implemented in April 2020 may have been helpful in limiting the impact on long-term care, although the protective impact did not extend through the second wave.

Politically, the Kenney government did not benefit from its relatively strong management of the first wave. Unlike other premiers, Kenney did not receive a "pandemic bump" in his approval numbers, which continued the slow decline that had started before the pandemic (for contrast, see Malloy chapter). In part, this may be due to the economic adversity that the province faced, with oil prices dropping sharply, prompting a panicked decision to spend $1.3 billion to prop up the doomed KXL pipeline (as discussed in Rioux's chapter).

Kenney's COVID Manifesto

As the first wave ended, governments had greater opportunity to come to terms with the challenge COVID presented and to develop a coherent policy response. A key stage of policy development is known as "framing." The way a problem is articulated can shape the subsequent policy response. Problem framing is inherently political. As McConnell and Stark observe, the diversity of frames that various governments have used for the COVID crisis "is the product of more than mere crisis pragmatism. It is also underpinned by political ideology, and perceptions of the legitimacy (or not) of state 'interference' and regulation of markets, as well as citizens' individual freedoms."[8]

The UCP's ideological commitment to individualism and personal freedom influenced the framing of COVID as a policy issue from May 2020 on. The party's founding principles refer to "a robust civil society made up of free individuals" and emphasize freedom of speech, worship and assembly, economic freedom, limited government, and fiscal responsibility.[9] The only countervailing pressure mentioned is the last item: "protecting public safety as a primary responsibility of government." The frames employed by the government for the pandemic focused on balancing concerns—"protecting lives and livelihoods"—and protecting the health care system. These can be contrasted to frames that emphasized minimizing or eliminating cases.

Figure 20.1 (a and b). Case and Death Rates, Alberta and
Canada

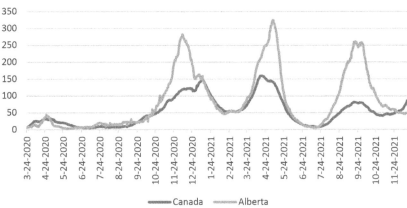

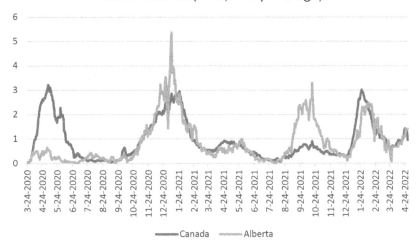

Sources: Calculated from Government of Canada, "COVID-19 Epidemiology Update," https://health-infobase.
canada.ca/covid-19/epidemiological-summary-covid-19-cases.html, (accessed 4 May 2022). Note that the case
rate figure is cut off in mid-December when Alberta stopped offering PCR testing.

Figure 20.2. Stringency Index

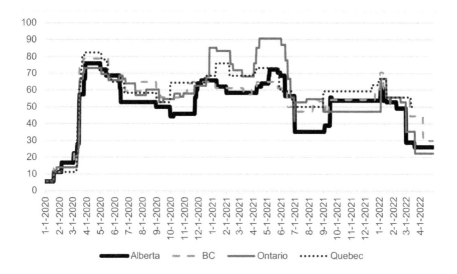

Sources: Calculated from Hale et al., "Oxford COVID-19 Government Response Tracker," https://www.bsg.ox.ac.uk/research/research-projects/covid-19-government-response-tracker. Data use policy: Creative Commons Attribution CC BY standard.

In Alberta, as elsewhere, conservatives opposed stringent public health restrictions and were more inclined to believe COVID did not pose a serious threat. As early as March 2020, Conservative Party voters at the national level were more likely than others to say that they thought the risks of COVID were "overblown."[10] This perception was central to the Kenney government's articulation of its approach going forward.

In late May, as the province began to re-open, Premier Kenney addressed the legislature, setting out what can now be seen as his manifesto for the remainder of the pandemic. He described COVID as "an influenza that does not generally threaten life apart from the most elderly, the immunocompromised, and those with comorbidities."[11] To refer to COVID as "an influenza" is not only incorrect in virological terms, but an effort to diminish the perceived threat posed by COVID to something similar to "the flu." The premier asserted that, for all but the elderly and the vulnerable, the risks associated with COVID infection were small and so the appropriate public health response should be "predicated on protecting the most vulnerable in the strongest and most discrete ways possible because we cannot continue indefinitely to impair the social and economic as well as the mental health and physiological health of the broader population for potentially a year." This framing minimized the potential health consequences of COVID other than death and articulated the policy problem as one of balance between a relatively non-lethal disease and economic, social, and other health considerations.

There are essentially three public health approaches to COVID: the "herd immunity" approach that lets the virus run its course, the "COVID-Zero" approach that tries to eliminate the virus from circulation in a population, and the mitigation approach, which falls between these two alternatives. Mitigation approaches vary considerably, with some focused on minimizing loss of life and others on ensuring health care systems are not overwhelmed (and thus accepting a certain number of deaths). The path the premier charted in his May speech to the legislature signalled an approach focused on mitigation, and one that would be likely to fall closer to the herd immunity end of the mitigation spectrum, as it gave considerable weight to the importance of keeping the economy going, and less to limiting cases.

The Second Wave (October 2020–January 2021)

The Kenney manifesto shaped the province's response to both the second and third waves of COVID. As they began, the government downplayed the public health threat, called on citizens to exercise personal responsibility, and refrained from imposing restrictions until the health system was at risk of being overwhelmed. Inaction and delayed action frequently pushed the burden of imposing restrictions onto municipalities and school boards. The premier's rationalizations for inaction in the days prior to action resulted in muddled messaging that undermined government action once it was taken.

Figure 20.1 shows the per-capita number of COVID cases in Alberta vastly exceeded the number for Canada as a whole through both waves. Deaths exceeded those in the rest of the country only during the second wave. Figure 20.2 shows that Alberta's COVID-related restrictions were less stringent than those in the three larger provinces.

As other jurisdictions prepared for the inevitable second wave in the fall of 2020, the Kenney government did relatively little. In July, it announced a plan for a "near-normal" return to school. Dismayed that masks were not required, the large urban school boards established their own requirements. In August, the province changed its plan to require teachers and students in grades 4–12 to wear masks in public areas. In the absence of a provincial mask mandate, both Calgary and Edmonton adopted mandatory indoor mask bylaws that took effect on 1 August.

Case numbers began to rise in early October, prompting calls to re-introduce restrictions. CMOH Hinshaw imposed a fifteen-person limit on private gatherings in Calgary and Edmonton, but restaurants, casinos, and other public places remained open. The contact-tracing system became overwhelmed, and effectively collapsed, with a backlog of over 20,000 cases by early December.[12] Among the calls for more stringent rules were four open letters to government signed by physicians.[13] Premier Kenney emphasized "personal responsibility" but avoided imposing any additional restrictions, even as case numbers and deaths increased. He disappeared for ten days in mid-November, making no statements or public appearances, virtual or otherwise.

During this period, there were reports of tension between the government and the CMOH and/or her organization. The CBC obtained leaked documents and recordings of meetings that revealed that the premier and cabinet sometimes overruled expert advice, and "pushed an early relaunch strategy that seemed more focused on the economy and avoiding the appearance of curtailing Albertans' freedoms than enforcing compliance to safeguard public health."[14] That a public servant leaked these materials to journalists speaks to the intensity of frustration in the CMOH's office. Longer term, the incident likely weakened the CMOH's ability to influence government. The day it was published, Dr. Hinshaw appeared at a news conference with the health minister and condemned the leak. From that point on, there were no indications from Dr. Hinshaw or her team of dissent from the government's approach.

In late November, the province declared a state of public health emergency, banned indoor social gatherings, and limited outdoor gatherings and places of worship. Students in Grades 7–12 were moved to online classes from the end of November until January, and employees were encouraged to work from home. Restaurants, bars, and casinos were permitted to stay open with some restrictions in place. Case numbers continued to rise. On 8 December, the premier announced a ban on indoor and outdoor social gatherings, a province-wide mask mandate, closure of restaurants/bars and personal services, limits on worship and retail, and a work-from-home order. Figure 20.2 shows this was the first time since June that Alberta's COVID response was as stringent as the three other large provinces. The case numbers began to decline almost immediately.

The delay in taking action can be attributed to the premier and governing party's reluctance to impose restrictions. In announcing these measures, the premier lamented the "crushed dreams and terrible adversity" the restrictions would produce for business owners, and spoke of the "Constitutionally protected rights and freedoms that are being suspended or abridged" in imposing them.[15] With this, the premier signalled both an acknowledgement to the voices within his party that these measures were not consistent with their fundamental beliefs, and his own personal reluctance to impose them. His words would be echoed in the months to come by his critics, some of whom would test his implausible argument that restrictions violated the constitution in court, with no success.

The premier and CMOH urged Albertans to celebrate the holidays at home, warning of the dangers of a post-Christmas spike in infections. But travel outside the province was surprisingly easy, facilitated by a federal-provincial pilot project allowing returning international travellers to Alberta a shorter quarantine if they tested negative for the virus.[16] The ease of international travel enticed a cabinet minister, several UCP MLAs, the premier's chief of staff, and some senior political staff to holiday abroad over the Christmas break.

In late December, journalists reported on these vacationers, leading to what became known as the "Alohagate" scandal. The premier held a press conference on 1 January, indicating he was "not happy" with the vacationers, that he believed they had "made a mistake," but that he took responsibility because he was "not absolutely clear" in his directive that senior officials not travel internationally. After four days of public rage from across the political spectrum, the premier reversed course and asked Minister Allard (who had vacationed in Hawaii) and his chief of staff (who had vacationed in the United Kingdom) to step down.

The travel itself suggests that the dominant belief within cabinet and the premier's office was that the threat posed by the pandemic was not so serious as to cancel a vacation. There also appeared to be a remarkable lack of understanding that senior government officials had to model and even exceed the sacrifices being asked of the general population during a crisis. And, perhaps most important, it signalled that the premier—who played a central and dominant role in the government—might not command the kind of respect and control within his government that had been assumed.

The scandal weakened Premier Kenney and his government. His approval rating, already dropping, fell further (see DeCillia chapter). A premier unable to deliver either the policy desired by his caucus or the promise of electoral success faces an uncertain political future. Having imposed a series of restrictions a segment of his caucus did not agree with and having bungled the Alohagate situation, the premier was weakened as he moved toward the third wave in the spring of 2021.

Third Wave and Caucus Revolt (March–June 2021)

The number of COVID cases declined steadily through January, and the premier announced a new reopening plan tied to the number of hospitalizations. Even as restrictions were being relaxed, case numbers began to rise, so by mid-March the reopening was paused, but not reversed. On 1 April, the eve of the Easter weekend, the premier acknowledged that the province was in a third wave. He announced no new restrictions but emphasized how well prepared the province was to cope with the wave, boasting of its ICU capacity. He pled with Albertans to follow guidelines and avoid indoor gatherings over the holiday, asking for patience and cooperation through this "final" wave of COVID and saying he believed the province would soon move into the "best summer in Alberta history."[17]

Five days later, Kenney once again took to the podium to announce new restrictions, saying "this is not an easy announcement to make." Predicting daily new case counts over 2,000 by the end of the month, he returned the province to restrictions similar to December, saying, "As Premier, my job is to make the tough choices, and to protect the lives and livelihoods of Albertans. The only responsible choice to save lives and protect our health care system is to take immediate action."[18] While announcing the change, the premier noted that the province had become polarized on the question of COVID restrictions. He positioned himself as a centrist, and the restrictions being imposed as a compromise between those who want more stringent rules and those who want to re-open more quickly. His characterization of Alberta as polarized on the issue was confirmed by polling data at the time, which showed that 45 per cent of Albertans believe that their provincial restrictions went too far, and 42 per cent believed they did not go far enough.[19]

Those who believed the provincial restrictions went too far included a significant portion of Kenney's caucus. The next day, fifteen UCP MLAs, none from Calgary or Edmonton, released a letter criticizing the decision to reinstate restrictions: "We have heard from our constituents and they want us to defend their livelihoods and freedoms as Albertans." The letter also hinted at internal strife in the caucus, saying, "For months, we have raised these concerns at the highest levels of government and unfortunately, the approach of the Government has remained the same."[20] This kind of public dissent is seldom tolerated in Canadian governing parties, but Premier Kenney called it "free speech" and did not punish the dissidents.

Despite the province's restrictions and actions by school boards, cases continued to increase. By early May, the province was identifying over 2,000 new COVID cases each day; over 600 Albertans were hospitalized, and over 150 were in intensive care. The province's infection rate was by far the highest of any Canadian province, and was briefly higher than any American state.

Through March and April, a movement protesting COVID restrictions had gained momentum, marching through the streets and malls of Calgary and Edmonton most weekends. Several evangelical churches continued to hold in-person services, defying the provincial restrictions. In mid-April, after repeated violations, AHS erected fences around GraceLife Church outside of Edmonton. Protesters rallied around the church, tearing down the temporary fencing. "In an emailed statement, AHS said it was aware that some Albertans are "actively disobeying public health measures" but reiterated that enforcement remained a last resort.[21]

On 1 and 2 May, protesters organized an "Anti-Lockdown Rodeo" in direct and deliberate violation of the public health restrictions. While the government had apparently tolerated a considerable degree of non-compliance, the rodeo was the final straw. On Twitter, the premier wrote that

Figure 20.3. COVID-19 Vaccination Rates, Canada and Alberta (as of 24 April 2022)

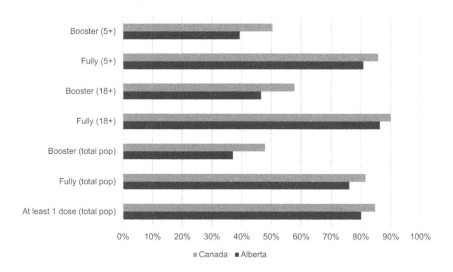

Sources: Government of Canada, "COVID-19 Vaccination in Canada," https://health-infobase.canada.ca/covid-19/vaccination-coverage/, (accessed 5 May 2022).

"It is disturbing to see large numbers of people gathering this weekend at Bowden in flagrant violation of COVID-19 public health measures."[22]

On 4 May, the premier announced new measures, including closing all K–12 schools until later in May, returning restaurants to take-out only, and restricting numbers for outdoor gatherings, religious worship, and weddings and funerals. The province employed the emergency alert system, so all cell phones lit up with a warning about COVID cases. Perhaps the most significant element of the announcement, though, had to do with enforcement. The premier stated that individuals ignoring the public health rules would not be tolerated. This signalled a change in approach in the province and resulted in more aggressive enforcement actions from AHS, including the arrest of several pastors who had defied restrictions and the closure of a non-compliant restaurant. Case numbers began to fall immediately and attention turned to the growing momentum of the vaccination campaign.

The measures announced in May met with further criticism from backbench UCP MLAs. Days after Kenney's May announcement, UCP Caucus Chair (and signatory on the April letter) Todd Loewen released a public letter of resignation that did not mention the COVID restrictions, but rather listed a series of other political failures and complained that the premier was unwilling to listen when caucus members brought their and their constituents' concerns to his attention. Loewen's letter prompted a lengthy meeting of the caucus, which voted to expel Loewen and Drew Barnes, the most outspoken critic of COVID measures in the caucus, leaving them to sit as independent MLAs.

Although he won the day when his caucus voted to expel the dissidents, Premier Kenney was further wounded politically. His delays in acting to address the third wave left him even more unpopular among those Albertans who believed action should be taken to limit the spread of COVID. And those who had followed the premier's own logic of diminishing the seriousness of the crisis had become critics, sometimes public, of the government's approach. The protests against the restrictions laid the foundation for a much more significant set of protests a year later. Faced with this political morass, the premier appeared increasingly desperate to get past the political quagmire of COVID.

The Vaccination Campaign

Throughout the third wave, the premier and the CMOH spoke about the "race" between the vaccines and the virus. For a government pursuing a mitigation strategy, effective vaccines are essential as they can reduce both the number of infections and the number of hospitalizations and deaths associated with the virus. Across Canada, vaccines were very scarce in the early months of 2021, but then started to become readily available through the spring.

Premier Kenney frequently complained about the scarcity of vaccines in the first months of 2021, blaming the federal government for inadequate procurement. In April, he said "I know many Albertans are looking around at states like Florida and Texas, where economies are pretty much fully open and life looks much more normal, and people are wondering why we can't just do what they're doing. Well, the answer is, it's because they have a huge head start over us on vaccination. If our federal government didn't put Canada at the back of the line for buying vaccines, we'd be where they are in those US states."[23] As vaccines became available, the provincial roll-out was generally well organized, using both vaccination sites and pharmacies to get the maximum possible number of shots in arms as quickly as possible. The premier offered no credit to the federal government once shortages were resolved.

Alberta's vaccination campaign faced two obstacles. The first was demographic: Alberta has the largest population twelve and under of any province, proportionately. As vaccines for children were not yet approved, the province had to vaccinate a larger share of the over-12 population to gain the same kind of protection. The second and more significant obstacle was attitudinal. As early as the summer of 2020, Albertans were more likely than other Canadians to say they had no intention of getting vaccinated against COVID-19 (16.4 per cent in Alberta versus 9.3 per cent nationally).[24] A survey of Albertans in the fall of 2021 found that respondents who were not vaccinated were more likely to have lower incomes, to favour far-right political parties, and to support the idea of Alberta separating from the rest of Canada.[25]

Given its ideological commitments to limited state intervention and the anti-vaccine views of some of its supporters, the Kenney government shied away from any hint that vaccinations would be required and passed legislation in April 2021 removing the province's authority to require immunization, on the ground that such a power was "unnecessary."[26] The province's advice to employers in the summer of 2021 advocated a "collaborative rather than mandatory" approach, stating "there is no intent to restrict the activities of those who choose not to immunize."[27] Though no public directive was issued, Alberta public institutions like health care facilities, school boards and post-secondary institutions all avoided imposing vaccine mandates of any kind, a pattern that suggests that there were informal directives from government telling them not to. And the premier frequently rejected the idea of "vaccine passports" despite the province's lagging rate of vaccinations. Instead, the province held a series of lotteries open only to the vaccinated, which had a minimal impact. Alberta's vaccination rates remained the lowest of any province, lagging the national rate by a substantial proportion (see Figure 20.3).

Stampeding into Summer

As cases declined sharply after more stringent restrictions were imposed in early May of 2021 and vaccination numbers grew, the government signalled a rapid and definitive end to COVID restrictions. In late May, three weeks after imposing stricter measures, the premier unveiled his government's re-opening plan, "Open for Summer." The key metric was vaccination rates, with hospitalizations as a secondary factor. Elimination of all restrictions required that 70 per cent of eligible Albertans have their first dose—and the premier projected that it would occur on 1 July, which it did. This paved the way for the Calgary Stampede to be held a week later.

At the time, medical experts and others cautioned that the province might be moving too quickly. With the more transmissible and deadly Delta variant in ascendance and the effective rate of vaccination in Alberta still relatively low, there was reason to be concerned that the early and aggressive reopening could trigger a fourth wave. The premier and his supporters dismissed these concerns, vilifying those voicing them as "not wanting the pandemic to end."[28] The premier's issues manager famously tweeted on 2 June that "The pandemic is ending. Accept it."[29]

After months of plummeting popularity and internal caucus strife, the premier wagered his political future on a successful reopening that would put COVID behind him and his government. With forced jollity, he pronounced that this would be the "best Alberta summer" and emphasized the symbolic importance of holding the Calgary Stampede. Maskless, he flipped pancakes, shook hands, and pronounced that the end of the pandemic at a series of events focused on shoring up his party's base of support. The premier's messaging emphasized that Alberta was the first province to end the pandemic, and his Twitter profile proclaimed "Focused on leading Canada out of the pandemic."

This "leadership" took a remarkable turn on 28 July. With case numbers once again increasing and only 63.8 per cent of the province's population fully vaccinated, CMOH Hinshaw held her first COVID update in a month. Viewers who expected to hear words of concern about rising case counts were astonished to hear her announce that over the month of August, virtually all residual restrictions would end, as COVID would no longer be treated as a pandemic, but rather as an "endemic" disease (like influenza). The public health fundamentals of test, trace, and isolate would be abandoned, as testing would occur only for severe cases, contact tracing would end, and self-isolation for close contacts *or individuals with COVID* would end.

In the days following this astonishing announcement, the premier and health minister deflected questions, claiming that Dr. Hinshaw came to the government with the plan and that cabinet merely approved her recommendation. In asserting this, the premier and health minister violated a norm that public servants' advice should remain confidential, so that public servants remain free to offer "fearless advice" to elected officials. The government doubled down on this stance the next week, having Dr. Hinshaw release an op-ed justifying the decision. In it, she wrote that "it is time, *in my opinion*, to shift from province-wide extraordinary measures to more targeted and local measures. . . . We will not eliminate COVID, which means that we need to learn to live with it."[30] (*emphasis added*).

It is impossible to know whether Dr. Hinshaw initiated the measures announced in late July, or whether government requested this specific advice, and she saw it as her duty to announce and support the decision. Her actions following the announcement suggest that she did not disagree with it; she did nothing to distance herself and permitted the op-ed with the words "in my opinion" to be published. Consequently, Hinshaw's credibility declined as COVID case counts rose. Regardless of the CMOH's advice and role, decisions about the management of public health are the responsibility of cabinet. It is difficult to see the decisions made about reopening and moving to "endemic" as anything other than a politically motivated bid to put the pandemic behind the beleaguered Kenney government.

Physicians who had been mobilized by the government's inaction during the second and third waves leapt to criticize the abandonment of test, trace, and isolate, and a segment of the public followed. Daily protests at the legislature and the government's offices in Calgary kept the issue alive. In the face of this criticism, Kenney and his communications staff reverted to sneering at their critics, accusing the media of fearmongering and critics of wanting lockdowns to go on indefinitely.[31]

The Fourth Wave & Caucus Revolt (August–November 2021)

The fourth wave of COVID was the worst public health failure of the pandemic in Alberta, and also the most damaging politically to the premier. Putting political considerations ahead of public health, the premier disappeared for three weeks as the fourth wave began. When he finally reappeared and intervened, he unleashed a caucus revolt that further destabilized his government. Over 900 Albertans died of COVID between 1 August and 30 November 2021 (see Figure 20.1).

The government knew that the number of COVID cases would rise through the summer, but expected that the availability of vaccinations would "decouple" cases from hospitalizations and other severe outcomes.[32] Two factors worked to foil these assumptions: the greater virulence of the Delta variant and the relatively low rate of vaccination in Alberta. Once Premier Kenney announced that the pandemic was behind the province, the number of vaccinations delivered fell sharply. As of 1 August, 76 per cent of eligible Albertans were fully vaccinated; this translated into 64 per cent of the full population. In early August, case numbers and hospitalizations continued to rise. On 13 August, three days before the test, trace, and isolate measures were to be removed, Dr. Hinshaw announced that the action would be postponed until the end of September.[33]

Aside from Dr. Hinshaw's 13 August news conference, she, the premier, and the minister of health were invisible as case numbers and hospitalizations increased. A federal election called on 15 August prompted conservative provincial premiers to keep a very low profile throughout the campaign. The premier was on vacation from 9 to 23 August at an undisclosed location, and subsequent reports indicated that the government was paralyzed during his absence.[34] A backbench MLA appeared on a Christian news show and expressed his hope that COVID numbers would spike and then fall, leading to speculation that the province's plan for the fall was to let the Delta variant rip through schools and the unvaccinated population.[35]

By the time the premier reappeared in early September, AHS was starting to cancel surgeries and other procedures because of pressure on ICUs. The premier held a news conference on 3 September where he announced the re-imposition of a province-wide mask mandate (except in schools, where boards could implement their own policies), as well as a recommendation that employers return to work-from-home and that the unvaccinated not gather socially. Calling the mounting crisis a "pandemic of the unvaccinated," the premier also announced an incentive program that offered $100 per shot for unvaccinated Albertans, sparking considerable outrage that the government would spend taxpayers' money to reward the unvaccinated to do what others had done willingly.

By mid-September, the province was within days of running out of staffed ICU beds. On 15 September, five days before the federal election, the premier appeared at a news conference to acknowledge that action was necessary. He was joined by Dr. Verna Yiu, president of AHS, who gravely presented a portrait of a health system in crisis facing the possibility of implementing triage measures. The premier declared a state of emergency and announced a "Restriction Exemption Program" that would allow businesses and other organizations to avoid limits on their activities if they verified that participants were vaccinated. This was a vaccine passport system in all but name, something that Kenney had repeatedly pledged he would never introduce.

At this news conference, in his prepared remarks, Kenney apologized, saying: "I know that we had all hoped this summer that we could put COVID behind us once and for all, that was certainly my hope and I said that very clearly. It is now clear that we were wrong, and for that I apologize." But when pressed by journalists after his statement, Kenney backtracked, saying "We were wrong in talking about moving this from pandemic management to endemic management in July and August. I frankly don't think we were wrong to lift public health restrictions in July."[36] The premier's inept apology and inability to accept responsibility for his mistakes did little to improve his standing with Albertans.

By declaring the state of emergency, the premier drew attention to the situation in the province. In the final days of the federal election, the Liberal campaign pointed to statements from Conservative Leader Erin O'Toole praising Premier Kenney's handling of the pandemic. This gave the Liberals momentum in a tight campaign and left O'Toole on the defensive, avoiding even mentioning the premier's name. The Conservatives lost the election and performed worse in Alberta than they had in 2019, losing

Figure 20.4. Percentage Who Have "A Lot" or "Full" Trust in the Premier and Chief Medical Officer of Health to Manage the Pandemic

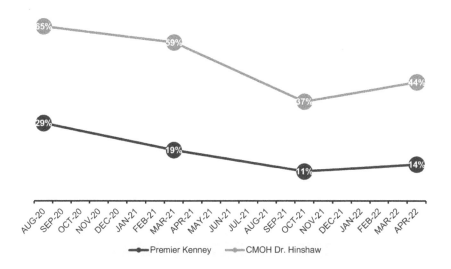

Sources: CommonGround. "Viewpoint Alberta Survey," October 2021 survey and April 2022 survey, https://www.commongroundpolitics.ca/covid-19trust.

three seats. In some conservative circles, the premier's decision to break his silence was seen not as an act of responsible leadership in a crisis, but as a betrayal of the conservative political cause.

Even before the federal ballots were counted, some MLAs were planning to oust the premier. The caucus meeting was scheduled for 22 September, two days after the federal election. Journalists reported that approximately twenty MLAs were prepared to vote non-confidence in Kenney as party leader.[37] The day prior to the caucus meeting, the premier made a surprise announcement that he was shuffling his cabinet. He indicated that he had accepted Health Minister Shandro's resignation, and had reassigned him to the labour portfolio, while bringing in Jason Copping as the new health minister, as it was time for a "fresh set of eyes" in the portfolio. The way in which the shuffle was announced was deliberately ambiguous, suggesting both that Shandro's resignation had been accepted as an acknowledgement that his handling of the pandemic had been unsatisfactory but also that the minister wanted to be reassigned to a new portfolio. When ministers resign because of poor performance, they are not normally appointed to another cabinet position.

When caucus met the next day, a call for a vote of non-confidence quickly collapsed when the party leadership insisted that it not be a secret ballot.[38] The caucus met for several hours and emerged claiming to be "more united than ever." To keep his job, the premier had both offered up the change in his cabinet and a promise that a leadership review would be held in spring of 2022.

In his first appearance as health minister, on 28 September, Copping announced that he would focus on three priorities: increasing vaccinations, increasing baseline ICU capacity, and preparing the system to deal with future waves of COVID. This avoided taking any kind of preventative actions like those advocated by many doctors and other health care professionals to institute a "firebreak" lockdown to slow the rate of transmission. The emphasis on increasing ICU capacity responded to a critique from some backbench MLAs that the policy problem facing the province was not too much COVID in circulation, but rather too few ICU beds for those afflicted with severe COVID.

Through September and into October, while the premier focused on his own political survival, the health care system operated under extraordinary stress. The 172 ICU beds normally available in the province were supplemented with enough additional beds to accommodate over 300 patients in ICU, the vast majority with COVID. Health care workers increasingly took to social media to tell stories of crowded hospital rooms filled with COVID patients, long shifts and understaffing, and experiences of abuse by unvaccinated patients who denied the existence of COVID.

Elements of the government's response appeared improvised. The Restriction Exemption Program was announced on a Thursday to come into force the next Monday, but the regulations were not issued until the weekend, and then were so unclear that businesses and other organizations struggled to cope. A website was set up to allow Albertans to download a printable pdf of their vaccination records, but the pdf was not locked, inviting the creation of fraudulent vaccination records. Weeks later, Albertans could download a QR code showing their vaccination status, but there was no app available for businesses to read the codes. It appears that the government had engaged in no contingency planning; they believed their own rhetoric that the pandemic was over.

The policies introduced throughout this period repudiated the government's prior stances. The government that had claimed vaccination passports were violations of privacy legislation found itself hastily devising a vaccination passport system. The government that had committed to a "collaborative rather than mandatory" approach to vaccination acquiesced to AHS and post-secondary institutions imposing vaccination mandates, and then imposed one for provincial employees. Despite the inconsistencies and poor implementation, these measures did prompt a modest increase in vaccination rates, although they continued to lag behind those in most other provinces.

By October 2021, a majority of Albertans had lost trust in both the premier and Dr. Hinshaw's management of the pandemic. Figure 20.4 shows that surveys of Albertans taken in August 2020, August 2021, and October 2021 show a marked decline in trust. Only one in ten Albertans expressed trust in the premier, a remarkably low rate. And between August and October, trust in Dr. Hinshaw dropped by over twenty percentage points, from 59 per cent to 37 per cent.

Fifth Wave & Freedom Convoy (December 2021– February 2022)

The emergence of the highly transmissible Omicron variant of COVID placed further stress on Alberta's beleaguered health care system and on the internally divided Kenney government. With the spring leadership review looming, the government made public health decisions shaped by its internal political pressures. The high-profile mobilization of "freedom" protesters accelerated the end of any pandemic restrictions and caused the provincial government to take its most firm stance against any further public health measures.

Through the fall of 2021, the fourth wave subsided and ICUs were gradually cleared of COVID cases. Albertans experienced a glimmer of hope that life was returning to normal. With a new health minister at the helm and chastened by the experience of taking the health care system to the brink of collapse, the provincial government between September and December consistently presented a cautious and conscientious approach to managing the pandemic.

This interlude was interrupted by news that a new and highly transmissible COVID variant—Omicron—had been identified. In mid-December, as other provincial governments tightened restrictions to slow the spread of the new variant, Alberta forged its own path and loosened restrictions on private gatherings in advance of the Christmas holiday.[39] The velocity of transmission of Omicron and the alarms being raised in Quebec and Ontario put the Kenney government once again in the position of defending an insufficiently proactive response. On 21 December, as Quebec entered a full lockdown and British Columbia announced additional restrictions on gatherings, Alberta did not reverse its decision to relax restrictions on gatherings, but put in place rules that venues with more than 1,000 seats would need to move to half occupancy, and could not allow food or drinks to be consumed.

Claiming that the provincial laboratories could not manage the volume of tests required, CMOH Hinshaw told Albertans to take rapid tests if they could source them, but to reserve public PCR (polymerase chain reaction) tests for health care and other essential workers. Even with reduced testing levels, the numbers of cases were staggering, with over 4,000 cases identified on New Year's Eve and a positivity rate over 30 per cent.

On 30 December, the cabinet committee met for several hours. The education minister stepped out of the meeting to announce that the holiday break for schools would be extended by a week to "give school authorities time to gather additional data to assess staffing implications and the potential operational impacts of the current COVID-19 situation."[40] But when the health minister appeared the next day, it was to announce that the mandatory isolation period for workers would be reduced from ten days to five, following a controversial decision made by the American Centers for Disease Control several days earlier. The contradiction between these two outcomes of the cabinet meeting are striking. The decision to postpone school reopening was consistent with the perception that Omicron posed a significant public health threat, or at least that it would make it difficult for schools to sustain operation, as had been the case during the third wave. The other decision was consistent with an approach that accepted widespread spread but tried to mitigate its impact on a return to normal, by reducing the time workers would need to isolate after testing positive. The apparent contradiction was resolved several days later when the education minister announced that schools would reopen on Monday, 10 January with mitigation measures in place—distribution of rapid tests to students' families and distribution of medical-grade masks to students.

Although the public health restrictions were limited, many organizations took actions to slow the spread. Many post-secondaries returned to online instruction for the first two months of 2022, and many employers encouraged work from home. Despite this, the Omicron variant swept through the Alberta population. Because testing was unavailable, the actual infection rate is unknown. University of Toronto epidemiologist Tara Moriarty, in an unpublished calculation, placed the infection rate in Alberta by 5 April 2022 as high as 77 per cent, albeit with a =/- error range of 20 per cent.[41] Between 1 December and 1 March, over 650 Albertans died of COVID. The province made booster shots available to all Albertans eighteen and over, but as Figure 20.3 shows, the uptake was limited.

Even as a record number of Canadians were being infected with the Omicron variant, ongoing protests against COVID restrictions were gaining momentum. Ostensibly triggered by the federal government's decision to require truckers crossing borders to be vaccinated or to quarantine, protesters from across the country descended on Ottawa in late January. Although this protest was national, many of its key organizers gave Alberta addresses after they were arrested. There were also parallel protests at various border crossings, including a major crossing at Coutts, Alberta. Protesters there closed the border crossing on 29 January.

On 1 February, the premier appeared at the weekly COVID briefing to say the situation was improving, and some restrictions would be lifted by the end of the month. He was explicit that pressure on hospitals would have to ease before restrictions could be lifted, and that the first restriction to go would be the vaccine passport system. Once again trying to straddle the divide between the public health imperative and the views of his party's base, he expressed sympathy with those who wanted restrictions lifted, but criticized the tactics of protesters who had closed the border crossing at Coutts.[42]

The next day, everything changed. The federal Conservative Party caucus, led by MPs sympathetic to the protesters occupying downtown Ottawa, voted to oust their leader. Energized by the protests in Ottawa and Coutts, rural UCP MLAs once again became restless and frustrated at the prospect of waiting weeks for restrictions to be dropped. Some surely felt jealous that their federal counterparts could dispose of a leader so easily while their efforts had been stymied. There were reports that they set out to end the border closure by reaching out to the protesters to "negotiate." The party quickly denied these reports.[43] Late in the day, various MLAs were letting it be known that the vaccine mandates would be dropped by Monday. With MLAs and even a cabinet minister—Jason Nixon—making statements either claiming the restrictions would be dropped, or advocating that they should be, the government once again appeared to be in chaos, with Kenney unable to stop open revolt.

After a hastily organized cabinet committee meeting, and exactly one week after saying that pandemic measures would start to be lifted at the end of February, the premier held a 5 p.m. briefing on Tuesday, 7 February and announced the end of pandemic measures on an accelerated timetable. The Restriction Exemption Program would be gone as of midnight. Mask mandates for schools would end on 14 February (even as the provincially provided masks were arriving for distribution), and children twelve and under would be exempted from any indoor mask mandate as of that date. Messaging around the decision focused heavily on children, saying that "kids must come first" and that children had "borne an unfair share of the burden." Stage 2 of the plan would begin on 1 March, and would remove virtually all remaining restrictions, including the provincial mask mandate, limits on social gatherings, or most capacity limits. A Stage 3 was tied to hospitalization rates falling (although no target level was specified) and would remove all remaining public health measures, including mandatory isolation. The government's rush to change its approach meant that it had not consulted with or informed affected organizations, including school boards, municipalities, or businesses. Organizations ranging from the Calgary Chamber of Commerce to Municipalities Alberta issued statements expressing their disappointment with the lack of consultation and notice.

The government pursued its new approach with vigour. The premier started to refer to public health measures his government had implemented as "damaging." The education minister released a letter to school boards indicating that they "would not be empowered" to impose their own restrictions and the minister of advanced education sent an open letter to the boards of post-secondary institutions communicating his "expectation" that as of 1 March all pandemic-related measures, including vaccine mandates and mask mandates, would cease at all institutions. When the legislature resumed sitting, the government amended the Municipal Government Act to prohibit municipalities from imposing COVID-related public health measures independent of the government. All of this was a significant departure from the government's prior approach, which allowed more stringent measures where there was an appetite for them.

In contrast to her willingness to drop restrictions in the summer of 2021, Dr. Hinshaw started to send signals that she was not supportive of the government approach. The first instance was on 10 January, when her response to a reporter's question was simply "Decisions about restrictions are not mine to make." On 3 February, when asked if she would feel as safe in a restaurant with a vaccine passport program as opposed to one that didn't have a program, Dr. Hinshaw replied that she had not eaten at a restaurant in two years. On 10 February, after the government had announced its timetable to end restrictions, Dr. Hinshaw was asked how the science had changed regarding the decision not to require children to mask in schools. Her reply: "I would defer to Minister Copping to answer that question."

Putting the Pandemic Behind Us and Leadership Review (March–May 2022)

Alberta, followed quickly by several other provinces, had decided to put the pandemic behind them. This approach was grounded in a shift in public opinion, with support for ongoing restrictions waning.[44] The virus continued to circulate in the province, with wastewater testing indicating another spike in April 2022. There were some 400 COVID deaths over this period. The Kenney government's focus shifted toward the impending leadership review, scheduled for 9 April in Red Deer, and then converted to a mail-in vote in May. As Sayers and Stewart discuss in their chapter, opposition to Kenney's leadership came from many sources, but COVID was central to the conflicts. The premier acknowledged this in his speech to party members on 9 April, calling COVID "the elephant in the room."

Many of the most vocal critics within caucus remained focused on the government's handling of the COVID pandemic. MLA Shane Getson on his Facebook page complained that, for the salaries that AHS executives were paid, the public deserved better outcomes, in particular more ICU beds.[45] The idea that the policy "problem" was not inadequate COVID mitigation, but rather insufficient numbers of ICU beds persisted in the anti-vax, anti-restrictions circles in the party. When Danielle Smith announced her intention to seek a party nomination in late March, she signalled a need for change at AHS, evoking this same critique.

And so, on 4 April, AHS announced that Dr. Verna Yiu would no longer be president and CEO of AHS. Yiu's contract had been extended in June 2021 for two years. But the AHS board terminated her contract, presumably at the behest of the government. The minister of health issued a statement indicating that "It's time to move forward with an ambitious agenda to improve and modernize the health system, and renewed leadership at Alberta Health Services will support delivering those changes."[46] The announcement came as a surprise. Yiu had joined the government's media availabilities through the fourth/Delta wave, calmly presenting information about the pressure on the health care system and ICUs in particular. Many AHS employees took to social media to express their admiration for Yiu, using the hashtag #ThankYiu.

Conclusion

Alberta's policy failure on COVID was not inevitable. Other provinces showed the way for a more measured response. Even if one argues that political culture or public opinion in Alberta drew the province toward a less interventionist approach, it is possible to identify specific moments where Alberta's greatest failure was delay: had it imposed restrictions or vaccine mandates a few weeks earlier, the number of cases and deaths would have been lower.

The political failure might have been more difficult to avoid. Public opinion in Alberta was divided from the outset of the pandemic and became more polarized as the waves crashed over the province. Thinking about the options available to the government, the political difficulties it faced are readily apparent. On one hand, had the government opted for the "Full Florida" response of minimizing the threat of COVID and maximizing "freedom" it would have pleased the backbench MLAs and the segment of the public they represented. But the outcry among the majority of Albertans would have been so overwhelming that the premier would likely have faced the same kind of rebellion from his urban MLAs (and perhaps cabinet ministers). As the health care system became utterly overwhelmed, with triage protocols employed to deny care to those unlikely to survive, the pressure to act would have been impossible to resist. Arguably, this is a version of what happened in September 2021.

On the other hand, had the province followed a stringent set of restrictions through 2020/21, more similar to those found in British Columbia or Ontario, there might have been an even stronger backlash from within the caucus and public opinion. But it is more difficult to sketch this scenario. Arguably, those who opposed the public health measures were not nuanced in their critiques, which became increasingly detached from reality. Perhaps the rebellion of the fifteen MLAs was the worst that this group had to offer. Had he imposed stronger discipline on those who criticized government actions, Kenney might have caused some of those MLAs to cross the floor (voluntarily or otherwise), thereby rendering his critics external to his party. Of course, this meant abandoning the idea that his conservative party was, in fact, united.

Was there a middle way? Perhaps. Kenney's approach to caucus management was high-handed. A leader with a different style might have been able to bring his critics along with him, convincing them of the necessity of action in the face of crisis, making them believe that they were active participants in charting the middle course. But perhaps these MLAs were not open to such persuasion, or could not resist pressure put on them by constituents enraged by the pandemic restrictions.

What is certain is that the pandemic exacerbated cleavages within Alberta politics and heightened political tensions. A brewing libertarian populist movement in the province appears to have gained strength, and now places its grievances at the door of both the provincial and federal governments. Public sector workers, particularly in health care and K–12 education, have suffered illness and moral injury. Some are responding by using their voices in the political sphere; others are exiting their professions or the province. Racialized Albertans, who bore a disproportionate burden through the pandemic, question the status quo. These forces and others unleashed during the pandemic will animate Alberta politics for years to come.

NOTES

1   The study estimated a ratio of reported to actual deaths in Alberta of between 1:41 and 1:96. Using these parameters with the May death toll, the estimates fall between 6093 and 8469. See COVID Excess Mortality Collaborators, "Estimating Excess Mortality Due to the COVID-19 Pandemic: A Systematic Analysis of COVID-19-Related Mortality, 2020–21," *The Lancet* 399, no. 10334 (16 April 2022): 1513–36. https://doi.org/10.1016/S0140-6736(21)02796-3.

2   Canada, "COVID-19 Epidemiology Update," https://health-infobase.canada.ca/covid-19/epidemiological-summary-covid-19-cases.html?stat=rate&measure=deaths&map=pt#a2, accessed 8 May 2022. Note that the COVID Excess Mortality Collaborators see Quebec's death reporting as much more accurate than other provinces'.

3   Ji Yoon Han and Charles Breton, "Have Provinces Put Schools First during COVID?" *Policy Options*, 1 February 2022, https://policyoptions.irpp.org/magazines/february-2022/have-provinces-put-schools-first-during-covid/.

4   For a discussion of the process of developing and issuing these public health orders, see Shaun Fluker and Lorian Hardcastle, "COVID-19 and Rule by Fiat under Alberta's *Public Health Act*," University of Calgary Faculty of Law (blog), 26 November 2020, https://ablawg.ca/2020/11/26/covid-19-and-rule-by-fiat-under-albertas-public-health-act/.

5   Jason Kenney, "Protecting Lives and Livelihoods: Premier Kenney Address," Premier Jason Kenney's address to Albertans on the COVID-19 pandemic, 7 April 2020, https://www.alberta.ca/release.cfm?xID=7003168647E46-E91D-4945-E9517ABC712B807E.

6   Alberta Health Services, "Meat Processing Plant COVID-19 Outbreaks," last updated 11 March 2021, https://www.albertahealthservices.ca/topics/Page17115.aspx.

7   It may, however, have been understated systematically. See T. Moriarty et al., *Excess All-Cause Mortality During the COVID-19 Epidemic in Canada* (Ottawa: Royal Society of Canada, 2021), https://rsc-src.ca/sites/default/files/EM%20PB_EN.pdf.

8   Allan McConnell and Alastair Stark, "Understanding Policy Response to COVID-19: The Stars Haven't Fallen from the Sky for Scholars of Public Policy," *Journal of European Public Policy* 28, no. 8 (25 June 2021): 1115–30, https://doi.org/10.1080/13501763.2021.1942518.

9   United Conservative Party, "Statement of Principles," https://www.unitedconservative.ca/about/, accessed July 2021.

10 Angus Reid Institute, "COVID-19 Carelessness: Which Canadians Say Pandemic Threat Is 'Overblown'? And How Are They Behaving in Turn?" https://angusreid.org/covid-19-serious-vs-overblown/, accessed July 2021.

11 Jason Kenney, Legislative Assembly of Alberta, Hansard Transcript 30th Legislature, 1st sitting, 27 May 2020, 802.

12 Julia Wong, "Contact Tracing in Alberta's 2nd Wave: Documents Show Huge Backlog, Staff Shortages," *Global News*, 30 May 2021. https://globalnews.ca/news/7885228/covid-19-contact-tracing-backlog-alberta-second-wave/.

13 Mark Villani, "Alberta doctors express serious concerns over 'uncontrollable spread' of COVID-19," *CTV News*, 12 November 2020, https://calgary.ctvnews.ca/alberta-doctors-express-serious-concerns-over-uncontrollable-spread-of-covid-19-1.5185822.

14 Jennie Russell and Charles Rusnell, "Secret recordings reveal political directives, tension over Alberta's pandemic response," *CBC*, 26 November 2020, https://www.cbc.ca/news/canada/edmonton/alberta-covid-19-response-tension-recordings-1.5814877.

15 CPAC, "COVID-19 in Alberta: Premier Jason Kenney Announces New Provincewide Restrictions," transcription of video, 8 December 2020, https://www.youtube.com/watch?v=ePG3bivLLkk.

16 Canada, "News Release: New COVID-19 Pilot Planned for International Travellers," 22 October 2020, https://www.canada.ca/en/intergovernmental-affairs/news/2020/10/new-covid-19-pilot-planned-for-international-travellers.html.

17 YourAlberta, "Update on COVID-19," transcription of video aired 1 April 2021, https://www.youtube.com/watch?v=zuudrJZKxaA.

18 YourAlberta, "Update on COVID-19," transcription of video aired 6 April 2021, https://www.youtube.com/watch?v=hT2heeCCmDU.

19 Angus Reid Institute, "Third Wave Drives Surge of Criticism for Kenney, Ford, and other Premiers," 9 April 2021, https://angusreid.org/covid-restrictions-ford-kenney/.

20 Text of the MLA letter can be found with this article: Lisa Johnson, "Quarter of UCP MLAs speak out against Alberta's latest COVID-19 restrictions," *Edmonton Journal*, 7 April 2021. https://edmontonjournal.com/news/politics/fifteen-ucp-mlas-say-kenneys-latest-covid-19-restrictions-move-alberta-backwards. A sixteenth MLA signed on the next day.

21 Wallis Snowdon, "Resistance to Alberta's COVID-19 Health Restrictions Is Growing, Experts Warn," *CBC*, 13 April 2021, https://www.cbc.ca/news/canada/edmonton/alberta-covid-enforcement-health-restrictions-1.5984275.

22 Jason Kenney (@jkenney), "Not only are gatherings like this a threat to public health, they are a slap in the face to everybody who is observing the rules to keep themselves and their fellow Albertans safe," Twitter, 2 May 2021, 3:37 p.m., https://twitter.com/jkenney/status/1388970946984173577.

23 YourAlberta, "Update on COVID-19," transcription, 1 April 2021.

24 Xuyang Tang et al., "COVID-19 Vaccination Intention during Early Vaccine Rollout in Canada: A Nationwide Online Survey," *The Lancet Regional Health—Americas* 2 (October 2021), https://doi.org/10.1016/j.lana.2021.100055.

25 Michelle Maroto, "Albertans and COVID-19 Vaccinations," Common Ground: Connecting Communities & Politics, 13 October 2021, https://www.commongroundpolitics.ca/covid-19-vaccine-ab.

26 Legislative Assembly of Alberta, "Bill 66: Public Health Amendment Act, 2021," https://www.assembly.ab.ca/assembly-business/bills/bill?billinfoid=11911&from=bills.

27 Alberta, "COVID 19 Immunization Program Employer Information," June 2021, https://open.alberta.ca/dataset/12b11198-d0f5-46a3-af8c-dd8d49f8de6a/resource/ac3f1f39-87a8-41cf-94fa-33f1cc82d2a0/download/covid-19-immunization-program-employer-information-2021-06.pdf.

28 Matt Wolf (@MattWolfAB), "Some in the media really don't want the pandemic to end," Twitter, 19 July 2021, 6:29 p.m., https://twitter.com/mattwolfab/status/1417280367329951748?lang=en.

29 Matt Wolf (@MattWolfAB), "The pandemic is ending. Accept it," Twitter, 2 June 2021, 2:09 p.m., https://twitter.com/mattwolfab/status/1400182922427043840?lang=en.

30 Deena Hinshaw, "Learning to Live with COVID-19," Alberta, 4 August 2021, https://www.alberta.ca/article-learning-to-live-with-covid-19.aspx.

31 For example: Jason Kenney (@jkenney), "It's time for the media to stop promoting fear when it comes to COVID-19 and to start actually looking at where we're at with huge vaccine protection," Twitter, 28 July 2021, 9:49 a.m., https://twitter.com/jkenney/status/1420411178287648772?lang=en.

32 Bill Macfarlane and Sarah Reid, "Hinshaw Says Government Knew Since Mid-August Hospital Demand Would Rise without Provincial Intervention," *CTV News*, 14 September 2021, https://calgary.ctvnews.ca/hinshaw-says-government-knew-since-mid-august-hospital-demand-would-rise-without-provincial-intervention-1.5584542.

33 See YourAlberta, "COVID-19 and Back to School," video, 42:34, 13 August 2021, https://www.youtube.com/watch?v=UHQcd8vTgzo.

34 Drew Anderson, "The Political Consequences of Kenney's 4th-Wave Vacation," *CBC*, 1 September 2021, https://www.cbc.ca/news/canada/calgary/alberta-premier-kenney-vacation-pandemic-1.6160176.

35 *Ibid.*

36 See YourAlberta, "Update on COVID-19," video, 1:22:56, 15 September 2021, https://www.youtube.com/watch?v=Q_tkbvlsOEo.

37 Kelly Cryderman, James Keller, and Emma Graney, "Alberta Changes Health Ministers amid Hospital Crisis and Challenges to Kenney's Leadership," *Globe and Mail*, 21 September 2021.

38 Don Braid, "Kenney Heads Off Caucus Revolt But Agrees to Leadership Review," *Calgary Herald*, 22 September 2021, https://calgaryherald.com/opinion/columnists/braid-kenney-heads-off-caucus-revolt-but-agrees-to-leadership-review.

39 YourAlberta, "Update on COVID-19," video, 1:05:31, 15 December 2021, https://www.youtube.com/watch?v=fG7_dm4YB3g.

40 Alberta, "Winter Break Extended for K–12 Students," 30 December 2021. https://www.alberta.ca/release.cfm?xID=806788B71C10B-FD14-1E3C-70163D5371BF71E0.

41 "Canadian Regions Risk of Future Severe Outcomes," https://docs.google.com/
spreadsheets/d/1XUbN-bZOoC87_GcJQQvLRdSsqmDxjZTMHzEelEtCr_8/
edit#gid=499971165, accessed 5 May 2022. This is consistent with wastewater testing
data, which showed rates three or more times higher during Omicron than during the
third and fourth waves: Centre for Health Informatics, "The COVID-19 Response:
Alberta Wastewater," Cumming School of Medicine, University of Calgary, https://
covid-tracker.chi-csm.ca/, accessed 5 May 2022.

42 CPAC, "Alberta Update on COVID-19," video, 1:09:17, 1 February 2022, https://www.
youtube.com/watch?v=BAD53XNKBv4.

43 Hannah Kost, "UCP denies reports of rural caucus negotiating with blockade protesters
after lanes opened in 'good faith,'" CBC, 2 February 2022, https://www.cbc.ca/news/
canada/calgary/alberta-blockade-breakthrough-coutts-1.6337148.

44 Angus Reid Institute, "As 24 Months of Pandemic Restrictions Lift, Are Canadians
Ready—or Reluctant—to Let Go?" 15 March 2022, https://angusreid.org/covid-
restrictions-precautions-masking-trudeau/.

45 Michelle Bellefontaine (@MBellefontaine), "UCP MLA Shane Getson posted this on
Facebook about the current crisis facing our health care system," Twitter, 25 September
2021, 1:26 p.m., https://twitter.com/MBellefontaine/status/1441846528193138698/
photo/1.

46 Alberta, "Statement on Dr. Verna Yiu: Minister Copping," 4 April 2022, https://www.
alberta.ca/release.cfm?xID=8227298EC2469-E4E8-DD13-A3885EEC12A056A7.

VIII.
Conclusion

21

Conclusion: States of Uncertainty

Duane Bratt and Richard Sutherland

When we were in the final stages of preparing *Orange Chinook* for publication in 2018 it was still a few months out from the election, but there were a few things that seemed clear. The contest would be between the incumbent New Democratic Party (NDP) under Rachel Notley and the newly formed United Conservative Party (UCP) led by Jason Kenney. Coming off a successful career in federal politics, as a leading minister in Stephen Harper's cabinet, Kenney was largely responsible for the creation of the UCP, formed with the express purpose of merging Alberta's two main right-of-centre parties, the Progressive Conservatives (PC) and the Wildrose. Polling had been relatively consistent, showing a strong lead for the UCP. Just as significantly, polling also showed that voting intentions had solidified around these two parties—there seemed no likelihood of splitting the vote on the left, as had happened so many times over the previous decades or on the right, as had been the case in 2015. In the event, as Brooks DeCillia's chapter shows, the UCP's margin of victory was even greater than the polls had suggested. The signals around the 2023 provincial election are far less clear—the UCP has been in turmoil for over a year, and polls have been much closer. However, we do know that Jason Kenney's time as leader of the UCP and premier of Alberta has reached its end. On October 6, 2022 Danielle Smith became the UCP leader and on October 11 she was sworn in as Alberta Premier.

On 18 May 2022, Kenney stood before a group of supporters at Spruce Meadows, just outside of Calgary, to announce his intention to step down as leader of the UCP. This, despite having just won his leadership review with 51.42 per cent of votes. As he explained, this tepid level of support was "clearly not adequate . . . to continue as leader."[1] The road to Kenney's resignation had been a long one, stretching back to at least late summer 2021. The NDP had been outpolling and outfundraising the UCP for some time even then. Kenney's dismal polling results suggested that his days as leader were numbered. But because Kenney pushed back so hard against the efforts of some members of his party and caucus to hold a review, it was not a foregone conclusion that he would, in fact, depart. Over the fall and winter, he was able to delay calls for a leadership review to April 2022. The party's controversial decision to hold a mail-in vote, pushed the announcement of the review's results even further back to mid-May. Kenney had suggested throughout the review process that a bare majority (50 per cent + 1 votes) would be sufficient for him to continue, even though earlier leaders, such as Ralph Klein, had taken higher levels of support as insufficient to continue as leader. But when the results were finally announced, it was clear that a bare majority was not enough.

Kenney's resignation is only one event in what has been a tumultuous decade for Alberta politics. The unexpected election in 2015 of the NDP government after forty-four consecutive years of PC governments was, perhaps, the most dramatic development (and the occasion for assembling *Orange Chinook*), but it was by no means the beginning. The fractures within the right wing of Alberta politics, and the efforts to overcome these divisions had already resulted in surprise wins for compromise candidates in leadership races in 2006 and 2011, as well as some extraordinary episodes, such as most members of the official opposition Wildrose Party, including then leader Danielle Smith, crossing the floor to join the PC government late in 2014. Such divisions were also at least partially responsible for the NDP's election win months later, and they have continued to drive events in Alberta politics.

As Lisa Young's chapter outlines, perhaps the greatest disruption of all has been the global COVID-19 pandemic. As of mid-2022 severe cases and hospitalizations are down. However, COVID is still circulating widely within many populations, and many members of the public remain cautious about resuming their usual habits of socializing and circulating from before the pandemic. Many governments, including Alberta's, have dropped most, if not all, health restrictions and testing requirements, but politicians remain wary of declaring a definitive end to the pandemic. And for good reason—the Kenney government, especially, knows all too well the risks of such premature declarations. As a political issue, COVID and, even more so, the measures to combat it became a point of division within Alberta's public generally, with a significant portion of the population resistant to both vaccination and to other health measures. The division was felt especially within the UCP, a party that, as Stewart and Sayers show in their chapter, was already divided on many issues. The Kenney government's response to the pandemic poured gasoline on the smouldering disagreements within the party and the caucus. Several (mostly rural) MLAs declared their opposition to almost every restriction imposed by the government. Kenney, despite trying every approach from tolerance of dissent to expulsion from caucus, was unable to contain the dispute. As time went on, however, he himself became increasingly the focus of discontent within the party.

Kenney's announcement offers a turning point, a break in the narrative, even if the UCP remains in power until at least the next provincial election. But, as with the pandemic, the end of Kenney's premiership has proved to be an attenuated process. Within hours of his announcement, it became clear that Kenney was not leaving just yet. On 19 May, after a full day of deliberation, the UCP caucus issued an announcement that Kenney would be staying on as premier until after a leadership race had selected his successor. There was even some speculation in the first few days after the announcement that Kenney might enter the race himself, as there was nothing in the party's by-laws preventing it. Kenney eventually quelled these rumours, announcing the following Saturday on his call-in radio show that he would not be running. Regardless, Kenney would continue to govern, presumably with an eye to continuing to pursue his government's agenda. An immediate departure would have provided the party a much earlier opportunity to move on under a more neutral leader, likely in a caretaker role. Instead, Kenney continued to be associated with the party for some time yet. His continuing presence in the premier's office also clearly conditioned the terms on which the leadership race took place. His lingering unpopularity was a challenge for any member of cabinet, such as finance minister Travis Toews, running for the leadership, requiring them to distance themselves from him, while still campaigning on their own records. On the other hand, Brian Jean and Danielle Smith, the last two leaders of the Wildrose Party and explicitly anti-Kenney candidates, had already declared themselves before the results of the leadership review had been decided.

Legacies

How will we look back on the events of the past four years? COVID-19's impacts on employment, inflation, and on political dynamics seem destined to outlast the actual pandemic. The consequences of shutting down the economy and then re-opening it has ignited discussions around long-term measures such as guaranteed basic income. Continued disruptions in the global supply chain have led to shortages of many consumer goods, possibly contributing to the highest inflation rates seen in decades. Employment in Alberta, particularly Calgary and Edmonton (already an issue prior to the pandemic) has been slow to recover, lagging most of Canada. Resistance to pandemic measures has offered a rallying point for the right, not only in Alberta, but across Canada and in other countries. COVID has changed the conversation about public health measures and individual rights.

However, although COVID has been by far the biggest issue confronting the Kenney government, there is more to the story. Regardless of whether the pandemic had happened, the UCP was already determined to be a disruptive force, taking on its perceived enemies forcefully and very publicly. The UCP came into government aiming at disruption, promising a very different approach, not only from the NDP, but also the most recent PC governments. The party aimed at challenging the status quo beyond Alberta's borders, promising to push back aggressively against the federal government under Trudeau's Liberals, and even further afield at environmental groups based outside of Canada. The "war room" (see Brad Clark's chapter) and the Fair Deal Panel (see Jared Wesley's chapter) were the two major elements of this more aggressive footing.

Much of this is reflected in Jason Kenney's confrontational political persona. When he entered Alberta politics, Jason Kenney was viewed as the solution—the right man to bring together the two parties, as well as to forcefully defend the interests of Alberta and its oil and gas industry. The blue Dodge Ram he chose as his vehicle is, as Chaseten Remillard and Tyler Nagle suggest, a very deliberately chosen symbol for this attitude. Initially this seemed to work as the UCP handily won a large majority in the ensuing election. Kenney's approval rate in the first months after the 2019 election was even higher than his party's share of the vote at 61 per cent.[2] However, both ratings began a sharp decline in November, as his party unveiled its first budget. It seems that voters quickly grew tired of Jason Kenney's style. As several authors in this volume point out, while every other political leader in Canada received at least some uptick in approval ratings as they dealt with the COVID-19 crisis, Kenney's only dropped. He remained amongst the least popular premiers in the country. Many of the leading members of his cabinet have displayed a similar penchant for incendiary political behaviour, particularly in response to critics. The response of staffers (most notably Matt Wolf, former issues manager, and Brock Harrison, director of communications) and cabinet ministers such as Tyler Shandro, Jason Nixon, or Devin Dreeshen has been to hit back at opponents with maximum force, intensifying or even precipitating political scandals. This approach has left lasting wounds within the UCP, and has, arguably, contributed to an increasing polarization within Alberta politics more generally.

Although the Kenney government may be remembered by many for its confrontational style and the political battles that consumed it, there are other, policy-related legacies that may have lasting effects. Many of the steep cuts in government spending in education, post-secondary learning, and other sectors may have lasting consequences, such as the loss of jobs and closures of schools or programs. These effects will persist regardless of whether funding is restored in future. Of course, much also depends on how Smith chooses to govern over the coming months, as well, of course, on which party wins the next provincial election in May 2023. It seems likely that an NDP win would see very different approaches in many policy areas, but a UCP under new leadership might also have different priorities and positions in terms of policy. However, even if there is policy continuity, it is likely that the new leader will bring a different tone.

In his chapter on climate policy, Duane Bratt notes the NDP's Climate Leadership Plan has demonstrated surprising policy resiliency, with most of its elements surviving the change in government, despite the loudly announced plans of the Kenney government. There were some surprising continuities between the Notley and Kenney governments, regardless of what either one might say publicly. Just as for Notley's NDP, there are some areas where the resiliency of the Kenney government policies seems dubious and other areas where we could easily suppose they will continue. And, as Bratt's analysis might suggest, we might also be surprised at what stays the same. As always, we should look at the gap between political rhetoric and policy action.

Should the NDP reclaim government they have signalled their intention to eliminate the UCP's performance-based funding model for higher education.[3] At the same time, it's worth remembering that the provincial mandates for post-secondary institutions that figured so largely in discussions of labour relations in the sector (see Lisa Young's chapter) were, in fact, introduced by the NDP, albeit with very different criteria. As for the cultural industries sector, while the NDP has promised to reinstate the Digital Interactive Media Tax Credit[4] that was eliminated by the UCP in its first budget (see Richard Sutherland's chapter), there is no indication it would revert to grants from the tax credits the UCP introduced for film and television production. The NDP have also stated, as Charles Webber notes in his chapter on education, that it will drop the UCP's controversial revised curriculum for K–12 students, reverting, presumably, to the revised curriculum they had developed while in office. But it is less clear what line they would take on other matters, such as the removal of the Alberta Teachers Association's disciplinary role. It also seems likely that the NDP would take a different approach to health care, relations with the federal government, or fiscal policy, and it is almost unimaginable that the Canadian Energy Centre would continue to exist under an NDP government. However, there have been no specific commitments in these areas. Finally, in environmental policy, it is unclear whether the NDP would move to reinstate the provincial economy-wide carbon tax. On the other hand, a new UCP government with a fresh mandate might be inclined to follow a very different path on environment policy. For instance, even if Danielle Smith retains much of Jason Kenney's rhetoric on climate change, she may choose very different policies from those his government has quietly pursued. Bratt's chapter should remind us that there is no guarantee that the UCP automatically offers more continuity in every respect with the Kenney's government than does the NDP.

Finally, one of the main legacies of Jason Kenney in Alberta's political career is, not only the creation of the UCP, but also the final destruction of the PC Party that had governed the province for forty-four years. Kenney, as the last leader of that party, explicitly campaigned for the leadership with the aim of merging it with the Wildrose Party. In doing so, he was attempting to replicate the merger of the right in federal politics that happened between the Canadian Alliance and Progressive Conservatives in 2003, which healed the split in the right-of-centre vote in the country and contributed to Stephen Harper's Conservative Party of Canada forming government in 2006 after thirteen years of Liberal rule. Initially Kenney's project followed the same script: the parties were successfully united with Kenney becoming the new party's leader and winning a general election not long after. However, maintaining Harper's success as a leader has proved more elusive. In the federal merger of the Canadian Alliance and the Progressive Conservatives there was a persistent sense that more moderate voices were sidelined, although it was also clear that more right-wing views were also held in check under Harper's leadership. Kenney faced a similar problem of keeping the centre and the right under the same tent, but he has not been able to manage this task.

As he leaves the leadership, it is unclear what lies ahead for the party he essentially founded. As discussed earlier, there are deep divisions within that have already claimed his leadership, and which threaten its stability in the longer term. The UCP do not seem to be especially united, based on the results of the leadership review's 50/50 split, as well as Smith winning the leadership with just 53.8 per cent after 6 ballots. This is more divided than the Progressive Conservatives were even under Stelmach or Redford, but perhaps less surprising if we remember that the UCP also includes the remnants of the Wildrose Party, the party Danielle Smith led between 2009 and 2014. It is debatable whether, under her leadership, the United Conservatives will be able to retain centrist, formerly Progressive Conservative voters, or essentially devolve into a revival of the Wildrose Party. It is also unclear whether a more moderate leader, particularly one associated with Jason Kenney as a member of his cabinet, would have been acceptable to more right-wing voters. Either way, Jason Kenney's major legacy, the United Conservative Party itself, seems less than assured.

NOTES

1   Dean Bennett and Collette Derworiz, "Alberta Premier Jason Kenney intends to step down as UCP leader after narrow leadership win," *Global News*, 18 May 2022. Accessed at: https://globalnews.ca/news/8846607/jason-kenney-ucp-leadership-vote-results-alberta/ on 27 May 2022.

2   Angus Reid Institute. "Premiers' Performance: Ford Continues to Fall in Approval, Houston Rides High on Strength of COVID 19 Handling," 17 January 2022. Accessed at: https://angusreid.org/premiers-performance-january-2022/ on 31 May 2022.

3   Alberta NDP Caucus. "Strengthening Post-Secondary for a Resilient Future (2022)." Accessed at: https://www.albertasfuture.ca/albertas-future/albertas-future-campaigns/post/strengthening-post-secondary-for-a-resilient-future on 27 May 2022.

4   Alberta NDP Caucus. "Technology and AI Proposal (2021)." Accessed at: https://www.albertasfuture.ca/albertas-future/albertas-future-campaigns/post/technology on 27 May 2022.

Contributors

DUANE BRATT is professor in the Department of Economics, Justice, and Policy Studies at Mount Royal University. He has published extensively in the areas of Alberta politics, Canadian nuclear policy, and Canadian foreign policy and was most recently co-editor of *Orange Chinook*. He is seen and heard regularly on TV and radio.

BRAD CLARK worked as a journalist for twenty years in both print and broadcasting before entering the academy. He teaches in the Broadcast Media Studies and Journalism and Digital Media programs in the School of Communication Studies at Mount Royal University. He's the author of *Journalism's Racial Reckoning: The News Media's Pivot to Diversity and Inclusion.*

BROOKS DECILLIA is an assistant professor with Mount Royal University's School of Communication Studies. For more than a decade, Brooks was a national reporter with CBC News. His reports regularly aired on CBC Television's *The National* and CBC Radio One programs. Brooks covered stories across Canada, South Asia, Europe, and the United States, and was embedded with Canadian Forces in Afghanistan.

ROGER EPP is professor emeritus of political science at the University of Alberta, where he served in a number of senior leadership roles, including that of founding dean of the Augustana Campus in Camrose. Over the past quarter century, he has written extensively about the rural West. His books include *We Are All Treaty People: Prairie Essays and Writing Off the Rural West* (co-edited with Dave Whitson).

DOUG KING's interest in law enforcement began as a research analyst with the Calgary Police Service in the mid-1980s. As a professor in the Department of Economic, Justice, and Policy Studies, Doug offers courses in policing, law, and restorative justice. He is frequently interviewed by news media on justice-related matters.

JONATHAN MALLOY is a member of the Department of Political Science at Carleton University, where he holds the Bell Chair in Canadian Parliamentary Democracy. He is co-editor of *The Politics of Ontario* and co-author of *Fighting For Votes: Parties, the Media, and Voters in an Ontario Election.*

TYLER NAGEL teaches journalism at the Southern Alberta Institute of Technology and communications at Royal Roads University. He is a PhD candidate at the University of Groningen. His research interests are in local journalism, online news, and community media.

CHASETEN REMILLARD teaches in the School of Communication and Culture at Royal Roads University. His research includes topics as varied as homelessness, the artist Bill Reid, hockey art, Trudeau's selfies, and shark films. Despite this eclecticism, he consistently interrogates how images gain and transmit meaning and how these meanings serve to reinforce particular "ways of seeing" ourselves and the world around us.

JEAN-SÉBASTIEN RIOUX taught political science and public policy for twenty years, most recently at the School of Public Policy, University of Calgary. His scholarly publications have been in the fields of Canadian foreign policy, energy policy, war, and geopolitics. His most recent book, *Triple Crown: Winning Canada's Energy Future*, was co-authored with the late Honourable Jim Prentice and was a *Globe & Mail* bestseller. His writing now focuses on fiction and thrillers.

PETER MALACHY RYAN teaches public relations at Mount Royal University. He is an accredited public relations (APR) professional through the Canadian Public Relations Society (CPRS), and an advisory board member for the Centre for Crisis and Risk Communication (CCRC). His published research focuses on the areas of issues management in Alberta and Canadian online politics.

ANTHONY M. SAYERS is a professor of political science at the University of Calgary whose research and publications analyze political parties and elections, representation, and federalism in Alberta, Canada, and Australia.

GILLIAN STEWARD is a Calgary-based journalist who has been covering Alberta politics since Peter Lougheed was elected premier. She currently writes a regular column for the Toronto Star. She was the managing editor at the *Calgary Herald* from 1987 to 1990. In 2000 she co-authored with Kevin Taft *Clear Answers: The Economics and Politics of For-Profit Medicine* a collaboration with The Parkland Institute. In 2014 she completed a PhD in Communication Studies at the University of Calgary.

DAVID K. STEWART is a professor of political science at the University of Calgary. He has published in the areas of provincial politics, Canadian politics, and political parties. He is the co-author of a book on leadership selection in Alberta.

RICHARD SUTHERLAND is associate professor in the Department of Economics, Justice, and Policy Studies at Mount Royal University. He has degrees from the University of Calgary (BA, 1987; MCS, 1998) and McGill University (PhD, 2009). He teaches public policy, as well as on politics and media. His research interests are primarily to do with Canadian cultural policy, particularly music industry policy.

DAVID TARAS (1950–2022) was professor in Communication Studies and Ralph Klein chair in Media Studies at Mount Royal University. He was co-editor of *Orange Chinook: Politics in the New Alberta*. Through a distinguished career, David was a respected scholar, public intellectual, and generous mentor.

MELANEE THOMAS is an associate professor in political science at the University of Calgary. Her research addresses the causes and consequences of gender-based political inequality, with a particular focus on political attitudes and behaviour. Her objectives are to identify how Canadians think about themselves in politics; explain how this is structured by gender, sexism, and racism; and then develop potential solutions that ameliorate and strengthen our democratic politics. Her work appears in *Politics & Gender, Electoral Politics, Political Behaviour, Political Communication,* and the *Canadian Journal of Political Science.*

GRAHAM THOMSON is a political columnist who has covered Alberta politics for a myriad of news outlets including the CBC, *Edmonton Journal, Toronto Star, Alberta Views Magazine,* and others. He arrived in Alberta more than thirty-five years ago planning to leave once the province's spirited politics grew boring. He is still here.

TREVOR TOMBE is a professor of economics at the University of Calgary and a research fellow at the School of Public Policy. He is also co-director of Finances of the Nation. His research focuses on public finances, macroeconomics, international trade, and fiscal federalism. In addition to his academic research, he actively promotes the public understanding of economics through policy and media engagement.

KATE TOOGOOD is a student in the Master of Arts in Professional Communication program at Royal Roads University. Her research focuses on how framing is used in communications by politicians on social media. She is a communication and marketing professional with over thirteen years of experience, both in Canada and globally, and has worked with organizations in the public and private sector. Now a private consultant, she is dedicated to using her skills and expertise to help her clients to make the world a better place.

CHARLES F. WEBBER teaches in the Department of Education at Mount Royal University. He has served as professor and dean in Alberta and British Columbia. His research and publications focus on educational governance in K–12 schools and postsecondary institutions. He is editor of a forthcoming book, *Teacher Leadership in International Contexts,* published by Springer.

JARED J. WESLEY is a professor of political science at the University of Alberta. A former director of intergovernmental relations for the Government of Alberta, he leads the Common Ground initiative and

Viewpoint Alberta project, shedding light on political culture and public opinion in Alberta. He is author of *Code Politics: Campaigns and Cultures on the Canadian Prairies.*

LORI WILLIAMS is an associate professor in the Department of Economics, Justice and Policy Studies at Mount Royal University. Her research and teaching interests include women and politics, law, Charter rights, political philosophy, ethics, power and technology, including social media. She regularly engages in analysis and commentary on radio and television.

LISA YOUNG is professor of political science at the University of Calgary, where she was also vice-provost and dean of graduate studies from 2011 to 2018. She has published extensively in the field of Canadian politics, focusing on political parties, election finance, women in politics, and graduate education. She frequently comments on Alberta and Canadian politics in the media.

Index

mask use, 12, 128, 130, 181, 349, 350, 380, 425, 428, 429, 443, 444, 450, 453, 458, 459, 460
masculinity, 7, 146, 165, 170–171, 176, 181–183
Maurice, Eddie, 6, 134–135, 142
Mavericks (Glenbow Museum exhibit), 173, 178, 183, 185
McAdams, Roberta, 387
McFee, Dale, 138, 144
McGuinty, Dalton, 419
McKinney, Louise, 387
McKinsey & Company, 161, 166, 371
media, iv, xiii, 4–5, 20, 22, 33, 35–36, 38–41, 43, 45–52, 54–57, 59, 61, 64, 72–73, 76–77, 79, 129–131, 134, 138–139, 158, 161, 164, 183, 193, 216, 234, 236–238, 240–242, 250 252, 254, 256, 293, 303, 305, 308, 311–312, 314–315, 317–318, 339, 345, 351, 379, 410–411, 451, 455, 461, 465, 474, 477–481. *See also Calgary Herald*; *Calgary Sun*; Facebook; Canadian Broadcasting Corporation (CBC); *New York Times*; Rebel Media; social media; Twitter; Western Standard; YouTube
Medicine Hat, AB, 198, 299, 332
Métis, 293, 346, 349, 352, 354
Mikisew Cree First Nation, 292–293
Milke, Mark, 242, 254, 255
minimum wage, 20, 25, 314, 391–393
Moe, Scott, 66, 197, 422, 429
Molnar, Christine, 331, 339, 395
Morton, Ted, 101, 108, 184, 316
Mount Royal University, ii, xii–xiii, 207, 380, 477–481
Mulroney, Brian, 417

N

Nagel, Tyler, viii, 7, 169, 419, 478
Nanos Survey, 63, 66
National Energy Board, 212, 218, 233
natural gas, xi, 2, 8, 9, 11, 34, 46, 94, 101, 105, 122, 145, 148, 149, 150, 156, 158, 189, 191, 192, 193–194, 195, 196, 197, 198, 199, 200–201, 207, 215, 216, 218, 219, 222, 224, 226, 227, 237–238, 239, 240, 241, 243, 244, 245, 246–247, 248, 251, 259, 260, 261, 266, 269, 286, 290, 291, 292, 293, 294, 301, 302, 312, 315, 352, 355, 376, 386, 399, 473
Nenshi, Naheed, 60, 141–142, 387
Netflix, 240–241, 254, 309
Neufeld, Mark, 130
New Brunswick, 31, 197, 205, 210, 219, 365
New Democratic Party (NDP) Alberta, xi–xii, 1–5, 7, 11, 13, 15, 19–22, 24–25, 28–30, 35–55, 59–60, 62, 64–65, 67, 68–70, 74–75, 84, 86–90, 98, 100, 145–146, 149–150, 154–156, 160,

162, 170, 173, 174, 177–178, 189–190, 192–193, 195–197, 200, 206, 212–213, 215–219, 222, 225, 235–236, 261–262, 270, 271–272, 287, 289, 293, 301, 303, 306–307, 310–315, 344, 346, 348–349, 353, 367–368, 385–387, 389–391, 394, 397, 401–402, 469–470, 473–474
New Democratic Party (NDP) British Columbia, 67, 217
New Democratic Party (NDP) Manitoba, 38
New Democratic Party (NDP) Saskatchewan, 38, 75
New York Times, 198, 239, 242, 253, 360
Newfoundland, 182, 365
Nixon, Jason, 71, 200–201, 209, 238–239, 459, 473
Northern Gateway, 8, 202, 212, 216, 219, 239
Notley, Rachel, 1–2, 4, 7–8, 10, 13, 15, 19–23, 25–33, 36–37, 40–41, 44–46, 53–54, 59–60, 68, 70, 77, 84, 145, 156, 158, 167, 170, 174, 176–177, 189–190, 192–195, 203, 206, 208, 212–213, 216–219, 221–222, 224–226, 228–229, 235–236, 250, 261, 287, 301, 334, 367–368, 385–387, 389–391, 405–407, 410, 420–421, 469, 474
nurses, 12, 52, 272, 278, 286, 288, 295, 322–325, 327, 333–334, 337, 385, 389–390, 392, 396–397, 399, 407, 409, 411. *See also* United Nurses of Alberta (UNA)

O

O'Toole, Erin, 453
Obama, Barack, 9, 72, 223
oil, viii, xi, 2, 8–9, 11, 20, 30–31, 33–34, 51, 75, 101, 105, 108, 115, 122, 125, 145, 148–150, 156, 158, 167, 170–171, 173–177, 181, 187, 189, 191, 193–208, 211–213, 215–222, 224, 226–230, 233–237, 239–252, 254–256, 259–263, 265–266, 269–270, 274, 276, 285–286, 290–293, 295, 297–299, 301–302, 312, 315, 321, 323, 352, 355, 360, 376–377, 384, 386–389, 403, 405, 438–439, 473. *See also* bitumen; crude; petroleum
oil sands, 25, 228–229, 234–236, 239–240, 244, 246–247, 249–250, 291
Okotoks, AB, 6, 134, 137, 140
Olsen, Tom, 236–240, 249, 253
Ontario, ix, 12, 14, 76, 101, 157, 191, 193, 197–198, 201, 205, 209–210, 251, 256, 276, 308, 311, 328, 347, 358, 363, 365, 367, 369, 371–373, 377–378, 381, 383–384, 388, 402, 406–407, 413, 415, 417, 419, 421–433, 439, 457, 462, 478
Ontario Provincial Police (OPP), 421
Orange Chinook, ii, xiii, 2, 11, 16, 42, 56, 60, 76, 78, 88, 100, 166–167, 207–208, 215, 228, 296, 389, 406–408, 469–470, 477, 479
Ottawa protests, 458, 459
Oyen, AB, 291, 293, 299

CPSIA information can be obtained
at www.ICGtesting.com
Printed in the USA
BVHW010019280223
659143BV00003B/6